Bean Equivalents and Yields

- 1 cup dried beans = 8 ounces
- 1 cup dried beans yields 2 to 3 cups cooked beans
- 1 pound dried beans yields 4 to 6 cups cooked beans
- One 10-ounce can cooked beans yields 1 cup drained beans
- One 15-ounce can yields 1½ cups drained beans
- One 16-ounce can yields 1¾ cups drained beans
- One 19-ounce can yields 2 cups drained beans

Rice Yields

- 1 cup raw white rice cooked in 2 cups liquid yields 3 cups cooked rice
- 1 cup raw brown rice cooked in 2½ cups liquid yields 4 cups cooked rice
- 1 cup quick-cooking rice cooked in 1 cup liquid yields 2 cups cooked rice

Flour Equivalents

Spoons and Cups =	Ounces =	Grams
1 tablespoon	¼ ounce	8.75 grams
¼ cup (4 tablespoons)	1¼ ounces	35 grams
⅓ cup (5 tablespoons)	1½ ounces	45 grams
½ cup	2½ ounces	70 grams
⅔ cup	3¼ ounces	90 grams
¾ cup	3½ ounces	105 grams
1 cup	5 ounces	140 grams
1½ cups	7½ ounces	210 grams
2 cups	10 ounces	280 grams
3½ cups	16 ounces (1 pound)	490 grams

American Medical Association

FAMILY

HEALTH

COOKBOOK

Good Food That's Good For You

American
Medical
Association

FAMILY
HEALTH
COOKBOOK

Good Food That's Good For You

Melanie Barnard and Brooke Dojny
with Mindy Hermann, RD and C. Wayne Callaway, MD
Illustrations by Patience Brewster

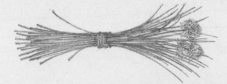

POCKET BOOKS
New York London Toronto Sydney Tokyo Singapore

A Janis A. Donnaud & Associates, Inc. Book

The recommendations and information in this book are appropriate for most people; however, they are not a substitute for advice from your physician. For specific information concerning your personal medical condition, the AMA suggests you consult a physician.

POCKET BOOKS, a division of Simon & Schuster, Inc.
1230 Avenue of the Americas, New York, NY 10020

Credits:
"USDA Dietary Guidelines for Americans" from *Nutrition and Your Health: Dietary Guidelines for Americans*. 4th ed. 1995. USDA and USDHHS; "Are You Overweight?" from *Report of the Dietary Guidelines Advisory Committee on the Dietary Guidelines for Americans*. 1995:23-24. USDA and USDHHS; "Calculating Your Waist-to-Hip Ratio" from Bray GA, Gray DS. Obesity: Pathogenesis. *Western Journal of Medicine*. 1988:149(part 1):429-441; "Calculating Your Body Mass Index" National Institutes of Health National Task Force on Prevention and Treatment of Obesity; "Moderate Amounts of Physical Activity" from *Physical Activity and Health: A Report of the Surgeon General Executive Summary*. 1996. USDHHS; "Appropriate Number of Daily Food Group Servings" from *Recommended Dietary Allowances*. 10th ed. 1992. Adapted from the Food Guide Pyramid Bulletin. USDA; "Food Guide Pyramid" USDA and USDHHS; "Nutrition Facts" (panel/label) USFDA; "Recommended Weight Gain in Pregnancy" from *Nutrition During Pregnancy*. 1990. National Academy of Sciences. Washington, DC: National Academy Press. Adapted with permission by the American College of Obstetrics and Gynecology.

ISBN: 0-671-53667-2

First Pocket Books hardcover printing November 1997

10 9 8 7 6 5 4 3 2 1

For orders other than by individual consumers, Pocket Books grants a discount on the purchase of 10 or more copies of single titles for special markets or premium use. For further details, please write to the Vice-President of Special Markets, Pocket Books, 1633 Broadway, New York, NY 10019-6785, 8th Floor.

For information on how individual consumers can place orders, please write to Mail Order Department, Simon & Schuster Inc., 200 Old Tappan Road, Old Tappan, NJ 07675.

A Janis A. Donnaud & Associates, Inc. Book

American Medical Association

Physicians dedicated to the health of America

FOREWORD

In recent years, both doctors and the public have been paying more attention to the vital connection between what we eat and our overall health. The role diet plays in preventing disease, helping to treat some diseases, and just making us feel and look our best has been the subject of exciting new research.

And the best news that doctors and food experts have for us is that foods that are good for us can also taste great. Today we are eating more fresh, whole foods seasoned with a variety of herbs, spices, and unusual ingredients that help us enjoy our meals even as we are cutting down on fat and cholesterol.

The *American Medical Association Family Health Cookbook* has been developed to help you make good food choices for yourself and your family every day in the grocery store, in your kitchen, and even at your favorite restaurant. A 50-page section about nutrition at the front of this book cuts through confusing findings and food fads to give you clear, reliable guidelines about how to eat more healthfully.

Of course at the heart of the *AMA Family Health Cookbook* are the recipes—more than 350 of them—each one developed to bring to your family's table food that is healthy, appealing, and delicious.

The physician members of the AMA bring you this nutrition reference and cookbook as part of their ongoing effort to keep you and your family healthy. Another valuable reference the AMA offers you is Physician Select: Online Doctor Finder—an online directory of licensed physicians nationwide—so you can easily get information about doctors in any specialty from your own home. Go to http://www.ama-assn.org to find Physician Select: Online Doctor Finder.

From the American Medical Association, here's to good health and good cooking for you and your family.

P. John Seward, MD
Executive Vice President

The American Medical Association

P. John Seward, MD, Executive Vice President

James F. Rappel, Group Vice President, Business and Management Services

Larry Jellen, Vice President and General Manager, Book and Product Group

M. Frances Dyra, Director, Product Line Development

Editorial Staff

C. Wayne Callaway, MD, Medical Editor

Mindy Hermann, RD, Writer and Nutritional Analyst

Dorothea Guthrie, Managing Editor

Pam Brick, Senior Editor

Robin Fitzpatrick Husayko, Editor

Debra Smith, Editorial Assistant

Acknowledgments

American College of Gynecology and Obstetrics

American Heart Association

National Cancer Institute

Stephen Blair, PED—Epidemiology/Fitness

Janis A. Donnaud & Associates, Inc.

Janis Donnaud, President

Judy Pray, Managing Editor

Melissa Holcombe, Production Editor

Wendy Palitz, Designer

Barbara Scott-Goodman, Design Associate

Laura Smyth, Typesetter

Contents

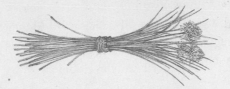

Chapter 1: Appetizers and Snacks 50

Mini Pita Pizza Wedges • Herbed Cheese Dip and Crudité Color
Wheel • Smoked Salmon Yogurt Cheese Dip with Winter Crudités •
Buffalo Chicken Strips • Pico de Gallo Salsa • Chile con Queso with
Dippers • Real Cajun Popcorn • Crispy Garlic Potato Skins • Baked
Herbed Pita Crisps • Spicy Baked Tortilla Chips • Tomatillo Salsa •
Black Olivade Crostini • Sun-Dried Tomato Crostini • Grilled Chicken
Satay • Sicilian Caponata • Spiced Baba Ghanouj • Pickled Vegetable
Medley • Three-Alarm Texas Black Bean "Caviar" • White Bean
"Pesto" with Garden Vegetables • Sweet Red Pepper Hummus

Chapter 2: Salads 72

Basic Vinaigrette • Basic Creamy Dressing • Easy Thousand Island
Dressing • Classic Southern Chicken Salad • Thai Grilled Chicken and
Broccoli on Napa Cabbage Salad • Wild Rice, Turkey, and Grape
Salad • Steakhouse Salad • Greek Barbecued Lamb and Spring
Greens Salad • Tzatziki Dressing • Marinated Scallop, Lima Bean, and
Corn Salad • Grilled Salad Niçoise • Grilled Shrimp, Black Bean, and
Mango Salad • Tropical Vinaigrette • Lemon, Tuna, and White Bean
Salad • Peppery Jambalaya Seafood Salad • Seashell Macaroni and

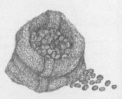

Thighs • All-American Barbecued Chicken • Chinese Grilled Five-Spice Chicken • Tuscan Grilled Chicken and Roasted Garlic Aioli • Roasted Garlic Aioli • Tandoor-Style Chicken Nuggets • Easy Chicken Cacciatore • Roasted Lebanese Chicken • Chicken Vindaloo • Chicken and Summer Vegetable Tagine • Chicken Adobo • Turkey Stir-Fry with Ginger and Mint • Basil Chicken and Sweet Pepper Packets • Turkey Cutlets and Cranberry-Kumquat Relish • Turkey and Tarragon Tomato Salsa • Garden Vegetable and Turkey Meat Loaf • Grilled Duck with Citrus Honey Salsa • Sesame Turkey and Asparagus Stir-Fry • Apple-Sage Glazed Game Hens

Tuna and Celery Bread Pudding • Crackling Fish Sticks • Lemon Tartar Sauce • Southern-"Fried" Lemon Pepper Catfish • Cape Cod Baked Stuffed Clams • Baltimore Crab Cakes • Crawfish and Tasso Jambalaya • Sausalito Cioppino • Sole Rolls Florentine • Poached Turbot with Sorrel Sauce • Sesame-Glazed Tuna • Broiled Citrus and Herb Trout • Sautéed Red Snapper Maque Choux • Skewered Swordfish and Summer Squash • Grilled Salmon with Dilled Cucumber Yogurt Sauce • Dilled Cucumber Yogurt Sauce • Grouper with Cantaloupe-Lime Salsa • Seafood Printemps en Papillotes • Vietnamese Steamed Fish in Spicy Broth • Scallops and Grapefruit Gratinée • Stir-Fried Scallops and Vegetables • Shrimp and Clams Espagnole • Herb-Steamed Mussels

Marrakech Orange and Spice-Braised Lamb Shanks • Tex-Mex Beef Pie with Cornmeal Biscuit Topping • Quick Spring Lamb Stew • Contemporary Shepherd's Pie • Marvelous Mustard Meat Loaf • Ginger-Sesame Beef and Broccoli Stir-Fry • Veal and Mushroom Stew in Acorn Squash Halves • Herb-Smoked Steak with Grilled Vegetables • Pork Chops Braised in Cider • Spiced Applesauce • Pork Pot Roast with Root Vegetables and Thyme • Maple-Mustard Pork on Mashed "Sweets" • Pork with Cranberry-Orange-Pear Sauce • Fiery Grilled Pork Tenderloin • Five-Alarm Firehouse Chili • Canadian Bacon and Garlic Greens • Lamb with White Beans and Rosemary • Curried Lamb and Fruit on Skewers • Teriyaki Flank Steak with Shiitakes • Moorish Lamb and Dried Fruit Tagine • Roast Pork Tenderloin with Lemon and Fennel • Savory Beef Stew with Paprika and Herbs • Apple and Pork Stir-Fry with Cashews and Ginger

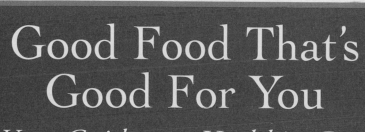

NUTRITION SECTION

Good Food That's Good For You

Your Guide to a Healthier Diet

Eating is simply a great pleasure. Today we know more than ever before about the crucial link between nutrition and health. But we still crave the look, smell, and taste of a delicious meal. The *American Medical Association Family Health Cookbook* will show you that good-tasting food can also be good for you. As a nutrition reference and a cookbook, it translates the facts about healthy eating into delicious meal choices that will appeal to your entire family.

The *American Medical Association Family Health Cookbook* advocates common-sense nutrition—widely accepted guidelines that are easy to adapt to your family's tastes. These guidelines suggest following a diet that is low in fat; includes plenty of whole grains, vegetables, and fruits; minimizes salt and sugar; supplies the right number of calories; and includes alcohol only in moderation if at all. This sensible pattern of eating follows the Dietary Guidelines for Americans, published jointly by the US Department of Agriculture (USDA) and the US Department of Health and Human Services (see page 4).

This book also stresses the importance of looking at your diet over the course of several days, not meal by meal. The nutrition information on food package labels and at the end of each recipe in this book can help you fit individual foods and dishes into your overall diet. Once you understand how to use these tools, you can get a feel for eating right, without having to count every ounce of protein or gram of fat.

Your family may have very specific or changing nutrition needs. Perhaps your child is overweight. You or your spouse might be pregnant or have high blood pressure. You may have a family history of heart disease or diabetes. All these conditions can be influenced by diet. That's why it's important for you to learn as much as you can about your own health profile and your family's. Then you can sit down with your doctor and talk about how you can use this knowledge to guide your family's food choices.

This book is packed with information about food, including the essentials of shopping for, storing, and preparing food in ways that are healthy, safe, and delicious. With the wide availability of prepared foods and the time constraints that many families face, cooking is disappearing from the American kitchen. This book puts the pleasure back into cooking by giving you recipes that are good tasting and easy to prepare. Many recipes, such as Spicy Baked Tortilla Chips (page 61) and Mini Pita Pizza Wedges (page 52), are so easy that you can make them with your kids, a great way to instill a love and understanding of food in the next generation. In every recipe, flavor is the most important ingredient. But, because the recipes comply with the most current Dietary Guidelines for Americans, they take the guesswork out of cooking healthfully.

One of the challenges of healthy cooking is creating great-tasting dishes without using too much fat, which enhances a food's flavor, texture, and moistness. Most of the recipes developed for this book are not fat free. Some are not even low fat in the strict definition of the term (3 grams or less per 100 grams of food and less than 30 percent of calories from fat). Recipes that call for a higher fat content, like Nantucket Clam Chowder (page 152), need that extra amount to maintain their taste. This book shows you how to fit those higher-fat recipes into the context of a balanced diet by budgeting your fat intake over the course of a few days.

Physical activity is another essential component of overall health—you can't assess what you eat without taking your activity level into account. When you exercise, you burn more calories, so you can eat more than if you were inactive. Just as important, physical activity can help prevent or control some of the most common chronic diseases—heart disease, high blood pressure, diabetes, and osteoporosis (bone thinning).

Every food you eat offers a different combination of nutrients, but no single food supplies all the nutrients you need. The key to overall good nutrition is eating a variety of foods. The *American Medical Association Family Health Cookbook* will help you and your family choose and enjoy an assortment of delicious and healthful dishes.

THE DIET/HEALTH CONNECTION

Ideas about food and health have changed dramatically in the last 100 years. During the early 1900s, public health efforts, such as the pasteurization of milk, focused on protecting food from contamination. This era also saw the creation of the Food and Drug Administration (FDA), which monitors food safety to this day. Back then, people were more concerned about sanitary food preparation and storage than about the basics of good nutrition. Many nutrients had not yet been discovered.

At the start of World War II, researchers tested large numbers of military recruits and found them to be lacking in key nutrients. This finding spurred research into nutrient deficiencies, resulting in the development of the Recommended Dietary Allowances (RDAs) and the concept of basic food groups. Except for calories, the RDAs exceed the requirements of most people, to allow for individual variations in needs and differences in the amount of nutrients in various foods.

In the last half of the 20th century, doctors and researchers began to explore the connection between diet and chronic diseases, such as heart disease, diabetes, and some types of cancer. Research showed that certain sensible dietary advice, such as that found in the Dietary Guidelines for Americans (see page 4) and the Food Guide Pyramid (see page 12), can lower the incidence of these diseases. These are the guidelines used here, in the *American Medical Association Family Health Cookbook.*

The Dietary Guidelines and the Food Guide Pyramid were designed as general advice for healthy people. You can tailor these recommendations to lower your personal risk of disease by "knowing your numbers"—your cholesterol level, blood pressure, blood sugar, body mass index, body fat distribution, and family history. You will need a physical examination by your doctor to determine some of these indicators. You can calculate others, such as the waist-to-hip ratio and body mass index (see page 6), yourself. Using this information, you and your doctor can find out which chronic diseases you are most at risk for. Then, working together, you can plan a diet (and exercise plan) that works best to reduce your personal risks.

The Dietary Guidelines for Americans

Eating right can help preserve your health and prevent disease. The most general, yet comprehensive, diet advice is offered in the Dietary Guidelines for Americans, published jointly by the US Department of Agriculture (USDA) and the US Department of Health and Human Services. These guidelines were developed to help people get the nutrients they need, lead healthier, more active lives, and reduce their risk of certain chronic diseases.

USDA Dietary Guidelines for Americans

- ◆ Eat a variety of foods.
- ◆ Balance the food you eat with physical activity—maintain or improve your weight.
- ◆ Choose a diet with plenty of grain products, vegetables, and fruits.
- ◆ Choose a diet low in fat, saturated fat, and cholesterol.
- ◆ Choose a diet moderate in sugars.
- ◆ Choose a diet moderate in salt and sodium.
- ◆ If you drink alcoholic beverages, do so in moderation.

Diet is one of the factors that contributes to obesity, heart disease, high blood pressure, stroke, diabetes, and some types of cancer. So eating healthfully is one of the best ways to reduce your risk of chronic disease. Practically all chronic conditions would be less common if we consumed a more healthful diet, increased our physical activity, moderated our alcohol intake, and stopped smoking.

Managing your weight

Maintaining your weight at a healthful level is one of the most important ways to feel better and protect your health. Many of the Dietary Guidelines help you accomplish this goal. Obesity is a risk factor for many diseases. A weight gain of more than 20 pounds during your adult years may increase these risks. That's why it's important to maintain your weight by balancing your food intake with physical activity.

The Dietary Guidelines include a chart of weight ranges for adults over age 19 (see page 5). These weights are based on a height-to-weight relationship called the body mass index (page 6). Although the chart includes a range of weights, you should not necessarily allow your weight to rise to the top of your range. Staying well within the range is a good way to keep your weight from climbing.

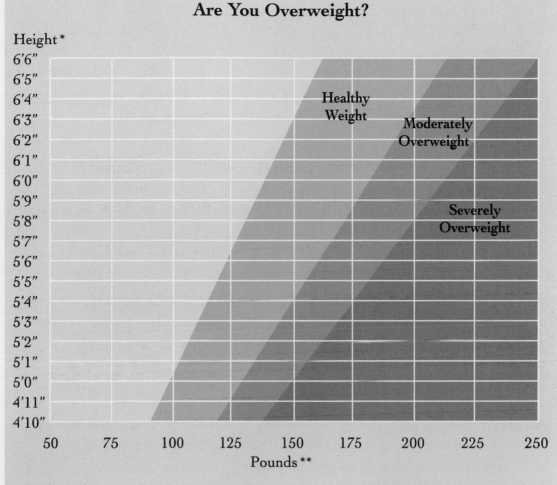

Are You Overweight?

Height *

* Without shoes.
**Without clothes. The higher weights apply to people with more muscle and bone, such as many men.

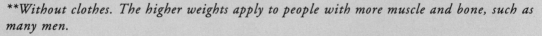

You do not need to lose weight for health reasons if your weight falls within the healthy range, you have gained less than 10 pounds during adulthood, and you are healthy. Conversely, you should lose weight if your weight is above the healthy range, you have too much fat in your abdominal area, or you have a weight-related medical problem.

To manage your weight, you need to balance the amount of food you eat with the energy you expend. If you consume more calories than you burn, you will gain weight. Neither extreme dieting nor excessive exercise is a healthful way to maintain or reduce your weight.

To prevent unhealthy weight gain or obesity, maintain your adult weight within the suggested range for your height. Don't put off trying to lose any amount of weight, because 5 or 10 pounds are often the easiest to take off. If your weight exceeds the upper limit of the range, go to a doctor, registered dietitian, or legitimate weight management program to help you lose those unwanted pounds. A loss of as little as 5 to 10 percent of your weight can improve your overall health, even if you are already in the acceptable range.

Where you carry weight on your body is an important indicator of your health risk. People who carry most of their weight on their hips and thighs (pear-shaped people) have a lower disease risk than people who carry most of their weight around the abdomen (apple-shaped people). An apple shape is more common in men and a pear shape is more common in women until after menopause.

Apple-shaped people have a higher risk for high blood pressure, diabetes, early heart disease, and certain types of cancer. The reasons for this higher risk are not fully understood, but apple-shaped people tend to have higher levels of LDL cholesterol (see page 23), the so-called "bad" cholesterol that increases heart disease risk. By measuring your waist-to-hip-ratio (see box below), you can find out your personal body shape.

Calculating Your Waist-to-Hip Ratio: Measure your waist at its narrowest point and your hips at their widest point. Divide your waist measurement by your hip measurement. You are at increased risk of chronic illness if your waist-to-hip ratio is greater than 0.80 if you are a woman and 0.95 if you are a man.

Calculating Your Body Mass Index: Divide your weight in pounds by 2.2. Multiply your height in inches by .0254 and then multiply this number times itself. Divide your converted weight by your converted height. A body mass index between 19 and 25 falls within the healthy range.

Lowering your risk of heart disease

Some risk factors for heart disease, such as a family history, are things you cannot change. But many risk factors, such as smoking, are within your control. A balanced diet that includes a variety of foods low in total fat, saturated fatty acids, and cholesterol can reduce heart disease risk. Doctors recommend a diet containing less than 30 percent of total calories from fat, with less than 10 percent of total calories from saturated fat, no more than 10 percent from polyunsaturated fat, and the remainder from monounsaturated fat (see page 21).

This 30 percent fat guideline is meant to apply over several days, not to just one day, one meal, or one dish. By following the principles of the Food Guide Pyramid (page 12), eating lower-fat foods more often, choosing recipes with less fat—for example, Baltimore Crab Cakes (page 358), which are baked instead of fried—and using high-fat extras sparingly, achieving the 30 percent goal can be surprisingly easy.

Two other nutrients to watch are cholesterol and sodium. Your daily intake of cholesterol varies, depending on whether you have eaten eggs, seafood, liver, or other high-cholesterol foods, but doctors recommend that most people with normal blood cholesterol levels consume no more than 300 milligrams of cholesterol per day. A useful guideline is to have no more than four whole eggs per week, a recommendation that may not be necessary if your blood cholesterol levels are normal. Sodium can elevate blood pressure in susceptible people. Check with your doctor about your personal situation.

A diet with plenty of high-fiber foods—whole grains, whole-grain breads and cereals, vegetables, and fruit—may help lower your blood cholesterol level. Foods rich in soluble fiber, such as oat bran, have cholesterol-lowering properties when they are part of a low-fat diet, but the best course of action is to include a variety of fiber-rich foods—such as in the Spiced Pear and Coconut Breakfast Couscous (page 249)—in your diet.

Reducing your risk of cancer

Maintaining your optimal body weight is important because being overweight elevates the risk of certain types of cancer, such as colon cancer (cancer of part of the large intestine), in men and women. Carrying a lot of weight in the abdomen has been linked to an increased risk of breast cancer in women.

A diet rich in fruits and vegetables appears to have a strong protective effect, lowering your risk of lung, prostate, stomach, and other cancers. The Food Guide Pyramid recommends that you have at least five servings of fruits, vegetables, or juice every day. High-fiber foods, including whole-grain cereals, dried peas and beans, vegetables, and fruits, may also help protect you against colon cancer. Try fiber-rich dishes such as Baked Potatoes with Spicy Chili Bean Topping (page 41).

To further reduce your risk of cancer, limit your intake of high-fat foods (especially from animal sources), choose foods that are low in fat, and limit consumption of meat, particularly high-fat meat. High-fat diets have been shown to increase the risk of several types of cancer, including breast, colon and rectal, endometrial, and prostate.

You should reserve alcohol for occasional and sparing use, if you choose to drink at all, because excessive drinking is connected to an increased incidence of liver and other cancers. Your risk of developing cancer of the mouth, throat, and esophagus may start to go up if you drink as few as two drinks per day. Breast cancer risk may increase with an intake of just a few drinks a week. However, the Dietary Guidelines recognize that alcohol, used in moderation, can be safe. Moderation is defined as no more than one drink per day for women and no more than two for men, with a typical drink being 12 ounces of regular beer, 5 ounces of wine, or 1½ ounces of 80-proof distilled spirits.

Reducing your risk of diabetes

A growing number of people are developing diabetes, but the reasons behind the increase are unclear. Doctors do know that obesity is a major contributor to type II diabetes, the most common form among adults, and that maintaining your weight within a healthy range may reduce your chances of developing diabetes. For some overweight people who have diabetes, weight loss normalizes blood sugar levels. Eating a high-fiber, low-fat diet is generally good advice because people with long-standing diabetes have a higher risk of heart disease, stroke, high blood pressure, and other diseases. Healthful eating might lower their risk. A high-fiber diet can help regulate blood sugar. But some diabetics achieve better control of their blood sugar with a diet that is slightly higher in fat and lower in carbohydrates than the type of diet recommended in the Dietary Guidelines. If you are diabetic or your blood sugar levels are elevated, work with your doctor to plan an individually tailored diet.

Exercise has several benefits for diabetics. It makes weight control easier by burning calories and building muscle. Exercise also improves your body's response to insulin, lowers your blood sugar, and may allow you to reduce your doses of diabetic medications.

The importance of physical activity

Our schedules are busier than ever, we've become dependent on cars, and our households are filled with labor-saving appliances. It's no surprise that we lead sedentary lives. Becoming more active could help enhance your feelings of well-being, control your weight, and improve the health of your heart.

Even a small increase in your activity level can have big health benefits, especially if you are currently inactive. If you are sedentary and become moderately active, you could cut your risk of death from heart disease by 50 percent. You should get a total of at least 30 minutes of moderate physical activity every day. Any type of activity counts, including heavy cleaning or yardwork, bicycling, or brisk walking.

Moderate Amounts of Physical Activity*

Washing and waxing a car for 45-60 minutes

Washing windows or floors for 45-60 minutes

Playing volleyball for 45 minutes

Playing touch football for 30-45 minutes

Gardening for 30-45 minutes

Wheeling self in wheelchair for 30-40 minutes

Walking 1¾ miles for 35 minutes (20 min/mile)

Basketball (shooting baskets) for 30 minutes

Bicycling 5 miles for 30 minutes

Dancing fast for 30 minutes

Pushing a stroller 1½ miles for 30 minutes

Raking leaves for 30 minutes

Walking 2 miles for 30 minutes (15 min/mile)

Water aerobics for 30 minutes

Swimming laps for 20 minutes

Wheelchair basketball for 20 minutes

Basketball (playing a game) for 15-20 minutes

Bicycling 4 miles for 15 minutes

Jumping rope for 15 minutes

Running 1½ miles for 15 minutes (10 min/mile)

Shoveling snow for 15 minutes

Stairwalking for 15 minutes

Less Vigorous, More Time

More Vigorous, Less Time

*A moderate amount of physical activity is roughly equivalent to physical activity that uses approximately 150 calories (kcal) of energy per day, or 1,000 calories per week. Some activities can be performed at various intensities; the suggested durations correspond to expected intensity of effort.

The amount of time you spend on each daily activity is cumulative; it all contributes to your goal of 30 minutes. Once you are getting moderate exercise on a regular basis, try to include some more vigorous exercise sessions into your schedule every week. More strenuous activity—rapid cycling, jogging, taking an aerobic exercise class, cross-country skiing—done several times a week, will build your heart and lung fitness even more.

Your personal health profile

Many chronic conditions result from a combination of diet, family history, environmental factors, and lifestyle. That's why diet alone may not prevent disease. For example, getting enough calcium from dairy products and high calcium ingredients, such as the tofu in Grilled Tofu Caesar Salad (page 91) and the yogurt in a Banana Berry Smoothie (page 446), may not prevent osteoporosis if you have a family history of the disease and are inactive, past menopause, or a smoker.

With your doctor's help and the information you find in these pages, you can get a clear sense of how you need to adjust your diet to improve your health. Your family health history is a good starting point. Create a family health tree that includes the health status, body size, and other relevant information about close family members, including grandparents, aunts and uncles, parents, siblings, and offspring. What you see on the family health tree—members who are overweight, who were diagnosed with heart disease at an early age, or who had cancer—can help you see into your potential health future so you can make preventive changes in your diet and lifestyle now.

THE FOOD GUIDE PYRAMID

The US Department of Agriculture (USDA) Food Guide Pyramid can help you choose the most healthful foods in the right proportions. It helps you plan meals without too much fat, saturated fat, and cholesterol, and with only moderate amounts of sugar and salt.

Understanding the Food Guide Pyramid

The Food Guide Pyramid is a graphic representation of healthy eating. The old four food groups represented a diet that guarded against nutrient deficiencies, but the Food Guide Pyramid symbolizes a balanced diet that also helps prevent disease. The Food Guide Pyramid's five food groups are arranged to depict their proportion in your diet. For example, the grain group is the largest portion because most of the food you eat should come from this group.

The Food Guide Pyramid reinforces three concepts of healthful eating: balance, variety, and moderation. Your diet will be balanced when you eat more foods from the groups toward the base of the Pyramid—such as Contemporary Pasta Carbonara (page 210) and Baked Herbed Polenta (page 281)—and fewer from food groups closer to the top. Variety means eating a variety of foods across Pyramid groups and a variety of foods within each group. Of course, moderation means neither too much nor too little of any one type of food.

Pyramid portions

The Pyramid suggests a range of recommended daily servings for each food group— for example, six to 11 servings of foods containing grains, such as bread, cereal, rice, and pasta. The lower number applies to children and sedentary adults. As calorie needs go up, so do the number of servings from each food group.

The portion sizes that the Pyramid uses to measure a serving may or may not reflect the actual amount of food you might eat at one meal. You may want to have two or three Pyramid-sized portions of rice—for example, the Herbed Brown Rice Pilaf (page 275)—at dinner. But you probably will eat only one apple—one Pyramid serving—at lunch. Portion

Approximate Number of Daily Food Group Servings

Daily Calorie Needs	Grains	Vegetables	Fruits	Dairy	Meat
1,300 calories for toddlers	6	3	2	2	2 (small)
1,600 calories for many sedentary women and some older adults	6	3	2	2	2 (5 ounce total)
2,200 calories for most children, teenage girls, active women, and many sedentary men	9	4	3	2-3	2 (6 ounce total)
2,800 calories for teenage boys, many active men, and some very active women	11	5	4	2-3	2 (7 ounce total)

size and number, as they are suggested in the Pyramid, are only a means of communicating how much food from a certain group you should consume in one day. They don't mean that you are allowed to eat only one serving of that type of food at one meal.

To cause further confusion, the serving sizes used on the nutrition labels required on all food packages are not the same as the serving sizes used on the Food Guide Pyramid. The portion sizes on food labels more closely reflect amounts that people actually eat at one meal.

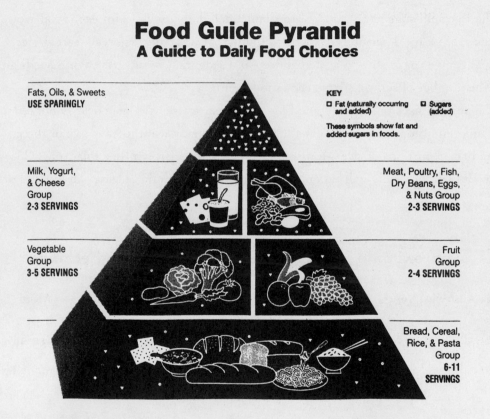

Food Guide Pyramid
A Guide to Daily Food Choices

Fats, Oils, & Sweets
USE SPARINGLY

KEY
☐ Fat (naturally occurring and added)   ☒ Sugars (added)

These symbols show fat and added sugars in foods.

Milk, Yogurt, & Cheese Group
2-3 SERVINGS

Meat, Poultry, Fish, Dry Beans, Eggs, & Nuts Group
2-3 SERVINGS

Vegetable Group
3-5 SERVINGS

Fruit Group
2-4 SERVINGS

Bread, Cereal, Rice, & Pasta Group
6-11 SERVINGS

The four levels of the pyramid

The Food Guide Pyramid's four levels illustrate the relative importance of certain foods in your diet. There are four levels, from the bottom of the Pyramid up.

The foundation: grains

The bread, cereal, rice, and pasta group makes up the largest section of the Pyramid, and grain foods should make up the largest portion of your diet. They supply complex

Bread, Cereal, Rice, and Pasta Group
6 to 11 servings daily

A serving is:
- ◆ 1 slice of bread
- ◆ ½ medium bagel or English muffin
- ◆ 1 tortilla
- ◆ 1 ounce of ready-to-eat cereal
- ◆ ½ cup of cooked cereal, rice, pasta, or grain

carbohydrates for energy, as well as B vitamins, minerals, and fiber.

Whole grains supply the most fiber. About half your grain group selections should be whole grains—for example, Honey-Orange Breakfast Oatmeal with Bananas (page 248) and Marvelous Multigrain Bread (page 112). Eating a diet that is high in fiber-containing grains may reduce your risks of some types of cancer and heart disease.

Level two: vegetables and fruits

Vegetables and fruits comprise the second-largest level of the Food Guide Pyramid. Grains, vegetables, and fruit make up the core of healthful eating. When you eat more of these foods, you have less room on your plate—and in your stomach—for foods that contain more calories and fat and fewer nutrients. Vegetables and fruits share some potential disease-lowering properties with grains. They are also a natural source of vitamin C and carotenoids (plant pigments like beta carotene) in your diet.

Vegetable Group
3 to 5 servings daily

A serving is:
- ◆ 1 cup of lettuce or other raw leafy greens
- ◆ ½ cup of cooked or raw vegetables
- ◆ ¾ cup of vegetable juice

Fruit Group
2 to 4 servings daily

A serving is:
- ◆ 1 medium apple, orange, pear, peach, or similar size fruit, or ½ average banana
- ◆ ½ cup of chopped, cooked, or canned fruit
- ◆ ¾ cup of fruit juice

The Food Guide Pyramid recommends more servings of vegetables than of fruits because most vegetables contain a wider assortment of vitamins and minerals than do fruits. Otherwise, the vegetable and fruit groups offer many similar nutrients: beta carotene (a plant pigment that can be converted into vitamin A), vitamin C, folic acid, potassium, and fiber. Both fruits and vegetables also supply carbohydrates, a source of energy. Try to enjoy a number of different fruits and vegetables every day for the greatest variety in taste and nutrition.

Level three: dairy and protein foods

The dairy and meat groups share a level near the top of the Pyramid. Dairy foods, meat, fish, and poultry should make up a smaller proportion of your diet, but they remain important.

Milk, Yogurt, and Cheese Group
2 to 3 servings daily

A serving is:
- ◆ 1 cup of milk or yogurt
- ◆ 1½ ounces of hard cheese
- ◆ 2 ounces of processed cheese
- ◆ ½ cup of part-skim ricotta cheese
- ◆ 1 cup of frozen yogurt

Meat, Poultry, Fish, Dry Beans, Eggs, and Nuts Group
**2 to 3 servings daily, totaling 5 to 7 ounces of meat,
poultry, or fish, or equivalent in dry beans, eggs, or nuts**

The following are equivalent to 1 ounce of cooked lean beef, lamb, pork, poultry, or fish:
- ◆ ½ cup of cooked or canned legumes (dried peas and beans)
- ◆ 1 egg
- ◆ 2 tablespoons of peanut butter

The milk, yogurt, and cheese group is packed with nutrients like calcium, protein, and riboflavin, a B vitamin. Dairy foods contain more calcium than almost any other food. Yet many Americans consume fewer than two daily servings of dairy products. Teens, pregnant women, and postmenopausal women need at least three servings per day to meet their calcium requirements.

Dairy foods made from whole milk can be a major source of fat, saturated fat, and cholesterol in your diet. While you do not have to eliminate these higher-fat dairy products entirely, you may need to cut back on fat elsewhere in your diet to keep your total fat "budget" within the Dietary Guidelines. For example, if you choose to use whole milk in a recipe, as in Sweet Corn and Shrimp Chowder (page 155), serve a lower-fat salad dressing or skip the margarine or butter on your bread. Nonetheless, fat budgeting is easiest when you choose low-fat or nonfat dairy products in the first place.

Meat, beans, eggs, nuts, and dairy products appear together in the protein group because they all supply protein and similar vitamins and minerals. Animal proteins are the best source of zinc and readily absorbable iron, while dried beans and peas and nuts supply fiber, which is not present in meat. You can get all the protein you need by eating two or three small portions of meat, fish, or poultry—2 to 3 ounces cooked, a piece about the size of your palm—along with the protein you get from vegetables, dairy products, and grains.

Fat Content of Cheeses

◆ **Full-fat** cheeses, like Cheddar, Gouda, Monterey Jack, and Swiss, are made from whole milk. Each has between 7 and 9 grams of fat per ounce.

◆ **Naturally lower-fat** cheeses, such as whole-milk mozzarella and feta, have about 6 grams of fat per ounce.

◆ **Reduced-fat** cheeses by law must contain at least 25 percent less fat than their full-fat versions. In general, they have much the same texture and melting properties as full-fat cheeses.

◆ **Low-fat** cheeses have no more than 3 grams of fat per ounce. They may not melt as well as full-fat cheeses and have a different flavor and texture.

◆ **Non-fat** cheeses supply less than ½ gram of fat per ounce. They are usually bland, more rubbery in texture, and do not melt well.

Like dairy foods, meats can be a source of fat, saturated fat, and cholesterol, so choose lean meat and eat poultry without the skin. Use lower-fat cooking methods, such as grilling and broiling, often.

The tip of the Pyramid: fats, oils, and sweets

Fats, oils, and sweets are the extras that contribute flavor and enjoyment to food, but you need to use them sparingly. The amount of fat you consume should reflect your calorie needs and the fat trade-offs that you make. For example, by choosing a lower-fat main course—Poached Turbot with Sorrel Sauce (page 362), Tuscan Grilled Chicken and Roasted Garlic Aioli (page 334), or Turkey and White Bean Chili Verde (page 314)—you can use the fat you save for extras like an occasional higher-fat salad dressing or dessert.

The Food Guide Pyramid recommends sparing use of sugar and sugary foods because sugar contains many calories but few nutrients. Sugary calories can add up quickly. For example, a 12-ounce soft drink contains about 9 teaspoons of sugar, the equivalent of more than 140 calories. An 8-ounce carton of sweetened, fruit-flavored yogurt derives about half of its calories from added sugar.

Overall, you can fit most foods into a healthful diet at least occasionally. The secret is to learn how to balance your food choices using the Food Guide Pyramid.

UNDERSTANDING FOOD LABELS

It's easy to plan healthy meals and snacks—if you read labels. Since May 1994, the federal government has required food manufacturers to label their products with specific and understandable nutrition and ingredient information.

Food labels contain a lot of information that can help you choose healthy foods when shopping and planning meals. Package labels provide useful facts about ingredients, key nutrients, and how a food fits into a balanced diet.

The ingredient list

Every food package displays a list of ingredients in descending order of weight. The ingredient that weighs the most is listed first and the one that weighs the least is listed last.

The nutrition facts panel

The nutrition facts panel (see right) is probably the most important part of any food package label. It lists a serving size, which is roughly the amount of the food a person would typically eat. (Remember that this serving size may not correspond to a Food Guide Pyramid serving.) The panel also lists the number of servings contained inside the package.

The nutrition facts panel shows the number of calories in a serving and displays the amount and percent of daily values of a number of important nutrients: total fat, saturated fat, cholesterol, sodium, and carbohydrate. (There are no daily values for protein and sugar because no minimum requirements have been

The Nutrition Facts Panel

Nutrition Facts

Serving Size 1 cup (228g)
Servings Per Container 2

Amount Per Serving

Calories 260   Calories from Fat 120

	% Daily Value*
Total Fat 13g	**20%**
Saturated Fat 5g	**25%**
Cholesterol 30mg	**10%**
Sodium 660mg	**28%**
Total Carbohydrate 31g	**10%**
Dietary Fiber 0g	**0%**
Sugars 5g	
Protein 5g	

Vitamin A 4%	•	Vitamin C 2%	
Calcium 15%	•	Iron 4%	

* Percent Daily Values are based on a 2,000 calorie diet. Your daily values may be higher or lower depending on your calorie needs:

	Calories:	2,000	2,500
Total Fat	Less than	65g	80g
Sat Fat	Less than	20g	25g
Cholesterol	Less than	300mg	300mg
Sodium	Less than	2,400mg	2,400mg
Total Carbohydrate		300g	375g
Dietary Fiber		25g	30g

Calories per gram:
Fat 9 • Carbohydrate 4 • Protein 4

set for them.) The panel also lists the percent of daily values for vitamins A and C, and for iron and calcium. In other words, if the panel says "Vitamin C 60%," it means that the food in the package contains 60 percent of your recommended daily intake of vitamin C.

Focus your attention on those nutrients that are most important to your health. Calories from fat, total fat, and saturated fat, and milligrams of cholesterol and sodium might be of most interest if you have a family history of heart disease. A woman concerned about osteoporosis could use the information on calcium to help her choose rich food sources of that nutrient.

The Nutrition Facts Panel—A Definition of Key Terms

Serving size: a standard size serving (not necessarily the same as a Food Guide Pyramid serving).

Servings per container: the number of standard servings.

Calories: the number of calories in one serving.

Calories from fat: compare this number to calories to get a sense of how high in fat a food is.

% daily value: the amount of a nutrient as compared to the recommended amount in a 2,000 calorie diet.

Explanatory chart: this section helps you determine your daily allowance of fats, sodium, carbohydrates, and fiber. The allowances are given for diets totaling either 2,000 or 2,500 calories per day.

Nutrient content claims

Some food labels make claims that the food inside the package is "fat free," "light," or "high in fiber." Food manufacturers can make such claims on labels only if the food in the package meets strict government guidelines (see chart on page 18).

Nutrient content claims are not permitted on packaged foods that are high in fat, saturated fat, cholesterol, or sodium.

Health claims

Science continually discovers new ways foods can reduce your risk of disease and improve your health, but most findings are not conclusive enough to merit a health claim on a food package. So the government allows food manufacturers only a limited number of health claims on labels. As of this writing, food labels can make only these specific claims:

◆ A diet with enough calcium may reduce osteoporosis risk.

◆ A diet low in sodium may reduce the risk of high blood pressure.

◆ A diet low in fat may reduce the risk of some types of cancer.

◆ A diet low in saturated fat and cholesterol may reduce heart disease risk.

◆ A low-fat diet that is rich in fiber-containing grain products, vegetables, and fruits may reduce the risk of some types of cancer.

◆ A diet low in fat, saturated fat, and cholesterol and rich in fiber-containing fruits, vegetables, and grain products may reduce heart disease risk.

◆ Low-fat diets that are rich in fruits and vegetables may reduce the risk of some types of cancer.

◆ Adequate amounts of folic acid (a B vitamin) consumed daily throughout a woman's childbearing years may reduce her risk of having a child with a birth defect such as spina bifida.

◆ Soluble fiber from oatmeal, as part of a low–saturated fat, low-cholesterol diet, may reduce the risk of heart disease.

Nutrient Content Claims

Claim	Usual Meaning
Free	None or an insignificant amount.
Low	Varies by nutrient: low fat is 3 grams or less and low cholesterol is 20 milligrams or less per serving.
Reduced/less/lower	At least 25 percent less than the amount in a comparable food that has not been modified.
Light	Must state percent reduction in fat and calories.
No added sugars	Sugars are not added during processing.
High/rich/excellent source	Contains at least 20 percent of the daily value.
Good source/contains/provides	Supplies from 10 to 19 percent of the daily value.

THE BUILDING BLOCKS OF NUTRITION

Most foods are made of carbohydrates, fat, or protein. Carbohydrates are your body's major fuel, so they should supply the bulk of your calories—about 50 to 60 percent of your daily intake. Fat should supply no more than 30 percent, with protein providing the rest.

Carbohydrates

Carbohydrates are the sugars, starches, and fiber found in plant foods. Fiber cannot be digested by your body, but helps keep your digestive system healthy.

Carbohydrates can be simple or complex. Complex carbohydrates consist of the starches or fibers in grain foods (rice, pasta, breakfast cereal, and bread), certain vegetables (such as potatoes), legumes (such as beans), and some fruits (such as bananas).

Most simple carbohydrates taste sweet and are easy to digest and absorb. Examples include granulated white table sugar, the fructose in most fruits, and the lactose found in milk.

Most of the carbohydrates you eat should be complex carbohydrates from grains, vegetables, and whole fruits with skins. Complex carbohydrates are absorbed more slowly than simple carbohydrates, giving your body a more continuous source of energy. Complex carbohydrates may also have a steadying effect on your blood sugar levels, causing them to rise and fall less rapidly than if you eat simple carbohydrates.

Fiber

A diet that is rich in fiber from whole grains, fruits, and vegetables may help reduce your risk of heart disease and certain types of cancer. Try high-fiber recipes such as Black Bean Patties with Dill (page 289) and Chicken and Summer Vegetable Tagine (page 339). Fiber also helps prevent constipation and some digestive system diseases. Fiber comes in two forms, soluble and insoluble, which have different effects on your body. Both can be important for overall health so, as with all foods, it's best to eat foods containing a variety of types of fiber.

Eating foods rich in fiber is better than taking a fiber supplement, such as plain bran. Whole foods provide a broader range of fiber and other nutrients not found in plain bran. Also, concentrated fiber supplements can impede the absorption of iron and other minerals. A balanced diet with plenty of whole grains, fruits, and vegetables can easily provide the recommended 25 grams of fiber per day.

Sugar and other sweeteners

We are born with a love of sweet flavors. Breast milk has a noticeably sweet taste that appeals to infants. Desserts, candy, and sweetened beverages are popular because they taste good. All sugars are virtually identical nutritionally and supply about 4 calories per gram, or 16 calories per teaspoon, but they are "empty" calories because sugar contains few nutrients. Sugar is available raw, white, or light and dark brown—the latter have molasses added for flavor, color, and texture. (Molasses is the syrup that remains after sugar has been crystallized from sugar cane.) As a sweetener, honey is higher in calories than sugar and offers no nutrition benefits.

Protein

If carbohydrates and fats are your body's main fuels, then protein acts as the mechanic that tunes up the body and repairs tissue. Protein also transports hormones and vitamins in the bloodstream and builds muscle. Proteins consist of combinations of 21 different chemicals called amino acids. Some amino acids are essential; your body cannot manufacture them and must get them from food. Your body forms nonessential amino acids from the essential ones.

Growing children have the highest protein requirements per pound. Infants need close to 300 percent more protein per pound and children need 150 percent more than do adults. Adult protein requirements are surprisingly low. The Recommended Dietary Allowance (RDA) for protein is 63 grams for an adult male and 50 grams for a woman— less than 0.4 grams of protein per pound of body weight. Meeting the RDA is easy—eat a total of 6 ounces of meat, chicken, or fish and drink two glasses of milk, and you've already exceeded the RDA for women and almost hit the RDA for men without even counting the protein you get from grains and vegetables. If you somehow don't eat enough protein, your body will break down muscle and other organs for the amino acids that it requires. But most Americans eat more protein than they need.

Sources of protein other than meat, poultry, and fish include eggs, legumes, nuts, and dairy products. Breads, cereals, grains, and vegetables also supply some protein. Unlike animal protein, plant protein foods supply fiber, have no cholesterol, and usually have little fat. Animal proteins are high in essential amino acids so they are called complete proteins. Vegetable proteins contain fewer essential amino acids and are known as incomplete proteins. Until recently, nutrition experts thought people had to eat a combination of plant proteins, such as rice and beans, at the same meal to obtain the right mix of essential amino acids. But now they know that, unless your overall protein intake is inadequate (which is unlikely), you don't need to combine plant proteins at a given meal as long as your total diet is balanced.

Neither animal nor vegetable sources of protein are pure protein. Meat, poultry, higher-fat fish, eggs, and nuts also supply fat, which can be the source of a lot of their calories. Legumes (peas and beans), with the exception of soybeans, have little or no fat. Instead, they contain carbohydrate in the form of starch and fiber.

Fats

Fat is more than just padding in your body—it's also a concentrated source of energy. Vitamins A, D, E, and K cannot be absorbed by the body unless they are carried in fat. Your body also uses the building blocks of fat, called fatty acids, to manufacture hormones, such as the female hormone estrogen and the male hormone testosterone. Just as important, fats carry flavor and help make foods taste good.

Eating too much fat has been linked to heart disease, some types of cancer, and other chronic diseases. For this reason, the Dietary Guidelines for Americans and many doctors recommend limiting the total fat in your diet to no more than 30 percent of calories. This amount translates into about 65 grams of fat (16 teaspoons total from all foods) per day in a 2,000 calorie diet. You should also limit saturated fat to less than 10 percent of your total calories, and cholesterol to an average of 300 milligrams or less per day. You can exceed these percentages on a given day as long as the numbers even out over time.

All fats are not the same

Fat can be saturated, polyunsaturated, or monounsaturated. Foods that contain fat usually have all three types in varying proportions, but some foods are higher in one type of fat than in others. For example, olive oil is high in monounsaturated fat, but also contains some saturated and some polyunsaturated fat.

Trans fatty acids are not a naturally occurring type of fat. They are created during food processing when polyunsaturated vegetable oils are processed with hydrogen gas to make them hard. Food manufacturers "hydrogenate" margarine, for example, to give it firmness. Hydrogenated fats can raise your blood cholesterol if consumed in high quantities.

The chart on page 22 explains the differences between the main types of fat and shows how each affects your blood cholesterol levels.

The effect any type of fat may have on your blood cholesterol depends on your overall diet, how much total fat you eat, and inherited factors.

Don't consume any fats, including monounsaturated and polyunsaturated fats, excessively. Try to follow a diet that derives no more than 30 percent of calories from fat: less than 10 percent from saturated fat, no more than 10 percent from polyunsaturated fat, and the rest from monounsaturated fat.

Know Your Fats

Type of Fat	Description	Foods Found In	Possible Effects on Blood Cholesterol
Saturated	Solid at room temperature	Red meat, butter, cheese, coconut oil, palm oil	Raises
Polyunsaturated (omega 6 and omega 3)	Liquid at room temperature	Omega 6—vegetable oils (corn, safflower); omega 3—fish, seafood	Lowers total cholesterol but also lowers HDL ("good cholesterol")
Monounsaturated	Liquid at room temperature	Olive oil, canola oil, meat, fish, poultry	May help lower total cholesterol without lowering HDL
Trans fatty acids	Solid at room temperature	Margarine, processed foods like crackers	Raises

Fat versus calories

In the past, if you were health conscious and concerned about maintaining your weight, you counted calories. Today you probably count fat grams instead. But this focus can be misleading. Calories still count. While we have trimmed some of the fat from our diets, we have compensated for it by eating extra carbohydrates. The result is that, for many people, their calorie intake and their weight have gone up.

Extremely low-fat diets, which can be extremely high in carbohydrates, may actually be harmful for people who have high triglycerides (see page 23), low HDL cholesterol, and high blood sugar, the classic picture of insulin resistance, a precursor of diabetes that occurs in up to 25 percent of adults. That's why you should not go on any kind of extreme diet unless you talk to your doctor. If you want to lose 5 or 10 pounds, just lower your calorie intake and exercise more until you reach your goal. Otherwise, stick with the Dietary Guidelines; they were written to provide the best advice for healthy people.

Cholesterol

Cholesterol is found only in foods of animal origin. Foods that are high in cholesterol are not necessarily high in fat or saturated fat, and vice versa. Vegetable oils, for example, are 100 percent fat but do not contain cholesterol.

Your body makes most of the cholesterol circulating in your blood from the saturated fat that you eat, although some comes from the cholesterol that is present in foods. How much dietary cholesterol affects blood cholesterol varies widely from person to person. For many people, the amount of cholesterol they eat has little effect on the level of cholesterol in their blood. But for others, especially people who already have high levels of blood cholesterol, dietary cholesterol can raise blood cholesterol levels even further. High levels of cholesterol in the blood, primarily cholesterol attached to low-density lipoproteins (LDL cholesterol, see below), is linked to an increased risk for heart attacks and strokes.

If your blood cholesterol is high (greater than 240 or greater than 200 if you have other heart disease risk factors or heart disease itself), your doctor may tell you to limit the amount of cholesterol you eat as well as the amounts of total and saturated fat.

Certain proteins, called lipoproteins, carry cholesterol in your blood. Low-density lipoproteins (LDLs)—the so-called "bad cholesterol"—carry cholesterol to cells throughout your body. Very low-density lipoproteins (VLDLs) also carry some cholesterol to cells. High-density lipoproteins (HDLs)—the so-called "good cholesterol"—transport cholesterol away from your cells back to your liver, which recycles or eliminates the cholesterol. Your doctor may need to check all three types of lipoproteins if your total cholesterol is high.

Your LDL and HDL levels say a lot about your risk of heart disease. Your risk goes up when your LDL cholesterol level is too high or if your HDL cholesterol is too low. A high total cholesterol level (the amount carried on all of the lipoproteins) usually, but not always, means a greater risk of heart disease as well. Higher HDL cholesterol levels lower your risk of heart disease.

Less is known about the relationship between high triglyceride levels and heart disease. Triglycerides are fats transported in the bloodstream on VLDL cholesterol. They can come from the fat you eat or be manufactured by your liver, especially from excess sugars. High triglycerides (greater than 200) frequently accompany low HDL cholesterol levels and may be an early warning sign for underlying resistance to insulin and an increased risk of diabetes, high blood pressure, and heart disease. That's why your doctor may measure your triglycerides when assessing your overall risk.

The best way to lower the fat, saturated fat, and cholesterol in your diet is to eat plenty of fruits, vegetables, and grains. In their natural form, most of these foods have little or no fat and all are cholesterol free. Getting more of your calories from vegetables, fruits, and grains means you will need and want fewer foods containing fat.

As you cook, you'll need to use some fat for taste. Use it where it really makes a taste difference. For example, add a touch of butter for flavor at the end of your cooking instead of using a lot of it simply to lubricate the frying pan.

Sources of Fat and Cholesterol

Foods with Cholesterol and Fat	Foods with Cholesterol But Little Fat	High-fat Foods with No Cholesterol
Bacon	Chicken breast (skinless)	Margarine
Butter	Flounder	Nuts
Dairy products	Liver	Oil
Eggs	Lobster	Olives
Meat and poultry	Shrimp	
	Sole	

Vitamins

Vitamins are a group of chemicals essential for normal functioning of the body. With a few exceptions, such as vitamin D, which is produced in the skin when exposed to sunlight, your body cannot manufacture vitamins, so you need to get them from the foods that you eat.

Vitamin deficiencies are relatively uncommon in this country. Most of us get enough vitamins from the foods we eat. The benefits of taking vitamin supplements in amounts that exceed the RDAs remain uncertain.

Much attention has focused on the antioxidant nutrients—vitamin C, beta carotene (which is converted to vitamin A in the body), and vitamin E. Research findings on disease prevention and the antioxidant vitamins are far from conclusive. The best way to get adequate amounts of all vitamins and any other potentially beneficial components of food is to eat a wide variety of foods, including at least five servings of fruits and vegetables a day.

Minerals

Plants absorb minerals through soil or water; then you consume the minerals when you eat plant foods. Minerals are essential to human nutrition, but your body needs only small amounts of each mineral. In fact, the requirement for some minerals—such as iron, iodine, chromium, or copper—is so small that the minerals are commonly known as "trace elements."

Many common minerals play important roles in your body. Calcium is the major mineral in your bones and teeth. The iron in red blood cells helps carry oxygen from your lungs to every cell in your body. Your muscles also need iron to obtain energy from the food you eat. Other minerals work behind the scenes to regulate your heartbeat and the fluid balance in your tissues.

Some trace minerals have well-understood functions and minimum daily requirements. For others, the minimum requirements are not known. Intake recommendations have been established for only eight trace minerals—chromium, copper, fluoride, iodine, manganese, molybdenum, selenium, and zinc.

Food versus supplements

Vitamin and mineral requirements are commonly expressed in terms of their Recommended Dietary Allowances (RDAs). Not meeting your RDA every day does not mean that you are on the road to poor nutrition. The RDA for each nutrient is set well above the amount known to prevent a deficiency. Some people think that extra amounts of certain vitamins and minerals, far in excess of their RDAs, can help keep them healthier, but research has not yet proven this assumption for most vitamins.

Most people do not need to take vitamin and mineral supplements if they eat a balanced diet. Exceptions include children living in areas without fluoridated water, pregnant and breast-feeding women, people on very low-calorie weight-loss diets, some vegetarians, and people taking drugs that interfere with vitamin or mineral absorption. If you fall into one of these groups, talk to your doctor about whether you should take a vitamin or mineral supplement. For other people, a daily multivitamin may serve as a form of nutrition "insurance," although usually an unnecessary one. In fact, large amounts of individual vitamins and minerals may interfere with your absorption and use of other nutrients. This possibility is less likely when you consume nutrients in foods.

Know Your Vitamins

Vitamin	Functions	Food Sources
Biotin	Helps release energy from food	Egg yolks; liver
Folic acid	Helps to produce DNA; protects against neural tube birth defects	Oranges; green, leafy vegetables; legumes; liver
Pantothenic acid	Helps release energy from food	Animal proteins; fresh vegetables
Vitamin A	Necessary for normal vision; keeps skin and hair healthy; helps form bones and teeth; bolsters the immune system	Foods containing vitamin A—liver; eggs; butter; fortified milk; fortified margarine: foods containing beta carotene, which is converted to vitamin A—carrots; sweet potatoes; cantaloupe; other orange vegetables and fruits; leafy greens
Vitamin B_1 (thiamine)	Helps produce energy from food; needed by the brain, nervous system, and muscles	Pork; dried beans and peas; whole grains; enriched flour
Vitamin B_2 (riboflavin)	Helps produce energy from food; maintains body tissues; builds red blood cells; keeps skin healthy	Milk and other dairy products; animal proteins; fortified cereals; green, leafy vegetables
Vitamin B_3 (niacin)	Helps release energy from food; helps ensure the health of the skin, nervous system, and digestive tract	Animal proteins; enriched breads, cereals, and grain products
Vitamin B_6	Needed for healthy nervous and immune systems and for normal red blood cells	Chicken; fish; pork; organ meats; nuts; whole grains; dried peas and beans
Vitamin B_{12}	Helps manufacture red blood cells and DNA; maintains healthy nervous system	Animal foods (including meat, organ meats, clams, and oysters)
Vitamin C	Builds collagen (a protein that helps support bone); "glues" cells together; helps heal wounds	Citrus fruits; kiwi fruit; berries; melon; potatoes; broccoli; cabbage; other fruits and vegetables
Vitamin D	Promotes calcium absorption; builds and maintains normal bones and teeth	Fortified milk; liver; egg yolks; fatty fish (such as eel, herring, and salmon)
Vitamin E	Prevents cell damage; needed by red blood cells, muscle, and other tissues	Nuts; vegetable oils; whole grains; green, leafy vegetables
Vitamin K	Promotes blood clotting; helps maintain normal bones	Spinach; kale; other green, leafy vegetables

Water

Water is the most abundant nutrient in your body. It makes up about 75 percent of the weight of your muscles, is the predominant liquid in all your body fluids, and is a part of every cell, organ, bone, and tissue. You could not survive more than a few days without drinking water.

Water performs a variety of essential functions. Like the fluid in your car's radiator, water circulates in your bloodstream to cool your body—the water that evaporates through your skin helps keep your temperature steady. Water also carries nutrients to your cells and transports waste out of your body.

The popular recommendation that adults drink at least eight, 8-ounce glasses of water daily is a bit arbitrary. Your actual fluid requirements vary depending on climate, activity, and your body size. Thirst is a good indicator that you need water. Avoid trying to quench your thirst with caffeinated or alcoholic beverages, because they actually cause your body to lose water.

Fluoridated water helps protect your teeth from tooth decay. The water in some regions of the United States naturally supplies fluoride, and many municipalities add fluoride to their water supplies. Fluoridation has proven to be an effective and safe means of preventing dental cavities.

The safety of American drinking water is regulated by the federal government. In 1974, the government passed the Safe Water Drinking Act and set standards for drinking water purity. Most public water supplies meet these standards. But bacteria and other water contaminants occasionally reach unsafe levels when municipal water treatment systems break down. In such cases, local water treatment facilities usually advise you to boil your tap water before drinking it or using it for cooking.

Drinking water can also become contaminated with lead that leeches into it from plumbing pipes, solder, and faucets, or from well pumps. To reduce the lead in your tap water, run the water for several minutes before using it and always use cold water for cooking because hot water can draw lead out of pipes and fixtures. Other options that eliminate not only bacteria, but also lead and chemicals, include home water filtration systems or bottled water that has been distilled or filtered.

Other ingredients in food

Alcohol and caffeine are two substances that can have significant effects on the body. It's best to use both in moderation, if at all.

Know Your Minerals

Mineral	Functions	Food Sources
Calcium	Builds bone; helps control blood pressure; enables muscles to contract	Milk and dairy products; canned sardines or salmon with bones; tofu (soybean curd) made with calcium; oysters; dark green, leafy vegetables
Chromium	Helps the hormone insulin move blood sugar into your cells	Whole grains; processed meats; some fortified breakfast cereals
Copper	Needed for bone formation and nerve protection	Shellfish; whole grains; dried peas and beans; organ meats
Fluoride	Strengthens bones and teeth	Fluoridated water; tea
Iodine	Helps regulate metabolism	Seafood; iodized salt; seaweed
Iron	Helps carry oxygen in the bloodstream	Beef; pork; dark-meat poultry and organ meats; dried peas and beans; enriched cereals and grains; green, leafy vegetables
Magnesium	Helps muscles relax after contractions; helps regulate heartbeat	Grains; vegetables; meat; dairy products
Manganese	Starts up several enzyme processes; needed for production of sex hormones	Whole grains; nuts; dried peas and beans; tea
Molybdenum	Works with several enzymes	Dairy products; dried peas and beans; organ meats
Phosphorus	Works with calcium, magnesium, and fluoride in bone growth; helps protect cells	Meat; poultry; fish; dairy products
Potassium	Maintains fluid balance inside and outside of cells; helps regulate blood pressure	Bananas; potatoes; oranges; dried fruit; other fruits and vegetables
Selenium	Helps vitamin E protect cells from damage	Seafood; organ meats; red meat; whole grains grown in selenium-rich soil
Sodium	Maintains fluid balance inside and outside of cells; helps regulate blood pressure	Table salt; processed foods; baked goods
Zinc	Essential for normal cell growth and wound healing	Shellfish; whole grains; beef; dried peas and beans

Food Allergies and Intolerances

Food allergies

True food allergies are not as common as you might think. They are most prevalent in children and tend to diminish as they get older. Foods that are most likely to cause allergic reactions, particularly in young children, include egg whites, nuts, shellfish, and milk. Talk to your pediatrician if, after eating certain foods, your child consistently vomits or wheezes, or has diarrhea, difficulty breathing, a runny nose, a rash, or hives.

Lactose intolerance

You get stomach cramps and gurgling after drinking a glass of milk. Do you have lactose intolerance? Lactose intolerance develops when the lining of the intestine no longer makes enough of an enzyme (lactase) that digests milk sugar (lactose). This change usually happens after weaning. Production of the enzyme tends to drop as you get older and can also be affected by illness, medication, or periods of time when you stop drinking milk. Lactose intolerance is common among most of the world's people after adolescence. Only people of Northern European descent keep their ability to digest milk sugar throughout adulthood; even in them this ability declines with age.

If you are lactose intolerant, your symptoms—cramps, stomach gurgling, gas, or diarrhea—develop shortly after you've had milk (although many people can drink small amounts of milk without problems). You will probably be better able to tolerate yogurt because its live, active bacteria cultures partially break down milk sugar. Cheese too is more digestible because most varieties have only a fraction of the lactose found in milk.

The increasing variety of low-lactose and lactose-free dairy products enables lactose-intolerant people to enjoy the taste and nutrition benefits of milk and other dairy foods without the side effects. Lactase enzyme is available in tablets, which you can take before, during, or immediately after eating a lactose-containing food, or in enzyme drops you can add to a carton of milk.

Getting enough calcium may be a challenge, so use lactose-reduced products. Try smaller portions of milk instead of a glassful at a time. Have yogurt and cheese, which you may tolerate well. Calcium-rich foods (such as sardines), calcium-fortified juices, and supplements are acceptable alternatives but lack many of the other nutrients supplied by dairy products.

Food sensitivities

Food or ingredient sensitivities are different from allergies because they do not cause an immune system reaction. A sensitivity to sulfites, a food preservative used in wine and processed foods, can trigger asthmalike symptoms, shortness of breath, a rash, chest and throat tightness, or headaches. Chinese restaurant syndrome refers to the headache, flushing, and other symptoms thought to affect a small number of people who consume monosodium glutamate (MSG), a flavor enhancer commonly used in Chinese cooking. But recent research shows that the link between MSG and these symptoms is questionable. Migraine headaches may be triggered by such foods as red wine, aged cheese, and chocolate. Your doctor can help you identify the foods that trigger your sensitivity so you can avoid them.

Alcohol

Alcohol supplies calories but not much else nutritionally. Alcoholic drinks contain varying amounts of alcohol. Hard liquors are about 40 to 50 percent alcohol (80 to 100 proof), while beer and wine are about 4 and 14 percent alcohol, respectively. Alcohol that you use in cooking evaporates when you simmer foods uncovered.

One drink per day may help some people to reduce their heart disease risk, according to recent scientific research. But drinking alcoholic beverages is not recommended as a preventive measure because of its other health risks. So, if you don't drink, don't start. If you do drink, you should limit your consumption of alcoholic beverages to no more than one drink a day for a woman and two drinks a day for a man.

You may have heard that the French have lower rates of heart disease than do Americans in spite of the fact that they eat an extremely high-fat diet. Some experts have speculated that this lower incidence of heart disease is linked to the widespread consumption of red wine in France. But others believe heart disease rates may be lower because the French eat many more fresh fruits and vegetables than do people in the United States. Additionally, the rates of alcoholism and liver disease are much higher in France than in the United States.

Alcohol affects women differently from men because women generally weigh less and have less body water than men. A woman will feel the effects of alcohol sooner because blood alcohol levels become more concentrated in women's smaller bodies. Alcohol also remains in a woman's body for a longer time because the female hormone estrogen slows down the liver's metabolism of alcohol.

Excess alcohol consumption increases your risk of accidents, violence, suicide, and overall death. It can also cause cirrhosis (severe scarring) of the liver, inflammation of the pancreas, and damage to the brain and heart. Heavy drinking has also been linked with an increased risk of heart disease, fetal alcohol syndrome (birth defects caused by a mother's high alcohol consumption), and several types of cancer (see page 8).

Overconsumption of alcohol can also cause nutritional problems, including nutrient deficiencies and general malnutrition. Alcohol can interfere with the way your body absorbs, stores, and uses nutrients.

Caffeine

Caffeine is a bitter, addictive chemical found in coffee, tea, cola, cocoa, and several other beverages and foods, and some pain relievers. In your body, caffeine acts as a stimulant to make you feel more alert and energetic, at least initially. People who drink several cups of coffee per day or their equivalent can develop a tolerance to caffeine and may not feel its stimulant effect unless they drink excessive amounts. Long-term, excessive use of caffeine can cause fatigue. Extremely high doses of caffeine can

Sources of Caffeine

Common Beverages and Foods	Caffeine Content
Brewed coffee, 8 ounces	100-150 milligrams
Cola, 12 ounces	45 milligrams
Tea, 5 ounces	20-50 milligrams
Iced tea, 12 ounces	22-36 milligrams
Decaffeinated coffee, 8 ounces	6 milligrams
Bittersweet chocolate, 1 ounce	5-35 milligrams
Hot cocoa, 8 ounces	7 milligrams
Milk chocolate, 1 ounce	6 milligrams
Chocolate milk, 8 ounces	5 milligrams

cause heart palpitations and increase feelings of anxiety. Caffeine also causes your body to excrete water.

Moderate caffeine consumption averages roughly 280 milligrams per day, about 2 to 3 cups of coffee. Your doctor may recommend that you avoid caffeine if you have a history of heart disease or irregular heartbeats. You may also want to cut down or eliminate caffeine if you experience caffeine-related symptoms, such as anxiety, insomnia, rapid heartbeat, or headaches when you skip your morning cup of coffee. Weaning yourself from caffeine should be a gradual process. First, identify all sources of caffeine in your diet, including soft drinks listing caffeine as an ingredient, and pain relievers and other caffeine-containing medications. Then gradually cut out caffeine-containing foods, beverages, and medications over several weeks to minimize the severe headaches and other symptoms that occur during withdrawal.

GOOD NUTRITION AT EVERY AGE

It's never too early in life—or too late—to start eating healthfully. Of course, a lifetime of good nutrition conveys the most benefits, but improving your diet now will also improve your health in the future. This section shows you how to eat healthfully from childhood into your senior years.

Infants and children

An infant grows more rapidly during the first year of life than at any other time. To meet the demands of this rapid growth, an infant needs close to three times as many calories per pound as do its parents.

Pediatricians recommend breast-feeding during a child's first several months of life. In addition to its nutritional benefits, breast milk also supplies antibodies to help infants fight off infections. But a mother who chooses not to breast-feed can rest assured knowing that commercial infant formulas will adequately meet her child's nutritional needs.

One nutrient that infants may not get enough of is iron. Infants typically are born with enough iron to last up to 6 months, so breast milk supplies only small amounts. But by the sixth month, most infants begin eating iron-fortified cereals and other foods with iron. Unless your child is a poor eater, you shouldn't worry whether or not he or she is getting enough iron.

Your pediatrician will guide you through the transition from breast milk or formula to solid food. Generally, you should feed infants cereal first, then introduce puréed vegetables, fruit, and protein foods at monthly intervals. Protein foods and some fruits can cause allergies in young children, so introduce them one at a time in case any allergic reactions occur.

By 1 year of age, a child is usually eating table food and drinking cow's milk in place of baby food and formula. Unless your child's pediatrician tells you otherwise, do not give your child cow's milk until after his or her first birthday because it is too concentrated, and may cause allergies in younger children.

Fussiness is the hallmark eating behavior of toddlers and preschoolers. Children of this age may become less interested in food as their growth slows. Activities suddenly become more important to them than eating. They also use eating as a way to exert their newfound independence. The end result is children who refuse to eat, do not appear to be eating enough, or insist on eating only certain foods.

The best news for parents is that when young children are hungry they will eat. Offer a variety of foods at each meal without forcing your child to eat any of them. Include at least one food that you know your child will eat, like fruit or bread, and don't fill him or her up with juice, watered down children's drinks, or soda pop. (Limit juice consumption to 8 ounces per day.) Serve food in child-size portions—about 1 tablespoon of each food per year of age. Stock up on nutritious snacks, because young children need to snack to consume enough calories. Ride out your child's food "jags" and chances are that he or she will tire of eating the same foods over and over. Most importantly, set a good example for your child with the foods that you eat.

Once your child is eating table foods, offer him or her tastes of dishes that you've made for the rest of the family. It may help to start with foods like pastas that you can serve your child with the sauce or spicy ingredients on the side. Remember that many toddlers prefer their foods separate from each other instead of mixed together in a dish. You can serve many of the salad recipes in this book with ingredients in separate bowls so that toddlers and preschoolers can decide which to eat and how to eat them.

Your child can begin the transition to the adult Dietary Guidelines after his or her second birthday. In the first two years of life, your child needs fat as a concentrated source of calories to ensure normal growth and development. When your child switches from higher-fat to lower-fat foods depends on his or her eating habits and growth. Picky eaters and slow growers may need the additional fat calories until their eating habits improve. By about the age of 5 years, or the beginning of elementary school, your child should be following adult food recommendations.

A growing number of children are overweight, from too little physical activity and too many calories. Encourage your kids to engage in indoor and outdoor activities with friends and family. Avoid forcing them to eat less. Instead, help your child to sense what it feels like to be full and to decide when to stop eating. Prepare and serve nutritious dishes, and limit, but don't eliminate, higher-fat and higher-sugar foods. Serve plenty of grains, vegetables, and fruits, along with low-fat dairy and protein foods. Send your child to school with a satisfactory but low-fat lunch (see page 175). Work with your pediatrician to ensure that an overweight child will get the nutrients he or she needs to grow and develop while losing weight.

Adolescents

It's tough to make sure your teenagers are eating the right foods. Your adolescents' calorie and nutrient needs increase virtually overnight to support this period of rapid growth and maturation. Yet their eating habits, which are heavily influenced by their friends rather than their parents, may have little to do with their nutritional needs.

Two minerals that are extremely important for growing teenagers—especially girls— are calcium and iron. Calcium is crucial to support rapid bone growth and build strong bones during adolescence. Good bone development during these years helps ensure healthy, strong bones in adulthood. The recommended calcium intake for adolescents is 1,200 milligrams per day, or the equivalent of four cups of milk. While teenage boys usually meet this requirement easily, girls are often more concerned with calories than calcium and may refuse to consume the amount of high-calcium foods that they need. Skim milk, nonfat yogurt, calcium-fortified juice, foods like broccoli, sardines, and tofu, and dishes made with dairy products—Whole-Wheat Yogurt Waffles (page 134), Mediterranean-Style Tuna Melt (page 181), or Huevos Rancheros Tostadas (page 190)— can all help supply your adolescent girl with enough calcium.

Adolescents need extra iron because the body's volume of blood increases during the teenage years. Teens also build muscle, another process that requires iron. Girls need more iron than boys because of menstrual blood loss. Iron is most abundant in and easily absorbed from dark-colored animal proteins like beef, lamb, liver, and dark-meat poultry. Dried peas and beans and iron-fortified breakfast cereals can also be good sources of iron, especially for teens who choose not to eat meat.

Adults

Your nutrient needs level off after about age 25 and remain stable into your senior years. But sound eating habits are as important as ever during adulthood. Adopting a healthful lifestyle now—eating a low-fat, high-fiber diet with plenty of grains, fruit, and vegetables; getting regular exercise; and stopping smoking—can help reduce your risk of chronic diseases like heart disease, high blood pressure, cancer, and diabetes later in life.

Weight control should be a top priority during your adult years because excessive weight gain can increase your risk of heart disease, certain types of cancer, diabetes, and other chronic illnesses. As we age, most of us need fewer calories. Most people become less active as they get older and, with less activity, muscles get smaller. Regular exercise, which burns calories and preserves and builds muscle, is an essential element of good health in adulthood.

Every adult should accumulate at least 30 minutes of moderately intense physical activity on most days. Activities can include walking, gardening, or cycling (see page 9). You can do them in 10-minute blocks if you cannot devote a full 30 minutes at a time. This kind of activity can translate into as much as an additional 200 calories burned each day.

Adult women have unique needs at different stages of their reproductive lives. Calcium and iron are as important to women during adulthood as they were in adolescence. A diet that includes at least 800 milligrams of calcium per day helps preserve bone mass and protects bone strength once a woman's bones begin to lose calcium in her late 30s. Premenopausal women lose iron monthly, so they need to consume iron in their diet.

Pregnant and breast-feeding women

During pregnancy, a woman's energy requirements increase. Many doctors prescribe prenatal vitamin supplements because many pregnant women find it difficult to meet their increased vitamin and mineral requirements through diet alone. Women of childbearing age, even if they are not pregnant, need to more than double their intake of folic acid, through foods—orange juice, spinach and other leafy greens, dried peas and beans, and whole grains—or supplementation. Folic acid helps reduce the risk of birth defects, such as spina bifida, that develop in the first few weeks of pregnancy, often before a woman knows that she is pregnant.

Recommended Weight Gain in Pregnancy	
Condition	Weight Gain (pounds)
Underweight	28-40
Normal weight	25-35
Overweight	15-25
Carrying twins	35-45

Food cravings are common during pregnancy. Women crave many foods to satisfy thirst, to reduce nausea, or for no discernible reason. Talk to your doctor if you crave nonfoods like laundry starch, dirt, or toothpaste. This type of craving may signify a nutrient deficiency.

Breast-feeding requires about 500 to 700 extra calories per day and increased amounts of most nutrients. Plan your meals and snacks to ensure that the additional calories come from foods rich in vitamins and minerals. Many women continue taking prenatal vitamins during breast-feeding.

Menopausal women

A woman's nutritional needs change after menopause. Fat accumulates in the abdominal area, increasing disease risk, and weight control may become more difficult. Iron loss is no longer an issue after menstruation has stopped, but loss of calcium from bones accelerates. Osteoporosis (thinning of bones) affects millions of older women. It develops when bone mineral diminishes at a faster rate than it can be replaced, resulting in weak bones that break easily.

Lowering your risk of osteoporosis is a lifelong process. A diet that is adequate in calcium—two or three daily servings of dairy products for children through age 10 and at least four servings for adolescents and young adults—can help optimize bone mass when you are young. Physical activity, especially weight-bearing exercise, is essential to maintain bone.

Bone building and maintenance call for calcium. The Recommended Dietary Allowance (RDA) for calcium is 1,200 milligrams daily (three dairy servings) up to age 25 and 800 milligrams after age 25, but many experts recommend as much as 1,500 milligrams after menopause if the woman does not take estrogen through hormone replacement therapy. That amount is just about impossible to get from diet alone, so many doctors prescribe a calcium supplement.

Also important to bone health is vitamin D, which your body manufactures from sunlight. Vitamin D helps your body absorb calcium. But your vitamin D levels may be low if you live in the northern part of the country, where late fall, winter, and early spring sunlight is weak. Vitamin D is found in fortified milk, eggs, liver, and some kinds of fish. You should talk to your doctor about a vitamin D supplement if you are not often exposed to the sun and you don't eat foods that contain vitamin D.

Hormone replacement therapy at menopause provides the greatest protection against osteoporosis because bone loss speeds up when estrogen production falls. Nonhormonal medication to treat osteoporosis is also available. If you are a postmenopausal woman, work with your doctor to plan the combination of diet, exercise, medication, and calcium supplementation that is best for you.

The senior years

Your metabolism drops by about 10 percent per decade after age 50 and your calorie needs go down as well. But your vitamin and mineral requirements remain the same; they may even go up, as in the case of calcium. That's why you need to choose foods that deliver the most nutrition bang for your bite.

Sound eating habits can be a challenge if physical conditions like arthritis, diminished eye sight, tooth loss or ill-fitting dentures, a deteriorating sense of taste and smell, food intolerances, and appetite loss make eating difficult and less enjoyable. For some people,

Osteoporosis Risk Factors

- ◆ Being female
- ◆ Having a family history of osteoporosis
- ◆ Early menopause without estrogen replacement therapy
- ◆ Being inactive
- ◆ Not consuming sufficient amounts of calcium
- ◆ Drinking excessive amounts of alcohol
- ◆ Extreme dieting or overexercising
- ◆ Being slender
- ◆ Smoking
- ◆ Having a fair complexion

loneliness, grief, boredom, and feelings of isolation make mealtime a low priority. Limited finances sometimes affect food choices. Medications can also interfere with appetite and food tolerance.

Older people can take advantage of local community programs to manage these common problems. Senior centers offer low-cost meals and fellowship and senior volunteer programs often cover expenses such as meals. Home-delivered meals can improve the nutrition of older people who are homebound, while food stamps can help low-income seniors. Churches and adult day care offer additional options. Ask your doctor or pharmacist whether the drugs you are taking can interact with any foods. Talk to a dietitian at a local hospital or senior center about simple meal and nutrition planning.

People with special nutritional needs

Some people—athletes, vegetarians, smokers—may have unique nutritional needs. They should plan their diets carefully to make sure they are getting all the nutrients they need for good health.

Athletes

Athletes need more calories than less active people. In fact, endurance athletes may require more than 5,000 calories per day. High-calorie snacks and beverages can supplement a basic, balanced diet.

The practice of "carbohydrate loading" has become popular among runners and other endurance athletes but extreme forms of the practice, combined with exercising to exhaustion, can cause muscle damage and may affect your kidney function. Unless you are exercising at Olympic levels, carbohydrate loading is of little benefit.

Many high-school athletes, weight lifters, and bodybuilders believe that they need more protein than less active people. But, although their protein requirements may be slightly higher, such athletes can more than meet them by eating more food overall. Protein supplements and excessive amounts of high-protein foods do not build extra muscle.

An athlete needs adequate fluids before, during, and after any workout or athletic event. Drink plenty of fluids before a competition, 4 to 8 ounces at 15-minute intervals during a competition, and at least 8 ounces every half hour for a couple of hours afterward. One way to find out how much water you should drink after an athletic event is to step on a scale before and after. For every pound you lost, you should drink 2 cups of fluid.

Water is the best choice, but many athletes prefer to drink sports beverages. Sports drinks are easily absorbed and replenish the sodium, potassium, and other minerals lost in perspiration during intense exercise. It is debatable whether these beverages benefit anyone other than athletes exercising continuously for over an hour or in hot temperatures. But their flavor is appealing and their slight saltiness may increase thirst, prompting an athlete to drink more.

Children can become so caught up in athletics that they forget to drink fluids. They can become dehydrated faster than adults because they have a proportionally large skin surface area. Encouraging young athletes to become dehydrated so they can qualify for a lower weight class in wrestling or other sports is extremely dangerous. Young athletes also need to get enough calories to both support their growth and to supply energy for their activities.

Sports anemia occurs often in runners and other endurance athletes. One reason is that the athlete's increased blood volume lowers the concentration of iron in the blood. Iron supplements usually are not necessary as long as the athlete eats a balanced diet. But, if you feel unusually tired—one of the symptoms of anemia—you should see your doctor.

Some athletes take certain vitamins, minerals, and other compounds touted for their supposed ability to improve athletic performance. None has been proven to be effective in people eating an adequate diet

Vegetarians

A well-planned vegetarian diet can supply all the nutrients that you need. In fact, some studies show that vegetarians are less likely to develop heart disease, high blood pressure, and obesity than people who eat meat. But because animal protein is a major source of iron, vitamin B_{12}, vitamin D, calcium, zinc, and other essential vitamins and minerals, vegetarians are at greater risk of deficiencies of these nutrients than are meat eaters.

People can practice vegetarianism at three levels of strictness: ovolactovegetarianism, lactovegetarianism, and veganism. Ovolacto is the least restrictive level—eggs and dairy products are included in the diet, along with plant foods. Planning a nutritionally adequate ovolacto diet is relatively easy because eggs and dairy foods supply many essential nutrients. But you should realize that an ovolacto diet that incorporates a lot of full-fat dairy products can be higher in calories, fat, saturated fat, and cholesterol than a diet that contains meat. Lactovegetarians consume dairy products, along with foods of plant origin, but not eggs. The exclusion of eggs eliminates a source of easily absorbed iron and zinc. A vegan diet excludes all animal foods, even eggs and dairy products. Such a diet lacks vitamin B_{12}, which is present only in animal foods, and can also be deficient in iron, calcium, and vitamin D. Vegans may benefit from taking vitamin B_{12} supplements.

The diets of children who are vegetarians require careful planning. Vegetable- and grain-based foods can fill your child up without supplying adequate calories for normal growth and development. Children who are vegans must rely on fortified soy milk, tofu, leafy greens, or other nondairy foods for calcium. Foods that supply iron—dried peas and beans, enriched cereals and grain products, leafy greens, and nuts—should be a daily part of your child's vegetarian diet. Tell your pediatrician if your child is on a vegetarian diet so that he or she can monitor your child's growth and health.

This same need for careful planning applies to pregnant and breast-feeding women, athletes (because of their increased need for calories), and older adults who consume a vegetarian diet.

Smokers

Aside from its other extremely harmful effects, cigarette smoking can lower blood levels of vitamin C and may also depress levels of other vitamins in your body. Stopping smoking is one of the most important steps you can take to improve your health.

THE HEALTHY GROCERY CART

Getting to know your grocery store is essential for a health-conscious shopper. You should become familiar with the location of the foods you buy and know what foods are stocked in the greatest variety. Always read labels (see page 16) to locate the best nutrition picks. Most importantly, make a shopping list to make sure you get what you need to eat healthfully all week long.

Shopping by the Pyramid

Use the Food Guide Pyramid (see page 12) to help you fill your grocery cart as well as plan your meals. A healthy shopping cart contains a balance of foods selected in Pyramid proportions: a multitude of grain foods, vegetables, and fruits; a moderate amount of dairy and protein foods; and only a small number of foods that are high in fat, sugar, or salt.

Shopping for freshness and safety

Careful shopping can ensure that the foods you select are as fresh as possible. Pay attention to expiration dates, particularly on perishables such as packaged vegetables, dairy items, packaged meats, poultry, eggs, and frozen foods. Items with the latest expiration dates are usually at the back or bottom of the case, where they stay the coldest and foods stay fresher longer. Purchase only as much as you and your family can consume before the expiration date.

The "fresh" designation on poultry and fish does not guarantee that they have not been frozen and defrosted. The law allows poultry and fish to be held at 32 degrees and still be called "fresh." Unless you are certain that your purchase is fresh, avoid refreezing it because its quality will be affected.

Bringing Home Fresh Foods

- ◆ Keep packages of raw meat and poultry away from other foods in the grocery cart and have them bagged separately to prevent raw juices, which contain bacteria, from contaminating other foods.
- ◆ Buy uncracked eggs that have been kept at a temperature no higher than 45 degrees Fahrenheit.
- ◆ Avoid dented cans, which may have a pinhole opening that allows bacteria to enter the can. Swollen cans could be a sign of contamination with a toxin that can cause botulism, a potentially fatal form of food poisoning.
- ◆ Select jars with a depressed safety "button" on the lid. If the safety button has popped up, the vacuum seal on the jar has been broken.
- ◆ Avoid most moldy foods, with the exception of some salamis and certain cheeses. You can cut mold away from hard cheeses, but do not touch the knife surface to the mold. Avoid all other cheeses with visible mold, except those where mold is expected, like Roquefort and blue.

Plan your shopping so that you buy perishables last to minimize the time they spend out of refrigeration. Bring fresh foods home immediately or store them in a cooler in the car if you can't return home right away.

Even the most health-conscious shoppers will bring home some processed foods, to supplement the whole foods in their diet. The most common methods of processing foods include canning, bottling, and milling. Processed foods can differ greatly from fresh foods and usually are packaged with added ingredients.

Commercial canning prevents food spoilage by heating the food at temperatures high enough to kill bacteria. No preservatives are needed. Canned foods can be kept safely for at least 2 years without a loss of nutrients or taste if stored in a cool, dry place, such as a pantry.

Processed foods, especially packaged main dishes, side dishes, and convenience foods, can be high in fat. Check the ingredient list on the label for high-fat ingredients and buy foods that have fats low on the list. The nutrition facts panel (see page 16) can help you figure out how much fat you will get in one serving, compared to your daily value.

Processed foods may also be high in sodium and sugar. Sodium watchers should buy mainly fresh foods. Packaged items with less sodium are usually labeled "reduced sodium," "light in sodium," or "low sodium." When you buy products that are not low in sodium, compare labels to identify brands with the least amount of sodium and select items with salt- or sodium-containing ingredients farthest down on the ingredient list. To find out how much sugar a packaged food contains, check for sugar and other sweeteners like corn syrup on the ingredient list. The nutrition facts panel lists every food's sugar content; 4 grams equals 1 teaspoon of sugar.

THE HEALTHY KITCHEN

A healthy kitchen is characterized by more than just good food—it also includes proper storage, safe food handling, and cleanliness.

Storing perishables

Meat, poultry, fish, dairy foods, and fresh fruits and vegetables deteriorate rapidly if not handled properly. When you bring these items home from the supermarket, refrigerate or freeze them as soon as possible. At room temperature or in a warm trunk, quality suffers and harmful bacteria can proliferate.

Adequate refrigerator and freezer temperatures maintain top food quality. Keep your refrigerator temperatures below 40 degrees Fahrenheit to retard bacterial growth. Bacteria in frozen foods may survive but do not grow or proliferate at a freezer temperature of 0 degrees Fahrenheit or below.

Certain foods require special handling. Store eggs in their carton on a shelf in the refrigerator. The temperature of the egg section on your refrigerator door fluctuates when you repeatedly open and close the door and may become too warm. Fresh fruits can remain unrefrigerated until they are ripe; refrigeration slows further ripening and retards spoilage. Store refrigerated fruits and vegetables unwashed—with a few exceptions, they spoil more rapidly if washed and then refrigerated. Rinse lettuce and other greens to remove dirt and insects, then dry and store them loosely in a bag in the refrigerator. Tomatoes do not need to be refrigerated. Bread keeps best at room temperature, if eaten within a couple of days. Otherwise, store it in the freezer. Refrigeration dries out bread.

Refrigerating Foods

Food	Use Within
Fresh fruit	3 to 7 days, depending on the fruit
Lettuce and leafy greens	5 days
Root vegetables (beets, carrots, radishes, turnips)	2 weeks
Hard cheese	1 month
Milk	1 week after opening
Uncooked meat, poultry, and fish	2 days
Eggs	1 to 3 weeks (check expiration date)

Stocking staples

Keep plenty of staple ingredients on hand so that you can put healthy meals together in a snap. Periodically check the expiration dates of dry packaged foods and discard any that are stale or past their expiration date.

Stock items from this handy checklist of kitchen staples. Be sure to add them to your shopping list as they run out.

Bread, cereal, rice, and pasta group

- Whole-grain breads (keep a loaf or two in the freezer)
- Dried pasta of all shapes and sizes
- Rice (brown, white, long grain, arborio)
- Grains (bulgur, couscous, barley, cornmeal)
- Ready-to-eat and hot cereals

Vegetable group

- Vegetables that keep a long time (onions, garlic, shallots, potatoes, root vegetables)
- Frozen vegetables (peas, corn kernels, mixed vegetables, greens)
- Canned tomatoes (whole, crushed, diced, stewed, sauces, pastes)
- Sun-dried tomatoes
- Dried mushrooms

Fruit group

- Fruits canned in water or juice
- Bottled, canned, or frozen fruit juices
- Frozen berries
- Dried fruit

Milk, yogurt, and cheese group

- Milk (fresh, powdered, canned)
- Reduced-fat hard cheeses for the freezer
- A well-wrapped chunk of imported Parmesan to keep in the refrigerator

Meat, poultry, fish, dry beans, eggs, and nuts group

- Lean beef, pork, veal, and poultry for the freezer
- Water-packed tuna, salmon, and sardines
- Beans (canned, dry)
- Peanut butter
- A variety of nuts

Fats, oils, and sweets group

- Cooking oil in a neutral flavor
- Olive oil
- Flavorful oils (walnut, hazelnut)
- Butter and margarine
- Sugar, honey, and other sweeteners
- Nonstick cooking oil spray

Seasonings, condiments, and baking ingredients

- Broths (low-sodium chicken, beef, vegetable)
- Vinegars (red and white wine, balsamic, cider, rice, herb infused)
- Mustards (regular yellow, grainy, Dijon, mustard powder)
- Pickles, olives, and hot sauces
- Baking ingredients, including all-purpose, whole-wheat, whole-grain flours; white and brown sugar, molasses, maple syrup; baking powder and baking soda; vanilla and other extracts

Using herbs and spices

Herbs and spices enhance the flavor of foods and can help make up for lower amounts of fat or sugar. Fresh herbs such as parsley, dill, and basil add a light, delicate flavor. They are generally less potent than dried herbs and taste quite different. Fresh herbs are most commonly added at the end of a recipe, while dried herbs are cooked with other recipe ingredients.

Cooking with Herbs and Spices

When Preparing:	Try One or More of These Herbs and Spices:
Bread	Caraway, oregano, poppy seeds, thyme
Fruit	Cinnamon, cloves, ginger, mint
Vegetables	Basil, chives, dill, parsley
Salads	Basil, chives, garlic, tarragon
Soups	Bay leaves, marjoram, rosemary, tarragon
Beef	Chives, cumin, garlic, rosemary
Pork	Coriander seeds, cumin, ginger, sage
Poultry	Garlic, oregano, rosemary, sage
Fish	Chervil, dill, tarragon, thyme

Look for fresh herbs in your supermarket, at a produce store, or in the refrigerator case of a gourmet shop. Parsley, basil, and chives are easy to grow on a sunny windowsill or in a garden. When a recipe calls for fresh herbs but you have to substitute dried, use about one third the amount that you would use if the herbs were fresh. For example, you could replace 1 tablespoon of fresh oregano with 1 teaspoon of dried. Crushing or crumbling dried herbs helps release their flavor.

The most useful savory herbs to stock in your cupboard include oregano, basil, thyme, rosemary, and sage. The most popular sweet spices are cinnamon, nutmeg, cloves, and allspice. You will need a more varied spice supply to create your favorite ethnic and international recipes.

Keep bottled herbs in a cool, dark place because light can shorten their shelf life. Buy dried herbs and spices in small amounts; many lose their flavor after about a year. Smell herbs and spices before you use them to check for freshness.

Safe food handling

Safe food handling begins at the grocery store and does not end until the last leftovers are finished because at every step you need to minimize the risks of contamination and spoilage. You may not be able to detect food that has become contaminated with bacteria;

you could eat some without realizing it. Food that has spoiled is easier to detect; it looks, smells, and tastes bad. When in doubt, throw it out.

Preventing food contamination

Many people who think they have "stomach flu" never realize that food poisoning is to blame for their symptoms. The most common causes of food poisoning are contamination of foods from other foods, such as uncooked meats, poultry, or eggs touching cooked foods; undercooking meats, poultry, or eggs; poor handwashing; and leaving either cooked or uncooked foods out at room temperature when they should be either refrigerated or frozen or kept hot (for instance, at a buffet table or a cafeteria).

Cleanliness is extremely important. Always wash your hands thoroughly before preparing food. Make sure that your cutting boards are clean and that you do not use a board used for cutting meat and poultry for other foods. Poultry is a major source of salmonella. After handling poultry, wash all cutting surfaces, knives, the kitchen sink (if you rinsed the poultry before cooking), and your hands with hot, soapy water.

Store raw meat for no more than 3 to 5 days and poultry for no more than 2 days. Separate all uncooked meat, poultry, and fish from other items in the refrigerator.

The refrigerator is the safest place to defrost foods because it maintains a temperature that is cold enough to keep bacteria from growing. Allow at least 12 to 24 hours to defrost foods. If time is short, use the microwave to defrost the food and then cook it immediately.

Know when to discard foods. Don't refreeze frozen foods that have been defrosted (with the exception of bread); you must either eat them promptly or throw them away. Don't eat foods that have an offensive smell or that are off-color. Cans that bulge or hiss and spurt out their contents when you open them may be contaminated and cause botulism, although some hissing may occur if a can has been vacuum sealed.

Do not eat raw or undercooked beef, chicken, fish, or eggs—they may harbor harmful bacteria. You must cook these foods at temperatures above 140 degrees Fahrenheit to kill the bacteria. (Raw fish from a sushi restaurant may also be harmful; make sure the restaurant is reputable.) Remember that bacteria can proliferate after cooking if the food is held for too long at temperatures above 40 degrees Fahrenheit. Cook eggs until the whites are set and the yolks thicken to ensure that any bacteria are killed.

Refrigerate cooked foods as soon as possible after a meal. Transfer them to a shallow pan to cool more rapidly. Eat leftovers within 2 or 3 days, or store them in the freezer.

Leftovers to be stored in the freezer should be wrapped well and frozen quickly, in a freezer kept at 0 degrees. When you reheat foods in the microwave, stir them often to distribute the heat evenly and to ensure that all of the food is hot before serving.

For additional information on food safety, call the USDA Meat and Poultry Hotline at 1-800-535-4555, the American Dietetic Association Consumer Nutritional Hotline at 1-800-366-1655, or your county Cooperative Extension office (see your phone book or call directory assistance).

THE HEALTHY TABLE

How do you set a healthy table? Start with a well-planned menu that combines dishes in an appealing and nutritionally balanced way. Choose quality ingredients. Follow the rules of safe food handling. Present the food in an attractive way. And allow enough time to taste and enjoy every bite.

The social aspects of food

Meals eaten in the company of family or friends supply much more than just nutrition. Social meals communicate cultural, ethnic, and family customs. Children learn about food and table manners through the examples set by their parents. Even such subtle learning as how much to eat and when to stop gets transmitted during social meals. Healthy food and healthy eating habits are learned from others.

If you have young children at home, involve them in cooking from an early age. Young children can handle simple tasks, such as rinsing and tearing lettuce. As your child gets older, delegate harder but still age-appropriate jobs—cutting fruit with a plastic knife for fruit salad, stirring together cookie ingredients, making sandwiches. The kitchen can become a family learning center where you can teach lessons on food, nutrition, science, math, and history.

Planning healthy meals

Don't judge your eating habits by one food, one meal, or even one day. What counts is the way that you balance what you eat over the course of a week, a month, a year, or even a lifetime. Successful meal planning includes variety while keeping the overall diet within the guidelines of healthy eating.

Pair dishes from the different food groups to make up a complete meal. Make foods from the grain group the foundation of your meal. Build on that foundation by combining bread, rice, or pasta with foods from other food groups. For example, serve Buckwheat Buttermilk Silver Dollar Pancakes (page 139) with yogurt and an assortment of fruit. Pair the Contemporary Club Sandwich (page 174), layered atop slices of Super Sandwich Bread (page 114), with Shredded Carrot, Jicama, and Currant Slaw (page 96). Dinner can include something like Spicy Mixed Bean Soup with Turkey Sausage (page 162) accompanied by Yogurt Corn Bread (page 125).

Many families fall back on the same foods and dishes every week. Think variety when you plan your menus. Seasonal recipes, like Garden Patch Gazpacho (page 144), offer an opportunity to use ingredients you can get only during a particular time of year. Leave blanks in your menu and on your shopping list so you can fill in with those fruits, vegetables, and other items that look most appealing once you get to the store.

Moderate your intake of calories, fat, sugar, and salt by making meal-to-meal trade-offs. If you choose to spend more calories on a large Sunday brunch of Light-and-Easy Turkey Tetrazzini (page 212) and Orange Marmalade–Glazed Cheesecake (page 464), eat a dinner that's smaller than usual and centered on fresh fruits, vegetables, and grains. A dish that is somewhat high in fat—Shrimp and Tofu Pad Thai (page 240) or Antipasto Pan Pizza (page 197)—can be offset by low-fat selections at the same meal or during the same day. Balancing your fat, sugar, or salt budget does not have to be a daily requirement, but too many days of excess will take their toll on your diet and eventually on your health.

Healthy cooking from the pantry and freezer

A thoughtfully stocked kitchen makes it easier to eat healthfully. A busy person rushing to get dinner on the table after work is less apt to turn to take-out food (which may be loaded with sodium and fat) if the kitchen is stocked with healthy foods that can be turned into a simple, quick meal. For example, quick-cooking brown rice tossed with colorful frozen stir-fry vegetables and slivers of cooked turkey combine to produce Turkey Stir-Fry with Ginger and Mint (page 342). A can of salmon, some cooked dried pasta, and diced vegetables mixed with reduced-fat mayonnaise become Seashell Macaroni and Salmon Salad (page 90) in no time. For the exotic Cuban Black Beans and Rice (page 299), canned black beans get zip from garlic and other seasonings, are simmered for a few minutes, and then get ladled over rice.

Make good use of your freezer. Package and freeze leftovers in convenient portion sizes for later use (for the best flavor, use within 3 to 6 months). You can freeze breads and baked goods up to 2 months. However, after 1 month, some items—especially those low in fat—

can dry out and pick up an unpleasant "frozen" flavor. Raw meat can remain frozen for up to 6 months.

Keep a supply of freezer containers so you can turn a family recipe into meals for one or two. Making a double recipe saves cooking time later. It's a good way to stock your freezer for those times when you're not in the mood to cook. Fill containers soon after cooking, and freeze immediately. Label your freezer containers with the name of the dish and the date it was cooked. Frozen dishes should be eaten within a few months. Salads and other recipes made with fresh fruits and vegetables or with dressing do not withstand freezing. Make only half if you cannot eat the full recipe within 1 to 2 days.

Healthy cooking tips

Any dish can fit into a healthy diet, but some recipes fit more easily than others. Recipes that call for the right-sized portions of key ingredients take the guesswork out of portion sizing. For example, Greek Chicken, Artichokes, and Brown Rice (page 269) includes 3 ounces of cooked chicken per person, the per-meal protein portion suggested in the Food Guide Pyramid.

When updating your own favorite recipes at home, change ingredients to make the dishes more healthful. For example, use ground turkey or chicken in place of ground beef to lower the total fat and saturated fat content of a dish.

When adjusting recipes, replace some of the fat with a bit of additional liquid, such as broth or fruit juice. You can defat commercial broth and stock (page 142) with no sacrifice in flavor. Sauté onions or garlic in just a tiny amount of oil, or steam them in a little broth or water to release their flavor before adding other ingredients. Keep in mind that fat carries flavor, so, when you reduce it, you must amplify the other flavors. Be extra generous with garlic, onions, citrus juices and peels, herbs and spices, hot peppers, ginger, vinegars, and mustards.

Recipes for baked goods, such as quick breads and cakes, are harder to adapt because their success depends on a precise and balanced formula. Some of the recipes in this book have been developed and tested as low-fat recipes. To modify your own favorite recipes from other sources, try reducing the amount of fat by up to one third, then add a bit more liquid in the form of skim milk, skim buttermilk, or applesauce. If you want to lower the cholesterol in baked goods, replace half of the eggs with egg whites—instead of two eggs, use one whole egg and one egg white.

Lower-fat substitutions

With the abundance of reduced-fat and fat-free products on the market, you could find a substitute for almost any fat-containing food or ingredient you eat but you would end up getting rid of most of the taste. The lower-fat substitutions in the box below work well in many recipes.

Low-Fat Substitutions for Common Ingredients

Substitute:	For:
Reduced-fat mayonnaise	Regular mayonnaise
Canned broth with the fat skimmed off	Broth straight from the can
Low-fat or nonfat yogurt in dips and as a topping	Sour cream
Whole, low-fat, or skim milk	Cream or half-and-half
Reduced-fat Cheddar, Swiss, Monterey Jack, or other hard cheeses	Full-fat hard cheese
Part-skim ricotta or mozzarella cheeses	Whole-milk ricotta or mozzarella
Light cream cheese	Regular cream cheese

Keep trying low-fat or fat-free products to find the brands you like best. Foods with fat replacements are also available. Manufacturers are developing new ways all the time to deliver taste and texture without fat.

Now it's time to put the basics of healthful eating into practice by trying the recipes presented in the following chapters. Choose from more than 350 delicious main-course and side-dish recipes that showcase grains, vegetables, and fruits, along with lean meats and other protein sources in proportions recommended by the Food Guide Pyramid. Tasty and versatile dishes, such as Pasta with Lightened Pesto Sauce (page 208) and Turkey and White Bean Chili Verde (page 314), will nourish your family members and satisfy their taste for something new. Desserts like Updated Old-Fashioned Chocolate Pudding (page 468) are smooth, rich, and nutritious without being high in fat. Once you sample these recipes, you'll find that eating a healthy, balanced diet can be easier and more enjoyable than you think.

CHAPTER ONE

Appetizers and Snacks

The sight, aroma, and first taste of an appetizer rank among the most pleasurable aspects of eating a meal. Your mouth waters in anticipation of the variety of tastes and textures to come. You experience a clarity of flavor unlike that of any other course because foods taste best when you are most hungry. Appetizers are meant to be delicious treats that whet your appetite and ready your body for the meal that follows.

But appetizers have a well-founded reputation for being extremely high in fat. It's difficult to find low-fat appetizers on the traditional list of chips and dips, nuts, pastry-wrapped meats, and cheeses. One or two small, high-fat nibbles might not affect your overall fat intake much, but you have to decide whether more than one or two are worth the significant fat "budgeting" required to fit them into a healthful eating pattern.

The tasty array of American and international favorites in this chapter present a new world of healthy yet delicious appetizers that are lower in fat and calories than traditional appetizers. Tortilla chips, pita wedges, and potato skins are baked to a crisp instead of fried. Dips like the Herbed Cheese Dip (page 53) and Chile con Queso (page 58) have shed many of their high-fat ingredients while retaining the seasoning that makes their flavors distinct. Buffalo Chicken Strips (page 56) feature broiled pieces of skinless chicken breast, instead of fried chicken wings, and are dipped in a lightened-up but piquant blue cheese dressing.

Nutrient-packed, flavorful ingredients abound in this chapter's recipes. Low-fat yogurt serves as a tangy, smooth, and higher-calcium alternative to sour cream or mayonnaise. Legumes like white beans and chickpeas impart a rich taste while providing lots of fiber and vitamins. Olives, peanut butter, sesame paste, and other higher-fat ingredients, used in moderate amounts, enhance flavor without adding too much fat.

When you plan a meal that includes appetizers, balance your appetizer selections with the meal that will follow. For example, vegetable-based appetizers like Tomatillo Salsa (page 62) served with a raw vegetable platter or Pickled Vegetable Medley (page 68) are ideal starters for a large or heavy meal. Appetizers that feature ingredients from the protein group—Grilled Chicken Satay (page 65) or Sweet Red Pepper Hummus (page 71)—can be paired with main courses that have smaller protein portions, like meatless soups or vegetable-based stews. This thoughtful planning helps balance an entire meal so you can serve your family or guests a variety of foods that both taste good and follow the principles of healthful eating.

Parents may cringe at the thought of children making a meal out of high-fat appetizers like fried zucchini, stuffed potato skins, and tortilla chips topped with melted cheese. Yet, if chosen wisely, appetizers like the ones in this chapter make terrific meals for children. Appetizers are just the right portion size for kids, can be eaten with the fingers, and come in appealingly bright colors. To create an all-appetizer children's meal, include as many food groups as possible, create a palette of food colors for maximum nutritional value, and select appetizers that are not too highly seasoned. Baked Herbed Pita Crisps (page 61), White Bean "Pesto" with Garden Vegetables (page 70), and any of the chips also make tasty snacks for kids—and adults.

Travel the new world of appetizers. Whether you choose Mexican, Italian, Mediterranean, or American, you'll broaden your experience—but not your waistline.

Mini Pita Pizza Wedges

Makes 8 servings

Pita, the traditional Middle Eastern flatbread, makes a terrific base for these colorful, vegetable-strewn mini pizzas. They're simple enough for a weeknight family snack and festive enough for a sophisticated party.

2 tablespoons extra-virgin olive oil	1 small red onion, thinly sliced
1 garlic clove, finely chopped	1 small yellow bell pepper, seeded
1/4 teaspoon salt	and thinly sliced
1/8 teaspoon cayenne pepper	1/4 cup slivered fresh basil or
4 whole-wheat or white pitas,	2 teaspoons dried
6 to 7 inches in diameter	4 teaspoons grated Parmesan
3 medium plum tomatoes, very	cheese
thinly sliced	

1. In a small bowl, combine the oil, garlic, salt, and cayenne. Set aside and let steep for 10 minutes.

2. Using a sharp knife, split the pitas all the way around the perimeter. Place the pitas cut side up on two baking sheets. Arrange the sliced tomatoes, onion, and bell pepper on the cut pitas and sprinkle with the basil. (The ingredients in this recipe can be prepared up to this point several hours ahead. Cover and refrigerate.)

3. Preheat the broiler. Dip a small brush in the oil and drizzle over the pita halves. Sprinkle with the cheese.

4. Broil about 5 inches from the heat source, until the pitas are lightly toasted and the vegetables slightly charred, 1 to 2 minutes.

5. Cut each round into 6 wedges, arrange on a platter, and serve warm.

◆ *PER SERVING: About 138 cals, 43 cals from fat, 5g total fat, 1g sat fat, 1mg chol, 258mg sodium, 21g total carbs, 0g fiber, 4g prot*

HOW TO CRUSH A GARLIC CLOVE

First, separate an individual clove from the bulb of garlic. Put the clove on a cutting board and place the flat side of a broad chef's knife blade over the garlic clove. Lean on the blade with the heel of your hand to crush the clove. (Be sure you use a knife with a blade wide enough so you will not cut yourself.) The skin of the garlic will separate from the flesh and you can easily slip it off. Use the crushed clove as is (to flavor the oil for the Mini Pita Pizza Wedges, for example) or chop as needed.

Herbed Cheese Dip and Crudité Color Wheel

Makes 2 cups (about 12 servings)

The contrasting colors and shapes of vegetables on a platter make a gorgeous crudité color wheel. Feel free to substitute whatever vegetables look freshest for any of those in this recipe. A wider variety of color usually means a wider variety of vitamins and minerals.

Herbed Cottage Cheese Dip:

2 cups low-fat (1 percent) cottage cheese

3 tablespoons reduced-fat mayonnaise

1 tablespoon coarse Dijon mustard

1 tablespoon fresh lemon juice

½ cup chopped scallions

2 tablespoons chopped parsley, preferably flat leaf, plus 1 tablespoon

½ teaspoon salt

⅛ teaspoon black pepper

Crudité Color Wheel:

4 carrots, peeled and cut into sticks

2 large celery ribs, cut into sticks

1 red bell pepper, seeded and cut into strips

1 yellow bell pepper, seeded and cut into strips

2 small zucchini, cut into diagonal slices

1 cucumber, cut into sticks or slices

1. For the dip, combine the cottage cheese, mayonnaise, mustard, and lemon juice in a food processor or blender. Process, using short pulses, until the mixture is smooth, scraping down the bowl once if necessary.

2. Transfer to a medium mixing bowl and stir in the scallions, 2 tablespoons of the parsley, and salt and pepper. Cover and refrigerate for at least 15 minutes.

3. Before serving, sprinkle with the remaining 1 tablespoon of parsley.

4. Place the bowl of dip in the center of a platter. Arrange the vegetables around the dip like the spokes of a wheel.

◆ *PER SERVING: About 67 cals, 17 cals from fat, 2g total fat, 1g sat fat, 2mg chol, 320 mg sodium, 7g total carbs, 1g fiber, 6g prot*

DO-AHEAD CRUDITÉS

Crudités are fresh, raw, cut-up vegetables usually served with some type of dipping sauce. Vegetables taste and look freshest and retain their nutritional value best if they're cut up shortly before serving. When you need to prepare them ahead of time, keep the vegetables crisp by wrapping them in damp paper towels. Put the vegetables in sealable plastic bags and store them in the refrigerator for up to 6 hours.

Smoked Salmon Yogurt Cheese Dip with Winter Crudités

Makes 1 cup (about 6 servings)

Yogurt that has been strained overnight produces a thick, rich, tangy, yogurt "cheese," which makes a delicious base for a variety of spreads and dips that have less fat and calories (but more calcium) than those made with sour cream or mayonnaise. Here, the yogurt cheese is enhanced with just a bit of potently flavored chopped smoked salmon, enlivened with fresh dill, and served with a selection of green and white winter vegetables.

Smoked Salmon Yogurt Cheese Dip:

2 cups low-fat or nonfat plain yogurt

2 ounces smoked salmon

2 teaspoons fresh lemon juice

½ teaspoon grated lemon peel

½ teaspoon Dijon mustard

1½ tablespoons chopped fresh dill
  or 1½ teaspoons dried

⅛ teaspoon black pepper

Dill sprigs for garnish

Winter Crudités:

2 cups broccoli florets

2 cups small brussels sprouts

1 head fennel, cut in strips

2 small white turnips, peeled and cut into thin slices

1. Line a large strainer with a double layer of dampened cheesecloth. Spoon in the yogurt, place the strainer over a bowl, and refrigerate, loosely covered, for about 6 hours

or overnight. (Alternatively, strain the yogurt through a coffee filter set over a bowl or through a yogurt strainer available in specialty shops.) Discard the liquid (the whey) left in the bowl. You should have about 1 cup of yogurt cheese.

2. Using a food processor, finely chop the smoked salmon. Add the yogurt cheese, lemon juice, lemon peel, and mustard and process until well mixed. Stir in the dill and pepper. Or use a large knife to finely chop the smoked salmon and combine with the remaining dip ingredients in a medium mixing bowl. (This recipe can be prepared to this point 2 days ahead. Cover and refrigerate.)

3. Blanch the broccoli in a large pot of lightly salted boiling water until crisp-tender, 3 to 4 minutes. Remove with a slotted spoon and transfer immediately to a bowl of cold water to stop the cooking and set the color. Drain well on paper towels. Cook the brussels sprouts in the same pot of water until just tender, 7 to 9 minutes. Drain in a colander and rinse under cold water. Drain well on paper towels. Use immediately or wrap in dry paper towels and store in plastic bags in the refrigerator (up to 6 hours).

4. Spoon the dip into a decorative bowl and garnish with the dill sprigs. Serve surrounded by the vegetables.

◆ *PER SERVING: About 114 cals, 19 cals from fat, 2g total fat, 1g sat fat, 7mg chol, 191mg sodium, 18g total carbs, 4g fiber, 10g prot*

LOWER-FAT CHEESE SNACK CHOICES

Cheese is an excellent source of calcium and it can make a healthful addition to a snack platter. Some of the best naturally lower-fat cheeses are French-style goat cheese (except the dry, concentrated crottins, which are higher in fat) and Greek feta cheese made from sheep's milk. Part-skim cheeses, such as mozzarella and ricotta, and Neufchâtel (a reduced-fat cream cheese) are also excellent choices. Some types of cheddar and Monterey Jack cheeses are now available in reduced-fat versions. They generally contain one-third less fat than regular cheese. When including cheese as part of a snack platter, figure on a portion of about 1 ounce per person. Be sure to offer it with a variety of other snacks so that people have plenty to eat besides just cheese.

Buffalo Chicken Strips

Makes 6 servings

The legendary original recipe for Buffalo wings, concocted in 1964 in a bar near Buffalo, New York, was made with deep-fried chicken wings. This slimmed-down version calls for strips of lean boneless chicken breast quickly seared in a hot skillet and, like the original, is doused with liquid hot pepper sauce. The spiciness is tamed and cooled by the crunch of celery sticks and the rich taste of this lower-fat blue cheese dipping sauce.

Blue Cheese Dip:
- ⅔ cup nonfat plain yogurt
- 2 tablespoons reduced-fat mayonnaise
- 2 ounces crumbled blue cheese
- 3 tablespoons finely chopped scallions
- ¼ teaspoon coarsely ground black pepper

Chicken Strips and Celery Sticks:
- 1 teaspoon vegetable oil
- ½ pound skinless boneless chicken breasts, cut crosswise into ¼-inch strips
- ¼ teaspoon salt
- 2 teaspoons butter
- 1 tablespoon liquid hot pepper sauce
- 5 celery stalks, cut into 3-inch sticks

1. In a small bowl, whisk together the yogurt, mayonnaise, and blue cheese. Stir in the scallions and pepper and set aside while preparing the chicken. Cover and refrigerate. (This recipe can be made 1 day ahead to this point.)

2. Heat the oil in a large, preferably nonstick skillet. Season the chicken with the salt. Cook the chicken over medium-high heat, stirring frequently, until lightly browned and cooked through, 3 to 4 minutes. Remove the skillet from the heat. Add the butter and hot pepper sauce to the pan and swirl until the butter melts and the sauce coats the chicken.

3. Serve the chicken and celery sticks along with the blue cheese dip. Provide toothpicks for spearing the chicken and dipping it in the sauce.

◆ *PER SERVING: About 136 cals, 64 cals from fat, 7g total fat, 3g sat fat, 33mg chol, 363mg sodium, 5g total carbs, 0g fiber, 13g prot*

TO MAKE YOGURT

It's easy and economical to make your own yogurt, and you don't need any special equipment. Yogurt is a remarkably versatile addition to your diet. Not only is it an excellent replacement for higher-fat ingredients such as mayonnaise and sour cream in sauces, dips, and salad dressings, but it's also refreshing and delicious eaten on its own. The addition of nonfat dry milk to this recipe (to thicken the yogurt) actually boosts the yogurt's calcium content.

To make 1 quart of yogurt, combine 3½ cups of 1 percent or skim milk with ⅓ cup of nonfat dry milk in a heavy saucepan or double boiler. Heat, stirring frequently, until steam rises and the milk is scalded (about 160 degrees). Remove the milk from the heat, cover loosely, and cool to lukewarm (about 98 degrees). Whisk in 1 tablespoon of plain nonfat or low-fat yogurt and transfer to a covered container. Let the mixture rest in a warm place—either a turned-off oven with a pilot light or a cooler filled about halfway with warm tap water—for 6 hours, until thickened. For tangier yogurt, let rest 1 to 2 hours longer. Store in the refrigerator.

Pico de Gallo Salsa

Makes about 2 cups (about 6 servings)

This chunky salsa, which is a great source of vitamin C, makes a delicious appetizer served with Spicy Baked Tortilla Chips (page 61) or as a topping or condiment to all sorts of tacos or burritos. Jicama makes a wonderfully crunchy addition but, if you can't find it, use additional bell pepper, or even corn kernels.

¾ pound fresh plum tomatoes, seeded and finely diced (about 1½ cups)
½ cup finely diced yellow or green bell pepper
⅓ cup finely diced red onion
⅓ cup finely diced jicama
3 tablespoons chopped cilantro
1 garlic clove, finely chopped
1 tablespoon fresh lime juice
1 tablespoon defatted lower-sodium chicken broth
½ teaspoon salt
¼ teaspoon grated lime peel

In a mixing bowl, stir together all the ingredients. Refrigerate for at least 30 minutes (up to 6 hours) before using.

◆ *PER SERVING: About 42 cals, 3 cals from fat, 0g total fat, 0g sat fat, 0mg chol, 274mg sodium, 9g total carbs, 1g fiber, 2g prot*

Chile con Queso with Dippers

Makes 2¼ cups (about 8 servings)

This spicy, cheesy dip makes a festive party hors d'oeuvre. It looks spectacular in a chafing dish surrounded by Spicy Baked Tortilla Chips (page 61) and the vegetables.

Chile con Queso:

¾ cup chopped onion

1 garlic clove, finely chopped

1½ teaspoons chili powder

8 ounces reduced-fat cream cheese, such as Neufchâtel

1 can (4½ ounces) chopped green chiles, drained

½ cup dry white wine or water

1½ cups chopped fresh tomato

¼ teaspoon liquid hot pepper sauce, or to taste

Dippers:

4 carrots, peeled and cut in sticks

1 red bell pepper, seeded and cut in strips

1 green bell pepper, seeded and cut in strips

1 small jicama, peeled and sliced

1. In a large, preferably nonstick skillet, combine the chopped onion and 3 tablespoons water. Cover and cook over medium-low heat, stirring frequently, until the onion is softened, about 5 minutes. Add the garlic and chili powder and cook, stirring, until the chili powder is fragrant, about 1 minute.

2. Reduce the heat to low. Break the cream cheese into several chunks and add it, along with the green chiles and wine, to the skillet. Stir until the cheese melts and the mixture is smooth, about 5 minutes. Stir in the chopped tomato and season with the hot pepper sauce. (This recipe can be made 1 day ahead and refrigerated. Remelt by stirring it in a saucepan over low heat or by heating it in a microwave.)

3. Serve the dip warm, surrounded by chips and vegetables for dipping.

◆ *PER SERVING: About 122 cals, 48 cals from fat, 5g total fat, 3g sat fat, 10mg chol, 312mg sodium, 14g total carbs, 3g fiber, 5g prot*

SNACK MEALS FOR KIDS

As a change of pace, or on those evenings when a sit-down dinner isn't possible, create mini meals by setting out a selection of appealing appetizers and let the kids concoct their own supper.

Include some of the following choices: reduced-fat, multigrain crackers with Herbed Cheese Dip (page 53); plain yogurt; cut-up, fresh vegetables and fruits; small rice cakes; pretzels; raisins; pop-

corn; whole-grain and multigrain cereal; peanut butter; reduced-fat cheeses; reduced-fat chips; and skim milk. Suggest that the kids create "sundaes" by sprinkling cereal or fruit on top of yogurt.

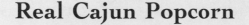

Real Cajun Popcorn

Makes 12 servings

If you order Cajun popcorn in New Orleans, you will get deep-fried crawfish tails. This recipe is more literal—it uses real popcorn tossed with peppery Cajun spices. The spices make this recipe a great adult party snack. For kids, try one of the other flavored toppings listed at the bottom of the page.

1 cup raw popcorn	½ teaspoon dried thyme
2 tablespoons vegetable oil	½ teaspoon dried oregano
1 teaspoon salt	½ teaspoon paprika
½ teaspoon garlic powder	¼ teaspoon black pepper
½ teaspoon ground cumin	¼ teaspoon cayenne pepper

1. Use a hot-air popper to pop the corn, then place the popcorn in a large bowl.

2. Heat the oil in a small saucepan. Add the salt and all of the spices, along with 1 tablespoon of water. Cook over medium heat, stirring, for 1 minute.

3. Drizzle the spice mixture over the warm popcorn and toss with your hands until the coating is evenly distributed. Serve warm.

◆ *PER SERVING: About 53 cals, 25 cals from fat, 3g total fat, 0g sat fat, 0mg chol, 178mg sodium, 7g total carbs, 0g fiber, 1g prot*

POPCORN BASICS

High in carbohydrates and relatively low in calories, popcorn makes a terrific snack for kids of all ages—unless it's drenched with high-fat toppings, including butter or margarine. Plain, unflavored kernels popped in a hot-air popper are the best choice and you can also control what goes on top. If you opt for bags of microwave popcorn or buy popcorn ready-made in the snack section of the supermarket, read the labels carefully and look for those marked reduced fat.

Looking for new ideas for popcorn flavorings? Adjust the Real Cajun Popcorn recipe as follows:

◆ Add a clove of minced fresh garlic to the oil and heat. Drizzle over the popcorn along with a sprinkle of salt.

◆ Stir a teaspoon of chili powder into the oil and heat as directed.

◆ Toss the popcorn with 1 tablespoon of grated Parmesan cheese.

◆ Add 1½ teaspoons of curry powder to the oil, heat as directed, and drizzle it over the corn. Sprinkle with salt.

Crispy Garlic Potato Skins

Makes 4 servings

Turns out that Mom was right, as usual. The skin of a potato is not only full of flavor, but also a source of nutrients such as vitamin C, fiber, and iron. Make these crispy snacks on a night when you're serving Fabulous Garlic Mashed Potatoes (page 419) in your dinner menu. This dish is great as is, but it can be served with a bowl of salsa for dipping.

Vegetable oil spray
2 tablespoons extra-virgin olive oil
1 garlic clove, very finely chopped
6 large (about 12 ounces each) russet potatoes
½ teaspoon dried oregano, crumbled
¼ teaspoon salt
¼ teaspoon freshly ground black pepper

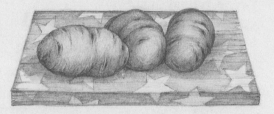

1. Preheat the oven to 425 degrees. Lightly coat two baking sheets with vegetable oil spray.

2. In a small bowl, combine the olive oil with the garlic.

3. Wash the potatoes. With a peeler or small sharp knife, remove large strips of skin from the potatoes approximately 2 inches long and ⅛ inch thick. (Use the potatoes for another dish such as mashed potatoes.) Arrange the skins on the baking sheet, white sides up. Brush with the garlic oil and sprinkle with the oregano, salt, and pepper.

4. Bake until golden and crisp around the edges, 18 to 20 minutes, and serve hot.

◆ *PER SERVING: About 110 cals, 62 cals from fat, 7g total fat, 1g sat fat, 0mg chol, 142mg sodium, 11g total carbs, 3g fiber, 2g prot*

TO ROAST GARLIC

Preheat the oven to 400 degrees. (A small toaster oven works well for this purpose.) Use a large knife to slice about ½ inch off the top of a head of garlic. Rub the excess papery skin off with your hands. Place the garlic on a small sheet of aluminum foil, sprinkle it with 2 teaspoons of water, and pinch the edges of the foil together to seal. Place the packet in the oven and roast for 45 to 60 minutes or until the cloves are very soft when pierced with the tip of a sharp knife. Unwrap the aluminum foil, let the garlic cool slightly, and squeeze the cloves out of their skins. Spread the mellow, buttery-soft flesh on small pieces of crusty bread as a tasty fat-free hors d'oeuvre or use as a flavor enhancer in soups, stews, sauces, and other recipes.

Baked Herbed Pita Crisps

Makes 4 servings

These crisps make great scoops for all kinds of dips but they are especially delicious with Sweet Red Pepper Hummus (page 71) and Spiced Baba Ghanouj (page 67).

Olive oil spray
2 whole-wheat pitas
   (6 to 7 inches in diameter)
1 teaspoon mixed dried herbs
   (such as oregano, basil, and

thyme) or Italian seasoning mix
¼ teaspoon salt
¼ teaspoon coarsely ground black
   pepper

1. Preheat the oven to 375 degrees. Coat a baking sheet with the olive oil spray.

2. With a sharp knife, cut around the perimeter of each pita, separate into two rounds, and cut each round into 8 triangles. Arrange, cut sides up, on the baking sheet. Spray with the olive oil spray and sprinkle with the herbs. Season with salt and pepper.

3. Bake in the preheated oven until the bread is crisp and golden, 5 to 7 minutes.

4. Serve warm or at room temperature. (The crisps can be stored in a plastic bag at room temperature for 1 day. To recrisp, heat in a 350-degree oven for about 5 minutes.)

◆ *PER SERVING: About 86 cals, 8 cals from fat, 1g total fat, 0g sat fat, 0mg chol, 303 mg sodium, 18g total carbs, 0g fiber, 3g prot*

Spicy Baked Tortilla Chips

Makes 4 servings

A sprinkle of chili powder adds color and zing to these chips. If they're served with a dip or salsa with plenty of its own heat, such as Three-Alarm Texas Black Bean "Caviar" (see page 69), omit the chili powder and just make the chips plain. By baking your own chips instead of buying commercially fried ones, you cut both fat and calories significantly.

Vegetable oil spray
6 corn tortillas (5 to 6 inches
   in diameter)

½ teaspoon chili powder
¼ teaspoon salt

continued

1. Preheat the oven to 400 degrees. Lightly coat a baking sheet with vegetable oil spray.

2. Cut each tortilla into eight triangles and spread them on the baking sheet. Spray the tortillas lightly with the vegetable oil spray and sprinkle with the chili powder and the salt.

3. Bake until crisp and lightly toasted, about 5 minutes.

4. Serve warm or at room temperature. (The chips can be made a day ahead and stored in a well-sealed plastic bag. To recrisp, heat in a 350-degree oven for about 5 minutes.)

◆ *PER SERVING: About 85 cals, 9 cals from fat, 1g total fat, 0g sat fat, 0mg chol, 197mg sodium, 18g total carbs, 0g fiber, 2g prot*

Tomatillo Salsa

Makes 2 cups (about 6 servings)

Fresh tomatillos, sometimes called Mexican green tomatoes, have a refreshing lemony flavor. If you can't find them, substitute two cans (10 ounces each) of cooked tomatillos, drained, rinsed, and puréed. This salsa is also good spooned over grilled fish or chicken.

1 pound tomatillos
¾ cup coarsely chopped onion
2 garlic cloves, peeled and coarsely chopped
2 fresh or canned jalapeño peppers, seeded,
    if desired, and coarsely chopped
½ teaspoon salt
½ cup chopped cilantro
2 tablespoons lime juice
Pinch of sugar

1. Remove the papery brown husks from the tomatillos. Place in a saucepan, cover with water, and bring to a boil. Reduce the heat to medium and cook, uncovered, until just tender, about 5 minutes. Drain and rinse under cold running water to stop the cooking.

2. In a food processor or blender, combine the tomatillos, onion, garlic, jalapeños, and salt. Process, using long pulses, until the mixture becomes a textured purée. Add the cilantro and lime juice and process to mix. Season with the sugar.

3. Serve at room temperature. (The salsa can be refrigerated for 1 day. Return to room temperature before serving. If it has thickened, stir in a tablespoon or two of water to thin to the right consistency.)

◆ *PER SERVING: About 38 cals, 8 cals from fat, 1g total fat, 0g sat fat, 0mg chol, 204mg sodium, 7g total carbs, 0g fiber, 1g prot*

Black Olivade Crostini

Makes about 6 servings

Black olive paste (olivade) is wonderful on grilled fish or chicken and you can also turn it into a great pasta sauce. Spread on toasted Italian bread (crostini), olivade is a superb appetizer. Dress up these canapés by garnishing each one with a single leaf of Italian parsley or basil, or crisscross yellow and red bell pepper slivers on top.

¼ pound (about ⅔ cup) gaeta or
   kalamata olives, pitted and rinsed
2 anchovy fillets
2 teaspoons drained capers
2 teaspoons extra-virgin olive oil
1 small garlic clove, peeled
1 loaf (8 ounces) Italian or French
   bread, cut into 24 slices

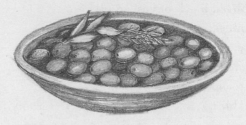

1. In a food processor or blender, combine the olives, anchovies, capers, and olive oil. With the motor running, drop the garlic in. Process, using long pulses, to a fairly smooth purée, scraping down the sides of the bowl if necessary. Or chop the ingredients by hand until they become a paste. (The olivade can be stored in the refrigerator for up to 1 week.)

2. Preheat the oven to 400 degrees. Arrange the bread in a single layer on a baking sheet. Bake 5 to 8 minutes, turning the bread once, until it is pale golden on both sides. (The crostini can be stored at room temperature in a sealed plastic bag for 8 hours, or frozen. Thaw to room temperature before using.)

3. Spread each toast with 1 teaspoon of olivade and serve.

◆ *PER SERVING: About 140 cals, 45 cals from fat, 5g total fat, 1g sat fat, 1mg chol, 468mg sodium, 20g total carbs, 0g fiber, 4g prot*

ABOUT OLIVES

With the explosion of interest in Mediterranean foods, olives appear in staggering variety.

Green olives are harvested unripe, processed to remove bitterness, and then pickled in brine. Examples include picholine from France and sicilian and calabrese from Italy.

Black olives are picked ripe and then cured for several months to remove bitterness. Dry curing, in which black olives are imbedded in coarse salt, produces wrinkled olives with a concentrated flavor. Some of the most popular black olive varieties are Italian gaeta, Greek kalamata, Spanish alfonso, and French niçoise. In addition to canned black olives, California now produces some of its own European-style olives.

All types of olives contain about 9 calories a piece.

Sun-Dried Tomato Crostini

Makes about ⅔ cup (about 8 servings)

This lovely brick-red, sun-dried tomato paste is also wonderful (in small spoonfuls) as a sauce for hot cooked pasta or steamed vegetables.

12 dry-packed sun-dried tomato halves (not oil packed)
1 small ripe tomato (about 6 ounces),
   seeded and coarsely chopped
4 pitted black olives, any type
1 tablespoon extra-virgin olive oil
1 teaspoon drained capers
1 garlic clove, peeled
¼ teaspoon cayenne pepper
1 tablespoon chopped parsley, preferably flat leaf
1 loaf (10 ounces) Italian or French bread, cut into 32 slices

1. Place the sun-dried tomatoes in a small bowl. Pour ⅓ cup boiling water over them, cover them with a sheet of plastic wrap, and set aside for 20 minutes. Drain in a colander, pressing to squeeze out liquid.

2. In a food processor, combine the rehydrated tomatoes, fresh tomato, olives, olive oil, and capers. With the motor running, drop the garlic through the feed tube. Process, using long pulses, to a textured paste, scraping down the side of the bowl once or twice. Stir in the cayenne and parsley. (The spread can be stored for up to 5 days in the refrigerator.)

3. Preheat the oven to 400 degrees. Arrange the bread in a single layer on a baking sheet and bake it for 5 to 8 minutes, turning once, until pale golden brown. (The crostini can be stored at room temperature in a sealed plastic bag for up to 8 hours, or frozen.)

4. Spread the crostini with the sun-dried tomato paste and serve.

◆ *PER SERVING: About 136 cals, 30 cals from fat, 3g total fat, 1g sat fat, 0mg chol, 248mg sodium, 23g total carbs, 0g fiber, 4g prot*

PITTING OLIVES

Most European-style black olives are sold unpitted. To use them in recipes, you must first remove their stones. Spread the olives in a single layer on a work surface. Then, using a large mallet, rolling pin, or the bottom of a large pot, press down hard on the olives. The pits should pop out of the olives, leaving the flesh in slightly ragged halves.

ABOUT SUN-DRIED TOMATOES

Originally a specialty of Calabria, Italy, sun-dried tomatoes are ripe plum tomatoes that have been dried in the sun or dehydrated by another method. The result is a chewy, intensely flavored tomato—sweet and slightly salty. Like fresh tomatoes, they are rich in the plant pigments known as carotenoids (which may have health benefits) and in vitamin C. Sun-dried tomatoes are sold packed either dry or in oil. The oil-packed tomatoes are already softened, but the dry-packed ones need to be rehydrated before using; cover them with boiling water and steep for about 20 minutes. (Save the liquid and add it to soups and stews.) For a fat-free choice, opt for the dry-packed sun-dried tomatoes. They should be soft and easy to chew—not so dehydrated that they're brittle or leathery hard. To chop dried tomatoes, cut them with kitchen shears or a large chef's knife.

Grilled Chicken Satay

Makes 18 skewers (about 6 servings)

Indonesian-style satays, which are bite-size cubes of meat grilled on skewers and served with a spicy peanut sauce, have become extremely popular as hors d'oeuvres. Be sure to soak the bamboo skewers in water so they don't burn on the grill.

1½ tablespoons creamy peanut butter

1½ tablespoons nonfat plain yogurt

1½ tablespoons reduced-sodium soy sauce

1 tablespoon lime juice

2 teaspoons minced fresh ginger

2 teaspoons sugar

¼ teaspoon dried red pepper flakes

½ pound skinless boneless chicken breasts, cut into 1-inch cubes

⅔ cup finely chopped scallions

1. In a medium bowl, whisk together the peanut butter, yogurt, soy sauce, and lime juice until smooth. Stir in the ginger, sugar, and red pepper flakes. Add the chicken and stir to coat completely. Cover and refrigerate at least 30 minutes or up to 6 hours. Soak 16 bamboo skewers in cold water for at least 30 minutes.

2. Prepare a hot barbecue fire or light a gas grill. Remove the chicken from the marinade, but do not pat dry. Thread two pieces of chicken onto each skewer. Place the skewers around the outside edges of the grill so that the ends are not exposed to direct heat, and grill, turning occasionally and basting with the remaining marinade, until browned outside and white in the center, about 5 minutes.

3. Roll the skewers of chicken in the scallions and serve on a platter.

◆ *PER SERVING: About 79 cals, 23 cals from fat, 3g total fat, 1g sat fat, 22mg chol, 179mg sodium, 4g total carbs, 0g fiber, 10g prot*

Sicilian Caponata

Makes 2½ cups (about 10 servings)

This caponata makes a great hors d'oeuvre on crackers or melba toast. It also works well as part of an antipasto platter, as a pizza topping, or even as an omelet filling.

1 medium-large (about 1 pound) eggplant, peeled and cut into ¾-inch dice
1 teaspoon salt
2 tablespoons extra-virgin olive oil
1 large onion, chopped
1 celery rib, chopped
1 small red bell pepper, seeded and chopped
2 garlic cloves, chopped
½ pound fresh tomatoes, seeded and chopped
¼ cup sliced black olives (such as kalamata)
1 tablespoon red wine vinegar
2 teaspoons sugar
1 teaspoon chopped fresh thyme or ¼ teaspoon dried
1 tablespoon chopped fresh basil or 1 teaspoon dried
1 bay leaf, broken in half
2 tablespoons chopped parsley
1 tablespoon drained capers
¼ teaspoon black pepper

1. Place the eggplant in a colander, sprinkle with the salt, and set aside for 30 minutes. Rinse well under cold water, drain, and pat dry with several layers of paper towels.

2. In a large, preferably nonstick skillet, heat the oil over medium heat. Add the eggplant, onion, celery, and red pepper and cook until softened, about 6 minutes. Add the garlic, and cook, stirring, for 1 minute. Stir in the tomatoes, olives, vinegar, sugar, thyme, basil, and bay leaf. Cover the pan and cook over medium-low heat, stirring occasionally, until the vegetables are very soft, about 20 minutes.

3. Uncover and continue to cook until any remaining liquid evaporates, 5 to 10 minutes. Stir in the parsley and capers and season with the pepper. Remove from the heat and cool. Discard the bay leaf. (The caponata can be stored in the refrigerator for up to 3 days. Return to room temperature before serving.)

4. Transfer caponata to a serving bowl and surround with crackers or toast.

◆ *PER SERVING: About 61 cals, 31 cals from fat, 3g total fat, 0g sat fat, 0mg chol, 183mg sodium, 7g total carbs, 2g fiber, 1g prot*

Spiced Baba Ghanouj

Makes about 3 cups (about 10 servings)

The simplicity of the ingredient list belies the exotic flavor of this deservedly famous Middle Eastern dip or spread. One secret is that the eggplant is slow roasted in the oven, giving it a subtle smoky flavor. Another is tahini, a sesame seed paste now readily available in the gourmet section of most supermarkets. Serve the baba ghanouj with untoasted pita triangles or pieces of lavash or other flatbread for dipping or scooping.

2 large (1¼ pounds each) eggplants

¾ teaspoon whole cumin seed
  (see note)

1 tablespoon tahini

1 medium plum tomato (about 3
  ounces), seeded and finely chopped

2 tablespoons fresh lemon juice

1 large garlic clove, finely chopped

½ teaspoon salt

¼ teaspoon black pepper

1 tablespoon chopped parsley

2 teaspoons extra-virgin olive oil

1. Preheat the oven to 425 degrees. Cut the eggplants in half lengthwise and score the flesh with a small knife in several places. Place cut sides down on a lightly oiled baking sheet and bake until the eggplant is very soft and starts to collapse, 30 to 40 minutes.

2. Meanwhile, toast the cumin seed in a small skillet over medium heat, stirring frequently, until dark brown and fragrant, about 3 minutes. When cool, crush it with a mortar and pestle or grind it in a spice grinder.

3. When the eggplant is cool enough to handle, place the halves flesh side up and, using a small spoon, scrape out and discard as many of the bitter seeds as possible. Scoop the rest of the flesh into a large bowl. Add the tahini and cumin, and use a large fork to mash the eggplant to a coarse purée. Stir in the chopped tomato, lemon juice, garlic, salt, and pepper. (The baba ghanouj can be refrigerated for 3 to 4 days.)

4. Transfer to a bowl, sprinkle with the parsley, and drizzle with the olive oil. Serve with bread or crackers.

◆ *PER SERVING: About 39 cals, 13 cals from fat, 1g total fat, 0g sat fat, 0mg chol, 114mg sodium, 6g total carbs, 3g fiber, 1g prot*

Note: You can substitute the same quantity of ground cumin for the cumin seed. To bring out its flavor, toast it in a small skillet as instructed for the whole seed.

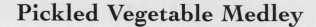

Pickled Vegetable Medley

Makes 10 servings

The vegetables in this recipe make a lovely presentation, but you can substitute others, such as cucumbers, fennel, and any color of bell pepper. Avoid using broccoli, asparagus, or peas because the vinegar in the pickling liquid tends to diminish their green color.

1½ cups cauliflower florets

2 carrots, peeled and cut into 1½-inch sticks

2 medium zucchini (6 ounces each), sliced ¼ inch thick

1 large red bell pepper, seeded and cut into 1-inch dice

2 cups cider vinegar

1 cup sugar

1 teaspoon whole cloves

1 teaspoon whole allspice berries (see note)

1 teaspoon whole black peppercorns

1 cinnamon stick, broken in half

1 slice fresh ginger

1. In a large pot of boiling water, blanch the cauliflower and carrots for 1 minute. Drain into a colander and rinse under cold water until cooled. Transfer to a large mixing bowl. Add the raw zucchini and red pepper.

2. In a medium-sized saucepan, combine the vinegar, sugar, and ½ cup of water. Tie the cloves, allspice, and peppercorns in a cheesecloth bag. Add to the pan along with the cinnamon stick and ginger. Bring to a boil, stirring to dissolve the sugar, and simmer for 2 minutes. Let cool for 5 minutes, then pour the pickling liquid over the vegetables. If the vegetables are not quite covered, add more water. Stir to blend well. Let the vegetables cool to room temperature, then cover and refrigerate for at least 4 hours. (The vegetables can be soaked in the refrigerator for up to 24 hours.)

3. To serve, remove the spice bag and use a slotted spoon to transfer the vegetables to a serving bowl. Spoon some of the liquid over the vegetables and serve.

◆ *PER SERVING: About 39 cals, 1 cal from fat, 0g total fat, 0g sat fat, 0mg chol, 11mg sodium, 9g total carbs, 1g fiber, 1g prot*

Note: If allspice berries aren't available, substitute ⅛ teaspoon of ground allspice.

Three-Alarm Texas Black Bean "Caviar"

Makes 2½ cups (about 8 servings)

This Texas version of "caviar" tastes every bit as good as the high-priced delicacy. In true Texas style, this dish is hot enough to make your lips sting, so tame it down with a bit less cayenne pepper if you like. Serve the caviar surrounded with Spicy Baked Tortilla Chips (page 61), or use it as a piquant relish for cold meats.

1 can (15 to 16 ounces) black beans, rinsed and drained, or 1¾ cups cooked black beans	2 tablespoons sugar
1 medium onion, chopped	1 teaspoon chili powder
1 small red bell pepper, seeded and chopped	½ teaspoon dried savory
1 pickled jalapeño pepper, finely chopped	½ teaspoon ground cumin
1 garlic clove, finely chopped	½ teaspoon salt
¼ cup red wine vinegar	¼ teaspoon black pepper
	¼ teaspoon cayenne pepper
	⅛ teaspoon white pepper
	2 teaspoons fresh lemon juice

1. In a large mixing bowl, combine the beans, onion, red pepper, jalapeños, and garlic.

2. In a medium saucepan, combine the vinegar, sugar, chili powder, savory, cumin, salt, black pepper, cayenne, and white pepper. Bring to a boil, stirring until the sugar is dissolved. Add the beans, return the mixture to a boil, and simmer for 1 minute. Using the back of a spoon, mash about a quarter of the beans against the side of the saucepan. (This will help thicken the mixture.) Remove from the heat and stir in the lemon juice. Transfer to a bowl, cool to room temperature, and refrigerate for at least 1 hour (up to 5 days).

3. Return to room temperature before serving. Serve in a bowl, accompanied by chips for scooping.

◆ *PER SERVING: About 80 cals, 3 cals from fat, 0g total fat, 0g sat fat, 0mg chol, 163mg sodium, 16g total carbs, 3g fiber, 4g prot*

White Bean "Pesto" with Garden Vegetables

Makes 1¼ cups (about 8 servings)

Use cannellini or Great Northern beans to make this simple and delicious fiber-rich dip that's reminiscent of Italian pesto. It seems especially appropriate surrounded by spring and summer vegetables, but of course you can substitute any other vegetables available in the grocery store year-round.

1 can (15 to 16 ounces) white beans, rinsed and drained,
    or 1¾ cups cooked white beans
¾ cup packed fresh basil leaves, plus
    additional for garnish
1 large garlic clove, peeled
2 tablespoons extra-virgin olive oil
½ teaspoon salt
¼ teaspoon black pepper
½ pound sugar snap peas, strings removed
½ pound asparagus, trimmed
1 bunch radishes, trimmed
1 long European cucumber, scored and cut on a sharp diagonal
1 yellow bell pepper, seeded and cut in strips

1. In a food processor, combine the beans and basil. With the motor running, drop the garlic down the feed tube. Process to a coarse purée. Pour the olive oil through the feed tube and process until smooth. Season with salt and pepper. Refrigerate for at least 1 hour to blend the flavors. (The dip can be stored in the refrigerator for 1 day. Return to room temperature before serving.)

2. Blanch the sugar snap peas in a large pot of lightly salted boiling water until bright green, about 1 minute. Remove with a slotted spoon and transfer to a bowl of cold water to stop the cooking and set the color. Blanch the asparagus in the same pot of water until crisp-tender, about 3 minutes. Place in a colander and run under cold water. Pat the peas and asparagus dry on paper towels.

3. To serve, transfer the dip to a bowl and garnish with basil leaves. Place the bowl on a platter and surround with the sugar snap peas, asparagus, and other vegetables.

◆ *PER SERVING: About 115 cals, 34 cals from fat, 4g total fat, 1g sat fat, 0mg chol, 141mg sodium, 16g total carbs, 4g fiber, 6g prot*

Sweet Red Pepper Hummus

Makes 1½ cups (about 8 servings)

Roasted red peppers add color and sweetness to traditional Middle Eastern hummus. You can serve it with cut-up raw vegetables or Baked Herbed Pita Crisps (page 61).

1 can (15 to 16 ounces) chickpeas, rinsed
    and drained, or 1½ cups cooked chickpeas
4-ounce jar roasted red peppers, drained
3 tablespoons fresh lemon juice
1½ tablespoons tahini
1 garlic clove, peeled
½ teaspoon ground cumin
½ teaspoon cayenne pepper
¼ teaspoon salt
1 tablespoon chopped parsley

1. In a food processor, combine the chickpeas, red peppers, lemon juice, tahini, garlic, cumin, cayenne, and salt. Process, using long pulses, to a fairly smooth, slightly fluffy, purée, scraping down the sides of the bowl once or twice. Transfer to a serving bowl and refrigerate for at least 1 hour. (The hummus can be made up to 3 days ahead and refrigerated. Return to room temperature before serving.)

2. Sprinkle the hummus with the chopped parsley and serve surrounded by vegetables or the suggested crisps for dipping.

◆ *PER SERVING: About 64 cals, 12 cals from fat, 1g total fat, 0g sat fat, 0mg chol, 87mg sodium, 10g total carbs, 0g fiber, 3g prot*

CHAPTER TWO

Salads

Gone are the days when the word "salad" conjured up thoughts of a side dish of chilled iceberg lettuce drenched in dressing. Salad making has undergone a revolution. Choices are limitless— colorful lettuces, sharply flavored leafy greens, vegetables, pastas, grains, and protein-rich ingredients that include beans, beef, chicken, and fish. Dressings go far beyond Italian and blue cheese, with fresh flavors from herbs and international flair from ingredients like ginger and mint. The end result is that today's salads have more flavor and higher nutritional benefits than ever before. No longer just a side dish, salad makes a satisfying and stylish main course.

The vegetable group of the Food Guide Pyramid is the traditional salad starting point. Because each cup of lettuce or greens, or half cup of any other vegetable, counts as one vegetable serving, salads can take you a long way toward the recommended three to five servings per day. Deep green and leafy vegetables—like broccoli, kale, arugula, and spinach—have plenty of carotenoids (plant pigments that may have health benefits) and vitamin C, along with other essential nutrients. Lighter-colored lettuce, such as iceberg, contains fewer nutrients than the deep green varieties but still supplies vitamins like folic acid and balances out the stronger flavor of the deeper greens. For the most variety in nutrition and taste, mix different vegetables in a single salad and serve different types of salads during the course of a week.

Salads can contain more than just vegetables. Adding fruit to a vegetable salad offers flavor and color contrast and often boosts the salad's fiber and vitamin C content. An ingredient from the grain group, such as the tabbouleh in our Herbed and Spiced Tabbouleh (page 101) or the bread in the Tuscan Bread and Roasted Pepper Salad (page 102), enhances nutrition, texture, and flavor. Toss in a selection from the protein group—lean beef, as in the Steakhouse Salad (page 80); chicken, as in the Thai Grilled Chicken and Broccoli on Napa Cabbage Salad (page 77); or beans, found in the Four-Bean Ranch Salad (page 94)—and you've created a salad with even more essential nutrients, including protein, iron, and zinc. The more varied and diverse a salad's ingredient list, the greater the nutrition value.

The basic ingredients of a salad—vegetables, fruit, grains, lean meat, poultry, or fish— are naturally low in fat. Whether a salad retains its low-fat personality depends on how you dress it. Cloaked in a standard oil-based or mayonnaise dressing, salad can be extremely high in fat and calories. A 2-tablespoon serving of regular dressing may be the major calorie source in an all-vegetable salad. Try substituting a lighter dressing that does away with the classic mayonnaise base or three-parts-oil-to-one-part-vinegar salad dressing formula. The dressings you'll find in this chapter successfully trim fat and calories with creamy substitutes like plain yogurt and reduced-fat mayonnaise. Compared to standard dressings, ours have at least 25 percent and up to 50 percent less fat and calories per serving. Flavor-enhancing dressing ingredients, like shallots, citrus juices, and chili sauce, bring out the best in a salad.

This chapter demonstrates the versatility of salads as a regular menu item. Make salads as simple or as complex as you like. Vary ingredients to change a salad's personality—try different types of lettuce or beans, substitute seasonal vegetables, or switch to another dressing. Use salads as the opener for a meal, serve them along with customary partners like soup, sandwiches, or pizza, or create an entire meal with larger portions of salad as the main course, accompanied by nothing more than good bread.

Basic Salad Dressings

Unlike the heavy Thousand Island and creamy garlic dressings of yesteryear, today's salad toppings are light and elegant and they have great taste. Though a good dressing must contain a bit of oil to carry the flavor and cling to the leaves, the real spark comes from imaginative ingredients, such as fruit juices, flavored vinegars, broths, herbs, and dairy products, such as low-fat yogurt.

BASIC VINAIGRETTE

Makes about ¾ cup (six 2-tablespoon servings)

Defatted lower-sodium chicken broth or canned vegetable broth is one of the secrets of a lower-fat yet flavorful vinaigrette. The other is the use of high-quality ingredients, such as freshly ground pepper and fine-grade vinegar and olive oil. Because this vinaigrette is relatively low in oil, it should be used on a leafy green salad just before serving to prevent wilting and sogginess.

4 tablespoons fresh red or white wine vinegar or balsamic vinegar

4 tablespoons defatted lower-sodium chicken broth or vegetable broth

4 tablespoons extra-virgin olive oil

1 teaspoon Dijon mustard

1 tablespoon chopped fresh shallots

½ teaspoon salt

¼ teaspoon freshly ground pepper

1 garlic clove, finely chopped (optional)

1. In a small bowl, whisk together the vinegar, broth, oil, mustard, shallots, salt, and pepper. If desired, whisk in the garlic.

2. Use the vinaigrette immediately or refrigerate up to 2 days. Just before serving, whisk or shake the vinaigrette in a covered jar to blend it.

Per serving (without garlic): About 90 cals, 82 cals from fat, 9g total fat, 1g sat fat, 0mg chol, 208mg sodium, 1g total carbs, 0g fiber, 0g prot

BASIC VINAIGRETTE VARIATIONS

◆ Add 1 tablespoon of chopped fresh herbs, such as tarragon, chives, thyme, marjoram, cilantro, or dill.

◆ Substitute lemon or lime juice for the vinegar, or use half each of citrus juice and vinegar.

◆ For a fruit-salad vinaigrette, use a fruit vinegar or lemon juice, substitute orange juice for the chicken or vegetable broth, and add 1 teaspoon of honey.

◆ For a nutty-tasting vinaigrette, use 3 tablespoons of vegetable oil and 1 tablespoon of walnut or hazelnut oil in place of the olive oil.

◆ Increase the mustard to 1 tablespoon for a more assertive vinaigrette.

BASIC CREAMY DRESSING

Makes about 1 cup (eight 2-tablespoon servings)

Because this versatile, rich, and creamy dressing keeps for several days, it can be a staple in your refrigerator.

⅓ cup reduced-fat mayonnaise	7 tablespoons low-fat buttermilk	½ teaspoon salt
¼ cup nonfat plain yogurt	1 tablespoon fresh lemon juice	¼ teaspoon fresh ground pepper

In a small bowl, whisk together all ingredients until smooth. Refrigerate until ready to use, up to 3 days.

Per serving: About 43 cals, 31 cals from fat, 3g total fat, 1g sat fat, 1mg chol, 225mg sodium, 2g total carbs, 0g fiber, 1g prot

BASIC CREAMY DRESSING VARIATIONS

◆ Increase the amount of pepper to 1 teaspoon for a ranch-style dressing.

◆ Add 1 tablespoon chopped fresh herbs, such as tarragon, cilantro, or dill.

◆ Add 1 teaspoon of grated orange peel and 1 tablespoon of honey for a fruit-salad dressing.

◆ Add 1 tablespoon tomato paste.

◆ Dissolve ¼ teaspoon saffron in 2 teaspoons of hot water and add to the dressing, along with a pinch of ground cumin and curry powder, for an exotic dressing that tastes especially good on a tomato salad.

EASY THOUSAND ISLAND DRESSING

Makes about 1 cup (eight 2-tablespoon servings)

This versatile, low-fat dressing is delicious spooned over a chef's salad or as a dressing for chicken or crabmeat. It's also a terrific dress-up for a simple romaine lettuce salad. But, best of all, it contains less than half the calories and a third of the fat of commercial Thousand Island dressing.

½ cup nonfat plain yogurt	2 tablespoons minced onion	½ teaspoon freshly ground
⅓ cup reduced-fat mayonnaise	1 tablespoon bottled sweet	black pepper
¼ cup bottled chili sauce	pickle relish	¼ teaspoon salt

Whisk all ingredients together in a mixing bowl. Use immediately or store in the refrigerator up to 4 days.

Per serving: About 53 cals, 30 cals from fat, 3g total fat, 1g sat fat, 0mg chol, 266mg sodium, 5g total carbs, 0g fiber, 1g prot

Classic Southern Chicken Salad

Makes 4 main-dish servings

A really good, classic chicken salad recipe is an important basic in any cook's repertoire. Dill gives this salad a Scandinavian flavor that goes well with rye bread. If you use tarragon, serve the salad with French bread. In either case, round out the meal with some colorful cooked or raw vegetables, such as Summer Harvest Ratatouille (page 426).

2½ cups cubed cooked skinless
  boneless chicken breasts
  (about ¾ pound)
2 tablespoons fresh lemon juice
¼ cup reduced-fat mayonnaise
¼ cup nonfat plain yogurt
1 tablespoon reduced-fat
  sour cream
2 tablespoons chopped fresh dill or
  1 tablespoon chopped fresh
  tarragon
½ teaspoon salt

¼ teaspoon black pepper
⅔ cup thinly sliced celery
½ cup diced fresh pineapple or
  canned unsweetened pineapple,
  drained
½ cup thinly sliced scallions
Lettuce leaves
Tomato wedges, hard-boiled egg
  wedges, gherkins, dill or
  tarragon sprigs, black olives,
  edible flower blossoms
  (optional)

1. In a medium mixing bowl, toss the chicken with the lemon juice. Refrigerate for about 30 minutes. In a small bowl, whisk together the mayonnaise, yogurt, sour cream, dill, salt, and pepper.

2. Add the celery, pineapple, and scallions to the chicken in the mixing bowl. Add the dressing and stir to blend well. Refrigerate the salad for about 30 minutes or up to 4 hours before serving. Spoon into lettuce leaves and garnish as desired.

◆ *PER SERVING (without garnishes): About 233 cals, 84 cals from fat, 9g total fat, 2g sat fat, 75mg chol, 476mg sodium, 7g total carbs, 1g fiber, 29g prot*

CHICKEN SALAD SERVING SUGGESTIONS

◆ Hollow out a tomato and spoon the salad inside. Sprinkle the top with freshly ground pepper.
◆ Slice the top off a seedless orange. Scoop out and dice the pulp and add to the salad in place of the pineapple. Spoon the salad into the orange shell and make a lid from the top.
◆ Add the pulp of a pineapple to the salad, then spoon the salad into the hollowed-out pineapple.
◆ Finely chop the salad ingredients before combining them. Use the salad as a sandwich filling, garnished with lettuce.
◆ Spread finely chopped chicken salad onto firm bread or miniature bagel halves and garnish with fresh herbs or a dash of paprika.

Thai Grilled Chicken and Broccoli on Napa Cabbage Salad

Makes 4 main-dish servings

The lemongrass in this recipe has a distinctive flavor that is characteristic of Thai cooking. If you can't find it, use grated lemon peel instead. Napa cabbage has an elongated shape and a mild flavor; you can substitute regular green or savoy cabbage. Fish sauce is available at many large supermarkets and in Asian markets.

3 tablespoons defatted lower-sodium chicken broth

3 tablespoons fresh lemon juice

1 tablespoon fish sauce (nam pla)

1 tablespoon minced fresh lemongrass
   or 1 teaspoon grated lemon peel

2 teaspoons Thai hot chili sauce
   or Chinese chili paste with garlic

2 teaspoons honey

2 teaspoons grated fresh ginger

2 garlic cloves, finely chopped

½ tablespoon peanut oil, plus 1½ tablespoons

1 pound skinless boneless chicken breasts,
   cut into 1½-inch chunks

Salt to taste

½ pound broccoli florets

6 thick scallions, trimmed and cut into 2-inch pieces

4 cups shredded napa cabbage

1 small cucumber, peeled, seeded, and thinly sliced

¼ cup thinly sliced radishes

2 tablespoons chopped roasted peanuts

1. In a small bowl, whisk together the chicken broth, lemon juice, fish sauce, lemongrass, chili sauce, honey, ginger, garlic, and ½ tablespoon of the oil. Pour about half of the marinade into a shallow dish just large enough to hold the chicken. Add the chicken, turning to coat. Whisk the remaining 1½ tablespoons of oil into the remaining marinade and season lightly with salt. Reserve to use as the salad dressing. Cover the chicken and the salad dressing and refrigerate for 1 hour, turning the chicken once or twice.

continued

2. Prepare a medium-hot barbecue fire or preheat a gas grill. If you are using bamboo skewers, soak them in cold water for 30 minutes. Remove the chicken from the marinade. Add the broccoli and scallions to the marinade, stirring to coat. Alternate the broccoli, scallions, and chicken on skewers. Grill, turning once or twice, until the outside of the chicken is browned and the inside is white throughout, about 6 minutes.

3. In a mixing bowl, toss the cabbage with all but 1 tablespoon of the reserved salad dressing. Transfer to a serving platter or four plates. Arrange the skewers on top of the cabbage. Drizzle with the remaining dressing. Garnish the salad with the sliced cucumber, sliced radishes, and chopped peanuts.

◆ *PER SERVING: About 242 cals, 76 cals from fat, 8g total fat, 1g sat fat, 66mg chol, 254mg sodium, 12g total carbs, 4g fiber, 31g prot*

Wild Rice, Turkey, and Grape Salad

Makes 4 main-dish servings

This is a great salad to take to an autumn tailgate party. Using smoked turkey, which is extremely low in fat, leaves room for small amounts of flavorful high-fat ingredients like nuts and nut oil.

¼ cup hazelnut or walnut pieces

1 cup raw wild rice

1½ cups defatted lower-sodium chicken broth, plus ¼ cup

3 tablespoons reduced-fat mayonnaise

1½ tablespoons white wine vinegar, preferably tarragon flavored

1½ tablespoons hazelnut or walnut oil

1 tablespoon chopped fresh tarragon or 1 teaspoon dried

¼ teaspoon salt, plus additional to taste

¼ teaspoon black pepper, plus additional to taste

½ pound smoked turkey, cut into ½-inch cubes

1½ cups mixed red and green grapes, plus grape clusters for garnish

⅔ cup chopped celery

½ cup chopped red onion

1 small head green leaf lettuce

1 head radicchio, separated into leaves

1. Preheat the oven to 350 degrees. Toast the nuts on a small baking sheet, stirring once or twice, until golden and fragrant, about 5 minutes. (If using hazelnuts, rub them in a kitchen towel to remove most of the skins.) Let the nuts cool, then coarsely chop them. (The nuts can be toasted up to 2 days ahead and stored, covered, at room temperature.)

2. Rinse the rice in a colander. In a medium saucepan, bring 1½ cups of the broth and 1 cup of water to a boil. Add the rice, cover the pan, reduce the heat to low, and simmer until the liquid is absorbed and the rice softens and splits, 40 to 45 minutes. Spoon the rice into a mixing bowl and let it cool slightly.

3. In a small bowl, whisk together the remaining ¼ cup of broth with the mayonnaise, vinegar, oil, tarragon, salt, and pepper. Toss the dressing with the warm rice, and let the rice cool to room temperature. Gently stir the turkey, grapes, celery, and onion into the salad. Season to taste with additional salt and pepper. Refrigerate for at least 30 minutes or up to 6 hours before serving.

4. At serving time, arrange a bed of leaf lettuce on four serving plates. Arrange two radicchio leaves into a cup on each plate. Spoon the salad into the radicchio cups and sprinkle the top with the toasted nuts. Garnish each salad with small grape clusters.

◆ *PER SERVING: About 422 cals, 152 cals from fat, 17g total fat, 2g sat fat, 10mg chol, 68mg sodium, 50g total carbs, 4g fiber, 23g prot*

HOW TO CHOOSE SALAD GREENS

Greens are interchangeable within the following categories, so you can freely substitute or mix the best of the daily pick from the garden or the produce stand. In general, darker greens are richer in vitamins, fiber, and carotenoids. For example, romaine lettuce gives you a much bigger hit of nutrients—folic acid, vitamin A, and vitamin C—than iceberg lettuce. Look for salad greens that are vibrant and crisp and have no signs of browning or rotting. Mesclun is a mix of tender young greens from all categories.

MILD

BIBB: soft, small heads with large, pale green outer leaves

BOSTON: fluffy, loose heads with soft, pale green leaves

ICEBERG: compact, crisp, globular head with very pale green leaves

LOOSE LEAF: large, loose, soft medium green or red and green leaves

MÂCHE (LAMBS' LETTUCE): small, tender, medium green leaves

OAKLEAF: curly edged, tender, red leaf (a type of loose leaf)

ROMAINE: long, crisp, medium green leaves

SPINACH: deep green, heart-shaped leaves, crisp if large and tender if small

BITTER

CHICORY (CURLY ENDIVE): elongated, crisp, medium green, curly leaves

DANDELION: pointed edge, dark green, young leaves; use tender, young leaves raw; cook older leaves before eating

ENDIVE: small, elongated heads with tightly attached, pale green leaves with yellow or red edges

ESCAROLE: large, soft, green leaves with pale centers; cook outer dark leaves

FRISÉE: smaller, milder, softer green cousin to chicory

RADICCHIO: ruby red leaves in small, tight, globular heads

PEPPERY

ARUGULA (ROCKET): tender, very dark green leaves

WATERCRESS: small, shiny, dark green leaves on tender stems

THE UPDATED CHEF'S SALAD

Today's chef's salad can be tastier, quicker, much lower in fat, and much more imaginative than the boiled ham, American cheese, and baked turkey combo of yesteryear. Here are some ideas:

◆ Double the amount of greens for your salad "bed," and add some extra color with a few radicchio leaves and some shredded carrots.

◆ Try reduced-sodium, reduced-fat meats, or higher-quality turkey "ham."

◆ Use smaller amounts of smoked turkey and smoked chicken, which have more flavor than roast turkey.

◆ Use smaller amounts of full-flavored cheeses, such as Gouda or fontina, or shavings of good Parmesan.

◆ Blanch fresh green vegetables, such as broccoli, green beans, or asparagus. They contribute flavor, color, and nutrients.

◆ Garnish the salad with croutons made from toasted rye or other flavorful bread.

◆ Sprinkle your salad with crunchy beans, such as chickpeas.

◆ Top the salad with a sprinkling of fresh herbs, such as thyme, tarragon, basil, or dill.

Steakhouse Salad

Makes 4 main-dish servings

Serious steakhouses have limited menus—beef, potatoes, bread, and green salads. In this delicious salad-on-a-stick, you can dress up the menu at home by adding tasty artichokes and mushrooms. Lean red meat, such as beef tenderloin, is one of the best sources of iron.

¼ cup balsamic vinegar

¼ cup defatted lower-sodium beef broth

4 teaspoons Dijon mustard

1 tablespoon chopped fresh thyme or 1 teaspoon dried

½ teaspoon freshly ground black pepper

½ tablespoon extra-virgin olive oil, plus 1 tablespoon

2 garlic cloves, divided

¾ pound trimmed beef tenderloin or sirloin, cut into 1-inch chunks

¼ teaspoon salt

4 small artichokes, trimmed (see note)

8 small red-skinned potatoes (about ½ pound), scrubbed and halved

4 medium portobello mushrooms, stems removed and caps quartered

4 slices Italian bread

2 bunches arugula, washed, dried, and torn (about 10 cups)

1 cup torn radicchio leaves

1. In a small bowl, whisk together the vinegar, beef broth, mustard, thyme, pepper, and ½ tablespoon of the oil. Mince one of the garlic cloves and add to the mixture. In a shallow dish just large enough to hold the meat, combine the beef and about half of the marinade.

Toss to coat. Whisk the salt and remaining 1 tablespoon of oil into the remaining marinade and reserve to use as the salad dressing. Refrigerate the beef and the salad dressing for 1 to 3 hours, stirring the beef once or twice.

2. Meanwhile, cook the artichokes in a pot of boiling salted water until just tender, 10 to 15 minutes. Drain well. When cool enough to handle, cut the artichokes lengthwise into quarters. Remove the fuzzy, inedible choke with a paring knife or small melon baller. Cook the potatoes in a large pot of boiling salted water until just tender, about 6 minutes. Drain. (The vegetables can be prepared several hours ahead and refrigerated.)

3. Prepare a medium-hot barbecue fire. Remove the meat from the marinade and thread onto metal skewers. Add the artichokes, potatoes, and mushrooms to the remaining marinade in the dish and toss to coat. Thread them onto separate metal skewers.

4. Grill the meat until browned, 6 to 8 minutes for medium-rare. Grill the vegetables until lightly blackened and tender, 10 to 12 minutes. During the last couple of minutes, toast the bread at the edge of the grill for about 30 seconds per side. Cut the remaining garlic clove in half and rub the cut sides onto the grilled bread slices.

5. In a large salad bowl, toss the arugula and radicchio with all but 2 tablespoons of the reserved salad dressing. Remove the beef and vegetables from the skewers and arrange on top of the greens. Drizzle with the remaining dressing. Garnish with the grilled toasts.

◆ *PER SERVING: About 381 cals, 114 cals from fat, 13g total fat, 3g sat fat, 48mg chol, 536mg sodium, 45g total carbs, 3g fiber, 27g prot*

Note: Four canned or frozen cooked artichoke hearts can be substituted for fresh. They do not need to be cooked before grilling.

"ATTACKING" AN ARTICHOKE

Artichokes, with their sharply pointed tips and convoluted interiors, can be intimidating to the uninitiated. But they're actually quite easy to conquer, and worth the effort. One artichoke has a moderate amount of fiber and it's also a good source of folic acid and magnesium. To prepare an artichoke for cooking, first wash it by swishing it up and down in cold water. Then, using a stainless steel knife or scissors (carbon blades can discolor the artichoke), trim off about ¾ inch from the pointed top and tips of the prickly outer leaves. If you are going to use the artichoke whole, slice off the stem so that the base will sit flat. Rub all cut sides with lemon juice or soak the whole artichoke in water and lemon juice (2 or 3 tablespoons of lemon juice to each quart of water) for an hour or two before cooking. Steam or boil the artichoke in water with lemon juice until you can pierce the base with a knife tip and the outer leaves pull off easily, 20 to 40 minutes, depending upon the size of the artichoke.

Greek Barbecued Lamb and Spring Greens Salad

Makes 6 main-dish servings

This sophisticated but simple main-course salad is perfect for spring entertaining. Complete the meal with orzo or rice pilaf and additional pitas. The deep green leaves of the watercress and arugula are good sources of vitamins A and C and calcium.

12 small loin lamb chops (about
   1½ pounds), cut about ¾ inch
   thick

3 whole-wheat pitas, split

1 garlic clove, cut in half

¼ teaspoon ground cumin

¼ teaspoon ground coriander

Salt and pepper

2 bunches watercress

1 bunch arugula, torn

¼ cup sliced mint leaves

1½ cups Tzatziki Dressing
   (recipe follows)

1 cup alfalfa sprouts

1. Prepare a hot barbecue fire. Rub the lamb and the cut sides of the pitas with the cut sides of the garlic. Sprinkle the lamb with the cumin, coriander, salt, and pepper. Grill the lamb, turning once, to desired degree of doneness, 3 to 4 minutes per side for medium. Grill the pitas, cut sides down, until lightly toasted, about 1 minute.

2. In a shallow bowl, toss together the watercress, arugula, and mint. Add ½ cup of the Tzatziki Dressing and toss. Divide the greens among six serving plates. Top with the grilled lamb chops. Spoon the remaining Tzatziki Dressing over the lamb. Sprinkle with the sprouts. Cut each toasted pita into three wedges and use to garnish the salads.

◆ *PER SERVING (without dressing): About 222 cals, 70 cals from fat, 8g total fat, 2g sat fat, 34mg chol, 227mg sodium, 19g total carbs, 1g fiber, 20g prot*

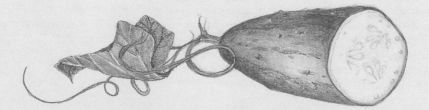

TZATZIKI DRESSING

Makes about 1½ cups (about six 3-tablespoon servings)

Tzatziki is a Greek dip made from drained, thickened yogurt and cucumbers. Here, the yogurt is not drained so it will remain thin enough to pour as a salad dressing. To use as a dip, simply let the yogurt drain and thicken for about 2 hours in a strainer lined with cheesecloth, then mix with the other ingredients.

1 cup low-fat plain yogurt
1 large garlic clove,
   finely chopped

2 teaspoons fresh lemon
   juice
¼ teaspoon salt

½ cucumber (about 4 ounces),
   peeled and seeded

1. In a mixing bowl, stir together the yogurt, garlic, lemon juice, and salt. Cut the cucumber into matchstick strips, about 1x¼ inch (about ½ cup). Stir into the yogurt.
2. Use the dressing immediately or refrigerate it up to 4 hours before using.

Per serving: About 28 cals, 6 cals from fat, 1g total fat, 0g sat fat, 2mg chol, 116mg sodium, 3g total carbs, 0g fiber, 2g prot

FRESH VERSUS DRIED HERBS

Both fresh and dried herbs have an important place in cooking. They deliver loads of taste, which means that you can use less fat. Add fresh herbs toward the end of cooking or use them in uncooked soups or salads or as a garnish; their delicate flavor tends to diminish with long cooking. Herbs best used fresh include basil, cilantro, dill, and parsley. Dried herbs reconstitute during long simmering, but you can intensify their flavor by rubbing them between your fingers for a few seconds before adding to a

dish. Bay leaves and oregano are especially good dried.

One tablespoon of chopped fresh herbs is equivalent to 1 teaspoon of dried. Fresh and dried herbs can taste quite different; add both to give a more varied taste to a dish. Herbs that work well both fresh and dried are marjoram, rosemary, sage, tarragon, and thyme.

To dry your own herbs, you can tie a bunch of sprigs or branches together and hang them in a cool dry place for several days or weeks until they are dried. This method

works particularly well for sturdy herbs, such as rosemary and bay leaves. Using the microwave oven is quicker. Place individual sprigs or leaves on a paper towel in a single layer and microwave on high heat for no more than a few minutes. Test the herbs every 30 seconds by rubbing them between your fingers until they feel dry. Crumble the dried herbs and store them in airtight containers in a cool, dry place. Use the herbs within a couple of months for the best flavor.

IS ORGANIC PRODUCE WORTH THE COST?

People sometimes purchase organic produce because they think it is pesticide-free. But foods labeled "organic" may still be treated with so-called natural pesticides or may have been exposed

to chemicals from adjacent growing fields or water supplies. Also, the definition of organic varies from state to state. Organic produce may or may not have a higher nutrient content than nonorganic

produce. Freshness and proper handling from picking to purchase are the most important factors in the nutritional content of any vegetables or fruits.

Marinated Scallop, Lima Bean, and Corn Salad

Makes 6 main-dish servings

This truly American dish combines New England succotash ingredients with Southwest seasonings for a sophisticated make-ahead salad. Don't overcook the scallops—they need only a brief heating in an aromatic liquid. Toasting the cumin seed deepens its flavor.

½ teaspoon cumin seed

2 cups dry white wine or 1 cup bottled
    clam juice and 1 cup water

1½ pounds bay scallops

⅓ cup fresh lime juice

3 tablespoons olive oil

2 teaspoons grated lime peel

½ teaspoon salt, plus additional to taste

2 garlic cloves, finely chopped

1 to 2 jalapeño peppers, seeded and minced

1 red bell pepper, seeded and coarsely chopped

1 celery rib, thinly sliced

1 sweet onion, such as Vidalia, thinly sliced

¾ cup cooked frozen baby lima beans

¾ cup cooked fresh or frozen corn kernels or drained canned corn

½ cup chopped flat-leaf parsley

1 head radicchio, separated into leaves

1. In a small skillet, toast the cumin seeds over medium heat, stirring constantly until fragrant, 1 to 2 minutes. Remove the seeds from the pan immediately and let them cool slightly, then crush them with a mortar and pestle or in a spice grinder.

2. In a saucepan, bring the wine and scallops to a simmer and remove from the heat. Cover the pan and let it stand for 5 minutes. Transfer the scallops and liquid to a glass bowl and stir in the lime juice, oil, peel, salt, garlic, jalapeños, and crushed cumin seed. Stir in the bell pepper, celery, onion, lima beans, corn, and parsley. Salt to taste.

3. Refrigerate the salad for at least 1 hour or up to 24 hours. To serve, arrange two or three radicchio leaves on individual plates. Spoon the salad onto the leaves.

◆ *PER SERVING: About 290 cals, 72 cals from fat, 8g total fat, 1g sat fat, 38mg chol, 409mg sodium, 20g total carbs, 3g fiber, 23g prot*

Grilled Salade Niçoise

Makes 6 main-dish servings

For this recipe, buy anchovies packed in olive oil so you can use the flavorful oil in the marinade. If you don't feel like grilling, substitute 1 can (12½ ounces) of drained water-packed tuna, boiled potatoes, and raw onions for the grilled items.

1 tin (2 ounces) anchovies packed in olive oil

1 tablespoon extra-virgin olive oil

⅓ cup bottled clam juice or chicken broth

¼ cup balsamic vinegar

3 garlic cloves, chopped

1½ tablespoons chopped fresh rosemary or 1½ teaspoons dried

½ teaspoon black pepper

1 pound fresh tuna steak, cut into 1½-inch chunks

1½ pounds small red potatoes, scrubbed

½ pound green beans, trimmed

1 large red onion, cut into 8 pieces

12 cups mâche lettuce or other small-leaf lettuce

12 cherry tomatoes

12 niçoise or 6 kalamata olives

1 hard-boiled egg, sliced

1 tablespoon drained capers

1. For the marinade, measure 2 tablespoons of oil from the tin of anchovies and place in a small bowl along with the olive oil. Add three anchovies to the oil in the bowl and use the back of a spoon to mash the anchovies into the oil. (Transfer remaining anchovies to a small container and store in the refrigerator for another use.) Add the clam juice, vinegar, garlic, rosemary, and pepper. Whisk until smooth.

2. Pour 3 tablespoons of the marinade into a shallow dish just large enough to hold the tuna. Add the tuna, turning to coat. Cover and refrigerate for at least 20 minutes or up to 1 hour. Reserve the remaining marinade to use as the vinaigrette.

3. Cook the potatoes in a large pot of boiling salted water until barely tender, about 6 minutes. Remove the potatoes with a slotted spoon and set aside. Add the beans to the boiling water and cook until just crisp-tender, about 3 minutes. Drain and rinse under cold water to stop the cooking and set the color.

4. Prepare a medium-hot barbecue fire or preheat the broiler. Remove the tuna from the marinade. Add the onion and potatoes to the marinade, turning gently to coat. Thread the potatoes, onions, and tuna onto six metal skewers, placing the vegetables in the center of the skewers. Grill or broil, turning once or twice, until the vegetables are slightly blackened and the tuna is cooked through, about 10 minutes.

continued

5. Toss the mâche with ¼ cup of the reserved dressing and place on a large platter. Toss the green beans with 2 tablespoons of the dressing and scatter over the lettuce. Place the grilled tuna and vegetables still on the skewers on top of the salad. Garnish with the cherry tomatoes, olives, sliced egg, and capers. Drizzle with the remaining dressing.

◆ *PER SERVING: About 338 cals, 82 cals from fat, 9g total fat, 1g sat fat, 71mg chol, 218mg sodium, 41g total carbs, 3g fiber, 25g prot*

FLAVORED OILS AND VINEGARS

In the past, we had only plain vegetable oil and white or cider vinegar to choose from. Now dozens of oils and vinegars offer almost unlimited options for flavored vinaigrettes. You can make your own flavored vinegars by simply steeping fruit or herbs in wine vinegar for several days. But it's difficult to make flavored oils safely at home, because bacteria growing on the herbs thrive in the oils' low-acid environment. To be on the safe side, keep commercially flavored oils in the refrigerator once the bottle has been opened. Both vinegars and oils are now more reasonably priced and readily available than ever before. Brands differ in their potency and flavor, so try several to find your favorites. But remember that no amount of flavoring will cover up an inferior oil or vinegar base.

Grilled Shrimp, Black Bean, and Mango Salad

Makes 6 main-dish servings

The vibrant pink shrimp mixed with the orange, red, green, and black of the other ingredients make a dazzling presentation. You don't have to avoid shrimp, even though they are relatively high in cholesterol, because they are extremely low in total and saturated fat.

2 cans (16 ounces each) black
  beans, rinsed and drained,
  or 4 cups cooked black beans
1 red bell pepper, seeded and
  chopped
1 ripe but firm mango, peeled and
  cut into ½-inch dice
½ cup thinly sliced scallions,
  plus ¼ cup

½ cup chopped cilantro
½ cup Tropical Vinaigrette
  (recipe follows), plus ¼ cup
1 pound (about 24) large shrimp,
  peeled and deveined
6 cups torn spinach leaves

1. In a mixing bowl, combine the beans, bell pepper, mango, ½ cup of scallions, and cilantro with ½ cup of the Tropical Vinaigrette. Refrigerate for at least 30 minutes or up to 6 hours.

2. Prepare a medium-hot barbecue fire or preheat a broiler. In a shallow dish, toss the shrimp with the remaining Tropical Vinaigrette. Refrigerate for 15 to 30 minutes. Thread the shrimp onto metal skewers and grill, turning once or twice, until lightly charred on the outside and cooked through, 4 to 5 minutes.

3. Divide the spinach among six plates. Spoon the bean and mango salad onto the spinach, top with the shrimp, and sprinkle with the remaining ¼ cup of scallions.

◆ *PER SERVING (without dressing): About 260 cals, 18 cals from fat, 2g total fat, 0g sat fat, 87mg chol, 135mg sodium, 38g total carbs, 8g fiber, 24g prot*

TROPICAL VINAIGRETTE

Makes about ¾ cup or six 2-tablespoon servings

This light, fresh, and piquant dressing is wonderful drizzled over a salad of fruit and greens. It also makes a fine marinade for chicken or shrimp.

¼ cup fresh lime juice
¼ cup fresh orange juice
3 tablespoons extra-virgin
  olive oil

1 tablespoon white wine vinegar
2 teaspoons grainy Dijon
  mustard
2 garlic cloves, minced

2 teaspoons ground cumin
2 teaspoons chili powder
¼ teaspoon black pepper
Salt to taste

In a small bowl, whisk together all of the ingredients. Use immediately or refrigerate up to 2 days.

Per serving: About 77 cals, 65 cals from fat, 7g total fat, 1g sat fat, 0mg chol, 53mg sodium, 3g total carbs, 1g fiber, 1g prot

HOW TO MANAGE A MANGO

The mango, a prized fruit in the tropics, is now widely available in supermarkets. It is in season in spring and early summer—just the right time for making salsas and salads. Mangoes are naturally high in carotenoids and vitamin C and are a good source of fiber. Look for fruit with golden skin tinged with red or bright pink to assure the best flavor. Like an avocado, a ripe mango yields to gentle pressure, but is not soft or shriveled. A mango that is firm but not rock-hard will ripen in a few days if left on the counter or overnight in a brown paper bag.

The best way to cut a mango is to stand it on its end and make two wide slices on either side of the pit. Then use a sharp knife to peel the skin away from the flesh. If some flesh clings to the pit, just scrape it off or eat it right around the seed—it will be messy but worth it.

Lemon, Tuna, and White Bean Salad

Makes 4 main-dish servings

Canned tuna and white beans make this salad easy to prepare, which is especially nice for a weeknight dinner. The cannellini beans provide iron and some calcium.

2 cans (16 ounces each) cannellini beans
   or other white beans, rinsed and drained,
   or 4 cups cooked cannellini beans
1 medium red onion, chopped
2 tablespoons fresh lemon juice
2 tablespoons bottled clam juice
2 tablespoons extra-virgin olive oil
2 teaspoons chopped fresh thyme
   or ½ teaspoon dried
2 teaspoons chopped fresh oregano
   or ½ teaspoon dried
½ teaspoon grated lemon peel
¼ teaspoon black pepper
1 can (6 ounces) water-packed tuna
½ cup chopped flat-leaf parsley
Salt to taste
1 bunch arugula, rinsed and dried
2 tomatoes, cut into wedges

1. In a mixing bowl, combine the beans and onion. In a small bowl, whisk together the lemon juice, clam juice, oil, thyme, oregano, lemon peel, and pepper. Add the dressing to the beans and onion, and toss to mix. Add the tuna and parsley and stir gently to combine, just enough to break the tuna into clumps. Taste and add salt if desired.

2. Let the salad stand for 10 minutes to blend the flavors or refrigerate up to 1 hour before serving. To serve, spoon over a bed of arugula and garnish with tomato wedges.

◆ *PER SERVING: About 400 cals, 74 cals from fat, 8g total fat, 1g sat fat, 12mg chol, 186mg sodium, 53g total carbs, 10g fiber, 30g prot*

Peppery Jambalaya Seafood Salad

Makes 6 main-dish servings

Readily available shrimp and crabmeat are used in this Louisiana-style recipe, but any other cooked seafood, such as lobster or swordfish, will work just as well.

⅓ cup bottled clam juice
3 tablespoons red wine vinegar
3 tablespoons extra-virgin olive oil
1½ tablespoons Dijon mustard
1½ teaspoons liquid hot pepper
   sauce
2 garlic cloves, minced
1½ teaspoons dried oregano
1 teaspoon dried thyme
¼ teaspoon cayenne pepper
6 cups cooked brown or white rice
¾ pound plum tomatoes, seeded
   and diced

½ pound (about 18) cooked
   medium shrimp
6 ounces smoked ham, cut into
   ½-inch dice (about 1½ cups)
1 large green bell pepper, seeded
   and chopped
1 cup thinly sliced celery
1 cup thinly sliced scallions
⅔ cup chopped flat-leaf parsley
½ pound lump crabmeat, picked
   over to remove all shell
   and cartilage

1. In a small mixing bowl, whisk together the clam juice, vinegar, olive oil, mustard, and hot pepper sauce. Whisk in the garlic, oregano, thyme, and cayenne pepper.

2. In a large mixing bowl, stir together the rice, tomatoes, shrimp, ham, bell pepper, celery, scallions, and ½ cup of the parsley. Add the dressing and toss to combine well. Add the crabmeat and stir gently to combine, without breaking up the crabmeat too much.

3. Serve the salad immediately or refrigerate up to 3 hours. Sprinkle with the remaining parsley just before serving.

◆ *PER SERVING: About 423 cals, 101 cals from fat, 11g total fat, 2g sat fat, 106mg chol, 927mg sodium, 51g total carbs, 4g fiber, 29g prot*

LOW-FAT SALAD TOPPERS

Instead of the usual packaged croutons or cheese, get creative with healthful salad toppers:

◆ Unsweetened cereal

◆ Small, plain, low-fat crackers
◆ A variety of different sprouts
◆ Raisins or dried fruits, such as cranberries or cherries, on fruit salads

◆ Unsalted pretzels
◆ Chopped fresh apples, pears, orange segments, or frozen grapes

Seashell Macaroni and Salmon Salad

Makes 6 main-dish servings

Canned salmon is convenient, tasty, and a good source of calcium. In this recipe, salmon is the centerpiece of a main-course macaroni salad that is sure to please the whole family.

½ cup reduced-fat mayonnaise

½ cup nonfat plain yogurt

3 tablespoons Dijon mustard

1½ tablespoons fresh lemon juice

¼ cup chopped fresh dill, plus dill sprigs for garnish

½ teaspoon salt

¼ teaspoon cayenne pepper

1 pound medium shell macaroni

2 cups broccoli florets

1 large red bell pepper, seeded and coarsely chopped

1 cup coarsely chopped celery

1 cup thinly sliced scallions

2 cans (6½ ounces each) pink salmon, drained

6 cherry tomatoes, halved

Paprika for garnish

1. In a small bowl, whisk together the mayonnaise, yogurt, mustard, lemon juice, dill, salt, and pepper. Refrigerate until ready to use, up to 2 days.

2. Cook the macaroni in a large pot of boiling salted water until nearly al dente, about 8 minutes. Add the broccoli florets to the boiling water and cook until the broccoli is crisp-tender, about 2 minutes. Pour the macaroni and broccoli into a colander to drain, then rinse under cold water to stop the cooking and set the color of the broccoli.

3. In a large mixing bowl, combine the macaroni and broccoli, bell pepper, celery, and scallions. Add the salad dressing and toss to blend. Gently stir in the salmon. Cover the salad and refrigerate for at least 30 minutes (up to 4 hours) before serving.

4. Garnish the salad with the dill sprigs, cherry tomato halves, and a dusting of paprika.

◆ *PER SERVING: About 502 cals, 120 cals from fat, 13g total fat, 3g sat fat, 27mg chol, 888mg sodium, 68g total carbs, 4g fiber, 27g prot*

Grilled Tofu Caesar Salad

Makes 4 main-dish servings

For other variations on this protein-rich Caesar salad, substitute shrimp or chicken for the tofu, if you wish. (See the note at the end of the recipe.)

1 tin (2 ounces) anchovies packed
   in olive oil

1½ tablespoons lower-sodium
   chicken broth

1½ tablespoons fresh lemon juice

1 teaspoon Worcestershire sauce

2 garlic cloves

¾ pound firm tofu, patted dry and

cut into four lengthwise slices

½ teaspoon coarsely ground black
   pepper

8 slices French bread, each
   about ½ inch thick

8 cups torn romaine lettuce

¼ cup (1 ounce) coarsely grated
   pecorino Romano cheese

1. Measure and reserve 2 tablespoons of oil from the anchovies. Place one of the anchovies in a small bowl. (Cover and refrigerate the remaining anchovies for another use.) Add the oil to the anchovy and mash with the back of a spoon. Whisk in the broth, lemon juice, and Worcestershire sauce. Cut one of the garlic cloves in half and reserve it. Finely chop the remaining garlic and add it to the anchovy dressing. (The dressing can be made up to 1 day ahead and refrigerated.)

2. Prepare a medium-hot barbecue fire or preheat the broiler. Brush about a quarter of the dressing over the tofu, then sprinkle with the pepper. Rub the cut sides of the bread with the cut sides of the ½ clove of garlic, then chop the garlic and add it to the dressing.

3. Grill the tofu until golden, turning once during the cooking time, 6 to 8 minutes. Grill the bread for about 1 minute, turning once, until toasted.

4. In a bowl, toss the romaine with about half of the remaining dressing and half of the grated cheese. Transfer to serving plates. Slice the tofu, and arrange on top of the salads. Drizzle with the remaining dressing and sprinkle with the remaining cheese. Garnish with the grilled bread slices.

◆ *PER SERVING: About 357 cals, 147 cals from fat, 16g total fat, 3g sat fat, 8mg chol, 448mg sodium, 34g total carbs, 3g fiber, 22g prot*

Note: Instead of tofu, ¾ pound peeled and deveined large shrimp or four small skinless, boneless chicken breasts can be grilled. The shrimp should be threaded on skewers and grilled until opaque, 4 to 5 minutes. Chicken breasts should be grilled until white through-out, 8 to 10 minutes, and sliced before adding to the salad.

Tortellini and Cilantro Pesto Salad

Makes 4 main-dish servings

The cilantro and chili powder give a pleasing Southwestern twist to this traditional Italian pasta salad.

½ cup defatted lower-sodium chicken broth, plus ¼ cup
1 ounce (about ¼ cup) sun-dried tomatoes
1 pound refrigerated or frozen cheese tortellini
½ cup Cilantro Pesto (recipe follows)
1 tablespoon red wine vinegar
1 teaspoon chili powder
1 yellow crookneck squash, halved
  lengthwise and sliced
1 yellow bell pepper, seeded and diced
1 tablespoon toasted pine nuts (see note)

1. Bring ½ cup of the broth to a boil in a small pan. Remove from the heat and add the sun-dried tomatoes. Let the tomatoes stand until they are softened and have absorbed most of the liquid, about 15 minutes. Drain off and discard any excess liquid. Thinly slice the tomatoes.

2. Cook the tortellini in a large pot of boiling water according to package directions. Drain well and transfer to a mixing bowl.

3. In a small bowl, stir together the Cilantro Pesto, remaining ¼ cup broth, vinegar, and chili powder. (This recipe can be made to this point a day ahead and refrigerated, but the salad should be dressed no more than 2 hours before serving.)

4. To serve, add the dressing, squash, bell pepper, and sun-dried tomatoes to the pasta and toss to coat. Sprinkle with the pine nuts. Let the salad stand for at least 15 minutes or refrigerate up to 2 hours before serving at room temperature.

◆ *PER SERVING (without pesto): About 405 cals, 88 cals from fat, 10g total fat, 3g sat fat, 53mg chol, 582mg sodium, 62g total carbs, 1g fiber, 20g prot*

Note: To toast the pine nuts, place them in a small skillet set over medium-high heat. Cook, stirring constantly, until golden and fragrant, about 3 minutes. Remove immediately from the pan.

CILANTRO PESTO

Makes about ½ cup (about four 2-tablespoon servings)

The tart, lemony flavor of cilantro makes a wonderful substitute for basil in this potent and fresh-tasting pesto. Most people don't think of herbs like cilantro as leafy greens, but, in quantities like these, herbs pack a broad range of nutrients.

1 cup lightly packed cilantro sprigs

1 cup lightly packed flat-leaf parsley sprigs

3 large garlic cloves

¼ cup grated Parmesan or hard Monterey Jack cheese

2 tablespoons defatted lower–sodium chicken broth

2 tablespoons extra-virgin olive oil

1. Place the cilantro and parsley in the work bowl of a food processor. With the motor running, drop in the garlic cloves and process until all ingredients are finely chopped. Add the cheese and process about 5 seconds until well blended. With the motor running, pour in the broth and oil. Process, stopping to scrape down the sides of the bowl, until a thick, rough purée forms.
2. Use the pesto immediately, refrigerate up to 2 days, or freeze up to 6 months.

Per serving: About 103 cals, 80 cals from fat, 9g total fat, 2g sat fat, 5mg chol, 136mg sodium, 3g total carbs, 0g fiber, 4g prot

Old-Fashioned Potato Salad

Makes 8 side-dish servings

A good potato salad is simple, unfussy, and tasty. An important ingredient is thin-skinned, waxy potatoes, because they don't need to be peeled, and the skin adds color to the salad. If you can find them, try using Yukon Gold potatoes, which have a lovely golden hue.

2 pounds Yukon Gold or red potatoes, cut into rough 1½- to 2-inch chunks

2 tablespoons reduced-fat sour cream

1 tablespoon white wine or lemon juice

1 medium bell pepper, seeded and chopped

½ cup thinly sliced celery

⅓ cup thinly sliced scallions

¼ cup reduced-fat mayonnaise

¼ cup nonfat plain yogurt

3 tablespoons sweet pickle relish

1½ tablespoons Dijon mustard

½ teaspoon salt

¼ teaspoon freshly ground pepper

2 tablespoons chopped parsley

1 hard-boiled egg, sliced (optional)

1. Cook the potatoes in a large pot of lightly salted boiling water until tender, about 10 minutes. Drain well and turn into a mixing bowl. Use a small knife to cut each chunk in

continued

half. Add the sour cream and wine to the warm potatoes and toss to coat. Let cool to room temperature, then add the bell pepper, celery, and scallions to the bowl.

2. In a small bowl, whisk together the mayonnaise, yogurt, pickle relish, mustard, salt, and pepper. Pour over the vegetables and toss gently but thoroughly to coat.

3. Refrigerate the potato salad for at least 1 hour or up to 8 hours. Just before serving, sprinkle the potato salad with the parsley and sliced egg, if desired.

◆ *PER SERVING (without egg): About 162 cals, 28 cals from fat, 3g total fat, 1g sat fat, 1mg chol, 324mg sodium, 31g total carbs, 0g fiber, 3g prot*

Four-Bean Ranch Salad

Makes 8 side-dish servings

You can make this recipe with fresh black beans and fresh lima beans, but the convenience of canned and frozen beans is especially welcome in the summertime, when this salad becomes the perfect picnic dish.

½ pound fresh green beans
½ pound fresh yellow string or wax beans
1 package (10 ounces) frozen baby lima beans
1 can (16 ounces) black beans, rinsed and drained,
    or 2 cups cooked black beans
1 medium red onion, coarsely chopped
¼ cup white wine vinegar
2 tablespoons vegetable oil
1½ tablespoons sugar
1 to 2 teaspoons finely chopped jalapeño
    pepper, to taste
1 teaspoon ground cumin
½ teaspoon salt
½ teaspoon freshly ground pepper

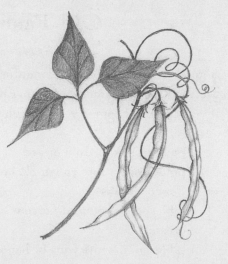

1. Trim the green and string beans and cut them diagonally into pieces about 1½ inches long. Cook the lima beans in a large pot of boiling salted water for 3 minutes. Add the green and string beans and cook until the limas are tender and the green and string beans are crisp-tender, about 3 minutes longer. Drain all the beans in a colander, then rinse under cold water to stop the cooking and set the color. Turn the beans into a large mixing bowl. Add the black beans and the onion.

2. In a small bowl, whisk together the vinegar, oil, sugar, jalapeños, cumin, salt, and pepper until the sugar is dissolved. Pour the mixture over the beans and toss to coat completely.

3. Let the beans stand for at least 30 minutes or refrigerate up to 4 hours before serving at room temperature.

◆ *PER SERVING: About 165 cals, 36 cals from fat, 4g total fat, 1g sat fat, 0mg chol, 155mg sodium, 26g total carbs, 6g fiber, 8g prot*

Family Reunion Macaroni Salad

Makes 10 side-dish servings

This all-American macaroni salad is great for summer parties. The addition of so many vegetables makes this a hit in the nutrient department, too. The ingredients can be prepared ahead but, for optimum color and texture, toss the salad shortly before serving.

1 pound elbow or other similarly shaped macaroni
3 tablespoons defatted lower-sodium chicken broth
1½ cups finely diced or coarsely shredded carrots
1 cup finely diced celery
1 large red bell pepper, seeded and diced
1 medium-sized zucchini, diced
½ cup thinly sliced scallions
⅓ cup chopped parsley, preferably flat leaf
½ cup reduced-fat mayonnaise
⅓ cup nonfat plain yogurt
¼ cup reduced-fat sour cream
2 tablespoons Dijon mustard
½ teaspoon salt
½ teaspoon black pepper
Halved cherry tomatoes for garnish

1. Cook the macaroni in a large pot of boiling salted water until al dente, 10 to 12 minutes. Drain well, rinse under cold water, and transfer to a large mixing bowl. Toss the macaroni with the chicken broth to coat. Add the carrots, celery, bell pepper, zucchini, scallions, and parsley to the macaroni. In a small bowl, whisk together the mayonnaise, yogurt, sour cream, mustard, salt, and pepper. (This recipe can be prepared up to 6 hours ahead to this

continued

point. Refrigerate salad and dressing separately.)

2. About 30 minutes (up to 2 hours) before serving, add the dressing to the macaroni mixture in the bowl and toss to blend well. Garnish with cherry tomato halves.

◆ *PER SERVING: About 246 cals, 50 cals from fat, 6g total fat, 1g sat fat, 2mg chol, 300mg sodium, 41g total carbs, 2g fiber, 8g prot*

Shredded Carrot, Jicama, and Currant Slaw

Makes 6 side-dish servings

This updated version of grated carrot salad replaces some of the traditional ingredients with crunchy jicama and colorful red cabbage.

2 cups coarsely grated carrots	2 tablespoons fresh lemon juice
2 cups coarsely grated jicama	1 tablespoon white wine vinegar
1 cup coarsely shredded red cabbage	2 teaspoons honey
	1 teaspoon Dijon mustard
¼ cup dried currants	¼ teaspoon salt
3 tablespoons reduced-fat mayonnaise	⅛ teaspoon black pepper

1. In a mixing bowl, combine the carrots, jicama, cabbage, and currants. In a small bowl, whisk together the mayonnaise, lemon juice, vinegar, honey, mustard, salt, and pepper. Pour the dressing over the salad and toss to mix well.

2. Cover the salad and refrigerate it for at least 1 hour (up to 4 hours) before serving.

◆ *PER SERVING: About 93 cals, 24 cals from fat, 3g total fat, 1g sat fat, 0mg chol, 180mg sodium, 17g total carbs, 2g fiber, 1g prot*

HANDLING JICAMA

Jicama (pronounced HEEK-a-ma) is a root vegetable often used in Mexican cuisine that can be eaten raw or cooked. In texture and taste it is somewhat like a very crunchy, giant water chestnut. Jicama is a good source of vitamin C; ½ cup supplies 25 percent of the daily requirement. Jicamas vary in size from several ounces to more than a pound and will keep in the refrigerator for at least a week. To prepare, use a small sharp knife to peel away the thick brown outer skin and the white fibrous layer underneath. Use the peeled vegetable immediately or store it in water to which a teaspoon of lemon juice has been added to retain color and crispness. Diced jicama is great in vegetable salads and adds crunch to salsas and sandwiches. It can also be used like water chestnuts in a stir-fry. Shredded jicama works well in a slaw or as a garnish for gazpacho.

Calico Coleslaw

Makes 8 side-dish servings

Coleslaw should be made at least an hour before serving so that the vinegar in the dressing can tenderize the cabbage a bit.

4 cups coarsely shredded green
   cabbage
3 cups coarsely shredded red
   cabbage
2 carrots, coarsely grated
1 small onion, finely chopped
⅓ cup reduced-fat mayonnaise

⅓ cup nonfat plain yogurt
2 tablespoons cider vinegar
2 teaspoons sugar
¾ teaspoon salt
½ teaspoon celery seeds
½ teaspoon black pepper

1. Place the cabbages, carrots, and onion in a large mixing bowl. In a small bowl, whisk together the mayonnaise, yogurt, vinegar, sugar, salt, celery seeds, and pepper until the sugar dissolves. Pour the dressing over the vegetables and toss to mix thoroughly.

2. Refrigerate the coleslaw for at least 1 hour (up to 8 hours) before serving.

◆ *PER SERVING: About 72 cals, 32 cals from fat, 4g total fat, 1g sat fat, 0mg chol, 297mg sodium, 9g total carbs, 2g fiber, 2g prot*

PICNIC SAFETY: KEEP IT HOT—KEEP IT COLD

Picnics are a traditional part of summer. But ants aren't the only buggy invaders to watch out for at a picnic. The warm temperatures are also ideal for bacterial growth in food. So it's important to follow these safety tips:

◆ Keep hot foods hot. Use a thermos for soups and other hot liquids. Put solids, such as baked beans, in sturdy foil containers wrapped in many layers of newspaper or in a thermal blanket that can later be used as a tablecloth.

◆ Keep cold foods cold. Carry them in a cooler that has been rinsed down in cold water, then lined with frozen cold packs or ice in heavy plastic bags. You can use the ice later for beverages.

◆ Be especially careful with raw or cooked meats or poultry, cheeses and other dairy products, and salad dressings. These foods spoil very quickly.

◆ To make sure that hot and cold foods remain safe to eat, repack them as soon as the meal has been served.

◆ When you get home, promptly refrigerate leftovers that have been kept at the right temperature and discard anything that may have become contaminated.

Chunked Tomato, Fennel, and Chickpea Salad

Makes 6 side-dish servings

Chickpeas, also called garbanzo beans, retain their firmness when cooked so they give a salad an especially good texture. If you have access to garden-fresh cucumbers, you can use them unpeeled. Otherwise, buy the long, unwaxed, thin-skinned seedless English variety.

1 can (19 ounces) chickpeas, rinsed and drained,
    or 2 cups cooked chickpeas
2 cups seeded and roughly chopped tomatoes
    (about 2 medium)
2 cups seeded and diced unpeeled cucumber
⅔ cup diced fennel (about 1 small bulb)
1 large red onion, coarsely chopped
¼ cup chopped fresh mint, plus ¼ cup
3 tablespoons fresh lemon juice
2 tablespoons defatted lower-sodium
    chicken broth
2 tablespoons extra-virgin olive oil
1¼ teaspoons ground cumin
1¼ teaspoons paprika
½ teaspoon salt
½ teaspoon black pepper
½ teaspoon cayenne pepper
Mint sprigs for garnish

1. In a mixing bowl, toss together the chickpeas, tomato, cucumber, fennel, onion, and ¼ cup of the chopped mint. In a small bowl, whisk together the lemon juice, broth, oil, cumin, paprika, salt, and black and cayenne peppers. Pour the dressing over the salad and toss to mix well. Let the salad stand for at least 15 minutes or refrigerate up to 4 hours before serving at room temperature.

2. Just before serving, add the remaining chopped mint to the salad and toss to combine. Serve garnished with mint sprigs.

◆ *PER SERVING: About 197 cals, 58 cals from fat, 6g total fat, 1g sat fat, 0mg chol, 328mg sodium, 29g total carbs, 2g fiber, 8g prot*

Minted Couscous Greek Salad

Makes 6 side-dish servings

This salad looks great, it's easy to eat, and it tastes terrific. It's also low in fat and the red peppers are an excellent source of vitamin C.

2 cups vegetable broth or defatted lower-sodium chicken broth

1½ cups packaged raw couscous

1 small red bell pepper, diced

1 small yellow bell pepper, diced

1 celery rib, diced

¾ cup sliced scallions plus ¼ cup

1 cup (10-ounce can) chickpeas (garbanzo beans), drained and rinsed

1½ cups fresh, frozen, or canned artichoke hearts, cooked and quartered

⅓ cup (about 1½ ounces) crumbled feta cheese

3 tablespoons thinly sliced kalamata or other similar olives

¾ cup Mint Vinaigrette (recipe follows)

Romaine lettuce leaves for serving

1. Bring the broth and ¼ cup water to a boil in a medium pot. Stir in the couscous, remove the pot from the heat, cover, and let stand for 5 minutes. Transfer the couscous to a large mixing bowl and fluff with a fork. Let stand for 5 minutes, then fluff again.

2. Add the red and yellow bell peppers, celery, ¾ cup of the scallions, chickpeas, artichokes, feta cheese, and olives. Toss gently with a fork. Add the Mint Vinaigrette and toss again until mixed. (The salad can be made and refrigerated up to 4 hours ahead. Fluff with a fork before serving.)

3. To serve, line a shallow serving bowl or rimmed platter with romaine lettuce leaves. Spoon the salad into the bowl. Sprinkle with the remaining ¼ cup of scallions.

◆ *PER SERVING (without vinaigrette): About 285 cals, 38 cals from fat, 4g total fat, 1g sat fat, 6mg chol, 337mg sodium, 51g total carbs, 13g fiber, 12g prot*

MINT VINAIGRETTE

Makes about 1 cup (eight 2-tablespoon servings)

This accompaniment to the Minted Couscous Greek Salad (page 99) also would be a well-chosen dressing for spinach salad with sliced oranges, or any other green salad that needs a lemony-mint lift.

8 tablespoons defatted lower-sodium chicken or vegetable broth
4 tablespoons extra-virgin olive oil

5 tablespoons fresh lemon juice
1 teaspoon grated lemon peel
1 large garlic clove, finely chopped
¼ cup chopped fresh mint

1 tablespoon chopped fresh marjoram or 1 teaspoon dried
½ teaspoon freshly ground pepper
Salt to taste

1. Whisk together the broth, oil, lemon juice, peel, and garlic until well blended. Whisk in the mint, marjoram, and pepper. Taste and add salt, if desired.
2. Use immediately or cover and refrigerate up to 1 day.

Per serving: About 66 cals, 61 cals from fat, 7g total fat, 1g sat fat, 0mg chol, 5mg sodium, 1g total carbs, 0g fiber, 0g prot

PRECUT VEGGIES—DO THEY ALSO CUT OUT NUTRIENTS?

Precut vegetables, whether in commercial packages or in salad bars, are highly susceptible to the loss of water-soluble nutrients. Because they are cut up, more of their surfaces are exposed to air, light, and water—all of which can destroy nutrients or cause them to leach out. If the vegetables are not fresh or not properly stored, even more nutrients will be lost. But, if they are properly chosen and handled, the convenience of precut veggies can also mean convenient, high-quality nutrition. Here's what to look for:

FRESHNESS: Look for crisp, richly colored pieces that have no brown spots or white film. Shop at stores with high volume and rapid turnover and buy precut bags well before their expiration dates.
TEMPERATURE: The refrigerated case or salad bar should be nicely chilled, like a refrigerator. Test for coldness by putting your hand on the case or the package.
SIZE: Larger pieces, such as tomato wedges (rather than chopped tomatoes) at a salad bar, will retain more vitamins because they have less exposed surface.
MOISTURE: Veggies allowed to sit in water, whether in bags or bins, will lose nutrients in the water and may have higher bacterial counts on their surfaces. Always look for dry containers.

Herbed and Spiced Tabbouleh

Makes 4 generous side-dish servings

A classic Lebanese dish, tabbouleh should be piquant with parsley, tart with lemon juice, and peppery enough to be interesting. The customary chopped ripe tomatoes should be added just before serving so they keep their texture. Bulgur, or cracked wheat, is the essential ingredient in tabbouleh; it's rich in many essential nutrients.

1 cup raw bulgur
⅓ cup fresh lemon juice
¼ cup defatted lower-sodium chicken broth
2 tablespoons extra-virgin olive oil
½ teaspoon ground cumin
½ teaspoon ground coriander
½ teaspoon salt, plus additional to taste
⅛ teaspoon ground cinnamon
⅛ teaspoon cayenne pepper, plus
   additional to taste
½ cup chopped parsley, preferably flat leaf
½ cup chopped scallions
⅓ cup chopped mint leaves
½ pound seeded and diced plum tomatoes

1. Place the bulgur in a large heat-proof mixing bowl and pour 1½ cups of boiling water over it. Cover the bowl with plastic wrap and let it stand for about 20 minutes until the liquid is absorbed and the grains are puffy. Drain off any excess water.

2. Meanwhile, in a small bowl, whisk together the lemon juice, broth, oil, cumin, coriander, salt, cinnamon, and cayenne. Pour it over the bulgur and toss to mix well. Add the parsley, scallions, and mint, and toss again. Let the salad stand at room temperature for 30 minutes or refrigerate up to 2 hours.

3. Just before serving, toss in the tomatoes and season to taste with salt and cayenne.

◆ *PER SERVING: About 206 cals, 69 cals from fat, 8g total fat, 1g sat fat, 0mg chol, 377mg sodium, 32g total carbs, 9g fiber, 6g prot*

Tuscan Bread and Roasted Pepper Salad

Makes 8 side-dish servings

Bread salad is a Tuscan specialty that makes good use of the crusty, unsalted peasant bread for which the region is famous. It's a great use for leftover Italian bread in America, too. If you add a little prosciutto to the salad, you can easily turn it into a main course. The peppers add more than bright color—they dish up lots of vitamin C.

3 tablespoons fresh lemon juice

¼ cup defatted lower-sodium chicken broth

3½ tablespoons extra-virgin olive oil

1½ tablespoons red wine vinegar

2 garlic cloves, finely chopped

2 teaspoons chopped fresh marjoram or ½ teaspoon dried

½ teaspoon salt

½ teaspoon freshly ground pepper

6 cups day-old crusty Italian bread, torn into 1-inch pieces

¼ pound cubed fresh mozzarella cheese

½ pound tomatoes, seeded and diced

1 small green bell pepper, roasted and peeled (see page 103)

1 small yellow bell pepper, roasted and peeled (see page 103)

½ cup coarsely chopped sweet onion, such as Vidalia

⅓ cup chopped parsley, preferably flat leaf

⅓ cup slivered fresh basil

1 bunch arugula, washed and dried

¼ cup shaved pecorino Romano cheese

1. In a large mixing bowl, whisk together the lemon juice, broth, oil, vinegar, garlic, marjoram, salt, and pepper. Add the bread to the vinaigrette in the bowl. Let the bread stand for 30 minutes at room temperature, stirring occasionally.

2. Add the mozzarella cheese, tomatoes, roasted peppers, onion, parsley, and basil to the bread and toss again. Let stand at least 15 minutes (up to 1 hour). Do not refrigerate the salad. Thinly slice about half of the arugula and toss into the salad along with about half of the Romano cheese.

3. To serve, make a bed of the remaining arugula leaves on six serving plates. Spoon the salad over the arugula, then sprinkle with the remaining cheese.

◆ *PER SERVING: About 201 cals, 97 cals from fat, 11g total fat, 2g sat fat, 15mg chol, 381mg sodium, 20g total carbs, 0g fiber, 7g prot*

ROASTING PEPPERS

Roasting a bell pepper softens and sweetens the flesh and gives it a distinctive, yet subtle, smoky flavor. To roast on a grill, halve the peppers, remove the seeds, and place, cut side down, on the oiled grill rack over a medium fire. Roast, turning once or twice, until softened and lightly charred. To roast over an indoor gas stove flame, push a metal skewer through a whole pepper and roast, turning over the flame, until the skin is blistered and blackened. To roast in an electric broiler, place the whole pepper on a baking sheet and set it about 4 inches below the heat source, turning occasionally until the skin is charred. Roasting will take from 5 to 8 minutes. Immediately place the hot roasted pepper in a brown paper bag and let the pepper steam in its own heat for about 10 minutes to loosen the skin. Peel off the blackened skin with your fingers and a small, sharp knife. Use the peppers immediately or refrigerate them for up to 2 days before serving.

Chicory, Arugula, and Orange Salad Siciliana

Makes 8 side-dish servings

If they are available, use blood oranges, which are native to Sicily and southern Italy, in this salad. Their brilliant red pulp makes a dramatic (and delicious) addition to this dish.

4 small blood or navel oranges

2 tablespoons balsamic vinegar

1 tablespoon finely chopped shallots

1 teaspoon Dijon mustard

½ teaspoon salt

½ teaspoon freshly ground black pepper

2 tablespoons extra-virgin olive oil

1 bunch arugula, washed and stems trimmed (about 4 cups)

1 small head chicory, washed and torn (about 4 cups)

1 small red onion, thinly sliced

1. Grate 2 teaspoons of peel from one of the oranges and squeeze ¼ cup of juice. Peel and thinly slice the remaining three oranges. Reserve. In a small bowl, whisk together the orange juice and peel, vinegar, shallots, mustard, salt, and pepper. Whisk in the oil to blend. (The vinaigrette can be made 2 days ahead and refrigerated.)

2. In a mixing bowl, toss together the arugula and chicory. Separate the onion into rings and scatter the rings and the orange slices over the greens. At the table, drizzle the vinaigrette over the salad and toss.

◆ *PER SERVING: About 90 cals, 35 cals from fat, 4g total fat, 1g sat fat, 0mg chol, 195mg sodium, 13g total carbs, 6g fiber, 3g prot*

Curried Waldorf Salad

Makes 6 side-dish servings

Curry powder adds wonderful color and an exotic flavor to this updated classic American salad. Each of the three different kinds of apple included in this recipe has its own distinctive taste. Use the best of your local apple varieties. If you wish, you can substitute 2 slices of cooked and crumbled bacon for the ham.

¼ cup walnut pieces

3 tablespoons reduced-fat
  mayonnaise

3 tablespoons nonfat plain yogurt

1½ tablespoons fresh lemon juice

¼ teaspoon grated lemon peel

2 teaspoons curry powder

¼ teaspoon salt

¼ teaspoon black pepper

⅛ teaspoon cayenne pepper

1 golden Delicious or other yellow-
  skinned apple

1 red Delicious, McIntosh, or
  other red-skinned apple

1 Granny Smith or other tart
  green apple

1 cup chopped celery

⅓ cup dried currants

2 ounces (about ½ cup) diced
  smoked ham

1 head Bibb lettuce

1. Preheat the oven to 350 degrees. Toast the walnuts on a small baking sheet, stirring once or twice, until golden and fragrant, about 5 minutes. Let cool. (The nuts can be toasted up to 2 days ahead and stored, covered, at room temperature.)

2. In a small bowl, whisk together the mayonnaise, yogurt, lemon juice and peel, curry powder, salt, pepper, and cayenne. (The dressing can be made and refrigerated up to 2 days ahead.)

3. Core the apples, but do not peel them. Cut the apples into ¾-inch dice and place in a mixing bowl along with the celery and currants. Add the dressing and toss to coat completely. Refrigerate the salad for at least 30 minutes (up to 2 hours). Just before serving, stir in the ham.

4. Serve the salad spooned into Bibb lettuce leaves. Sprinkle with the toasted walnuts.

◆ *PER SERVING: About 164 cals, 57 cals from fat, 6g total fat, 1g sat fat, 6mg chol, 270mg sodium, 26g total carbs, 4g fiber, 5g prot*

Vietnamese Grilled Vegetable Salad

Makes 6 side-dish servings

Vegetables are fantastic when grilled, and these are among the best. To turn this into a main-dish salad, marinate a steak or chicken for an hour in half of the marinade, then grill along with the vegetables. If you don't want to grill the vegetables, roast them in the oven. Japanese eggplants are available in large supermarkets and Asian grocery stores.

1 tablespoon sesame seeds

¼ cup defatted lower-sodium chicken broth

3 tablespoons fresh lime juice

2 tablespoons fish sauce (nam pla)

2 tablespoons sesame oil

1 tablespoon reduced-sodium soy sauce

1 tablespoon honey

2 garlic cloves, finely chopped

1 teaspoon minced jalapeño pepper

2 tablespoons chopped fresh basil, preferably Asian basil

3 Japanese eggplants (about ¼ pound each)

1 medium zucchini (about 6 ounces)

1 medium crookneck squash (about 6 ounces)

¼ pound shiitake mushrooms, stems trimmed and large mushrooms cut in half

9 cups torn red and green leaf lettuces

1. In a small skillet set over high heat, toss the sesame seeds until they become fragrant, about 2 minutes. Immediately remove the seeds from the pan and let them cool. In a small bowl, whisk together the broth, lime juice, fish sauce, sesame oil, soy sauce, honey, garlic, and jalapeño pepper. Pour about half of the marinade into a shallow dish just large enough to hold the vegetables. Add the basil and toasted sesame seeds to the remaining marinade and reserve to use as a vinaigrette.

2. Prepare a medium barbecue fire or preheat the oven to 500 degrees. Trim the eggplants and both squashes, then cut them all into lengthwise slices slightly less than ½ inch thick. Place the sliced vegetables and the mushrooms in the marinade and turn to coat. Grill the vegetables directly on the grill rack or roast them in the oven in a single layer on a baking sheet, turning once and brushing with the marinade, until tender, 6 to 8 minutes.

3. In a bowl, toss the lettuces with half of the reserved vinaigrette, then transfer to plates. Arrange the vegetables on the lettuce, then drizzle with the remaining vinaigrette.

◆ *PER SERVING: About 89 cals, 40 cals from fat, 4g total fat, 1g sat fat, 0mg chol, 259mg sodium, 12g total carbs, 3g fiber, 3g prot*

Using Herbs

Every serious English garden has a carefully cultivated herbal section. Americans have also come to love the way fresh herbs can enhance and enliven the simplest of recipes. If you grow your own herbs, be sure to pinch them back regularly so that they won't go to seed. When buying fresh herbs, look for bright green coloring and leaves that give off a lot of fragrance when you pinch them. To keep dried herbs potent, store them in a cool, dry, dark place and replace them every few months because they lose their potency over time.

NAME	FLAVOR	USAGE	HERBS THAT COMPLEMENT
Basil	Lightly sweet anise and clove-like flavor	Use fresh in Italian dishes—with tomatoes or pesto. Add near the end of cooking time or sprinkle on top before serving.	Marjoram, oregano, lemongrass
Bay leaves	Potent woodsy, lightly cinnamon flavor	Use fresh or dried in soups or stews or with poached fruits. Break dried leaves in half before adding and remove before serving. Look for small, deep green, fresh leaves.	Thyme, marjoram, sage
Chervil	Subtle tarragon or celery flavor	Use fresh in salads and delicate seafood or egg dishes. Add near the end of cooking or sprinkle on top before serving.	Tarragon, dill, chives
Chives	Mild garlic and onion flavor	Use fresh in egg, poultry, fish, and cheese dishes. Chop or snip with scissors. Use small purple flowers as edible garnish.	Parsley, mint, tarragon
Cilantro (coriander)	Astringent, lemony-mint flavor	Leaves and stems are cilantro. Dried seeds are coriander. Use fresh in Asian and Latin American dishes. Add leaves near the end of cooking or sprinkle on top before serving.	Basil, chives
Dill	Subtle caraway flavor	Use fresh in salad, soup, vegetable, cheese, poultry, and seafood dishes. Add fresh near the end of cooking or sprinkle on top before serving. Use dried seeds in pickles, stews, and soups.	Chives, parsley
Fennel	Anise flavor	Use diced or sliced bulb raw in salads or cooked in soups or stews. Lacy fronds can be used as an attractive garnish. Dried seeds have a potent licorice flavor.	Oregano, thyme
Lemongrass	Unique lemony flavor	Use fresh in Thai and Vietnamese soups, curries, and poultry dishes. Discard outer leaves of stalks; chop woody inner stalk.	Basil, chives

NAME	FLAVOR	USAGE	HERBS THAT COMPLEMENT
Marjoram	Mild oregano flavor	Use in soups, stuffings, or vegetables. Good both fresh and dried.	Oregano, basil
Mint	Cool, refreshing flavor	Use fresh in chicken, lamb, vegetable, fruit, and dessert dishes and in beverages. Dozens of varieties are available including pepper-mint, spearmint, apple mint, and lemon mint.	Lemongrass, parsley
Oregano	Intense marjoram flavor	Use in Italian and Mexican dishes. A partner to basil in tomato sauces. Good both fresh and dried.	Marjoram, basil, savory
Parsley	Mild celery flavor	Use in soups, stews, sauces, vegetables, and salad dressings and as garnish. Flat leaf has more flavor; curly is a pretty garnish.	Nearly any other herb
Rosemary	Bittersweet, slightly resiny pine flavor	Use in meat, game, poultry, and potato dish-es. Chop fresh leaves. Whole branches can be used as a flavorful basting brush. Dried can develop a soapy taste over time.	Mint, parsley
Sage	Aromatic, dusky mint flavor	Use in poultry stuffings and in meat, veg-etable, soup, stew, and apple dishes. Good fresh and dried. Crumbled dried leaves are much more potent than fresh.	Savory, thyme, or marjoram
Savory	Aromatic pepper flavor	Use in meatloaf and in poultry, rice, and egg dishes. Summer variety is milder and best fresh; winter variety is stronger and good dried or fresh.	Thyme, sage
Tarragon	Pungent anise flavor	Use in chicken, egg, cheese, seafood, and veg-etable dishes. Particularly good with mush-rooms. Good fresh or dried, but fresh has a subtler flavor.	Chives, parsley
Thyme	Pleasantly astringent, mintlike flavor	Use in soups or stews or in any meat, poultry, or vegetable dish. Good fresh and dried. Versatile in its many varieties, such as lemon, orange, English, and French.	Mint, marjoram, chives

Oils

An ever-growing variety of both traditional and specialty oils appears on super-market shelves. Mildly flavored oils like canola and corn allow the flavor of other dressing ingredients to shine through, while stronger oils like olive, hazelnut, and sesame impart their own characteristic flavor.

All oils contain about 14 grams of fat and 125 calories per tablespoon. Like all fats, oils are made up of a mixture of polyunsaturated, monounsaturated, and saturated fat. Doctors recommend cutting down on saturated fat to reduce your risk of heart disease. So you should choose oils with a high percentage of polyunsaturated or monounsaturated fat rather than highly saturated oils. Make sure you use all oils only in moderation.

COMMONLY USED OILS

NAME	MONO-UNSAT. FAT	POLY-UNSAT. FAT	SAT. FAT	CHARACTERISTICS
Canola (rapeseed)	8g	4g	1g	Very mild flavor; colorless; used in sautéing, salad dressings, and baking.
Corn	3.3g	8g	1.7g	Mild corn flavor and pale-to-bright gold color; used in sautéing.
Cottonseed	2.4g	7g	3.5g	Flavorless and colorless; used in sautéing.
Olive	9.9g	1.1g	1.8g	Flavor ranges from very mild to distinctly olive to sometimes peppery. Color varies from nearly clear to deep green or amber. Extra-virgin oil, from the first cold pressing, is most expensive and used primarily as an accent flavor in vinaigrettes or sauces. Pure olive oil, processed from the pulp left after the first pressing and lighter in flavor than virgin oil, is used for cooking but not for high-temperature frying because it tends to scorch at high heat.

NAME	MONO-UNSAT. FAT	POLY-UNSAT. FAT	SAT. FAT	CHARACTERISTICS
Peanut	6.2g	4.3g	2.3g	Mild peanut flavor; very pale golden color. Used in sautéing and salad dressings. Often used in stir-fries.
Safflower	1.6g	10.1g	1.3g	Flavorless and colorless; used in sautéing, salad dressings, and baking.
Soybean	5.9g	5.1g	2g	Flavorless and colorless; used in sautéing and salad dressings.
Sunflower	6.2g	5.5g	1.4g	Flavorless and colorless; used in sautéing, salad dressings, and baking.

SPECIALTY OILS

NAME	MONO-UNSAT. FAT	POLY-UNSAT. FAT	SAT. FAT	CHARACTERISTICS
Grapeseed	2.2g	9.5g	1.3g	Mild grape flavor; nearly colorless; used primarily as a flavoring or in sautéed Mediterranean dishes.
Hazelnut	10.6g	1.4g	1g	Nutty hazelnut flavor; pale brown color. Used primarily as an accent in vinaigrettes, sauces, and baking, but not for frying because it tends to scorch at high heat.
Sesame	5.4g	5.7g	2g	Nutty flavor, from mild to intensely spicy; colorless (toasted sesame oil is dark brown with a strong flavor). Used in Asian cooking and stir-fries, but not for frying because it tends to scorch at high heat.
Walnut	3.1g	8.6g	1.2g	Nutty walnut flavor; pale gold color. Used primarily as an accent in vinaigrettes, sauces, and baking, but not for frying because it tends to scorch at high heat.

CHAPTER THREE

Breads

Breads—whether yeast breads or quick breads, pitas, tortillas, pancakes, or flat breads—hold a singular place in the human diet. Bread is fundamental. It's the center around which much of the world's nutrition has been based. And with good reason. Who can resist the blissful fragrance and warm goodness of a loaf just out of the oven?

Bread belongs to the Food Guide Pyramid's bread, cereal, pasta, and rice group, along with grains and foods made from grain. This food group remains the foundation of a healthful diet because it is abundant in complex carbohydrates, one of the best energy sources. Although you should choose a variety of grain foods to make up the recommended 6 to 11 daily servings, you can get all the necessary grain nutrients by eating only bread, as long as at least half of it is whole grain.

Whole-grain bread, thought of as less desirable than white bread until just recently, is enjoying a surge in popularity. It usually has at least twice the fiber of bread made with only refined white flour. Because whole grains retain their nutrient-rich outer husk, breads (such as multigrain, whole wheat, buckwheat, barley, and oat) made with some whole-grain flour offer more vitamins B_6 and E as well as zinc, copper, and other minerals than do breads made with only white flour. White flour may be enriched with iron and B vitamins in amounts similar to those in whole-grain flour, however.

Whole-grain breads usually have a richer flavor than white breads, and the intensity of the flavor depends on the amount of unrefined flour in the recipe. In general, these breads taste best when made with about half unrefined flour and half white flour. Breads made with only whole-grain flours tend to be too dense and heavy to rise well.

Each of your meals should include at least 2 servings from the bread group. Remember that a Food Guide Pyramid serving—a slice or piece weighing approximately 1 ounce—is less than the total portion you ordinarily would eat at a meal. The recipes for Steamed Boston Brown Bread (page 122) and Coffee Cake with Oat and Nut Streusel Topping (page 132), for example, yield portions equal to 1 bread group serving, while a slice of Super Sandwich Bread (page 114) is closer to 2 bread group servings.

Most of the breads in this chapter, as with almost all commercial bread, contain small amounts of fat. Muffins need vegetable oil for moistness and a tender crumb. Oil in the batter of waffles and pancakes helps prevent sticking. Nuts and seeds add flavor and texture. You can keep overall fat in check by serving breads, pancakes, waffles, and muffins with fruit-based or lower-fat dairy toppings in place of butter or margarine.

The beauty of the recipes in this chapter lies in their adaptability. Any bread can be used to make Oven-Baked Orange French Toast (page 133). Add flavored instead of plain yogurt in a recipe to give a bread a different taste. In a muffin recipe, substitute applesauce or ripe mashed peaches, apricots, or bananas for other fruit. Experiment with your own flavor combinations to vary your experience of the wholesome goodness of bread.

Marvelous Multigrain Bread

Makes 2 loaves (12 slices each)

Chock-full of grains, this chewy bread is even better when toasted and served with marmalade or Fresh Berry Jam (recipe follows) for breakfast. The toasted whole grains in this loaf have a wonderfully nutty flavor and contribute a variety of nutrients to your family's diet. This is a marvelous all-purpose bread.

⅓ cup cracked wheat
⅓ cup rolled oats, regular or quick
⅓ cup raw unprocessed wheat bran
3 cups white bread flour, plus additional
  for kneading
2 cups whole-wheat flour
⅓ cup toasted wheat germ
¼ cup coarsely chopped sunflower seeds
2 teaspoons salt
2 packages (¼ ounce each) quick-rising yeast
  (see note)
1¼ cups very warm water (110 to 120 degrees)
1 cup low-fat or nonfat yogurt brought to room temperature
3 tablespoons vegetable oil
3 tablespoons maple syrup
Vegetable oil spray

1. Preheat the oven to 350 degrees. Place the cracked wheat, rolled oats, and wheat bran on a rimmed baking sheet. Stir to mix together, then spread out to make an even layer on the baking sheet. Toast the grains for 3 to 5 minutes until just fragrant and lightly browned, stirring once or twice. Let cool.

2. In a large mixing bowl, whisk together the white and whole-wheat flours, wheat germ, sunflower seeds, salt, and yeast. Mix in the toasted cracked wheat mixture. Make a well in the center and pour in the water, yogurt, oil, and maple syrup. Mix with a wooden spoon or the paddle of an electric mixer until a dough forms, about 5 minutes. Turn onto a lightly floured surface and knead by hand for 10 minutes, or knead in the mixer bowl with a dough hook for 5 minutes.

3. Lightly coat a large mixing bowl and two 4½ x 8½-inch loaf pans with vegetable oil spray. Place the dough in the bowl, cover lightly with a towel, and let rise at room temperature until doubled in bulk, about 45 minutes. Punch the dough down. Divide in half and form each half into a loaf; place in the prepared loaf pans. Cover again and let rise until doubled, about 30 minutes.

4. Bake until the loaves are well risen, appear browned, and sound hollow when tapped, 40 to 45 minutes. Turn the loaves out of the pan onto a rack to cool completely before slicing. (This bread is best eaten within a day of baking although it can be frozen up to 1 month.)

◆ *PER SLICE: About 156 cals, 31 cals from fat, 3g total fat, 1g sat fat, 1mg chol, 186mg sodium, 26g total carbs, 3g fiber, 6g prot*

Note: Regular dry yeast can be substituted for quick-rising yeast. Rising times will be about doubled.

THE YEAST RACE—REGULAR VERSUS QUICK RISE

You can use quick-rising yeast interchangeably with regular dry yeast in these recipes. Quick-rising yeast is made from a special strain of yeast that works faster than its regular cousin. The long, slow rise characteristic of regular yeast gives a more yeasty flavor, which is especially good in classic Italian and French breads. Compressed fresh yeast, once the only commercially available choice, is used far less often these days because it is so perishable and must be refrigerated.

FRESH BERRY JAM
Makes about 5 half-pints

Uncooked berry jam is not "put up" or preserved in the traditional sense, but this very easy-to-make jam will keep in the refrigerator for 3 weeks or in the freezer for up to a year. It isn't as thick as commercial jams, but tastes far fresher.

1 quart very ripe berries, such as strawberries, blueberries, raspberries, or blackberries	4 cups sugar 1 pouch (3 ounces) liquid fruit pectin	2 tablespoons lemon juice

1. Thoroughly wash 5 half-pint freezer containers or jelly jars in hot water.
2. Use a potato masher or the back of a spoon to mash enough berries to make 2 cups. (If you wish, you can strain out the seeds by pressing the mashed mixture through a strainer, but remember that you need to end up with a total of 2 cups of mashed fruit.)
3. In a mixing bowl, stir together the berries and sugar, and let the mixture stand for 10 minutes. In a small bowl, stir together the pectin and lemon juice, then add to the berries. Stir for a full 3 minutes.
4. Ladle the jam into the containers to within ¼ inch of the tops. Cover with lids and let stand at room temperature until set, up to 24 hours. (Store the jam in the refrigerator up to 3 weeks or freeze up to 1 year.)

Per tablespoon serving: About 41 cals, 0 cals from fat, 0g total fat, 0g sat fat, 0mg chol, 1mg sodium, 11g total carbs, 0g fiber, 0g prot

Super Sandwich Bread

Makes 1 loaf (16 slices)

The fiber from whole-wheat flour and the moist goodness of mashed potatoes make this bread super for sandwiches. You can use leftover mashed potatoes, if you beat in a little warm water or milk.

1 large Idaho potato (about ½ pound),
　peeled and cut into 1½-inch chunks
3 to 4 tablespoons skim milk
2 cups white bread flour, plus additional
　for kneading
2 cups whole-wheat flour
1 package (¼ ounce) quick-rising yeast
¼ cup nonfat dry milk powder
1 teaspoon salt
2 tablespoons honey
Vegetable oil spray

1. Cook the potato in lightly salted boiling water until very tender, about 15 minutes. Drain off the cooking water but reserve 1½ cups of it. Let the water cool to very warm, 110 to 120 degrees. Mash the potato with the milk to make moderately soft mashed potatoes. Let cool to lukewarm. Measure ¾ cup for the bread and reserve any extra for other uses.

2. In a large mixing bowl, whisk together the white and whole-wheat flours, yeast, dry milk powder, and salt. Make a well in the center and pour in the reserved potato water, honey, and mashed potatoes. Mix with a wooden spoon or the paddle of an electric mixer until a dough forms, about 5 minutes. Turn onto a lightly floured surface and knead by hand for 10 minutes, or knead in the mixer bowl with a dough hook for 5 minutes until smooth and elastic.

3. Lightly coat a large mixing bowl and a 5x9-inch loaf pan with vegetable oil spray. Place the dough in the bowl, cover lightly with a towel, and let rise at room temperature until doubled in bulk, about 40 minutes. Punch the dough down, form into a loaf, and place in the prepared pan. Cover again and let rise until doubled, about 25 minutes.

4. Preheat the oven to 350 degrees. Bake until the loaf is browned and sounds hollow when tapped, 45 to 50 minutes. Remove from the pan and cool on a rack. (This bread is best eaten within a day of baking although it can be frozen up to 1 month.)

◆ *PER SLICE: About 139 cals, 5 cals from fat, 1g total fat, 0g sat fat, 0mg chol, 143mg sodium, 29g total carbs, 3g fiber, 5g prot*

SUPER SANDWICH BREAD VARIATIONS

◆ For a lighter-textured loaf, omit the mashed potatoes and use fresh water or water saved from cooking vegetables for the liquid in the dough. Increase the dry milk to ⅓ cup.

◆ Make cinnamon raisin bread by kneading ½ cup of raisins into the dough, then roll dough into a 9x12-inch rectangle. Sprinkle with a mixture of 2 tablespoons of sugar and 1 teaspoon of ground cinnamon. Roll up from the short side to form a loaf about 9 inches long. Place,

seam side down, in the prepared pan, let rise, and bake as directed.

◆ Substitute 1 cup of rye flour for 1 cup of whole-wheat flour.

◆ For dinner rolls, divide the dough into 16 pieces after the first rising. Form each into a smooth ball and place, about 2 inches apart, on a lightly oiled baking sheet. Cover and let rise as directed, then brush with a mixture of 1 egg beaten with 1 tablespoon of water. Bake at 375 degrees for about 20 minutes or until golden.

◆ For soft poppy seed or Parmesan breadsticks, divide the dough into 16 pieces after the first rising. Pull or roll each piece into a 12-inch rope. Twist each rope several times, then place on a large, lightly oiled baking sheet. Brush the breadsticks with a mixture of 1 egg beaten with 1 tablespoon of water, and sprinkle with 2 teaspoons of poppy seeds or 2 tablespoons of grated Parmesan cheese. Bake at 400 degrees for about 16 minutes until golden.

Braided Semolina Bread

Makes 1 large braided loaf (16 slices)

This circular, braided Italian bread looks intricate, but it's actually easy to shape. Semolina flour, also called pasta flour, gives the bread a golden color and chewy texture.

2½ cups white bread flour, plus
    additional for kneading
1½ cups semolina flour
1 cup whole-wheat flour
2 teaspoons salt
2 packages (¼ ounce each) quick-
    rising yeast

1¾ cups very warm water
    (110 to 120 degrees)
Vegetable oil spray
1 tablespoon yellow cornmeal
1 egg white beaten with
    2 teaspoons water for glaze
1 tablespoon sesame seeds

1. In a large mixing bowl, whisk together the white, semolina, and whole-wheat flours with the salt and yeast. Make a well in the center and pour in the water. Mix with a wooden spoon or the paddle of an electric mixer until a dough forms, about 5 minutes. Turn onto a lightly floured surface and knead by hand for 10 minutes, or knead in the mixer bowl with a dough hook for 5 minutes until dough is smooth and elastic.

2. Lightly coat a large mixing bowl and a large baking sheet with vegetable oil spray. Place the dough in the bowl, cover lightly with a towel, and let rise at room temperature until doubled in bulk, about 45 minutes. Punch the dough down, and divide into three parts. Use your hands to roll and stretch each part into a 26-inch-long rope. Sprinkle the

continued

baking sheet with the cornmeal, then lay the dough ropes on the baking sheet and braid them. Form the braid into a circle with a 3-inch hole in the center; pinch the ends together to seal. Cover lightly with a towel and let rise until doubled, 20 to 30 minutes.

3. Preheat the oven to 475 degrees. Brush the top of the braid with the egg white glaze, then sprinkle with the sesame seeds. Bake until the loaf is golden brown and sounds hollow when tapped, about 30 minutes. Let it cool on a rack before slicing. (The bread ring is best eaten on the day of baking but can be frozen up to 1 month.)

◆ *PER SLICE: About 158 cals, 9 cals from fat, 1g total fat, 0g sat fat, 0mg chol, 271mg sodium, 31g total carbs, 2g fiber, 6g prot*

Note: The dough can also be fashioned into two 14-inch-long, freestanding loaves on the baking sheet. The baking time will be about the same. One package of regular dry yeast can be substituted for quick-rising yeast. Rising times will be about doubled.

Basic Pizza Dough

Makes enough for one 14-inch-round pizza (4 servings)

Homemade pizza dough is so easy that you'll want to make it often. If you use quick-rising yeast and a food processor, the pizza will be ready in about 45 minutes—just about as long as it takes to order from the pizzeria. All you really need to add is a tossed salad and some fruit for dessert to make a complete and tasty meal. Keep in mind that 1 serving of this pizza equals 4 Food Guide Pyramid grain servings.

1¼ cups white bread flour, plus
   additional for kneading
½ cup semolina flour or additional
   white bread flour
½ cup whole-wheat flour
¼ cup yellow cornmeal, plus
   2 teaspoons

¾ teaspoon salt
1 package (¼ ounce) quick-rising
   yeast (see note)
1 cup very warm water
   (110 to 120 degrees)
1 tablespoon olive oil
Vegetable oil spray

1. In a large mixing bowl, whisk together the white, semolina, and whole-wheat flours, ¼ cup of the cornmeal, salt, and yeast. Make a well in the center and pour in the water and oil. Mix with a wooden spoon or the paddle of an electric mixer until a dough forms, about 5 minutes. Turn onto a lightly floured surface and knead by hand for 10 minutes, or knead in the mixer bowl with a dough hook for 5 minutes until smooth and elastic. (Alternatively, mix the dry ingredients in the work bowl of a food processor. With the motor running, pour in the water and oil. Process to mix and knead for about 45 seconds.)

2. Lightly coat a mixing bowl and a baking sheet or pizza pan with vegetable oil spray. Place the dough in the bowl, cover lightly with a towel, and let rise at room temperature until doubled in bulk, about 30 minutes. Punch the dough down. Sprinkle the baking sheet with the remaining 2 teaspoons of cornmeal. Using a rolling pin and your hands, roll and stretch the dough on the baking sheet to form a 14-inch circle. Top the pizza according to individual recipe instructions, then bake in a preheated 450-degree oven until browned and crisp, 10 to 12 minutes. Cut the pizza with a sharp knife or pizza-cutting wheel.

◆ *PER SERVING: About 339 cals, 43 cals from fat, 5g total fat, 1g sat fat, 0mg chol, 402mg sodium, 63g total carbs, 5g fiber, 11g prot*

Note: Regular dry yeast can be substituted for quick-rising yeast. Rising times will be about doubled. For extra flavor, add 2 teaspoons of dried herbs, such as oregano or sage, to the dough.

YEAST BREAD TERMINOLOGY

KNEADING strengthens the protein in flour so it can support the bread as it rises. To knead by hand, place the dough on a lightly floured surface, and flour your hands. Use the heels of your hands to flatten and push the dough away from you. Fold the dough over toward you, rotate a quarter-turn and repeat the process for 5 to 10 minutes until the dough feels smooth and elastic. You may need to add additional flour in the begin-ning to keep the dough from stick-ing. Dough can be kneaded in about half the time with a heavy-duty electric mixer with a dough hook. Dough with 3 cups or less of flour can be kneaded in a minute or so in a food processor with the plastic or steel blade.

DOUBLED IN SIZE is self-explanatory. Test for it by pressing the tips of two fingers about ½ inch into the dough. If the dents remain, the dough has doubled in size.

PUNCHING DOWN means just that. Use your fist to punch the middle of the risen dough so that it deflates. This step is done after a first rise to eliminate excess car-bon dioxide and to redistribute the yeast before a second rising or shaping.

SOUNDS HOLLOW WHEN TAPPED is a way to test for doneness for yeast breads. The top of the loaf in the pan should be firm and sound hol-low when tapped with the fingertips.

HIGH ALTITUDE YEAST

Because of lower atmospheric pressure, yeast dough rises faster at altitudes over 3,000 feet, so you may need to use up to 25 percent less yeast. Check often to see if breads have risen in less time than the recipe calls for.

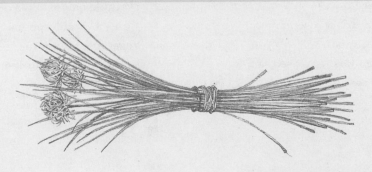

SIFTING THROUGH THE FLOUR TYPES

ALL-PURPOSE WHITE FLOUR is milled from a mixture of hard and soft wheat that performs well in a wide range of baking. Both the germ and bran of the wheat have been removed. The flour may then be "enriched" to put back the nutrients that were taken out during processing. The enrichment replaces the vitamin content but the flour still lacks the natural fiber found in whole grains.

WHITE BREAD FLOUR is better for yeast breads when you want an elastic texture. It is also slightly higher in protein than all-purpose white flour. White bread flour is usually made from nearly 100 percent unbleached flour, with a small amount of malted barley flour added.

CAKE OR PASTRY FLOUR is best when you want a delicate texture and is rarely used in breads. Both white and whole-wheat varieties are available. Self-rising cake flour has baking powder and salt added, but you can't substitute it for regular cake flour without recipe adjustments.

WHOLE-WHEAT FLOUR comes from the whole kernel of wheat so it has more fiber and higher amounts of vitamins and minerals (such as magnesium, manganese, potassium, zinc, and vitamins B_6 and E)

than white flour. It's often used with all-purpose white flour or white bread flour to produce appealingly light baked goods.

SEMOLINA FLOUR is made from hard or durum wheat; it's the preferred flour for homemade pasta. Used in some Italian breads, semolina has a light golden color and produces a chewy, crisply crusted loaf.

RYE, SOY, RICE, CORN, OAT, AND BUCKWHEAT FLOURS must be used with all-purpose white flour or white bread flour to assure the rising of yeast breads and quick breads. They are much higher in fiber than all-purpose white flour.

Herbed Focaccia

Makes 1 focaccia (12 squares)

Focaccia is a simple, rustic Italian bread that is often flavored with herbs or pepper. To give the top of the risen dough its typically dimpled appearance, lightly press the dough with your fingertips, then brush the dough with a little oil and sprinkle it with more herbs or a dusting of coarse salt.

2 to 2¼ cups white bread flour, plus
　　additional for kneading
1 cup whole-wheat flour
1 package (¼ ounce) quick-rising
　　yeast (see note)
1 teaspoon dried rosemary,
　　plus 1 teaspoon
¾ teaspoon kosher or sea salt,
　　plus ¼ teaspoon

½ teaspoon coarsely ground black
　　pepper, plus ¼ teaspoon
1 cup very warm water
　　(110 to 120 degrees)
1½ tablespoons olive oil,
　　plus 1½ tablespoons
Vegetable oil spray
1 tablespoon yellow cornmeal

1. In a large mixing bowl, whisk together the white and whole-wheat flours, yeast, 1 teaspoon of the rosemary, ¾ teaspoon of the salt, and ½ teaspoon of the pepper. Make a well in the center and pour in the water and 1½ tablespoons of the oil. Mix with a wooden spoon or the paddle of an electric mixer until a dough forms, about 5 minutes. Turn onto a lightly floured surface and knead by hand for 10 minutes, or knead in the mixer bowl with a dough hook for 5 minutes until smooth and elastic. (Alternatively, mix the dry ingredients in the work bowl of a food processor. With the motor running, pour in the liquids. Process to mix and knead for about 45 seconds.)

2. Lightly coat a mixing bowl and a 9x13-inch baking pan with vegetable oil spray. Place the dough in the bowl, cover lightly with a towel, and let rise at room temperature until doubled in bulk, about 30 minutes. Punch the dough down. Sprinkle the baking pan with the cornmeal. Place the dough in the prepared pan, patting and stretching to fill the bottom of the pan. Cover lightly and let the dough rise again until doubled, 20 to 30 minutes.

3. Preheat the oven to 400 degrees. Use your fingers to make light indentations in the risen dough. Brush with the remaining 1½ tablespoons of oil, then sprinkle with the remaining 1 teaspoon of rosemary, ¼ teaspoon of salt, and ¼ teaspoon of pepper. Bake until the focaccia is a rich golden brown and well risen, 25 to 35 minutes. Turn the focaccia onto a rack to cool slightly, then cut into squares. (Although best eaten warm, the focaccia can be frozen up to 1 month. To reheat, wrap in foil and bake in a 350-degree oven for 5 minutes, then unwrap and heat another 5 minutes to recrisp.)

◆ *PER SQUARE: About 157 cals, 36 cals from fat, 4g total fat, 1g sat fat, 0mg chol, 179mg sodium, 26g total carbs, 2g fiber, 5g prot*

Note: Regular dry yeast can be substituted for quick-rising yeast. Rising times will be about doubled.

HERBED FOCACCIA VARIATIONS

Focaccia can be even more delicious with these additions:

◆ Substitute dried sage or marjoram for the rosemary.
◆ Knead ¼ cup chopped black olives, such as kalamata, gaeta, or niçoise, into the dough.

◆ Knead ¼ cup finely chopped, sun-dried tomatoes into the dough.
◆ Add 2 tablespoons of grated Parmesan cheese to the dough, then sprinkle 2 additional tablespoons over the dough before baking.
◆ Add 2 finely minced garlic cloves

to the oil that you mix into and brush over the dough.
◆ Top the focaccia with ½ cup very thinly sliced onions sautéed in 2 teaspoons of olive oil until softened.

Caraway-Currant Soda Bread

Makes 1 loaf (about 14 slices)

Traditional Irish soda bread is made without yeast. This large, round loaf has a crisp, chewy crust and a moist, tender interior. Try it toasted and spread with jam for breakfast, as a sandwich bread at lunch, or accompanying soup or salad for dinner.

Vegetable oil spray
1 cup all-purpose white flour, plus additional for kneading
1 cup whole-wheat flour
2 tablespoons packed dark brown sugar
1½ teaspoons caraway seeds
1½ teaspoons baking powder
½ teaspoon baking soda
½ teaspoon salt
2 tablespoons cold butter
½ cup dried currants
1 egg
2 tablespoons vegetable oil
¾ cup nonfat buttermilk

1. Preheat the oven to 375 degrees. Lightly coat a baking sheet with vegetable oil spray.

2. In a large bowl, combine the white and whole-wheat flours, brown sugar, caraway seeds, baking powder, baking soda, and salt. Stir with a whisk to mix well. Cut the butter into small pieces and use your fingers to rub it into the flour until the butter is the size of small peas. Stir in the currants. In a small bowl, whisk the egg with the oil until smooth. Whisk in the buttermilk.

3. Add the buttermilk mixture to the dry ingredients and stir until a stiff dough forms. Gather into a ball, turn onto a lightly floured board, and knead until smooth, 2 to 3 minutes. Transfer to the baking sheet and shape into a slightly domed disk about 6 inches in diameter. Use a sharp knife or razor blade to cut a large crisscross about ¼ inch deep in the top of the dough to allow for even rising.

4. Bake until the loaf is golden and sounds hollow when tapped, 40 to 50 minutes.

5. Cool on a rack before cutting into slices. Serve warm or at room temperature. (This soda bread is best served on the same day it is made but can be frozen up to 2 weeks.)

◆ *PER SLICE: 127 cals, 39 cals from fat, 4g total fat, 1g sat fat, 20mg chol, 197mg sodium, 20g total carbs, 2g fiber, 3g prot*

Maple-Oat Buttermilk Quick Bread

Makes 1 loaf (about 14 slices)

Quick breads, which are leavened with baking powder and/or baking soda, take less time to make than yeast breads because the dough does not need to rise before baking. This relatively nonsweet quick bread is appetizing served alongside a bowl of hearty wintertime soup. It also makes a great breakfast bread when lightly toasted and spread with jam.

Vegetable oil spray
1¼ cups all-purpose white flour
½ cup whole-wheat flour
1 teaspoon baking powder
½ teaspoon baking soda
¾ teaspoon salt
1 egg
4 tablespoons vegetable oil
½ cup maple syrup
3 tablespoons packed light brown
   sugar
1½ cups nonfat buttermilk
¾ cup regular or quick rolled oats
½ cup raisins (optional)

1. Preheat the oven to 350 degrees. Lightly coat a 4½ x 8½-inch loaf pan with vegetable oil spray.

2. In a large bowl, whisk together the white flour, whole-wheat flour, baking powder, baking soda, and salt. In a medium bowl, whisk the egg with the oil until smooth. Whisk in the maple syrup, brown sugar, and buttermilk. Stir in the oats. Stir in the raisins, if using.

3. Add the buttermilk mixture to the flour mixture and stir to combine. Scrape the batter into the prepared pan, smooth the top, and bake until the bread is golden brown, the edges pull away slightly from the sides of the pan, and a tester inserted in the center comes out clean, 60 to 65 minutes.

4. Cool in the pan for 10 minutes, turn onto a rack, and cool completely before slicing. (This bread can be wrapped and refrigerated for 1 day or frozen for up to 2 weeks.)

◆ *PER SLICE (without raisins): About 165 cals, 45 cals from fat, 5g total fat, 1g sat fat, 16mg chol, 231mg sodium, 27g total carbs, 1g fiber, 4g prot*

Steamed Boston Brown Bread

Makes 1 loaf (about 10 slices)

This fat- and cholesterol-free bread is traditionally served with baked beans on Saturday night in New England. Steamed rather than baked, the loaf acquires an amazingly fine, tender texture. You will need a clean 13- to 14-ounce coffee can to use as a mold.

Vegetable oil spray
⅓ cup whole-wheat flour
⅓ cup cornmeal
⅓ cup rye flour
¾ teaspoon baking soda

½ teaspoon salt
¾ cup nonfat buttermilk
¼ cup molasses
½ cup raisins (optional)

1. Lightly coat the coffee can with vegetable oil spray.

2. In a large mixing bowl, whisk together the whole-wheat flour, cornmeal, rye flour, baking soda, and salt until blended. In a small bowl, combine the buttermilk and molasses. Mix in the raisins, if desired. Pour the buttermilk mixture into the flour mixture and whisk just until blended. Do not overmix.

3. Scrape the batter into the prepared coffee can and cover tightly with aluminum foil, pinching to seal well. Place the coffee can in a large pot with a lid and add boiling water to about halfway up the sides of the can. Cover the kettle, and steam over low heat until the bread rises and is firm to the touch, about 1½ hours (a tester should come out clean). Remove the can from the steamer and place on a rack until cool enough to handle.

4. Tap the bread out of the can or remove the bottom of the can and push the bread out. Serve warm or at room temperature. (The bread can be refrigerated for 1 day or frozen for 2 weeks. Reheat in a steamer before serving.)

◆ *PER SLICE (without raisins): About 70 cals, 3 cals from fat, 0g total fat, 0g sat fat, 1mg chol, 222mg sodium, 15g total carbs, 1g fiber, 2g prot*

CHEMICAL LEAVENING AGENTS

Baking soda, or sodium bicarbonate, is a chemical compound that produces carbon dioxide gas when combined with an acidic liquid, such as buttermilk, yogurt, citrus juice, or molasses. Baking soda is usually called for in bread recipes using any of these ingredients. Baking powder is a commercial mixture of baking soda, an acid such as cream of tartar, and a moisture-absorbing filler such as cornstarch. Today, almost all baking powder is double acting, which means it begins to work as soon as it comes in contact with liquid, but has a second burst of energy when exposed to the heat of the oven. Because both kinds of leavening begin to work as soon as they get wet, it's important to have all of your ingredients ready and to bake the bread batter as soon as you've mixed it.

Spiced Zucchini Tea Bread

Makes 1 loaf (about 14 slices)

Toasted walnuts add richness to this sweet, moist bread. It's good at teatime, either plain or made fancy with powdered sugar sprinkled over the top.

Vegetable oil spray
¼ cup chopped walnuts
1½ cups all-purpose white flour
1 teaspoon baking powder
¼ teaspoon baking soda
¾ teaspoon salt
1¼ teaspoons ground cinnamon

¼ teaspoon ground cloves
1 egg
½ cup packed dark brown sugar
¼ cup skim milk
3 tablespoons vegetable oil
1½ cups packed shredded zucchini
 (from ½ pound zucchini)

1. Preheat the oven to 350 degrees. Lightly coat a 4½ x 8½-inch loaf pan with vegetable oil spray.

2. Spread the nuts in a metal pie plate and toast, stirring once, until golden and fragrant, about 5 minutes. Set aside.

3. In a medium bowl, combine the flour, baking powder, baking soda, salt, cinnamon, and cloves. Whisk to combine.

4. Use an electric mixer to beat the egg with the brown sugar in a large bowl until smooth. Beat in the milk and oil. With the mixer on a low speed, add the shredded zucchini and the flour mixture, beating just until no specks of flour are visible. Stir in the nuts.

5. Transfer the batter to the prepared pan and smooth the top. Bake until golden brown and a tester inserted in the center comes out clean, 55 to 60 minutes.

6. Cool in the pan for 10 minutes, turn onto a rack, and cool completely. (Use immediately or refrigerate up to 24 hours. This bread can also be frozen up to 2 weeks.)

◆ *PER SLICE: About 127 cals, 42 cals from fat, 5g total fat, 1g sat fat, 15mg chol, 173mg sodium, 19g total carbs, 1g fiber, 3g prot*

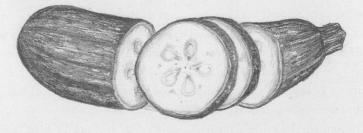

Cranberry Pumpkin Bread

Makes 1 loaf (about 14 slices)

This deliciously dense, moist pumpkin bread is studded with tart, ruby red cranberries and has a little cornmeal added for texture. It's a festive bread to include on the Thanksgiving table and makes a terrific tea bread all autumn long.

Vegetable oil spray
1 cup whole raw cranberries, fresh or frozen
1½ cups all-purpose white flour
¼ cup yellow or white cornmeal
1⅓ cups granulated sugar
1 teaspoon baking soda
¼ teaspoon baking powder
¾ teaspoon salt
½ teaspoon ground cinnamon
½ teaspoon ground ginger
¼ teaspoon ground cloves
1 egg
1 cup canned pumpkin purée
4 tablespoons vegetable oil
2 teaspoons grated orange rind

1. Preheat the oven to 350 degrees. Lightly coat a 4½ x 8½-inch loaf pan with vegetable oil spray.

2. In the work bowl of a food processor, process the cranberries until coarsely chopped. Remove and set aside. Do not wash the work bowl.

3. Add the flour, cornmeal, sugar, baking soda, baking powder, salt, cinnamon, ginger, and cloves to the work bowl and process briefly to blend. In a medium mixing bowl, whisk the egg with the pumpkin purée until smooth. Mix in the oil and orange rind. Add to the flour mixture in the work bowl and process just until blended, about 3 seconds. Add the cranberries and process to mix. Scrape the batter into the prepared pan. (Alternatively, you can chop the cranberries by hand and mix the bread in the traditional manner by combining the dry and liquid ingredients in separate bowls and then blending them together.)

4. Bake until the bread has shrunk slightly away from the sides of the pan and a tester inserted in the center comes out clean, 55 to 60 minutes.

5. Cool in the pan for 10 minutes, turn onto a rack, and cool completely before slicing.

(The pumpkin bread is best if used immediately but can be refrigerated up to 24 hours or frozen for up to 2 weeks.)

◆ *PER SLICE: About 182 cals, 41 cals from fat, 5g total fat, 1g sat fat, 15mg chol, 217mg sodium, 34g total carbs, 1g fiber, 2g prot*

FREEZING BREAD

Most breads freeze reasonably well. Freshly baked breads should be completely cooled, then wrapped tightly in foil or placed in plastic freezer bags. Breads that are relatively low in fat tend to dry out, so freeze them for no more than 1 month. Thaw the bread in the wrapping, then unwrap and let it stand for at least 30 minutes to prevent sogginess. If you want to serve a bread warm, reheat (soft breads loosely wrapped in foil and crisp loaves or bread sticks unwrapped) at 325 degrees for 5 to 10 minutes.

Yogurt Corn Bread

Makes 12 pieces

A basket of fragrant, golden corn bread squares, hot out of the oven, turns an ordinary meal into something special. This recipe—which substitutes yogurt for the butter usually included in a more traditional corn bread—is easy, quick, and scrumptious.

Vegetable oil spray
¾ cup yellow cornmeal
¾ cup all-purpose white flour
1 tablespoon sugar
1½ teaspoons baking powder
½ teaspoon baking soda

½ teaspoon salt
1 egg
1 cup nonfat plain yogurt
2 tablespoons skim milk
3 tablespoons vegetable oil

1. Preheat the oven to 425 degrees. Coat an 8-inch-square baking pan with vegetable oil spray.

2. In a large bowl, mix the cornmeal, flour, sugar, baking powder, baking soda, and salt until blended. In a small bowl, using a whisk, blend the egg with the yogurt, milk, and oil until smooth. Stir the yogurt mixture into the dry ingredients and whisk gently, until the batter has no lumps. Pour into the pan and smooth the top with a spoon or spatula.

3. Bake in the center of the oven until the corn bread is golden brown on top and begins to pull away from the sides of the pan, about 20 minutes.

4. Cut into 12 squares and serve hot.

◆ *PER PIECE: About 112 cals, 37 cals from fat, 4g total fat, 1g sat fat, 18mg chol, 208mg sodium, 15g total carbs, 1g fiber, 3g prot*

YOGURT CORN BREAD VARIATIONS

You can easily change the taste or the shape of corn bread with these variations.

◆ Add 2 teaspoons of coarsely ground black pepper to the batter.
◆ Add 1 can (4 ounces) of drained chopped green chiles to the batter.
◆ Add 1 to 2 teaspoons of dried herbs to the batter.
◆ Make cornsticks by spraying a cast-iron cornstick pan with vegetable oil spray and heating the empty pan in a 425-degree oven for 5 minutes until sizzling hot. Pour the batter level to the top and bake for about 12 minutes until golden brown. Remove from pan and cool on rack. Repeat to make about 15 cornsticks. Serve warm.
◆ Make corn muffins by coating 12 muffin tins with vegetable oil spray. Fill each tin about ⅔ full with batter and bake for 15 to 18 minutes until golden. Remove from pan and serve warm.

Moist Banana Muffins

Makes 12 muffins

Kids love these tasty, fragrant banana muffins. Make them when you have super-ripe bananas on hand—the riper the fruit, the sweeter the muffins.

Vegetable oil spray
2 cups all-purpose white flour
1½ teaspoons baking powder
¾ teaspoons baking soda
½ teaspoon salt
1 teaspoon ground cinnamon
1½ cups mashed ripe bananas (from about 4 bananas)
1 egg
4 tablespoons vegetable oil
⅔ cup packed dark brown sugar
½ cup unsweetened applesauce
1 teaspoon vanilla extract

1. Preheat the oven to 375 degrees. Line 12 muffin cups with paper liners or lightly coat with vegetable oil spray.

2. In a large bowl, whisk the flour with the baking powder, baking soda, salt, and cinnamon. In another large bowl, whisk the mashed bananas with the egg until smooth. Whisk in the oil, brown sugar, applesauce, and vanilla.

3. Add the banana mixture to the flour mixture and whisk just until blended. Do not overmix. Spoon into the prepared muffin cups, filling them almost full.

4. Bake until the muffins have risen and turned golden brown, 22 to 25 minutes. Remove to a rack. Serve warm or at room temperature. (The muffins are best eaten on the day they are made, but can be frozen for up to 2 weeks.)

◆ *PER MUFFIN: About 202 cals, 48 cals from fat, 5g total fat, 1g sat fat, 18mg chol, 224mg sodium, 36g total carbs, 1g fiber, 3g prot*

Molasses Raisin Bran Muffins

Makes 12 muffins

A good bran muffin should be moist and chewy, with a deep, dark color and robust flavor. This one fits the bill perfectly, and is packed with fiber and whole grains to boot.

Vegetable oil spray

1¼ cups unprocessed wheat bran

½ cup whole-wheat flour

½ cup all-purpose white flour

1 teaspoon baking soda

¼ teaspoon baking powder

½ teaspoon salt

¼ teaspoon ground ginger

1 egg

4 tablespoons vegetable oil

¼ cup molasses

¼ cup honey

1 cup nonfat buttermilk

½ cup raisins

1. Preheat the oven to 375 degrees. Lightly coat 12 muffin cups with vegetable oil spray or line with paper liners.

2. In a large bowl, whisk together the bran, whole-wheat and white flours, baking soda, baking powder, salt, and ginger. In a medium bowl, whisk the egg with the oil until smooth. Whisk in the molasses, honey, and buttermilk. Stir in the raisins.

3. Pour the liquid ingredients into the dry ingredients and stir just until no specks of flour remain. Do not overbeat. Spoon into the muffin cups, filling them about ⅔ full.

4. Bake until the muffins are a dark, golden brown, 18 to 22 minutes. Serve warm or at room temperature. These muffins can be refrigerated for 1 day or frozen for 2 weeks.

◆ *PER MUFFIN: About 143 cals, 50 cals from fat, 6g total fat, 1g sat fat, 19mg chol, 230mg sodium, 23g total carbs, 2g fiber, 3g prot*

Morning Glory Breakfast Muffins

Makes 12 muffins

It's a good idea to make this recipe every few weeks so you can keep a ready supply of these moist, carrot- and sunflower-packed muffins in the freezer. Rich in vitamins (C from the orange juice, A from the carrots, and E from the sunflower seeds), they're a great way to begin the day served either plain or spread with berry jam or preserves.

Vegetable oil spray
⅔ cup hulled roasted sunflower
   seeds (see note)
¾ cup whole-wheat flour
¾ cup all-purpose white flour
1 teaspoon baking powder
½ teaspoon baking soda
½ teaspoon salt
1 teaspoon ground cinnamon
1 egg
2 tablespoons vegetable oil
¾ cup grated carrot
   (about 2 medium-sized carrots)
½ cup unsweetened applesauce
½ cup packed dark brown sugar
½ cup orange juice
1 teaspoon vanilla extract
½ cup raisins

1. Preheat the oven to 375 degrees. Lightly coat 12 muffin cups with vegetable oil spray or line with paper liners.

2. In a large bowl, whisk together the sunflower seeds, whole-wheat and white flours, baking powder, baking soda, salt, and cinnamon until blended. In a medium bowl, whisk the egg with the oil until smooth. Add the grated carrot, applesauce, brown sugar, orange juice, and vanilla and whisk until blended. Stir in the raisins.

3. Add the carrot mixture to the flour mixture and whisk just until combined. Do not overmix. Spoon into the prepared muffin cups, filling them almost full.

4. Bake until the muffins have risen slightly and are golden brown, 25 to 30 minutes.

Remove from the muffin cups. Serve warm or at room temperature. (You can refrigerate the muffins for 1 day or freeze them for 2 weeks.)

◆ *PER MUFFIN: About 192 cals, 63 cals from fat, 7g total fat, 1g sat fat, 18mg chol, 185mg sodium, 30g total carbs, 2g fiber, 5g prot*

Note: If the sunflower seeds are raw, spread them out in a pie plate and toast them in a 375-degree oven, stirring once, until one shade darker, about 5 minutes.

DRIED CRAN-RASPBERRY QUICK JAM
Makes ½ cup (about 8 servings)

Sweetened dried cranberries are increasingly available nationwide. When combined with fresh raspberries, they produce a delicious, slightly tart "instant" jam.

½ cup dried sweetened cranberries	1 cup fresh ripe raspberries 2 tablespoons corn syrup	1 teaspoon fresh lemon juice

1. Cook the cranberries in ⅓ cup water in a small covered saucepan over medium-low heat until softened and most of the water is absorbed, 3 to 5 minutes. If any water remains, drain it off.

2. In the work bowl of a food processor, combine the cranberries, raspberries, corn syrup, and lemon juice. Process, using long pulses, to make a coarse purée.

3. Transfer the mixture to a covered container and refrigerate for at least 1 hour to blend flavors. The jam can be stored in the refrigerator for up to 1 week.

Per serving: About 45 cals, 1 cal from fat, 0g total fat, 0g sat fat, 0mg chol, 4mg sodium, 3g fiber, 0g prot

ABOUT MUFFINS

A good muffin has a rough, rounded top and a moist, slightly crumbly interior. To achieve these results, prepare the batter just before baking. Mix the liquids into the dry ingredients lightly, just until everything is moistened—it's fine if there are a few lumps left in the batter. Overmixing produces a compact texture or oddly pointed tops. Most muffin recipes call for standard-size muffin cups that hold between ⅓ and ½ cup of batter—fill no more than ¾ full to allow for rising. You can grease the tins with a coating of nonstick vegetable spray or use paper liners. Don't grease any cups that won't be used, and place a couple of tablespoons of water into the unused cups before baking so that the pan won't warp. Muffins taste best warm from the oven, but can be frozen for up to 1 month.

Blueberry Corn Muffins

Makes 12 muffins

Blueberries and cornmeal seem to have a natural affinity, showcased beautifully in these crunchy muffins.

Vegetable oil spray
1⅓ cups all-purpose white flour
⅔ cup yellow cornmeal
1 tablespoon baking powder
¼ teaspoon salt
1 teaspoon ground cinnamon
1 cup fresh or frozen blueberries (see note)
1 egg
4 tablespoons vegetable oil
½ cup honey
½ cup skim milk
1 teaspoon sugar

1. Preheat the oven to 400 degrees. Lightly coat 12 muffin cups with vegetable oil spray or line with paper liners.

2. In a large bowl, whisk together the flour, cornmeal, baking powder, salt, and cinnamon. Add the blueberries and toss to coat with the flour mixture. In a small bowl, whisk the egg with the oil until smooth. Whisk in the honey and milk.

3. Add the milk mixture to the flour mixture and stir gently just until blended, trying not to break the blueberries. Spoon into the prepared muffin tins and sprinkle the tops with the sugar.

4. Bake until the muffins are golden and well risen, and a tester inserted in the center comes out clean, 18 to 22 minutes. Serve warm, or cool the muffins on a rack and serve at room temperature. (Freeze for up to 2 weeks.)

◆ *PER MUFFIN: About 181 cals, 48 cals from fat, 5g total fat, 1g sat fat, 18mg chol, 148mg sodium, 31g total carbs, 1g fiber, 3g prot*

Note: If using frozen blueberries, do not thaw them. Simply rinse off any ice crystals and pat dry gently on paper towels. Toss separately with about 2 tablespoons of the flour, then stir them in after adding the liquid to the batter.

Feather-Light Buttermilk Drop Biscuits

Makes 16 biscuits

These delicate biscuits are made with about half the usual fat and are wonderful hot, straight out of the oven. If you want to do some advance preparation, blend the flour mixture and milk mixture in separate bowls ahead of time, then mix the dough and shape the biscuits just before they go into the oven.

Vegetable oil spray
2 cups all-purpose white flour
2 teaspoons baking powder
½ teaspoon baking soda
¾ teaspoon salt

3 tablespoons cold solid vegetable
 shortening
1 tablespoon cold butter
1 cup nonfat buttermilk

1. Preheat the oven to 425 degrees. Lightly coat a baking sheet with vegetable oil spray.

2. In a large bowl, combine the flour, baking powder, baking soda, and salt. Whisk to combine. Cut the shortening and butter into small pieces and use your fingers to rub them into the flour until they are about the size of small peas.

3. Pour the buttermilk into the flour mixture and stir until a soft, sticky dough forms. Drop by heaping tablespoons onto the prepared baking sheet and flatten the biscuits with your fingertips to about ½ inch thick. (See note.)

4. Bake until flecked golden brown, 12 to 14 minutes. Transfer to a napkin-lined basket and serve immediately.

◆ *PER BISCUIT: About 91 cals, 31 cals from fat, 3g total fat, 1g sat fat, 2mg chol, 208mg sodium, 13g total carbs, 0g fiber, 2g prot*

Note: To make rolled biscuits, use 2 tablespoons less buttermilk. Turn the dough onto a lightly floured board and knead until smooth, about 10 times. Roll or pat to a thickness of ½ inch. Use a 2-inch cutter or an upside-down drinking glass to cut biscuits, rerolling and cutting the scraps once.

BISCUIT VARIATIONS

◆ Add 1 teaspoon of dried herbs or 1 tablespoon of chopped fresh herbs to the dough.

◆ Add 2 tablespoons of finely chopped scallions to the dough.
◆ For sweet biscuits, add 1 tablespoon of sugar to the dough, then sprinkle the biscuits with 2 teaspoons of sugar before baking.

Coffee Cake with Oat and Nut Streusel Topping

Makes 1 cake (24 squares)

This special streusel-topped coffee cake is ideal for Sunday morning brunch.

Vegetable oil spray

Streusel Topping:
**2 tablespoons coarsely chopped
walnuts or pecans**
**3 tablespoons packed dark brown
sugar**
**3 tablespoons regular or quick
rolled oats (not "instant")**
¾ teaspoon cinnamon

Coffee Cake:
**¾ cup regular or quick rolled oats
(not "instant")**
½ cup granulated sugar
1¼ cups white cake flour
1 teaspoon baking powder
1 teaspoon baking soda
½ teaspoon salt
1 egg
3 tablespoons vegetable oil
1 cup orange juice
2 teaspoons grated orange rind
1 teaspoon vanilla extract

1. Preheat the oven to 350 degrees. Lightly coat a 9-inch-square baking pan with vegetable oil spray.

2. For the topping, process the nuts and brown sugar in the work bowl of a food processor until the nuts are chopped medium-fine. Add the rolled oats and cinnamon and process briefly to combine. Transfer to a bowl and set aside. Do not wash the work bowl.

3. For the cake, process the rolled oats with the sugar in the work bowl until the oats are evenly ground to a medium-fine meal. Add the flour, baking powder, baking soda, and salt and process briefly to blend. In a small bowl, whisk the egg with the oil until smooth. Whisk in the orange juice, orange rind, and vanilla. With the food processor motor running, pour the orange juice mixture through the feed tube and process just until blended, about 3 seconds. (Alternatively, you can chop the topping by hand and make the cake traditionally by mixing the liquid and dry ingredients in separate bowls and then combining.) Scrape the batter into the prepared pan and sprinkle evenly with the topping.

4. Bake until the topping is browned, the cake shrinks from the sides of the pan, and a tester inserted in the center comes out clean, 30 to 35 minutes. Serve warm or at room temperature. (The cake is best made and eaten on the same day but can be kept at room temperature for 8 hours before serving.)

◆ *PER SQUARE: About 83 cals, 23 cals from fat, 3g total fat, 0g sat fat, 9mg chol, 116mg sodium, 14g total carbs, 0g fiber, 1g prot*

Oven-Baked Orange French Toast

Makes 8 slices (about 4 servings)

French toast is usually fried in butter, but in this recipe it's oven-baked to a crusty golden goodness and then drizzled with a sweet orange-flavored syrup.

Toast:
Vegetable oil spray
8 slices (about ½ pound) day-old, whole-grain bread
2 eggs
1 egg white
2 tablespoons granulated sugar
1 cup low-fat (1 percent) milk
1 teaspoon vanilla extract
½ teaspoon ground cinnamon

Syrup:
⅔ cup orange juice
⅓ cup packed light brown sugar
1 teaspoon grated orange rind
1 teaspoon butter
2 thin orange slices cut in half, for garnish

1. Coat a jelly roll pan (a 10x15-inch pan with 1-inch sides) with vegetable oil spray. Arrange the bread slices in a single layer on the pan.

2. In a mixing bowl, whisk the eggs, egg white, and sugar until blended. Whisk in the milk, vanilla, and cinnamon. Pour the milk mixture evenly over the bread and let stand until absorbed, 10 to 20 minutes.

3. Preheat the oven to 400 degrees.

4. Bake the bread until it is firm and lightly toasted on top and dark and crusty on the bottom, 15 to 18 minutes. Change the oven setting to broil and place the pan a few inches from the heat source. Broil until golden on top, about 1 minute.

5. Meanwhile, in a small saucepan, combine the orange juice and sugar, whisking until smooth. Bring to a boil, reduce the heat to medium, and simmer for 3 minutes. Remove from the heat and stir in the orange rind and butter.

6. Use a large flexible spatula to remove the French toast from the pan, being careful to remove each piece of toast with the browned bottom crust intact. Serve on plates, crusty sides up. Pour the syrup over the toast and garnish each plate with an orange slice.

◆ *PER SERVING (two slices): About 337 cals, 43 cals from fat, 5g total fat, 2g sat fat, 112mg chol, 243mg sodium, 63g total carbs, 3g fiber, 12g prot*

GRATING CITRUS PEEL

The peel of citrus fruits, such as lemons, limes, oranges, and grapefruits, lends a concentrated flavor to baked goods. Use a standard kitchen grater or a special citrus grating tool, but be sure to wash the fruit before you begin. Grate only the outer, colored portion. The inner white pith is very bitter. Grated citrus peel, or zest, is best used right away when it is still soft and the oils are most fragrant, but the peel can also be refrigerated or frozen. If using both peel and juice in a recipe, grate the peel first. In fact, it's a good idea to always grate the peel of citrus fruit, even if you don't plan to use it right away. It's a great way to perk up all sorts of foods, from canned soups to bottled pasta sauces and salsas.

Whole-Wheat Yogurt Waffles

Makes 4 waffles

Made with whole-wheat flour, these waffles have a rich, nutty flavor. Each serving supplies almost one quarter of the daily value for calcium from the milk and yogurt.

Vegetable oil spray
1¼ cups all-purpose white flour
¾ cup whole-wheat flour
1 teaspoon baking powder
½ teaspoon baking soda
½ teaspoon salt

1 egg
1 egg white
1 cup nonfat plain yogurt
3 tablespoons sugar
3 tablespoons vegetable oil
1½ cups skim milk

1. Heat a waffle iron, preferably one with nonstick grids. If necessary, coat lightly with vegetable oil spray.

2. In a large bowl, whisk together the white and whole-wheat flours, baking powder, baking soda, and salt. In a medium bowl, whisk the egg and egg white until frothy. Whisk in the yogurt, sugar, and oil until smooth. Whisk in the milk. Add the milk mixture to the flour mixture and stir just until blended and few lumps remain.

3. For 8-inch waffles, ladle about 1 cup of batter onto the waffle iron, and bake according to the machine's instructions. (Adjust the amount of batter for other sizes.)

4. Serve hot, with maple syrup or other toppings.

◆ *PER WAFFLE: About 433 cals, 113 cals from fat, 13g total fat, 2g sat fat, 56mg chol, 637mg sodium, 65g total carbs, 4g fiber, 16g prot*

PINEAPPLE AND COTTAGE CHEESE TOPPING

Makes 1 cup (about 8 servings)

Spoon this creamy topping over waffles and pancakes or serve it as a dipping sauce for fresh berries. You can use either fresh or canned unsweetened pineapple.

1 cup nonfat cottage cheese
½ cup chopped fresh pineapple
or canned unsweetened
crushed pineapple, drained

1 tablespoon orange all-fruit
marmalade

⅛ teaspoon ground cinnamon

1. Process the cottage cheese in a food processor until smooth.
2. Transfer to a small bowl and stir in the pineapple, marmalade, and cinnamon. Use immediately or refrigerate up to 2 days.

Per serving: About 29 cals, 0 cals from fat, 0g total fat, 0g sat fat, 1mg chol, 76mg sodium, 4g total carbs, 0g fiber, 4g prot

WAFFLE TIPS

◆ Use a nonstick waffle iron or season the waffle iron with oil according to the manufacturer's directions. Reseason it if you haven't used the waffle iron in several months. A light coating of nonstick vegetable spray is a good precaution, even for nonstick irons.

◆ To prevent sticking, be sure the iron is thoroughly preheated before spooning in the batter.
◆ Don't be tempted to open the waffle iron during the first minute or so. The unset batter will stick and the waffle will fall apart.
◆ Let the iron reheat for a couple of minutes before adding batter.
◆ Use a fork to lift the cooked waffle from the iron.
◆ Although waffles taste best right from the iron, they can be kept warm or reheated on a baking sheet in a 350-degree oven, or in a wide-slot toaster.

Crunchy Oat Waffles

Makes 4 waffles

If you've never tried oat waffles, you're in for a treat. Rolled oats lend a natural sweetness to the batter, and the waffles emerge from the iron with a pleasing light crunch.

Vegetable oil spray

1 cup boiling water

¾ cup regular or quick rolled oats

1¼ cups all-purpose white flour

1½ teaspoons baking powder

½ teaspoon baking soda

½ teaspoon salt

3 tablespoons vegetable oil

2 tablespoons sugar

1 egg

1 egg white

1¼ cups nonfat buttermilk

1. Heat a waffle iron, preferably one with nonstick grids. If necessary, coat lightly with vegetable oil spray.

2. In a medium bowl, pour the boiling water over the oats. Stir to combine and set aside for 3 minutes.

3. In a large bowl, whisk together the flour, baking powder, baking soda, and salt.

4. Whisk the oil and sugar into the oat mixture. Add the egg and egg white and whisk until blended. Whisk in the buttermilk. Add the oat mixture to the flour mixture and stir just until blended.

5. For 8-inch waffles, ladle about 1 cup of batter into the waffle iron. (Adjust the amount of batter for other sizes.) Bake according to the machine's instructions.

6. Serve the waffles hot, with maple syrup or other toppings.

◆ *PER WAFFLE: About 370 cals, 121 cals from fat, 13g total fat, 2g sat fat, 56mg chol, 671mg sodium, 51g total carbs, 1g fiber, 11g prot*

BUTTERMILK AND YOGURT IN BAKING

The milk solids and natural acids in buttermilk (what's left after butter is churned) and plain yogurt give a tenderness to baked goods, and their flavor adds a light and pleasing tang to offset the sugars in sweet breads. You can use both the low-fat and nonfat kinds of buttermilk and yogurt in baking and you can also substitute one for the other. Dry buttermilk powder is also available and can be reconstituted at the ratio of ¼ cup of powder to 1 cup of water. You can also substitute clabbered milk for buttermilk. Make clabbered milk by placing 1 tablespoon of vinegar or lemon juice in a liquid measuring cup, then add enough milk to make 1 cup. Let it stand for 5 minutes to thicken.

HONEY-ORANGE RICOTTA TOPPING

Makes 1 cup (about 8 servings)

This topping is especially delicious spooned over Crunchy Oat Waffles (page 136) or spread on toast.

1 cup part-skim ricotta cheese
2 tablespoons orange juice

2 tablespoons honey

1 teaspoon grated orange rind

Combine all the ingredients in a small bowl and blend until smooth. Use immediately or cover and refrigerate up to 2 days.

Per serving: About 61 cals, 22 cals from fat, 2g total fat, 2g sat fat, 10mg chol, 39mg sodium, 6g total carbs, 0g fiber, 4g prot

A SPOONFUL OF HONEY AND OTHER LIQUID SWEETENERS

Honey, molasses, and maple syrup all have roughly the same nutritional qualities, though honey is slightly higher in calories. They can often be used interchangeably, but molasses is more acidic so you need to increase the baking soda in the recipe to neutralize the acid. Blackstrap molasses is higher in nutrients than regular molasses, but has a strong flavor you don't always want in delicate baked goods. Here are some tips for using liquid sweeteners in baking:

◆ In general, it isn't a good idea to substitute solid sweeteners, such as granulated sugar, for liquid ones in baking because the balance of liquids in the recipe will be upset.

◆ If a recipe also calls for oil, measure the oil first, then measure the honey, molasses, or maple syrup in the same unwashed container. The oil coating will allow the sticky sweetener to slide out easily.

◆ Honey and maple syrup tend to crystallize in their jars, and they thicken when refrigerated. To reliquefy them, place the jar in a pot of very hot water for about 5 minutes, or open the jar and microwave it from several seconds to a minute.

Giant Cornmeal Flapjacks

Makes 12 large pancakes (about 6 servings)

A bit of cornmeal gives these delectable, golden pancakes a slight crispness, and the all-purpose, fortified flour makes them a good source of iron. Of course, you can make the flapjacks any diameter you want, but the large size turns breakfast into a special event.

Vegetable oil spray
1¼ cups all-purpose white flour
½ cup yellow or white cornmeal
2 teaspoons baking powder
¾ teaspoon baking soda
¾ teaspoon salt
1 egg
3 tablespoons vegetable oil
1 tablespoon granulated sugar
2 cups nonfat buttermilk

1. Preheat a pancake griddle or large, heavy frying pan. If the pan is not well seasoned, coat lightly with vegetable oil spray. The griddle will be hot enough when a drop of water dances around on the surface.

2. In a large mixing bowl, whisk together the flour, cornmeal, baking powder, baking soda, and salt. In a medium bowl, whisk the egg with the oil and sugar until smooth. Whisk in the buttermilk. Pour the milk mixture into the flour mixture and whisk just until blended.

3. Using about ⅓ cup for each pancake, ladle the batter into the pan. When the edges of the pancake are dry and the bottom is golden, turn it over and cook until the bottom is lightly browned, 3 to 4 minutes total.

4. Serve the flapjacks hot, with syrup or other toppings.

◆ *PER SERVING (two pancakes): About 244 cals, 72 cals from fat, 8g total fat, 2g sat fat, 39mg chol, 642mg sodium, 35g total carbs, 1g fiber, 7g prot*

Buckwheat Buttermilk Silver Dollar Pancakes

Makes 36 small pancakes (about 4 servings)

Kids love these silver dollar–sized pancakes, and the finely ground buckwheat flour even gives the flapjacks a slightly silvery hue. Because they're made with only egg whites, these pancakes are very low in cholesterol.

Vegetable oil spray	½ teaspoon salt
¾ cup all-purpose white flour	2 egg whites
¼ cup buckwheat flour	1 tablespoon sugar
1 teaspoon baking powder	3 tablespoons vegetable oil
¾ teaspoon baking soda	1 cup nonfat buttermilk

1. Preheat a pancake griddle or large, heavy frying pan. If the pan is not well seasoned, coat lightly with vegetable oil spray. The griddle will be hot enough when a drop of water dances on the surface.

2. In a medium mixing bowl, whisk together the white and buckwheat flours, baking powder, baking soda, and salt. In another medium bowl, whisk the egg whites until frothy, about 2 minutes. Whisk in the sugar, oil, and buttermilk. Pour the milk mixture into the flour mixture and whisk just until blended.

3. Using about 1 tablespoon for each pancake, spoon the batter into the pan. When the edges are dry and the bottoms golden, turn the pancakes over and cook until they are lightly browned, 2 to 3 minutes total.

4. Serve the pancakes hot, with syrup or jam.

◆ *PER SERVING (nine pancakes): About 242 cals, 95 cals from fat, 11g total fat, 2g sat fat, 2mg chol, 686mg sodium, 30g total carbs, 2g fiber, 7g prot*

CHAPTER FOUR

Soups

Many of our coziest memories relate to soup, one of the hallmark "comfort" foods. The first whiff of autumn leaves and the smoke from crackling fires spark recollections of fall harvest soups made from squash and potato. A bracing sea breeze makes one hunger for a cup of thick chowder from a waterfront stand, and chilled soups always bring to mind hot summer days. Hot or cold, thick or thin, soup is a part of our collective memory.

The key to good soup is a good flavor base. Some soup recipes call for a particular type of broth or stock. You can make your own chicken stock (page 142), fish stock (page 143), or vegetable broth (page 143) when you have the time and ingredients. Or you can just use canned chicken, beef, or vegetable broth, available in both regular and lower-sodium versions. Lower-sodium canned broth is much less salty, somewhat lower in fat, and even a bit richer in flavor than regular broth. Recipes without broth contain other ingredients—tomatoes, wine, or onions, for example—that establish a flavor theme.

Small amounts of highly flavorful ingredients go a long way in soup because it simmers so long. Soup is the ideal dish for small amounts of higher-fat ingredients—bacon, sausage, and other smoked meats—that deliver lots of flavor. Try bacon and sausage made from poultry because they are considerably lower in calories and fat than those made from pork; the flavor and texture are just as good.

The way you mix and match ingredients also enhances flavor. Some pairings are naturals—the smoky ham and sweet creamy split peas in the Split Pea Soup with Ham Bits and Dilled Yogurt (page 160) or the beef and tomatoes in the Family-Style Vegetable Beef Alphabet Soup (page 151). Other combinations—the cranberry added to the Sweet Potato and Squash Soup (page 163)—create unexpected flavor pairings that add punch to your everyday meals.

Today's soups contain a wide array of ingredients that produce a creamy texture without all the fat found in cream-based soups. Potatoes lend smoothness and whole milk contributes a distinct dairy flavor to the Sweet Corn and Shrimp Chowder (page 155), while plain yogurt supplies the needed creaminess in the Creamy Iced Cantaloupe Soup (page 145).

The appetizer or first course is the traditional spot on the menu for soup. Some credit the French for this practice; many a French menu starts with a clear soup called consommé that wakes up the appetite. Soup works best as an appetizer when it readies you for the meal without being too filling. That's one reason why broth-based, fruit, or vegetable soups are such natural first courses. A soup appetizer takes the edge off your appetite so you can better control how much you eat at the meal. And, of course, an appetizer-sized cup of soup is the ideal lunch partner for half a sandwich or a salad.

Soup as the main dish is very different. It is heartier and packed with more ingredients. While an appetizer-sized soup might include ingredients from just one Food Guide Pyramid group (vegetables, for example), a main-course soup can contain two or three Food Guide Pyramid groups. Meal-sized soups also demand larger portions and a larger bowl—a cup hardly holds enough soup to make a meal. Use main-dish soups as a way of boosting your grain and vegetable intake. Fill them with pasta, rice, and an array of colorful veggies.

When soup is the main course, round out your menu with foods from other food groups to create a complete meal. Baskets of bread, rolls, crackers, or breadsticks are natural accompaniments. Add a salad or vegetable dish when you serve a soup that doesn't have many vegetables. And if it's meat, beans, or other protein ingredients that are missing from the soup, serve a sandwich on the side.

Winter, spring, summer, or fall—the season's always right for soup.

Basic Soup Stocks

Stock is the liquid you get when you simmer various ingredients—meat, poultry, fish, vegetables, bones—in water to extract their essence. Use stock as a base for soups, stews, and sauces. Quality stock supplies a lot of flavor; use it to enrich the taste of low-fat dishes.

BASIC CHICKEN STOCK

Makes about 8 cups

Although you can now buy several good brands of regular and lower-sodium canned chicken broth, you can control the intensity of flavor as well as the amounts of sodium and fat if you make your own stock. Quantities can be increased for a larger yield.

3 pounds chicken backs, necks, wing tips, or any other chicken parts except the liver
1 large onion, quartered

1 celery stalk with leafy top, coarsely chopped
1 large carrot, peeled and coarsely chopped
½ cup parsley sprigs with stems

6 branches fresh thyme or 1 teaspoon dried thyme
1 bay leaf, broken in half
5 peppercorns
Salt to taste

1. Rinse the chicken parts and place them in a large soup pot. Add 12 cups of cold water. Bring to a boil and simmer for 20 minutes, skimming off the foam that rises to the surface.
2. Add the onion, celery, carrot, parsley, thyme, bay leaf, and peppercorns. Cook uncovered at a gentle simmer, adding small amounts of water as necessary to keep the chicken covered, until the flavor is extracted from the meat, about 1½ hours.
3. Let the broth cool slightly and then strain it, pushing on the solids to extract as much liquid as possible. Spoon off any excess fat or refrigerate the stock and lift the fat off after it has congealed on the top. Add salt to taste. (This stock can be refrigerated for up to 3 days or frozen for 2 months.)

Per cup: About 34 cals, 20 cals from fat, 2g total fat, 0g sat fat, 7mg chol, 85mg sodium, 0g total carbs, 0g fiber, 3g prot

DEFATTING CANNED BROTH

Some food manufacturers make defatted canned broths, but most canned broth contains some fat. Because fat rises to the surface, it can quite easily be spooned off the top of an opened can of broth. To do an even more thorough job, chill the can (or place it in the freezer for about 30 minutes if you're short of time), then spoon out the almost solid, congealed fat.

BASIC FISH STOCK

Makes about 8 cups

Fish stock is delicious. You won't believe how often you will use it once you've tasted it. Almost any type of fish will make good stock, with the exception of the oiliest varieties of fish, such as mackerel or bluefish.

2 pounds fish trimmings and
  bones, preferably with heads
  included
1 large onion, sliced

1 large carrot, peeled and
  sliced
1 large celery rib with leafy top,
  sliced

1 bay leaf, broken in half
1 clove
6 peppercorns
Salt to taste

1. Rinse the fish trimmings and place them in a large soup pot with 9 cups of cold water. Bring to a boil, skimming any foam that rises to the surface. Add the onion, carrot, celery, bay leaf, clove, and peppercorns and simmer uncovered for 30 minutes.

2. Strain through a sieve and discard the solids. Season the stock with salt. Use immediately, refrigerate for up to 2 days, or freeze for up to 2 months.

Per cup: About 22 cals, 5 cals from fat, 1g total fat, 0g sat fat, 2mg chol, 154mg sodium, 0g total carbs, 0g fiber, 4g prot

BASIC VEGETABLE BROTH

Makes about 8 cups

While good commercial vegetable broth is now available in cans, this nutritious homemade version is simple to make and freezes well. You can also add a bit of nutritional punch by saving the water from ordinary cooked vegetables, and adding it to this broth, or using it instead of broth.

4 carrots, peeled and sliced
2 large onions, sliced
2 leeks, with about 4 inches of
  green tops, washed and thinly
  sliced

2 celery stalks with leafy tops,
  sliced
2 garlic cloves, crushed
6 branches fresh thyme or
  1 teaspoon dried

4 parsley sprigs
1 bay leaf, broken in half
8 peppercorns
Salt to taste

1. In a large soup pot, combine all the ingredients except the salt with 9 cups of cold water. Bring to a boil, reduce the heat, and simmer uncovered for 35 to 40 minutes, until the vegetables are very tender.

2. Let the broth cool slightly and then strain it, pressing hard on the solids to extract as much liquid as possible. Season the broth with salt to taste. (This broth can be refrigerated for 2 days or frozen up to 2 months.)

Per cup: About 35 cals, 0 cals from fat, 0g total fat, 0g sat fat, 0mg chol, 82mg sodium, 8g total carbs, 0g fiber, 1g prot

STOCK TIPS

In America, the terms "stock" and "broth" are used more or less interchangeably, although broth tends to be a slightly milder, thinner, and lighter liquid. "Bouillon" is simply the French term for a strong stock or broth, while canned "consommé" has been thickened and concentrated, usually by adding gelatin.

◆ You can easily obtain bones for fish stock at a fish market.
◆ Although you can make beef broth at home, you will find that the parts required—such as beef and veal bones, shank, plate, and knuckle—are becoming increasingly difficult to obtain at supermarkets, and the cooking and browning process takes several hours.
◆ When seasoning stock with salt, add the salt at the end of the cooking time. To make a completely salt-free stock, concentrate the flavors by boiling the stock uncovered for an additional 30 minutes.
◆ Stock and broth should be cooled, uncovered, in the refrigerator. If the pot is covered tightly while cooling, the trapped heat may cause the stock to spoil and turn sour.

◆ Stock freezes extremely well. To save space in the freezer, reduce the volume of chicken stock by boiling the strained stock for an additional 30 minutes or so; then freeze it in small portions and dilute it with water after thawing.
◆ To extract the most flavor from ingredients when making stock, start with cold water, then bring it slowly to a boil. Skim the impurities off the top and simmer the stock gently so it does not become cloudy.
◆ You can safely store stock for 2 days in the refrigerator or freeze it for up to 2 months.

Garden Patch Gazpacho

Makes 8 side-dish servings

This cold soup, full of fiber and vitamin C, is the perfect height-of-summer recipe. There's no cooking involved, and you can take advantage of the vine-ripe tomatoes, piquant basil, and crunchy peppers overflowing from gardens and farm stands.

4 medium tomatoes, cored and cut into 2-inch chunks

3 large slices firm bread such as Super Sandwich Bread (page 114), about 1½ ounces each, torn into 2-inch pieces

1 large garlic clove, peeled

3 tablespoons red wine vinegar

4 tablespoons extra-virgin olive oil

3 cups chilled tomato juice

2 cups chilled defatted lower-sodium chicken or vegetable broth

3 tablespoons thinly sliced fresh basil leaves or 2 teaspoons dried

1 large green bell pepper, seeded

1 medium onion, peeled

1 cucumber, peeled, halved, and with seeds scooped out

2 teaspoons Worcestershire sauce

½ teaspoon liquid hot pepper sauce

Black pepper to taste

1½ cups whole-wheat or white bread croutons

1. In a food processor or blender, combine the tomatoes, bread, and garlic. Pulse until roughly puréed. With the motor running, pour the vinegar and oil through the feed tube or into the blender and process until smoothly puréed. Combine the purée with the chilled tomato juice and broth in a large bowl or container, stir in the basil, and refrigerate. (This recipe can be made to this point up to 1 day ahead.)

2. Chop the vegetables medium-fine by hand or cut into 2-inch chunks and pulse in a food processor until chopped. Add to the tomato mixture. Season with the Worcestershire, hot pepper sauce, and pepper to taste. Refrigerate for at least 1 hour or up to 4 hours before serving.

3. Pour into small bowls, top with the croutons, and serve.

◆ *PER SERVING: About 194 cals, 70 cals from fat, 8g total fat, 1g sat fat, 0mg chol, 397mg sodium, 26g total carbs, 2g fiber, 6g prot*

Creamy Iced Cantaloupe Soup

Makes 8 side-dish servings

This refreshing soup, which can also be made with honeydew or Persian melon, makes a superb starter for a summer luncheon or supper. For a lovely extra touch, try floating a nasturtium blossom atop each serving as a peppery-sweet garnish. Did you know that cantaloupe has more vitamin A than almost any other fruit?

8 cups chilled cubed cantaloupe (from a 3-pound melon)
⅓ cup honey
2 tablespoons lime juice
2 teaspoons grated lime peel
1 cup pineapple juice
1½ cups low-fat plain yogurt
½ teaspoon freshly ground pepper
¼ teaspoon salt

In a food processor or blender, purée the melon, honey, lime juice, and peel, in batches if necessary, until smooth. Add the pineapple juice and process a few seconds to blend. Add the yogurt, pepper, and salt and process briefly to blend. Serve immediately or refrigerate up to 4 hours.

◆ *PER SERVING: About 145 cals, 10 cals from fat, 1g total fat, 0g sat fat, 3mg chol, 112mg sodium, 32g total carbs, 1g fiber, 4g prot*

THE BIG CHILL

To quickly cool a hot puréed soup base that you want to serve cold, transfer it to a bowl and set the bowl in a larger bowl filled with ice and water. Stir until cold. Or stir some ice cubes into the hot purée, adjusting the amount of liquid you add later.

Very Cool Beet and Berry Borscht

Makes 8 side-dish servings

Cold borscht is a refreshing treat on a hot summer day. Beets, a great source of the B vitamin folic acid, give the soup a lovely magenta hue, while buttermilk smooths it and adds a pleasing tang. Serve with a salad such as Marinated Scallop, Lima Bean, and Corn Salad (page 84).

1 tablespoon vegetable oil

1 medium onion, coarsely chopped

1 pound potatoes, peeled and coarsely chopped

1 pound beets (from about 1¾ pounds beets with tops), tops removed, peeled and coarsely chopped (see note)

1 tablespoon sugar

1 teaspoon salt

½ teaspoon dill seed

1 pint strawberries, hulled

2½ cups nonfat buttermilk

2 teaspoons lemon juice

¼ teaspoon white pepper

Dill sprigs for garnish, if desired

1. Heat the oil in a large saucepan or soup pot. Add the onion and cook over medium heat, stirring frequently, until it begins to soften, about 5 minutes. Add 2 cups water and the potatoes, beets, sugar, salt, and dill seed. Cover the pot and cook over medium-low heat until the vegetables are tender, 20 to 25 minutes.

2. In a food processor or blender, purée the vegetable mixture with the strawberries, in batches if necessary, pulsing until smooth. Refrigerate for at least 1 hour or until cold. (This recipe can be made to this point up to 2 days before serving.)

3. Whisk in the buttermilk and season with the lemon juice and pepper. Serve the soup cold, garnished with dill sprigs if desired.

◆ *PER SERVING: About 137 cals, 18 cals from fat, 2g total fat, 1g sat fat, 3mg chol, 395mg sodium, 26g total carbs, 2g fiber, 5g prot*

Note: A 16-ounce can of drained and rinsed beets can be substituted for fresh beets. Add them with the potatoes in step 1.

ABOUT BORSCHT

Borscht is the national soup of both Russia and Poland and, like many peasant soups, there are almost as many recipes for it as there are cooks. The only ingredient common to all borschts is beets. While some versions of borscht are hearty, chunky winter-time concoctions made with beef and chopped vegetables, others are smooth, delicate purées served cold.

Day-After-Thanksgiving Turkey Noodle Soup

Makes 4 main-dish servings

When the turkey carcass has been stripped of most of its meat, recycle your Thanksgiving bird into this hearty soup. This recipe is particularly flexible, so just use whatever vegetables happen to be leftover from the feast.

1 turkey carcass from a 12- to 16-pound turkey

1 large onion, coarsely chopped

1 large carrot, peeled and coarsely chopped

1 celery rib, coarsely chopped

1 bay leaf

4 to 5 sprigs parsley, including stems

3 branches fresh herbs, such as thyme, sage, tarragon, or savory

4 whole peppercorns

Up to 2 cups defatted reduced-sodium chicken broth, if needed

1 can (16 ounces) stewed tomatoes

1½ cups medium-fine dried noodles, preferably cholesterol free

3 tablespoons chopped fresh herbs, such as thyme, sage, tarragon, or savory (see note)

4 cups cooked vegetables, such as peas, carrots, broccoli, green beans, cubed sweet potatoes, or chopped creamed onions (see note)

2 cups (8 ounces) cubed cooked turkey, preferably dark meat

2 tablespoons chopped parsley

Salt to taste

Black pepper to taste

1. Break the turkey carcass in half or cut it with shears so it will fit into a large soup kettle. Add cold water to cover (approximately 10 cups), bring to a boil over high heat, and skim off any foam that rises to the surface. Add the onion, carrot, celery, bay leaf, parsley sprigs, herb branches, and peppercorns, reduce the heat to medium-low, and cook at a gentle simmer, partially covered, for 1½ hours, until the flavor is extracted from the bones. Cool slightly and then strain through a sieve, discarding the bones and vegetables. Measure the broth back into the pot, adding canned chicken broth if necessary to make 8 cups.

continued

2. Add the tomatoes to the broth, breaking up any large chunks with the side of a spoon. Bring to a boil, add the noodles and chopped herbs, and cook uncovered until the noodles are almost tender, about 8 minutes.

3. Add the cooked vegetables and turkey and simmer until the noodles and vegetables are tender, about 5 minutes. Stir in the chopped parsley. Salt and pepper to taste. (This recipe can be made several hours ahead and refrigerated. Reheat before serving.)

◆ *PER SERVING: About 420 cals, 66 cals from fat, 7g total fat, 2g sat fat, 60mg chol, 726mg sodium, 55g total carbs, 5g fiber, 34g prot*

Note: Instead of the chopped fresh herbs, you can also use about ¾ teaspoon each of dried thyme, sage, tarragon, and savory. If you don't have any leftover vegetables, you can use any type of frozen vegetables, such as peas, carrots, broccoli, or green beans, and simmer until tender.

"KID FRIENDLY" SOUP TIPS

◆ Most children love such familiar favorites as Family-Style Vegetable Beef Alphabet Soup (page 151), Tortellini Soup with Greens and Mushrooms (page 166), and Classic Wonton Soup (page 171).

◆ Many children are also partial to smooth soups such as Creamy Broccoli and Leek Bisque (page 150), Sweet Potato and Squash Soup (page 163), or Creamy Iced Cantaloupe Soup (page 145).

◆ Sometimes a food that your child has refused when you served it separately (peas or carrots, for example) will be happily eaten when added to a soup.

◆ You can customize a soup recipe to your family's taste preferences. For example, substitute pasta with a different shape if you know your child prefers it. If a particular herb or seasoning is not a favorite (cilantro or hot pepper, for example), omit it from the recipe or serve it on the side.

◆ Many cooked vegetables, including potatoes, broccoli, carrots, and winter squash, can be puréed with a bit of liquid and added to soups to boost nutrition.

◆ Serve soups with a "topping bar" that includes small bowls of croutons, grated cheeses, yogurt, chopped cooked potato, cooked rice, grated carrots, chopped tomato, chopped onion, or diced bell peppers.

Favorite Neoclassic Chicken Noodle Soup

Makes 6 main-dish servings

In grandma's day, chicken soup was made with a stewing hen set to simmer on the back burner for several hours. This version uses a young broiler or fryer which cooks to flavorful tenderness in under an hour. When you add vegetables and noodles, you get a deliciously satisfying chicken soup—the quintessential comfort food.

1 chicken (about 3 pounds) cut
  into 8 parts
4 cups defatted lower-sodium
  chicken broth, such as Basic
  Chicken Stock (page 142)
1 onion, quartered
1 carrot, coarsely chopped
1 celery rib, coarsely chopped
¼ cup parsley sprigs, including
  stems
1 teaspoon dried thyme plus
  1 teaspoon

4 whole peppercorns
4 whole cloves
½ teaspoon salt
½ teaspoon pepper
2 cups thinly sliced carrots
2 cups dried medium-wide noodles,
  preferably cholesterol free
2 cups frozen peas
½ cup thinly sliced scallions,
  including green tops
¼ cup chopped parsley, preferably
  flat leaf

1. In a large soup pot or Dutch oven, combine the chicken, broth, and 8 cups of water. Bring to a boil, skimming off any foam that rises to the top. Add the onion, chopped carrot, celery, parsley, 1 teaspoon thyme, peppercorns, cloves, salt, and pepper. Reduce the heat to medium-low and simmer, partially covered, until the chicken is tender, about 45 minutes. Remove the chicken from the broth and pull off and discard the skin and chop the meat into 1- to 2-inch chunks. Strain the broth, pressing on the solids to extract as much flavor as possible. Skim off and discard the fat, or refrigerate the stock and then lift the fat off the top. (The stock can be refrigerated for 3 days or frozen for up to 2 months.)

2. Return the stock to the pot. Add the sliced carrots and simmer until almost tender, about 8 minutes. Add the noodles, peas, and remaining teaspoon of thyme. Simmer uncovered until the noodles are tender, about 8 minutes. Return the chicken to the pot to heat through. Stir in the scallions and chopped parsley and adjust seasonings if necessary. (Serve immediately or refrigerate for up to 6 hours.)

◆ *PER SERVING: About 332 cals, 74 cals from fat, 8g total fat, 2g sat fat, 70mg chol, 374mg sodium, 34g total carbs, 6g fiber, 31g prot*

Creamy Broccoli and Leek Bisque

Makes 8 side-dish servings

This versatile, all-season puréed soup tastes equally delicious served hot or cold. In winter, try it with Chicory, Arugula, and Orange Salad Siciliana (page 103), and in summer with a tomato salad and toasted pita.

1 tablespoon vegetable oil
4 leeks, white and pale green parts only, washed and thinly sliced
3 garlic cloves, chopped
4 cups vegetable broth or defatted lower-sodium chicken broth plus 2 cups
2 pounds all-purpose or russet potatoes, peeled and sliced
1 pound broccoli, coarsely chopped
1 teaspoon sugar
⅓ cup parsley sprigs, preferably flat leaf
¼ teaspoon grated nutmeg
1 cup low-fat (1 percent) milk
1 tablespoon fresh lemon juice
½ teaspoon green or red liquid hot pepper sauce
Salt and pepper to taste
Thin lemon slices, cut in half for garnish, if desired

1. Heat the oil in a large saucepan or soup pot. Add the leeks and garlic and cook over medium heat, stirring, for 1 minute. Add 2 tablespoons water, cover, and cook over low heat for 5 minutes until somewhat softened. Add the 4 cups broth, potatoes, broccoli, and sugar. Cook, covered, over medium-low heat, until the vegetables are tender, about 15 minutes.

2. In a food processor or blender, purée the vegetable mixture along with the parsley, in batches if necessary, pulsing until smooth. Stir in the nutmeg. (This recipe can be made to this point up to 2 days ahead and kept refrigerated.)

3. To serve cold, whisk the remaining 2 cups of broth and the milk into the cold soup base. To serve hot, return it to a saucepan, whisk in the broth and milk, and reheat gently, stirring frequently.

4. Season with the lemon juice, hot pepper sauce, salt, and pepper, and serve topped with a lemon slice if desired.

◆ *PER SERVING: About 205 cals, 23 cals from fat, 3g total fat, 0g sat fat, 1mg chol, 118mg sodium, 41g total carbs, 5g fiber, 6g prot*

LEEK LESSONS

◆ Although leeks look like huge, overgrown scallions, they are one of the milder members of the onion family, with a sweet, slightly earthy taste. Leeks are particularly well suited for use in soup. Their tough texture softens with long simmering and their distinctive flavor adds depth and interest to many soups.

◆ Buy leeks with long green stalks that look fresh and with their root ends still attached.

◆ To prepare leeks for cooking, trim off the rootlets and all but about 3 inches of the tough green tops.

◆ Because of the way they grow, leeks almost always harbor sand and grit between their tightly packed layers. To clean them, first cut crosswise 2 or 3 inches into the green ends. Hold under running water, while "riffling" the stalks like a deck of cards so the grit washes out.

◆ Cut the cleaned leeks in half lengthwise and place on a cutting board, flat sides down. Slice the white and pale green parts only, discarding any remaining dark green leaves.

◆ The dark green leaves, though too fibrous to eat, are full of flavor, and can be added to any simmering broth or stock. Don't forget to wash them well before using and remove them before serving.

Family-Style Vegetable Beef Alphabet Soup

Makes 4 main-dish servings

This soup is a great way to entice kids—and adults—to eat their vegetables. You can make it in less than half an hour. A basket of warm Yogurt Corn Bread (page 125) makes a particularly homey accompaniment.

¾ pound lean ground beef

1 large onion, coarsely chopped

2 garlic cloves, chopped

2 teaspoons mixed dried Italian herb seasoning (see note)

1 can (16 ounces) stewed tomatoes with juice

4 cups defatted lower-sodium beef broth

4 cups frozen mixed vegetables

½ cup alphabet macaroni or other small pasta

½ teaspoon black pepper

Salt to taste

4 tablespoons minced parsley, preferably flat leaf

1. In a large saucepan or soup pot, cook the ground beef, onion, and garlic over medium heat, stirring frequently, until the meat loses its pink color, about 8 minutes. Spoon off any excess fat. Add the dried herb seasoning and cook, stirring, for 1 minute.

2. Add the tomatoes to the pot and use the side of a spoon to cut them into smaller chunks. Add the beef broth, along with 2 cups water, and bring to a boil. Reduce the heat to medium and simmer, partially covered, for 10 minutes to blend flavors.

continued

3. Add the vegetables and the macaroni. Simmer uncovered over medium heat until the pasta and vegetables are tender, 10 to 12 minutes.

4. Season the soup with the pepper and salt to taste and stir in the parsley. (This recipe can be made a day or two ahead, but the pasta will absorb liquid, so thin the soup with additional broth or water when you reheat it.)

◆ *PER SERVING: About 525 cals, 113 cals from fat, 13g total fat, 4g sat fat, 52mg chol, 1133mg sodium, 75g total carbs, 8g fiber, 29g prot*

Note: Italian seasoning is a mixture of several dried herbs, including marjoram, thyme, rosemary, and oregano. You can make your own blend, or substitute another mixture, such as herbes de Provence.

Nantucket Clam Chowder

Makes 4 main-dish servings

Less rich than some traditional versions, which call for salt pork, half-and-half, and butter, this milky potato-laden New England–style chowder makes for an immensely satisfying lunch or supper when paired with soda crackers and a salad of dark, leafy greens. Try to find Yukon gold potatoes because they make the chowder an attractive yellow.

2 slices (about 1 ounce) bacon
1 large onion, chopped
1 large celery rib, thinly sliced
2 cups chopped clams with juice (see note)
Up to 1 cup bottled clam juice or fish stock, as needed
1½ pounds Yukon gold or all-purpose potatoes,
   peeled and diced roughly into ¾-inch pieces
   (about 4 cups)
1½ tablespoons chopped fresh thyme or
   2 teaspoons dried thyme
2 parsley sprigs, with stems
1 bay leaf, broken in half
4 cups whole milk
Freshly ground black pepper to taste

1. In a large saucepan or soup pot, cook the bacon over medium-low heat, stirring occasionally, until browned and crisp, about 6 minutes. Remove the bacon from the pot with a slotted spoon, drain on paper towels, then crumble the bacon into small bits. Reserve it for garnishing the chowder. Pour off and discard the bacon drippings in the pan, leaving only the amount that clings to the bottom. Add the onion and celery, raise the heat to medium, and cook, stirring often, until softened, about 5 minutes.

2. Drain the clam juice into a large glass measuring cup and add enough additional bottled clam juice to make 2 cups. Add the clam juice to the saucepan, along with the potatoes, thyme, parsley, and bay leaf. Bring to a boil, reduce the heat to low, and cook, covered, until the potatoes are tender, 10 to 15 minutes. Add the clams and slowly stir the milk into the chowder. Cook over medium-low heat, stirring occasionally, until the chowder is heated through, about 5 minutes. Use the back of a large spoon to mash about one quarter of the potatoes against the side of the pot to lightly thicken the chowder. (This recipe can be made up to 2 days ahead and refrigerated. Reheat gently before serving.)

3. Discard the parsley sprigs and bay leaf. Ladle the chowder into bowls, sprinkle with the reserved bacon, and grind pepper over the top.

◆ *PER SERVING: About 405 cals, 101 cals from fat, 11g total fat, 6g sat fat, 127mg chol, 382mg sodium, 55g total carbs, 3g fiber, 25g prot*

Note: Use chopped fresh clams in juice from the fish market or 2 cans (10½ ounces each) chopped clams in juice.

BAY LEAF ADVICE

Bay leaves, from the bay laurel tree, are readily available in dried form. Short, oval, olive green Turkish bay leaves have a more subtle flavor than the longer, narrower, usually brighter green California variety. Bay leaves are added to a soup or stew whole or broken in half to speed up the release of flavor. Be sure to remove the leaf—or the two halves of a broken leaf—before serving. Bay leaves never soften, and if one is accidentally eaten, it makes an unpleasant, sharp-edged, indigestible mouthful and can even cut the inside of your throat.

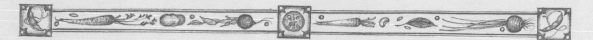

Clam Chowder Manhattan Style

Makes 4 main-dish servings

A medley of delicious vegetables contributes wonderful color, flavor, and texture to this soup—as well as a variety of nutrients not found in traditional New England–style chowders. Dried red pepper flakes make this soup somewhat peppery, so adjust the amount in accordance with your family's "heat index."

2 teaspoons olive oil

2 tablespoons minced lean cooked ham

1 large onion, chopped

1 large celery rib, thinly sliced

1 large carrot, peeled and thinly sliced

2 garlic cloves, chopped

1½ teaspoons dried oregano

2 cups chopped clams, drained, with juice reserved (see note)

1 can (14 to 16 ounces) plum tomatoes with juice

½ cup dry white wine or water

1 pound all-purpose potatoes, peeled and roughly chopped into ¾-inch dice (about 3 cups)

¼ to ½ teaspoon dried red pepper flakes

2 tablespoons chopped parsley

Salt to taste

Black pepper to taste

1. In a large saucepan or soup pot, heat the oil, add the ham, and cook over medium heat for about 3 minutes, stirring, until lightly browned. Add the onion, celery, and carrot and cook, stirring occasionally, until the vegetables are quite soft, about 8 minutes. Add the garlic and oregano and cook, stirring, for 1 minute.

2. Measure the clam juice and add enough water to make 4 cups. Add the liquid to the soup pot along with the tomatoes, wine, potatoes, and pepper flakes. Bring to a boil, breaking up any large chunks of tomato with the side of a spoon, reduce the heat to medium-low, and cook, partially covered, until the potatoes are tender, 10 to 15 minutes.

3. Add the reserved clams and simmer, uncovered, until heated through. Stir in the parsley and season with salt and black pepper to taste. (The chowder can be made up to 2 days ahead and refrigerated. Reheat gently before serving.)

◆ *PER SERVING: About 278 cals, 44 cals from fat, 5g total fat, 1g sat fat, 95mg chol, 351mg sodium, 41g total carbs, 4g fiber, 18g prot*

Note: Two 10½-ounce cans of chopped clams can be substituted for fresh chopped clams.

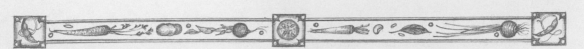

Sweet Corn and Shrimp Chowder

Makes 4 main-dish servings

Succulent fresh pink shrimp and golden corn kernels turn a homey chowder into something special. Although it can be made with frozen corn, this chowder is particularly delicious during the summer, made with sweet, fresh corn "off the cob." Serve it with a crusty bread and thickly sliced ripe tomatoes heavily sprinkled with chopped fresh basil.

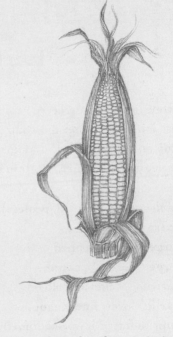

2 slices (about 1 ounce) bacon

1 large onion, chopped

2 garlic cloves, finely chopped

2 cups fish stock (page 143) or bottled clam juice

¾ pound red-skinned potatoes, roughly
   chopped into ¾-inch dice (about 2 cups)

1 tablespoon chopped fresh thyme or
   2 teaspoons dried thyme

1 bay leaf, broken in half

3 cups corn kernels (see note)

4 cups whole milk

¾ pound (about 18 to 20) medium shrimp,
   shelled and deveined

⅛ teaspoon grated nutmeg

Freshly ground black pepper to taste

1. In a large saucepan or soup pot, cook the bacon over medium-low heat, stirring occasionally, until browned and crisp, about 6 minutes. Remove the bacon from the pot with a slotted spoon and drain on paper towels. Crumble the bacon into small bits and reserve. Pour off and discard the bacon drippings in the pan, leaving only the amount of fat that clings to the bottom. Add the onion, raise the heat to medium, and cook, stirring often, until softened, about 5 minutes. Add the garlic and cook, stirring, for 1 minute.

2. Add the fish stock, potatoes, thyme, and bay leaf. Bring to a boil, reduce the heat to medium-low, and cook covered for 5 minutes. Add the corn and continue to cook until the potatoes and corn are tender, 8 to 10 minutes.

3. Slowly stir the milk into the chowder and bring it to a simmer, stirring frequently. Add the shrimp and simmer gently, uncovered, until they turn pink, about 3 minutes. Season with the nutmeg. (The chowder can be made 1 day ahead and refrigerated. Reheat gently before serving.)

continued

4. Discard the bay leaf. Ladle the chowder into shallow bowls, sprinkle with the reserved bacon, and grind pepper over the top.

◆ *PER SERVING: About 461 cals, 102 cals from fat, 11g total fat, 6g sat fat, 135mg chol, 358mg sodium, 63g total carbs, 4g fiber, 30g prot*

Note: To cut corn kernels, stand a husked ear of corn, raw or cooked, on its blunt end and use a sharp knife to cut the kernels and milky pulp away from the cob. One medium-sized ear of corn yields about ½ cup of kernels.

Herbed Minestrone

Makes 6 main-dish servings

Minestrone has a well-deserved reputation as one of the world's classic soups. Though the ingredient list looks daunting, the soup goes together quite quickly, and the result is immensely satisfying and rich in fiber, vitamins, calcium, and iron. A basket of Italian bread and a salad of dark, leafy greens turn this into a favorite supper any time of year.

2 tablespoons olive oil, preferably extra virgin
1 large onion, chopped
1 large celery rib, sliced
2 carrots, peeled and sliced
2 garlic cloves, finely chopped
3 cups defatted lower-sodium beef broth
1 can (14 to 16 ounces) diced tomatoes
¾ pound all-purpose potatoes, peeled and diced
2 teaspoons dried marjoram
½ pound green beans, trimmed and cut in 1-inch slices

2 cups thinly sliced cabbage
2 cans (16 ounces each) cannellini or Great Northern beans, rinsed and drained, or 3½ cups cooked white beans
½ cup (4 ounces) ditali or other small tubular pasta
½ cup chopped fresh basil (see note)
¼ cup chopped parsley, preferably flat leaf
Salt to taste
Black pepper to taste
⅓ cup grated Parmesan cheese

1. Heat the oil in a very large saucepan or soup pot. Add the onion, celery, carrot, and garlic and cook over medium heat, stirring occasionally, until the vegetables begin to soften, about 5 minutes. Add 3 cups of water along with the broth, tomatoes, potatoes, and marjoram. Bring to a boil over high heat, reduce the heat to low and cook covered for 10 minutes.

2. Add the green beans, cabbage, cannellini, and pasta. Simmer uncovered over medium heat until the vegetables and pasta are tender, about 15 minutes. (This recipe can be made several hours ahead. Reheat before serving, adding additional liquid if necessary.)

3. Stir in the fresh basil and parsley and season with salt and pepper to taste. Ladle into bowls and pass the Parmesan cheese at the table.

◆ *PER SERVING: About 355 cals, 71 cals from fat, 8g total fat, 2g sat fat, 4mg chol, 547mg sodium, 60g total carbs, 10g fiber, 15g prot*

Note: If fresh basil is unavailable, use 2 teaspoons dried basil and add it with the marjoram.

Quick Cuban Black Bean Soup with Garnishes

Makes 4 main-dish servings

A touch of honey amplifies the hidden depths of flavor in this velvety black bean soup, and the garnishes add a welcome dimension of color, crunch, and taste.

1 tablespoon olive oil
1 onion, chopped
1 celery rib, chopped
2 garlic cloves, chopped
2 teaspoons dry mustard
3 cans (16 ounces each) black
  beans, rinsed and drained, or
  6 cups cooked black beans
1 teaspoon honey
3 cups vegetable or defatted
  lower-sodium chicken broth

2 tablespoons dry sherry
  (optional)
½ teaspoon liquid hot pepper sauce
Salt to taste
Black pepper to taste
1 cup chopped tomato
1 cup chopped sweet onion
1 cup nonfat plain yogurt
½ cup chopped cilantro

1. In a large, heavy saucepan, heat the oil over medium heat. Add the onion, celery, and garlic and cook, stirring occasionally, until the vegetables begin to soften, about 5 minutes. Stir in the mustard and cook for 1 minute.

2. Add the beans, honey, and 3 cups of water to the pot. Bring to a boil, reduce the heat to medium-low, and simmer uncovered until the vegetables are very tender and the liquid is somewhat reduced, about 20 minutes.

3. Purée the soup base in a food processor or blender, in batches if necessary, until smooth. Return the purée to the cooking pot, stir in the broth, and simmer over medium heat until heated through, about 5 minutes. The soup should be quite thick but not so thick

continued

that it mounds on a spoon. Add more liquid to thin if necessary. (This recipe can be made 3 days ahead and refrigerated or frozen. Reheat before serving.)

4. Stir in the optional sherry and season with the hot pepper sauce, and salt and pepper to taste. Serve the tomato, onion, yogurt, and cilantro at the table as garnishes.

◆ *PER SERVING (without sherry): About 487 cals, 51 cals from fat, 6g total fat, 1g sat fat, 1mg chol, 1033mg sodium, 83g total carbs, 13g fiber, 29g prot*

ALCOHOL IN SOUP

When wine or other alcohol is added to a soup early in the cooking process and the soup is simmered uncovered in a large pot for a long time, most of the alcohol evaporates, leaving behind only the concentrated flavor of the wine. If a recipe calls for wine but you would rather not use it, try broth, nonalcoholic wine, unsweetened grape juice, or a combination of one part lemon juice mixed with three parts water or broth, depending on the soup.

Moroccan Lamb, Chickpea, and Vegetable Soup

Makes 6 main-dish servings

In Morocco, where this soup is called "harira," the traditional long-simmering version is made with lamb shanks and served to break the fast of Ramadan. This updated recipe calls for lean lamb and chicken breast meat, and takes less than an hour to make. Chock full of legumes, grains, vegetables, and meats, the soup is spiced with intriguing flavors, making it taste as delicious as it is nutritious.

3 cups defatted lower-sodium chicken broth
1 small whole chicken breast (about 1¼ pounds), split
½ cup dried lentils, rinsed and picked over
1 cinnamon stick, broken in half
1 teaspoon extra-virgin olive oil
½ pound lean lamb, cut in 1-inch cubes
½ teaspoon salt, or more to taste
¼ teaspoon black pepper
1 large onion, chopped
2 garlic cloves, finely chopped

1½ teaspoons curry powder
1 teaspoon turmeric
½ teaspoon powdered ginger
2 cans (14 to 16 ounces) diced tomatoes
1 can (19 ounces) chickpeas, rinsed and drained, or 2 cups cooked chickpeas
½ cup (4 ounces) small dried pasta such as tubettini
2 tablespoons fresh lemon juice
¼ cup chopped parsley, preferably flat leaf
¼ cup chopped cilantro

1. In a large soup pot, combine the broth, chicken breast, lentils, cinnamon stick, and 4 cups of water. Bring to a boil, reduce the heat to low, and cook covered until the lentils are tender and the chicken is no longer pink near the bone, about 25 minutes. Remove the chicken to a plate and, when cool enough to handle, shred the meat with a fork, discarding the skin and bones. Return the chicken meat to the pot with the lentils and skim off any excess fat from the broth.

2. In a large skillet, heat the oil over medium-high heat. Season the lamb with the salt and pepper and cook until brown on all sides, about 5 minutes. Reduce the heat to medium, add the onion, and cook, stirring frequently, until it softens and is lightly browned, about 5 minutes. Stir in the garlic, curry powder, turmeric, and ginger and cook, stirring, for 1 minute. Scrape the lamb mixture into the soup pot.

3. Add the tomatoes, chickpeas, and pasta to the soup. Bring to a boil over high heat, reduce the heat to medium-low, and cook partially covered until the pasta is tender, about 15 minutes. Adjust the liquid, adding more broth or water if the soup is too thick. (This recipe can be made several hours ahead and refrigerated or frozen. See note. Reheat before proceeding.)

4. Shortly before serving, stir in the lemon juice, parsley, and cilantro. Taste and adjust the seasonings if necessary. Ladle into shallow bowls and serve.

◆ *PER SERVING: About 394 cals, 58 cals from fat, 6g total fat, 1g sat fat, 57mg chol, 799mg sodium, 52g total carbs, 7g fiber, 33g prot*

Note: If you plan to freeze the soup, omit the pasta in step 3, and add it when the soup is reheated. Cook about 15 minutes or until the pasta is tender.

TOMATOES IN SOUP

In a recipe that calls for tomatoes, you can substitute one type for almost any other. Fresh tomatoes, canned whole tomatoes (regular or plum), stewed tomatoes, diced tomatoes, "recipe-ready" chopped and seasoned tomatoes, crushed tomatoes, and tomato sauce can all be used more or less interchangeably.

Split Pea Soup with Ham Bits and Dilled Yogurt

Makes 4 main-dish servings

Simmer a pot of this savory split pea soup on the back burner in wintertime for a truly satisfying lunch or supper. The recipe calls for a small amount of finely chopped, lean ham which adds flavor but not as much fat as traditional recipes for this kind of soup. A final swirl of dill-flecked yogurt contributes calcium as well as a welcome tart flavor contrast.

2½ cups dried split green peas, rinsed
4 cups defatted lower-sodium chicken broth
1 bay leaf
1 large onion, chopped
3 carrots, peeled and chopped
1 large celery rib, chopped
2 garlic cloves, chopped

2 tablespoons chopped parsley, preferably flat leaf, plus 1 tablespoon
1½ tablespoons chopped fresh dill plus 1½ teaspoons
1 cup (4 ounces) finely cubed lean smoked ham
¼ teaspoon black pepper
Salt to taste
⅔ cup nonfat plain yogurt

1. In a large soup kettle, combine the split peas with the broth, bay leaf, and 4 cups of water. Bring to a boil over high heat, skimming off any foam that rises to the surface, reduce the heat to low, and cook covered until the peas are almost tender, about 1 hour.

2. Add the onion, carrots, celery, garlic, 2 tablespoons of parsley, and 1½ tablespoons dill. Simmer uncovered over medium-low heat until the split peas and vegetables are tender, 30 to 40 minutes. Discard the bay leaf.

3. Process the soup in a food processor or blender, in batches if necessary, pulsing to make a textured (not completely smooth) soup. Stir in the cubed ham, season with the pepper, and add salt to taste. Adjust the amount of liquid, adding more broth or water if necessary. (This recipe can be made up to 3 days ahead and refrigerated or frozen. Reheat before proceeding.)

4. In a small bowl, whisk the yogurt with the remaining 1 tablespoon parsley and 1½ teaspoons dill.

5. Ladle the soup into bowls and top with a spoonful of yogurt. Use the tip of a sharp knife to swirl the yogurt into the soup.

◆ *PER SERVING: About 371 cals, 30 cals from fat, 3g total fat, 1g sat fat, 16mg chol, 520mg sodium, 57g total carbs, 10g fiber, 29g prot*

Tuscan Cannellini and Escarole Soup

Makes 4 main-dish servings

In this Tuscan classic, the leafy green escarole is blanched separately to remove some of its bitterness. The result is an intriguing interplay of flavors and colors, with the pale, neutrally flavored beans playing off the pleasant bite of garlic and greens, and finished with a sprinkle of Parmesan cheese. This fiber-packed soup is Italian comfort food at its best!

1 head escarole (1¼ to 1½ pounds), washed and torn or cut into bite-size pieces (about 11 cups)

2 tablespoons olive oil

5 garlic cloves, finely chopped

1½ teaspoons dried oregano

¼ teaspoon dried red pepper flakes

7 cups defatted lower-sodium chicken broth

2 cans (19 ounces each) white beans such as cannellini or Great Northern, rinsed and drained, or 4 cups cooked white beans

Salt to taste

Black pepper to taste

½ cup freshly grated Parmesan cheese, preferably Parmigiano-Reggiano

1. Blanch the escarole in a large pot of lightly salted boiling water until tender, about 5 minutes. Drain into a colander.

2. Meanwhile, heat the oil in a large saucepan or soup pot. Add the garlic, oregano, and red pepper flakes and cook over medium heat, stirring, until fragrant, about 1 minute.

3. Add the broth, beans, and escarole. Bring to a boil, reduce the heat to medium, and simmer uncovered until the broth is slightly reduced and the flavors are blended. Salt and pepper to taste. (This recipe can be made up to 2 days ahead and refrigerated. Reheat before serving, adding additional liquid if necessary.)

4. Ladle into shallow bowls and pass the Parmesan cheese at the table.

◆ *PER SERVING: About 367 cals, 116 cals from fat, 13g total fat, 1g sat fat, 11mg chol, 682mg sodium, 43g total carbs, 15g fiber, 23g prot*

TO REDUCE FAT AND SALT IN SOUP RECIPES

◆ Substitute defatted, lower-sodium broth for regular chicken or beef broth in a recipe.

◆ Soup becomes saltier as it cooks down, so salt it toward the end of the cooking time. Begin

by adding the minimum amount of salt called for, and season to taste.

◆ If a recipe calls for whole milk, try substituting low-fat or skim milk.

◆ If a recipe calls for regular sour cream or yogurt, you can usually substitute low-fat sour cream or low-fat or nonfat yogurt.

Spicy Mixed Bean Soup with Turkey Sausage

Makes 6 main-dish servings

Prepackaged bean mixes are perfect for soup because the larger, harder beans (such as kidney beans and chickpeas) tend to stay whole, while the smaller varieties (such as lentils) dissolve into the soup, enriching and thickening it.

1 pound packaged mixed dried beans, rinsed and picked over
½ pound smoked turkey sausage such as turkey kielbasa
1 large onion, chopped
1 celery rib, chopped
1 bay leaf
1 can (14 to 16 ounces) stewed tomatoes
2 tablespoons brown sugar
1 tablespoon chili powder
1 teaspoon ground cumin
½ teaspoon dry mustard
¾ teaspoon dried oregano
1 tablespoon red wine vinegar
¼ teaspoon liquid hot pepper sauce, or to taste
Salt to taste

1. Cover the beans in cold water and soak them for 4 hours or overnight. Drain into a colander. In a large soup pot, bring 10 cups of water to a boil. Add the beans, reduce the heat to low, and simmer covered for 1 hour.

2. Add the whole sausage, onion, celery, and bay leaf and cook for 30 minutes longer.

3. Add the stewed tomatoes, breaking up any large pieces with the side of a spoon. Add the brown sugar, chili powder, cumin, mustard, and oregano. Continue to cook, covered, until the beans are tender, 30 to 60 minutes. Remove the sausage, cut into thin slices, and return it to the soup. Adjust the thickness of the soup by simmering longer if too thin and adding liquid if too thick. (This recipe can be made up to 3 days ahead and refrigerated. Reheat before serving.)

4. Discard the bay leaf, stir in the vinegar and hot pepper sauce, and season with salt to taste if necessary. Ladle into bowls and serve.

◆ *PER SERVING: About 384 cals, 70 cals from fat, 8g total fat, 0g sat fat, 20mg chol, 571mg sodium, 58g total carbs, 4g fiber, 23g prot*

Sweet Potato and Squash Soup

Makes 6 side-dish servings

This smooth, golden soup topped with scarlet puréed cranberry epitomizes the flavors and colors of the autumn season. It can be made ahead, and makes a lovely first course for Thanksgiving dinner.

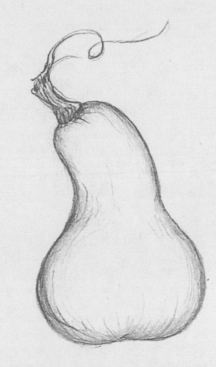

1 tablespoon butter
1 medium-large onion, sliced
2 cups defatted lower-sodium chicken
    broth plus 2 cups
1½ pounds peeled and cubed
    butternut squash
    (from 1 medium-sized squash)
½ pound peeled and cubed sweet potato
    (from 1 large potato)
2 large carrots, peeled and sliced
1½ teaspoons crumbled dried sage
½ teaspoon ground mace
½ teaspoon ground ginger
½ teaspoon liquid hot pepper sauce
Salt to taste
¼ cup sugar
1 cup fresh cranberries (see note)
2 tablespoons orange juice

1. Heat the butter in a large saucepan or soup pot. Add the onion and cook over medium-low heat, stirring frequently, until softened and golden brown, about 10 minutes. Add 2 cups of the broth and the squash, sweet potato, carrots, sage, mace, and ginger. Bring to a boil, cover, and cook over low heat until the vegetables are very tender, 20 to 25 minutes.

2. In a food processor or blender, purée the vegetable mixture, in batches if necessary, pulsing until smooth. (This recipe can be made to this point up to 2 days ahead and refrigerated or frozen for 1 month.)

3. Return the purée to the saucepan and whisk in the remaining 2 cups of broth. Simmer gently until heated through. Season with the hot pepper sauce and salt to taste.

4. In a small saucepan, combine the sugar with ⅓ cup water. Bring to a boil, stirring until the sugar dissolves, and add the cranberries. Cook uncovered over medium heat, stirring

continued

occasionally, until the cranberries soften and burst, about 10 minutes. Cool slightly. In a food processor or blender, purée the cranberries with the orange juice until smooth. (The cranberry purée can be made 3 days ahead and refrigerated.)

5. Ladle the hot soup into bowls. Top with a spoonful of cranberry purée and draw the tip of a knife through the purée to create a decorative swirl, or pipe the purée through a pastry bag using a small tip.

◆ *PER SERVING: About 150 cals, 24 cals from fat, 3g total fat, 1g sat fat, 5mg chol, 83mg sodium, 30g total carbs, 4g fiber, 3g prot*

Note: You can substitute ½ cup of canned whole-berry cranberry sauce for the cooked cranberry and sugar mixture. Purée it with the orange juice as directed in step 4.

SOUP FREEZING TIPS

◆ Most soups freeze very well. You can double or triple the original recipe and freeze the soup in amounts suited to your family's needs.

◆ Some milk- and buttermilk-based soups do not freeze well. Check individual recipes for specific freezing instructions.

◆ Sometimes soup that has been frozen needs reseasoning. After you reheat the soup, taste it carefully and adjust the seasonings if necessary.

◆ When freezing soup in plastic containers, leave about ¾ inch at the top of the container because liquid expands as it freezes.

◆ To freeze soup in freezer-weight plastic bags, place the bag inside a bowl, pour in the soup, then seal. Carefully place the filled bag upright in the freezer and freeze until solid.

TO PURÉE SMOOTH SOUPS

◆ To avoid splashes and possible burns, do not fill a blender container more than two thirds full when puréeing hot liquids. Place the lid on the machine firmly, then hold your hand on it to prevent the lid from popping off. Begin blending at low speed, gradually increasing to high. Starting the blender at high speed can force hot liquid up and out of the blender, scalding your hands or face.

◆ If a liquid is too thin, it will be difficult to purée smoothly in a blender or a food processor. You will see that most puréed soups in this book use only part of the liquid in the recipe at the puréeing stage; the remainder is added later to thin the thick, puréed base.

◆ Smaller amounts generally purée to a smoother consistency.

◆ Puréed soups thicken as they cool and might need thinning with additional liquid before serving.

Scottish Turkey, Leek, and Barley Soup

Makes 4 main-dish servings

This dish is a modern take on that famous Scottish soup quaintly known as "cock-a-leekie," which contains leeks, barley, prunes, and a hen simmered for hours. This quick and delectable version uses flavorful turkey meat—an excellent way to use up leftover turkey.

2 teaspoons butter

4 large leeks (about 2 pounds), white and pale green parts only, washed and thinly sliced (about 5 cups)

6 cups defatted lower-sodium chicken broth

4 carrots, peeled and thinly sliced (about 1¾ cups)

1 cup raw pearl barley

1 cup chopped pitted prunes

2 cups (8 ounces) cubed leftover cooked turkey or chicken (see note)

2 tablespoons chopped parsley, preferably flat leaf, plus 2 tablespoons

1 tablespoon fresh lemon juice

Salt to taste

Black pepper to taste

1. Melt the butter in a large, heavy saucepan or soup pot. Add the leeks, stir to coat with butter, and add ¼ cup of water. Cover and cook over low heat, stirring occasionally, until the leeks are softened and very lightly browned, 10 to 15 minutes.

2. Add the broth, along with 2 cups of water, and bring to a boil over high heat. Add the carrots, barley, and prunes, reduce the heat to low, and cook covered for 20 minutes. Add the turkey and 2 tablespoons of the parsley and simmer uncovered until the barley is tender, 5 to 10 minutes. Adjust the liquid, if necessary. The soup should be quite thick. (This recipe can be made up to 2 days ahead and refrigerated. Reheat before serving, adding more liquid if necessary.)

3. Season with the lemon juice, salt, and pepper to taste. Ladle into bowls and sprinkle with the remaining 2 tablespoons parsley.

◆ *PER SERVING: About 548 cals, 72 cals from fat, 8g total fat, 2g sat fat, 51mg chol, 668mg sodium, 101g total carbs, 16g fiber, 24g prot*

Note: If you don't have cooked turkey or chicken on hand, substitute ½ pound of cubed raw turkey or chicken breast and add it to the soup during the last 15 minutes of cooking.

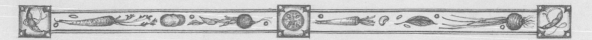

Tortellini Soup with Greens and Mushrooms

Makes 4 main-dish servings

In this recipe, frozen tortellini, a deservedly popular convenience food, is simmered in broth laden with shredded fresh spinach and slivered mushrooms, and spiked with oregano and lots of garlic. Braided Semolina Bread (page 115) and a red-leaf lettuce salad are all you need for a quick-and-easy weeknight supper.

1 teaspoon olive oil
4 ounces shiitake or other fresh mushrooms,
   thinly sliced
4 large garlic cloves, finely chopped
1 teaspoon dried oregano
8 cups defatted lower-sodium chicken broth
1 pound frozen chicken-filled tortellini
12 ounces spinach leaves, thinly sliced
   (6 to 7 cups)
3 tablespoons grated Parmesan cheese
Salt to taste
Freshly ground black pepper to taste

1. Heat the oil in a large soup pot. Add the mushrooms, and cook over medium-high heat, stirring frequently, until somewhat softened, about 5 minutes. Add the garlic and oregano and cook, stirring, for 1 minute. Add the chicken broth and bring to a boil over high heat. Add the tortellini, reduce the heat to medium, and cook, partially covered, until the pasta is tender but still firm, 6 to 8 minutes.

2. Add the spinach and simmer until it wilts and becomes tender, about 2 minutes. Stir in the cheese and season with salt and pepper. Ladle into shallow bowls and serve.

◆ *PER SERVING: About 466 cals, 130 cals from fat, 14g total fat, 4g sat fat, 65mg chol, 585mg sodium, 62g total carbs, 5g fiber, 24g prot*

PASTA AND RICE IN SOUP

Do not add rice or pasta to soup that you want to store in the refrigerator or freeze. Add the pasta or rice while reheating the soup before serving. Pasta— particularly softer noodles that are not made with semolina flour— absorbs liquid and becomes mushy when frozen, while rice grains can split and begin to disintegrate. You will need to add some extra liquid when reheating smaller amounts of leftover soup containing rice or pasta to return them to their proper soupy consistency.

Hot and Sour Tofu and Rice Soup

Makes 4 main-dish servings

Although tofu is not low in fat, it is cholesterol free and has very little saturated fat. It can be an excellent source of calcium (check the labels). This tofu and rice soup is not only soothing, it also provides an invigorating kick from fresh ginger. Vinegar adds a pleasing sourness, while the subtly smoky flavor of toasted sesame oil smooths and finishes the soup.

6 cups defatted lower-sodium
   chicken broth
1 cup raw white rice
2 cups thinly sliced green cabbage
   (about 8 ounces)
1 pound firm tofu, cut in ½-inch cubes

1 tablespoon minced fresh ginger
1 tablespoon toasted sesame oil
1 tablespoon rice wine vinegar or
   distilled white vinegar
¾ cup thinly sliced scallions,
   including green tops, plus ¼ cup

1. In a large pot, bring the broth and 3 cups of water to a boil over high heat. Add the rice, reduce the heat to low, and cook covered for 5 minutes. Add the cabbage and continue to cook for 10 minutes.

2. Add the tofu, ginger, sesame oil, vinegar, and ¾ cup scallions. Simmer uncovered over medium heat until the rice is tender, about 5 minutes. (This recipe can be made 1 day ahead and refrigerated. Reheat before serving, adding more broth or water if necessary.)

3. To serve, ladle the soup into bowls and sprinkle with the remaining ¼ cup scallions.

◆ *PER SERVING: About 412 cals, 134 cals from fat, 15g total fat, 2g sat fat, 0mg chol, 123mg sodium, 47g total carbs, 3g fiber, 25g prot*

SOUP TOPPINGS AND GARNISHES

Garnishes add visual appeal, nutritional value, and flavor to soups. Easy garnishes include:

◆ Crisp, toasted whole-grain bread croutons

◆ Crumbled reduced-fat tortilla chips
◆ Chopped fresh herbs, herb blossoms, or other edible flowers
◆ Snipped chives or scallions
◆ Thin slices of lemon or lime

◆ Reduced-fat sour cream or non-fat yogurt
◆ A dusting of paprika
◆ Shredded sharp cheddar or Parmesan cheese or chopped roasted peanuts

Cambodian Chicken, Rice, and Garlic Soup

Makes 4 main-dish servings

The flavors of the Far East enliven this satisfying and nutritious iron- and vitamin C–rich chicken and rice soup. Lemongrass, if you can get it, adds a unique perfume, but the soup is also delicious with grated lemon rind.

1 tablespoon vegetable oil, preferably peanut oil
6 garlic cloves, finely chopped
6 cups defatted lower-sodium chicken broth
1 cup jasmine rice (see note)
½ pound skinless boneless chicken breast,
   cut in ¼-inch strips
1 tablespoon bottled fish sauce (nam pla)
1 tablespoon sugar
1 teaspoon finely minced lemongrass or grated lemon rind
2 cups bean sprouts
½ cup thinly sliced scallions, including green tops
⅓ cup chopped cilantro
1 lime, cut in wedges

1. In a large soup pot, heat the oil over medium heat. Add the garlic and cook, stirring, for 1 minute. Add the broth, along with 2 cups of water, and bring to a boil. Add the rice, reduce the heat to low, and cook covered for 10 minutes.

2. Add the chicken, fish sauce, sugar, and lemongrass. Simmer the soup uncovered over medium heat until the rice is tender and the chicken is cooked through, about 10 minutes. (This recipe can be made to this point up to 1 day ahead and refrigerated. Reheat before serving, adding more liquid if necessary.)

3. Place the bean sprouts, scallions, and cilantro in small dishes or on a single platter. Ladle the soup into bowls and pass the garnishes at the table. Finish with a squeeze of lime.

◆ *PER SERVING: About 367 cals, 72 cals from fat, 8g total fat, 1g sat fat, 33mg chol, 370mg sodium, 49g total carbs, 1g fiber, 25g prot*

Note: Jasmine rice is a very soft, fragrant rice imported from Asia. It is increasingly available in supermarkets but, if you cannot get it, substitute the same quantity of regular long-grain white rice.

Japanese Vegetable Noodle Soup with Wasabi

Makes 4 main-dish servings

Wasabi is called "Japanese horseradish." It is usually sold as a green powder, packed in cans, and mixed with an equal amount of water to make a paste. It packs a powerful wallop, so as a condiment for this plain noodle soup, it provides terrific flavor contrast. If you can't find daikon, the mild Japanese white radish, substitute finely chopped celery or jicama.

2 cups defatted lower-sodium
  chicken broth
2 cups fish stock (page 143) or
  bottled clam juice
4 tablespoons reduced-sodium soy
  sauce
2 tablespoons rice wine vinegar or
  distilled white vinegar
1 tablespoon sugar

1 pound fresh Japanese udon
  noodles or fresh linguine
½ pound thinly sliced roast beef,
  cut in slivers
¼ cup thinly sliced scallions plus
  ¼ cup
1½ cups shredded carrots
¾ cup shredded daikon
1 tablespoon reconstituted wasabi

1. In a large saucepan, combine the chicken broth, fish stock, and 1 cup water. Bring to a simmer over medium heat. Add the soy sauce, vinegar, and sugar, and simmer until the sugar dissolves, about 1 minute. Cover and keep warm over low heat.

2. Bring a large pot of lightly salted water to a boil. Add the noodles and cook until tender but still firm, 3 to 5 minutes. Drain in a colander.

3. Add the beef and ¼ cup of scallions to the broth mixture and simmer until heated through. Add the noodles and stir to combine.

4. Ladle the soup into bowls and pass the rest of the scallions and the carrots, daikon, and wasabi at the table so each person can stir them into the soup.

◆ *PER SERVING: About 529 cals, 106 cals from fat, 12g total fat, 3g sat fat, 47mg chol, 724mg sodium, 74g total carbs, 5g fiber, 33g prot*

Spicy Thai Noodle Soup with Shrimp and Lime

Makes 4 main-dish servings

Look for packages of dried Asian noodles in the ethnic food section of your supermarket. Some noodles are curly, others are straight; either shape works fine as long as the noodles are relatively thin. This scrumptious soup is a good source of calcium and is also rich in vitamin C and iron.

2 tablespoons bottled fish sauce (nam pla)

1 tablespoon tomato paste

1 tablespoon vegetable oil, preferably peanut oil

1 tablespoon sugar

2 garlic cloves, finely chopped

½ teaspoon cayenne pepper

6 cups defatted lower-sodium chicken broth

12 ounces thin dried Chinese noodles or vermicelli (see note)

1 pound small or medium shrimp, shelled and deveined

3 celery ribs, thinly sliced on a sharp diagonal

½ cup chopped cilantro

1 large or 2 small limes, cut in wedges

1. To make the sauce, stir together the fish sauce, tomato paste, oil, sugar, garlic, and cayenne in a small bowl. Set aside for at least 30 minutes to blend the flavors. (This part of the recipe can be made several days ahead and refrigerated. Return to room temperature before using.)

2. In a large soup pot, bring the broth and 4 cups of water to a boil over high heat. Add the noodles and simmer uncovered over medium heat until they are almost tender, about 5 minutes. Add the shrimp and celery and cook until the shrimp turn pink, 2 to 3 minutes. Stir in the cilantro.

3. Ladle the soup into bowls. Pass the sauce and the lime wedges at the table so that each person can season the soup to taste.

◆ *PER SERVING: About 456 cals, 58 cals from fat, 6g total fat, 1g sat fat, 131mg chol, 1177mg sodium, 70g total carbs, 1g fiber, 29g prot*

Note: If you're watching your sodium intake, use American vermicelli, which tends to be less salty than Asian noodles.

Classic Wonton Soup

Makes 4 main-dish servings (8 wontons per serving)

Now that wonton wrappers are sold in supermarkets (usually in the produce section), wonton soup is much easier to make at home. It can be a fun family project and the results are delicious. Try experimenting with other fillings, substituting ground turkey or chicken for the pork, or using different seasonings such as five-spice powder or other Asian spices.

½ pound lean boneless pork, cut
    into cubes

3 water chestnuts

1 tablespoon reduced-sodium soy
    sauce

1 tablespoon dry sherry

1 tablespoon coarsely chopped
    fresh ginger

1 garlic clove, peeled

¼ teaspoon cayenne pepper

32 wonton wrappers

8 cups defatted lower-sodium
    chicken broth

⅓ cup thinly sliced scallions,
    including green tops

1. In the bowl of a food processor, combine the pork, water chestnuts, soy sauce, sherry, ginger, garlic, and cayenne. Process, using long pulses, to make a smooth paste. (The filling can be made 1 day ahead and refrigerated.)

2. Line up about 6 wonton wrappers on a work surface, keeping the remainder covered with plastic wrap. Spoon 1 teaspoon of filling onto the center of each square. Dip a pastry brush in water or use a wet finger to lightly moisten the edges of the dough. Fold each wonton diagonally into a triangle and press the edges to seal well. To make a traditional wonton shape, bring the two bottom points of the triangle together and pinch to join. Repeat with the remaining dough and filling. (The wontons can be placed on a baking sheet, covered lightly, and refrigerated for 12 hours, or frozen. To freeze, arrange on a baking sheet, freeze until firm, then transfer to a plastic bag and store in the freezer.)

3. To make the soup, bring the chicken broth to a boil in a large saucepan or soup pot. Add the wontons and simmer over medium heat, partially covered, until the dough is tender and the filling loses its pink color, 5 to 8 minutes.

4. Ladle the soup into bowls, sprinkle with the scallions, and serve.

◆ *PER SERVING: About 311 cals, 54 cals from fat, 6g total fat, 1g sat fat, 34mg chol, 650mg sodium, 42g total carbs, 0g fiber, 20g prot*

CHAPTER FIVE

Sandwiches, Burgers, Pizzas, and Tacos

It's hard to find a food that is more popular than the sandwich. Whether they're burgers, filled pita breads, or burritos, sandwiches appear on almost every restaurant menu. They're perfect for the modern lifestyle—quick, portable, informal, cross-cultural, and open to creative interpretation.

Ask a child how to make a sandwich and the response will be "First you take some bread. . . ." Bread is what makes a sandwich a sandwich. But in the past, the flavor emphasis of a sandwich rested on the filling, and the sole function of the fluffy, bland white sandwich bread was to serve as an unobtrusive holder. Now breads vary so much in flavor and texture that they, not the filling, are often the star of the sandwich.

Like the Food Guide Pyramid, sandwiches are best built from the bottom up. A hearty, whole-grain sandwich bread, like Marvelous Multigrain Bread (page 112), lays a tasty and fiber-rich foundation. Choose a bread with a milder flavor when you want the taste of the filling to take the lead. Breads with international roots—pita, tortillas, lavash, and many others now in the American sandwich mainstream—can lend an exotic touch to what might otherwise be just another sandwich.

What you put inside the bread determines how light or substantial your sandwich is. Fill a sandwich with vegetables, as in the Roasted Vegetable Baguette (page 199), and there's room for soup or another side dish to fill out the meal. But pack the bread with meat and plenty of vegetables, like the lamb, red onion, zucchini, spinach, and tomato in the Athenian Lamb Gyros (page 201) and you've got a satisfying meal.

Until recently, high-fat sandwich fillings, such as luncheon meats, fillings dressed in mayonnaise such as tuna salad or chicken salad, and cheese, were the norm. The explosion of reduced-fat alternatives to traditional fillings is good news for sandwich lovers. Whether you choose leaner ham, lower-fat cheese, or turkey cold cuts, you can build a flavorful sandwich without breaking the fat bank on one meal. (Be sure to compare labels on luncheon meats made from poultry because some are almost as high in fat as their beef and pork counterparts. They may also be higher in sodium.) The recipes in this chapter abandon the traditional deli-sized sandwich overflowing with meat. Instead, the meat and poultry fillings in these sandwiches conform to the 2- or 3-ounce portion recommended in the Food Guide Pyramid.

Today's sandwiches may not fit the standard bread-filling-bread model. Consider the tostada, quesadilla, and fajita, three "sandwiches" from south of the border. All feature a distinctive type of bread, the tortilla, along with a filling, such as steak and onions in the Steak and Charred Onion Fajitas (page 192) or cheese and beans in the Baked Cheese and Bean Quesadillas (page 194). Italian favorites, such as pizza, bruschetta, and calzone may not look like sandwiches but they are just as portable, versatile, and nutritionally balanced as their distant American sandwich cousins.

While there is no limit to what your imagination can create in a sandwich, only so much can fit between two slices of bread. An over-stuffed sandwich will lose much of its filling when you try to pick it up. So, instead of trying to pack everything into your sandwich, serve side dishes that will make your sandwich part of a complete meal.

It is virtually impossible to get tired of sandwiches. Change the bread and you have a new meal. Add new ingredients to a sandwich classic—for example, the chopped vegetables in the Summer Sloppy Joes (page 182)—and you've given it new life. Scan this chapter for sandwich ideas and let your imagination soar.

Contemporary Club Sandwich

Makes 4 sandwiches

Like the hamburger, the club sandwich is quintessentially American. The combination of bacon, tomato, turkey, lettuce, and mayo is just this side of sandwich heaven. This version is brought up to date with the use of some of today's new and tasty reduced-fat foods.

3 tablespoons reduced-fat
   mayonnaise
2 tablespoons bottled chili sauce
12 thin slices Super Sandwich
   Bread (page 114) or whole-wheat
   bread, toasted
½ pound thinly sliced smoked
   turkey breast
8 slices reduced-fat turkey bacon,
   cooked crisp and drained
1 bunch watercress or arugula
2 tomatoes, sliced
8 pickle slices or cornichons for
   garnish
8 small radishes for garnish

1. In a small bowl, stir together the mayonnaise and chili sauce. Spread 1 side of the toasts with the mayonnaise. Prepare 4 triple-decker sandwiches by layering the turkey, bacon, watercress, and tomatoes between 3 thinly cut slices of bread per sandwich.

2. Cut each sandwich into quarters and secure with toothpicks. Garnish with the pickle slices and/or radishes.

◆ *PER SERVING: About 391 cals, 98 cals from fat, 11g total fat, 2g sat fat, 30mg chol, 1271mg sodium, 49g total carbs, 5g fiber, 26g prot*

BUYING BREAD

Smart bread buying means reading labels or asking your local baker for the ingredients used in bakery breads. If you prefer white bread, look for enriched flour in the ingredient list. Whole-grain breads, which do not need enriching and have more fiber, should list a whole-grain flour, such as wheat, as the first or second ingredient. Note that fancy bakery breads may not contain enriched flour, especially if the flours used are organic.

LUNCHBOX SAFETY

A brown bag lunch that sits for hours in a warm school locker is a veritable laboratory of unfriendly bacteria. Think of your child's brown bag or boxed lunch as a picnic, and apply the same safety rules.

◆ Keep cold foods cold. Add a small freezer pack or frozen individual juice container to the lunch-box. Either one will slowly thaw out and keep sandwiches cool until lunchtime, and the juice box can become a sippable treat.

◆ Keep hot foods hot. Before filling a thermos with hot soup or chili, "preheat" it by rinsing it with very hot tap water.

◆ Snacks such as grapes, cookies, or muffins can be frozen ahead, then popped into the bag or lunchbox to thaw gradually.

◆ If you know that a sandwich is likely to become warm, stick with peanut butter and jelly. Avoid meat- or poultry-based fillings, which are more likely to be a breeding ground for bacteria. Some sandwiches, notably peanut butter and jelly, turkey breast, and roast beef, are freezeable.

PEANUT BUTTER AND...

Peanut butter and jelly is the sandwich of choice for the lunchbox set. There's no rival to this sacred combo, but other foods team up deliciously and nutritiously with peanut butter. Here are some ways to enhance the basic peanut butter sandwich.

◆ Mix 2 tablespoons of peanut butter with a tablespoon of apple-sauce; crushed pineapple with juice; chopped prunes or other dried fruit; grated carrot or apple; mashed banana; or fruit yogurt.

◆ Spread peanut butter on whole-wheat or rye bread and layer with sliced dill pickles; oatmeal bread, homemade bread such as Super Sandwich Bread (page 114), or cinnamon rice cakes, then layer with apple butter or thick applesauce; or bagel halves and top with orange slices.

◆ Cut a fruit muffin crosswise in thirds, then make a "triple-decker" muffinwich with peanut butter.

◆ Toss a small container of peanut butter in your child's lunchbox along with pretzel logs for dipping.

◆ Two tablespoons of peanut butter supply about as much protein as 1 ounce of meat, poultry, or fish, but have about 190 calories and 16 grams of fat, more than twice that found in a lean protein source. A 2-tablespoon portion of peanut butter provides almost $\frac{1}{4}$ of the daily value for vitamin E and is an excellent source of the minerals niacin and magnesium. Commercial peanut butter is made from peanuts, sweetener, salt, and a little vegetable oil to prevent separation. Natural or "old-fashioned" peanut butters lack the extra oil, and tend to separate. Nutritionally, both types are about equal. Reduced-fat peanut butters have the same number of calories, but about 25 percent less fat because soy protein and sweeteners replace some of the peanuts. They have a stickier texture than regular peanut butter.

Egg Salad Bagelwich

Makes 4 sandwiches

You'll never notice that this excellent egg salad is missing a couple of yolks, reducing the cholesterol content. The soft texture of this salad goes well with toasted bagels, but Super Sandwich Bread (page 114) or any toasted whole-wheat bread makes a fine sandwich, too.

2 tablespoons reduced-fat mayonnaise
1 tablespoon plain nonfat yogurt
2 tablespoons sweet pickle relish
4 hard-cooked eggs, chopped
2 hard-cooked egg whites, chopped
½ cup finely chopped celery
⅓ cup finely chopped scallions
2 tablespoons slivered radishes
¼ teaspoon salt
¼ teaspoon black pepper
⅛ teaspoon cayenne pepper
4 standard-size whole-wheat bagels, sliced in half and toasted
4 leaves soft Bibb or Boston lettuce

1. In a mixing bowl, combine the mayonnaise, yogurt, and relish. Add the eggs, egg whites, celery, scallions, radishes, salt, pepper, and cayenne. Mix well. (The egg salad can be made a day ahead and refrigerated.)

2. Make the sandwiches by spooning the egg salad onto the toasted bagel bottoms. Add the lettuce leaves, then the bagel tops.

◆ *PER SERVING: About 324 cals, 81 cals from fat, 9g total fat, 2g sat fat, 213mg chol, 735mg sodium, 44g total carbs, 1g fiber, 16g prot*

EGG TIPS

◆ Use large eggs for baking, unless the recipe specifies otherwise. All of the recipes in this book use large eggs.

◆ Brown- and white-shelled eggs are equal in nutritional value and taste.

◆ If you can't remember whether an egg is hard-cooked or not, spin it on a countertop. A cooked egg will roll evenly while a raw egg will wobble.

◆ Eggs separate better when cold, but egg whites beat better when they have been brought to room temperature. Whole eggs also cook better and more evenly when they have been brought to room temperature.

◆ The freshest eggs are best for scrambling, but eggs about a week old will separate better and are easier to peel when soft- or hard-cooked.

Panfried Fish Po' Boy

Makes 4 sandwiches

New Orleans' contribution to sandwich cuisine is the fried fish po' boy. This panfried version is considerably lower in fat than the traditional recipe. Any lean, white fish fillet will make a good po' boy, but catfish is particularly well suited.

2 tablespoons flour

2 tablespoons yellow cornmeal

½ teaspoon salt

½ teaspoon black pepper

1 pound firm white fish fillets, such as catfish

1 tablespoon vegetable oil

1 tablespoon fresh lemon juice

¼ cup reduced-fat mayonnaise

2 tablespoons plain nonfat yogurt

1 tablespoon drained small capers

1 tablespoon sweet pickle relish

½ teaspoon grated lemon peel

4 hoagie, Kaiser, or other large sandwich rolls, sliced in half lengthwise

2 cups shredded romaine lettuce

1 large tomato, seeded and coarsely chopped

1. In a shallow dish, combine the flour, cornmeal, salt, and pepper. Dampen the fish under cold water, shake off the excess water, then dip the fish into the flour mixture to coat on all sides.

2. Heat the oil in a large, preferably nonstick skillet, and fry the fish over medium-high heat until it becomes a rich golden brown, about 5 minutes. Use a spatula to carefully turn the fish and cook until the other side is browned, 4 to 5 minutes more.

3. Remove the fish from the pan. Remove the pan from the heat, add the lemon juice, and stir to scrape up any browned bits clinging to the bottom of the pan. Gently stir in the mayonnaise, yogurt, capers, relish, and lemon peel.

4. Spread the warm sauce over the cut sides of the rolls. Add the fish, then top with the lettuce and tomatoes to make 4 sandwiches.

◆ *PER SERVING: About 457 cals, 179 cals from fat, 20g total fat, 4g sat fat, 53mg chol, 866mg sodium, 43g total carbs, 1g fiber, 26g prot*

EGG COOKING TIPS

Overcooked eggs become tough and rubbery, but undercooked eggs can harbor dangerous bacteria, notably salmonella. Here's how to properly cook an egg.

◆ To soft- or hard-cook an egg in the shell: Place a single layer of eggs in a saucepan large enough to keep the eggs from knocking against each other. Add enough water so that the eggs are covered with 2 inches of water. Cover the pan, and set it over medium heat. Allow the water to just come to a boil. Remove the covered pan from the heat and let it stand for about 4 minutes for soft-cooked eggs, and 14 to 17 minutes for hard-cooked eggs. Drain off the hot water, then cover the eggs with ice water to cool them quickly. Peel soft-cooked eggs as soon as they are cool enough to handle. Wait until hard-cooked eggs cool completely, then roll them on a countertop to create hairline cracks. You can then peel the eggs easily.

◆ To scramble eggs: Break them into a bowl and whisk them with a small amount of water or milk (about 1 teaspoon per egg) until just blended, but not too frothy. Cook in a nonstick skillet, or a regular skillet coated with vegetable oil spray or a few drops of oil, or a double boiler set over hot water. Set over low or medium-low heat, stirring gently but frequently with a wooden spoon, until the eggs are set and no longer runny, 7 to 10 minutes.

◆ To make an omelet: Whisk the eggs as you would for scrambled eggs, but cook them in a slope-sided skillet over medium heat without stirring, until they form a flat "pancake" of eggs that you can roll over a filling. Omelets cook quickly, often in a minute or so.

Ideas for fillings are endless and are a great way to use leftovers, such as bits of meat or fish, vegetables or fruit, and grated hard cheese or soft cheeses like ricotta or cottage cheese. Add a sprinkling of fresh herbs to enhance the flavor.

◆ To fry eggs: Crack the eggs into a nonstick skillet or a regular skillet coated with a film of oil, set over medium-high heat. Immediately reduce the heat to low, then cover the pan to speed up cooking and fry the eggs evenly.

◆ It's possible to microwave eggs out of the shell, but they tend to cook unevenly, so it isn't recommended. Don't even try to microwave an egg in the shell—cleaning up the inevitable eggy explosion in the microwave teaches a powerful lesson.

Western Omelet Sandwich

Makes 4 servings

A classic Western or Denver omelet is speckled with bits of ham, green pepper, and onion. Here, scrambled eggs are spooned onto bagels or English muffins to create a new classic. Carrots and red pepper load this sandwich with vitamins.

3 whole eggs (see note)

3 egg whites

2 tablespoons skim milk

¼ teaspoon salt

2 teaspoons olive oil

⅓ cup chopped carrot

⅓ cup chopped red bell pepper

⅓ cup chopped scallions

¼ cup chopped lean smoked ham

¼ to ½ teaspoon liquid hot pepper sauce

4 whole-wheat English muffins or bagels, split and toasted

¼ cup bottled chili sauce or ketchup

1. In a small bowl, whisk together the eggs, egg whites, milk, and salt. Reserve. In a large, preferably nonstick skillet, heat the oil and cook the carrot, bell pepper, and scallions, covered, over medium-low heat until the vegetables are softened, about 5 minutes. Add the egg mixture and ham. Continue to cook, uncovered and stirring often, until the eggs are softly scrambled and set, about 5 minutes. Stir in the hot pepper sauce.

2. Spoon the eggs over the toasted halves of the English muffins or bagels. Top each with a small spoonful of chili sauce and serve immediately.

◆ *PER SERVING: About 268 cals, 72 cals from fat, 8g total fat, 2g sat fat, 165mg chol, 963mg sodium, 35g total carbs, 1g fiber, 16g prot*

Note: One cup of commercial fat-free and cholesterol-free liquid egg product can be substituted for the eggs, egg whites, and milk.

WHOLE EGG SUBSTITUTES

The recipes in this book call for large eggs, which generally measure about ¼ cup each. In most scrambled egg or omelet recipes, you can use liquid egg substitute, which is mostly egg whites, in equal quantities. You cannot always use egg substitute when baking, however. You can reduce the number of yolks in some recipes by substituting 2 egg whites and 2 whole eggs for 3 whole eggs. This works especially well when making omelets and scrambled eggs and sometimes when baking, where at least 3 whole eggs are called for. Powdered egg whites can be substituted for fresh egg whites as directed on the package.

Roast Beef Lavash Rolls

Makes 4 sandwiches

Thinly sliced deli roast beef works well in this recipe because it is tender and easy to roll onto lavash, which are large, soft flatbreads. Fresh dill, horseradish, and mustard give the rolls a slightly Scandinavian flavor, which also goes well with flour tortillas if you can't find the lavash flatbreads.

6 tablespoons plain nonfat yogurt
2 tablespoons reduced-fat
    mayonnaise
2 tablespoons Dijon mustard
1 tablespoon prepared horseradish
¼ cup chopped fresh dill

2 soft lavash (6 or 7 ounces each)
¾ pound very thinly sliced cooked
    roast beef
½ teaspoon freshly ground pepper
3 cups shredded romaine or other
    deep green lettuce

continued

1. In a small bowl, stir together the yogurt, mayonnaise, mustard, horseradish, and dill. Spread one side of each lavash with the flavored yogurt mixture, leaving a ½-inch margin around each edge. Layer each lavash with the roast beef slices, then sprinkle with the pepper and top with the lettuce.

2. Roll up each lavash into a cylinder and use a sharp knife to cut each roll crosswise into 2 sandwiches.

◆ *PER SERVING: About 392 cals, 87 cals from fat, 10g total fat, 3g sat fat, 66mg chol, 1062mg sodium, 47g total carbs, 14g fiber, 34g prot*

Tuna Salad Roll-Ups

Makes 4 sandwiches

Soft lavash flatbreads add a touch of the exotic to tuna salad sandwiches. Lavash are available in many large supermarkets and Middle Eastern grocery stores but, if you can't find them, make individual rolls using flour tortillas.

2 tablespoons reduced-fat mayonnaise
2 tablespoons plain nonfat yogurt
2 cans (6 ounces each) tuna packed in
　water, drained
1 cup finely chopped celery
¼ cup chopped pimiento
¼ cup finely chopped onion
Salt and black pepper to taste
2 soft lavash (6 or 7 ounces each)
2 cups alfalfa sprouts

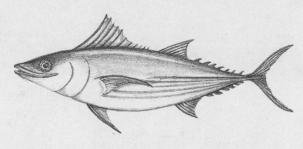

1. In a large mixing bowl, stir together the mayonnaise and yogurt. Add the tuna, celery, pimiento, and onion and stir gently to mix and break up the tuna. Season with salt and pepper to taste.

2. Spread the lavash with the tuna salad, leaving a ½-inch margin around each edge. Sprinkle with the sprouts.

3. Roll up each lavash into a cylinder and use a sharp knife to cut each roll crosswise into 2 sandwiches.

◆ *PER SERVING: About 334 cals, 43 cals from fat, 5g total fat, 1g sat fat, 35mg chol, 1134mg sodium, 47g total carbs, 15g fiber, 32g prot*

Mediterranean-Style Tuna Melt

Makes 4 sandwiches

Pan Bagna is a Provençal French sandwich, typically made up of tuna, anchovies, peppers, and tomato stuffed into a hollowed-out French bread loaf. These same savory ingredients work equally well as a tuna melt, with provolone or mozzarella cheese.

1 can (2 ounces) anchovies rolled around capers

1 can (6 ounces) tuna packed in water, drained

1 jar (7 ounces) roasted red peppers, drained and sliced

1 garlic clove, minced

1 tablespoon red wine vinegar

1 tablespoon chopped fresh marjoram or 1 teaspoon dried

½ teaspoon black pepper

4 whole-wheat English muffins, split and lightly toasted

1 large tomato, thinly sliced

1 small red onion, thinly sliced

2 ounces (½ cup) shredded reduced-fat mozzarella or provolone cheese

Sprigs of fresh marjoram (optional)

1. Drain the anchovies, reserving 2 teaspoons of the oil. Coarsely chop the anchovies and capers and place in a mixing bowl along with the tuna, roasted peppers, and garlic. Add the reserved oil, vinegar, marjoram, and pepper. Stir gently to mix.

2. Let the filling stand 10 minutes at room temperature. Preheat the broiler. Spoon the filling onto the toasted English muffin halves. Add the tomato and onion slices, then sprinkle with the cheese.

3. Broil, about 4 inches from the heat source, until the cheese melts and the filling becomes warm, 1 to 2 minutes. Garnish with a fresh marjoram sprig, if desired.

◆ *PER SERVING (without garnish): About 278 cals, 61 cals from fat, 7g total fat, 1g sat fat, 27 mg chol, 1138mg sodium, 32g total carbs, 0g fiber, 25g prot*

Summer Sloppy Joes

Makes 8 sandwiches

Here's a summery version of a kid-pleasing American standby. When you can't get good fresh tomatoes, use 2 cans (about 14 ounces each) of diced tomatoes. The fresh veggies provide plenty of vitamin C. This recipe serves a crowd and can be made ahead, so it's terrific for informal entertaining. Team it with a big bowl of Family Reunion Macaroni Salad (page 95).

2 teaspoons olive oil
1½ pounds ground turkey
2 medium onions, chopped
1 green bell pepper, chopped
4 garlic cloves, minced
1½ tablespoons chili powder
1½ pounds ripe meaty tomatoes, peeled, seeded,
   and diced (about 3 cups)
½ cup bottled chili sauce
⅓ cup defatted lower-sodium chicken broth
1 tablespoon red wine vinegar
2 teaspoons Worcestershire sauce
½ teaspoon liquid hot pepper sauce
⅓ cup chopped parsley
8 sandwich buns

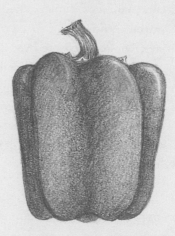

1. In a large, preferably nonstick skillet, heat the oil and cook the turkey, onion, bell pepper, and garlic, stirring often over medium heat, until the turkey loses its pink color and the vegetables are softened—about 5 minutes. Add the chili powder and stir for 1 minute.

2. Add the tomatoes, chili sauce, broth, vinegar, and Worcestershire. Simmer, uncovered, over medium-low heat until the mixture thickens slightly, about 20 minutes. (The recipe can be prepared to this point up to 2 days ahead and refrigerated. Reheat before proceeding.) Stir in the hot pepper sauce and parsley.

3. Serve the sloppy joes spooned onto the buns.

◆ *PER SERVING: About 356 cals, 92 cals from fat, 10g total fat, 1g sat fat, 69mg chol, 615mg sodium, 42g total carbs, 1g fiber, 24g prot*

Sage and Onion Turkey Burgers

Makes 6 sandwiches

Cranberry-orange ketchup is just the right condiment for these burgers, which are filled with seasonings reminiscent of Thanksgiving.

1¼ pounds ground turkey
⅔ cup fresh whole-wheat bread crumbs, from about 1½ slices of bread
½ cup finely chopped onion
⅓ cup finely chopped celery
1 egg white
1 teaspoon dried rubbed sage

½ teaspoon dried leaf thyme
½ teaspoon dried summer savory
½ teaspoon salt
¼ teaspoon black pepper
6 whole-wheat hamburger buns
⅔ cup Cranberry-Orange Ketchup (recipe follows)

1. Prepare a medium-hot barbecue fire, or preheat a gas grill or broiler.

2. In a large mixing bowl, use your hands to mix together the turkey, bread crumbs, onion, celery, egg white, sage, thyme, savory, salt, and pepper. Form into 6 patties, each about ½ inch thick.

3. Grill or broil the burgers, turning once carefully with a spatula, until browned on both sides and white throughout, about 10 minutes total. Place the buns, cut sides down, at the edge of the grill to toast lightly, about 1 minute.

4. Serve the burgers on the toasted buns, spread with Cranberry-Orange Ketchup.

◆ *PER SERVING (without ketchup): About 306 cals, 85 cals from fat, 9g total fat, 2g sat fat, 76mg chol, 562mg sodium, 33g total carbs, 0g fiber, 24g prot*

CRANBERRY-ORANGE KETCHUP

Makes about ⅔ cup (6 servings)

Use this piquant ketchup variation anytime you want a change from the usual condiment.

⅓ cup canned whole-berry cranberry sauce

⅓ cup bottled chili sauce

1 tablespoon grated orange peel

In a small bowl, stir together all ingredients until well blended. Cover and store in the refrigerator until ready to use, up to 1 week.

Per serving: About 38 cals, 0 cals from fat, 0g total fat, 0g sat fat, 0mg chol, 181mg sodium, 9g total carbs, 0g fiber, 0g prot

Black Bean and Radish Burgers

Makes 6 sandwiches

Made with black beans instead of meat, these spicy burgers are low in fat and virtually free of cholesterol. They supply iron, and plenty of fiber, calcium, and vitamin C. But the best news is that they taste great. If you don't want to grill or broil them, fry them in 1 tablespoon of oil in a nonstick skillet.

¾ cup plain nonfat yogurt plus 2 tablespoons

3 tablespoons prepared mango chutney plus 2 tablespoons

1½ tablespoons fresh lime juice

1 jalapeño pepper, seeded and chopped

2 cans (16 ounces each) black beans, drained and rinsed, or 3½ cups cooked black beans

¾ cup chopped red onion

½ cup plain dry bread crumbs

¼ cup coarsely grated radishes

2 teaspoons curry powder

1 teaspoon ground cumin

½ teaspoon ground cardamom

½ teaspoon ground coriander

¼ teaspoon ground ginger

6 pitas, 6 or 7 inches in diameter, opened to form pockets

1 cup radish sprouts or alfalfa sprouts

¼ cup chopped cilantro

1. In a small bowl, mix together ¾ cup yogurt, 3 tablespoons chutney, the lime juice, and the jalapeño. Cover and refrigerate until ready to use, up to 3 days.

2. In a food processor or large mixing bowl, place the beans, onion, bread crumbs, radishes, curry powder, cumin, cardamom, coriander, ginger, the remaining 2 tablespoons yogurt, and the remaining 2 tablespoons chutney. Process or mash with a potato masher to blend the ingredients and partially purée the beans.

3. Prepare a barbecue fire, or preheat a gas grill or the broiler. Use your hands to form the bean mixture into 6 patties, each 3 or 4 inches in diameter. Grill or broil the patties, turning once carefully with a spatula, until browned and crusty on both sides, about 10 minutes total.

4. Spoon about 1 tablespoon of the chutney yogurt into each pita pocket. Add the burgers, then garnish with the remaining chutney yogurt, sprouts, and cilantro.

◆ *PER SERVING: About 417 cals, 19 cals from fat, 2g total fat, 0g sat fat, 1mg chol, 486mg sodium, 81g total carbs, 6g fiber, 19g prot*

Falafel Pitas with Chutney and Yogurt

Makes 4 servings

Fried, mashed chickpea patties are the tasty "street food" of the Middle East. They are stuffed into pita pockets and served with both spicy tomato-based and creamy yogurt sauces, chopped tomatoes, and shredded lettuce or sprouts.

1 medium onion, cut in chunks
2 garlic cloves
½ cup parsley sprigs, preferably flat leaf
1 can (16 ounces) chickpeas, drained and rinsed, or 1¾ cups cooked chickpeas
1 teaspoon grated orange peel
1 teaspoon ground cumin
¾ teaspoon ground coriander
¼ teaspoon cayenne pepper
¼ teaspoon ground turmeric
¼ teaspoon ground cinnamon
¼ teaspoon ground allspice
¼ teaspoon salt
2 tablespoons olive oil
1 cup Tomato-Lemon Chutney (recipe follows)
8 small (about 4 inches in diameter) whole-wheat pitas, opened to form pockets
⅔ cup Tahini Yogurt (recipe follows)
1 cup alfalfa sprouts

1. Chop the onion in a food processor. With the motor running, drop the garlic through the feed tube, and process about 5 seconds to chop. Add the parsley, chickpeas, orange peel, cumin, coriander, cayenne, turmeric, cinnamon, allspice, and salt. Process briefly until the chickpeas are coarsely ground and the spices are blended into the mixture.

2. Form the chickpea mixture into 8 patties, each about ½ inch thick. In a large, preferably nonstick skillet, heat the oil and fry the patties over medium heat, turning once, until browned on both sides, about 10 minutes total.

3. Spoon about 2 tablespoons of the chutney into each pita. Add a falafel patty, some Tahini Yogurt, more chutney, and sprouts. Serve any remaining chutney on the side.

◆ *PER SERVING (without chutney or yogurt): About 338 cals, 93 cals from fat, 10g total fat, 1g sat fat, 0mg chol, 683mg sodium, 54g total carbs, 5g fiber, 11g prot*

TOMATO-LEMON CHUTNEY

Makes about 1 cup (4 servings)

Chutney, which originated in India, is probably the forerunner of the relishes, salsas, and other condiments we use today. Chutney can be either raw or cooked, simple or complex, and often combines vegetable and fruit tastes along with potent herbs and spices. This is a simple, uncooked chutney that complements any grilled meat, chicken, or seafood recipe.

1 cup diced, seeded, fresh plum tomatoes	⅛ cup chopped shallots	¼ teaspoon salt
1½ tablespoons chopped fresh mint	1 tablespoon fresh lemon juice	⅛ teaspoon black pepper
	1 teaspoon grated lemon peel	⅛ teaspoon cayenne pepper
	1 teaspoon extra-virgin olive oil	

In a mixing bowl, combine all ingredients. Let stand at least 15 minutes or refrigerate up to 8 hours before serving.

Per serving: About 27 cals, 12 cals from fat, 1g total fat, 0g sat fat, 0mg chol, 232mg sodium, 4g total carbs, 1g fiber, 1g prot

TAHINI YOGURT

Makes about ⅔ cup (4 servings)

Tahini, or sesame seed paste, is so potent that you need only a little to impart a lot of flavor. This seasoned yogurt is excellent as a condiment for Greek– or Middle Eastern–style dishes, or as a spread on chicken or roast beef sandwiches.

1 tablespoon tahini	1 garlic clove, minced	⅛ teaspoon cayenne pepper
1 tablespoon fresh lemon juice	¼ teaspoon salt	½ cup plain nonfat yogurt

1. In a small mixing bowl, whisk or stir together the tahini and lemon juice until blended and smooth. Stir in the garlic, salt, and cayenne, then stir in the yogurt until blended.
2. Cover and refrigerate until ready to use, up to 2 days.

Per serving: About 39 cals, 17 cals from fat, 2g total fat, 0g sat fat, 1mg chol, 156mg sodium, 4g total carbs, 0g fiber, 2g prot

THE CONTEMPORARY CONDIMENT CUPBOARD

The condiment shelf of yesteryear contained mostly yellow mustard, tomato ketchup, mayonnaise, and pickle relish, but today's pantry is bursting with all kinds of exotic condiments. Dozens of mustards—ranging from sweet, honey mustard to fiery, grainy varieties—now stand on supermarket shelves. Bottled salsa has become as popular as ketchup. Condiments from the Far East, such as chutney, fish sauce, and wasabi, abound. So do many Middle Eastern, European, and Latin American condiments, from tahini to olive paste to chipotles in adobo. Commercial mayonnaise is available in flavored varieties, as well as good low-fat versions that are interchangeable with standard mayonnaise.

Many condiments are low in fat, or are fat free. Use them as flavorsome replacements for fat in sandwiches, salad dressings, soups, stews, and gravies. Those watching their sodium intake should be aware that some condiments, even ketchup and mustard, are high in sodium.

Springtime Chicken and Watercress Sandwich

Makes 4 servings

This sandwich is so elegant that it makes a great main course for weekend dinners with friends. Serve with Curried Waldorf Salad (page 104) and end the meal with strawberries dusted with powdered sugar to make a meal that truly celebrates spring.

¾ **pound thinly sliced chicken breast cutlets**
¾ **teaspoon coarsely ground black pepper**
¾ **teaspoon dried thyme**
½ **teaspoon salt**
1 **tablespoon olive oil plus ½ tablespoon**
1 **large garlic clove, minced**
¼ **cup dry white wine (see note)**
2 **tablespoons reduced-fat mayonnaise**
2 **tablespoons Dijon mustard**
2 **tablespoons chopped chives plus 2 tablespoons**
8 **slices French bread, lightly toasted**
1 **bunch watercress**
4 **cherry tomatoes, halved**

1. Sprinkle both sides of the chicken with the pepper, thyme, and salt. Heat 1 tablespoon of the oil in a medium skillet and cook half of the chicken over medium-high heat until golden on both sides and white throughout, about 5 minutes. Remove from the pan, add the remaining ½ tablespoon of oil, and cook the remaining chicken in the same way. Remove from the pan.

2. Add the garlic and cook for 1 minute, then add the wine and cook, scraping up any browned bits on the bottom, until reduced to a glaze, about 3 minutes. Remove the pan from the heat and stir in the mayonnaise, mustard, and 2 tablespoons of the chives.

3. Spread one side of the toasts with some of the mustard sauce. Top with the watercress sprigs and then the chicken. Spoon the remaining sauce on top and garnish with the cherry tomatoes and the remaining 2 tablespoons of chives.

◆ *PER SERVING: About 334 cals, 98 cals from fat, 11g total fat, 2g sat fat, 49mg chol, 873mg sodium, 29g total carbs, 1g fiber, 26g prot*

Note: Three tablespoons of defatted lower-sodium chicken broth plus 1 tablespoon of lemon juice can be substituted for the wine.

MUSTARD

Mustard, a spice that has been used for thousands of years, varies in color from yellow to white, and brown to black. It has a wide range of potency and flavor, depending on the seed type. You can buy mustard in seed form, as a powder, or as a prepared sauce. You can also grind your own mustard seeds to a powder with a mortar and pestle to concoct your own prepared mustard. There are hundreds of prepared mustards on the market, but they are not interchangeable in recipes, because each has a distinctive flavor. Many mustards are high in sodium, but this is rarely a problem because the condiment is used in such small quantities. Most mustards contain about 12 calories per tablespoon.

AMERICAN MUSTARD gets its canary-yellow color primarily from the addition of turmeric and is generally quite mild and rather sweet. **ENGLISH MUSTARD** is also yellow, but is much more potent, sharper, and hotter. **DIJON MUSTARD** originated in Dijon, France, but is now widely produced elsewhere. It is a good all-purpose hot mustard for mixing with mayonnaise or yogurt, or for making sauces.

GERMAN MUSTARD is dark brown from added spices, and tastes acidic because it is processed with vinegar.

CHINESE MUSTARD can be bought in prepared form, but is often sold as a powder. After mixing with water, let it stand for about 15 minutes so it can reach its peak potency. It diminishes in intensity after a couple of hours, so mix only as much as you need at one time.

Grilled Portobello Mushroom and Arugula Sandwich

Makes 4 sandwiches

Portobello mushrooms have as much meaty flavor and body as a tender grilled steak, and make a delicious sandwich.

2 tablespoons reduced-fat mayonnaise

2 tablespoons plain nonfat yogurt

1 tablespoon chopped fresh rosemary or 1 teaspoon dried

2½ tablespoons extra-virgin olive oil

2 teaspoons lemon juice

½ teaspoon grated lemon peel

2 garlic cloves, minced

¾ pound portobello mushrooms, wiped clean

8 slices Braided Semolina Bread (page 115) or Italian bread

Salt and freshly ground pepper to taste

1 tablespoon balsamic vinegar

4 slices tomato

1 small bunch arugula

1. For the spread, stir together the mayonnaise, yogurt, and rosemary in a small bowl. Cover and refrigerate until ready to use, up to 3 days. In another small bowl, combine the oil, lemon juice and peel, and garlic.

2. Prepare a medium barbecue fire, or preheat a gas grill or broiler. Brush or rub all sides of the mushrooms with the flavored oil. Grill, turning once, until tender, about 8 minutes total. Cut the mushrooms on the diagonal into ¼-inch slices. Set the bread at the edge of the grill to lightly toast on one side, about 30 seconds.

3. Spread the untoasted sides of the bread with the flavored mayonnaise. Heap the mushrooms onto half of the breads. Sprinkle with salt, pepper, and vinegar. Add the tomato and arugula, then top with the remaining bread, untoasted side down.

◆ *PER SERVING: About 464 cals, 123 cals from fat, 14g total fat, 2g sat fat, 0mg chol, 615mg sodium, 72g total carbs, 6g fiber, 15g prot*

Soft Tacos with Turkey

Makes 4 servings

Strips of well-seasoned, low-fat turkey breast fill these tasty soft tacos. Turkey, a native American bird, was once a common game bird in the Southwest, so it just might be a more authentic taco filling than beef.

¾ **pound thinly sliced turkey breast cutlets**	1 **tablespoon tomato paste**
1 **teaspoon chili powder**	8 **flour tortillas (7 to 9 inches in diameter)**
¾ **teaspoon ground cumin**	2 **cups Pico de Gallo Salsa (page 57) or good-quality bottled chunky salsa**
2 **teaspoons vegetable oil**	
1 **medium onion, chopped**	
2 **garlic cloves, finely chopped**	2 **cups shredded romaine lettuce**
¼ **cup defatted lower-sodium chicken broth**	2 **ounces (½ cup) shredded reduced-fat Monterey Jack cheese**

1. Cut the turkey across the grain into ¼-inch strips. Sprinkle it with the chili powder and cumin. Heat the oil in a medium, preferably nonstick frying pan and cook the turkey and onion over medium heat, stirring often until the onion is nearly softened—about 3 minutes. Add the garlic and cook for 30 seconds. Stir in the broth and tomato paste. Cover the pan and simmer over medium-low heat for 8 minutes. (The taco filling can be made early in the day and refrigerated. Reheat before proceeding.)

continued

2. Heat the tortillas in a 350-degree conventional oven for about 6 minutes, or wrap in plastic wrap and heat in a microwave oven for about 1 minute.

3. Assemble the tacos by spooning the filling into the center of the tortillas, then top with the salsa, lettuce, and cheese. Fold the edges over and serve.

◆ *PER SERVING (without salsa): About 407 cals, 96 cals from fat, 11g total fat, 3g sat fat, 63mg chol, 497mg sodium, 45g total carbs, 2g fiber, 31g prot*

Huevos Rancheros Tostadas

Makes 4 servings

Huevos rancheros, or ranch-style eggs, are a breakfast favorite throughout the Southwest. This recipe uses fewer egg yolks than in most scrambled eggs, but is every bit as flavorful as the original chuck-wagon classic. If you don't want to make the Warm Fruit Salsa, simply heat up some good bottled salsa and stir in a diced nectarine.

8 corn tortillas (5 or 6 inches in diameter)
Vegetable oil spray
5 whole eggs (see note)
3 egg whites
3 tablespoons nonfat skim milk
1 small jalapeño pepper, minced
¼ teaspoon salt
¼ teaspoon black pepper
1 teaspoon vegetable oil
2 ounces (½ cup) shredded reduced-fat Monterey Jack cheese
2 cups Warm Fruit Salsa (recipe follows) or 1½ cups bottled
    salsa plus 1 small nectarine, diced
¼ cup chopped cilantro

1. Preheat the oven to 375 degrees. Lightly spray both sides of the tortillas with vegetable oil spray. Place the tortillas in a single layer on a baking sheet. Bake, turning once, until the tortillas are crisp, about 8 minutes.

2. While the tortillas are baking, whisk the eggs, egg whites, milk, jalapeño, salt, and pepper in a mixing bowl until blended. Heat the oil in a large skillet, add the egg mixture, and cook over medium-low heat, stirring often, until softly scrambled and set, about 5 minutes. Add the cheese and stir gently until melted.

3. Warm the salsa in a saucepan over low heat. Spread about 2 tablespoons of the salsa onto each warm tortilla. Top with the scrambled eggs, then sprinkle with the cilantro. Serve the remaining salsa on the side.

◆ *PER SERVING (without salsa): About 276 cals, 101 cals from fat, 11g total fat, 4g sat fat, 277mg chol, 531mg sodium, 25g total carbs, 0g fiber, 18g prot*

Note: You can substitute 1¼ cups of commercial fat- and cholesterol-free liquid egg product for the eggs, egg whites, and milk.

WARM FRUIT SALSA
Makes about 2 cups (4 servings)

High in vitamin C and lower in sodium than most commercial salsas, this salsa lends a delicate flavor to any egg dish. It's also good as a sauce for plain grilled chicken, pork, or fish steaks.

1 tablespoon defatted lower-sodium chicken or vegetable broth
1 teaspoon vegetable oil
1 medium onion, chopped
2 garlic cloves, minced
1 tablespoon chili powder

1 teaspoon dried oregano
1 can (4 ounces) chopped mild green chiles
1 can (14½ ounces) diced tomatoes or 2 cups (1 pound) diced fresh plum tomatoes
1 tablespoon fresh lime juice

1 nectarine, pitted and diced
Salt and black pepper to taste

1. Heat the broth and oil in a medium skillet and cook the onion and garlic, uncovered over medium-low heat, stirring often, until the onion is softened, about 5 minutes. Stir in the chili powder and oregano and cook for 1 minute. Stir in the chiles and tomatoes and simmer, stirring often, for 3 minutes. Add the lime juice and nectarine and simmer, stirring, until the fruit begins to soften, about 2 minutes. Season to taste with salt and pepper.
2. Use the salsa immediately, or let it cool and refrigerate it up to 8 hours. Rewarm gently to use.

Per serving: About 80 cals, 19 cals from fat, 2g total fat, 0g sat fat, 0mg chol, 130mg sodium, 14g total carbs, 3g fiber, 2g prot

TORTILLAS

Tortillas (from the Spanish "torta" or "round cake") are unleavened flatbreads indigenous to North and Central America.

Corn tortillas are unleavened round cakes of ground cornmeal baked on a hot stone. Most corn tortillas are nearly fat free and lower in calories than flour tortillas, containing about 50 to 60 calories each. They may also be a bit higher in calcium because they are treated with calcium-containing lime. Commercial corn tortilla chips vary in fat content from fat-laden fried varieties to nearly fat-free baked ones.

Flour tortillas are especially popular in northern Mexico and parts of the southwestern United States, where wheat is a common crop. Flour tortillas are higher in B vitamins and iron than corn tortillas if made with enriched flour.

The average flour tortilla has about 114 calories and about 2 to 3 grams of fat. Low-fat, fat-free, and whole-wheat flour tortillas are now available. In the past, flour tortillas were made with lard, but now most national and regional brands use vegetable shortening instead. Flour tortillas are especially good used in quesadillas or as wrappers for a variety of spicy fillings.

Steak and Charred Onion Fajitas

Makes 4 fajitas

Fajitas are traditionally made with skirt steak, cut from the "skirt" or diaphragm of the cow. Skirt steak is very juicy and cooks quickly. If you can't find it, thinly sliced round steak—often called sandwich steak—is a good substitute. In either case, be sure to slice the cooked meat across the grain for maximum tenderness.

¼ cup plain nonfat yogurt

¼ cup low-fat sour cream

½ teaspoon ground cumin

3 tablespoons fresh lime juice

2 teaspoons vegetable oil

½ teaspoon grated lime peel

¼ teaspoon salt

1 small jalapeño pepper, seeded
  and minced

¾ pound skirt or thin-sliced round
  steak, cut into 4 pieces

1 large sweet onion, such as Vidalia
  or Walla Walla, sliced about ¼
  inch thick

1 green bell pepper, seeded and cut
  into quarters

4 large flour tortillas
  (9 or 10 inches in diameter)

1 cup Pico de Gallo Salsa (page 57)
  or bottled chunky salsa

1. In a small bowl, gently stir together the yogurt, sour cream, and cumin. Refrigerate until ready to use, up to 8 hours. In a shallow dish just large enough to hold the meat, combine the lime juice, oil, lime peel, salt, and jalapeño pepper. Add the meat, turning to coat. Refrigerate for 1 to 2 hours.

2. Prepare a barbecue fire or preheat a gas grill or broiler. Remove the meat from the marinade. Add the onion and bell pepper to the marinade left in the dish, turning and brushing to coat.

3. Grill the meat and vegetables over medium-hot coals, turning once or twice, until the vegetables are lightly charred and tender, and the meat is cooked to the desired degree of doneness, 6 to 7 minutes for medium doneness. Wrap the tortillas in foil and heat at the edge of the grill just until warm, about 2 minutes.

4. Remove the meat and vegetables to a cutting board. Thinly slice the meat across the grain. Thinly slice the peppers and separate the onion into rings. Toss the meat and vegetables together and fill the tortillas with them. Roll up the tortillas to enclose the filling, garnish with the salsa and the seasoned yogurt and sour cream, and serve.

◆ *PER SERVING (without salsa): About 367 cals, 85 cals from fat, 9g total fat, 2g sat fat, 59mg chol, 372mg sodium, 41g total carbs, 2g fiber, 27g prot*

Pork and Unfried Bean Burritos

Makes 4 servings

Grilled turkey or chicken breast cutlets can be substituted for the pork in this recipe, if you prefer. You can also replace the pork with ½ pound of shredded, reduced-fat, Monterey Jack cheese, which will partially melt when folded into the warm burrito.

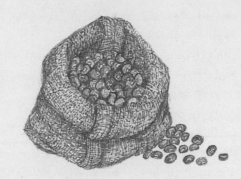

- 2 tablespoons lime juice
- 2 teaspoons vegetable oil
- ½ teaspoon grated lime peel
- ¼ teaspoon salt
- ⅛ teaspoon cayenne pepper
- 1 small pork tenderloin, about 10 ounces
- 8 flour tortillas (7 to 9 inches in diameter)
- 2 cups Unfried Beans (page 291), at room temperature
- 1 cup Pico de Gallo Salsa (page 57) or bottled chunky salsa
- 2 cups shredded romaine lettuce

1. In a shallow dish just large enough to hold the meat, combine the lime juice, oil, lime peel, salt, and cayenne. Cut the pork into ½-inch diagonal slices and add to the marinade, stirring to coat. Cover and refrigerate for 1 to 2 hours.

2. Prepare a medium-hot barbecue fire, or preheat a gas grill or the oven broiler. Wrap the tortillas together in foil. Set the tortillas at the edge of the grill to heat through, about 5 minutes, or warm them under the broiler, about 2 to 3 minutes. Grill or broil the pork, turning once or twice, until lightly charred and cooked through, 5 to 7 minutes total. Cut the pork crosswise into thin slices.

3. To assemble the burritos, spread about ¼ cup of the Unfried Beans onto each warm tortilla. Add the pork, some salsa and lettuce, and roll into a loose cylinder to serve.

◆ *PER SERVING (without beans or salsa): About 328 cals, 74 cals from fat, 8g total fat, 2g sat fat, 50mg chol, 405mg sodium, 40g total carbs, 0g fiber, 22g prot*

Baked Cheese and Bean Quesadillas

Makes 4 servings

Much easier to prepare than the usual grilled version, baked quesadillas make a simple and tasty supper. They're also great for calcium- and iron-rich after-school snacks. Black, red, pink, or white beans can be substituted for the pinto beans, and reduced-fat cheddar cheese works well in place of Monterey Jack—making this an easy recipe that uses whatever you have on hand.

**8 ounces (2 cups) shredded reduced-fat
    Monterey Jack cheese
1 can (16 ounces) pinto beans, rinsed
    and drained
½ cup chopped onion
¼ cup chopped cilantro
1 tablespoon lime juice
8 flour tortillas (7 to 9 inches in diameter)
1½ cups Pico de Gallo Salsa (page 57)
    or bottled chunky salsa**

1. Preheat the oven to 375 degrees. In a mixing bowl, stir together the cheese, beans, onion, cilantro, and lime juice. Place 4 of the tortillas on a large baking sheet (or 2 sheets if necessary). Divide the bean mixture among the tortillas, spreading over each and leaving a ¾-inch border all around. Top with the remaining tortillas, and press the edges together to lightly seal.

2. Bake the tortillas until the cheese is melted and the tortillas are golden brown. If you're using 2 baking sheets on 2 levels of your oven, reverse them halfway through baking time.

3. Use a pizza wheel or sharp knife to cut the quesadillas into quarters for serving. Serve the salsa separately for dipping or spooning onto the quesadilla quarters.

◆ *PER SERVING (without salsa): About 466 cals, 139 cals from fat, 15g total fat, 7g sat fat, 41mg chol, 986mg sodium, 54g total carbs, 4g fiber, 28g prot*

MEXICAN-FOOD TERMINOLOGY

BURRITO: A soft flour tortilla filled with meat, beans, or cheese and rolled into a loose cylinder. A burro is simply a large burrito.

CHIMICHANGA: A large flour tortilla wrapped like a burrito, then deep-fried until crisp.

ENCHILADA: A rolled corn tortilla filled with meat or beans, then often baked in a sauce.

EMPANADA: A fried or baked turnover made from pastry dough and filled with meat or fruit.

FLAUTA: A corn or flour tortilla wrapped tightly around a filling to form a "flute" shape, then deep-fried until crisp.

NACHOS: Crisp fried or baked corn tortilla chips covered with melted cheese, beans, peppers, or other garnishes.

QUESADILLA: A flat or folded corn or flour tortilla topped or filled with cheese, chiles, or beans and then grilled, fried, or baked until hot.

TACO: A crisp-fried or soft corn or flour tortilla filled with meats, chicken, beans, or vegetables.

TAMALE: Fresh cornmeal dough rolled in a corn husk and filled with savory or sweet fillings, then steamed until the cornmeal becomes firm. A good deal of fat is often added when making the dough.

TOSTADA: A flat, deep-fried corn tortilla, heaped high with meat or beans, cheeses, and garnishes to resemble an open-face taco.

Basil and Ripe Tomato Bruschetta

Makes 4 servings

This exceedingly simple bruschetta is best made when you can get really good, flavorful tomatoes and fresh basil. It is the essence of summer and also provides plenty of iron, vitamin C, and fiber.

1 pound ripe tomatoes

4 ounces (about 1 cup) diced reduced-fat mozzarella cheese

2 tablespoons chopped fresh basil plus 2 tablespoons

2 tablespoons extra-virgin olive oil

1 tablespoon balsamic vinegar

¼ teaspoon dried hot red pepper flakes

2 garlic cloves, peeled

8 slices Braided Semolina Bread (page 115) or seeded Italian bread

8 basil leaves

1. Submerge the tomatoes in a pot of boiling water for about 30 seconds to loosen the skins. Remove the tomatoes from the water and use your fingers and a small knife to slip off the skins. Cut the tomatoes in half crosswise and gently squeeze to remove the seeds. Dice the tomatoes and place them in a mixing bowl. Stir in the cheese, 2 tablespoons chopped basil, oil, vinegar, and pepper flakes. Cut one of the garlic cloves in half and reserve one half. Mince the remaining 1½ garlic cloves and add to the tomatoes. Let the mixture stand for 10 to 30 minutes at room temperature.

continued

2. Preheat the broiler. Broil the bread, turning to toast both sides lightly. Rub one side of the toasts with the reserved garlic clove half. Place the toasts, rubbed side up, on 4 serving plates. Stir the remaining 2 tablespoons of chopped basil into the tomatoes and spoon the mixture over the toasts. Garnish with the whole basil leaves.

◆ *PER SERVING: About 469 cals, 110 cals from fat, 12g total fat, 1g sat fat, 10mg chol, 697mg sodium, 69g total carbs, 5g fiber, 21g prot*

BRUSCHETTA VARIATIONS

Bruschetta is grilled, thickly sliced, country-style bread that is rubbed with the cut side of a garlic clove, then brushed or drizzled with a little olive oil and sprinkled with salt and pepper. The rough toasted bread surface releases the flavor of the garlic and the heat from the grill disperses the fragrance of the oil. Bruschetta is one of the simplest and most sublime dishes in Italian cooking. In American restaurants,

the basic bruschetta is most often dressed with chopped tomatoes and slivered basil leaves. Here are some other options:

◆ Spread the bread with mashed, warmed cannellini beans seasoned with a little chopped red onion and sprinkled with torn arugula leaves.
◆ Spread with low-fat ricotta cheese mixed with a little grated Parmesan and top with cooked broccoli rabe.

◆ Layer with grilled eggplant and other vegetables and sprinkle with paper-thin shavings of Romano or Parmesan cheese.
◆ Spread with nonfat or low-fat ricotta cheese and top with thinly sliced prosciutto, fresh fig quarters, and a sprinkling of thyme.
◆ Rub the grilled bread with a thick slice of tomato, and top with grilled shrimp and a few drops of fresh lemon or lime juice.

Personalized Pita Pizzas

Makes 4 servings

With just a little supervision, even small children can create their own personal pizzas and, with assorted vegetables as toppings, they'll get lots of vitamins A and C. An adult should have an array of topping ingredients ready and, of course, should operate the oven.

4 whole-wheat pitas (6 to 7 inches in diameter)
1 cup bottled marinara or pizza sauce
2 cups assorted fresh vegetables, such as thinly sliced bell peppers, carrots, tomatoes, cooked green beans, broccoli florets, and onions
2 ounces (½ cup) thinly sliced turkey salami
6 ounces (1½ cups) shredded reduced-fat mozzarella cheese

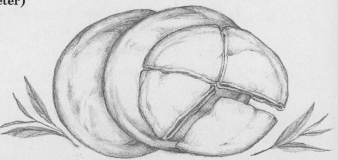

1. Preheat the broiler. Use your fingers or a small knife to split the pitas in half. Place the pitas, split sides up, on a baking sheet. Broil, about 4 inches from the heat source, until lightly toasted, about 1 minute. Spread about 2 tablespoons of marinara sauce on each pita half. Top the pita halves with the vegetables and salami, then sprinkle with the cheese.

2. Broil until the cheese is melted and the toppings are bubbly, about 1 minute.

◆ *PER SERVING: About 332 cals, 71 cals from fat, 8g total fat, 1g sat fat, 23mg chol, 1298mg sodium, 48g total carbs, 1g fiber, 22g prot*

Antipasto Pan Pizza

Makes 4 servings

Like a good antipasto, the toppings in this recipe can be varied according to taste and season. The options here are quick and easy, but you can use other cooked vegetables, such as broccoli, asparagus, snow peas, carrots, onions, or bell peppers. Mozzarella, reduced-fat cheddar, or Swiss cheese can stand in for the fontina.

1 tablespoon yellow cornmeal
1 recipe Basic Pizza Dough
    (page 116) or 1 tube (10 ounces)
    refrigerated pizza dough
1 jar (6 ounces) marinated
    artichokes
1 jar (7½ ounces) roasted peppers,
    sliced

1 cup sliced celery
¼ cup sliced black or green olives
    or a mixture
4 ounces (1 cup) grated fontina
    cheese
¼ cup chopped fresh basil

1. Preheat the oven to 400 degrees. Sprinkle the bottom of a 9x13-inch baking pan with the cornmeal. Roll or pat the pizza dough to fit the bottom and extend about ½ inch up the sides of the pan. Drain and quarter the artichokes, reserving 1 tablespoon of the liquid. Brush the reserved liquid over the pizza dough, then sprinkle with the artichokes, peppers, celery, olives, cheese, and basil.

2. Bake the pizza until it is golden brown and crisp on the edges, 15 to 20 minutes, and the topping is bubbly. Let the pizza cool for about 3 minutes, then cut it into squares before serving.

◆ *PER SERVING: About 536 cals, 182 cals from fat, 20g total fat, 7g sat fat, 33mg chol, 813mg sodium, 71g total carbs, 8g fiber, 20g prot*

HEALTHY PIZZA TOPPINGS

Pizza is an all-American food but, depending on the toppings, it can be a nutritional asset or liability. In Italy, pizza is a flatbread lightly topped with fresh vegetables and just a touch of highly seasoned meat such as prosciutto and strong cheese such as Parmesan. In America, pizza has become laden with heavy cheese and fatty sausage or pepperoni. But you can experiment with healthier toppings. When ordering pizza from a restaurant or pizza parlor, request whole-wheat crust, choose vegetable toppings including spinach, broccoli, and eggplant, and ask them to go easy on the cheese. At home, follow the same rules, but try reduced-fat cheeses and allow only 1 to 1½ ounces per serving.

New Mexican White Clam Pizza

Makes 4 servings

The original white clam pizza is a specialty of New Haven, Connecticut, where Yalies and locals alike have revered the nontomato, clam-studded pizzas for generations. The original is seasoned with dried hot red pepper flakes and chopped basil. This version takes a Southwestern twist with jalapeños and cilantro, but remains true to its nontomato roots. Because it contains so little cheese, it is lower in fat than most pizzas.

1 can (10 ounces) chopped clams or 1 cup chopped fresh clams
2 tablespoons olive oil, preferably extra virgin
2 large garlic cloves, minced
1 tablespoon chopped pickled jalapeño pepper
1 teaspoon dried oregano
1 recipe Basic Pizza Dough (page 116) or
　1 tube (10 ounces) refrigerated pizza dough
1 tablespoon yellow cornmeal
½ cup thinly sliced scallions
⅓ cup chopped fresh cilantro
2 tablespoons grated Parmesan cheese

1. Drain the clams and reserve 1 tablespoon of the juice. Combine the reserved juice with the oil, garlic, jalapeño, and oregano.

2. Preheat the oven to 450 degrees for Basic Pizza Dough and 425 degrees for refrigerated pizza dough. Sprinkle a 14-inch pizza pan or large baking sheet with the cornmeal. Roll or pat the pizza dough into a 14-inch circle for the pizza pan or an 11x14-inch rectangle for the baking sheet. Brush the dough with half of the flavored oil. Sprinkle with the clams, scallions, and cilantro. Sprinkle with the remaining oil, then with the cheese.

3. Bake the pizza until the crust is golden brown and crisp, about 15 minutes. Cut the pizza into wedges for serving.

◆ *PER SERVING: About 489 cals, 121 cals from fat, 13g total fat, 2g sat fat, 29mg chol, 564mg sodium, 69g total carbs, 5g fiber, 23g prot*

Roasted Vegetable Baguette

Makes 6 servings

The vegetables in this recipe can be roasted or grilled, and you can vary them according to the season. The vegetables used here are available practically year-round; they make an especially colorful presentation. There now are many tasty herb- and garlic-flavored reduced-fat cheese spreads on the market for you to choose from.

3 tablespoons extra-virgin olive oil

1 large garlic clove, minced

1 red bell pepper, seeded and cut into 6 strips

1 yellow bell pepper, seeded and cut into 6 strips

1 medium zucchini (about 6 ounces), cut on a long diagonal into

  6 lengthwise strips

1 small eggplant or 2 baby eggplants (about ¾ pound total), cut into ½-inch slices

1 medium red onion, cut into crosswise slices slightly less than ½ inch thick

1 French baguette (about ¾ pound), cut in half lengthwise

4 ounces (about 1 cup) reduced-fat spreadable garlic and herb cheese

18 fresh basil leaves

1. Preheat the oven to 500 degrees. In a small bowl, combine the oil and garlic. Rub or brush the cut sides of the vegetables with the oil. Place the vegetables in a single layer on 1 or 2 baking sheets. Roast them, turning them once, until they are softened and lightly charred, 6 to 8 minutes. (If using 2 baking sheets on 2 levels of your oven, reverse the pan positions halfway through baking time.)

2. Remove the vegetables from the oven and change the oven setting to broil. Broil the baguette halves, cut side up, until lightly toasted, about 30 seconds.

3. Spread the cut sides of the baguettes with the cheese, then arrange the vegetables on top. Cut each baguette half into 3 portions and garnish each with 3 basil leaves. Serve warm.

◆ *PER SERVING: About 319 cals, 116 cals from fat, 13g total fat, 3g sat fat, 13mg chol, 413mg sodium, 40g total carbs, 3g fiber, 12g prot*

Spinach and Cheese Calzone

Makes 4 servings

Calzone are actually pizza turnovers, often filled with a seasoned cheese mixture. This one takes its flavor cue from the Greek spinach and cheese pie called spanakopitta.

1 teaspoon olive oil

1 small onion, chopped

1 garlic clove, minced

3 cups (about 4 ounces) coarsely chopped fresh spinach

1 cup low-fat ricotta cheese

½ teaspoon ground nutmeg

½ teaspoon salt

¼ teaspoon cayenne pepper

1 egg yolk

½ cup (2 ounces) crumbled feta cheese

1 tablespoon yellow cornmeal

1 recipe Basic Pizza Dough (page 116) or 1 tube (10 ounces) refrigerated pizza dough

1 cup bottled marinara sauce (optional)

1. Heat the oil in a large skillet and cook the onion, covered, over medium-low heat, stirring until softened, about 5 minutes. Stir in the garlic and cook, uncovered, for 1 minute. Stir in the spinach and cook, stirring until the spinach is wilted, about 2 minutes. Transfer the vegetables to a mixing bowl and stir in the ricotta, nutmeg, salt, and cayenne. Then stir in the egg yolk and feta until blended. (The filling can be made several hours ahead and refrigerated. Return to room temperature before using.)

2. Preheat the oven to 375 degrees. Sprinkle a large baking sheet with the cornmeal. On a flat surface, roll or pat the pizza dough to a rough 12- or 14-inch square. Use a sharp knife or pizza wheel to cut the dough into 4 equal squares. Divide the filling among the dough squares, spooning it onto one diagonal half of each square and leaving about a ½-inch margin all around. Fold the top over to make a triangle and seal the edges by pressing with the tines of a fork. Use a small knife to make 3 slashes in the top of each calzone to allow steam to escape.

3. Place the calzone on the prepared baking sheet and bake until a rich golden brown, 25 to 30 minutes. Serve warm with heated marinara sauce for dipping, if desired.

◆ *PER SERVING (without marinara sauce): About 495 cals, 113 cals from fat, 13g total fat, 3g sat fat, 66mg chol, 1140mg sodium, 73g total carbs, 7g fiber, 22g prot*

Athenian Lamb Gyros

Makes 4 sandwiches

Some say the American "hero" sandwich is from the Greek "gyro," which is pronounced similarly. Both have the same appeal—meat and vegetables heaped onto bread. You can broil the skewered gyros, but they are most authentic when grilled.

¾ cup plain nonfat yogurt

3 tablespoons fresh lemon juice

1 tablespoon chopped fresh
    rosemary or ½ teaspoon dried

1 tablespoon chopped fresh
    oregano or ½ teaspoon dried

1 teaspoon grated lemon peel

¼ teaspoon dried hot red pepper
    flakes

1 large garlic clove, minced

¾ pound lean boneless lamb, cut
    into 1-inch cubes

1 large red onion, cut into rough
    1-inch chunks

1 medium zucchini, cut into rough
    1-inch chunks

4 whole-wheat pitas, 7 inches in
    diameter, opened to form pockets

2 cups thinly sliced fresh spinach

1 cup chopped fresh tomato

1. In a small bowl, stir together the yogurt, lemon juice, rosemary, oregano, lemon peel, pepper flakes, and garlic. Pour about half of this marinade into a shallow dish just large enough to hold the meat. Reserve the rest to use as a sauce. Add the lamb to the marinade in the dish, turning to coat. Cover and refrigerate 2 to 6 hours.

2. Prepare a medium-hot barbecue fire, or preheat a gas grill or the broiler. Remove the meat from the marinade. Add the onion and zucchini chunks to the marinade remaining in the dish and stir to coat. Thread the lamb and vegetables onto 4 large skewers, alternating them to make a colorful presentation.

3. Grill or broil, turning once or twice, until the lamb and vegetables are lightly charred and the lamb is cooked to the desired degree of doneness, 6 to 8 minutes for medium.

4. Serve the lamb and vegetables on the skewers, and allow each person to assemble his or her sandwich by spooning the reserved sauce into the pitas and stuffing each with the lamb and vegetables. Garnish with the remaining sauce, spinach, and tomato.

◆ *PER SERVING: About 331 cals, 54 cals from fat, 6g total fat, 2g sat fat, 43mg chol, 516mg sodium, 48g total carbs, 2g fiber, 25g prot*

CHAPTER SIX

Pasta

Who doesn't love pasta? While most of us call this popular member of the grain group by its Italian name, the Chinese probably ate "pasta" long before the Italians did. Travel around the world and you will be hard pressed to find a cuisine that does not feature at least one form of pasta or noodles.

Like other foods in the grain group, pasta is rich in complex carbohydrates, B vitamins, and protein. Pastas made from a simple dough of flour and water contain no fat. Egg noodles, and fresh pasta made with egg, supply small amounts of fat and about 50 milligrams (about 17 percent of the Daily Value) of cholesterol per cup, not a bad trade-off for their distinct flavor. As an added nutrition bonus, most commercial brands of pasta or noodles are made with iron-fortified flour, making them a good source of iron.

Many people make a meal out of pasta. Kids often eat unadorned noodles with pleasure, while their parents might add olive oil or butter and garlic. But pasta cries out for the flavor companionship of other ingredients. It also needs to be paired with foods from other food groups—such as vegetables and meat, poultry, fish, or beans—to form a nutritionally complete meal. For example, the recipe for Rigatoni and Savory Bean Sauce (page 233) tops pasta with a creamy bean and vegetable sauce and can be served with a tossed green salad.

How much pasta should you eat at a meal? The standard portion listed on package labels is 2 ounces dry, or about 1 cup cooked—the equivalent of two grain servings on the Food Guide Pyramid. (By this measure, 1 pound of dry pasta should make eight servings.) Most of the recipes in this chapter offer 1-cup pasta portions. Diners with bigger appetites can either increase their portion size or pair their pasta with other foods.

Many of the pasta dishes and sauces in this chapter include ingredients and seasonings derived from Italian cuisine. Tomatoes, a standard pasta partner, are featured in both the Basic Marinara Sauce (page 205) and Angel Hair Arrabbiata (page 217). In addition to their distinct flavor, tomatoes and sauces made from tomatoes supply plenty of vitamins A and C. Canned tomatoes are a flavorful alternative when fresh, ripe tomatoes are not available. They are about equal in vitamins, as long as you use the juice from the can in the recipe. When using canned tomatoes, don't add salt until you've tasted the sauce; most canned tomato products already have ample amounts of salt. Sodium watchers may need to use salt-free products, like tomatoes canned without salt. Fat watchers can rest assured that most tomato and clam sauces contain only small amounts of fat. (Olive oil and commercially prepared "white" sauces, such as cream or Alfredo, are the highest in fat and calories.)

As you stock your pantry with pasta, fill your condiment shelves with the herbs, spices, and sauces you'll need to create an international array of pasta dishes—sweet spices like cinnamon and nutmeg to turn egg noodles into Fruited Noodle Kugel (page 226); pungent curry powder to flavor Curried Penne with Cauliflower and Peas (page 232); and rice wine vinegar and sweet-and-sour sauce so you can turn ordinary noodles and chicken into the Asian-inspired Hot-and-Sour Chicken Noodle Stir-Fry (page 242).

It's a rare person who says basta ("enough") to pasta. Pasta and noodle dishes are quick. They're easy to make. And, most importantly, they're delicious.

Basic Pasta Sauces

Pasta can be sauced in unlimited ways, but the most popular sauces are tomato based. Though you can buy good-quality seasoned tomato sauces, making your own is more economical and certainly more creative. For example, you can change the herbs in Basic Marinara Sauce (page 205), or personalize the hot pepper quotient in Basic Bolognese Sauce (page 205). Double Tomato Sauce (below) is wonderful over any pasta or polenta dish or even as a pizza sauce. While store-bought pesto sauces are good, Basil Pesto (page 206) and Sun-Dried Tomato Pesto (page 207) are easy to make and infinitely better.

DOUBLE TOMATO SAUCE

Makes about 5½ cups (4 servings)

Spoon this spicy sauce over Baked Herbed Polenta (page 281), or ladle it over hot cooked spaghetti and sprinkle with freshly grated Parmesan cheese.

1 tablespoon extra-virgin olive oil	1 large can (32 ounces) crushed plum tomatoes in purée	½ teaspoon paprika
1 large onion, chopped	⅓ cup dry white wine	¼ teaspoon cayenne pepper
1 small green bell pepper, seeded and chopped	½ cup slivered sun-dried tomatoes	¼ teaspoon black pepper
3 garlic cloves, finely chopped	2 teaspoons brown sugar	Salt to taste
		¼ cup chopped parsley, preferably flat leaf

1. Heat the oil in a large, heavy skillet or Dutch oven. Add the onion and green pepper and cook over medium heat, stirring frequently, until the vegetables soften and begin to brown, about 8 minutes. Add the garlic and cook, stirring, for 1 minute more.

2. Add the canned tomatoes, wine, sun-dried tomatoes, brown sugar, and paprika. Bring to a boil, reduce the heat to medium-low, and simmer uncovered until the sauce is slightly reduced and thickened, about 20 minutes. Season with cayenne pepper, black pepper, and salt to taste, and stir in the parsley.

3. Serve over fresh or dried cooked pasta. (This recipe can be refrigerated up to 2 days or frozen up to 3 months.)

Per serving: About 178 cals, 34 cals from fat, 4g total fat, 1g sat fat, 0mg chol, 706mg sodium, 28g total carbs, 5g fiber, 6g prot

HOW TO PEEL AND SEED A TOMATO

Place the tomato in a pot of boiling water for 10 to 15 seconds. Remove with tongs and let cool until you can handle it. Then use your fingers and a small knife to slip off the skin. Cut the tomato in half crosswise and gently squeeze out the seeds.

BASIC MARINARA SAUCE

Makes about 4 cups (4 servings)

Marinara is a classic, quick-cooking sauce that dresses fresh or dried pasta nicely. This basic recipe can be endlessly varied with herbs—such as basil, oregano, or tarragon, and with spices—such as red pepper flakes, chili powder, or cumin.

2 teaspoons olive oil, preferably extra virgin
1 small onion, chopped
2 garlic cloves, minced
3 pounds peeled, seeded, and diced fresh plum tomatoes or 3 cans (14½ ounces each)

diced tomatoes with juice
½ cup red wine, white wine, chicken broth, vegetable broth, or water
1 teaspoon dried herbs, such as basil or oregano
½ teaspoon salt

¼ teaspoon pepper
¼ cup chopped parsley, preferably flat leaf
2 tablespoons chopped fresh herbs, such as basil or oregano (optional)

1. In a medium saucepan, heat the oil and cook the onion and garlic over medium-low heat, stirring often until the onion has softened, about 4 minutes. Add the diced tomatoes, wine, herbs, salt, and pepper. Partially cover the pan and simmer over medium-low heat, stirring occasionally, for 20 minutes. Stir in the parsley and optional fresh herbs.

2. Serve over cooked pasta. (This sauce can be refrigerated up to 5 days or frozen up to 3 months.)

Per serving: About 109 cals, 33 cals from fat, 4g total fat, 0g sat fat, 0mg chol, 290mg sodium, 15g total carbs, 0g fiber, 4g prot

BASIC BOLOGNESE SAUCE

Makes about 6 cups (6 servings)

In the region around Bologna, Italy, the classic ragù or meat sauce has as many variations as there are cooks. In America, we have simplified this sauce with a wide array of canned tomato products. Vary the seasonings according to your preferences.

1 teaspoon olive oil
1 pound ground turkey
1 ounce prosciutto or smoked ham, chopped
1 medium onion, chopped
1 medium carrot, chopped
1 small celery rib, chopped

2 garlic cloves, minced
1½ teaspoons dried oregano
1 teaspoon dried basil
¾ teaspoon dried thyme
½ teaspoon salt
¼ teaspoon dried hot red pepper flakes

1 can (28 ounces) Italian-style tomatoes in purée
1 can (14½ ounces) diced tomatoes in juice
½ cup red wine, white wine, chicken broth, or vegetable broth

1. In a large saucepan, heat the oil and cook the turkey, prosciutto, onion, carrot, celery, and garlic over medium-low heat, stirring often, until the turkey is white throughout and the vegetables are softened, about 8 minutes. Drain off any accumulated fat.

2. Stir in the oregano, basil, thyme, salt, and pepper flakes. Add the canned tomatoes and the wine. Bring to a simmer, then cook partially covered over medium-low heat for 30 minutes, stirring often. Use the back of a spoon to break up the tomato pieces.

3. Serve over cooked pasta. (This sauce can be refrigerated up to 3 days or frozen up to 3 months.)

Per serving: About 184 cals, 59 cals from fat, 7g total fat, 1g sat fat, 64mg chol, 811mg sodium, 12g total carbs, 2g fiber, 18g prot

BASIL PESTO

Makes about ½ cup (about four 2-tablespoon servings)

It's a breeze to grow basil in a pot on the windowsill or in your garden. The trick is to keep cutting it back, which promotes growth. All those cuttings mean more pesto. Fresh basil from the supermarket should be very fragrant—otherwise it's not really fresh. Pesto freezes nicely, so make it in quantity.

2 cups lightly packed fresh
   basil leaves
3 garlic cloves
1 tablespoon toasted pine nuts
   (see note)

¼ cup grated Parmesan
   cheese, preferably imported
3 tablespoons defatted lower-
   sodium chicken or vegetable
   broth

1½ tablespoons extra-virgin
   olive oil

1. Place the basil in the workbowl of a food processor. With the motor running, drop in the garlic cloves and pine nuts, and process until all ingredients are finely chopped. Add the cheese and process about 5 seconds until well blended. With the motor running, pour in the broth and oil. Process, stopping to scrape down the sides of the bowl, until a thick, chunky purée forms.
2. Toss with ¾ pound of fresh or dried cooked pasta. (This recipe can be refrigerated up to 2 days or frozen up to 1 month.)

Per serving: About 93 cals, 74 cals from fat, 8g total fat, 2g sat fat, 5mg chol, 120mg sodium, 2g total carbs, 0g fiber, 4g prot

Note: Toast the pine nuts by tossing them in a small skillet set over medium heat until lightly colored and fragrant, about 2 minutes. Immediately remove the pine nuts from the skillet and cool. You must have a food processor to make this pesto; the recipe will not work in a blender.

COOKING GREAT PASTA

The most common mistake people make when cooking pasta is to overcook it, which causes the pasta to turn mushy. Every brand varies slightly in cooking directions, so test the pasta after the minimum recommended cooking time by tasting a strand. Perfectly cooked pasta will be tender, with a center that remains a bit firm to the bite, "al dente" in Italian.

Fresh pasta cooks in a fraction of the time it takes dried pasta to cook. Very fresh homemade pasta will cook in under a minute because its moisture content is very high. If the pasta has been allowed to dry out or has been frozen, add a couple of minutes to the cooking time. Fresh commercial pasta also cooks quickly. For example, fettucine takes only about 2 minutes, while filled pastas, such as ravioli and tortellini, may take up to 9 minutes, depending on the size.

To cook dried pasta, use at least 4 quarts of water for each pound of pasta to allow plenty of room for the pasta to "swim" in the water. Add 1 to 2 teaspoons of salt to the boiling water, then allow the water to return to a boil. Add the pasta, stirring to break up any clumps. Cover the pan to allow the water to return quickly to a boil, then uncover and cook the pasta until it's al dente, stirring occasionally to keep it from sticking together. Drain immediately into a colander or strainer. Unless the recipe specifically directs, do not rinse the pasta under cold water because much of the starch will rinse off and your sauces will not cling. (See page 244 for average cooking times for various pasta shapes.) Use cooked pasta right away.

SUN-DRIED TOMATO PESTO

Makes about ½ cup (about four 2-tablespoon servings)

For best results, choose sun-dried tomatoes that are soft and pliable. Tough, very dry tomatoes have less flavor and will not soften properly. Basil gives an Italian or Provençal cast to the pesto, but try using cilantro or dill for a different twist.

¾ cup defatted lower-sodium chicken or vegetable broth
½ cup (about 1½ ounces) coarsely chopped sun-dried tomatoes

3 garlic cloves
1 tablespoon toasted pine nuts (see note on page 206)
¼ cup grated Parmesan cheese, preferably imported

½ cup lightly packed fresh basil leaves
1 tablespoon fresh lemon juice

1. In a small saucepan, bring the broth to a boil. Remove from the heat and add the tomatoes to the pan. Cover and let stand until the tomatoes are softened and cooled, 30 minutes to 1 hour. Drain, reserving 3 tablespoons of the liquid.

2. Place the tomatoes in the workbowl of a food processor. With the motor running, drop in the garlic cloves and pine nuts, and process until all ingredients are finely chopped. Add the cheese, basil, and lemon juice. Process until the basil is finely chopped, about 10 seconds. With the motor running, pour in the reserved tomato liquid, and process until smooth.

3. Serve over cooked pasta. (This recipe can be refrigerated up to 2 days or frozen up to 1 month.)

Per serving: About 67 cals, 30 cals from fat, 3g total fat, 1g sat fat, 5mg chol, 270mg sodium, 6g total carbs, 0g fiber, 5g prot

DRIED VS FRESH VS HOMEMADE

Dried pasta is usually made from semolina, a flour milled from durum wheat and water. It has strength and body and its slightly rough surface (from commercial pasta machines) holds sauce well. Stored airtight in a cool, dry place, dried pasta will stay fresh for up to 2 years.

Fresh pasta is sold refrigerated or frozen. The most common fresh pastas are made from white flour and eggs, resulting in a tender, delicate dough that is softer and more porous than semolina pasta. Common shapes are flat strands such as linguine and stuffed pastas such as tortellini and ravioli. If you are substituting fresh pasta for

dried in a recipe, note that about 1 pound of cooked, fresh pasta, which doesn't absorb as much liquid during cooking, equals ¾ pound of cooked dried pasta. Fresh pasta cooks in a fraction of the time that dried pasta cooks. When buying fresh pasta, check the expiration date on the package.

When making homemade pasta, you can personalize the dough with herbs, spices, and other flavorings. Though time consuming, making pasta at home can be fun, especially if you involve your family. You can mix the dough by hand or in a food processor, then roll it out and shape it with

either a rolling pin or a hand-cranked pasta machine. Electric pasta machines can mix the dough for you and produce many different pasta shapes.

Dried and fresh semolina pasta are just about equal nutritionally. Both have insignificant amounts of fat. Egg pasta is, of course, higher in cholesterol and fat; 1 cup of cooked fresh egg pasta can supply up to 25 percent of the Daily Value for cholesterol. One pound of dry pasta generally yields about 8 cups of cooked pasta, and serves four to six people. But 1 pound of fresh pasta usually equals only 6 cups of cooked pasta, serving about four people.

Pasta with Lightened Pesto Sauce

Makes 4 servings

If you have pesto on hand, this stylish pasta dish is unbelievably quick and easy. Choose a pesto, then complete your menu with compatible side dishes. For example, round out linguine and Basil Pesto with a cherry tomato salad and sesame breadsticks. Finish capellini and Cilantro Pesto with a spoonful of salsa, a romaine salad, and corn tortillas. And complement vermicelli and Sun-Dried Tomato Pesto with an arugula salad and crusty bread.

¾ pound thin-strand pasta, such as linguine,
   vermicelli, or capellini
⅔ cup canned lower-sodium defatted
   chicken broth or pasta cooking water
½ cup Basil Pesto (page 206),
   Sun-Dried Tomato Pesto
   (page 207), or Cilantro Pesto (page 93)
   at room temperature
¼ cup low-fat ricotta cheese
Salt and freshly ground black
   pepper to taste

1. Cook the pasta in a large pot of boiling, salted water until al dente, 8 to 10 minutes for linguine, 5 to 7 minutes for vermicelli, and 4 to 5 minutes for capellini. Drain well, reserving ⅔ cup of the cooking water if desired.

2. Toss the pasta with the reserved broth or cooking water, the pesto, and the cheese. Season to taste with salt and pepper.

◆ *PER SERVING: About 427 cals, 92 cals from fat, 10g total fat, 2g sat fat, 5mg chol, 203mg sodium, 67g total carbs, 0g fiber, 17g prot*

Freshened Fettuccine Alfredo

Makes 6 servings

With only 17 percent of its calories from fat, here's a fettuccine Alfredo with a lightened heart and soul. The creaminess is achieved with a white sauce made from low-fat milk, but the real key to great flavor is to use the best and most full-flavored imported Parmesan cheese you can find.

1 pound fettuccine

3 tablespoons all-purpose flour

$\frac{1}{3}$ cup low-fat (1 percent) milk, plus 3 cups

1 tablespoon unsalted butter

$\frac{1}{2}$ teaspoon freshly ground pepper

$\frac{1}{4}$ teaspoon grated nutmeg

$\frac{2}{3}$ cup grated Parmesan cheese, preferably imported

$\frac{1}{4}$ cup chopped parsley, preferably flat leaf

1. Cook the fettucine in a large pot of boiling salted water until al dente, 8 to 10 minutes. Drain well.

2. Meanwhile, stir the flour into $\frac{1}{3}$ cup of the milk until dissolved. In a large, preferably nonstick skillet, melt the butter over medium heat and stir in the flour and milk paste. Cook, stirring, for 1 minute. Slowly whisk in the remainder of the milk and cook, stirring constantly, until the sauce comes to a boil and thickens. Reduce the heat to medium-low and add the pepper and nutmeg. Simmer, stirring occasionally, for 3 minutes.

3. Toss the pasta with the sauce. Add the Parmesan cheese and toss again. Sprinkle with the parsley and serve immediately.

◆ *PER SERVING: About 420 cals, 72 cals from fat, 8g total fat, 4g sat fat, 20mg chol, 284mg sodium, 67g total carbs, 0g fiber, 19g prot*

WHO IS AL DENTE?

Overcooked pasta is mushy and unappetizing. That's why most recipes call for pasta to be cooked "al dente," which means "to the tooth" in Italian. Al dente pasta retains a slightly firm bite, although it is cooked through without any hardness in the center. It takes a little practice to get a feel for al dente pasta, but the general rule is to taste a piece early and often during cooking. If you need to cook a pasta further, such as in baked lasagne, undercook it slightly first.

Contemporary Pasta Carbonara

Makes 6 servings

Pasta Carbonara is Italy's answer to our bacon and eggs. The story goes that an American soldier in World War II asked the Carbonara restaurant in Rome to create a dish that would remind him of his favorite American breakfast. This recipe offers a lighter version of the traditional sauce. Serve it with romaine wedges drizzled with light vinaigrette and garnished with roasted pepper strips. Last-minute cooking is particularly important in this dish—it's mainly the heat of the skillet and the hot pasta that cook the eggs.

1 pound thick pasta such as bucatini or perciatelli

1 tablespoon extra-virgin olive oil

6 ounces pancetta or Canadian bacon, diced or cut into thin strips

2 eggs

2 egg whites

½ cup defatted lower-sodium chicken broth

½ cup dry white wine or additional chicken broth

¼ cup grated Parmesan cheese, plus 2 tablespoons, preferably imported

¼ cup chopped flat-leaf parsley, plus 2 tablespoons

¼ cup chopped fresh basil, plus 2 tablespoons

1 teaspoon coarsely ground pepper

1. Cook the pasta in a large pot of boiling salted water until al dente, 9 to 11 minutes. Drain well.

2. Meanwhile, in a very large, preferably nonstick skillet or Dutch oven, heat the oil over medium heat and cook the pancetta until golden, about 4 minutes. Reduce the heat to low.

3. In a small bowl, whisk together the eggs, egg whites, broth, and wine. Add the drained, hot pasta to the hot skillet. Add the egg mixture and toss the pasta and sauce over low heat for 2 to 3 minutes, until the eggs are cooked. Add ¼ cup each of the cheese, parsley, and basil. Add the pepper and toss again. Sprinkle with the remaining 2 tablespoons each of cheese, parsley, and basil. Serve immediately.

◆ *PER SERVING: About 409 cals, 78 cals from fat, 9g total fat, 3g sat fat, 86mg chol, 446mg sodium, 58g total carbs, 0g fiber, 20g prot*

Pasta Primavera with Mustard Cream

Makes 6 servings

The "cream" in this recipe is really a light white sauce made with skim milk and lots of Dijon mustard. Vary the vegetables and herbs according to the season, but keep in mind that a kaleidoscope of colors is most appetizing. For a springtime touch, serve this dish with a tender baby lettuce salad with whole-wheat croutons for crunch.

1 pound fettuccine or other long-strand pasta

1 teaspoon butter

¼ pound (about 1 cup) diced smoked ham

⅓ cup defatted lower-sodium chicken broth, plus ¾ cup

3 medium carrots, cut into thin, matchsticklike slices

1 red bell pepper, seeded and cut into thin strips

2 leeks, white and light green parts only, thinly sliced

½ pound thin asparagus, trimmed and cut into 1½-inch diagonal lengths

1½ tablespoons all-purpose flour

3 tablespoons grainy Dijon mustard

1⅓ cups low-fat (1 percent) milk

1 cup frozen baby peas

¼ cup grated Parmesan cheese, preferably imported

Salt and freshly ground black pepper to taste

1. Cook the pasta in a large pot of boiling salted water until al dente, 8 to 10 minutes. Drain well.

2. Meanwhile, in a large, preferably nonstick skillet, melt the butter and cook the ham over medium heat, stirring until golden, about 4 minutes. Add ⅓ cup of the broth and the carrots. Cover and cook over medium heat for 2 minutes. Add the bell pepper, leeks, and asparagus. Cover and cook until the vegetables are crisp-tender, about 3 minutes.

3. Whisk in the flour and mustard. Cook, stirring, for 1 minute. Add the milk, the remaining ¾ cup of broth, and the peas. Cook, stirring over medium-high heat until slightly thickened and bubbly, about 2 minutes.

4. Pour the sauce over the pasta in the cooking pot or a large bowl. Add the cheese and toss to mix. Season to taste with salt and pepper. Serve immediately.

◆ *PER SERVING: About 443 cals, 48 cals from fat, 5g total fat, 2g sat fat, 18mg chol, 553mg sodium, 78g total carbs, 4g fiber, 22g prot*

Light-and-Easy Turkey Tetrazzini

Makes 6 servings

Turkey is traditional for Thanksgiving, and tetrazzini should be traditional for the leftovers. This delicious but light version takes only 18 percent of its calories from fat. Made with wild mushrooms and good Madeira, this buffet dish is worthy of your fanciest dinner party. Complete the menu with Garlicky Broccoli Rabe (page 413) and fresh seasonal fruits with tiny cookies.

Vegetable oil spray
¾ cup (1½ ounces) dry-packed sun-dried tomatoes
1 cup defatted lower-sodium chicken broth,
    plus ¼ cup, plus 1¼ cups
¾ pound white or green fettuccine or linguine
1 tablespoon unsalted butter
½ pound sliced fresh mushrooms, preferably
    any variety wild mushroom
1 cup thinly sliced scallions
2 garlic cloves, minced
3 tablespoons all-purpose flour
¼ cup chopped fresh basil or 1 tablespoon dried
2 tablespoons chopped fresh marjoram
    or 1½ teaspoons dried
½ teaspoon black pepper
1 cup low-fat (1 percent) milk
¾ pound (about 3 cups) cooked boneless
    turkey meat, cubed
¼ cup Madeira or dry sherry
Salt to taste
¼ cup grated Parmesan cheese, preferably imported
2 tablespoons seasoned dry bread crumbs

1. Coat a shallow 2½-quart (about 9x12-inch) baking dish with vegetable oil spray. Place the tomatoes in a small heatproof bowl. In a small pan, bring 1 cup of the broth to a boil and pour over the tomatoes. Let stand until the tomatoes are softened, about 30 minutes. Drain and slice the tomatoes, discarding the soaking liquid. Cook the pasta in a large pot of boiling salted water until al dente, 8 to 10 minutes. Drain well.

2. Meanwhile, melt the butter with ¼ cup of the broth in a large, preferably nonstick skillet over medium heat and cook the mushrooms, stirring often until softened, about 5 minutes. Add the scallions and garlic, and cook 2 minutes longer. Stir in the flour and cook for 2 minutes, stirring. Add the basil, marjoram, and pepper. Whisk in the remaining 1¼ cups of broth and the milk. Cook, stirring over medium heat, until the sauce is thick and bubbly, about 5 minutes. Stir in the turkey, Madeira, and sun-dried tomatoes. Simmer for 1 minute. Stir in the pasta. Taste and season with salt. Spoon the tetrazzini into the prepared baking dish. Sprinkle with the cheese and bread crumbs. (This recipe can be made to this point several hours ahead and refrigerated.)

3. Preheat the broiler or the oven to 400 degrees. If the tetrazzini is freshly made and hot, simply set under the broiler until the top is flecked with brown and the cheese is melted, about 2 minutes. If it has been refrigerated, cover with foil and bake until nearly heated through, about 20 minutes. Uncover and bake until the top is flecked with brown, 10 to 15 minutes longer.

◆ *PER SERVING: About 436 cals, 79 cals from fat, 9g total fat, 3g sat fat, 53mg chol, 333mg sodium, 56g total carbs, 1g fiber, 31g prot*

COLORED AND FLAVORED PASTAS

Fresh and dried pastas come in a rainbow of colors and flavors. Green pasta is colored with puréed spinach, red pepper turns it pink, and whole wheat makes pasta a nutty brown. Pastas flavored with basil are flecked with green, while hot pepper pastas are speckled with red. None of the additions contribute much in the way of nutritional value, but they do add to the variety and appeal of pasta. Be aware that most colored pastas are a bit softer in texture, so don't overcook them.

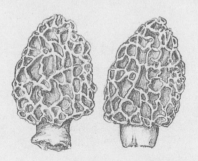

Summer Formal Bow Ties

Makes 6 servings

This elegant little dish is perfect for summer entertaining. The sauce is "cooked" by the heat of the pasta only, so you will be in and out of the kitchen in a flash. Yellow cherry tomatoes, now often available during the summer, make a colorful addition to the recipe.

1 pound cherry tomatoes, preferably a mix of red and yellow	½ cup vegetable broth
	3 tablespoons balsamic vinegar
6 ounces smoked mozzarella cheese, preferably fresh, cut into small cubes	2 tablespoons extra-virgin olive oil
	2 garlic cloves, minced
⅓ cup slivered fresh basil	¼ teaspoon dried hot red pepper flakes
	1 pound bow-tie pasta

1. Stem the tomatoes and cut them in half over a large mixing bowl to catch the juices. Place the tomatoes in the bowl. Add the cheese, basil, broth, vinegar, oil, garlic, and pepper flakes. Stir to mix, then let stand at least 15 minutes (up to 1 hour) at room temperature.

2. Cook the pasta in a large pot of boiling salted water until al dente, about 8 minutes. Drain well and return to the cooking pot. Add the sauce and toss. Cover the pot and let stand for 2 minutes to partially melt the cheese, then toss again and serve immediately.

◆ *PER SERVING: About 428 cals, 109 cals from fat, 12g total fat, 4g sat fat, 22mg chol, 123mg sodium, 63g total carbs, 0g fiber, 16g prot*

GARLIC TIPS

In spite of its pungent aroma, garlic, an unassuming member of the onion family, has worldwide appeal. It's so popular that you can buy it in many forms—ground, dehydrated, crushed in oil, and even pre-peeled. But no form is better (or cheaper) than plain fresh garlic. Here are some garlic tips:

◆ Look for firm, plump bulbs with dry, papery skins.
◆ Store the bulbs in a cool dry place, not in the refrigerator where they will pick up moisture and spoil.
◆ Peeling garlic is easier if you first flatten the unpeeled cloves with the broad side of a chef's knife. The skin will separate from the clove.
◆ If you are using a garlic press, do not peel the cloves first. The crushing process will separate the garlic from the skin. Crushed garlic is more potent than sliced or chopped because more of the pungent oils are released.

◆ Garlic chopped with a little salt won't stick to the knife blade. Just make sure that you use slightly less salt in the recipe.
◆ When cooking garlic, do not let it brown, or it will taste bitter.
◆ To remove garlic odor from your fingers or a chopping board, rub with a little lemon juice or a paste of baking soda and water.
◆ To remove garlic odor from your breath, chew on a little parsley or a few fennel seeds, or eat something with fresh lemon juice in it.

Straw and Hay with Peas and Pancetta

Makes 6 servings

The "straw and hay" in this classic dish are the regular and green fettuccine. You can use dried pasta, but this recipe is a nice showcase for fresh fettuccine. A delicate white sauce replaces the cream usually found in this dish, but a touch of Parmesan cheese and sour cream ensure a rich, satisfying flavor.

1 tablespoon olive oil	½ teaspoon dried thyme
4 ounces pancetta or smoked ham, diced	2¼ cups low-fat (1 percent) milk
¼ cup dry white wine or defatted lower-sodium chicken broth	1½ cups frozen baby peas
10 ounces sliced fresh mushrooms, preferably wild mushrooms, such as shiitake	½ pound fresh spinach fettuccine or 6 ounces dried
⅓ cup chopped shallots	½ pound fresh egg fettuccine or 6 ounces dried
2 tablespoons all-purpose flour	¼ cup grated Parmesan cheese, preferably imported
½ teaspoon freshly ground black pepper, plus additional	2 tablespoons reduced-fat sour cream

1. Heat 1 tablespoon of the oil in a large, preferably nonstick skillet and cook the pancetta over medium-high heat, stirring until golden. Use a slotted spoon to remove the pancetta to a plate. Add the wine, reduce the heat to medium, and cook the mushrooms and shallots, stirring often, until the mushrooms are softened, about 5 minutes. Stir in the flour, pepper, and thyme. Cook, stirring, for 2 minutes. Whisk in the milk and cook, stirring constantly, until the sauce is thick and bubbly. Add the peas and simmer for 2 minutes.

2. While the sauce is simmering, cook both pastas together in a large pot of boiling salted water until al dente, about 2 minutes for fresh pasta and 8 to 10 minutes for dried. Drain well.

3. Toss the pasta with the sauce. Stir in the cheese and sour cream and toss again. Spoon onto plates, and grind additional pepper over the top. Serve immediately.

◆ *PER SERVING: About 386 cals, 80 cals from fat, 9g total fat, 2g sat fat, 62mg chol, 405mg sodium, 57g total carbs, 2g fiber, 22g prot*

Modern Macaroni and Cheddar

Makes 6 servings

Everyone in the family will love this calcium- and protein-rich, meatless meal. For the best flavor, be sure to use a good-quality reduced-fat cheddar cheese. Broccoli teams up well with cheddar, so this dish is a tasty way to get your kids to eat broccoli. Sliced tomatoes and a basket of crusty whole-wheat rolls complete this appealing meal.

1 cup low-fat (1 percent) cottage cheese
¾ pound elbow macaroni or other short
   tube-shaped pasta
½ pound broccoli florets
Vegetable oil spray
2 teaspoons olive oil
1 small red bell pepper, seeded and chopped
⅔ cup thinly sliced scallions, plus ⅓ cup
1 tablespoon all-purpose flour
1½ teaspoons dry mustard
¼ teaspoon cayenne pepper
2 cups skim milk
1½ cups shredded reduced-fat cheddar cheese,
   plus ½ cup (about ½ pound total)
1 tablespoon Worcestershire sauce
1 teaspoon paprika

1. Process the cottage cheese in a blender or food processor just until smooth, about 15 seconds. Set aside. Cook the pasta in a large pot of boiling salted water for 7 minutes. Add the broccoli to the pasta and cook until the pasta is al dente and the broccoli is crisp-tender, about 3 minutes more. Drain the pasta and broccoli well and return to the cooking pot. Coat a shallow 2-quart baking dish or a 7x11-inch baking dish with vegetable oil spray.

2. In a large, preferably nonstick skillet, heat the oil over medium-low heat and cook the bell pepper for 3 minutes. Add ⅔ cup of the scallions and cook until the peppers are softened, about 2 minutes more. Stir in the flour, mustard, and cayenne and cook for 1 minute, stirring constantly. Slowly whisk in the milk and cook, stirring constantly, until thickened and bubbly, about 5 minutes. Reduce heat to low and whisk in the cottage cheese and 1½ cups of cheddar cheese until the cheese is melted and smooth. Stir in the Worcestershire.

3. Add the cheese sauce to the pasta and broccoli in the cooking pot and stir to combine well. Spoon into the prepared baking dish, then sprinkle with the remaining cheddar cheese and the paprika. (This recipe can be made up to 4 hours ahead to this point and refrigerated. Return to room temperature before baking.)

4. Preheat the broiler or preheat the oven to 400 degrees. If the recipe is freshly made and hot, set under the broiler until the top is flecked with brown and the cheese is melted, about 2 minutes. If the recipe has been made ahead and looks a little dry, you may need to add up to ¼ cup water to the baking dish. Cover with foil and bake until nearly heated through, about 20 minutes. Uncover and bake until the top is flecked with brown and the cheese is melted, about 10 minutes longer. Garnish with the remaining scallions and serve immediately.

◆ *PER SERVING: About 415 cals, 89 cals from fat, 10g total fat, 5g sat fat, 30mg chol, 422mg sodium, 54g total carbs, 2g fiber, 27g prot*

Angel Hair Arrabbiata

Makes 4 servings

Arrabbiata means "enraged" in Italian, and this peppery tomato sauce will indeed enrage your taste buds. But the soothing texture of the angel hair pasta will calm them right down. In the summer, you can substitute 2 pounds of seeded and diced plum tomatoes for the canned tomatoes. A plate of seasonal fruits is a balanced finish to this spicy meal.

1 tablespoon extra-virgin olive oil
2 ounces prosciutto or smoked
  ham, chopped
1 large onion, chopped
3 garlic cloves, minced
¼ cup chopped, drained, and
  rinsed, bottled or canned hot
  cherry peppers
2 cans (14½ ounces each)
  diced tomatoes
⅔ cup red wine or tomato juice

1 tablespoon chopped fresh
  rosemary or 1 teaspoon dried
¼ to ½ teaspoon dried hot
  pepper flakes
1 pound angel hair or capellini
  pasta
¼ cup grated Parmesan cheese,
  preferably imported
¼ cup chopped parsley, preferably
  flat leaf

1. In a large, preferably nonstick skillet, heat the oil and cook the prosciutto over medium-high heat, stirring until golden, about 3 minutes. Remove the prosciutto with a slotted spoon. Reduce the heat to medium and add the onion and garlic. Cook, stirring often, until the onion is softened, about 5 minutes. Add the cherry peppers, then stir in the
continued

undrained tomatoes, wine, rosemary, and pepper flakes. Simmer, uncovered, until lightly thickened, 5 to 8 minutes. Return the prosciutto to the pan.

2. Meanwhile, cook the pasta in a large pot of boiling salted water until al dente, 4 to 5 minutes. Drain well.

3. Toss the pasta with the sauce. Add the cheese and parsley, toss again, and serve immediately.

◆ *PER SERVING: About 575 cals, 72 cals from fat, 8g total fat, 2g sat fat, 13mg chol, 1183mg sodium, 102g total carbs, 1g fiber, 23g prot*

Cincinnati Chili Spaghetti

Makes 6 servings

Cincinnati chili has become a national sensation. Usually made with ground beef, this highly spiced dish is equally delicious with ground turkey. In Cincinnati, chili comes three-way (spaghetti, sauce, cheese), four-way (add onions), or five-way (add beans), and you never leave out the chocolate. Here is a version favored by real aficionados. A tossed salad with Basic Creamy Dressing (page 75), a basket of rolls, and Updated Old-Fashioned Chocolate Pudding (page 468) complete the meal.

2 teaspoons olive oil
1 pound ground turkey
1 large onion
2 large garlic cloves, minced
2 tablespoons chili powder
1 teaspoon dried oregano
1/4 teaspoon cayenne pepper
1/4 teaspoon ground cinnamon
1/8 teaspoon ground allspice
1/8 teaspoon ground cloves
1 large bay leaf, broken in half
1 can (16 ounces) tomato sauce

1 can (14 1/2 ounces) defatted lower-sodium beef broth
1 tablespoon cider vinegar
1/2 ounce unsweetened chocolate, chopped
Salt to taste
1 pound spaghetti
1 1/2 cups grated cheddar cheese (optional)
1 1/2 cups chopped onion (optional)
1 can (16 ounces) kidney beans, drained and rinsed (optional)

1. In a medium saucepan, heat the oil and cook the turkey, onion, and garlic over medium-low heat, stirring often until the onion is tender and the turkey is white, 5 to 7 minutes. Drain off drippings. Add the chili powder and cook, stirring, for 1 minute longer. Stir in the oregano, cayenne, cinnamon, allspice, cloves, and bay leaf. Add the tomato sauce, broth, vinegar, and chocolate. Bring to a boil over medium heat, then reduce the heat to medium-low and cover the pot. Simmer for 30 minutes. Uncover and simmer until the sauce is the consistency of a thin chili, 10 to 15 minutes longer. Discard the bay leaf and season to taste with salt. (This recipe can be prepared up to 2 days ahead to this point and refrigerated. Reheat to a simmer before serving.)

2. Cook the spaghetti in a large pot of boiling salted water until al dente, 7 to 9 minutes. Drain well.

3. Place the spaghetti on a serving platter or individual plates. Ladle the sauce over the spaghetti and serve with the optional cheese, onion, and bean garnishes.

◆ *PER SERVING (without garnishes): About 467 cals, 91 cals from fat, 10g total fat, 2g sat fat, 61mg chol, 585mg sodium, 68g total carbs, 3g fiber, 26g prot*

YOUR CANNED TOMATO PANTRY

Your supermarket contains a veritable garden of canned tomato products. Canned tomatoes have a high amount of acid, so you should not store tomatoes in the can once they have been opened. Instead, transfer the contents to a nonmetallic container and refrigerate up to 3 days. You can buy canned tomatoes salted or unsalted. The added salt is for flavor only. When you use several canned ingredients containing salt together (as in a soup), the end result may be overly salty.

CANNED TOMATOES IN JUICE can be drained and used in place of fresh tomatoes. In general, replace 2 pounds of fresh tomatoes with one 28-ounce can or two 14- to 16-ounce cans of tomatoes. Look for imported or domestic plum tomatoes for the best flavor.

CANNED TOMATOES IN PURÉE are used undrained as part of a recipe for homemade tomato sauce.

TOMATO PURÉE is puréed fresh peeled and seeded tomatoes that have been lightly cooked during the canning process. The purée is usually then cooked further when you use it in a recipe, such as in a sauce.

TOMATO SAUCE is tomato purée that has been simmered to a thicker consistency. You can use it without further cooking. Tomato sauce is available plain, unsalted, and in several flavored varieties.

TOMATO PASTE is tomato purée that has been cooked down to a thick paste. Available both in cans and in tubes, tomato paste adds potent flavor to sauces, and is usually diluted with other liquids.

STEWED TOMATOES are canned tomatoes that have been cooked with a touch of sugar and other flavorings, such as onions and green peppers. They are available whole and sliced, as well as in a variety of flavors from Italian to Cajun. Use them undrained.

BOTTLED AND CANNED TOMATO-BASED PASTA SAUCES come in dozens of varieties and flavors. Some are fat and sodium free, while others pack a hefty amount of both. Check the labels for contents.

PIZZA SAUCES are like pasta sauces, but are thickened with a starch so that they can be spread on a pizza crust.

Shellfish Lasagne

Makes 8 servings

This contemporary, sophisticated lasagne bakes very briefly so that all of the ingredients retain their freshness. You can also bake eight individual lasagnes in small baking dishes. Vary the shellfish according to availability and your preference—options include scallops, lump crabmeat, or even lobster if you are feeling extravagant. A salad of delicate lettuces and chilled asparagus spears is a fitting accompaniment.

½ cup dry-packed sun-dried
   tomatoes
1 tablespoon olive oil, preferably
   extra virgin
1 medium onion, coarsely chopped
1 medium fennel bulb (about ½
   pound), trimmed, cored, and
   coarsely chopped (see note)
2 large garlic cloves, minced
2 pounds fresh plum tomatoes,
   seeded and coarsely chopped, or
   2 cans (1 pound each) plum
   tomatoes in juice, drained and
   coarsely chopped
½ cup chopped parsley, preferably
   flat leaf
½ teaspoon dried red pepper flakes
1 cup bottled clam juice
1 cup dry white wine
¾ pound (about 20) medium
   shrimp in the shell

24 small clams in the shell (about 3
   pounds), scrubbed
24 mussels in the shell (about 1½
   pounds), scrubbed and debearded
½ pound cleaned squid,
   thinly sliced
¼ cup chopped fresh basil
2 tablespoons anise-flavored
   liqueur (optional)
Salt and freshly ground pepper
   to taste
¾ pound dried green or white
   lasagna noodles or 1 pound fresh
   (about 12 noodles)
Vegetable oil spray
¼ cup grated Parmesan cheese,
   preferably imported
Basil or parsley sprigs for
   garnish (optional)

1. In a small bowl, cover the sun-dried tomatoes with boiling water. Let stand until the tomatoes are softened, about 15 minutes. Drain and thinly slice the tomatoes.

2. In a large, preferably nonstick skillet, heat the oil and cook the onions, fennel, and garlic over medium-low heat, stirring often until softened, about 5 minutes. Add the fresh or canned tomatoes, chopped parsley, and pepper flakes. Simmer, stirring gently, until the liquid is nearly evaporated, about 15 minutes.

3. Meanwhile, in a large pot, bring the clam juice and wine to a boil. Add the shrimp, reduce heat to medium, cover the pot, and simmer until the shrimp turn pink, about 2 minutes. Remove the shrimp with a slotted spoon. Add the clams and mussels to the pot. Cover and steam until the shells open, about 5 minutes. Use a slotted spoon to transfer the shellfish to the bowl with the shrimp. If desired, set aside and refrigerate eight each of the shrimp, clams, and mussels to use as garnish. Peel the remaining shrimp, and remove the remaining clams and mussels from the shells. Discard the shells. Strain the shellfish cooking liquid through a colander lined with cheesecloth and measure out 1½ cups.

4. Add the 1½ cups of cooking liquid to the tomato sauce along with the squid. Simmer, uncovered, until the squid is cooked through, about 4 minutes. Stir in the peeled shrimp, shelled clams and mussels, chopped basil, anise liqueur, and salt and pepper to taste. (The sauce can be prepared a day ahead to this point and refrigerated. Reheat gently, along with any shellfish set aside for garnish, before assembling the lasagne.)

5. Cook the lasagna noodles in a large pot of boiling salted water until al dente, 11 to 13 minutes for dried pasta, 1 to 2 minutes for fresh. Drain well, then rinse under cold water to stop the cooking and keep the noodles from sticking together. Lightly coat a shallow 3-quart casserole or eight individual casseroles with vegetable oil spray.

6. Spread a thin layer of the tomato sauce over the bottom of the prepared baking dish or dishes. Make a layer of one third of the pasta, then spoon in half of the shellfish sauce. Make another similar layer, ending with the pasta. (This recipe can be prepared up to 8 hours ahead to this point, covered, and refrigerated.)

7. Preheat the oven to 450 degrees. Uncover the lasagne(s) if refrigerated, sprinkle with the cheese, and bake until heated through, 10 to 20 minutes, depending on size of dish. Place any reserved shellfish still in the shell on top and heat for 3 minutes longer. Serve the individual lasagnes immediately. Let the large lasagne stand for 5 to 10 minutes before cutting it into squares and serving. (The lasagne should be quite juicy.) Garnish with basil or parsley sprigs, if desired.

◆ *PER SERVING: About 313 cals, 61 cals from fat, 7g total fat, 1g sat fat, 138mg chol, 391mg sodium, 31g total carbs, 2g fiber, 27g prot*

Note: To prepare the fennel, trim off the fronds, quarter the bulb, and cut out and discard the core. Chop the fennel bulb coarsely.

IS PASTA FATTENING?

At 200 calories and almost no fat per cup, cooked pasta hardly can be called fattening. Even a relatively large portion of pasta—2 cups cooked—easily fits into a healthful diet equaling four Pyramid servings from the grain group. Of course, oversized portions of any food can add unwanted extra calories—and pounds—so keep an eye on pasta and other portion sizes, particularly when dining out. Also, choose your pasta sauce wisely. Traditional Alfredo, cream-based, and even olive oil and garlic sauces are teeming with calories and fat.

Roasted Summer Vegetable Lasagne

Makes 8 servings

You can substitute lots of other roasted vegetables, such as asparagus and other peppers and summer squash, for the ones used here.

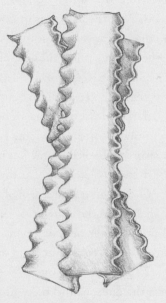

3 tablespoons olive oil, preferably extra virgin

2 large garlic cloves, minced

⅓ cup all-purpose flour

½ cup low-fat (1 percent) milk, plus 3½ cups

1 tablespoon chopped fresh tarragon or 1 teaspoon dried

¾ teaspoon salt

¼ teaspoon cayenne pepper

¼ teaspoon grated nutmeg

2 cups grated Swiss cheese, plus 1 cup
   (about ¾ pound total)

Vegetable or olive oil spray

1 large red bell pepper, seeded and quartered

1 large green bell pepper, seeded and quartered

1 small bunch broccoli, cut into spears

1 large red onion, cut crosswise into ¼-inch slices

2 medium yellow crookneck squash, cut lengthwise into ¼-inch slices

3 large tomatoes, seeded and cut crosswise into ½-inch slices

Salt and pepper to taste

¾ pound dried lasagna noodles or 1 pound fresh (about 12 noodles)

1. In a small bowl, combine the oil and garlic. Let stand at least 15 minutes or up to 2 hours.

2. In a medium saucepan, whisk the flour and ½ cup of milk until smooth. Whisk in the remaining 3½ cups of milk, tarragon, salt, cayenne, and nutmeg. Bring to a boil, stirring constantly. Cook, stirring, for 1 minute. Remove from heat and add 2 cups of the cheese, stirring until melted and the sauce is smooth.

3. Preheat the oven to 500 degrees. Coat two large baking sheets with vegetable oil spray. Place the vegetables in a single layer on the baking sheets and brush them with the garlic oil. Roast all the vegetables until lightly charred and softened, removing each vegetable as it softens, and reversing the position of the baking sheets once. The tomatoes and squash will take about 5 minutes, while the bell peppers, broccoli, and onion will take about 10 minutes. Season the vegetables lightly with salt and pepper. Slice the red and green peppers, cut the broccoli into bite-sized pieces, and separate the onion into rings.

4. Cook the pasta in a large pot of boiling salted water until just al dente, 11 to 13 minutes for dried pasta, 1 to 2 minutes for fresh. Drain well and rinse under cold water to stop the cooking and keep the noodles from sticking together.

5. Coat a shallow 3-quart baking dish with vegetable oil spray. Make a layer of one third of the lasagna noodles, spread with half of the cheese sauce, then layer with half of the vegetables. Repeat the layering, ending with the pasta. Sprinkle with the remaining 1 cup of cheese. Cover the baking dish with aluminum foil. (This recipe can be made up to 2 days ahead to this point and refrigerated. Return to room temperature before baking.)

6. Preheat the oven to 350 degrees. Bake the lasagne, covered, for 25 minutes. Uncover, increase the oven temperature to 425 degrees and bake until the top is lightly golden, about 10 minutes longer. Let the lasagne stand for 10 minutes before cutting into squares to serve.

◆ *PER SERVING: About 347 cals, 100 cals from fat, 11g total fat, 1g sat fat, 27mg chol, 470mg sodium, 41g total carbs, 6g fiber, 23g prot*

Santa Fe Spaghetti Pie

Makes 8 servings

This dish is a great way to use up leftover spaghetti. The noodles become the "crust" for a savory "pie" that can be seasoned with any herb or cooked meat filling. Good accompaniments would be a spinach and diced pineapple salad, and a basket of baked tortilla chips.

Vegetable oil spray
½ pound uncooked spaghetti or
  3½ cups cooked spaghetti
2 egg whites
½ cup low-fat (1 percent) milk
2 tablespoons grated Romano
  cheese, preferably imported
2 teaspoons olive oil
1 pound ground turkey
1 large onion, chopped
1 large green bell pepper, seeded
  and chopped
2 garlic cloves, minced

1 small fresh or pickled jalapeño
  pepper, minced
1½ tablespoons chili powder
½ teaspoon ground cumin
½ teaspoon dried oregano
¼ teaspoon cayenne pepper
1 can (16 ounces) tomato sauce
1 can (19 ounces) kidney beans,
  drained and rinsed, or 2 cups
  cooked kidney beans
2 cups (½ pound) grated reduced-
  fat Monterey Jack cheese

continued

1. Lightly coat a shallow 2½- or 3-quart casserole or 9x12-inch baking dish with vegetable oil spray. Cook raw spaghetti in a large pot of boiling salted water until al dente, about 8 minutes. Drain well. (If using cooked spaghetti, reheat it in a microwave or regular oven until warm.) In a large mixing bowl, whisk the egg whites with the milk until frothy, then stir in the hot pasta and Romano cheese. Spread the pasta over the bottom and halfway up the sides of the baking dish.

2. In a large, preferably nonstick skillet or Dutch oven, heat the oil and cook the turkey, onion, and green pepper, stirring often over medium heat, until the turkey is white and the vegetables are softened, about 7 minutes. Add the garlic, jalapeño pepper, and chili powder, and cook for 1 minute. Stir in the cumin, oregano, cayenne, tomato sauce, and beans. Spread the mixture over the pasta "crust." Sprinkle the Monterey Jack cheese evenly over the filling. Cover with aluminum foil. (The recipe can be prepared up to 8 hours ahead to this point and refrigerated. Return to room temperature before baking.)

3. Preheat the oven to 375 degrees. Bake the covered casserole for 20 minutes. Uncover and bake until the cheese is melted and golden brown, and the casserole is bubbly, about 20 minutes longer. Let stand for 10 minutes before cutting into squares to serve.

◆ *PER SERVING: About 388 cals, 107 cals from fat, 12g total fat, 4g sat fat, 68mg chol, 690mg sodium, 40g total carbs, 4g fiber, 30g prot*

RECYCLING PASTA

Leftover pasta has intriguing possibilities. Use it in frittatas, such as Dilled Salmon and Pasta Frittata (page 230); puddings, such as Fruited Noodle Kugel (page 226); and savory "pie crusts," such as Sante Fe Spaghetti Pie (page 223). Your microwave oven does the best job of reheating leftover pasta. Simply place it in a microwave-safe dish, add a tablespoon or so of liquid, cover, and reheat. If you don't have a microwave, place the pasta in a steamer basket set over simmering water to reheat.

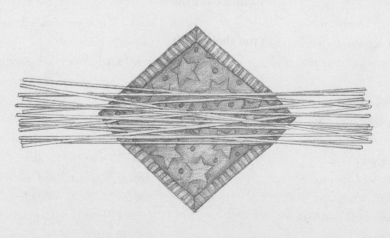

Spinach and Two-Cheese Stuffed Shells

Makes 6 servings

You can also use this versatile cheese filling to fill manicotti or cannelloni tubes. Flavor it with cilantro and jalapeño chiles for a Southwestern twist.

24 to 30 jumbo pasta shells (about ¾ pound)
2 cups (about 1 pound) low-fat (1 percent) cottage cheese
1 egg
1 package (10 ounces) frozen chopped spinach,
    thawed and squeezed of excess moisture (see note)
2 ounces (about ½ cup) finely diced smoked ham
¼ cup finely chopped shallots
¼ cup grated Romano cheese, plus ¼ cup
½ teaspoon black pepper
¼ teaspoon grated nutmeg
3 cups Basic Marinara Sauce (page 205) or bottled chunky
    pasta sauce flavored with basil

1. Cook the pasta in a large pot of boiling salted water until just al dente, 11 to 14 minutes. Drain well. In a large bowl, use a spoon to blend together the cottage cheese, egg, spinach, ham, shallots, ¼ cup of the Romano cheese, pepper, and nutmeg. Spoon 1 heaping tablespoon of the filling into each shell.

2. Spread about half of the pasta sauce over the bottom of a shallow 2- or 2½-quart baking dish. Arrange the shells in a single layer on top of the sauce. Pour the remaining sauce over and around the shells. Sprinkle the shells with the remaining ¼ cup of Romano cheese. (This recipe can be made up to 24 hours ahead to this point, covered, and refrigerated. Return to room temperature before baking.)

3. Preheat the oven to 350 degrees. Bake, covered, for 30 minutes. Uncover and bake 10 minutes longer. Let stand for 5 minutes before serving.

◆ *PER SERVING: About 402 cals, 65 cals from fat, 7g total fat, 3g sat fat, 54mg chol, 712mg sodium, 56g total carbs, 0g fiber, 26g prot*

Note: You can substitute ⅔ cup of very well-drained and squeezed, chopped fresh spinach (about ½ pound uncooked spinach leaves) for the frozen spinach.

Fruited Noodle Kugel

Makes 6 main-dish or 8 side-dish servings

Noodle kugel is a traditional Eastern European Jewish pudding. It's so good that it can stand alone as a main dish for brunch or supper, accompanied by colorful salads such as marinated beets and tossed greens. By adding ¼ cup more sugar, you can turn this versatile recipe into dessert.

Vegetable oil spray
6 ounces medium egg noodles
1 ripe firm pear, peeled, cored, and diced
1 tablespoon sugar
½ cup chopped mixed dried fruit or chopped dried pears
1 tablespoon all-purpose flour
½ teaspoon ground cinnamon
½ teaspoon grated nutmeg

½ teaspoon salt
¼ teaspoon white pepper
2 eggs
2 egg whites
1½ cups low-fat (1 percent) cottage cheese
1½ cups low-fat (1 percent) milk
½ cup reduced-fat sour cream
3 tablespoons sliced almonds

1. Coat a 2- or 2½-quart shallow baking dish with vegetable oil spray. Cook the noodles in a large pot of boiling salted water until al dente, about 8 minutes. Drain well.

2. In a medium mixing bowl, toss together the pear and sugar, then mix in the dried fruit, flour, cinnamon, nutmeg, salt, and pepper.

3. In a large mixing bowl, whisk together the eggs and egg whites. Blend in the cottage cheese, milk, and sour cream. Stir in the fruit mixture along with the noodles. Spoon the pudding into the prepared baking dish and sprinkle with the almonds. (This recipe can be prepared up to 4 hours ahead to this point and refrigerated. Return to room temperature before baking.)

4. Preheat the oven to 350 degrees. Bake uncovered, until the kugel is set and the top is golden, 45 to 55 minutes. Let it stand for 10 minutes, then cut into squares to serve.

◆ *PER MAIN-DISH SERVING: About 309 cals, 67 cals from fat, 7g total fat, 2g sat fat, 107mg chol, 496mg sodium, 43g total carbs, 2g fiber, 18g prot*

Linguine with Herbed Clam Sauce

Makes 4 servings

Clams are surprisingly rich in iron, so this delicious and classic dish should become a regular in your family's pasta repertoire. Serve this pasta in shallow soup bowls, accompanied by a big basket of crusty Braided Semolina Bread (page 115). There will be plenty of delicious, garlicky broth to sop up after the pasta is gone.

2 cups chopped fresh clams with juice or 2 cans
   (10 ounces each) chopped clams
1 cup bottled clam juice
¾ pound linguine, preferably spinach linguine
2 tablespoons extra-virgin olive oil
½ cup thinly sliced scallions, plus ¼ cup
4 large garlic cloves, minced
1 cup dry white wine
¾ teaspoon dried marjoram
¼ teaspoon dried red pepper flakes
½ cup chopped flat-leaf parsley
¼ cup chopped fresh basil

1. Drain the clams, reserving the juice. Add enough bottled clam juice to make 1½ cups.
2. Cook the linguine in a large pot of boiling salted water until al dente, 8 to 10 minutes. Drain well.
3. Meanwhile, in a large, preferably nonstick skillet, heat the oil and cook ½ cup of the scallions and the garlic over medium-low heat, stirring for 2 minutes. Add the reserved clam juice, wine, marjoram, and pepper flakes. Simmer over medium heat for 5 minutes. Add the clams, parsley, and basil, and simmer for 2 minutes.
4. Toss the pasta with the sauce and remaining ¼ cup of scallions, and serve.

◆ *PER SERVING: About 494 cals, 89 cals from fat, 10g total fat, 1g sat fat, 88mg chol, 217mg sodium, 70g total carbs, 0g fiber, 24g prot*

Calamari Fra Diavolo

Makes 6 servings

Americans are becoming more familiar with calamari (squid), the wonderful briny mollusk that has always been popular in Italy. If you can't get calamari, substitute 1½ cups of drained, chopped, fresh clams or 2 cans (10 ounces each) of chopped clams, drained—both calamari and clams have very little fat. Fra diavolo (or "brother of the devil") sauce lends just the right spicy touch.

2 tablespoons extra-virgin olive oil
1 medium onion, chopped
3 large garlic cloves, minced
1 bay leaf, broken in half
1½ teaspoons dried oregano
¾ teaspoon dried thyme
½ teaspoon dried red pepper
   flakes
1 can (28 ounces) Italian-style
   tomatoes in purée

½ cup bottled clam juice
½ cup dry red wine or additional
   clam juice
1 pound perciatelli or spaghetti
1 pound cleaned calamari, cut into
   ¼-inch rings with tentacles left intact
¼ cup chopped flat-leaf parsley
Salt and freshly ground pepper
   to taste

1. In a large, preferably nonstick skillet, heat the oil and cook the onion over medium-low heat, stirring often until softened, about 5 minutes. Add the garlic and cook for 1 minute. Stir in the bay leaf, oregano, thyme, pepper flakes, tomatoes in purée, clam juice, and wine. Break up the tomatoes with the side of a spoon, then simmer uncovered over medium-low heat until lightly thickened, about 15 minutes. Discard the bay leaf. (This recipe can be made up to 2 days ahead to this point and refrigerated. Return to a simmer before proceeding.)

2. Cook the pasta in a large pot of boiling salted water until al dente, about 10 minutes. Drain well.

3. While the pasta is cooking, add the calamari to the simmering sauce. Cover the pan and simmer until the calamari is tender and opaque, 3 to 5 minutes. (Do not overcook the calamari.) Stir in the parsley and season with salt and pepper to taste.

4. Place the pasta on a serving platter. Ladle the sauce over the pasta and serve.

◆ *PER SERVING: About 443 cals, 62 cals from fat, 7g total fat, 1g sat fat, 176mg chol, 317mg sodium, 66g total carbs, 1g fiber, 23g prot*

Shrimp, Feta, and Minted Orzo Pilaf

Makes 4 servings

Orzo, or rice-shaped pasta, makes an irresistible pilaf, especially used as a bed for savory broiled or grilled shrimp. If you omit the shrimp, you can serve the pilaf as a side dish for eight—a nice addition to a dinner of broiled chicken or roasted lamb.

1½ tablespoons extra-virgin olive oil

1 medium red onion, chopped

2 garlic cloves, minced

1 teaspoon dried oregano

½ teaspoon coarsely ground black pepper

½ pound peeled and deveined large shrimp (about 12 shrimp)

½ cup bottled clam juice

½ cup dry white wine or additional clam juice

¼ cup chopped fresh mint, plus 2 tablespoons

¼ cup sliced black olives, preferably Greek olives

1½ cups (about ½ pound) orzo

1 cup frozen baby peas

1 cup (about ¼ pound) feta cheese, crumbled

1. Preheat the broiler or prepare a barbecue fire.

2. In a large, preferably nonstick skillet, heat the oil and cook the onion over medium-low heat, stirring often until softened, about 5 minutes. Add the garlic, oregano, and pepper and cook for 1 minute. Remove the pan from the heat, add the shrimp, and toss them in the oil mixture to lightly coat. Thread the shrimp onto four metal skewers and set aside. Add the clam juice and wine to the skillet and simmer until lightly reduced, about 5 minutes. Stir in the mint and olives.

3. Meanwhile, cook the pasta in a large pot of boiling salted water until nearly tender, about 7 minutes. Add the peas and cook until the pasta is al dente and the peas are cooked, about 2 minutes longer. Drain well and add to the sauce in the skillet.

4. Broil or grill the shrimp about 4 inches from the heat source, turning once until cooked through, about 5 minutes.

5. To serve, add the feta to the orzo and toss lightly to mix. Remove the shrimp from the skewers and arrange on top of the orzo pilaf.

◆ *PER SERVING: About 438 cals, 110 cals from fat, 12g total fat, 3g sat fat, 100mg chol, 410mg sodium, 54g total carbs, 2g fiber, 24g prot*

Dilled Salmon and Pasta Frittata

Makes 4 servings

Because you can make this recipe with nearly any pasta shape, a wide variety of vegetables, and several other cheeses, you'll find that it's a creative and tasty way to use leftovers. You can use zucchini, broccoli, cauliflower, or peas in place of the red pepper and asparagus. Reduced-fat cheddar or mozzarella cheese works well in place of Swiss. The eggs and egg whites can be replaced by 1½ cups of liquid egg substitute. Almost any fresh herb can stand in for the dill.

½ pound thin asparagus, trimmed and cut into 1-inch diagonal pieces

2 teaspoons olive oil

1 red bell pepper, seeded and chopped

1 medium onion, chopped

2 cups cooked vermicelli

4 eggs

4 egg whites

½ cup low-fat (1 percent) cottage cheese

4 ounces smoked salmon, chopped or slivered

¼ cup chopped fresh dill, plus 1 tablespoon

1 tablespoon lemon juice

½ teaspoon grated lemon peel

¼ teaspoon cayenne pepper

1 cup (¼ pound) shredded reduced-fat Swiss cheese

1. Steam the asparagus over boiling water until crisp-tender, about 2 minutes. Place the asparagus in a strainer, rinse under cold water to stop the cooking, and set aside.

2. In an ovenproof 10- or 11-inch, preferably nonstick skillet, heat the oil and cook the pepper and onion over medium heat, stirring often until the vegetables become soft, about 5 minutes. Add the pasta and stir. Remove the pan from the heat.

3. In a large mixing bowl, whisk together the eggs and egg whites. Stir in the cottage cheese until blended. Stir in the salmon, ¼ cup of the dill, lemon juice, lemon peel, and cayenne. Pour over the pasta and vegetables in the skillet, and stir gently to combine.

4. Preheat the broiler. Cover the skillet and cook on the stovetop over medium-low heat, without stirring, until the eggs are nearly set and sides of the frittata begin to brown, about 10 minutes. Uncover, sprinkle with the Swiss cheese and place under the broiler, about 4 inches from the heat source, until the cheese is melted and speckled with brown and the eggs are set, 1 to 2 minutes. Let the frittata stand for 5 minutes before serving. (The frittata can also be made an hour or two ahead and served at room temperature.)

◆ *PER SERVING: About 395 cals, 131 cals from fat, 15g total fat, 5g sat fat, 238mg chol, 519mg sodium, 30g total carbs, 3g fiber, 34g prot*

Radiatore with Peppers, Chard, and Gorgonzola

Makes 6 servings

This is a great winter holiday dish because of its bright red and green colors. Vary the vegetables to suit the season, using asparagus and yellow peppers in spring, cherry tomatoes and summer squash in summer, or green peppers and cubed butternut squash in the fall.

¾ pound Swiss chard
2 tablespoons extra-virgin olive oil
1 large red bell pepper, seeded and
  diced
3 garlic cloves, minced
½ cup vegetable broth
½ cup dry white wine or additional
  vegetable broth

1 pound radiatore or other stubby
  pasta shape
1 cup (¼ pound) crumbled
  Gorgonzola cheese
Freshly ground pepper to taste

1. Separate the Swiss chard leaves. Thoroughly rinse and pat them dry, then slice the ribs and leaves crosswise into ½-inch strips.

2. In a large, preferably nonstick skillet, heat the oil and cook the red pepper over medium heat, stirring often, until it begins to soften, about 3 minutes. Stir in the garlic and Swiss chard, and cook for 1 minute. Add the broth and wine, partially cover the pan and simmer for 5 minutes.

3. Meanwhile, cook the pasta in a large pot of boiling salted water until al dente, 10 to 12 minutes. Drain well.

4. Toss the pasta with the sauce. Add the Gorgonzola and pepper to taste. Toss again and serve immediately.

◆ *PER SERVING: About 446 cals, 103 cals from fat, 11g total fat, 4g sat fat, 14mg chol, 643mg sodium, 69g total carbs, 5g fiber, 19g prot*

Curried Penne with Cauliflower and Peas

Makes 6 servings

Cooks in southern Italy commonly add currants, raisins, and cauliflower to pasta sauces, teamed with tube or stubby pasta shapes, such as penne or ear-shaped orrechiette. Serve this sophisticated, meatless pasta with Lemon and Honey-Glazed Baby Carrots (page 430). Lemon sherbet would be a refreshing dessert.

½ cup dried currants or raisins	1 teaspoon curry powder
¼ cup dry white wine or water	1 can (16 ounces) tomato sauce
¼ cup fresh whole-wheat bread crumbs (about ½ slice of bread)	1 cup vegetable broth
3 tablespoons pine nuts	½ teaspoon dried hot pepper flakes
¼ cup grated Parmesan cheese	1 cup frozen green peas
2 tablespoons extra-virgin olive oil	¾ pound penne or other stubby pasta
4 cups cauliflower florets	1 can (10 ounces) chickpeas, drained and rinsed, or 1 cup cooked chickpeas
3 garlic cloves, minced	
2 anchovies, optional	

1. In a small bowl, soak the currants in the wine until plumped, about 30 minutes. In a small dry skillet, toast the bread crumbs and pine nuts over medium heat until golden and fragrant, 2 to 4 minutes, and immediately spoon into a small bowl. Let cool, then toss with the cheese and set aside.

2. In a large, preferably nonstick skillet, heat the oil and cook the cauliflower, stirring over medium-high heat until lightly colored, about 3 minutes. Add the garlic, the anchovies if desired, and the curry, and cook, stirring, for 2 minutes. Add the currants and soaking liquid, tomato sauce, vegetable broth, and pepper flakes. Simmer, uncovered, until the cauliflower is tender and the sauce is slightly reduced, about 10 minutes. Add the peas and simmer for 2 minutes.

3. Meanwhile, cook the pasta in a large pot of boiling salted water until al dente, about 10 minutes. Drain well.

4. Toss the pasta with the sauce, chickpeas, and half of the bread crumb mixture. Transfer the pasta to a serving dish or six plates and sprinkle with the remaining bread crumb mixture. Serve immediately.

◆ *PER SERVING: About 461 cals, 92 cals from fat, 10g total fat, 2g sat fat, 3mg chol, 631mg sodium, 77g total carbs, 3g fiber, 18g prot*

Rigatoni and Savory Bean Sauce

Makes 6 servings

Use white cannellini beans in this recipe because they soften well and help to thicken the sauce. Even a tiny bit of smoky bacon packs big flavor, so buy the best. This easy, nutrition-packed, and flavorful recipe is sure to become a family favorite.

3 slices bacon
1 large onion, coarsely chopped
1 large green bell pepper, seeded and coarsely chopped
1 carrot, coarsely chopped
2 garlic cloves, minced
2 cans (14½ ounces each) stewed tomatoes, undrained
1 can (19 ounces) cannellini or white beans,
    drained and rinsed, or 2 cups cooked cannellini or white beans
½ cup dry white wine or tomato juice
1½ teaspoons dried savory
1 teaspoon dried oregano
½ teaspoon salt
½ teaspoon black pepper
¾ pound rigatoni or other similar pasta shape
¼ cup chopped parsley, preferably flat leaf, plus 2 tablespoons
¼ cup grated Parmesan cheese, preferably imported

1. In a large skillet, cook the bacon over medium heat until crisp. Drain the bacon on paper towels, crumble, and reserve. Pour off all but 1½ tablespoons drippings. Add the onion, bell pepper, and carrot. Cook, stirring over medium-low heat until the vegetables soften, about 5 minutes. Add the garlic and cook for 1 minute. Add the undrained tomatoes, beans, wine, savory, oregano, salt, and pepper. Partially cover the pan and simmer until slightly thickened, about 10 minutes. (The sauce can be prepared up to 8 hours ahead and refrigerated. Return to a simmer before continuing.)

2. Cook the pasta in a large pot of boiling salted water until al dente, 8 to 10 minutes. Drain well. Toss the pasta with the sauce, ¼ cup of the parsley, cheese, and reserved bacon. Sprinkle with the remaining 2 tablespoons of parsley. Serve immediately.

◆ *PER SERVING: About 522 cals, 66 cals from fat, 7g total fat, 3g sat fat, 9mg chol, 1072mg sodium, 95g total carbs, 8g fiber, 20g prot*

GRATING CHEESES

Pasta is unimaginable without Parmesan cheese. But you can also use other firm, ripened cheeses, such as Romano and Asiago, in most recipes. Although these cheeses are relatively high in fat and sodium, they have such a potent flavor that you need to use only a little. Hard grating cheeses make such a difference in pasta recipes that you should buy the very best quality and grate it yourself. Good domestic cheeses are on the market, but, in general, the Italian imports are consistently of a better quality. Look for cheese labeled Parmigiano-Reggiano, the authentic cheese from Parma, for example. Pecorino is a high-quality Italian Romano cheese. Visit a cheese shop with a frequent turnover and buy the cheese freshly cut from a large piece if you can, or check the expiration date on the package. Store grated cheese tightly covered in the refrigerator for up to 2 days.

Ziti with Roasted Potatoes, Tomatoes, and Leeks

Makes 6 servings

For this intensely flavored, easy vegetarian pasta main course, you need to first roast the potatoes, tomatoes, and leeks, then roast the sauce itself.

2 tablespoons extra-virgin olive oil

½ pound red potatoes, unpeeled, cut into ¾-inch cubes

½ pound plum tomatoes, seeded and cut into ½-inch slices

2 leeks, white and light green parts only, cut into ½-inch slices

1 tablespoon fresh chopped rosemary or 1 teaspoon dried

1 can (14½ ounces) Italian-style stewed tomatoes

1½ cups vegetable broth or defatted reduced-sodium chicken broth

½ cup dry white wine or additional broth

¼ teaspoon salt

¼ teaspoon black pepper

1 pound ziti or other similar pasta shape

4 ounces thinly sliced or shredded reduced-fat mozzarella cheese

¼ cup grated Parmesan cheese

1. Preheat the oven to 450 degrees. Pour the olive oil into a shallow 3-quart casserole or 9x13-inch baking dish. Add the potatoes, tomatoes, and leeks. Toss to coat the vegetables with the oil, then spread them out to cover the bottom of the pan. Sprinkle with the rosemary. Roast the vegetables, stirring occasionally, until just tender and lightly colored, 10 to 15 minutes. Add the stewed tomatoes, broth, wine, salt, and pepper and stir gently to mix. Reduce the oven temperature to 350 degrees and bake, uncovered, until the sauce is slightly reduced and the vegetables are tender, 25 to 30 minutes.

2. Meanwhile, cook the pasta in a large pot of boiling salted water until just al dente, about 10 minutes. Drain well. Stir the pasta into the sauce. Sprinkle with both cheeses.

3. Bake until the cheese is melted and bubbly, about 10 minutes longer.

◆ *PER SERVING: About 481 cals, 84 cals from fat, 9g total fat, 2g sat fat, 10mg chol, 440mg sodium, 80g total carbs, 1g fiber.*

Orrechiette with Broccoli Rabe and Beans

Makes 6 servings

The flowers, stems, and leaves—all edible—of the broccoli rabe are cooked together in this classic Tuscan pasta and garlicky bean dish. Orrechiette, or "little ears," is the traditional shape, but you can use any other short, fat pasta such as penne or ziti.

2 tablespoons extra-virgin olive oil
6 garlic cloves
1 cup defatted reduced-sodium chicken broth
1 cup dry white wine
2 cans (14 to 16 ounces each) cannellini
  or white beans, rinsed and drained, or 3 cups
  cooked cannellini or white beans
¾ teaspoon dried savory
¾ pound orrechiette
1 bunch broccoli rabe (about 1½ pounds),
  cut into rough 1-inch pieces
⅓ cup grated Parmesan cheese
Freshly ground black pepper to taste

1. In a large, preferably nonstick skillet, heat the oil and cook the garlic over medium-low heat for 1 minute. Stir in the broth, wine, beans, and savory. Simmer, uncovered, until slightly reduced, about 5 minutes.

2. Meanwhile, cook the pasta in a large pot of boiling salted water until almost al dente, about 9 minutes. Add the broccoli rabe and cook until the pasta is al dente and the broccoli rabe is crisp-tender, 2 to 4 minutes more. Drain well.

3. Toss the pasta and broccoli rabe with the sauce. Add the cheese and pepper to taste. Toss again and serve immediately.

◆ *PER SERVING: About 437 cals, 72 cals from fat, 8g total fat, 2g sat fat, 4mg chol, 161mg sodium, 66g total carbs, 9g fiber, 21g prot*

Whole-Wheat Fettuccine with Mushrooms

Makes 4 main-dish or 6 side-dish servings

This elegant pasta preparation, made with nutritious whole-wheat fettucine, makes a lovely first course, a delicious side dish, or a satisfying main course that needs only a salad and a basket of crusty French bread to accompany it. Nearly any mix of mushrooms will work.

1 cup defatted lower-sodium
   chicken broth
1 ounce dried mushrooms, such as
   morels or shiitake
2 tablespoons extra-virgin olive oil
¾ pound sliced fresh mushrooms,
   a mix of domestic and wild,
   such as porcini or shiitake
⅓ cup chopped shallots
2 garlic cloves, minced
1 tablespoon chopped fresh
   tarragon or 1 teaspoon dried

½ cup dry white wine, or
   additional chicken broth and
   1 tablespoon lemon juice
¼ cup Madeira or dry sherry
Salt and freshly ground pepper to
   taste
¾ pound whole-wheat fettuccine
   or other strand pasta
¼ cup reduced-fat or "light" sour
   cream

1. In a medium saucepan, bring the chicken broth to a boil. Remove the pan from the heat and add the dried mushrooms. Cover the pan and let stand until the mushrooms soften, about 15 minutes. Drain the mushrooms, reserving the liquid and allowing the sediment to settle. Slice the mushrooms.

2. In a large, preferably nonstick skillet, heat the oil and cook the fresh mushrooms, shallots, and garlic over medium-low heat, stirring often until the onion softens and the mushrooms have released their liquid, about 8 minutes. Stir in the tarragon and cook for 3 minutes, until most of the liquid evaporates. Add the dried mushrooms and the soaking liquid, leaving any sediment behind. Add the wine and Madeira. Simmer over medium-low heat until the sauce is slightly thickened, about 8 minutes. Season to taste with salt and pepper.

3. Meanwhile, cook the pasta in a large pot of boiling salted water until al dente, 8 to 10 minutes. Drain well. Toss the pasta with the hot sauce. Add the sour cream and toss again. Serve immediately.

◆ *PER MAIN-DISH SERVING: About 471 cals, 97 cals from fat, 11g total fat, 1g sat fat, 5mg chol, 40mg sodium, 76g total carbs, 3g fiber, 18g prot*

Penne with Sausage and Autumn Vegetables

Makes 6 servings

To get the most flavor from this recipe, use a really smoky sausage. The starch from the sweet potato and the beans helps to thicken this nicely herbed sauce so that it resembles a stew—perfect fare for an early autumn supper.

1 tablespoon olive oil
¼ pound reduced-fat or turkey kielbasa, thinly sliced
1 large onion, sliced
2 garlic cloves, minced
2 cans (14½ ounces each) stewed tomatoes
1½ cups vegetable broth
1 large sweet potato (about ½ pound),
  peeled and diced
1 can (1 pound) black beans, rinsed
  and drained, or 1¾ cups cooked black beans
1½ teaspoons dried rosemary
1 teaspoon dried thyme
1 pound whole-wheat or regular penne
1 zucchini (about ½ pound), diced
¼ cup grated Parmesan cheese, preferably imported
¼ cup chopped parsley, preferably flat leaf
Salt and freshly ground pepper to taste

1. In a large saucepan, heat the oil and cook the sausage over medium-high heat, stirring until golden. Use a slotted spoon to remove the sausage from the pan, leaving the pan drippings. Reduce the heat to medium-low, add the onion to the pan, and cook until the onion softens, about 5 minutes. Add the garlic and cook for 1 minute longer. Add the stewed tomatoes, broth, sweet potato, beans, rosemary, thyme, and the sausage. Cover the pan and simmer until the sweet potatoes are tender, 10 to 12 minutes.

2. Meanwhile, cook the pasta in a large pot of boiling salted water until nearly al dente, about 10 minutes. Drain well, then add the pasta to the sauce along with the zucchini. Simmer, covered, for 2 minutes. Stir in the cheese and parsley. Season to taste with salt and pepper, and serve immediately.

◆ *PER SERVING: About 499 cals, 79 cals from fat, 9g total fat, 1g sat fat, 3mg chol, 568mg sodium, 91g total carbs, 9g fiber, 21g prot*

Fusilli with Moroccan Lamb and Chickpeas

Makes 6 servings

Lamb and chickpeas contribute to this distinctive pasta dish reminiscent of a meal you might enjoy in Morocco. The fusilli adds a new twist. Baby eggplant are free of the bitterness that sometimes comes through in a large eggplant. If you can't find them, look for a small regular eggplant.

2 tablespoons olive oil
$\frac{3}{4}$ pound lean boneless lamb, cut into 1-inch cubes
2 baby eggplants (about 4 ounces each), unpeeled and cut into 1-inch cubes, or 1 small regular eggplant, peeled and cubed
1 large onion, chopped
2 garlic cloves, minced
$1\frac{1}{2}$ teaspoons ground cumin
$\frac{1}{2}$ teaspoon salt
$\frac{1}{4}$ teaspoon ground cinnamon

$\frac{1}{4}$ teaspoon cayenne pepper
$\frac{1}{4}$ teaspoon ground ginger
1 tablespoon grated orange rind
2 cans ($14\frac{1}{2}$ ounces each) stewed tomatoes
$\frac{1}{2}$ cup red wine or orange juice
1 can (10 ounces) chickpeas, rinsed and drained, or 1 cup cooked
$\frac{1}{4}$ cup sliced black olives, preferably Moroccan olives
1 pound fusilli
$\frac{1}{4}$ cup chopped parsley

1. In a large, preferably nonstick skillet, heat the oil and cook the lamb over medium-high heat, turning until browned on all sides, about 5 minutes. Reduce the heat to medium and add the eggplant, onion, and garlic. Cook, stirring often until the vegetables soften, about 5 minutes. Stir in the cumin, salt, cinnamon, cayenne, ginger, and orange rind. Then stir in the tomatoes and wine. Partially cover the pan and simmer until the sauce is slightly reduced and the lamb is quite tender, about 5 minutes. Uncover, add the chickpeas and olives. Simmer for 5 minutes. (The sauce can be made up to a day ahead to this point and refrigerated. Reheat to a simmer before continuing.)

2. Cook the fusilli in a large pot of boiling salted water until al dente, about 10 minutes. Drain well. Toss the sauce and the parsley with the pasta, and serve immediately.

◆ *PER SERVING: About 621 cals, 94 cals from fat, 10g total fat, 2g sat fat, 29mg chol, 1337mg sodium, 103g total carbs, 8g fiber, 25g prot*

Cold Sesame Noodles

Makes 6 servings

Soba are Japanese buckwheat noodles. You can find them in larger supermarkets and Asian grocery stores. They are worth seeking out for their earthy flavor but you can substitute conventional strand pasta, such as vermicelli or linguine. Reduced-fat peanut butter works well in this recipe because its slight sweetness nicely offsets the spicy garlic and ginger. If you have leftover cooked chicken or pork, you can shred about 1 cup and toss it in.

¼ cup sesame seeds

6 tablespoons smooth reduced-fat peanut butter

½ cup defatted lower-sodium chicken broth, plus ¼ cup

3 tablespoons rice wine vinegar

3 tablespoons reduced-sodium soy sauce

1½ tablespoons minced fresh ginger

1 teaspoon Thai hot pepper sauce

½ cup thinly sliced scallions, plus ¼ cup

¼ pound small snow peas

3 carrots

1 pound Japanese soba noodles or vermicelli or linguine

1 tablespoon sesame oil

1. In a small, dry skillet, toss the sesame seeds over medium heat until lightly colored and fragrant, about 2 minutes. Immediately remove from the pan and let cool.

2. In a food processor or blender, process the peanut butter, ½ cup of the broth, the vinegar, soy sauce, ginger, hot pepper sauce, and ½ cup of the scallions until well blended, about 30 seconds. Scrape down the sides of the workbowl once or twice during processing.

3. Remove the strings from the snow peas and cut each in half on the diagonal. Thinly slice the carrots. In a medium skillet, heat the remaining ¼ cup of broth, add the snow peas and carrots, and toss over medium-high heat, until just crisp-tender, about 2 minutes.

4. Cook the pasta in a large pot of boiling salted water until al dente, 6 to 8 minutes. Drain well, transfer to a large mixing bowl, and toss with the sesame oil. Add the sauce and vegetables. Toss to mix.

5. Serve at room temperature sprinkled with the remaining ¼ cup of scallions.

◆ *PER SERVING: About 498 cals, 128 cals from fat, 14g total fat, 2g sat fat, 0mg chol, 539mg sodium, 78g total carbs, 8g fiber, 15g prot*

Shrimp and Tofu Pad Thai

Makes 6 servings

The fish sauce known as nam pla is a potent anchovy-based condiment used in many authentic Thai recipes. Although shrimp and tofu are an especially delicious combination in this dish, you can also substitute chicken, pork, or even beef.

8 to 10 ounces Asian rice noodles
¼ cup bottled fish sauce
  (nam pla)
3 tablespoons tomato paste
1½ tablespoons sugar
1 tablespoon rice wine vinegar
1 tablespoon lime juice
1 tablespoon minced jalapeños,
  fresh or pickled, plus 2
  tablespoons
1 cup defatted lower-sodium
  chicken broth

2 tablespoons peanut oil
6 ounces extra-firm tofu, cut into
  ½-inch dice
¾ pound medium shrimp, peeled
  and deveined
1 cup thinly sliced scallions
2 cups bean sprouts
1 small head of romaine lettuce,
  shredded (about 6 cups)
½ cup chopped cilantro
⅓ cup chopped dry-roasted peanuts
2 small limes, cut into wedges

1. Cook the rice noodles in a large pot of boiling unsalted water for 3 minutes until swollen and tender. Drain well.

2. In a small bowl, whisk together the fish sauce, tomato paste, sugar, vinegar, lime juice, and 1 tablespoon jalapeño pepper. Whisk in the broth.

3. In a large, preferably nonstick skillet or wok, heat the oil and fry the tofu over high heat for 2 minutes, stirring carefully to keep it from breaking up too much. Remove the tofu with a slotted spoon. Add the shrimp to the same pan and stir-fry until the shrimp turn pink, 1 to 2 minutes. Add the sauce mixture and cook, stirring until it comes to a boil, about 1 minute.

4. Reduce the heat to medium, and add the drained rice noodles, tofu, scallions, and bean sprouts to the pan. Toss until the noodles are coated with sauce and heated through, 2 to 3 minutes.

5. Serve the pad thai on a bed of shredded romaine. Serve the cilantro, peanuts, and lime wedges in small bowls so your family can sprinkle them onto the pad thai.

◆*PER SERVING: About 276 cals, 110 cals from fat, 12g total fat, 2g sat fat, 44mg chol, 802mg sodium, 29g total carbs, 3g fiber, 16g prot*

Sizzling Pork and Black Bean Sauce

Makes 6 servings

Chinese black bean sauce is dark and rich, with preserved black beans, ginger, sesame, sherry, and garlic. It is the secret ingredient in this recipe and worth visiting an Asian market or a large supermarket to find. While you are there, pick up a package of the Asian rice noodles called mi-fun and you will have the basics for an authentic Chinese dish.

1 pound pork tenderloin	**1 tablespoon toasted sesame oil**
8 to 10 ounces Asian rice noodles	**1 tablespoon rice wine vinegar**
1 tablespoon peanut oil	**4 teaspoons sugar**
¾ teaspoon freshly ground pepper	**½ cup chopped cilantro**
⅓ cup bottled Chinese black bean sauce	**1 cup thinly sliced scallions**
2 tablespoons reduced-sodium soy sauce	**⅓ cup chopped dry-roasted peanuts**

1. Cut the pork into thin slices, then cut the slices into strips. Cook the noodles in a large pot of boiling unsalted water for 3 minutes until swollen. Drain well.

2. Heat the peanut oil in a large skillet or wok. Season the pork with pepper and stir-fry over medium-high heat until the meat is just cooked through, about 3 minutes. Reduce the heat to medium. Add the black bean sauce, soy sauce, sesame oil, vinegar, sugar, and 1¼ cups of water. Cook, stirring until the sugar dissolves, about 2 minutes.

3. Add the noodles to the sauce and stir until coated, about 2 minutes. Place the cilantro, scallions, and peanuts in bowls for sprinkling at the table and serve.

◆ *PER SERVING: About 296 cals, 103 cals from fat, 11g total fat, 2g sat fat, 54mg chol, 563mg sodium, 27g total carbs, 1g fiber, 20g prot*

ASIAN NOODLES

Pasta has always been a part of Asian cuisines. Now Asian-style noodles are becoming popular in our country, too. Here are some common ones to look for:

SOBA NOODLES are made from buckwheat flour. Soba are traditionally used in cold sesame noodle dishes. Don't overcook them or they will become soft and mushy. Whole-wheat or regular spaghetti and vermicelli are good substitutes.

RICE NOODLES or rice sticks, also called mi-fun, are made from rice flour and water. They cook quickly, keep their shape, and work well in soups and stir-fry dishes.

CHINESE NOODLES are often made from wheat flour with or without eggs. You will find them both dried and fresh, in a range of widths. Substitute regular noodles of similar size.

BEAN THREAD, CELLOPHANE, OR GLASS NOODLES, also called sai-fun, are made from mung bean starch and water. When cooked, they become slippery in texture. Use them in soups and stir-fries.

Hot-and-Sour Chicken Noodle Stir-Fry

Makes 6 servings

Sweet-and-sour chicken is a popular but high-fat Chinese restaurant dish. This very low-fat version combines the convenience of bottled sweet-and-sour sauce and canned pineapple with the freshness of crunchy vegetables that are packed with vitamin C.

¼ cup cornstarch

½ teaspoon pepper

¼ teaspoon salt

2 egg whites

1 pound skinless boneless chicken breasts, cut into ¾-inch chunks

¾ pound vermicelli or thin linguine

1½ tablespoons vegetable oil, plus ½ tablespoon

1 large onion, cut into 12 wedges

1 large red bell pepper, seeded and cut into 1-inch squares

3 cups broccoli florets

1 can (5 ounces) sliced water chestnuts, drained

1 large firm tomato, seeded and cut into rough 1-inch chunks

1 can (8 ounces) pineapple chunks in juice, undrained

1 cup bottled sweet-and-sour sauce

½ cup defatted lower-sodium chicken broth

3 tablespoons rice wine vinegar

1 tablespoon Asian garlic hot chili sauce

1. In a plastic bag, shake together the cornstarch, pepper, and salt. In a small bowl, whisk the egg whites until frothy. Dip the chicken into the egg white a few pieces at a time, then place them in the plastic bag and shake to coat.

2. When you are ready to stir-fry, cook the pasta in a large pot of boiling salted water until al dente, about 8 minutes. Drain well.

3. Meanwhile, in a large, preferably nonstick skillet or wok, heat 1½ tablespoons of the oil and stir-fry the chicken over medium-high heat until golden brown and crisp, about 5 minutes. Use a slotted spoon to remove the chicken from the pan. Add the remaining ½ tablespoon of oil to the wok and stir-fry the onion, bell pepper, and broccoli for 2 minutes. Add the water chestnuts, tomato, pineapple with juice, sweet-and-sour sauce, broth, vinegar, and chili sauce. Simmer for 2 minutes. Return the chicken to the pan and simmer until heated through, about 1 minute.

4. Turn the pasta onto a large platter or six plates. Ladle the sauce over the pasta.

◆ *PER SERVING: About 517 cals, 64 cals from fat, 7g total fat, 1g sat fat, 44mg chol, 361mg sodium, 84g total carbs, 5g fiber, 31g prot*

Simplified Sukiyaki

Makes 4 servings

This is a simple, quick version of a Japanese classic. It will be easier to slice the meat if you place it in the freezer for about an hour until it is partially frozen. Sukiyaki is delicious alongside a salad dressed with a light vinaigrette sparked with grated fresh ginger, and a basket of rice cakes. Mirin is sweetened sake. Dry sherry is a good substitute.

6 to 8 ounces Asian rice noodles

¾ pound boneless beef round

½ tablespoon vegetable oil, plus ½ tablespoon

1 red bell pepper, diced

1 cup thinly sliced scallions

¼ pound fresh shiitake mushrooms, thinly sliced

1½ cups defatted lower-sodium beef broth

¼ cup reduced-sodium soy sauce

¼ cup mirin or dry sherry

¼ cup rice wine vinegar

2 teaspoons sugar

1½ teaspoons toasted sesame oil

¼ cup chopped cilantro

1. Cook the noodles in a large pot of boiling unsalted water for 3 minutes until swollen. Drain well.

2. Cut the meat across the grain into thin slices, then cut the slices into ½-inch strips. Heat ½ tablespoon of the vegetable oil in a large skillet or wok, and stir-fry the meat over high heat for 2 minutes. Remove from the pan with a slotted spoon. Add the remaining ½ tablespoon of oil to the pan, reduce the heat to medium-high, and stir-fry the bell pepper, scallions, and mushrooms for 2 minutes. Return the meat to the pan along with the broth, soy sauce, mirin, vinegar, sugar, and sesame oil. Simmer for 5 minutes.

3. Toss the sauce with the noodles. Add the cilantro, toss again, and serve.

◆ *PER SERVING: About 354 cals, 117 cals from fat, 13g total fat, 3g sat fat, 82mg chol, 582mg sodium, 25g total carbs, 2g fiber, 31g prot*

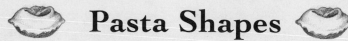

Pasta Shapes

Y ou can find hundreds of pasta shapes in any grocery store these days. It's fun to try new and whimsical shapes, but, if you don't have the one the recipe calls for, substitute a similar shape. Each pasta is interchangeable within its family.

NAME	TRANSLATION / DESCRIPTION	COOKING TIME FOR DRIED PASTA

THIN STRANDS

Best suited to light fresh tomato or broth-based sauces like Basic Marinara Sauce (page 205). Since these pastas are delicate when cooked, they can stick together if not well moistened. Thin strands are usually sold dried, but thicker ones are sometimes available fresh.

Capellini	"Fine hair."	2 to 5 minutes
Capelli d'angelo	"Angel hair."	2 to 5 minutes
Vermicelli	"Little worms"; a thin spaghetti.	5 to 6 minutes
Spaghettini	Similar to vermicelli in size.	6 to 7 minutes
Spaghetti	The thickest thin-strand pasta; works well with both light and sturdy sauces.	7 to 9 minutes
Linguine	Narrow oval ribbons; available in plain, spinach, and whole wheat.	7 to 9 minutes

THICK STRANDS

Well suited to sturdy tomato and meat sauces, such as Basic Bolognese Sauce (page 205), or cream sauces, such as the sauce used in Freshened Fettuccine Alfredo (page 209). Remains slightly chewy. Strands stay separate after cooking. Sauce does not need to have much liquid. Flat-strand pasta is sold fresh and flavored; also available dried.

Bucatini	Thick round spaghetti that is hollow in the center.	9 to 10 minutes
Perciatelli	Slightly thicker version of bucatini.	10 to 11 minutes
Fettuccine	Flat ribbon pasta available in both egg and spinach versions; sold fresh and dried.	8 to 10 minutes
Pappardelle	Wide, flat-strand pasta.	8 to 10 minutes
Fusilli	Long, corkscrew-shaped strand.	9 to 11 minutes
Malfaldi	¾-inch-wide flat ribbon with ruffled edges.	9 to 11 minutes
Lasagna	Very wide ribbon; may have ruffled edges.	10 to 13 minutes

TUBES

Remain sturdy and retain their shape when cooked. Good with hearty sauces and popular in baked dishes, such as Modern Macaroni and Cheddar (page 216). Usually sold dried.

Elbow macaroni or pipette	"Small pipe"; the most common macaroni shape.	8 to 10 minutes
Penne	"Quill" or "feather"; refers to the sharp, diagonal end cuts of the hollow tubes; penne rigate has a ribbed exterior; penne lisce is large; pennette is small.	10 to 13 minutes
Mostaccioli	"Little mustaches"; looks like penne.	10 to 13 minutes
Rigatoni	Similar to penne rigate, but slightly curved with vertical cut ends.	10 to 13 minutes
Ziti	"Bridegrooms"; narrower and often longer than penne; slightly curved; shaped like a big bucatini; cut into 2- or 3-inch lengths.	9 to 11 minutes

NAME	TRANSLATION / DESCRIPTION	COOKING TIME FOR DRIED PASTA

NOOKS AND CRANNIES

Short pasta shapes with curves and/or crevices to hold chunky vegetable or tomato sauces. Good served cold because they remain chewy and attractive. Described in recipes here as stubby or compact. Usually sold dried.

NAME	TRANSLATION / DESCRIPTION	COOKING TIME FOR DRIED PASTA
Rotini, short fusilli, or rotelle	Short, fat spirals.	10 to 14 minutes
Conchiglie	"Shells"; come in several sizes: small (for soup), medium (for salads), and jumbo (can be stuffed and baked).	8 to 15 minutes depending on size
Cavatelli	Similar to shells, but with a ruffled edge.	10 to 13 minutes
Farfalle	"Butterflies"; bow ties available in several sizes, including small for soup.	6 to 12 minutes depending on size
Orrechiette	"Little ears"; fat little disks that are folded.	10 to 12 minutes
Radiatore	"Radiators."	10 to 13 minutes
Ruote	"Wagon wheels."	10 to 13 minutes

FILLED

Filled pastas usually sold fresh or frozen; can be stuffed with cheese, meat, vegetables, or seafood.

NAME	TRANSLATION / DESCRIPTION	COOKING TIME FOR DRIED PASTA
Ravioli	Filled squares.	8 to 14 minutes depending on size
Tortellini	Resemble little hats; filled with cheese, chicken, or vegetables.	8 to 14 minutes depending on size
Manicotti or cannelloni	Large tubes usually cooked, stuffed, and baked.	10 to 16 minutes

MINIATURES

Tiny pasta shapes best suited to soups. Some mimic other grains, such as rice. Nearly always sold dried.

NAME	TRANSLATION / DESCRIPTION	COOKING TIME FOR DRIED PASTA
Pastina	Very tiny grains of pasta; a bit larger than couscous.	5 to 7 minutes
Tubettini	"Little tubes."	6 to 8 minutes
Ditalini	"Little thimbles"; larger tubettini.	8 to 10 minutes
Stellini	"Little stars."	5 to 7 minutes
Orzo or rosamarini	Rice-shaped pasta used like rice.	9 to 10 minutes
Alphabets	Usually used in soup.	7 to 10 minutes

NOODLES

Often made with egg pasta dough, but egg-free noodles are available. Vary from very fine strands (best suited to soups) to short ribbons more than an inch wide (used in casseroles). Can be flat or curly.

NAME	TRANSLATION / DESCRIPTION	COOKING TIME FOR DRIED PASTA
Soba	Used in cold noodle dishes.	6 to 8 minutes
Mi-fun	Rice noodles; used in soups and stir-fries.	3 minutes
Chinese noodles	Made from wheat flour with or without eggs.	5 to 7 minutes
Sai-fun	Made from mung bean starch and water.	Cover and let stand in boiling water for 5 minutes.

CHAPTER SEVEN

Rice and Other Grains

G rains are essential staples in our diet. Almost all grains, from the better-known wheat, oats, rice, corn, and rye to the exotic triticale and quinoa, are actually the fruit, or seed, of a grass plant. Because grains are seeds, designed to support new plant growth, they are loaded with several key nutrients, such as complex carbohydrates, B vitamins, and many essential minerals.

Foods made from whole or processed grain belong to the Bread, Cereal, Rice, and Pasta Group of the Food Guide Pyramid. All whole grains are naturally low in fat, but their fiber content differs greatly, depending on how—and how much—they were processed. For example, white rice, which is highly milled to remove its bran layer, has only a fraction of the fiber found in brown rice. But oats that are crushed or "rolled" retain most of their fiber.

In many cuisines around the world, grains form the centerpiece of the plate, while meat and other high-protein foods serve as mere adornment. The characteristic grain of a region often defines its cuisine. For Indian food, fragrant basmati rice comes to mind. What would Moroccan food be without couscous? Plan a Middle Eastern meal, and bulgur is invariably on the menu. Exotic grains are now so widely available that you could serve a different one every day and not run out of choices for well over a week.

The Dietary Guidelines and the Food Guide Pyramid emphasize the importance of grains. So, as you plan your menus, try selecting the grain of the meal first, instead of the meat, poultry, or fish. For example, you could serve rice on Monday and Thursday, couscous on Tuesday, and so on. Then flip through this chapter for menu ideas using that grain.

As shown in this chapter, grains combined with vegetables and a selection from the protein group make a nutritionally balanced main course. Side-dish grains served with vegetables and a portion of protein create a nutritionally balanced meal. Either way, a 1-cup portion of cooked grain (the equivalent of two Pyramid servings) should take up about half the space on your plate. Meat, chicken, or another form of protein should occupy no more than a quarter of the plate, a far cry from the meat-based meals we've been used to.

Grains go hand-in-hand with low-fat eating. You can make many grain dishes with very little fat—just enough to bring out the flavor when you cook onions or garlic. Some grain dishes that have only moderate amounts of fat even give the illusion of being extremely rich. Your first bite of Wild Mushroom and Herb Risotto (page 262) will introduce you to the natural creaminess of cooked grains such as short-grain rice.

The simplicity and versatility of grains allow you to become enormously creative. Make this chapter's recipes "by the book," or vary the grain to create an entirely new dish. The recipe for Barley "Risotto" with Clams and Tomatoes (page 259) is a dish in which the traditional grain, arborio rice, has been replaced by one that imparts similar creaminess but a different flavor.

Don't overlook grains as a delicious breakfast food. Your first thoughts might conjure up the familiar oatmeal, granola, and ready-to-eat cereals, but these are just the beginning. Try Spiced Pear and Coconut Breakfast Couscous (page 249), or top rice leftovers with chopped dried fruit or a warm fruit compote. Any leftover grain can become the next day's breakfast. Just warm it up with milk and add your favorite toppings.

Stock your kitchen with a bounty of grains. You can store white rice, couscous, pearl barley, degerminated cornmeal, and other processed grains almost indefinitely in your cupboard. The refrigerator or freezer is best for stone-ground cornmeal, brown rice, bulgur, and other whole grains because the oil in their bran becomes rancid more rapidly at warmer temperatures. Like any food, fresh is best, so check expiration dates on packages.

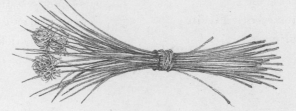

Honey-Orange Breakfast Oatmeal with Bananas

Makes 2 servings (about 3 cups)

Orange juice, a banana, and a touch of honey turn ordinary oatmeal into a refreshing and nutritious morning treat. A dusting of fresh nutmeg adds the final touch.

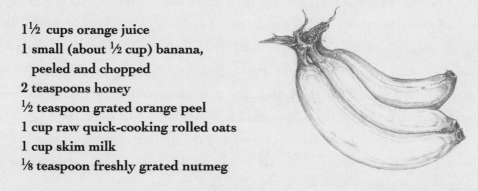

1½ cups orange juice
1 small (about ½ cup) banana,
  peeled and chopped
2 teaspoons honey
½ teaspoon grated orange peel
1 cup raw quick-cooking rolled oats
1 cup skim milk
⅛ teaspoon freshly grated nutmeg

1. In a medium saucepan, combine the juice, banana, honey, and orange peel and bring to a boil over high heat. Add the oats and cook over medium heat for 1 minute.

2. Remove from the heat, cover, and let stand until thickened, about 3 minutes. Spoon into bowls, pour the milk around the cereal, and dust with grated nutmeg.

◆ *PER SERVING: About 345 cals, 28 cals from fat, 3g total fat, 1g sat fat, 2mg chol, 67mg sodium, 69g total carbs, 1g fiber, 12g prot*

Fruited Barley and Rice Breakfast Bake

Makes 4 main-dish servings (6 side-dish servings)

This easy barley and brown rice casserole makes a tasty and fiber-rich addition to a festive brunch buffet. Mixed dried fruits come in packages that usually contain apples, apricots, pears, and prunes. This recipe takes a little while to cook so plan ahead.

¾ cup raw long-grain brown rice
½ cup raw pearl barley
1 cup chopped mixed dried fruits
½ cup orange juice

1 teaspoon grated orange peel
2 teaspoons butter
¾ teaspoon salt
1 cinnamon stick, broken in half

1. Preheat the oven to 350 degrees. In a 2-quart baking dish, combine the rice, barley, and dried fruits.

2. In a saucepan, combine the orange juice, orange peel, butter, salt, and cinnamon stick with 3 cups of water. Bring to a boil, stirring until the butter melts. Pour the liquid over the rice mixture, stir once with a fork, and cover the baking dish tightly with a sheet of foil.

3. Bake in the preheated oven for 60 to 70 minutes, until the rice and barley are tender and the liquid has been absorbed. (The recipe can be made ahead to this point and kept warm in a turned-off oven for about 30 minutes.)

4. Before serving, discard the cinnamon stick and fluff the casserole with a fork.

◆ *PER MAIN-DISH SERVING: About 334 cals, 31 cals from fat, 3g total fat, 1g sat fat, 5mg chol, 431mg sodium, 72g total carbs, 9g fiber, 6g prot*

Spiced Pear and Coconut Breakfast Couscous

Makes 4 servings (about 4 cups)

This sweetly spiced couscous offers a welcome change of pace for breakfast. You can make it the night before and pop it into the microwave to reheat for breakfast.

1 cup apple juice	¼ teaspoon ground cardamom
1 medium-large firm pear, cored and chopped	⅛ teaspoon grated nutmeg
1 tablespoon fresh lemon juice	1 cup raw couscous
½ teaspoon salt	3 tablespoons sweetened or unsweetened shredded coconut
¾ teaspoon ground cinnamon	2 cups skim milk, warmed

1. In a large saucepan, combine the apple juice, chopped pear, lemon juice, salt, cinnamon, cardamom, and nutmeg with ¾ cup water. Bring to a boil, reduce the heat to low, and cook, covered, until the pear becomes tender, about 5 minutes.

2. Add the couscous, stir once with a fork, and remove the pan from the heat. Let stand until the couscous softens and absorbs the liquid, about 5 minutes. (The couscous can be made a day ahead and reheated in the microwave.)

3. In a small skillet, toast the coconut over medium-low heat, stirring frequently, until pale golden, about 3 minutes.

4. Spoon the couscous into bowls, top with the coconut, and serve with warmed milk.

◆ *PER SERVING: About 299 cals, 21 cals from fat, 2g total fat, 2g sat fat, 2mg chol, 350mg sodium, 59g total carbs, 9g fiber, 11g prot*

Homemade Crunchy Granola

Makes 10 servings (about 5 cups)

You can make granola with different dried fruits—dried cherries and cranberries are particularly delicious—or other types of nuts, such as chopped pecans. This recipe has a lot less sugar and sodium than commercial low-fat granola.

Vegetable oil spray
2½ cups uncooked regular or quick-
   cooking rolled oats
½ cup preferably unsweetened flaked
   or shredded coconut
½ cup sliced natural unblanched almonds
¼ cup raw untoasted sunflower seeds
¼ cup honey
¼ cup molasses
½ teaspoon ground cinnamon
½ cup golden raisins
½ cup chopped pitted dates
1 teaspoon vanilla extract

1. Preheat the oven to 325 degrees. Spray a 10x15-inch jelly roll pan or two large 7x11-inch baking dishes with vegetable oil spray.

2. In a large bowl, combine the oats, coconut, almonds, and sunflower seeds. In a small bowl, blend the honey, molasses, and cinnamon with 3 tablespoons of hot water. Pour the liquid over the oat mixture and use your clean hands or two large spoons to combine the mixture until the dry ingredients are evenly coated with the honey-molasses mixture. Transfer to the prepared baking sheet, spreading out in an even layer.

3. Bake in the preheated oven, stirring thoroughly every 5 minutes, until the granola turns a rich, dark brown, 30 to 35 minutes. Watch carefully during the last few minutes to make sure it doesn't burn.

4. Remove from the oven, stir in the raisins, dates, and vanilla, and let cool completely. The granola will crisp as it cools.

5. Transfer to an airtight container and store at room temperature for up to 2 weeks.

◆ *PER SERVING: About 239 cals, 64 cals from fat, 7g total fat, 2g sat fat, 0mg chol, 5mg sodium, 41g total carbs, 2g fiber, 6g prot*

Turkish Bulgur with Chicken and Eggplant

Makes 4 main-dish servings

This aromatically spiced bulgur, chicken, and vegetable dish makes a quick, one-dish supper. Serve it with warm flatbreads and a cooling salad made with chopped tomatoes and cucumbers.

¾ pound skinless boneless chicken thighs, cut in rough 2- to 3-inch pieces

½ teaspoon salt, plus additional to taste

¼ teaspoon black pepper, plus additional to taste

2 teaspoons olive oil, plus 1 teaspoon

1 medium onion, chopped

1 red bell pepper, seeded and coarsely chopped

1 medium-small (about ¾ pound) eggplant, peeled and cut into 1-inch cubes

¾ teaspoon ground cumin

¾ teaspoon ground cinnamon

¼ teaspoon dried red pepper flakes

⅛ teaspoon ground cloves

1 cup defatted lower-sodium chicken broth, plus 1¼ cups

2 tablespoons tomato paste

1 cup uncooked bulgur

1. Sprinkle the chicken with salt and pepper. Heat 2 teaspoons of the oil in a large, preferably nonstick skillet or in a Dutch oven with a lid. Add the chicken and cook over medium-high heat until browned on both sides, about 5 minutes. Remove to a plate.

2. Add the remaining 1 teaspoon of oil to the pan. Add the onion, pepper, and eggplant and cook over medium heat, stirring frequently, until softened, about 6 minutes. Stir in the cumin, cinnamon, pepper flakes, cloves, 1 cup of the broth, and the tomato paste. Return the chicken to the pan, cover, and simmer over low heat until the chicken is no longer pink, 5 to 10 minutes.

3. Add the remaining 1¼ cups of broth, bring to a boil, and stir in the bulgur. Reduce the heat to low and cook, covered, for 5 minutes. Remove the pan from the heat and let it stand until the bulgur becomes tender and absorbs the liquid, about 15 minutes.

4. Rewarm over low heat if necessary and season to taste with salt and pepper before serving.

◆ *PER SERVING: About 383 cals, 118 cals from fat, 13g total fat, 3g sat fat, 76mg chol, 384mg sodium, 39g total carbs, 12g fiber, 29g prot*

Spinach and Mushroom Polenta "Lasagne"

Makes 4 main-dish servings

Here's a new twist on an old favorite that layers ricotta cheese and a spinach filling with cooked polenta instead of lasagna noodles. Like traditional lasagne, this casserole makes wonderful party fare because you can assemble it well ahead and then bake it just before the guests arrive. A big salad of radicchio and other mixed lettuces and a basket of Herbed Focaccia (page 118) make terrific accompaniments.

Olive or vegetable oil spray

3 cups defatted lower-sodium chicken or vegetable broth

1½ cups yellow cornmeal

½ teaspoon salt, plus additional to taste

2 teaspoons olive oil, preferably extra virgin

¾ pound fresh mixed wild or domestic mushrooms, cleaned and sliced

3 garlic cloves, finely chopped

2 tablespoons all-purpose flour

½ cup dry vermouth, white wine, or nonalcoholic wine

1½ cups low-fat (1 percent) milk

1 package (10 ounces) frozen chopped spinach, thawed and squeezed dry

½ cup slivered dry-pack sun-dried tomatoes

1 teaspoon dried oregano

¼ teaspoon cayenne pepper

⅛ teaspoon grated nutmeg

1 cup part-skim ricotta cheese

¾ cup shredded part-skim mozzarella cheese

1. Lightly coat a 7x11-inch baking dish with olive or vegetable oil spray.

2. In a large, heavy saucepan, bring the broth to a boil over high heat. In a mixing bowl, whisk the cornmeal and ½ teaspoon salt into 2 cups of water. Whisk the cornmeal mixture into the simmering broth, reduce the heat to medium, and cook, stirring almost constantly with a wooden spoon, until the polenta has thickened to about the consistency of mashed potatoes and begins to pull away from the sides of the pan, about 10 minutes. Scrape into the prepared pan and smooth the top. Place the dish in the freezer for 20 minutes or refrigerate for at least 30 minutes, or until cold and firm enough to slice.

3. Heat the oil in a large, preferably nonstick skillet. Add the mushrooms and garlic and cook over medium-high heat, stirring frequently, until the mushrooms soften, about 5 minutes. Sprinkle with the flour and cook, stirring, for 1 minute. Stir in the vermouth and cook, stirring, until the mixture is very thick, about 2 minutes. Add the milk and cook, stirring, until the sauce becomes smooth and thickened, about 3 minutes. Stir in the spinach, sun-dried tomatoes, oregano, cayenne, and nutmeg and season with salt to taste.

4. Preheat the oven to 350 degrees.

5. Invert the cold polenta onto a work surface. Using a long knife, cut through the polenta cake horizontally to make two sheets of polenta. (It doesn't matter if they're not in one piece or completely even.)

6. To assemble, place one sheet of polenta back in the bottom of the baking dish. Spread evenly with the ricotta and then with the spinach filling. Place the second layer of polenta over the spinach filling and sprinkle with the shredded mozzarella. (The recipe can be made 1 day ahead to this point and refrigerated. Return to room temperature before baking.)

7. Place the baking dish in the center of the preheated oven and bake, uncovered, until the cheese melts, the top is golden brown, and the edges brown, 35 to 40 minutes.

8. Cut into squares to serve.

◆ *PER SERVING: About 507 cals, 134 cals from fat, 15g total fat, 6g sat fat, 35mg chol, 726mg sodium, 62g total carbs, 3g fiber, 27g prot*

ABOUT POLENTA

Polenta is the Italian version of cornmeal mush. It can be made from special coarse-ground cornmeal (called polenta meal) sold in specialty food stores, from "instant" (precooked) polenta, or from regular yellow cornmeal. Yellow cornmeal is readily available in supermarkets, cooks faster than coarse polenta meal, and has a better texture and flavor than fine-grained instant polenta.

To cook polenta, use one part cornmeal to three parts liquid. To prevent lumping, stir the raw cornmeal into about half of the liquid before adding it slowly to the remaining boiling liquid in a heavy-bottomed saucepan. Cook the polenta until the cornmeal loses its raw taste, about 10 to 15 minutes. To make creamy, soft polenta, use a bit more liquid; for firm polenta that can be shaped, use a little less liquid. Store leftover polenta in the refrigerator. Reheat in a microwave oven.

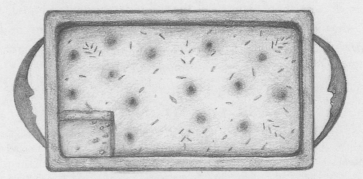

Cajun "Dirty" Rice

Makes 4 main-dish servings (8 side-dish servings)

Though its name is not glamorous, this delectable down-home rice dish presents Cajun country food at its best. It makes a great main dish served with stewed tomatoes and a big green salad, or a flavorful accompaniment to roast chicken or turkey. In Louisiana, they pass a bottle of liquid hot pepper sauce at the table for an additional dose of heat.

¼ **pound chicken gizzards, rinsed**
½ **pound chicken livers, rinsed**
1 **tablespoon vegetable oil**
1 **onion, chopped**
3 **garlic cloves, finely chopped**
2 **cups raw long-grain white rice**

4 **cups defatted lower-sodium**
   chicken broth
½ **teaspoon salt**
½ **teaspoon black pepper**
¼ **teaspoon cayenne pepper**
1 **cup thinly sliced scallions**

1. Pulse the gizzards in the workbowl of a food processor until chopped. Transfer to a plate and pick through and discard the large pieces of tough membrane. Or, first trim off the tough membrane of the gizzards and then finely chop them with a large knife. Pulse the livers in the food processor until chopped, or chop them by hand and set aside.

2. Heat the oil in a large, preferably nonstick saucepan with a lid or in a Dutch oven. Add the onion and the chopped gizzards and cook over medium heat, stirring almost constantly, until the meat begins to brown, about 4 minutes. Add the chicken livers and the garlic and cook, stirring, until browned, about 2 minutes. Add the rice and stir until coated with oil. Add the broth, salt, pepper, and cayenne. Bring to a boil, reduce the heat to low, and cook, covered, until the rice becomes tender and absorbs the liquid, 18 to 20 minutes.

3. Transfer the rice to a serving bowl, sprinkle with the scallions, and serve.

◆ *PER MAIN-DISH SERVING: About 492 cals, 67 cals from fat, 7g total fat, 1g sat fat, 254mg chol, 367mg sodium, 81g total carbs, 2g fiber, 23g prot*

LIVER—LOVE IT OR LEAVE IT

The human race seems to be divided into liver lovers and liver haters. In recent years, many people have avoided liver because of reports of a poor nutritional profile. But, although liver is relatively high in cholesterol, it is extremely low in both saturated and total fat, so that it may have little effect on blood cholesterol. Liver also contains many nutrients, such as B vitamins, folic acid, vitamin D, iron, and zinc. Some people avoid liver because they are concerned that it may contain harmful substances, such as heavy metals, ingested by the animal from which the liver came. But any potential toxins would appear in such minute amounts that the health risk would be insignificant.

Garlic-Lemon Rice with Shrimp and Snow Peas

Makes 4 main-dish servings

Not only does this garlicky rice and shrimp dish taste good, it's also a quick-and-easy meal in a single pot. And, if you add a loaf of crusty French bread and a tomato and watercress salad, you've created a meal special enough for company.

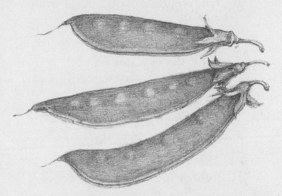

4 teaspoons olive oil, preferably extra virgin
1 small red bell pepper, seeded and
    coarsely chopped
5 garlic cloves, finely chopped
1¼ cups raw long-grain white rice
2 cups fish stock or bottled clam juice
½ cup dry white wine or white grape juice
¼ teaspoon dried red pepper flakes
1 pound (about 25 to 30) shelled and
    deveined medium shrimp
¼ pound (about 1 cup) snow peas, stems
    and strings removed
3 tablespoons fresh lemon juice
2 teaspoons grated lemon peel
Salt to taste
Freshly ground black pepper to taste

1. Heat the oil in a very large, preferably nonstick saucepan with a lid or in a Dutch oven. Add the red pepper and cook over medium heat, stirring frequently, until it begins to soften, about 2 minutes. Add the garlic and rice and cook, stirring, until the rice is coated with oil, about 2 minutes. Add the fish stock, wine, and red pepper flakes. Bring to a boil, reduce the heat to low, and cook covered for 15 minutes, until the rice is almost tender.

2. Add the shrimp, snow peas, lemon juice, and lemon peel and stir gently to distribute evenly. Cover and continue to cook until the rice is tender and the shrimp turn pink, 5 to 10 minutes. Season with salt and pepper to taste. (If using bottled clam juice, you may not need the salt.)

◆ *PER SERVING: About 433 cals, 65 cals from fat, 7g total fat, 1g sat fat, 176mg chol, 255mg sodium, 54g total carbs, 2g fiber, 31g prot*

Spoon Bread, Garlic Greens, and Smoked Ham

Makes 4 main-dish servings

The pleasing, sour tang of buttermilk adds a distinctive flavor to this southern-style baked cornmeal pudding. Curried Waldorf Salad (page 104) or Shredded Carrot, Jicama, and Currant Slaw (page 96), and crisp bread sticks would round out this supper beautifully.

Vegetable oil spray
1 pound young collard, mustard, or
　turnip greens, or Swiss chard, or
　1 package (10 ounces) frozen
　greens, thawed and drained
1 tablespoon butter
½ cup (2 ounces) diced lean
　smoked ham
3 garlic cloves, finely chopped

1 cup white or yellow cornmeal
½ teaspoon salt
1 cup low-fat or nonfat buttermilk
4 tablespoons grated Parmesan
　cheese
½ teaspoon liquid hot pepper
　sauce
2 whole eggs, separated
2 egg whites

1. Preheat the oven to 350 degrees. Lightly coat a 2-quart soufflé dish with vegetable oil spray.

2. If using fresh greens, wash them well. Discard the tough stems. In a large pot of boiling water, cook the greens until just tender, 5 to 7 minutes. Drain thoroughly, pressing out as much liquid as possible. Coarsely chop the greens.

3. Melt the butter in a large skillet. Add the ham, garlic, and greens and cook over medium heat until the garlic softens, 3 to 4 minutes. Spread the mixture in the bottom of the prepared dish.

4. In a heavy, medium-sized saucepan, bring 2 cups of water to a boil. Gradually whisk in the cornmeal and add the salt. Cook over medium heat, whisking almost constantly, until the mixture is very thick, begins to form a ball, and pulls away from the sides of the pan, about 5 minutes. Remove from the heat and whisk in the buttermilk, cheese, hot pepper sauce, and egg yolks.

5. Using an electric mixer, beat the 4 egg whites until stiff but not dry. Stir one third of the whites into the cornmeal mixture to lighten it, then fold in the remaining whites.

6. Spoon the batter over the greens and bake until puffed and lightly browned on top, 45 to 50 minutes. The spoon bread should be soft in the center and crusty around the edges.

7. Serve immediately.

◆ *PER SERVING: About 300 cals, 81 cals from fat, 9g total fat, 4g sat fat, 129mg chol, 707mg sodium, 39g total carbs, 6g fiber, 17g prot*

Herbed Broccoli and Rice Frittata

Makes 4 main-dish servings

You can use leftover broccoli and brown rice in this appetizing, herb-flecked frittata. Add a spinach salad and some whole-wheat rolls for a simply delicious Sunday supper.

2 teaspoons olive oil, preferably
  extra virgin
1 cup thinly sliced scallions,
  including green tops
1 large garlic clove, finely chopped
2 cups cooked brown rice
  (see note)
1 package (10 ounces) frozen
  chopped broccoli, thawed and
  drained, or 1½ cups chopped
  cooked broccoli

4 eggs (see note)
4 egg whites
½ cup part-skim ricotta cheese
1 teaspoon dried marjoram
½ teaspoon salt
¼ teaspoon cayenne pepper
3 tablespoons grated part-skim
  mozzarella cheese

1. Heat the oil in a large (10- or 11-inch) oven-proof skillet. Add the scallions and garlic and cook over medium heat, stirring, for 2 minutes. Add the rice and broccoli and cook, stirring, until heated through, about 2 minutes.

2. Whisk the eggs and egg whites with the ricotta cheese, marjoram, salt, and cayenne until well blended. Pour the egg mixture over the rice mixture in the pan, stir gently to combine, and cover. Cook over low heat until the eggs are almost set, 7 to 10 minutes.

3. Preheat the broiler.

4. Sprinkle the frittata with the mozzarella. Place under the broiler, about 5 inches from the heat source, and broil until the cheese melts and the top of the frittata is flecked golden brown, about 2 minutes. Watch carefully to prevent burning.

5. Cut into wedges to serve.

◆ *PER SERVING: About 298 cals, 104 cals from fat, 12g total fat, 4g sat fat, 225mg chol, 467mg sodium, 29g total carbs, 4g fiber, 19g prot*

Note: If you don't have leftover rice, cook ½ cup raw brown rice in 1¼ cups of lightly salted water until tender, about 45 minutes, or make 2 cups "instant" brown rice following package directions. You can substitute 1½ cups of liquid egg substitute for the fresh eggs.

Baked Grits Cakes with Shiitake Gravy

Makes 4 main-dish servings

For this dish, cooked hominy grits are seasoned with scallions, baked into a crusty cake, and topped with a delicious Madeira-spiked wild mushroom gravy.

Olive or vegetable oil spray

2 cups defatted lower-sodium chicken or vegetable broth, plus 1½ cups

1¼ cups quick-cooking grits (not instant)

½ teaspoon salt, plus additional to taste

1 cup thinly sliced scallions

¼ teaspoon black pepper

2 tablespoons grated Parmesan cheese, preferably imported

1½ tablespoons olive oil, preferably extra virgin

1½ pounds shiitake or other fresh mushrooms, wiped clean and thickly sliced

3 shallots, chopped

3 garlic cloves, finely chopped

4 teaspoons all-purpose flour

½ cup Madeira or dry sherry

1 tablespoon chopped fresh tarragon or 1 teaspoon dried

½ teaspoon cayenne pepper

3 tablespoons chopped fresh parsley, preferably flat leaf, plus 2 tablespoons

1. Preheat the oven to 425 degrees. Lightly coat a 9x9-inch baking dish with oil spray.

2. In a large, heavy saucepan, bring the 2 cups of broth and 2 cups of water to a boil over high heat. Gradually whisk in the grits, add the salt, and cook, covered, over low heat for 5 minutes. Uncover, and continue to cook, whisking almost constantly, until the grits are very thick, about 3 more minutes. Whisk in the scallions and pepper. Scrape the grits into the prepared baking dish, smooth the top, and sprinkle with the cheese. (The recipe can be prepared to this point several hours ahead and held at room temperature or refrigerated. Return to room temperature before baking.)

3. Bake the grits uncovered in the preheated oven until the top turns pale golden and the edges are browned and begin to pull away from the sides of the pan, 15 to 20 minutes. (The grits can be kept warm in a turned-off oven, loosely covered, for about 30 minutes.)

4. To make the gravy, heat the oil in a large, preferably nonstick saucepan. Add the mushrooms, shallots, and garlic and cook over medium-high heat, stirring frequently, until the mushrooms soften, about 5 minutes. Sprinkle with the flour and cook, stirring, for 1 minute. Stir in the Madeira and boil over high heat until most of the wine evaporates, about 2 minutes. Stir in the remaining 1½ cups of broth, add the tarragon, and bring to a boil. Cook, stirring, until the gravy is somewhat reduced and thickened, 3 to 4 minutes. Season with the cayenne, add salt to taste, and stir in the 3 tablespoons of parsley.

5. Cut the grits cake into eight pieces. Serve two pieces on each dinner plate, spoon on the mushroom gravy, and sprinkle with the remaining parsley.

◆ *PER SERVING: About 361 cals, 94 cals from fat, 10g total fat, 1g sat fat, 2mg chol, 395mg sodium, 50g total carbs, 0g fiber, 14g prot*

Barley "Risotto" with Clams and Tomatoes

Makes 4 main-dish servings

Risotto means rice in Italian, but creative chefs are breaking all the rules by applying the risotto cooking technique to a variety of other grains. And why not? The results are absolutely delicious. Here is a risotto using barley, combined with chopped tomatoes, basil, and black olives. Cooked greens flavored with garlic and warm Italian rolls would be perfect partners.

20 small hard-shell clams, scrubbed

1 bay leaf, broken in half

4 teaspoons extra-virgin olive oil

1 cup uncooked pearl barley

3 garlic cloves, finely chopped

¾ cup dry white wine

3½ cups defatted lower-sodium chicken broth

½ teaspoon salt, plus additional to taste

¼ teaspoon dried red pepper flakes

1½ cups chopped fresh plum tomatoes or 1 can (15 ounces) diced tomatoes, drained

½ cup sliced imported black olives, such as kalamata

3 tablespoons shredded fresh basil, plus 1 tablespoon

2 tablespoons fresh lemon juice

1 teaspoon grated lemon peel

1. In a large pot, combine the clams and bay leaf with 2 cups of water. Cover and bring to a boil over high heat. Reduce the heat to medium and cook the clams until they open, about 3 minutes. Remove the clams still in their shells with a slotted spoon and reserve. Carefully pour 1½ cups of the clam broth into a glass measuring cup, leaving behind any mud or grit. Reserve the broth, and place the broken bay leaf in it.

2. Heat the oil in a large, heavy saucepan with a lid or in a Dutch oven. Add the barley and garlic and cook over medium heat, stirring constantly, until the garlic is fragrant and the barley is coated with oil, about 1 minute. Add the wine and cook over high heat until most of the liquid evaporates, 1 to 2 minutes. Add the chicken broth, salt, and pepper flakes. Cover the pan, reduce the heat to low, and cook for about 40 minutes until the barley

continued

is tender and has absorbed most of the liquid. Every 10 minutes, stir the barley vigorously to release the starch and make a creamy sauce.

3. Discard the bay leaf halves and add the reserved 1½ cups of clam broth to the pot. Stir in the tomatoes, olives, 3 tablespoons of basil, lemon juice, and lemon peel. Arrange the cooked clams in their shells over the barley. Cover and cook until the clams are heated through, about 5 minutes. The barley should be tender, swollen, and swimming in thickened liquid. Adjust the amount of liquid if necessary and taste, adding salt if necessary.

4. Ladle into shallow soup bowls, sprinkle with the remaining basil, and serve.

◆ *PER SERVING: About 355 cals, 94 cals from fat, 10g total fat, 1g sat fat, 16mg chol, 618mg sodium, 48g total carbs, 9g fiber, 15g prot*

Fennel and Prosciutto Risotto

Makes 4 main-dish servings

Fennel lends its sprightly anise flavor to this elegant iron- and vitamin C–rich risotto. Serve it with a salad of radicchio and light lettuces, along with a loaf of seeded Italian bread to create a sophisticated yet lower-fat supper.

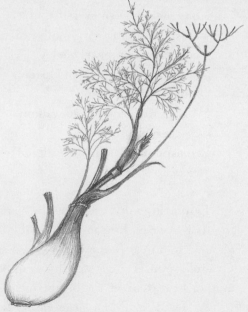

7 cups defatted lower-sodium chicken broth
1 cup dry white wine or nonalcoholic wine
½ teaspoon salt, plus additional to taste
2 teaspoons extra-virgin olive oil
1 medium onion, chopped
1 small fennel bulb, thinly sliced
  (about 2 cups)
2 cups raw arborio or other medium-
  or short-grain white rice
¾ cup (3 ounces) diced prosciutto
⅓ cup grated imported Parmesan cheese
2 tablespoons Pernod or other anise-flavored
  liqueur (optional)
Freshly ground black pepper to taste
½ cup chopped flat-leaf parsley

1. In a saucepan, combine the broth, wine, and salt. Set aside over low heat to warm.

2. Heat the oil in a large, heavy saucepan. Add the onion and fennel and cook over medium heat, stirring frequently, until the vegetables begin to soften and brown, about 5 minutes. Add the rice and cook, stirring, until the rice grains are coated with oil and slightly translucent, about 3 minutes.

3. Add all but 1 cup of the broth and wine mixture. Simmer uncovered, stirring every 4 to 5 minutes, until the rice is swollen, almost tender (yet still firm to the bite), and creamy, about 18 minutes total. Stir in the remaining cup of broth and add the prosciutto, cheese, and Pernod, if desired. Season with pepper and salt to taste.

4. Serve in shallow soup bowls and sprinkle with the parsley.

◆ *PER SERVING: About 542 cals, 65 cals from fat, 7g total fat, 2g sat fat, 19mg chol, 774mg sodium, 89g total carbs, 1g fiber, 19g prot*

ABOUT RISOTTO

When Italian risotto—rice cooked in a simmering liquid—is made correctly, the rice is tender, with just a hint of chewiness in the center. The flavorful, creamy liquid should have a consistency somewhere between a soup and a pilaf. Cooks usually make risotto with broth, wine, and Parmesan cheese. Beyond those basics, you can use your imagination to flavor your risotto with an assortment of ingredients, from asparagus to zucchini.

Arborio rice is best for making risotto. It is a short, roundish, pearl-centered rice grain that absorbs liquids well. It contains a lot of starch, which is released as you stir the risotto, producing a creamy sauce.

To make risotto, cook the rice in butter or olive oil to seal the grains and allow for slow absorption of the liquids you add later. The usual risotto proportions are about 3½ cups of liquid to 1 cup of rice. Risotto recipes that use less fat, including those in this book, can absorb up to 1 cup more liquid.

Most risotto recipes advise adding hot liquid to the rice a little at a time while stirring constantly. But you can achieve the same results by adding most of the liquid at the beginning of the cooking process, and then stirring vigorously every few minutes to release the starch in the rice. This method frees your hands so that you can do other things while the risotto is cooking.

Wild Mushroom and Herb Risotto

Makes 4 servings

The woodsy flavor and aroma of wild mushrooms—both dried and fresh—permeate this herb-flecked risotto. The Parmesan cheese in this dish is a source of calcium. Adding most of the liquid at the beginning of the cooking time, and then just stirring periodically, results in a creamy risotto that is equal to the traditional recipe that calls for constant stirring.

1 ounce dried wild mushrooms, any type

7 cups vegetable broth and/or defatted lower-sodium chicken broth

1½ cups dry white wine or water

2 teaspoons extra-virgin olive oil

½ pound fresh shiitake or other wild mushrooms, sliced

3 tablespoons chopped shallots

4 garlic cloves, finely chopped

2 cups raw arborio or other medium- or short-grain white rice

½ cup chopped flat-leaf parsley

2 tablespoons chopped fresh tarragon or 2 teaspoons dried

½ teaspoon black pepper

Salt to taste

½ cup grated Parmesan cheese

1. In a small bowl, pour 1 cup boiling water over the dried mushrooms and set aside to steep for 30 minutes. Remove the mushrooms with a slotted spoon, reserving the liquid, chop them, and set aside. Strain the soaking liquid through a coffee filter or several layers of cheesecloth and combine it with the broth and wine or water in a large saucepan. Set aside over low heat to warm.

2. In a large, heavy saucepan, heat the oil. Add the sliced fresh mushrooms and shallots and cook over medium heat until somewhat softened, about 4 minutes. Add the garlic and rice and cook, stirring, until the rice grains are coated with oil and slightly translucent, about 3 minutes.

3. Add the chopped dried mushrooms and all but 1 cup of the broth-wine mixture. Simmer, uncovered, stirring every 4 to 5 minutes, until the rice is almost tender (yet still firm to the bite) and creamy, about 18 minutes total. Stir in the remaining broth and the parsley, tarragon, and pepper. Season with salt to taste.

4. Serve in shallow soup bowls and sprinkle with the Parmesan cheese.

◆ *PER SERVING: About 539 cals, 82 cals from fat, 9g total fat, 3g sat fat, 10mg chol, 360mg sodium, 93g total carbs, 1g fiber, 19g prot*

Cuban-Style Saffron Rice with Smoked Ham and Peas

Makes 4 main-dish servings (6 generous side-dish servings)

There are many rice dishes in Cuban cuisine, and this saffron-flavored one typically reflects the island's Spanish heritage. Try serving Chicory, Arugula, and Orange Salad Siciliana (page 103) as an accompaniment.

1 tablespoon olive oil, preferably extra virgin
1 onion, chopped
1 small green bell pepper, seeded and chopped
3 garlic cloves, finely chopped
¾ cup (3 ounces) diced lean smoked ham
1 teaspoon ground cumin
½ teaspoon saffron threads or powdered turmeric
½ cup dry sherry
1½ cups raw long-grain white rice

3 cups defatted lower-sodium chicken broth
2 cups chopped fresh tomatoes or 1 can (15 ounces) diced tomatoes, drained
1 cup frozen green peas
2 tablespoons lime juice
Salt to taste
Freshly ground black pepper to taste
½ cup sliced pimiento-stuffed green olives

1. Heat the oil in a large, preferably nonstick saucepan with a lid. Add the onion and green pepper and cook over medium heat, stirring frequently, until the vegetables begin to soften, about 4 minutes. Add the garlic, ham, cumin, and saffron and cook, stirring, for 1 minute. Add the sherry and cook over high heat, uncovered, until most of the liquid evaporates, about 2 minutes.

2. Add the rice and cook, stirring, until the grains are coated with oil, about 1 minute. Add the broth, bring to a boil, cover, and cook over low heat for 15 minutes, until most of the liquid is absorbed.

3. Stir in the tomatoes and peas and continue to cook until the rice and peas are tender, about 5 minutes. Stir in the lime juice and season with salt and pepper to taste. Sprinkle with the olives before serving.

◆ *PER MAIN-DISH SERVING: About 463 cals, 72 cals from fat, 8g total fat, 1g sat fat, 12mg chol, 952mg sodium, 76g total carbs, 5g fiber, 15g prot*

SAFFRON LORE

Saffron, with its distinctive, pungent flavor and beautiful orange color, is an essential ingredient in Spanish paella and other rice dishes. It comes from the yellow-orange stigmas inside the petals of a small purple crocus. Known as the world's most expensive spice, saffron must be hand picked. It takes 14,000 tiny threads to make just 1 ounce. It is sold as whole threads or in powdered form, but powdered saffron can be easily adulterated and loses its flavor faster than do saffron threads. Keep saffron in a tightly covered jar in a dark place. Crush the threads just before using. Never use more saffron than the amount called for; in large quantities, saffron imparts a bitter, medicinal taste.

Classic Moroccan Chicken and Vegetable Couscous

Makes 8 main-dish servings

This is an updated version of the traditional North African dish. Heap some hot, cooked couscous in the center of a platter and spoon the savory meat, vegetable, and dried fruit stew over it to create some festive and exotic dinner-party fare. Pass the fiery sauce known as harissa or Moroccan Hot Pepper Sauce (recipe follows) separately.

2 tablespoons extra-virgin olive oil

1¾ pounds boneless chicken thighs or breasts, cut in rough 2-inch cubes

¾ teaspoon salt, plus additional to taste, plus 1½ teaspoons

½ teaspoon cayenne pepper

1 large onion, chopped

4 garlic cloves, finely chopped

2 teaspoons ground cumin

1 teaspoon curry powder

6 cups defatted lower-sodium chicken broth

2 cinnamon sticks, broken in half

1 pound (about 8) slender carrots, peeled and cut in 2-inch lengths

¾ pound white turnips, peeled and cut in 2-inch chunks

1 can (19 ounces) chickpeas, rinsed and drained, or 2 cups cooked chickpeas

1 slender zucchini, cut in 1-inch slices

1 red bell pepper, seeded and coarsely chopped

1½ cups pitted prunes

1 cup golden raisins

3 cups raw couscous

⅓ cup commercial harissa or 1 cup Moroccan Hot Pepper Sauce

1. Heat the oil in a very large, preferably nonstick skillet with a lid or in a Dutch oven. Season the chicken with the ¾ teaspoon of salt and the cayenne and cook over medium heat until lightly browned on all sides, about 5 minutes. Remove to a plate, leaving the drippings in the pan.

2. Add the onion and cook, stirring frequently, until it begins to soften, about 4 minutes. Add the garlic, cumin, and curry powder and cook, stirring, for 1 minute. Add the broth, cinnamon sticks, carrots, and turnips. Bring to a boil, reduce the heat to medium-low, and cook, covered, for 10 minutes to partially cook the vegetables.

3. Add the chickpeas, zucchini, red pepper, prunes, and raisins. Return the chicken to the stew and simmer uncovered over medium heat until the vegetables are tender and the chicken no longer looks pink in the center, about 20 minutes. Taste for seasoning and add more salt if necessary. (The recipe can be made several hours ahead to this point and refrigerated. Reheat gently before serving.)

4. For the couscous, bring 4½ cups of water to a boil in a large saucepan. Add the 1½ teaspoons of salt and stir in the uncooked couscous. Remove from the heat, cover, and let stand until the couscous is tender and the liquid is absorbed, 5 to 6 minutes.

5. Spoon out ½ cup of the stew liquid and blend it with the harissa.

6. Mound the cooked couscous in the center of a large, rimmed platter or on individual rimmed plates or shallow soup bowls. Spoon the chicken and vegetables around the outside of the couscous and ladle the broth over them. Pass additional hot sauce at the table.

◆ *PER SERVING: About 758 cals, 142 cals from fat, 16g total fat, 3g sat fat, 88mg chol, 1045mg sodium, 114g total carbs, 20g fiber, 42g prot*

MOROCCAN HOT PEPPER SAUCE
Makes about 1 cup (8 servings)

You can buy jars of harissa, the North African hot pepper paste, in some specialty food stores. If you can't find it, try this recipe. This sauce is seriously spicy, so warn your guests to use It sparingly.

3 tablespoons dried red pepper flakes	1¼ teaspoons ground cumin	3 garlic cloves, minced
1¼ teaspoons ground coriander seed	¾ teaspoon salt	½ cup defatted lower-sodium chicken broth or stew liquid (see recipe above)
	¼ cup boiling water	
	5 teaspoons olive oil	

1. In a small bowl, combine the red pepper flakes, coriander, cumin, and salt. Pour boiling water over the mixture and stir to combine. Mix in the olive oil and garlic. Set the mixture aside at room temperature to steep for 1 hour.

2. Whisk in the broth and serve. (The recipe can be made up to 3 days ahead and refrigerated. Return to room temperature before using.)

Per serving: About 37 cals, 30 cals from fat, 3g total fat, 0g sat fat, 0mg chol, 206mg sodium, 2g total carbs, 0g fiber, 1g prot

COUSCOUS CONFUSION

Couscous is not really a grain but a form of pasta made by mixing semolina flour with salted water to make tiny pellets. It originated in North Africa and has become increasingly popular here.

You can find quick-cooking couscous in the rice section of your supermarket. It reconstitutes in about 5 minutes when soaked in hot liquid.

Couscous is also the name of a Moroccan dish made by steaming couscous pellets in a special pot called a couscousière and serving them with a soupy stew made with vegetables, chicken, and/or fish.

Tunisian Couscous Pilaf with Chickpeas, Almonds, and Dates

Makes 4 main-dish servings (about 8 side-dish servings)

This couscous and chickpea pilaf, fragrant with the spices of Tunisia, stands on its own as a meatless main course, accompanied by a tomato and cucumber salad and a basket of warm flatbread. It also serves as an aromatic side dish for grilled meat or chicken.

2 tablespoons olive oil, preferably
　　extra virgin
1 onion, chopped
3 garlic cloves, finely chopped
1 teaspoon ground cumin
1 teaspoon paprika
½ teaspoon ground cinnamon
½ teaspoon ground coriander seed
½ teaspoon cayenne pepper
2½ cups defatted lower-sodium
　　chicken broth or vegetable broth,
　　plus ½ cup
4 tablespoons fresh lemon juice

1 teaspoon grated lemon peel
1 can (15 ounces) chickpeas, rinsed
　　and drained, or 1½ cups cooked
　　chickpeas
1 cup chopped pitted dates
1 box (10 ounces) or 1⅓ cups raw
　　couscous
½ teaspoon salt, plus additional
　　to taste
¼ cup sliced natural (unblanched)
　　almonds
Ground black pepper to taste
1 cup thinly sliced scallions

1. Heat the oil in a large, preferably nonstick saucepan with a lid or in a Dutch oven. Add the onion and cook over medium heat, stirring frequently, until lightly browned, about 8 minutes. Add the garlic, along with the cumin, paprika, cinnamon, coriander, and cayenne and cook, stirring, for 1 minute. Add the 2½ cups of broth, lemon juice, lemon peel, chickpeas, and dates. Bring to a boil, reduce the heat to low, and simmer, covered, for 5 minutes.

2. Add the couscous and salt, stir once with a fork, and remove the pan from the heat.

Set aside, covered, for 5 minutes, until the couscous absorbs the liquid and softens.

3. Meanwhile, toast the almonds in a small skillet set over medium heat, stirring often, until lightly brown and fragrant, 2 to 3 minutes.

4. Fluff the couscous with a fork and season with additional salt if necessary and pepper to taste. Stir in the remaining ½ cup of broth and heat through over low heat.

5. Turn the couscous onto plates. Sprinkle with the almonds and scallions and serve.

◆ *PER MAIN-DISH SERVING: About 615 cals, 118 cals from fat, 13g total fat, 1g sat fat, 0mg chol, 529mg sodium, 110g total carbs, 21g fiber, 18g prot*

Contemporary Paella

Makes 6 main-dish servings

With an updated balance of ingredients (more vegetables and rice, less meat), this paella represents Food Guide Pyramid eating at its best. And it makes a smashing presentation served with a salad of sliced blood oranges and red onion on romaine lettuce.

2 teaspoons extra-virgin olive oil
½ pound skinless boneless chicken thighs,
   cut in 1-inch chunks
½ teaspoon cayenne pepper
½ teaspoon salt, plus additional to taste
½ pound turkey kielbasa or other
   garlicky cooked sausage, cut in ½-inch slices
1 green bell pepper, seeded and coarsely chopped
4 garlic cloves, finely chopped
½ teaspoon saffron threads, crumbled
1½ cups raw medium- or long-grain white rice
2 cups defatted lower-sodium chicken broth
1 cup fish stock or bottled clam juice
1 can (15 or 16 ounces) diced tomatoes, drained
½ cup slivered dry-pack sun-dried tomatoes
1½ cups fresh or frozen green peas
1 teaspoon grated orange peel
12 hard-shell clams, scrubbed
Freshly ground black pepper to taste
½ cup chopped parsley, preferably flat leaf

continued

1. Heat the oil in a very large skillet with a lid, a Dutch oven, or a paella pan. Season the chicken with cayenne and ½ teaspoon salt and cook, along with the kielbasa, over medium-high heat, stirring frequently, until the meats are browned, 6 to 8 minutes. Add the green pepper, garlic, and saffron and cook, stirring, for 2 minutes. (The recipe can be made 1 day ahead to this point and refrigerated. Reheat before proceeding.)

2. Add the rice and cook, stirring, until the grains begin to turn translucent, about 3 minutes. Add the chicken broth, fish stock, canned tomatoes, and sun-dried tomatoes. Bring to a boil, reduce the heat to low, and cook, covered, for 15 minutes.

3. Gently stir in the peas and orange peel. Place the clams in the rice, hinge-side down, and push down until they are about half-embedded in the rice. Cover and continue to cook until the clams open and the rice and peas become tender and the liquid is absorbed, about 15 minutes.

4. Taste for seasoning, adding salt and pepper if needed. Serve the paella directly from the pot, sprinkled with parsley.

◆ *PER SERVING: About 426 cals, 103 cals from fat, 11g total fat, 1g sat fat, 60mg chol, 983mg sodium, 54g total carbs, 2g fiber, 26g prot*

ABOUT PAELLA

Paella is a traditional Spanish dish usually made with rice and saffron, seafood, chicken, sausage, and a variety of vegetables. But regional cooks often claim that only their own version is the true recipe. In the rice-growing areas of Spain, where the dish originated, locals make paella in a traditional large, shallow pan set over an open fire. Paella is a great party dish, particularly when customized with your own favorite ingredients.

Greek Chicken, Artichokes, and Brown Rice

Makes 4 main-dish servings

The flavors of the sunny Mediterranean saturate this "skillet-baked" meal-in-a-pot made with quick-cooking brown rice. A Greek salad of greens, tomatoes, and red onion sprinkled with crumbled feta cheese would accompany this dish nicely.

2 teaspoons olive oil, preferably extra virgin
¾ pound skinless boneless chicken
   breast meat, cut in thin strips
1 teaspoon dried oregano, plus ½ teaspoon
½ teaspoon salt, plus additional to taste
¼ teaspoon black pepper, plus additional
   to taste
1 medium red onion, sliced
3 garlic cloves, finely chopped
2½ cups defatted lower-sodium chicken broth
2½ cups raw quick-cooking brown rice
1 jar (6 ounces) marinated artichoke hearts,
   reserving liquid
½ cup chopped parsley, preferably flat leaf
4 thin lemon slices for garnish

1. Heat the oil in a very large, preferably nonstick skillet with a lid or in a Dutch oven. Sprinkle the chicken with 1 teaspoon of the oregano and the salt and pepper. Sauté the chicken, along with the onion, over medium-high heat until the chicken is golden brown and cooked through, 4 to 5 minutes. Add the garlic and cook, stirring, for 1 minute. Add the broth and rice and bring to a boil over high heat. Reduce the heat to low and cook, covered, according to the package directions, 5 to 10 minutes, or until the rice is tender and has absorbed the liquid.

2. Drain the artichoke hearts, reserving 2 tablespoons of the marinade. Stir the artichokes and the reserved marinade into the chicken and rice, add the remaining ½ teaspoon of oregano, and cook over medium heat until heated through, 2 to 3 minutes. Taste and season with additional salt and pepper if necessary.

3. Sprinkle with the parsley and garnish with the lemon slices before serving.

◆ *PER SERVING: About 628 cals, 98 cals from fat, 11g total fat, 2g sat fat, 49mg chol, 417mg sodium, 100g total carbs, 9g fiber, 33g prot*

Kasha with Lamb Tidbits

Makes 4 main-dish servings

Lamb complements the nutty, earthy flavor of kasha, also called buckwheat groats, in this tasty main dish. By toasting the kasha with an egg white, you will seal the grain so that it retains a pleasantly chewy texture as it cooks. Serve the kasha with a salad of romaine lettuce and sliced red cabbage topped by herbed croutons for crunch.

1 cup raw kasha
1 egg white
1 tablespoon olive oil, preferably extra virgin
¾ pound lean boneless lamb, cut into 1-inch cubes
½ teaspoon salt, plus additional to taste
¼ teaspoon pepper, plus additional to taste
1 medium onion, chopped

2 garlic cloves, finely chopped
1½ teaspoons dried rosemary, crumbled
1 teaspoon powdered ginger
2 cups defatted lower-sodium chicken broth, plus 1 cup
4 carrots, peeled and thinly sliced
1 celery rib, thinly sliced
½ cup chopped parsley, preferably flat leaf

1. Combine the kasha and egg white in a large, preferably nonstick skillet and stir until the grains are coated. Place the pan over medium heat and cook, stirring almost constantly, until the grains are separate and the kasha is fragrant and lightly toasted, about 4 minutes. Transfer to a bowl.

2. Heat the oil in the same skillet or in a Dutch oven. Season the lamb with the salt and pepper and sauté over medium heat, with the onion, until the meat is well browned on all sides, about 6 minutes. Add the garlic, rosemary, and ginger and cook, stirring, for 1 minute. Add the 2 cups of broth, carrots, and celery and bring to a boil over high heat.

3. Return the toasted kasha to the pan, cover, and cook over low heat until the kasha is tender and has absorbed the liquid, 25 to 30 minutes.

4. Stir in the remaining 1 cup of broth and heat through. Taste and season with additional salt and pepper if desired. Sprinkle with parsley before serving.

◆ *PER SERVING: About 338 cals, 82 cals from fat, 9g total fat, 2g sat fat, 43mg chol, 406mg sodium, 44g total carbs, 6g fiber, 23g prot*

Quinoa, Beef, and Sweet Potato Casserole

Makes 4 main-dish servings

Quinoa is a delicate South American grain with a nutty flavor. This dish combines quinoa with beef and sweet dried fruits in a savory casserole. You need to rinse quinoa before you cook it to remove a bitter coating. If you can't find quinoa, substitute the same quantity of white rice.

¾ pound lean ground beef
1 large onion, chopped
2 garlic cloves, finely chopped
½ teaspoon salt, plus additional
    to taste
¼ teaspoon pepper, plus additional
    to taste
1½ teaspoon ground coriander
    seed
1 teaspoon ground allspice
1 teaspoon ground cumin

¾ teaspoon powdered ginger
2 cups defatted lower-sodium
    chicken broth
1 cup uncooked quinoa, rinsed
¾ pound sweet potato, peeled and
    cut into ¾-inch cubes
⅓ cup dried cranberries
⅓ cup (about 2 ounces) quartered
    prunes
⅓ cup (about 2 ounces) quartered
    dried figs

1. Preheat the oven to 350 degrees.

2. In a large nonstick saucepan, cook the beef with the onion and garlic over medium-high heat, stirring to break up large pieces of meat, until the meat loses its pink color and browns, about 5 minutes. Drain the fat from the meat and season with the salt and pepper. Stir in the coriander, allspice, cumin, and ginger, add the broth, and bring to a boil over high heat. Remove from the heat.

3. Meanwhile, in a 2-quart baking dish, combine the quinoa, sweet potatoes, cranberries, prunes, and figs. (The recipe can be made several hours ahead to this point, covered, at room temperature. Reheat the meat and broth mixture before proceeding.)

4. Pour the hot meat and broth mixture over the ingredients in the baking dish and stir gently to distribute evenly. Cover the dish tightly with foil and bake in the preheated oven for 35 to 45 minutes, until the sweet potatoes are tender and the liquid has been absorbed.

5. Season with additional salt and pepper to taste before serving.

◆ *PER SERVING: About 495 cals, 137 cals from fat, 15g total fat, 4g sat fat, 52mg chol, 390mg sodium, 63g total carbs, 12g fiber, 26g prot*

Shredded Turkey and Chiles with Hominy Stew

Makes 4 main-dish servings

Hominy is corn with the hull and germ removed. You're probably most familiar with hominy ground and cooked as grits. In this recipe, the whole hominy kernel is simmered in a quickly made stew, along with turkey and two kinds of chili peppers. If you can't find chipotle peppers, substitute a small pickled jalapeño pepper.

2 teaspoons olive oil
1 medium onion, chopped
3 garlic cloves, finely chopped
2 teaspoons white or yellow
    cornmeal
2 teaspoons ground cumin
½ teaspoon dried oregano
2½ cups defatted lower-sodium
    chicken broth
1 can (15 to 16 ounces) stewed
    tomatoes with juice

1 can (4 ounces) chopped mild
    green chiles, drained
2 cans (15 ounces) cooked hominy,
    drained and rinsed
1 chipotle pepper in adobo sauce,
    minced
½ pound cooked turkey meat,
    shredded or diced
¼ cup chopped fresh cilantro
Salt to taste

1. Heat the oil in a large, preferably nonstick saucepan. Add the onion and cook over medium heat, stirring frequently, until it softens and begins to brown, 5 to 6 minutes. Add the garlic, cornmeal, cumin, and oregano and cook, stirring, for 1 minute.

2. Add the chicken broth and bring to a boil over high heat. Add the tomatoes, chiles, hominy, and chipotle pepper. Simmer, uncovered, over medium-low heat, breaking up the tomatoes into smaller chunks with the side of a spoon, until the liquid is slightly reduced and thickened, about 10 minutes. Add the turkey and cook another 5 minutes.

3. Shortly before serving, stir in the cilantro and season to taste with salt. Ladle into shallow soup bowls.

◆ *PER SERVING: About 383 cals, 71 cals from fat, 8g total fat, 2g sat fat, 46mg chol, 1657mg sodium, 58g total carbs, 6g fiber, 18g prot*

Quick Creamy Polenta

Makes 4 generous side-dish servings

When you cook cornmeal this way, you get a soft, creamy polenta that you can spoon right out of the pot onto a plate. It makes a marvelous accompaniment to all manner of "saucy" dishes such as Summer Harvest Ratatouille (page 426), leftover chili, or beef stew.

3 cups defatted lower-sodium
   chicken broth or vegetable broth
1¼ cups raw yellow or white
   cornmeal
½ teaspoon salt

2 tablespoons grated Parmesan
   cheese, preferably imported
Freshly ground black pepper to
   taste

1. In a large, heavy saucepan, bring the broth to a boil over high heat. In a mixing bowl, whisk the cornmeal with 2 cups of water and the salt.

2. Whisk the cornmeal mixture into the simmering broth. Return to a boil, reduce the heat to medium-low and cook, stirring almost constantly, until the polenta is very thick and begins to pull away from the sides of the pan, 10 to 15 minutes.

3. Stir in the cheese, season with black pepper to taste, and serve immediately.

◆ *PER SERVING: About 189 cals, 20 cals from fat, 2g total fat, 1g sat fat, 2mg chol, 374mg sodium, 35g total carbs, 2g fiber, 7g prot*

LEFTOVER POLENTA

Spoon leftover polenta into a small baking dish or ramekin, stirring in a few tablespoons of broth or water if the polenta is firm. Smooth the top of the polenta and refrigerate. To reheat, drizzle or brush it with a little olive oil or sprinkle it with grated cheese (any type), and bake, uncovered, in a 350-degree oven until heated through, about 20 minutes. You can also place the polenta in a microwave-safe dish and microwave it on high for a few minutes until hot.

Basic Baked Rice Pilaf

Makes 4 generous side-dish servings

Try baking rice when you are entertaining; it frees up a burner. You can also keep the finished rice warm in the oven if dinner gets delayed. This recipe works well with any type of white rice. To bake brown rice, just add ½ cup of broth and increase the cooking time to about 60 minutes.

2 teaspoons olive oil
1 medium onion, chopped
1½ cups raw white rice, any type
3 cups defatted lower-sodium
　　chicken broth

½ teaspoon salt, plus additional
　　to taste
¼ teaspoon black pepper

1. Preheat the oven to 350 degrees.

2. Heat the oil in a large saucepan. Add the onion and cook over medium heat, stirring frequently, until it begins to soften and brown slightly, about 5 minutes. Add the rice and cook, stirring, until the grains are coated with oil and the rice begins to turn translucent, about 3 minutes. In a saucepan, combine the broth and the salt and bring to a simmer.

3. Transfer the rice to a 2- to 2½-quart baking dish and pour the hot broth over the rice. Stir once with a fork and cover the dish tightly with foil or a lid. Bake in the preheated oven until the rice is tender and the liquid is absorbed, about 35 minutes. (The rice can be kept warm in the turned-off oven for about 30 minutes.)

4. Fluff with a fork and season with the black pepper and additional salt to taste.

◆ *PER SERVING: About 302 cals, 30 cals from fat, 3g total fat, 0g sat fat, 0mg chol, 320mg sodium, 59 total carbs, 1g fiber, 7g prot*

RICE COOKING TIPS

◆ Unless a recipe states otherwise, never stir rice while it's cooking. Stirring releases starch and makes rice sticky.
◆ You don't need to rinse rice before cooking unless it is imported and purchased in bulk. American rice is cleaned before packaging.
◆ Cook rice over very low heat. High heat can turn too much of the water into steam, leaving rice undercooked in the center.
◆ Lifting the lid while rice is cooking lets out valuable steam and lengthens cooking time.
◆ Rice and other grains cooked with highly acidic ingredients, such as tomatoes or lemon juice, often need a longer cooking time to become tender.
◆ If all of the liquid has been absorbed but the rice is still not tender, add a bit more liquid.
◆ If the rice seems done but there's still liquid left in the pan, drain off the liquid or cook the rice uncovered for a few more minutes until the liquid evaporates.
◆ Tossing hot, cooked rice with a fork before serving lets some steam escape and helps keep the grains separate.

Herbed Brown Rice Pilaf

Makes 4 generous side-dish servings

This dish is as versatile as it is delicious, because you can vary the fresh herbs depending on the rest of your menu or what's in the supermarket or garden. Browning the onions contributes sweetness and extra flavor to the pilaf.

2 teaspoons olive oil, preferably extra virgin
1 medium onion, chopped
1 garlic clove, finely chopped
1¼ cups raw long-grain brown rice (see note)
3¼ cups defatted lower-sodium chicken
    or vegetable broth, or a combination
    of broth and water
½ teaspoon salt, plus additional to taste
¼ cup chopped flat-leaf parsley
¼ cup chopped fresh herbs such as thyme,
    basil, tarragon, sage, dill, or chives, or a combination
Freshly ground black pepper to taste

1. In a large saucepan, heat the oil over medium heat. Add the onion and cook, stirring occasionally, until it softens and browns, about 8 minutes. Add the garlic and cook, stirring, for 1 minute. Add the rice and cook, stirring frequently, until the grains become coated with oil and begin to toast lightly, about 3 minutes.

2. Add the broth and the salt and bring to a boil. Reduce the heat to low and cook, covered, until the rice is tender and has absorbed the liquid, 40 to 45 minutes.

3. Use a fork to stir the parsley and other herbs into the rice. Season with black pepper and additional salt to taste.

◆ *PER SERVING: About 267 cals, 42 cals from fat, 5g total fat, 1g sat fat, 0mg chol, 327mg sodium, 49g total carbs, 4g fiber, 7g prot*

Note: To substitute quick-cooking brown rice, use 2 cups of rice and 2 cups of liquid. Follow the cooking directions on the package and stir in the herbs at the end.

Southwest Rice and Corn Pilaf

Makes 6 side-dish servings

This appealing corn-studded rice pilaf side dish rounds out almost any Southwestern-style meal. It's great with roast chicken, too.

1 tablespoon vegetable oil

1 cup chopped red onion

3 garlic cloves, finely chopped

1 teaspoon chili powder

¾ teaspoon ground cumin

¾ teaspoon dried oregano

1½ cups raw long-grain white rice

2 cups defatted lower-sodium chicken or vegetable broth

1 can (15 to 16 ounces) diced tomatoes, with juice

1 can (4 ounces) chopped green chiles, drained

1¼ cups frozen corn kernels

½ teaspoon liquid hot pepper sauce

½ cup chopped fresh cilantro

½ cup thinly sliced scallions

1. Heat the oil in a large saucepan with a lid. Add the onion and cook, stirring frequently, until it begins to soften, about 4 minutes. Add the garlic, chili powder, cumin, and oregano and cook, stirring, for 1 minute. Add the rice and stir until the grains are coated with oil.

2. Add the broth, canned tomatoes, and green chiles. Bring to a boil and add the corn. Reduce the heat to low and cook, covered, until the rice is tender, about 25 minutes. (The rice will take a little longer to cook than usual because of the acid in the tomatoes.)

3. Season with the hot pepper sauce. Transfer to plates or a serving bowl and sprinkle with the cilantro and scallions.

◆ *PER SERVING: About 261 cals, 29 cals from fat, 3g total fat, 0g sat fat, 0mg chol, 340mg sodium, 52g total carbs, 3g fiber, 6g prot*

TO STORE RICE

Uncooked white rice can be stored almost indefinitely in a cool, dry place with no loss of nutrients. Over time, the oil in the hull of brown rice slowly turns rancid at warm temperatures. Brown rice also gradually loses its vitamin E over time. You should store it in the refrigerator or freezer for up to 6 months.

You can store cooked white and brown rice, covered, in the refrigerator for up to 5 days or freeze it in airtight containers for up to 2 months.

Bulgur Pilaf with Leeks, Currants, and Pine Nuts

Makes 4 side-dish servings

Bulgur is whole wheat that has been cooked, dried, and then broken into coarse fragments. It's a very convenient staple for your pantry because, like couscous, it is ready to eat in minutes. Leeks, currants, and toasted pine nuts lend complementary flavors to this bulgur pilaf.

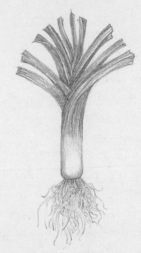

2 teaspoons olive oil, preferably extra virgin
2 cups thinly sliced leeks, white and pale
    green parts only
2 cups defatted lower-sodium chicken
    or vegetable broth
1¼ cups raw bulgur
¼ cup dried currants
2 tablespoons pine nuts
1 tablespoon fresh lemon juice
Salt to taste
Freshly ground black pepper to taste

1. Heat the oil in a medium-sized, preferably nonstick saucepan with a lid. Add the leeks and 2 tablespoons of the broth and stir to combine. Cover and cook over low heat, stirring frequently, until the leeks soften and become lightly browned, about 8 minutes.

2. Add the rest of the broth and bring to a boil over high heat. Add the bulgur, cover, and simmer over medium heat for 5 minutes. Remove the pan from the heat, add the currants, cover and let stand until the liquid is absorbed, about 15 minutes. (If any unabsorbed liquid remains, drain it off.)

3. Toast the pine nuts in a small skillet over medium heat, stirring frequently, until they are golden brown and fragrant, 2 to 3 minutes.

4. Stir the pine nuts and lemon juice into the bulgur with a fork. Season to taste with salt and black pepper.

◆ *PER SERVING: About 307 cals, 52 cals from fat, 6g total fat, 1g sat fat, 0mg chol, 65mg sodium, 59g total carbs, 13g fiber, 10g prot*

Braised Wild Rice with Cranberries

Makes 4 side-dish servings

Wild rice, an aquatic grass native to North America, has a unique flavor that is somehow both delicate and robust. The scarcity of wild rice makes it somewhat expensive, so save it for a special occasion or mix a little in with regular rice. This recipe adds the sweet but tart flavor of dried cranberries. It makes the perfect accompaniment to almost any roast meat.

2 teaspoons butter
1 medium onion, chopped
1 celery rib, chopped
1 garlic clove, finely chopped
2½ cups defatted lower-sodium chicken
   broth or vegetable broth, plus
    ½ cup if necessary
1 cup raw wild rice, rinsed
½ teaspoon salt, plus additional to taste
⅓ cup dried cranberries
1 tablespoon chopped fresh sage or
   ¾ teaspoon crumbled dried sage
1 teaspoon balsamic vinegar
Freshly ground black pepper to taste

1. Melt the butter in a large saucepan with a lid. Add the onion and celery and cook over medium heat, stirring frequently, until the vegetables begin to soften, about 4 minutes. Add the garlic and cook, stirring, for 1 minute. Add 2½ cups of broth along with the rice and the salt, stir once, and bring to a boil. Reduce the heat to low and cook, covered, until the rice grains begin to split apart. Depending on the rice, this could take 45 minutes to 1 hour. Check the level of the liquid once or twice and, if all the liquid has been absorbed before all the grains have split, add up to ½ cup more broth or water.

2. Add the cranberries and sage and continue to cook until most of the rice grains have split and all or most of the liquid has been absorbed, approximately 10 minutes. If excess liquid remains, drain it off.

3. Stir the vinegar into the rice and season it with black pepper and more salt to taste.

◆ *PER SERVING: About 223 cals, 27 cals from fat, 3g total fat, 1g sat fat, 5mg chol, 348mg sodium, 42g total carbs, 4g fiber, 8g prot*

WHY ARE WHOLE-GRAIN FOODS BETTER?

Whole-grain foods—such as whole-wheat breads and pasta, and brown rice—supply a variety of important nutrients, including B vitamins, vitamin E, fiber, and zinc, that foods containing milled grains do not. Most of these nutrients reside in the grain's outer hull, bran, and germ—all of which are lost when whole grains are milled. While some of the lost nutrients are restored when food manufacturers enrich their products, others, such as fiber, are lost forever. So, whenever you can, pass up that white bread and white rice and replace them with healthy, wholesome, whole-grain foods.

Curried Basmati Rice and Peas with Ginger

Makes 6 side-dish servings

Basmati rice, originally developed in India, is a long-grain rice with a delicious, toasty, almost popcornlike flavor. Texmati rice is a cross between basmati and regular long-grain rice and tastes similar to basmati. Use either one to make this spicy curried rice with peas.

2 teaspoons vegetable oil, preferably peanut oil

1 medium onion, chopped

2 garlic cloves, finely chopped

1 tablespoon minced fresh ginger

2 teaspoons curry powder

1 teaspoon chili powder

1½ cups raw basmati or Texmati rice

3 cups defatted lower-sodium chicken broth
or vegetable broth, or a mixture of broth and water

½ teaspoon salt, plus additional to taste

1½ cups frozen peas

1. Heat the oil in a large saucepan with a lid. Add the onion and cook over medium heat, stirring frequently, until softened, about 5 minutes. Add the garlic, ginger, curry powder, and chili powder and cook, stirring, for 1 minute. Add the rice and stir until the grains are coated with oil.

2. Add the broth and the salt. Bring to a boil, reduce the heat to low, and cook, covered, for 15 minutes.

3. Add the peas and continue to cook until the rice and peas are tender, about 5 minutes. Fluff with a fork and season with more salt if desired.

◆ *PER SERVING: About 238 cals, 22 cals from fat, 2g total fat, 0g sat fat, 0mg chol, 253mg sodium, 46g total carbs, 3g fiber, 7g prot*

Spicy Thai Rice with Chopped Peanuts

Makes 6 side-dish servings

This spicy, chili-flecked rice makes a superb accompaniment to grilled or broiled fish. Add a salad of tropical fruits and vegetables to make a colorful Asian-inspired meal.

2 teaspoons vegetable oil, preferably peanut oil

1 tablespoon minced fresh ginger

1 small fresh or pickled jalapeño or other hot pepper, finely chopped

2 teaspoons curry powder

1½ cups raw long-grain white rice

3 cups defatted lower-sodium chicken broth or vegetable broth

1 can (4 ounces) chopped green chiles, drained

½ teaspoon salt, plus additional to taste

⅔ cup thinly sliced scallions

½ cup chopped fresh cilantro

4 tablespoons honey-roasted peanuts, preferably reduced fat, chopped (see note)

1 lime, cut in wedges

1. Heat the oil in a large saucepan with a lid. Add the ginger, jalapeño, and curry powder and cook over medium heat, stirring, for 1 minute. Add the rice and cook, stirring, until it is coated with oil and begins to turn slightly translucent, about 3 minutes. Add the broth, green chiles, and the salt and bring to a boil over high heat. Reduce the heat to low and cook, covered, until the rice is tender and has absorbed the liquid, about 18 minutes.

2. Stir the scallions and cilantro into the rice and season it with salt if necessary. Serve the rice sprinkled with the chopped peanuts and pass lime wedges at the table to squeeze over the top.

◆ *PER SERVING: About 242 cals, 48 cals from fat, 5g total fat, 1g sat fat, 0mg chol, 387mg sodium, 42g total carbs, 2g fiber, 6g prot*

Note: Look for reduced-fat peanuts in the baking or snack section of the supermarket.

Baked Herbed Polenta

Makes 4 generous side-dish servings

A generous wedge of this herb-flecked, baked polenta makes a savory base for a flavorful tomato sauce, such as Double Tomato Sauce (page 204), Basic Marinara Sauce (page 205), or Basic Bolognese Sauce (page 205).

Olive oil or vegetable oil spray
2½ cups defatted lower-sodium
   chicken broth or vegetable broth
1¼ cups yellow or white cornmeal
½ teaspoon salt
1 tablespoon chopped fresh sage or
   1 teaspoon crumbled dried sage

1 teaspoon chopped fresh
   rosemary or ¾ teaspoon
   crumbled dried rosemary
1½ tablespoons grated Parmesan
   cheese, preferably imported,
   plus 1 tablespoon

1. Preheat the oven to 375 degrees. Coat a 9-inch cast iron skillet or 9-inch square baking dish with oil or oil spray.

2. In a large, heavy saucepan, bring the broth to a boil over high heat. In a mixing bowl, whisk the cornmeal with 1½ cups of water and the salt.

3. Whisk the cornmeal mixture into the simmering broth. Bring back to a boil, reduce the heat to medium-low and cook, stirring almost constantly, until the polenta thickens and begins to pull away from the sides of the pan, about 10 minutes. Whisk in the sage, rosemary, and 1½ tablespoons of the cheese. Scrape into the prepared pan, smooth the top, and sprinkle with the remaining tablespoon of cheese. (The polenta can be made several hours ahead to this point and refrigerated. Return to room temperature before baking.)

4. Bake, uncovered, until the polenta is firm and very lightly browned on top, and the edges have pulled away from the sides of the baking dish, 20 to 25 minutes. (The polenta can be kept warm, loosely covered, in a turned-off oven for 30 minutes.)

5. Cut into wedges to serve.

◆ *PER SERVING: About 191 cals, 22 cals from fat, 2g total fat, 1g sat fat, 3mg chol, 381mg sodium, 35g total carbs, 2g fiber, 7g prot*

Note: For softer polenta, use 2 cups of water. Spoon out of baking dish instead of cutting in wedges.

Grains

Grains and the foods made from them form the foundation of the Food Guide Pyramid. They are packed with complex carbohydrates—your best source of energy.

NAME	DESCRIPTION/USES	COOKING INSTRUCTIONS FOR 1 CUP RAW GRAIN
Barley	Usually sold pearled and with the hull, most of the bran, and some of the germ removed to shorten cooking time; flavor is mild and texture is slightly chewier than rice.	Cook 1 cup of barley in 2 to 3 cups of liquid, about 45 minutes. Yields 3 cups.
Bulgur	Wheat berries that have been partially cooked, then cracked; nutty whole-wheat taste.	Stir 1 cup of bulgur into 2 cups of boiling liquid and cook, covered, over low heat for about 15 minutes or remove from heat and let stand, 20 to 25 minutes. Yields 2½ to 3 cups.
Cornmeal (polenta)	Available as yellow, white, and blue; sold "degerminated," with germ and bran removed for longer shelf life (widely available in supermarkets), and stone ground, the whole-grain form. Sweet, cornlike flavor. Used in cornbreads and other baked goods.	To cook polenta as mush, stir 1 cup of cornmeal into 3 to 4 cups boiling liquid and cook 15 to 30 minutes. Yields 3 cups.
Couscous	Staple of North African and some Middle Eastern countries; a grain product rather than a grain, made from semolina wheat flour and salted water; tastes mild and neutral like pasta.	Combine 1 cup of quick-cooking dried couscous with 1½ cups boiling liquid, and let stand for 5 minutes. Yields 3 cups.
Cracked wheat	Similar to bulgur, but not precooked. Added to breads or muffins.	Cook 1 cup of cracked wheat in 2 cups water, 35 to 45 minutes, until soft. Yields 3 cups.
Grits	Coarsely ground meal from dried hominy; flavor is mild and neutral; staple cereal in southern United States. Available in regular, quick-cooking, and instant varieties.	For quick-cooking grits, stir 1 cup of grits into 4 cups of boiling water and cook, 5 to 7 minutes. Regular grits cook in about 20 minutes; instant grits cook in about 1 minute. Yields 3½ to 4 cups.
Hominy	Dried corn kernels from which the hull and germ have been removed; sold cooked, in cans, or dried; slightly sweet, firm texture; also called posole in Mexican cooking.	Simmer 1 cup of dried hominy in 4 cups of water for several hours to soften. Yields 2½ to 3 cups.
Kasha	The roasted, hulled seeds of the buckwheat plant—also called groats; technically not a grain, but an herb related to rhubarb and sorrel; staple in Russia; pungent, maltlike flavor.	Often coated with egg or egg white before cooking to seal the grains and keep them separate. Cook 1 cup of kasha in 2 cups of liquid, 20 to 30 minutes. Yields 3½ to 4 cups.

NAME	DESCRIPTION/USES	COOKING INSTRUCTIONS FOR 1 CUP RAW GRAIN
Millet	Small, round, yellow seed; sweet, grasslike flavor. Add to bread or muffins.	To cook as hot cereal, simmer 1 cup of millet in 2½ cups of water, about 20 minutes. Yields 4 cups.
Oats	American-style rolled oats are hulled, steamed, and flattened oat kernels; available in regular, quick-cooking, and instant varieties; slightly nutty, soft texture.	Simmer 1 cup of quick-cooking oats in 2 cups of boiling water, about 5 minutes. Regular oats cook in about 20 minutes; instant oats cook in about 1 minute. Regular oats yield about 2½ cups.
Quinoa	Pronounced "keen-wa"; was once the staple grain of the Incas of Peru; tiny round seed; pale yellow; slightly sweet, nutty flavor; soft and slightly chewy texture. Must always be rinsed to remove bitter-tasting natural coating before cooking.	Cook 1 cup of quinoa in 2 cups of liquid until tender, about 20 minutes. Yields 3 cups.
Triticale	A type of wheat obtained from an cross of durum wheat, hard red winter wheat, and rye. Used mostly ground as flour; produces flour that is higher in protein but lower in gluten than all-purpose flour.	Cook 1 cup of triticale in 3 cups of water until tender, about 45 minutes to 1 hour. Yields 3 cups.
Wheat	The world's largest cereal grass crop; usually ground into flour; contains relatively high amounts of gluten the protein that provides elasticity necessary for bread-baking. Three main types: hard wheat, high in protein, particularly suitable for yeast breads; soft wheat, lower in gluten and more suitable for tender baked goods; and durum wheat, the preferred choice for pasta.	Whole wheat berries are rarely cooked; (see bulgur, cracked wheat, and triticale).

Rice Varieties

All rice has an inedible husk that must be removed by milling before the rice can be consumed. Removing just the husk produces brown rice. Further milling or polishing to remove the bran layers produces white rice or polished rice.

Rice is available either long or short grained. Long-grain rice is at least four times longer than it is wide, has a low starch content, and produces light, dry grains that separate easily when cooked. Short-grain rice has fat, almost round grains with a high starch content. When cooked, the grains tend to stick together. Medium-grain rice, a type of short-grain rice, takes on some of the qualities of both long and short grain.

All types of rice supply complex carbohydrates, B vitamins, and small amounts of other vitamins and minerals. Brown rice has about three times more fiber than white rice and more minerals and vitamins because of its bran layer. Quick-cooking or "instant" rice is a bit lower in B vitamins than standard rices, while parboiled ("converted") rice is somewhat higher in some nutrients because its steaming process forces some nutrients from the outer hull into the grain. Fragrant rices, such as basmati and jasmine, are nutritionally identical to standard rices, but some imported brands of white rice—unlike domestic—are not enriched.

NAME	DESCRIPTION/USES	COOKING INSTRUCTIONS FOR 1 CUP RAW RICE
Arborio	Italian short-grained white rice; plump grains have a lot of starch in outer layer that dissolves when cooked to thicken broth. Center retains firm, chewy texture. The classic risotto rice.	Sauté in oil, then simmer, uncovered, in 3 to 4 cups of broth, stirring frequently to release the starch, about 20 minutes. Yields 3 cups.
Basmati	Long-grain white or brown rice with nutlike aroma and firm texture. Originally developed in foothills of the Himalayas in northern India, and grown in only a few areas of the world. Good in Indian dishes.	Cook, covered, in 2 cups of liquid, about 20 minutes. Yields 3 cups.
Brown	Unpolished rice with the outer hull removed and germ and bran layers intact. Nutlike flavor and chewy texture. Available in all size grains. A good all-purpose rice.	Cook, covered, in 2½ cups of liquid, 45 to 50 minutes. Yields 4 cups.
Glutinous	Also called sticky or sweet rice, although not sweet to the taste. A short-grain white rice with a high starch content. Good in many Asian dishes including dim sum, sushi, and desserts.	Soak overnight. Simmer, covered, in 1 cup of liquid, about 20 minutes. Yields 2½ cups.
Jasmine	An aromatic long-grain rice originally grown in Thailand. Available in both white and brown types. Has distinctive, flowery flavor and is soft and tender. Good in Asian foods, especially Thai and Vietnamese dishes.	Cook, covered, in 2 cups of liquid, about 20 minutes. Yields 3 cups.

NAME	DESCRIPTION/USES	COOKING INSTRUCTIONS FOR 1 CUP RAW RICE
Parboiled	Developed during World War II and commonly known as "converted," which is a proprietary name. Parboiled rice has been steamed and pressure cooked before milling to force nutrients into the grain, producing a slightly more nutritious product. The grains are hard and retain their shape well. A good all-purpose rice.	Cook, covered, in 2 cups of liquid, about 25 minutes. Yields 3½ cups.
Pecan and popcorn	Aromatic long-grain rices grown in Louisiana with a distinctive buttery or nutty fragrance. Available in both brown and white varieties. Their intense flavor makes them good choices as side dishes.	Cook, covered, in 2 cups of liquid, about 20 minutes. Yields 3 cups.
Quick cooking	Precooked, rinsed, and dehydrated before packaging, these products cook in a much shorter time than standard rice. Available in both white and brown varieties. The flavor and texture of quick-cooking white rice are not as good as standard white rice. Quick-cooking brown rice is a good substitute for regular brown rice.	Cook, covered, in 1 cup of water, about 5 minutes for white rice, 10 to 15 minutes for brown rice. Yields 2 cups.
Texmati	A hybrid of basmati and regular long-grain rice, grown in Texas. The flavor is like aromatic basmati rice, but slightly more delicate. A good rice for Indian or other Asian dishes.	Cook, covered, in 2 cups of liquid, about 20 minutes. Yields 3 cups.
Standard white	A long-grain rice that has been milled to remove the hull, germ, and most of the bran. This type is the most common rice used in the United States.	Cook, covered, in 2 cups of liquid, about 20 minutes. Yields 3 cups.
Wild	Not a true rice, wild rice is the grain of an aquatic grass native to North America. Originally found growing wild in Minnesota, most wild rice is now cultivated in California. Its limited supply keeps the price high. Excellent in side dishes and in stuffing for poultry.	Cook, covered, in 3 cups of liquid, 50 to 60 minutes. Yields 2½ cups.

CHAPTER EIGHT

Beans

When it comes to nutrition, flavor, and appearance, few foods can compare with dried beans. They make a beautiful presentation, with colors ranging from jet black to snow white and muted to speckled. Their flavor is both plain enough to complement other ingredients and strong enough to stand on its own. Most importantly, beans give tremendous nutritional "bang for the buck," providing protein, complex carbohydrates, fiber, and a variety of vitamins and minerals at almost the lowest price per pound of any food.

Dried beans and peas belong to the family of foods known as legumes. Sometimes they are part of the vegetable group of the Food Guide Pyramid because they offer many of the same nutrients found in vegetables. But, more commonly, they are part of the meat group. Like meat, legumes are a top source of protein, iron, and zinc—good news if you are trying to eat less meat. An added bonus—unlike meat, poultry, and other animal proteins, legumes contain very little fat and plenty of fiber.

Don't let the thought of soaking and boiling beans for hours scare you away from them. The most common types—kidney, garbanzo (chickpeas), pinto, cannellini (white), and black—are readily available canned. So, when you get the urge for chili, bean soup, or bean salad, just pop open a can. But when you have a bit more time, try dried beans. The varieties and combinations are endless, from heirloom varieties like the dappled Appaloosa bean to packaged bean mixes that are great in soups or salads. Remember that, unlike their bean cousins, dried split peas and lentils take very little time to cook.

Beans are usually canned with salt to help preserve their shape, texture, and flavor, so they may be high in sodium. If you are watching your sodium intake, look for beans canned without salt, or rinse and drain canned beans well before using. Beans canned without salt may not be as firm as those canned with salt.

Once you make dried beans and peas a regular part of your menu, you won't be able to imagine doing without them. Rice takes on a whole new personality when paired with lentils, as in Lentils and Rice with Blackened Onions (page 313) or with peas as in Spiced Split Peas on Jasmine Rice (page 304). Not only do they taste good together, but rice and beans are also a good nutrition match because together they form a complete protein. To get the benefit of a complete protein, you don't have to eat rice and beans together at the same meal, just make sure you eat them in the same day.

This chapter offers a tasty array of legume recipes inspired by classic American favorites. What would a barbecue be without baked beans? For a new twist, experience the subtle flavor of maple syrup combined with the smokiness of turkey bacon in the Mixed Baked Beans with Maple (page 293). A visit to New Orleans would be incomplete without red beans and rice, a traditional dish re-created here in French Quarter Red Beans and Rice (page 311). Meat loaf takes on new meaning when the meat is mixed with lentils and spinach as in Lentil, Spinach, and Meat Loaf (page 292). And to feed a crowd on a cold winter day, what could be better than chili? Try Smoky Black Bean and Pork Chili (page 294).

Legumes also fit all seasons. Cold winter days cry out for hot and hearty dishes like soups and stews made with beans, such as Lentil Stew with Rosemary (page 301). Lighter summer menus are the perfect place for dishes like Cuban Black Beans and Rice (page 299) or salads topped with beans.

Taste the way other cultures use legumes in their cuisine. Take a quick trip to Mexico with our Family-Style Bean and Tortilla Casserole (page 288). Travel to the Caribbean for legumes paired with rice and coconut in the Jamaican Rice and Beans with Thyme (page 298). Experience North Africa by preparing Tunisian Chickpea and Eggplant Stew (page 316).

It's never too late to start including a spectrum of dried beans and peas in your weekly menus.

Family-Style Bean and Tortilla Casserole

Makes 6 servings

Chilaquiles, a layered casserole popular in Mexico, is usually made with fried tortillas or tortilla chips. This deliciously updated, lower-fat version of the dish uses soft corn tortillas and a tomato and kidney bean sauce. It's a rich source of fiber, calcium, and vitamins A and C.

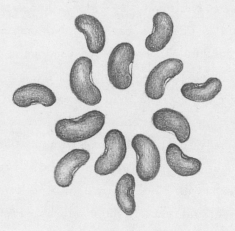

2 teaspoons olive oil
1 large onion, chopped
1 green bell pepper, seeded and chopped
½ cup shredded carrots
2 garlic cloves, chopped
4 teaspoons chili powder
1½ teaspoons dried oregano
1 can (28 ounces) crushed tomatoes
   with juice
1 can (16 ounces) kidney beans,
   rinsed and drained, or 1¾
   cups cooked kidney beans
1 cup vegetable broth or defatted
   lower-sodium chicken broth or water
1 teaspoon sugar
Salt and black pepper to taste
2 cups (8 ounces) shredded reduced-fat
   Monterey Jack cheese (see note)
1 cup reduced-fat sour cream
12 corn tortillas (5 to 6 inches in diameter),
   cut in quarters

1. Preheat the oven to 375 degrees. Heat the oil in a large, preferably nonstick skillet. Add the onion, green pepper, and carrots and cook over medium heat, stirring occasionally, until softened, about 5 minutes. Add the garlic, chili powder, and oregano and cook, stirring, for 1 minute. Stir in the tomatoes, beans, broth, and sugar and bring to a boil. Reduce the heat to medium-low and simmer the sauce, uncovered, for about 15 minutes until it is somewhat reduced and thickened. Season with salt and pepper to taste.

2. In a small bowl, whisk together the cheese and sour cream.

3. Spoon about half of the tomato-bean sauce into a shallow 2-quart baking dish. Layer with half the quartered tortillas and about one third of the cheese and sour cream mixture. Layer with the remaining tortillas, then the remaining sauce, and finally with the rest of the cheese mixture, spreading it over the sauce. (This recipe can be made to this point several hours ahead and refrigerated.)

4. If the casserole is freshly made, bake, uncovered, until bubbly around the edges, heated through, and browned on top, about 20 minutes. If it has been refrigerated, cover and bake until nearly heated through, about 20 minutes. Uncover and bake until the top is browned, about 10 minutes longer.

5. Cut into squares to serve.

◆ *PER SERVING: About 406 cals, 113 cals from fat, 13g total fat, 4g sat fat, 40mg chol, 871mg sodium, 52g total carbs, 7g fiber, 22g prot*

Note: To make the dish spicier, use Monterey Jack cheese with jalapeños.

Black Bean Patties with Dill

Makes 4 servings

You can substitute other soft, cooked beans, such as pinto or white beans, for the black beans in these tasty patties. Horseradish-spiked Chunky Yogurt Sauce (recipe follows) is a pleasantly piquant topping for these patties.

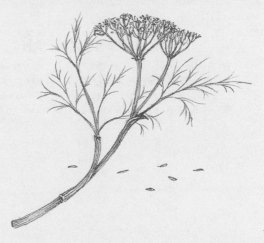

2 cans (19 ounces each) black beans,
   rinsed and drained, or
   4 cups cooked black beans
1 teaspoon olive oil, plus 2 teaspoons
2 garlic cloves, finely chopped
½ cup unseasoned dry bread crumbs
½ cup sliced scallions
¼ cup chopped fresh dill
¼ cup nonfat plain yogurt
2 teaspoons Worcestershire sauce
½ teaspoon liquid hot pepper sauce
Chunky Yogurt Sauce (recipe follows)

1. Use a potato masher or a large fork to mash the beans, or pulse them in a food processor to a coarse purée. Place the purée in a large bowl. *continued*

2. Heat 1 teaspoon of the oil in a large, preferably nonstick skillet. Add the garlic and cook over medium heat until it is fragrant, about 1 minute. Scrape into the bowl with the beans. Do not wash the pan.

3. Add the bread crumbs, scallions, dill, yogurt, Worcestershire, and hot pepper sauce to the bowl and stir to mix well. Shape into 8 patties, each about 3 inches in diameter. (The recipe can be made several hours ahead to this point and refrigerated.)

4. Heat the remaining 2 teaspoons of oil in the skillet. Cook the patties over medium heat, in two batches if necessary, until nicely browned on both sides and heated through, about 10 minutes.

5. Serve the bean patties with Chunky Yogurt Sauce.

◆ *PER SERVING: About 281 cals, 44 cals from fat, 5g total fat, 1g sat fat, 0mg chol, 942mg sodium, 46g total carbs, 12g fiber, 15g prot*

CHUNKY YOGURT SAUCE

Makes 2¹/₂ cups (4 servings)

This sauce is great spooned over Black Bean Patties with Dill (page 289).

1½ cups nonfat plain yogurt
1 medium-large tomato,
   seeded and chopped (1 cup)

¼ cup thinly sliced scallions
¼ cup chopped fresh dill

2 tablespoons prepared
   horseradish
¼ teaspoon black pepper

Combine all the ingredients in a small bowl. Serve immediately or refrigerate for up to 2 hours.

Per serving: About 64 cals, 3 cals from fat, 0g total fat, 0g sat fat, 2mg chol, 246mg sodium, 10g total carbs, 1g fiber, 6g prot

WHY RINSE AND PICK OVER DRIED BEANS?

Modern processing methods produce fairly clean, high-quality beans, but you should rinse beans before cooking to remove any traces of dust. Occasionally, you may find tiny stones, twigs, or other debris, particularly in imported dried legumes, so it's a good idea to sort through beans before cooking.

Unfried Beans

Makes 4 side-dish servings

Refried beans abound in Mexican and Tex-Mex cooking. This version, made without any added fat, tastes spicy and delicious. Team up these beans with almost any Mexican-style dish, or as a sandwich spread in burritos or tacos. You can make the beans spicier by adding extra jalapeño. Adjust the thickness of the final purée with more or less liquid.

2 teaspoons chili powder

1 teaspoon cumin

2 cans (16 ounces each) pinto beans, rinsed and drained, or 3½ cups cooked pinto beans

¾ cup chopped red onion

1 to 2 pickled jalapeño peppers, coarsely chopped

Salt and freshly ground black pepper to taste

1. Toast the chili powder and cumin in a small skillet over medium heat, stirring, until fragrant, 1 to 2 minutes.

2. In a blender or the workbowl of a food processor, combine the beans, onion, jalapeño(s), and toasted spices. Pulse to make a coarse purée. With the motor running, add 4 to 6 tablespoons of warm water to thin to a spreadable consistency. Season with salt and pepper to taste. (You can also mash the beans with the seasonings in a bowl, using a potato masher.)

3. Use immediately at room temperature as a sandwich spread or warm the beans in a saucepan over low heat, stirring, until heated through, about 5 minutes, and serve as a side dish.

◆ *PER SERVING: About 151 cals, 8 cals from fat, 1g total fat, 0g sat fat, 0mg chol, 448mg sodium, 28g total carbs, 1g fiber, 8g prot*

WHY RINSE AND DRAIN CANNED BEANS?

Canned beans usually contain more sodium than home-cooked dried beans. Rinsing them helps to remove some of the sodium added in the canning process, as well as the thick canning liquid.

Place canned beans in a sieve or colander and run them under a gentle stream of warm water, then drain.

Lentil, Spinach, and Meat Loaf

Makes 6 servings

Supplying both protein and fiber, this savory bean and meat loaf is also a source of iron and vitamins A and C. A big baked potato or Molasses and Pepper Grilled Sweet Potato Slices (page 424) would round out this meal beautifully. Serve Updated Old-Fashioned Chocolate Pudding (page 468) for dessert.

½ cup dried brown lentils, rinsed
   and picked over
1 teaspoon olive oil
1 medium onion, chopped
2 garlic cloves, finely chopped
¾ pound lean mixed ground meat,
   such as beef, veal, and pork
1 package (10 ounces) frozen
   chopped spinach, thawed and
   squeezed dry

3 tablespoons chili sauce or
   ketchup, plus 1 tablespoon
2 teaspoons Dijon mustard
2 teaspoons Worcestershire sauce
1½ teaspoons dried thyme
1 egg white, lightly beaten
Vegetable or olive oil spray

1. In a saucepan, bring 4 cups of lightly salted water to a boil. Add the lentils, reduce the heat to low, and simmer, covered, until tender, about 25 minutes. Drain the lentils well and set them aside. You should have about 1½ cups.

2. Preheat the oven to 350 degrees.

3. Heat the oil in a medium-sized, preferably nonstick skillet. Add the onion and cook over medium heat until softened, about 5 minutes. Add the garlic and cook, stirring, for 1 minute.

4. In a large bowl, combine the onion mixture with the reserved lentils, ground meat, spinach, 3 tablespoons chili sauce, mustard, Worcestershire, thyme, and egg white. Mix the ingredients together gently but thoroughly.

5. Spray a 9x5-inch loaf pan with vegetable oil spray. Transfer the lentil-meat mixture to the pan, pat it evenly into the pan, and brush with the remaining tablespoon of chili sauce. Bake, uncovered, until the loaf is brown on top and firm to the touch, and until the juices run clear when you pierce the center with the tip of a knife, 1 to 1¼ hours.

6. Let the loaf stand for 10 minutes before cutting it into slices and serving.

◆ *PER SERVING: About 184 cals, 53 cals from fat, 6g total fat, 2g sat fat, 35mg chol, 259mg sodium, 17g total carbs, 3g fiber, 16g prot*

Mixed Baked Beans with Maple

Makes 8 side-dish servings (4 main-dish servings)

This recipe is easy to double or triple and makes a terrific portable dish for a potluck supper or picnic.

2 slices (about 1 ounce) turkey
  bacon, coarsely chopped
1 large onion, chopped
2 garlic cloves, finely chopped
2 teaspoons dry mustard
1 teaspoon dried thyme
½ cup vegetable broth, defatted
  lower-sodium chicken broth,
  or water
½ cup maple syrup
⅓ cup chili sauce or ketchup
⅓ cup cider vinegar

1 tablespoon Worcestershire sauce
½ teaspoon liquid hot pepper
  sauce
1 can (15 to 16 ounces) black
  beans, rinsed and drained, or
  1½ cups cooked black beans
1 can (15 to 16 ounces) red kidney
  beans, rinsed and drained, or
  1½ cups cooked kidney beans
1 can (15 to 16 ounces) white
  beans, rinsed and drained, or
  1½ cups cooked white beans

1. Preheat the oven to 325 degrees.

2. In a large, preferably nonstick skillet or Dutch oven, cook the turkey bacon over medium heat until lightly browned, about 8 minutes. Add the onion and cook, stirring occasionally, until softened, about 5 minutes. Add the garlic, mustard, and thyme, and cook, stirring, for 1 minute. Stir in the broth, maple syrup, chili sauce, vinegar, and Worcestershire. Bring to a boil, cook for 1 minute, and stir in the hot pepper sauce.

3. Put the three types of beans into a 2- to 3-quart casserole dish, pour the sauce over them, and stir gently to combine. Cover and bake in the preheated oven for 1 hour. Uncover and check the sauce. If it is too liquid, continue to bake, uncovered, for about 10 minutes longer until the sauce becomes reduced and thickened. (This recipe can be prepared 1 day ahead and refrigerated. Reheat before serving.)

◆ *PER SERVING: About 188 cals, 11 cals from fat, 1g total fat, 0g sat fat, 3mg chol, 519mg sodium, 38g total carbs, 7g fiber, 8g prot*

STORING COOKED LEGUMES

You can cover and store cooled, cooked legumes in the refrigerator for up to 4 days. Cooked beans can be safely frozen in airtight containers for up to 6 months.

Smoky Black Bean and Pork Chili

Makes 8 servings

The smoky accent in this chili comes from both the chipotle peppers (dried and smoked jalapeños) and the toasted cumin seed. Although it requires a bit of extra effort, this chili is definitely in the "special enough for guests" category.

1 pound dried black beans, rinsed and picked over (see note)

¾ teaspoon salt, or to taste

2 tablespoons whole cumin seeds

¾ pound ground pork or mixed ground meat

2 medium onions, chopped

6 garlic cloves, finely chopped

1 can (28 ounces) crushed tomatoes with juice

3 cups defatted lower-sodium beef broth

2 teaspoons minced chipotle peppers in adobo sauce

½ cup fresh orange juice

2 teaspoons grated orange peel

Freshly ground pepper to taste

1. If you have time, soak the beans in water to cover for 4 hours or overnight, or use the "quick-soak" method (see page 312). Drain into a colander. In a large soup pot, bring 8 cups of water to a boil. Add the soaked or unsoaked beans and the salt. Cook, covered, over low heat until the beans are tender, 1 to 1½ hours. (If the beans have not been pre-soaked, they will take the longer time to cook.) Drain the cooked beans into a colander and reserve.

2. Toast the cumin seeds in a small skillet over medium-low heat, stirring frequently, until they turn a rich, golden brown, about 5 minutes. Coarsely grind the seeds in a spice grinder, with a mortar and pestle, or by chopping with a large knife. Set aside.

3. In a very large skillet or Dutch oven, cook the pork with the onions over medium heat, stirring frequently, until the meat loses its pink color, about 5 minutes. Spoon off any excess fat. Add the garlic and the cumin and cook, stirring, for 1 minute. Add the tomatoes, broth, chipotles, and cooked beans. Simmer uncovered, over medium-low heat, stirring occasionally, until quite thick, about 30 to 40 minutes.

4. Stir in the orange juice and peel and the salt and pepper to taste and serve.

◆ *PER SERVING: About 291 cals, 38 cals from fat, 4g total fat, 1g sat fat, 19mg chol, 498mg sodium, 43g total carbs, 8g fiber, 21g prot*

Note: You can substitute 6 cups (three 19-ounce cans) of rinsed and drained canned black beans for the dried black beans; add them to the chili at the same time as the tomatoes.

White Beans and Greens Casserole

Makes 4 servings

In this recipe, you can use either fresh turnip or mustard greens or frozen greens. Serve this garlicky meatless casserole with Lemon and Honey-Glazed Baby Carrots (page 430), crusty bread, and Amaretti Baked Pears (page 442) for dessert.

1 pound turnip or mustard greens, washed and torn, or 1 package (10 ounces) frozen greens, thawed and drained

2 tablespoons olive oil, preferably extra virgin

3 garlic cloves, finely chopped

1¾ cups defatted lower-sodium chicken broth or vegetable broth

2 cans (15 ounces) white beans, rinsed and drained, or 3 cups cooked white beans

2 cups chopped seeded tomatoes

1½ teaspoons crumbled dried sage

1 teaspoon dried thyme

½ teaspoon dried savory

½ teaspoon cayenne pepper

Salt to taste

1¼ cups fresh bread crumbs

½ teaspoon black pepper, preferably coarse ground

1. Cook fresh greens (just thaw frozen greens, if using) in a large pot of lightly salted boiling water until almost tender, 10 to 15 minutes. Drain into a colander, pressing on the greens to remove the excess water. Set aside.

2. Heat the oil in a large skillet or Dutch oven. Add the garlic and cook, stirring, for 1 minute. Stir in the broth and beans and bring to a simmer. Use a large spoon to mash about one quarter of the beans against the side of the pan to thicken the mixture.

3. Add the cooked fresh (or thawed frozen) greens along with the tomatoes, sage, thyme, savory, and cayenne to the bean mixture. Simmer, uncovered, over medium heat until the mixture becomes somewhat reduced and thickened, about 15 minutes. Season with salt to taste and transfer to a 2-quart baking dish. (The recipe can be made 1 day ahead to this point and refrigerated.)

4. Preheat the oven to 375 degrees. Sprinkle the crumbs and pepper evenly over the casserole. If the casserole is freshly made, bake, uncovered, until the casserole is heated through and the crumbs are lightly browned, about 25 minutes. If it has been refrigerated, cover the casserole with foil and bake until nearly heated through, about 20 minutes. Uncover and bake until it is hot and the crumbs are browned, 10 to 15 minutes longer.

◆ *PER SERVING: About 296 cals, 80 cals from fat, 9g total fat, 1g sat fat, 0mg chol, 631mg sodium, 43g total carbs, 12g fiber, 15g prot*

Quick Cassoulet

Makes 6 servings

You can quickly assemble this lightened and updated rendition of the famous French peasant dish for a weeknight supper. But it's sophisticated enough for a special dinner. The fresh thyme in the crumb crust adds a savory accent to this hearty bean stew.

½ pound skinless boneless chicken thighs
  or duck breast, cut in 1-inch cubes
6 ounces turkey kielbasa or other garlicky
  smoked sausage, thinly sliced (about 1½ cups)
1 large onion, chopped
1 celery rib, thinly sliced
4 garlic cloves, finely chopped
2 cans (19 ounces each) white beans, rinsed and
  drained, or 4 cups cooked white beans (see note)
1½ cups dry white wine
2 cups chopped seeded tomatoes or 1 can
  (16 ounces) chopped stewed tomatoes with juice
1½ cups defatted lower-sodium chicken
  broth or vegetable broth
¼ cup slivered dry-pack sun-dried tomatoes
1½ cups fresh bread crumbs (from about 3 slices
  white or whole-wheat bread)
3 tablespoons chopped fresh thyme or 2 teaspoons dried
½ teaspoon black pepper

1. In a very large, preferably nonstick skillet or Dutch oven, cook the chicken, kielbasa, onion, and celery over medium heat, stirring occasionally, until well browned, about 10 minutes. Add the garlic and cook, stirring, for 1 minute. Add the beans and wine, raise the heat to high, and boil until about half of the liquid is reduced and absorbed, about 3 minutes.

2. Add the chopped or canned tomatoes, broth, and sun-dried tomatoes, reduce the heat to medium-low, and simmer, uncovered, until the mixture has become reduced and thickened to a stewlike consistency, 15 to 20 minutes. Transfer it to a 2- to 2½-quart baking dish. (The recipe can be made 2 days ahead to this point and refrigerated. If the cassoulet seems dry, you can add up to ¾ cup broth before baking.)

3. Preheat the oven to 350 degrees. In a medium skillet, toss the crumbs over medium heat, stirring, until they are slightly dried but not toasted, about 2 minutes. Stir in the thyme and pepper and sprinkle the seasoned crumbs evenly over the bean mixture.

4. If the cassoulet is freshly made, bake the cassoulet uncovered in the preheated oven until the crumbs turn golden brown and the juices bubble around the edges, about 25 minutes. If it has been refrigerated, cover and bake until almost heated through, about 15 minutes. Uncover and continue to bake until the juices are bubbly and the crumbs brown, 15 to 20 minutes.

◆ *PER SERVING: About 317 cals, 65 cals from fat, 7g total fat, 2g sat fat, 53mg chol, 823mg sodium, 39g total carbs, 10g fiber, 26g prot*

Note: If you cook dry beans from scratch, use ½ pound Great Northern or navy beans. Soak them in water to cover at least 4 hours or overnight, if desired, then simmer, covered, in 5 cups of water with ½ teaspoon salt and a branch of fresh thyme, until tender, 1½ to 2 hours. Drain and use as directed.

TO "BEAN UP" DAILY MENUS

◆ To boost the nutrition content of everyday meals, you can add cooked beans to homemade or canned vegetable-style soups, meat stews, pasta sauces, and most types of salads, particularly those with vinaigrette dressings.
◆ Purée any type of well-cooked beans, season to your own taste, and serve them as a dip for crudités or crackers.
◆ Leftover bean dip makes a super sandwich spread.
◆ Add whole canned beans to any vegetable or meat sandwich filling for pita pockets.
◆ Mix coarsely mashed cooked beans with any type of ground meat to stretch burgers.
◆ Combine leftover cooked beans with spicy salsa for a terrific snack.

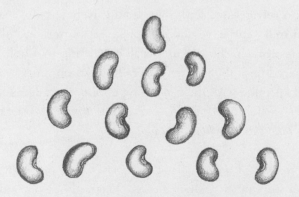

Jamaican Rice and Beans with Thyme

Makes 6 main-dish servings (10 side-dish servings)

This Jamaican classic needs the rich, sweet flavor of coconut milk to achieve the best-tasting (and most authentic) result. Look for canned, unsweetened coconut milk in the Asian ingredient section of your supermarket. You can use the lower-fat version but, because it's lighter, you will need a larger quantity to get the same flavor.

½ pound dried red kidney beans, rinsed and picked over (see note)

½ teaspoon salt, plus additional to taste

½ cup canned unsweetened coconut milk or ¾ cup lower-fat coconut milk

4 garlic cloves, finely chopped

3 tablespoons chopped fresh thyme or 1 tablespoon dried

1 small Scotch bonnet pepper or 2 jalapeño peppers, seeded and finely chopped

1 tablespoon butter

¼ teaspoon ground allspice

1½ cups raw long-grain white rice

¾ cup thinly sliced scallions, plus ¾ cup

1. If you have time, soak the beans in enough water to cover for 4 hours or overnight, or use the "quick-soak" method (page 312). Drain into a colander. In a large soup pot, bring 7 cups of water to a boil. Add the soaked or unsoaked beans and ½ teaspoon salt. Cover, reduce the heat to low, and simmer until the beans are almost tender, 1 to 1½ hours. (If the beans have not been presoaked, they will take the longer time to cook.) The beans can be cooked 2 days ahead and refrigerated with their liquid. Reheat before proceeding.

2. Add the coconut milk, garlic, thyme, hot peppers, butter, and allspice to the beans and simmer for 5 minutes. Stir in the rice and scallions, bring to a boil, reduce the heat to very low, and cook covered until the rice is tender, 20 to 25 minutes.

3. Salt to taste, and sprinkle with the remaining chopped scallions before serving.

◆ *PER MAIN-DISH SERVING: About 357 cals, 68 cals from fat, 8g total fat, 6g sat fat, 5mg chol, 206mg sodium, 61g total carbs, 3g fiber, 12g prot*

Note: You can substitute canned beans. Bring 4 cups of water or broth to a boil and add 3 cups of rinsed and drained canned kidney beans. Mash about one quarter of the beans against the side of the pan to add color to the finished dish. Stir in the coconut milk and proceed with the rest of the recipe as written.

Cuban Black Beans and Rice

Makes 4 servings

Black beans and rice (sometimes called "Moors and Christians") are a mainstay of the Cuban diet. This dish makes a scrumptious meatless main course, especially when finished with a generous spoonful of colorful Tropical Salsa (recipe follows).

1½ tablespoons olive oil
1 large onion, coarsely chopped
1 green bell pepper, coarsely chopped
3 garlic cloves, finely chopped
1½ teaspoons chili powder
1½ teaspoons ground cumin
2 cans (19 ounces each) black beans, rinsed and drained, or 4 cups cooked black beans
2½ cups vegetable broth or defatted lower-sodium chicken broth or a mixture of broth and water

1 to 2 fresh or pickled jalapeño peppers, minced
2 teaspoons honey
1 bay leaf, broken in half
1½ cups raw long-grain white rice
¾ teaspoon salt, plus additional to taste
2 teaspoons red or white wine vinegar
Tropical Salsa (recipe follows)

1. Heat the oil in a large skillet or Dutch oven. Add the onion and green pepper and cook over medium heat, stirring occasionally, until the vegetables begin to soften, about 5 minutes. Add the garlic, chili powder, and cumin and cook, stirring, for 1 minute until fragrant. Add the beans, broth, jalapeños, honey, and bay leaf. Bring to a boil, reduce the heat to medium-low, and simmer, uncovered, stirring occasionally, until the beans have thickened to a saucelike consistency, about 20 minutes. Remove the pieces of bay leaf. (The beans can be made 2 days ahead to this point and refrigerated. Reheat before proceeding.)

2. Meanwhile, bring 3 cups of water to a boil in a medium-sized saucepan. Add the rice and ¾ teaspoon salt. Reduce the heat to very low, and cook, covered, until the rice becomes tender and absorbs the water, about 20 minutes.

3. Stir the vinegar into the beans and season with salt to taste. To serve, ladle the beans over or alongside the rice. Pass a bowl of Tropical Salsa so everyone can spoon some over the top.

◆ *PER SERVING: About 584 cals, 90 cals from fat, 10g total fat, 1g sat fat, 0mg chol, 972mg sodium, 105g total carbs, 15g fiber, 19g prot*

TROPICAL SALSA

Makes about 2 cups (4 servings)

This vitamin C–rich papaya salsa enlivens Cuban Black Beans and Rice (page 299), and also makes a wonderful condiment for grilled fish or chicken. Use a larger quantity of hot pepper sauce if you prefer a spicier salsa.

1 medium-sized ripe papaya,
    peeled, seeded, and chopped
½ cup chopped red onion

¼ cup chopped fresh cilantro
2 tablespoons fresh lime juice
½ teaspoon grated lime peel

½ teaspoon salt
½ teaspoon liquid hot pepper
    sauce, or to taste

Combine all the ingredients in a small bowl. Let stand at room temperature for 10 minutes or up to 2 hours.

Per serving: About 73 cals, 2 cals from fat, 0g total fat, 0g sat fat, 0mg chol, 279mg sodium, 17g total carbs, 2g fiber, 1g prot

DRIED BEAN COOKING TIPS

◆ Begin cooking beans (presoaked or unsoaked, see page 312) in boiling water, which makes them cook much faster and more evenly than starting to cook them in cold water.

◆ Be sure to keep the pot tightly covered. An uncovered pot greatly lengthens cooking time.

◆ Do not boil beans; simmer them gently over very low heat so that the skins do not burst.

◆ High altitude and hard water may increase cooking time.

◆ You can add salt at any time in the cooking process without significantly affecting cooking time.

◆ Acidic foods such as tomatoes, citrus juice, and vinegar tend to retard cooking time, so add them toward the end of the cooking process.

◆ You can cook dried beans in a pressure cooker with some precautions. Beans produce foam that can clog the pressure vent, so cook only ½ pound at a time in an average-size pressure cooker. Follow the manufacturer's instructions, adding 1 tablespoon of cooking oil to help prevent foaming. Cook on high pressure (15 pounds) for about 7 minutes for lentils and split peas, 15 minutes for black beans and black-eyed peas, and 25 to 35 minutes for large beans such as kidney or pinto beans.

◆ You can cook dried beans in a slow cooker. Follow the manufacturer's directions.

◆ Do not try to cook dried beans in a microwave oven because the beans will not rehydrate evenly.

Lentil Stew with Rosemary

Makes 4 servings

Serve this tasty rosemary-scented lentil stew over Parsley-Parmesan Potato Cake (page 422) or with peasant bread. A green salad with radicchio or other bitter greens adds a welcome balance.

1½ tablespoons olive oil,
    preferably extra virgin
1 medium onion, chopped
2 carrots, peeled and thinly sliced
1 large celery rib, thinly sliced
2 garlic cloves, finely chopped
3 cups defatted lower-sodium
    chicken broth or vegetable broth
1½ cups dried green or brown
    lentils, rinsed and picked over
1 can (16 ounces) stewed tomatoes
    with juice

1 bay leaf, broken in half
½ teaspoon salt, or to taste
1½ teaspoons chopped fresh
    rosemary or 1 teaspoon dried
1½ teaspoons chopped fresh
    sage or 1 teaspoon dried
2 teaspoons balsamic vinegar
Freshly ground black pepper and
    salt to taste

1. Heat the oil in a medium-large saucepan. Add the onion, carrots, and celery, and cook over medium heat, stirring occasionally, until they begin to soften, about 5 minutes. Add the garlic and cook, stirring, for 1 minute. Add the broth, lentils, tomatoes, bay leaf, salt, and 2 cups of water. Bring to a boil, breaking the tomatoes into chunks with the side of a spoon if necessary. Reduce the heat to low, and cook, covered, until the lentils are tender but retain their shape, about 30 minutes. (Green lentils usually take about 15 minutes longer to soften.)

2. Uncover, stir in the rosemary and sage, and simmer until the lentils are thickened to a stewlike consistency, 5 to 10 minutes. Discard the pieces of bay leaf. Stir in the vinegar and season with black pepper and additional salt to taste.

◆ *PER SERVING: About 480 cals, 60 cals from fat, 7g total fat, 1g sat fat, 0mg chol, 1112mg sodium, 82g total carbs, 16g fiber, 26g prot*

Turkish Red Lentils and Rice

Makes 6 servings

Red lentils are a lovely saffron-orange color when dried. When cooked, their color pales, and they dissolve almost completely into a soft, delicately flavored purée. In this recipe, tomato paste and paprika help to keep the stewed lentils a rosy pink. Serve them the way they do in Turkey—over rice and garnished with yogurt, mint, and lemon wedges.

2 tablespoons olive oil
1 medium onion, coarsely chopped
1 carrot, peeled and sliced
1 celery rib, sliced
2 garlic cloves, finely chopped
1½ tablespoons sweet paprika,
   such as Hungarian paprika
¼ teaspoon cayenne pepper
5 cups defatted lower-sodium
   chicken or vegetable broth

1½ cups red lentils, rinsed and
   picked over
1 cup chopped seeded tomatoes
1½ tablespoons tomato paste
¾ teaspoon salt, plus additional to
   taste
1½ cups raw long-grain white
   rice
2 tablespoons chopped fresh mint
1 cup nonfat plain yogurt
1 lemon, cut into wedges

1. Heat the oil in a large saucepan or Dutch oven. Add the onion, carrot, and celery and cook over medium heat, stirring occasionally, until the vegetables begin to soften and brown, about 6 minutes. Add the garlic, paprika, and cayenne and cook, stirring, for 1 minute.

2. Stir in the broth and add the lentils, tomatoes, and tomato paste. Bring to a boil, reduce the heat to medium-low, and simmer, partially covered, until the lentils are very tender and almost completely dissolved, about 30 minutes. Adjust the liquid if necessary, adding more if needed to achieve the consistency of a very thick soup.

3. Meanwhile, in a medium-large saucepan, bring 3 cups of water to a boil. Add ¾ teaspoon salt and the rice. Return to a boil, reduce the heat to very low, and cook, covered, until the rice is tender, about 20 minutes.

4. Season the lentils with salt to taste. To serve, spoon the lentils over the rice and sprinkle with the mint. Serve the yogurt and lemon wedges in bowls for garnishing.

◆ *PER SERVING: About 451 cals, 54 cals from fat, 6g total fat, 1g sat fat, 1mg chol, 456mg sodium, 80g total carbs, 2g fiber, 20g prot*

Lentil, Spinach, and Potato Ragout

Makes 6 servings

This hearty, meatless stew, inspired by the flavors of the eastern Mediterranean, is accented with fresh lemon and chopped mint and then finished with a shower of crumbled feta cheese, which is big on flavor but doesn't add much fat.

2 tablespoons olive oil, preferably extra virgin
1 large onion, chopped
4 garlic cloves, finely chopped
4 cups defatted lower-sodium chicken
    broth or vegetable broth
1½ cups dried brown lentils,
    rinsed and picked over
1½ pounds red-skinned potatoes,
    sliced ¼ inch thick
1 pound torn fresh spinach leaves
    or 1 package (10 ounces)
    thawed frozen spinach
¼ cup fresh lemon juice
1 teaspoon grated lemon peel
½ teaspoon cayenne pepper
Salt to taste
½ cup chopped fresh mint
4 ounces (1 cup) crumbled feta cheese

1. Heat the oil in a large skillet with a lid or in a Dutch oven. Add the onion and cook, stirring occasionally, until it begins to soften, about 4 minutes. Add the garlic and cook, stirring, for 1 minute. Stir in the broth and lentils. Bring to a boil, reduce the heat to low, and cook, covered, for 15 minutes. Add the potatoes and cook until the lentils and potatoes are both tender, about 15 minutes longer.

2. Stir in the spinach and simmer, covered, until the spinach wilts and becomes tender, about 4 minutes. Add more liquid if needed to maintain a stewlike consistency.

3. Stir in the lemon juice, lemon peel, cayenne, salt to taste, and mint. Sprinkle with the crumbled feta before serving.

◆ *PER SERVING: About 431 cals, 91 cals from fat, 10g total fat, 4g sat fat, 17mg chol, 329mg sodium, 66g total carbs, 10g fiber, 23g prot*

Spiced Split Peas on Jasmine Rice

Makes 4 servings

In this recipe, dried split peas—either yellow or green—are seasoned with a heady mix of hot and fragrant Indian spices that will perfume your kitchen with aromas of the East. Serve the split peas in their thick, coconut-enriched sauce, over jasmine rice, accompanied by tart Cooling Cucumber Raita (recipe follows), which adds a piquant finish.

1 cup dried yellow or green split peas, rinsed
2 teaspoons olive oil
1 medium-large onion, coarsely chopped
2 garlic cloves, finely chopped
1 teaspoon curry powder
½ teaspoon ground cinnamon
½ teaspoon ground coriander seed
1½ cups vegetable broth or defatted
   lower-sodium chicken broth
1 medium-large tomato, seeded and chopped
3 tablespoons packaged grated sweetened coconut
1 fresh or pickled jalapeño pepper, finely chopped
¾ teaspoon salt, plus additional to taste
1½ cups raw jasmine rice
¼ cup chopped fresh cilantro, plus additional sprigs
   for garnish

1. Cook the split peas in about 6 cups of lightly salted water, covered, until tender, 40 minutes to 1 hour. Drain and set aside.

2. Heat the oil in a large, preferably nonstick skillet or Dutch oven. Add the onion and cook over medium heat, stirring frequently, until golden brown, about 8 minutes. Add the garlic, curry powder, cinnamon, and coriander and cook, stirring, for 1 minute. Add the broth, tomato, coconut, and jalapeño pepper. Bring to a boil over high heat and add the cooked split peas. Simmer, covered, over medium-low heat for 15 minutes to blend the flavors. Uncover and cook over medium heat until thickened to a saucelike consistency, adjusting the liquid if necessary. (This sauce can be made 2 days ahead and refrigerated. Reheat gently before serving.)

3. Meanwhile, bring 3 cups of water to a boil in a heavy saucepan. Add the ¾ teaspoon of salt, stir in the rice, and cook, tightly covered, over low heat until the rice becomes tender and absorbs the water, about 20 minutes. Fluff with a fork.

4. Stir the cilantro into the split peas and season with salt to taste. To serve, spoon the split pea sauce over the rice and garnish with additional cilantro sprigs if desired.

◆ *PER SERVING: About 440 cals, 44 cals from fat, 5g total fat, 2g sat fat, 0mg chol, 501mg sodium, 85g total carbs, 5g fiber, 14g prot*

COOLING CUCUMBER RAITA
Makes 2½ cups (4 servings)

Raita is a yogurt-based Indian sauce or condiment that provides a cool, refreshing balance to spicy foods.

1½ cups nonfat plain yogurt
¾ cup chopped seeded cucumber
1 small garlic clove, finely chopped

½ teaspoon ground cumin
¼ teaspoon ground coriander seed
1 teaspoon rice wine vinegar
1 teaspoon honey

½ teaspoon liquid hot pepper sauce
Salt to taste

Combine all the ingredients in a small bowl. Serve immediately or refrigerate for up to 2 hours.

Per serving: About 58 cals, 2 cals from fat, 0g total fat, 0g sat fat, 2mg chol, 69mg sodium, 9g total carbs, 0g fiber, 5g prot

BUYING AND STORING DRIED LEGUMES

When you are shopping for dried legumes, look for bright, uniform color and smooth, unbroken skins, which indicate freshness and quality. Buy them in packages or in bulk from a super-market with a high turnover to ensure freshness. Store dried beans in their original package or in a jar or canister in a cool, dark, dry location. Dried beans have an almost indefinite shelf life but, for the best quality, don't keep them for more than 1 year or they may not soften properly during cooking. Extremes of heat, light, and moisture affect storage life.

BEAN COUNTING

Dried legumes double or triple in volume as they cook, so be sure to use a large enough pot.

◆ 1 cup dried beans weighs about 8 ounces.

◆ 1 cup dried beans yields 2 to 3 cups cooked beans.
◆ 1 pound dried beans yields 6 to 7 cups cooked beans.
Cooked beans are sold in various-size cans that yield the following in drained beans.
◆ One 10-ounce can = 1 cup
◆ One 15-ounce can = 1½ cups
◆ One 16-ounce can = 1¾ cups
◆ One 19-ounce can = 2 cups

Black Bean and Yam Stew with Sofrito

Makes 4 servings

Sofrito refers to the cooked onions, garlic, and green pepper that form the basis for much of Spanish Caribbean cooking. This version, made with olive oil, produces a lighter stew than the traditional recipe, which calls for salt pork or bacon. This colorful dish is rich in fiber as well as vitamin C and iron.

1 tablespoon olive oil

1 medium onion, finely chopped

1 small green bell pepper, seeded and finely chopped

3 garlic cloves, finely chopped

1 pound yams or sweet potatoes, peeled and cut in ³/₄-inch dice (about 2½ cups)

2 teaspoons chili powder

1 teaspoon ground cumin

2 cans (19 ounces each) black beans, rinsed and drained, or 4 cups cooked black beans

2 cups chopped seeded tomatoes or 1 can (16 ounces) diced tomatoes, drained

3 tablespoons chopped fresh cilantro

1 tablespoon red wine vinegar

³/₄ teaspoon liquid hot pepper sauce, or to taste

Salt to taste

1. To make the sofrito, heat the oil in a medium-large skillet. Add the onion and green pepper and cook over low heat, stirring occasionally, until very soft, about 15 minutes. Stir in the garlic and cook for 1 minute. Set the sofrito aside.

2. Cook the yams in a saucepan full of lightly salted water just until tender, 8 to 10 minutes. Drain, reserving 1½ cups of the cooking water.

3. In a large skillet or Dutch oven, toast the chili powder and cumin over medium heat, stirring almost constantly, until fragrant and one shade darker, about 3 minutes. Add the beans, tomatoes, and reserved yam cooking water. Bring to a boil, breaking up the tomatoes into smaller chunks with the side of a spoon. Reduce the heat to medium-low and simmer, uncovered, until the mixture is somewhat reduced and thickened, about 10 minutes. Stir in the cooked yams and the sofrito—the onion and bell pepper mixture. (The stew can be made a day ahead and refrigerated. Reheat before proceeding.)

4. Stir in the cilantro, vinegar, and hot pepper sauce, and season with salt to taste.

◆ *PER SERVING: About 372 cals, 44 cals from fat, 5g total fat, 1g sat fat, 0mg chol, 656mg sodium, 70g total carbs, 16g fiber, 15g prot*

Fava Beans with Fennel and New Potatoes

Makes 4 servings

Fresh fava beans take a bit of time to prepare, but their unique, delicate flavor makes it worth the occasional effort. Make this dish in late winter or early spring when these prized seasonal ingredients are at their peak.

1¾ pounds fresh fava beans in pods or 2½ cups (about 1 pound) thawed frozen lima beans

2 tablespoons olive oil, preferably extra virgin

3 garlic cloves, finely chopped

4 cups vegetable broth or defatted lower-sodium chicken broth

1 cup dry white wine or nonalcoholic wine or ¼ cup lemon juice mixed with ¾ cup broth

1 pound red-skinned potatoes, diced (about 3 cups)

1 small fennel bulb, trimmed and thinly sliced (about 2 cups)

¾ pound slender asparagus spears, trimmed and cut in 1-inch lengths

2 tablespoons chopped fresh thyme or 2 teaspoons dried thyme

Salt to taste

Freshly ground black pepper to taste

1 cup fresh bread crumbs

3 tablespoons grated Parmesan cheese, preferably imported

1. If using fava beans, split the pods with your thumb and remove the beans. Cook the beans in a saucepan full of lightly salted boiling water until just tender, about 5 minutes. Drain into a colander and run under cold water to cool. Use a small, sharp knife to peel off the thick outer skins and set the peeled beans aside.

2. Heat the oil in a large skillet with a lid or in a Dutch oven. Add the garlic and cook over medium heat, stirring, for 1 minute. Add the broth, wine, potatoes, and fennel. Bring to a boil, reduce the heat to low, and simmer, covered, for 5 minutes until the potatoes begin to soften.

3. Add the asparagus, reserved favas, and thyme and simmer over medium heat, partially covered, until all the vegetables are tender, 5 to 8 minutes. Season with salt and pepper to taste.

4. In a small skillet, toss the bread crumbs over medium heat until they are lightly toasted, 3 to 4 minutes. Remove from the heat and toss with the cheese.

5. Serve the stew in shallow bowls and sprinkle with the toasted bread topping.

◆ *PER SERVING: About 443 cals, 85 cals from fat, 9g total fat, 2g sat fat, 4mg chol, 324mg sodium, 68g total carbs, 8g fiber, 16g prot*

Tuscan-Style Ribollita

Makes 6 servings

This savory peasant stew gets cooked twice. The vegetable mixture is delicious made from scratch, but if you have some leftover Herbed Minestrone (page 156), you can use it too. Simply ladle it into a baking dish, top with the bread and cheese, and bake.

2 tablespoons olive oil

1 large onion, coarsely chopped

2 carrots, sliced

2 celery ribs, sliced

1 small red bell pepper, seeded and coarsely chopped

1 small yellow crookneck squash, sliced

4 garlic cloves, chopped

2 teaspoons chopped fresh rosemary or 1 teaspoon dried

1 teaspoon dried thyme

2 cups defatted lower-sodium chicken broth or vegetable broth

1 can (15 ounces) diced tomatoes with juice or stewed tomatoes

2 cans (15 ounces each) white beans, rinsed and drained, or 3 cups cooked white beans

1 head (approximately 1¼ pounds) escarole, coarsely chopped or torn (about 5 cups)

Salt and black pepper to taste

8 to 12 ½-inch-thick slices (about 6 ounces) whole-wheat Italian bread

3 tablespoons grated Parmesan cheese, preferably imported

1. Heat the oil in a very large skillet with a lid. Add the onion and cook over medium heat, stirring occasionally, until soft, about 5 minutes. Add the carrot, celery, red pepper, and squash. Raise the heat to medium-high, and cook, stirring, until the vegetables are browned, 3 to 4 minutes. Stir in the garlic, rosemary, and thyme and cook, stirring, for 1 minute.

2. Add the broth, tomatoes, and beans. Bring to a boil, reduce the heat to medium-low, and cook, covered, until the carrots become tender, 10 to 15 minutes. Add the escarole and cook, covered, until the leaves wilt, about 3 minutes. Salt and pepper to taste. Transfer to a shallow 2-quart baking dish.

3. Preheat the broiler. Lightly toast the bread. Arrange the bread over the top of the stew, turning each piece so that both sides are well moistened with broth. (If the stew seems dry, add a bit more broth.) Sprinkle with the cheese.

4. Set the ribollita under the broiler until the top is golden brown and the cheese melts, about 2 minutes.

◆ *PER SERVING: About 307 cals, 71 cals from fat, 8g total fat, 1g sat fat, 2mg chol, 791mg sodium, 47g total carbs, 14g fiber, 15g prot*

Kentucky Bean and Vegetable Stew

Makes 4 servings

This savory stew is a vegetarian burgoo, a famous country recipe that originated in Kentucky. A traditional burgoo is made by braising the vegetables of the region—lima beans, corn, and okra—along with meat. This meatless rendition is every bit as satisfying, especially when served with a basket of Feather-Light Buttermilk Drop Biscuits (page 131) or corn muffins.

1 tablespoon vegetable oil

1 tablespoon butter

1 medium-large onion, chopped

3 garlic cloves, finely chopped

1 tablespoon all-purpose flour

2 cups defatted lower-sodium chicken
   broth or vegetable broth

½ pound red-skinned potatoes, diced
   (about 1½ cups)

1 carrot, peeled and sliced

1 package (10 ounces) frozen baby lima beans

2 teaspoons dried thyme

1 teaspoon dried sage

1 can (14 to 16 ounces) stewed tomatoes with juice

1 cup frozen or fresh corn kernels

1 cup sliced okra (see note)

1 tablespoon brown sugar

2 teaspoons Worcestershire sauce

2 teaspoons cider vinegar

½ teaspoon liquid hot pepper sauce

2 tablespoons chopped parsley, preferably flat leaf

1. Heat the oil and butter together in a large skillet with a lid or in a Dutch oven. Add the onion and cook over medium heat, stirring occasionally, until softened, about 5 minutes. Add the garlic and cook, stirring, for 1 minute. Add the flour and cook, stirring, until foamy and lightly browned, about 3 minutes. Gradually whisk in the broth and cook, stirring, until the sauce comes to a boil and becomes smooth and thick, about 2 minutes.

continued

2. Add the potatoes, carrots, lima beans, thyme, and sage. Reduce the heat to medium-low and cook, covered, for 10 minutes.

3. Stir in the tomatoes, corn, and okra and simmer, uncovered, stirring occasionally until all the vegetables are tender, about 15 minutes. Adjust the liquid if necessary to achieve a thick, stewlike consistency.

4. Stir in the brown sugar, Worcestershire, vinegar, and hot pepper sauce.

5. Serve in shallow soup bowls or rimmed plates and sprinkle with parsley.

◆ *PER SERVING: About 408 cals, 65 cals from fat, 7g total fat, 2g sat fat, 8mg chol, 845mg sodium, 76g total carbs, 11g fiber, 13g prot*

Note: If fresh okra pods are not available, use thawed frozen okra.

Hoppin' John with Colorful Garnishes

Makes 4 servings

Southerners believe that a plate of Hoppin' John eaten on New Year's Day ensures good luck in the coming year. The traditional dish—made with black-eyed peas and rice, and flavored with smoky bacon—gets a fresh new twist with the addition of chopped vegetable garnishes. Pass cruets of white wine vinegar and olive oil at the table.

3 slices (about 1½ ounces) bacon
1 large onion, chopped
1 large celery rib with leaves, chopped
3 garlic cloves, finely chopped
2 cups defatted lower-sodium chicken broth
2 packages (10 ounces each) frozen
   black-eyed peas (see note)
1 cup raw long-grain white rice
1 bay leaf, broken in half
½ teaspoon salt or to taste
½ teaspoon black pepper
½ teaspoon liquid hot pepper sauce or to taste
1 cup chopped seeded tomatoes
1 cup chopped seeded yellow bell peppers
¾ cup chopped red onion
White wine vinegar (optional)
Olive oil (optional)

1. In a large, heavy saucepan, cook the bacon over medium heat until lightly browned, about 8 minutes. Drain on paper towels and set aside, leaving the drippings in the pan.

2. Add the onion to the pan drippings and cook, stirring occasionally, until the onion becomes soft, about 8 minutes. Add the celery and garlic and cook, stirring, for 1 minute.

3. Raise the heat to high. Add the broth and 2 cups of water along with the black-eyed peas, rice, bay leaf, salt, and pepper. Bring to a boil, reduce the heat to low, and cook, covered, until the beans and rice are both tender, about 20 minutes. The Hoppin' John should be a little soupier than regular rice. Season with hot pepper sauce.

4. Discard the bay leaf. Crumble the reserved bacon over the Hoppin' John and serve.

5. Serve the tomatoes, peppers, and onion in bowls at the table and pass cruets of vinegar and oil, if desired.

◆ *PER SERVING: About 450 cals, 31 cals from fat, 3g total fat, 1g sat fat, 2mg chol, 474mg sodium, 86g total carbs, 11g fiber, 20g prot*

Note: Although the flavor and texture of frozen black-eyed peas is better than canned, you can substitute 2 cans (16 ounces each) of drained and rinsed black-eyed peas, or 4 cups of cooked dried black-eyed peas.

French Quarter Red Beans and Rice

Makes 6 servings

On wash-day Mondays in old New Orleans, a pot of well-seasoned red beans was set on the back burner to simmer all day to be served at the end of the work day over hot, steaming white rice. Smooth, medium-sized light red beans are the choice in Louisiana. If you can't find them, just use red kidney beans.

¾ pound (about 1½ cups) dried red beans or red kidney beans, rinsed and picked over (see note)

½ teaspoon salt, plus ¾ teaspoon

¾ pound turkey kielbasa or andouille sausage, sliced in 1-inch lengths (see note)

1 large onion, chopped

1 large green bell pepper, seeded and chopped

1 celery rib, sliced

½ cup thinly sliced scallions, plus ¼ cup

1 large bay leaf, broken in half

1 teaspoon dried thyme

1½ cups raw long-grain white rice

½ teaspoon liquid hot pepper sauce, plus additional to taste

Freshly ground black pepper to taste

continued

1. If you have time, soak the beans in water to cover for 4 hours or overnight, or use the "quick-soak" method (below). Drain into a colander. In a large soup kettle, bring 6 cups of water to a boil. Add the soaked or unsoaked beans and ½ teaspoon salt. Bring the water back to a boil, reduce the heat to low, and simmer, covered, until the beans are almost, but not quite, tender, 1 to 1½ hours. (If the beans have not been presoaked, they will take the longer time to cook.)

2. In a very large, preferably nonstick skillet or Dutch oven, cook the kielbasa, onion, pepper, celery, and scallions over medium heat, stirring frequently, until the kielbasa browns and the vegetables soften, about 8 minutes.

3. Add the red beans, along with 3 cups of the cooking liquid, to the sausage mixture. Add the bay leaf and thyme. Bring to a boil, reduce the heat to medium-low, and simmer uncovered until the beans become very tender, 30 to 45 minutes. (This recipe can be made 2 days ahead to this point and refrigerated. Reheat before proceeding.)

4. In a medium-large saucepan, bring 3 cups of water to a boil. Add ¾ teaspoon salt and the rice. Reduce the heat to low and cook, covered, until the rice becomes tender and absorbs the water, about 20 minutes.

5. To thicken the beans, mash about one quarter of the cooked beans against the side of the pan with a spoon. Season with the hot pepper sauce and black pepper and adjust the liquid if necessary. The beans should have a fairly thick, stewlike consistency. Discard the bay leaf pieces.

6. Spoon the beans over the hot, cooked rice, sprinkle with the remaining ¼ cup of scallions, and serve. Pass additional hot sauce at the table.

◆ *PER SERVING: About 424 cals, 45 cals from fat, 5g total fat, 1g sat fat, 38mg chol, 950mg sodium, 72g total carbs, 8g fiber, 24g prot*

Note: You can substitute 4 cups (two 19-ounce cans) of rinsed and drained canned beans for the dried beans. Add them to the kielbasa mixture in step 3, along with about 3 cups of water, and proceed with the recipe. You can also substitute a ham bone for the kielbasa. Simply simmer it along with the beans to extract its flavor. Then cut any meat off the bone, dice it, and add it to the finished beans. This substitution may increase the amount of fat in the recipe.

NO SOAK, QUICK SOAK, OR LONG SOAK?

You don't really need to presoak dried beans before cooking. The practice of presoaking beans in cold water for several hours or overnight (called the long-soak method) helps to rehydrate the beans, but it shortens overall cooking time by only 30 minutes or so. Quick-soaking dried beans (boiling them for 2 minutes, then letting them stand in the hot water for 1 hour) shortens the final cooking time by only about 15 minutes. So, unless you have lots of time, don't presoak. Just allow for a few minutes' more cooking time. But be sure to stop the cooking when the beans become tender; beans that have not been presoaked break apart more easily when they are overcooked.

Lentils and Rice with Blackened Onions

Makes 4 servings

Iron-rich lentils are among the oldest cultivated legumes; some say that their use goes back to biblical times. A generous dollop of yogurt finishes this dish, supplying calcium as well as a fresh, pleasing tang.

2 tablespoons olive oil, plus 1 tablespoon

1 medium onion, chopped, plus 2 large onions, sliced

3 garlic cloves, finely chopped

1 teaspoon ground cumin

½ teaspoon ground cinnamon

½ teaspoon ground allspice

3½ cups vegetable broth or water

1 cup dried lentils, rinsed and picked over

1 cup raw long-grain white rice

½ teaspoon salt, plus additional to taste

Freshly ground black pepper to taste

2 cups nonfat plain yogurt

1. Heat the 2 tablespoons of oil in a large, heavy saucepan or Dutch oven. Add the chopped onion and cook over medium heat, stirring occasionally, until softened, about 5 minutes. Add the garlic, cumin, cinnamon, and allspice and cook, stirring, for 1 minute.

2. Add the broth, bring to a boil over high heat, and add the lentils. Cover, reduce the heat to medium-low, and cook for 15 minutes.

3. Add the rice and ½ teaspoon salt and cook, covered, over low heat until the lentils and rice are tender, 20 to 25 minutes.

4. Meanwhile, heat the remaining tablespoon of oil in a medium-sized skillet. Add the two sliced onions and cook over medium heat, stirring occasionally, until the onions are well browned and tinged with black in some places, 15 to 20 minutes.

5. Season the lentils and rice with black pepper and additional salt if necessary. Serve topped with the blackened onions and the yogurt.

◆ *PER SERVING: About 593 cals, 104 cals from fat, 12g total fat, 2g sat fat, 2mg chol, 438mg sodium, 97g total carbs, 11g fiber, 26g prot*

Turkey and White Bean Chili Verde

Makes 4 servings

This quick, mild chili does not include tomatoes, but does have beans. Texans might balk at this heresy, but you won't once you taste it. Serve the tomatoes on the side, in a chunky salad tossed with slices of red onion and Basic Vinaigrette (page 74). Round out this fiber-rich meal with a basket of warm corn or flour tortillas and end with a Citrus Chiffon Cake (page 455).

2 teaspoons vegetable oil
1 pound ground turkey
1 medium onion, chopped
2 large garlic cloves, minced
1½ tablespoons yellow or white
   cornmeal
1½ tablespoons chili powder
1½ teaspoons ground cumin
1 teaspoon dried oregano

2½ cups defatted lower-sodium
   chicken broth
1 can (19 ounces) cannellini beans,
   drained and rinsed, or 2 cups
   cooked cannellini beans
1 can (4 ounces) green chiles,
   chopped
Salt and black pepper to taste
½ cup chopped scallions
⅓ cup chopped cilantro

1. Heat the oil in a large, preferably nonstick skillet, and cook the turkey and onion over medium heat, stirring often, until the turkey loses its pink color and the onion softens, 5 to 7 minutes. Add the garlic, cornmeal, and chili powder and cook, stirring, for 1 minute. Stir in the cumin and oregano. Add the broth and simmer, stirring often, over medium-low heat, for 10 minutes. Add the beans and chiles and simmer for 10 minutes. Season to taste with salt and pepper. (The recipe can be prepared a day ahead and refrigerated. Reheat gently before serving.)

2. When ready to serve, add the scallions and cilantro to the chili. Simmer for 3 minutes, then serve.

◆ *PER SERVING: About 336 cals, 107 cals from fat, 12g total fat, 2g sat fat, 92mg chol, 485mg sodium, 28g total carbs, 9g fiber, 30g prot*

Chickpea-Cilantro Stew with Cumin Croûtes

Makes 4 servings

Enlivened with fresh cilantro and lemon, this chickpea stew typifies the delicious, spicy food of the Mediterranean region. Spoon the stew over croûtes (literally crusts of French bread) that you have brushed with cumin-flavored oil and baked.

4 teaspoons extra-virgin olive oil,
   plus 1½ tablespoons
1 teaspoon ground cumin
4 ¾-inch-thick slices Italian or
   French bread (about 5 ounces)
1 large onion, chopped
4 garlic cloves, finely chopped
4 cups defatted lower-sodium
   chicken broth or vegetable broth

2 cans (19 ounces each) chickpeas,
   rinsed and drained, or 4
   cups cooked chickpeas
1 cup packed cilantro sprigs
3 tablespoons fresh lemon juice
1 teaspoon grated lemon peel
1½ cups chopped seeded fresh
   tomatoes
Salt and freshly ground black
   pepper to taste

1. Preheat the oven to 375 degrees. To make the croûtes, stir together the 4 teaspoons of olive oil with the cumin in a small bowl. Brush the flavored oil lightly over both sides of the bread slices and arrange on a baking sheet. Bake in the preheated oven for about 10 minutes, turning once, until toasted on both sides. Set aside.

2. Heat the remaining 1½ tablespoons of oil in a large skillet or Dutch oven. Add the onion and sauté over medium heat, stirring occasionally, until softened, about 5 minutes. Add the garlic and cook, stirring, for 1 minute. Stir in the broth and chickpeas and bring to a boil over high heat. Reduce the heat to low and cook, covered, for 20 minutes to blend the flavors.

3. In a blender or food processor, process about half of the chickpea and broth mixture with the cilantro, lemon juice, and lemon peel to make a smooth purée.

4. Return the puréed mixture to the pan with the remaining whole chickpeas and reheat gently, about 2 minutes. Stir in the chopped tomatoes and simmer until just heated through, about 2 minutes. Season with salt and pepper to taste. Serve immediately so that the colors remain bright.

5. Place the cumin croûtes in shallow soup bowls or on rimmed plates and spoon the stew over them.

◆ *PER SERVING: About 453 cals, 116 cals from fat, 13g total fat, 2g sat fat, 0mg chol, 978mg sodium, 69g total carbs, 13g fiber, 18g prot*

Tunisian Chickpea and Eggplant Stew

Makes 6 servings

This savory stew, fragrant with the sweet spices of Tunisia, is a breeze to put together. Serve it with sliced cucumbers drizzled with Basic Creamy Dressing (page 75) and flatbreads.

1 medium eggplant, about 1 pound
1 teaspoon salt, plus additional to taste
3 tablespoons olive oil
1 large onion, chopped
1 red bell pepper, seeded and coarsely chopped
4 garlic cloves, finely chopped
1 tablespoon ground cumin
1½ teaspoons ground cinnamon
1 teaspoon ground coriander seed
1 teaspoon powdered ginger
½ teaspoon cayenne pepper
1 can (28 ounces) crushed plum tomatoes with juice
2 cans (19 ounces each) chickpeas, rinsed
    and drained, or 4 cups cooked chickpeas
2 teaspoons honey
Freshly ground black pepper to taste
¼ cup chopped parsley, preferably flat leaf

1. Cut off the eggplant's cap and stem, but do not peel it. Cut it into rough ¾-inch cubes, place them in a colander, and toss with the salt. Set aside for 20 minutes to drain. Rinse well under cold water and pat dry on several layers of paper towels.

2. Heat the oil in a very large skillet or Dutch oven. Add the onion and cook over medium heat, stirring occasionally, until it begins to soften, about 4 minutes. Add the red pepper and garlic and cook, stirring, for 2 minutes. Stir in the cumin, cinnamon, coriander, ginger, and cayenne and cook for 1 minute.

3. Stir in the tomatoes, eggplant, and 1 cup of water. Bring to a boil, reduce the heat to low, and cook, covered, stirring occasionally, for 15 minutes.

4. Add the chickpeas and the honey, and simmer, uncovered, over medium heat until the eggplant is tender and the flavors blend, about 20 minutes longer. Salt and pepper to taste.

5. Sprinkle with the parsley and serve.

◆ *PER SERVING: About 313 cals, 91 cals from fat, 10g total fat, 1g sat fat, 0mg chol, 877mg sodium, 47g total carbs, 13g fiber, 11g prot*

Popular Bean Varieties

Beans are virtually fat free. They are high in protein, complex carbohydrates, and fiber. They are also a good source of iron, zinc, magnesium, and folic acid. One cup of beans contains about 225 calories and supplies about half of the recommended daily value for fiber.

You can find dozens of bean varieties to choose from. They differ most noticeably in color and shape, but also display subtle differences in flavor and texture. Look for more recipes containing beans in other chapters of this book.

NAME	DESCRIPTION, OTHER NAMES	USES
Black beans	Small, kidney shaped, shiny black. Sweet, earthy taste. Also known as turtle beans.	Available dried and canned. Widely used in Latin American and North American cuisines.
Black-eyed peas	Cream colored, with a small dark spot on one end. Fresh, sweet taste. Also known as cow peas.	Available fresh, frozen, dried, and canned. Used in African and southern US cooking (particularly in Hoppin' John recipes).
Chickpeas	Tan, bumpy, and round. Firm texture and mild, nutty flavor. Also known as garbanzo or ceci beans.	Available canned or dried. Popular in Mediterranean, Middle Eastern, and Indian cuisines. Main ingredient in hummus.
Fava beans	Large, pale green (fresh) or brown and wrinkled (dried). Delicate, earthy flavor. Similar but not identical to broad beans.	Available fresh in pods and dried. Used in Mediterranean and Middle Eastern cuisines.
Kidney beans	Large, sturdy, richly flavored. Dark red, light red, and white.	Available canned and dried. Widely used in chili. Light red are used in Louisiana red beans and rice recipes and white are the Italian cannellini.
Lentils	Small, disk-shaped. Many colors, including green, brown, and red.	Available dried only. Cook quickly, usually in less than 30 minutes. One of the world's oldest cultivated foods. Used in countless dishes all around the world.
Lima beans	Pale green and starchy. Available as baby limas and Fordhooks, which are large.	Available frozen and dried. Pale cream-colored limas are known as butter beans in the South. Used in succotash recipes.
Pinto beans	Large and kidney shaped. Beige with brownish streaks (like a pinto pony). Turns a uniform pale pink when cooked.	Available canned and dried. Widely used in Mexican and South American cooking.
Split peas	Available in both green and yellow. During processing, the peas are husked, dried, and split.	Available dried only. Used mostly in soups. Cook to a soft purée in less than an hour.
White beans	A color designation that includes navy or pea beans, Great Northern beans, and cannellini (white kidney beans).	Available both canned and dried. Used in several cuisines, including New England baked bean dishes (navy or great Northern beans) and many Italian dishes, particularly with pasta (cannellini beans).

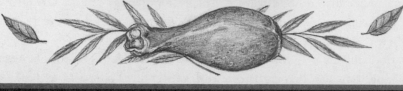

CHAPTER NINE

Poultry

Poultry appears regularly on America's tables. And it's no wonder—poultry is tasty, reasonably priced, versatile, and healthful. Always in abundant supply, poultry is an excellent, low-fat source of protein.

Poultry is more than just chicken, although chicken is easily the best known and most widely used type of poultry. Cornish hens are the closest to chicken in flavor and nutritional value. Turkey, no longer just for Thanksgiving, has a more assertive flavor and firmer texture. Duck deserves a more regular place on the menu because today's duck is bred to be lean and is distinct in flavor. Goose remains high in fat, and should be served only on the most special occasions.

Poultry is popular in large part because it is low in fat. As Americans have begun to understand the relationship between diet and heart disease, they have started to cut the fat out of their diets by eating less beef, pork, and other higher-fat meats. Poultry fills in the gap. Eaten without the skin, chicken is lower in both fat and saturated fat than beef and pork. Poultry stays moister when you cook it with the skin on, so leave the skin on while cooking, but remove it before you serve the dish. Turkey breast is among the lowest-fat sandwich fillings around. Poultry cold cuts, frankfurters, sausage, and burger patties offer variety, taste, and less fat than their red meat counterparts.

Poultry also can't be beat for convenience. Boneless, skinless breast or thigh cutlets are ideal when you're short on time. Dishes like Easy Chicken Cacciatore (page 336) and Basil Chicken and Sweet Pepper Packets (page 343) can go from cutting board to table in less than 30 minutes. Poultry sausage and ground poultry cook in a flash. Adding to the convenience factor, chicken, turkey, duck, and other poultry are interchangeable in many recipes.

You may have difficulty figuring out how much poultry to buy for a given dish. To begin with, parts vary in size. A drumstick from a small broiling chicken may be a fraction of a serving, while the same part from a roaster could yield as much as 5 or 6 ounces of meat. Also, in some families, certain parts are more popular than others. A 3-pound chicken doesn't serve six people if nobody likes dark meat. The chart on page 350 offers general guidelines that you can adjust to your family's preferences and whether or not you want to cook extra servings for leftovers. Packages of one type of part—for example, breasts, drumsticks, wings, or the "family" assortment of favorite parts—let you buy just those pieces that your family will eat.

Poultry is very popular, not only in the United States, but also around the world. What could be more American than All-American Barbecued Chicken (page 331) with its smoky flavor and tangy sauce? A stir-fry served over rice, like the Sesame Turkey and Asparagus Stir-Fry (page 348) typifies Chinese cuisine. For flavorful dishes inspired by the cuisines of the Middle East and India, look no further than this chapter's Roasted Lebanese Chicken (page 337), Chicken and Summer Vegetable Tagine (page 339), and Chicken Vindaloo (page 338).

What to do with leftovers? Few foods lend themselves to next-day dishes as well as poultry does. Use leftover poultry in a Classic Southern Chicken Salad (page 76) or Day-After-Thanksgiving Turkey Noodle Soup (page 147). Leftovers from Tandoor-Style Chicken Nuggets (page 334) or Tuscan Grilled Chicken and Roasted Garlic Aioli (page 333) make tasty sandwich fillings. And many hearty soups only get better with the addition of leftover chicken or turkey.

Convenient, versatile, healthy, and tasty, poultry well deserves its popularity.

Sunday Supper Roast Chicken

Makes 8 servings

Roast chicken is the classic Sunday dinner and a great way to stretch one chicken to serve the whole family. The Kale, Corn Bread, and Cranberry Dressing or the Exotic Fruit and Nut Bulgur Dressing (recipes follow) are delicious accompaniments for roasted chicken along with Molasses and Pepper Grilled Sweet Potato Slices (page 424). Removing the skin from the chicken lowers the fat content. You can cut even more fat by skipping the gravy.

1 whole roasting chicken
   (about 5 pounds), giblets reserved
Salt and freshly ground pepper
1 onion, quartered
1 bay leaf, broken in half
6 whole peppercorns
2 whole cloves
1½ tablespoons all-purpose flour

1. Preheat the oven to 400 degrees. Rinse the chicken inside and out, then pat it dry with paper towels. Sprinkle the chicken skin and cavity liberally with salt and pepper. Place the onion inside the chicken. Tie the chicken legs together with kitchen string for more even cooking. Place the chicken, breast side up, on a rack in a shallow roasting pan just large enough to accommodate it.

2. Roast the chicken for 30 minutes, reduce the heat to 350 degrees, and continue to roast until a thermometer inserted into the thigh registers 180 degrees, about 1½ hours longer.

3. While the chicken is roasting, place the neck, gizzard, bay leaf, peppercorns, and cloves in a saucepan and cover with about 3 cups of water. Bring to a boil, reduce the heat to medium-low, cover the pan, and simmer for 30 minutes. Strain the broth, discarding the solids. Let the broth cool slightly, then refrigerate it for at least 30 minutes to allow the fat to solidify. Scrape off and discard the fat. You should have between 2 and 2½ cups of broth.

4. Transfer the cooked chicken to a platter and let it stand, loosely covered with foil, for 15 minutes before carving. Pour the pan juices into a measuring cup and let them stand for 5 minutes to allow the fat to rise to the top. Skim off and discard the fat.

5. Remove the rack from the roasting pan. Do not wash the roasting pan. Sprinkle the flour over the bottom of the roasting pan. Cook on the stovetop, stirring over medium heat, until golden brown, about 2 minutes. Whisk in the defatted pan drippings and the defatted giblet broth. Bring to a boil, stirring constantly to dislodge any browned bits in the bottom of the pan. Cook the pan gravy, stirring often, until lightly thickened, 3 to 5 minutes. Salt and pepper to taste.

6. Carve the chicken, removing the skin before serving. Serve the chicken with the gravy.

◆ *PER SERVING: About 223 cals, 82 cals from fat, 9g total fat, 2g sat fat, 96mg chol, 107mg sodium, 2g total carbs, 0g fiber, 32g prot*

KALE, CORN BREAD, AND CRANBERRY DRESSING
Makes 8 servings

Kale and cranberry add flavor and color to this corn-bread dressing that complements pork chops or ham just as nicely as it does chicken or turkey. When baked alongside the bird, instead of in the cavity, the dressing remains colorful and absorbs no extra fat.

2 teaspoons unsalted butter
1 medium onion, chopped
1 large celery rib, chopped
⅓ cup defatted lower-sodium chicken broth, plus ½ to ⅔ cup
¾ pound fresh kale, trimmed and chopped, or 1 package (9 or 10 ounces) frozen chopped kale, thawed and drained
⅔ cup fresh cranberries, coarsely chopped
4 cups day-old low-fat corn bread, crumbled (such as Yogurt Corn Bread, page 125) (see note)
1 teaspoon crumbled dried sage
1 teaspoon crumbled dried thyme
1 teaspoon crumbled dried savory
¼ teaspoon salt
¼ teaspoon pepper

1. In a large skillet, heat the butter and cook the onion and celery, covered, over low heat until softened—about 5 minutes. Add ⅓ cup chicken broth and the kale. Cook, covered, and stir occasionally until the kale is tender, about 6 minutes for fresh kale and 3 minutes for frozen. Add the cranberries and cook, covered, for 3 minutes to soften somewhat. Add the corn bread, sage, thyme, savory, salt, and pepper and toss to combine. Add ½ cup of chicken broth and toss to moisten the dressing. Transfer the dressing to a large ovenproof baking dish and cover the casserole. (This recipe can be made several hours ahead to this point and refrigerated.)

2. Preheat the oven to 350 degrees. Bake the covered casserole until heated through, 20 to 25 minutes if freshly made, and 40 to 50 minutes if it has been chilled. If the dressing seems dry during baking, add a bit more chicken broth. If you prefer a crispy-topped dressing, uncover it during the last 15 minutes of baking.

3. Serve directly from the casserole dish.

Per serving: About 107 cals, 34 cals from fat, 4g total fat, 1g sat fat, 14mg chol, 221mg sodium, 15g total carbs, 3g fiber, 3g prot

Note: To dry out the corn bread, crumble and spread it on a baking sheet. Let it stand for 8 to 24 hours at room temperature. To dry it out in less time, toast it for 1 hour in a 200-degree oven.

EXOTIC FRUIT AND NUT BULGUR DRESSING

Makes 8 servings

Fiber-rich bulgur has a wonderful nutty flavor, which is enhanced in this dressing by toasted pecans. This unusual dish teams nicely with any roasted poultry and also pairs well with pork.

⅓ cup pecan pieces
1 tablespoon vegetable oil
1 large onion, chopped
2 celery ribs, chopped
2 carrots, chopped
2 garlic cloves, minced
1 teaspoon ground cumin

1 teaspoon paprika
½ teaspoon salt
¼ teaspoon cayenne pepper
1½ cups uncooked bulgur
1 cup chopped mixed dried fruit
2 teaspoons grated orange peel
½ cup orange juice

2 to 2¼ cups defatted
  lower-sodium chicken broth
⅓ cup chopped parsley,
  preferably flat leaf, plus
  2 tablespoons

1. Preheat the oven to 350 degrees. Toast the pecans on a small baking sheet, stirring once or twice, until they turn a shade darker and become fragrant, 5 to 7 minutes. Cool completely, then coarsely chop the nuts. Leave the oven on if you plan to bake the dressing right away.

2. In a medium saucepan, heat the oil and cook the onion, celery, and carrots, covered, over medium-low heat, stirring often, until very soft, about 8 minutes. Add the garlic, cumin, paprika, salt, and cayenne, and cook for 1 minute. Stir in the bulgur, dried fruit, orange peel and juice, and 2 cups of the broth. Transfer to a large ovenproof casserole dish. (This recipe can be made several hours ahead to this point and refrigerated. Return to room temperature before baking.)

3. Stir in ⅓ cup of chopped parsley. If the dressing has been made ahead, add the additional ¼ cup of broth. Bake, covered, in a 350-degree oven, for 45 minutes, until the liquid has been absorbed and the bulgur is tender.

4. Sprinkle the dressing with 2 tablespoons of chopped parsley and serve.

Per serving: About 217 cals, 50 cals from fat, 6g total fat, 1g sat fat, 0mg chol, 183mg sodium, 40g total carbs, 9g fiber, 6g prot

AN ENLIGHTENED THANKSGIVING

Try the side dishes and desserts listed below for a delicious—yet healthy—Thanksgiving dinner.

Kale, Corn Bread, and Cranberry
  Dressing (page 321)
Exotic Fruit and Nut Bulgur
  Dressing (above)
Spoon Bread, Garlic Greens,
  and Smoked Ham (page 256)

Braised Wild Rice with Cranberries
  (page 278)
Cranberry Pumpkin Bread
  (page 124)
Steamed Boston Brown Bread
  (page 122)
Fabulous Garlic Mashed Potatoes
  (page 419)
Glazed Gratin of Yams, Potatoes,
  and Turnips (page 423)
Gingered Carrot Purée (page 429)

Molasses and Pepper Grilled
  Sweet Potato Slices (page 424)
Lemon and Honey-Glazed Baby
  Carrots (page 430)
Deep-Dish Apple Pie (page 466)
Candied Gingerbread (page 462)
Pumpkin Pecan Bars (page 457)
Orange Marmalade–Glazed
  Cheesecake (page 464)
Cinnamon Raisin Bread
  Pudding (page 471)

Easy Amish Country Chicken Noodle Stew

Makes 6 servings

This Amish version of a chicken pot pie is really a stew with homemade noodles. This is a quick-and-easy interpretation that uses boneless chicken thighs and store-bought fresh pasta sheets or dried noodles. It tastes great, and it's rich in fiber, iron, and vitamins A and C.

7 cups defatted lower-sodium chicken broth

¼ teaspoon crushed saffron threads or ground turmeric

1 teaspoon dried thyme

1 teaspoon dried summer savory

½ teaspoon dried marjoram

½ teaspoon coarsely ground black pepper

¼ teaspoon grated nutmeg

½ pound potatoes, peeled and cut into 1-inch cubes

½ pound parsnips, peeled and cut into 1-inch cubes

2 carrots, cut into 1-inch chunks

2 celery ribs, cut into 1-inch chunks

1 onion, coarsely chopped

1 pound skinless boneless chicken thighs, cut into 1-inch chunks

½ cup fresh or frozen green peas

½ pound fresh pasta sheets or 4 ounces dried wide noodles

¼ cup chopped parsley

1. In a large Dutch oven or 5-quart pot, combine the broth, saffron, thyme, savory, marjoram, pepper, and nutmeg. Add the potatoes, parsnips, carrots, celery, and onion. Bring to a boil, then reduce the heat and simmer, partially covered, until the vegetables are tender, 20 to 30 minutes. Add the chicken and peas and simmer until the chicken is cooked through, about 10 minutes.

2. Cut the fresh pasta into 1x4-inch noodles. Drop the noodles into the simmering stew and cook, uncovered, until the noodles are tender, 1 to 3 minutes. (If using dried noodles, cook them for 8 to 10 minutes until tender.)

3. Serve the chicken, vegetables, noodles, and broth in wide, shallow soup bowls sprinkled with the parsley.

◆ *PER SERVING: About 396 cals, 87 cals from fat, 10g total fat, 2g sat fat, 100mg chol, 185mg sodium, 47g total carbs, 5g fiber, 29g prot*

Country-Style Chicken and Dumplings

Makes 6 servings

This dish is down-home cooking at its best. Dumplings are simply drop biscuits that cook in simmering broth. These herb-flecked biscuits impart a delicate flavor to the entire dish.

Chicken:

- 3 pounds chicken breasts and/or thighs, fat and skin removed
- 6 cups defatted lower-sodium chicken broth
- 1 large onion, thinly sliced
- 3 carrots, thickly sliced
- 2 celery ribs with leaves, thickly sliced
- 1 bay leaf, broken in half
- 1 teaspoon dried summer savory
- ½ teaspoon salt
- ½ teaspoon black pepper

Dumplings:

- 1 cup all-purpose flour
- 1 teaspoon baking powder
- ¼ teaspoon baking soda
- ¼ teaspoon salt
- 2 tablespoons vegetable shortening
- ½ cup nonfat buttermilk, plus 1 tablespoon
- 3 tablespoons chopped parsley, plus 1 tablespoon
- 3 tablespoons chopped chives, plus 1 tablespoon

1. In a Dutch oven or wide 4-quart pan, simmer the chicken in the broth along with the onion, carrot, celery, bay leaf, savory, salt, and pepper until the chicken is tender, about 30 minutes. Remove the chicken from the broth. When cool enough to handle, remove the chicken from the bones, cut it into chunks, and reserve. Discard the bones and bay leaf.

2. For the dumplings, combine the flour, baking powder, baking soda, and salt in a medium bowl. Rub the shortening into the flour mixture with your fingers until it resembles coarse crumbs. Stir in the buttermilk, 3 tablespoons chopped parsley, and 3 tablespoons chopped chives and mix to make a soft dough.

3. Return the broth to a simmer and add the reserved cooked chicken. Drop 12 dumplings by rounded tablespoons into the simmering broth to make a single layer. Cover the pot and simmer gently until the dumplings are cooked through and are no longer doughy, about 15 minutes.

4. Serve the chicken, broth, and dumplings in wide shallow soup bowls. Sprinkle with the remaining parsley and chives.

◆ *PER SERVING: About 329 cals, 79 cals from fat, 9g total fat, 2g sat fat, 75mg chol, 568mg sodium, 27g total carbs, 2g fiber, 34g prot*

Garlic-Braised Chicken and New Potatoes

Makes 6 servings

When slowly cooked, the whole garlic cloves in this recipe infuse the chicken and potatoes with a rich flavor, while the cloves themselves soften to a buttery consistency.

2 whole heads garlic (about 30 cloves)
3½ pounds chicken breasts and/or thighs,
   fat and skin removed
Salt and black pepper to taste
1 tablespoon olive oil, plus ½ tablespoon
1½ pounds red potatoes, cut into 1- to
   1½-inch chunks
1 tablespoon chopped fresh rosemary or
   1 teaspoon dried
1 cup defatted lower-sodium chicken broth
1 cup white wine or additional chicken broth
¼ cup chopped parsley, preferably flat leaf

1. Preheat the oven to 350 degrees. Separate the unpeeled garlic into cloves and trim the ends. Drop the garlic cloves into a pot of boiling water for about 15 seconds to loosen the skins. Remove with a slotted spoon, then slip off the garlic skins.

2. Season the chicken with salt and pepper. In a large, ovenproof Dutch oven, heat 1 tablespoon of the oil and cook the chicken over medium heat for 5 minutes. Turn and cook another 5 minutes until both sides are lightly browned.

3. Remove the chicken from the pan and add the remaining ½ tablespoon of oil along with the potatoes and the garlic. Cook the potatoes and garlic, tossing in the oil, until they just begin to turn golden, about 3 minutes.

4. Return the chicken to the pan, sprinkle with the rosemary, and add the broth and wine. Cover the pan tightly and bake until the chicken is cooked through, the juices run clear, and the potatoes and garlic are tender, 50 minutes to 1 hour.

5. Remove the chicken, potatoes, and garlic to a platter and spoon the pan juices on top. Sprinkle with the parsley and serve.

◆ *PER SERVING: About 363 cals, 66 cals from fat, 7g total fat, 2g sat fat, 86mg chol, 99mg sodium, 32g total carbs, 0g fiber, 35g prot*

Company Chicken and Wild Rice Bake

Makes 6 servings

This casserole can be assembled ahead, baked, and served out of a single dish, so it is a great party main course. Add a big green salad, a dish of Summer Harvest Ratatouille (page 426), and a basket of Marvelous Multigrain Bread (page 112) for a colorful and delicious buffet.

1 ounce dried mushrooms, any
   type
6 skinless boneless chicken breast
   halves (about 1½ pounds)
¼ teaspoon salt, plus ¼ teaspoon
¼ teaspoon freshly ground
   pepper, plus ½ teaspoon
1 teaspoon dried sage, plus
   1½ teaspoons
1 teaspoon dried thyme, plus
   1 teaspoon
1 tablespoon olive oil
3 cups (about 1¼ pounds)
   Hubbard or other winter squash,
   peeled and cubed

1 medium onion, chopped
1 cup raw brown rice
½ cup raw wild rice, rinsed
2 bay leaves, broken in half
Olive oil cooking spray
3 cups defatted lower-sodium
   chicken broth
½ cup white wine or
   2 tablespoons lemon juice and
   6 tablespoons additional chicken
   broth
⅓ cup chopped scallions

1. Soak the mushrooms in 2 cups of very hot water until softened, about 30 minutes. Drain the mushrooms, reserving the mushroom liquid and straining it through cheesecloth or a coffee filter to remove the sediment. If necessary, add additional water to make 1 cup. Coarsely chop the mushrooms, and reserve them and the liquid. Season the chicken with ¼ teaspoon each of salt and pepper, then sprinkle with 1 teaspoon each of the sage and thyme. Gently pat in the seasonings with your hand.

2. Preheat the oven to 350 degrees.

3. In a large, preferably nonstick skillet, heat the oil and cook the chicken over medium-high heat until it turns light golden on both sides, about 5 minutes total. Remove the chicken from the pan and add the squash and onion. Reduce the heat to medium and cook, stirring often, until the vegetables begin to soften, about 5 minutes. Stir in the reserved mushroom liquid, scraping up the browned bits clinging to the bottom of the pan. Stir in the brown and wild rice, bay leaves, ¼ teaspoon salt, ½ teaspoon pepper, 1½ teaspoons sage, 1 teaspoon thyme, and the mushrooms.

4. Lightly coat a 9x13-inch baking dish or other shallow 3-quart casserole with olive oil spray. Transfer the vegetable and rice mixture to the casserole. Stir in the broth and wine, and cover the casserole. (This recipe can be made up to 8 hours ahead to this point with the rice mixture and chicken refrigerated separately. Return to room temperature before baking.)

5. Bake the covered rice casserole for 45 minutes, until the rice is nearly done. Uncover and, if the rice seems dry, add up to ¼ cup water. Place the chicken breasts on the rice, pushing them down into the rice a bit. Cover the casserole and continue to bake until the chicken is cooked through and the rice is tender, about 15 minutes longer. Remove from the oven and discard the bay leaves.

6. Sprinkle with the scallions and serve.

◆ *PER SERVING: About 382 cals, 47 cals from fat, 5g total fat, 1g sat fat, 66mg chol, 203mg sodium, 47g total carbs, 4g fiber, 33g prot*

SAFE HANDLING OF POULTRY

Raw poultry sometimes contains salmonella organisms, which cause gastrointestinal illnesses. These organisms are destroyed at temperatures of 160 degrees or more, so thorough cooking of all poultry is the first line of defense against such problems. Proper handling of raw or cooked poultry, as well as knives, cutting boards, or anything else that comes in contact with the poultry, is also important.

◆ For maximum safety, all poultry should be cooked to the well-done stage. For whole birds, this rule means reaching an internal temperature of 180 degrees in the thigh and 170 degrees in the breast. For bone-in parts, the meat should reach 180 degrees for dark meat and 170 degrees for white meat. Boneless pieces should register at least 160 degrees.

◆ After handling raw poultry, use soap and hot water to thoroughly wash your hands, the counter or cutting board, and all utensils that have come into contact with the poultry. You can transfer bacteria to other food if you bring it in contact with raw birds. For maximum safety, designate a cutting board exclusively for poultry and meat.

◆ Never leave cooked poultry at room temperature for more than 2 hours. If you have to transport it, use an insulated container that will keep it below 40 degrees or above 140 degrees to retard bacterial growth.

◆ You can keep fresh poultry in the refrigerator for up to 2 days after purchase and you can safely store cooked poultry in the refrigerator for up to 3 days.

◆ Stuff a chicken or turkey just before roasting and promptly remove all stuffing from a cooked bird. Refrigerate leftovers separately.

Crusty Oven-Fried Chicken

Makes 4 servings

In this recipe, the oven does the frying, eliminating most of the fat, and all of the messy splatters of traditional panfrying. This quick-and-easy supper is sure to become a family favorite, especially if you pair it with Greens with Bacon and Onion (page 437), thickly sliced tomatoes, and a basket of warm Feather-Light Buttermilk Drop Biscuits (page 131).

4 skinless boneless chicken breast halves
    (about 1 pound total)
¾ cup nonfat buttermilk
1 teaspoon Worcestershire sauce
½ teaspoon liquid hot pepper sauce
Vegetable oil spray
¼ cup all-purpose flour
¼ cup yellow cornmeal
2 teaspoons grated lemon peel
¼ teaspoon salt
¼ teaspoon cayenne pepper
1 tablespoon vegetable oil
Lemon wedges

1. Use the palms of your hands to pat the chicken to an even thickness. In a shallow bowl, combine the buttermilk, Worcestershire, and hot pepper sauce. Add the chicken, turning to coat. Let the chicken soak in the sauce for 10 minutes.

2. Meanwhile, preheat the oven to 450 degrees. Lightly coat a baking sheet with vegetable oil spray. In a shallow dish, combine the flour, cornmeal, lemon peel, salt, and cayenne pepper. Remove the chicken from the buttermilk and dip it into the flour mixture to coat completely. Place the chicken on the prepared baking sheet, leaving at least 1 inch between each piece. Drizzle with the oil.

3. Bake the chicken until the coating is golden brown and crusty and the chicken is white throughout, about 20 minutes.

4. Serve the chicken garnished with the lemon wedges.

◆ *PER SERVING: About 226 cals, 47 cals from fat, 5g total fat, 1g sat fat, 67mg chol, 239mg sodium, 14g total carbs, 1g fiber, 29g prot*

Crispy Mustard Crumb Baked Chicken

Makes 6 servings

The mustard and mayonnaise in this recipe protect and flavor the chicken breasts during baking, and the whole-wheat crumbs add a pleasant nutty taste. This easy and delicious family dish is nicely completed by Gingered Carrot Purée (page 429), Southwest Rice and Corn Pilaf (page 276), and a spinach salad with Basic Creamy Dressing (page 75).

Vegetable oil spray

1½ pounds skinless boneless
   chicken breast halves or thighs

¼ cup Dijon mustard

¼ cup low-fat or light
   mayonnaise

¼ cup finely chopped scallions
   including green tops

1½ cups whole-wheat bread
   crumbs

½ teaspoon coarsely ground black
   pepper

1. Preheat the oven to 450 degrees. Lightly coat a baking sheet with vegetable oil spray. Use the palms of your hands to pat the chicken to an even thickness. In a shallow dish, stir together the mustard, mayonnaise, and scallions. In another shallow dish, combine the bread crumbs and pepper.

2. Dip the chicken into the mustard mixture to coat, then dredge in the crumbs to coat completely. Place the chicken in a single layer on the prepared baking sheet.

3. Bake until the coating is golden and crisp, and the chicken is white throughout, 17 to 20 minutes.

◆ *PER SERVING: About 198 cals, 48 cals from fat, 5g total fat, 1g sat fat, 69mg chol, 409mg sodium, 8g total carbs, 2g fiber, 28g prot*

HOW TO PICK A GOOD BIRD

◆ Poultry packages are dated for the last day of sale. Note the date before purchasing. Poultry can be refrigerated for about 2 days after purchase.

◆ Look for packages that have little or no liquid in them. If the bird is packaged with an absorbent pad underneath, check whether the pad is saturated with liquid. Excess liquid is a sign of freezing and thawing, which produces a dry bird when cooked. Government regulations require that chicken marked "fresh" should never have been frozen although the law allows poultry to be held at 32 degrees and still be called "fresh."

◆ The skin color of chicken and, to a lesser degree, turkey and game hens may vary from creamy white to golden yellow. This color variation does not necessarily indicate or affect quality; it's caused by the bird's diet.

◆ Free-range chickens usually cost more than standard supermarket chickens but may or may not taste better. The taste of a bird depends on what it is fed and how it has been handled.

Zesty Molasses Mustard Chicken Thighs

Makes 4 servings

Serve this summery meal with some other deliciously messy seasonal foods, such as corn on the cob and juicy sliced tomatoes; then add a pasta salad with vegetables. Enjoy watermelon wedges or Red, White, and Blueberry Shortcakes (page 452) for dessert.

⅓ cup maple syrup

¼ cup bottled chili sauce

3 tablespoons cider vinegar

2 tablespoons prepared horseradish

2 teaspoons dry mustard

1 pound skinless boneless chicken thighs

2 teaspoons vegetable oil

1. Prepare a medium-hot barbecue fire or preheat a gas grill or the oven broiler. In a small pan, heat together the maple syrup, chili sauce, vinegar, horseradish, and mustard, stirring to dissolve the mustard.

2. Rub the chicken with the oil. Grill or broil the thighs, turning once or twice and brushing with sauce, until the chicken is no longer pink, 15 to 18 minutes.

◆ *PER SERVING: About 214 cals, 89 cals from fat, 10g total fat, 2g sat fat, 53mg chol, 209mg sodium, 14g total carbs, 0g fiber, 18g prot*

WHEN IS POULTRY DONE?

There are several ways to make sure that poultry is cooked thoroughly:

◆ Insert a thermometer into the center of the bird or part, taking care to place it in a meaty area not touching a bone. The thigh is a good place to test doneness in a whole bird. The temperature will register within a few seconds. Pop-up timers in roasting chickens or turkeys are often unreliable.

◆ Check the juices. If the bird is done, its juices will run clear when you prick the bird with a knife.

◆ When roasting or panfrying poultry parts, add the breasts 5 to 10 minutes after the dark meat has begun to cook. Dark meat takes longer to cook than white meat and must reach a higher internal temperature.

◆ Cut into boneless cuts, especial-ly cutlets, with a knife because they are hard to test with a thermometer. The breast meat should be white throughout and the dark meat should have no traces of pink. There is a fine line between doneness and dryness in boneless chicken breasts, so test first after the minimum recommended cooking time.

All-American Barbecued Chicken

Makes 8 servings

This recipe keeps all of the flavor of traditional barbecued chicken, with less than 30 percent of the calories from fat. The secret is removing the skin from the chicken breasts. You can buy skinless chicken breasts if you are willing to pay quite a bit more, but it's easy to pull off the skin yourself.

½ cup defatted lower-sodium
　chicken broth
1 medium onion, finely chopped
2 garlic cloves, finely chopped
1 tablespoon dry mustard
¼ teaspoon celery seeds
¼ teaspoon cayenne pepper
1 bay leaf, broken in half
1 cup bottled chili sauce

1 cup beer or ginger ale
2 tablespoons molasses
1 tablespoon cider vinegar
1 tablespoon Worcestershire sauce
Salt and black pepper to taste
Vegetable oil spray
8 chicken breast halves (2 to 2½
　pounds), fat and skin removed
2 teaspoons vegetable oil

1. In a medium saucepan, bring the broth, onion, and garlic to a simmer. Cover the pan and simmer over medium-low heat until the onion and garlic are softened, about 5 minutes. Stir in the mustard, celery seeds, cayenne, and bay leaf. Then add the chili sauce, beer, molasses, vinegar, and Worcestershire. Simmer over medium-low heat, uncovered, until slightly thickened, about 30 minutes. Discard the bay leaf. Season to taste with salt and pepper.

2. Prepare a medium-hot barbecue fire. Lightly oil the grill rack or coat with nonstick vegetable oil spray. Rub the chicken with the 2 teaspoons of oil, then season lightly with salt and pepper.

3. Grill the chicken, meat side down, for 3 minutes. Turn with a spatula and grill 3 minutes more. Brush chicken with sauce. Grill, brushing and turning two or three times more, until the chicken is white throughout, 14 to 20 minutes. (The chicken should cook for 20 to 25 minutes total.)

4. Boil any remaining sauce for 3 minutes, then serve alongside the chicken.

◆ *PER SERVING: About 214 cals, 41 cals from fat, 5g total fat, 1g sat fat, 73mg chol, 495mg sodium, 14g total carbs, 0g fiber, 28g prot*

Chinese Grilled Five-Spice Chicken

Makes 6 servings

You can find Chinese five-spice powder in the spice section of most large supermarkets. It is a heady blend of ground fennel and anise seeds, ginger, cinnamon, and cloves, and adds a distinctive flavor to any dish. Complete this meal with steamed rice and a green salad tossed with a lemon vinaigrette or Vietnamese Grilled Vegetable Salad (page 105).

6 skinless boneless chicken breast
   halves (about 1½ pounds)
3 tablespoons reduced-sodium soy sauce
1½ tablespoons defatted lower-sodium
   chicken broth or dry sherry
1 tablespoon hot chili oil
4 teaspoons Chinese five-spice powder
1 large garlic clove, minced
12 thick scallions, trimmed to include
   2 inches of green parts

1. Use the palms of your hands to flatten the chicken to an even thickness. In a shallow dish just large enough to accommodate the chicken, stir together the soy sauce, chicken broth, chili oil, five-spice powder, and garlic. Place the chicken in the marinade, turning to coat both sides. Cover the dish with plastic wrap and refrigerate the chicken, turning once or twice for at least 30 minutes and up to 3 hours.

2. Prepare a medium-hot barbecue fire or preheat a gas grill or the oven broiler. Remove the chicken from the marinade and add the scallions to the marinade. Grill the chicken, turning once or twice, until the meat is white throughout, about 10 minutes. Grill the scallions, turning once, until lightly charred and softened, 2 to 3 minutes.

3. Serve the chicken with the scallions crisscrossed over the top.

◆ *PER SERVING: About 158 cals, 36 cals from fat, 4g total fat, 1g sat fat, 66mg chol, 343mg sodium, 2g total carbs, 0g fiber, 27g prot*

Tuscan Grilled Chicken and Roasted Garlic Aioli

Makes 4 servings

If you make the aioli (garlic-flavored sauce) ahead of time, this recipe turns into a quick-and-easy main course that looks and tastes like it came out of the finest restaurant kitchen. Try it for summer entertaining.

3 tablespoons fresh lemon juice
1 tablespoon extra-virgin olive oil
1 tablespoon chopped fresh thyme or
  1 teaspoon dried
1 tablespoon chopped fresh summer savory
  or 1 teaspoon dried
½ teaspoon salt
½ teaspoon coarsely ground black pepper
1 pound chicken breast cutlets, thinly sliced
4 slices Braided Semolina Bread (page 115)
  or Italian bread, each ½ to ¾ inch thick
½ cup Roasted Garlic Aioli (recipe follows)
1 large bunch arugula
1 tomato, cut into 8 slices

1. In a shallow dish just large enough to hold the chicken, combine the lemon juice, oil, thyme, savory, salt, and pepper. Add the chicken, turning to coat both sides. Cover the dish and refrigerate for 1 to 2 hours.

2. Prepare a medium-hot barbecue fire or preheat a gas grill or the oven broiler. Remove the chicken from the marinade and grill, turning once, until white throughout, 5 to 6 minutes total. Grill the bread slices at the edge of the grill, until lightly toasted on both sides, about 2 minutes total.

3. Spread one side of each piece of toast with some of the Roasted Garlic Aioli (recipe follows), then cut each toast in half. Arrange the arugula on the toasts and top with chicken, then a dollop of Roasted Garlic Aioli, and finally a garnish of overlapping tomato slices. Serve immediately.

◆ *PER SERVING: About 336 cals, 55 cals from fat, 6g total fat, 1g sat fat, 66mg chol, 634mg sodium, 35g total carbs, 3g fiber, 34g prot*

ROASTED GARLIC AIOLI

Makes about ¹/₂ cup

This roasted garlic sauce is smooth and mellow in taste. It's wonderful on bread, baked potatoes, or grilled poultry, meats, or seafood. Elephant garlic is larger and milder than regular garlic and provides an interesting change of pace when you can find it.

1 head garlic, separated into cloves or 6 cloves elephant garlic

2 teaspoons extra-virgin olive oil
¼ cup reduced-fat mayonnaise

3 tablespoons plain nonfat yogurt

1. Preheat the oven to 450 degrees or prepare a medium barbecue fire. Trim the tips off the garlic cloves, then drop the cloves into boiling water for about 15 seconds. Drain the garlic and, when cool enough to handle, slip off the skins. Place the peeled cloves in the center of a square of heavy-duty or a double thickness of regular aluminum foil. Drizzle with the olive oil. Wrap the garlic completely in the foil, sealing well. Roast in the oven or on the grill rack for 20 to 30 minutes until the garlic is soft.
2. Mash the garlic with the back of a spoon or purée in a mini food processor, then blend with the mayonnaise until nearly smooth. Stir in the yogurt to blend. Cover and refrigerate the aioli until ready to use, up to 24 hours.

Per serving: About 72 cals, 57 cals from fat, 6g total fat, 1g sat fat, 5mg chol, 24mg sodium, 3g total carbs, 0g fiber, 1g prot

Tandoor-Style Chicken Nuggets

Makes 6 servings

A tandoor is a clay oven used in parts of India to bake everything from chicken to bread. When marinated in a spiced yogurt sauce, foods cooked in a tandoor come out moist, tender, and flavorful. Even without a clay oven, you'll love this chicken and vegetable combo served over basmati or brown rice and accompanied by a spoonful of chutney.

2 cups large broccoli florets
2 cups large cauliflower florets
1½ cups low-fat plain yogurt
4 teaspoons fresh lemon juice
1½ tablespoons grated fresh ginger
2 large garlic cloves, minced
1 tablespoon ground cardamom
1 tablespoon ground cumin
¾ teaspoon ground turmeric
½ teaspoon salt

¼ teaspoon cayenne pepper
1 pound skinless boneless chicken breasts, cut into 1- to 1½ -inch chunks
1 large red bell pepper, cut into 1-inch strips
6 cups cooked basmati or brown rice
6 tablespoons prepared mango chutney

1. Blanch the broccoli and cauliflower florets in a large pot of boiling salted water for 1 minute. Drain and immediately immerse the vegetables in a bowl of cold water to set the color and stop the cooking. Drain well and set the vegetables aside.

2. In a shallow dish just large enough to accommodate the chicken, combine the yogurt, lemon juice, ginger, garlic, cardamom, cumin, turmeric, salt, and cayenne. Add the chicken, stirring to coat completely. Cover the dish with plastic wrap and refrigerate for 30 minutes to 1 hour, stirring once or twice. Remove the chicken from the marinade, then add the bell pepper strips and the broccoli and cauliflower florets to the marinade, stirring to coat.

3. Prepare a medium-hot barbecue fire or preheat a gas grill or oven broiler. Alternately thread the chicken, broccoli and cauliflower florets, and pepper strips onto 6 large metal skewers or 6 bamboo skewers that have been soaked in cold water for at least 20 minutes.

4. Grill the kebabs, turning 2 or 3 times, until the chicken is white throughout and the vegetables are tender and lightly charred.

5. To serve, lay the skewers directly on top of the rice or remove the chicken and vegetables from the skewers and arrange the food on the rice. Serve with the chutney.

◆ *PER SERVING: About 371 cals, 19 cals from fat, 2g total fat, 1g sat fat, 45mg chol, 125mg sodium, 62g total carbs, 3g fiber, 25g prot*

TO FREEZE OR NOT TO FREEZE

All poultry can be frozen, if well wrapped in freezer paper or heavy-duty plastic freezer bags, but the home freezing and thawing process can sometimes draw liquid from the bird, producing a change in texture and dry meat when cooked. Whole turkeys, ducks, and other game birds are often flash frozen under controlled conditions and, when thawed properly, do not suffer the same problems. Use home-frozen poultry in dishes that add moisture in the cooking process, such as braised, stewed, or poached dishes, or soups.

Thaw poultry in the refrigerator.

Thawing at room temperature can foster bacterial growth. Poultry parts thaw more quickly than whole birds, and should also be thawed in the refrigerator. Do not thaw poultry in the microwave because some parts will start to cook while others remain frozen.

Easy Chicken Cacciatore

Makes 6 servings

Cacciatore means "hunter's style" and this lusty Italian dish is sometimes made with rabbit or other small game. Dark chicken meat gives the fullest flavor in this contemporary rendition. The dish is easy to prepare in advance and you may think it's even better the second day.

2 pounds skinless chicken thighs
½ teaspoon salt
¼ teaspoon black pepper
2 teaspoons olive oil, plus
   1 teaspoon
1 large onion, chopped
3 garlic cloves, minced
½ pound wild or cultivated
   mushrooms or a combination,
   sliced
2 cans (14½ ounces each)
   Italian-style stewed tomatoes

½ cup red wine or defatted
   lower-sodium chicken broth
1 bay leaf, broken in half
1½ teaspoons grated lemon peel
1½ teaspoons dried rosemary
½ teaspoon dried marjoram
¼ teaspoon dried red pepper
   flakes
1 pound uncooked spaghetti
3 tablespoons chopped parsley,
   preferably flat leaf
6 small sprigs of fresh rosemary

1. Season the chicken with the salt and pepper. Heat the 2 teaspoons of oil in a large, preferably nonstick skillet and cook the chicken over medium-high heat, turning until all sides are golden, about 6 minutes. Use tongs to remove the chicken from the skillet.

2. Add the onion to the drippings in the pan, reduce the heat to medium, and cook, stirring often, until the onion begins to soften, about 3 minutes. Add the garlic and mushrooms and cook, stirring often, until the mushrooms are softened, about 5 minutes. Add the tomatoes, wine, bay leaf, lemon peel, rosemary, marjoram, and pepper flakes. Bring to a simmer. Return the chicken to the pan and simmer, partially covered, over medium-low heat for 25 to 30 minutes. Discard the bay leaf.

3. Cook the spaghetti in a large pot of boiling salted water until al dente, 8 to 9 minutes. Drain well.

4. Serve the chicken mixture ladled over the pasta. Sprinkle with the parsley and rosemary.

◆ *PER SERVING: About 605 cals, 138 cals from fat, 15g total fat, 4g sat fat, 101mg chol, 545mg sodium, 70g total carbs, 2g fiber, 41g prot*

Roasted Lebanese Chicken

Makes 6 servings

Lemon and garlic give this chicken lots of zip. Toasting and grinding the cumin and corian-der make a real taste difference in this dish. Tunisian Couscous Pilaf with Chickpeas, Almonds, and Dates (page 266) and Sautéed Zucchini Shreds with Herbed Yogurt (page 436) are attractive and tasty accompaniments.

2 teaspoons whole cumin seed

½ teaspoon whole coriander seed

¾ cup fresh lemon juice

6 large garlic cloves, coarsely chopped

2 tablespoons fresh thyme, finely chopped,
  or 2 teaspoons dried leaf thyme

1 tablespoon paprika

¾ teaspoon cayenne pepper

6 chicken breast halves (2 to 2½ pounds),
  fat and skin removed

2 teaspoons olive oil, preferably extra virgin

Salt and black pepper to taste

1 lemon, cut into wedges

6 sprigs fresh thyme (optional)

1. Toss the cumin and coriander seeds in a small skillet set over medium heat until they darken a shade and become fragrant, 1 to 2 minutes. Immediately remove the seeds from the pan and let them cool completely, then grind the seeds in a mortar and pestle or spice grinder.

2. In a shallow baking dish large enough to hold the chicken in a single layer, combine the lemon juice, garlic, thyme, paprika, cayenne, and the ground spices. Rub the chicken with the oil, then season lightly with salt and pepper. Place the chicken in the marinade, turning to coat both sides. Cover the dish with plastic wrap and refrigerate, turning the chicken two or three times, for at least 3 hours or up to 12 hours.

3. Preheat the oven to 425 degrees. Bake the chicken in the marinade, meat-side up and uncovered, basting occasionally with the marinade, until the chicken is golden and the meat is white throughout, 45 to 50 minutes.

4. Serve the chicken garnished with the lemon wedges, and thyme sprigs, if desired.

◆ *PER SERVING: About 170 cals, 43 cals from fat, 5g total fat, 1g sat fat, 69mg chol, 63mg sodium, 5g total carbs, 0g fiber, 26g prot*

Chicken Vindaloo

Makes 6 servings

Vindaloo, one of the hottest Indian dishes, has been slightly tamed in this rendition, which is equally good made with boneless cubed lamb. Typical accompaniments include mango chutney, Cooling Cucumber Raita (page 305), and warmed flatbreads.

1 tablespoon cumin seed

1 tablespoon coriander seed

1 tablespoon chili powder

6 tablespoons cider vinegar

2 tablespoons fresh lemon juice

6 large garlic cloves, minced

1 canned chipotle chili in adobo sauce, minced

1 tablespoon minced fresh ginger

¾ teaspoon ground cinnamon

¼ teaspoon ground cloves

¼ to ½ teaspoon cayenne pepper to taste

1½ pounds skinless boneless chicken thighs, cut into 1-inch chunks

1 tablespoon vegetable oil

1 pound red potatoes, cut into ¾-inch chunks

1 large onion, cut into ¾-inch pieces

1 red bell pepper, cut into ¾-inch pieces

1½ cups defatted lower-sodium chicken broth

½ cup canned tomato sauce

5 cups cooked basmati or brown rice

1. Toss the cumin and coriander seeds and the chili powder in a small skillet set over medium heat until they darken a shade, 1 to 2 minutes. Immediately scrape the mixture from the skillet and let it cool. Then grind it in a mortar and pestle or spice grinder.

2. In a blender, purée the spices with the vinegar, lemon juice, garlic, chipotle pepper, ginger, cinnamon, cloves, and cayenne. Place the chicken in a shallow dish. Pour the purée over the chicken, coating it completely. Cover and refrigerate, stirring occasionally, for 2 to 6 hours.

3. Remove the chicken from the marinade, scraping any excess marinade back into the dish. Reserve the marinade. In a Dutch oven, heat the oil and cook the chicken, potatoes, onion, and bell pepper over medium heat, stirring often, just until the vegetables soften, about 5 minutes. Stir in the broth, tomato sauce, and any reserved marinade.

4. Cover the pot, reduce the heat to medium-low and simmer, stirring occasionally, until the potatoes are very tender, 40 to 45 minutes. Serve the vindaloo spooned over the rice.

◆ *PER SERVING: About 543 cals, 134 cals from fat, 15g total fat, 4g sat fat, 101mg chol, 244mg sodium, 67g total carbs, 2g fiber, 36g prot*

Chicken and Summer Vegetable Tagine

Makes 6 servings

A tagine is a North African stew made with all sorts of meat, poultry, and vegetables braised with fragrant spices. The vegetables and the couscous make it a high-fiber, high-flavor dish, and an unusual and delicious way to use the summer garden bounty. Harissa is a Moroccan hot sauce you can find at Middle Eastern groceries, but any liquid hot pepper sauce can heat up the dish to your personal taste.

1 tablespoon olive oil, plus
  ½ tablespoon
3 pounds chicken thighs and/or
  drumsticks, fat and skin removed
¼ teaspoon salt, plus ¼ teaspoon
¼ teaspoon black pepper
1 large onion, chopped
4 garlic cloves, minced
1½ tablespoons grated fresh
  ginger
1 tablespoon ground coriander
1½ teaspoons ground cumin
1 teaspoon ground cinnamon
1 teaspoon ground turmeric
¼ teaspoon dried red pepper
  flakes
4 cups defatted lower-sodium
  chicken broth

1 pound fresh plum tomatoes,
  seeded and diced, or 1 can
  (14½ ounces) undrained diced
  plum tomatoes
3 tablespoons fresh lemon juice
1 teaspoon grated lemon peel
1 medium eggplant (about ¾
  pound), peeled and cut into
  1-inch cubes
¼ cup chopped dates
2 medium zucchini (about ¾
  pound), sliced about ½ inch thick
6 cups cooked couscous
¼ cup chopped fresh cilantro
Harissa or other liquid hot sauce
  (optional)

1. In a Dutch oven, heat 1 tablespoon of the oil. Season the chicken with ¼ teaspoon salt and the black pepper. Cook the chicken over medium-high heat, turning once or twice, until golden on both sides, about 8 minutes total. Remove the chicken from the pan. Add the remaining ½ tablespoon of oil and add the onion, reduce the heat to medium and cook, stirring often, until the onion is softened, about 5 minutes. Stir in the garlic, ginger, coriander, cumin, cinnamon, turmeric, and pepper flakes. Cook, stirring, for 1 minute. Add the chicken broth, tomatoes, lemon juice, and peel. Bring to a simmer, scraping up any brown bits clinging to the bottom of the pan.

2. Return the chicken to the pan, cover, and simmer for 30 minutes. Add the eggplant

continued

and dates. Cover and simmer for 15 minutes. Add the zucchini and simmer, uncovered, for 10 minutes. (This recipe can be prepared up to a day ahead and refrigerated. Reheat to serve.)

3. To serve, ladle the chicken, vegetables, and broth over the couscous. Sprinkle with the cilantro, and pass the harissa at the table.

◆ *PER SERVING: About 496 cals, 122 cals from fat, 14g total fat, 3g sat fat, 75mg chol, 311mg sodium, 61g total carbs, 12g fiber, 31g prot*

Chicken Adobo

Makes 6 servings

Adobos are distinctive marinades based on citrus fruits, garlic, herbs, and spices common throughout Mexico, Central America, and the Caribbean. This Cuban-inspired chicken adobo can be grilled or broiled, and tastes good served with Herbed Brown Rice Pilaf (page 275) and Chicory, Arugula, and Orange Salad Siciliana (page 103).

⅓ **cup fresh orange juice**
⅓ **cup fresh lime juice**
1 **teaspoon grated orange peel**
1 **teaspoon grated lime peel**
1 **teaspoon ground oregano**
1 **teaspoon ground cumin**
1 **teaspoon dried thyme**
½ **teaspoon salt**
¼ **teaspoon cayenne pepper**
4 **large garlic cloves, minced**
6 **skinless boneless chicken breast halves**
   (about 1½ pounds)
2 **teaspoons olive oil**
1 **seedless orange, peeled and thinly sliced**
3 **tablespoons chopped fresh cilantro**

1. In a shallow dish just large enough to hold the chicken, combine the orange and lime juices, orange and lime peels, oregano, cumin, thyme, salt, cayenne, and garlic. Rub the chicken with the oil, then add it to the marinade, turning to coat both sides. Cover the dish and refrigerate the chicken, turning occasionally, for 1 to 6 hours.

2. Prepare a medium-hot barbecue fire or preheat a gas grill or the oven broiler. Grill the chicken, turning once or twice and brushing with the marinade during the first half of grilling, until the chicken is white throughout, 12 to 15 minutes.

3. Serve the chicken garnished with the orange slices and sprinkled with the cilantro.

◆ *PER SERVING: About 154 cals, 27 cals from fat, 3g total fat, 1g sat fat, 66mg chol, 120mg sodium, 4g total carbs, 2g fiber, 27g prot*

GRILLING TIPS

Chicken remains the most popular bird for barbecue, and there are all sorts of ways to grill this all-time favorite. You can grill chicken with the skin on, but if you remove the skin after cooking to reduce the fat content of the chicken, you will lose much of the grilling flavor. Instead, try grilling chicken breasts, thighs, or drumsticks without the skin. Take care not to overcook chicken and brush it with a sauce or use a marinade to protect the delicate flesh. Here are some other tips that apply to grilling in general:

◆ Trim off all excess fat before cooking. Fat drips onto the coals and causes flare-ups.

◆ Reduce the oil in standard marinade recipes by replacing some of it with fruit juice or broth.

◆ Allow enough time to build a fire or preheat a gas grill to the right temperature. If you use chemical charcoal lighters, let the fire burn for at least 30 minutes before cooking to burn off the chemical taste and smell.

◆ Grill small cuts directly over the coals. Grill larger cuts that take a longer time over indirect heat by moving the coals to one side of the grill and placing the food on the other side.

◆ Lightly coat the grill rack with vegetable oil or vegetable oil spray before placing it over the coals to prevent food from sticking.

◆ Let the grill rack heat over the coals for about 10 minutes before placing the food on it. A cold rack will cause the food to stick.

◆ Avoid turning the foods more than necessary—once or twice is enough for burgers or boneless cuts of chicken or vegetables. Turn the food using a spatula or round-edge tongs. Try not to pierce the food because juices will escape into the fire.

◆ Brush on thick or sweet sauces during the last 10 minutes or so of cooking to prevent burning.

Turkey Stir-Fry with Ginger and Mint

Makes 4 servings

The combination of sour, hot, and sweet flavors in this recipe makes a wonderful, multicultural stir-fry. You can substitute other fruits and vegetables, from cantaloupe and pineapple to green peppers and carrots, but be sure to pick ones that present a colorful contrast.

⅔ cup papaya or pineapple juice

3 tablespoons rice wine vinegar

1½ tablespoons reduced-sodium
   soy sauce

1½ tablespoons grated fresh
   ginger

1 tablespoon brown sugar

⅓ cup chopped fresh mint, plus
   2 tablespoons

1 jalapeño pepper, seeded and
   finely chopped

1 pound turkey breast cutlets, cut
   crosswise into ½-inch strips

1 tablespoon cornstarch

2 tablespoons peanut or vegetable
   oil

¼ pound sugar snap peas,
   trimmed and halved on the
   diagonal

1 large red bell pepper, cut into
   thin strips

2 large garlic cloves, minced

1 papaya, peeled, seeded, and cut
   into 1-inch cubes

3 cups cooked white or brown rice

1. In a shallow dish just large enough to accommodate the turkey, combine the juice, vinegar, soy sauce, ginger, brown sugar, ⅓ cup of chopped mint, and the jalapeño. Add the turkey, stirring to coat completely. Cover the dish with plastic wrap and refrigerate for at least 30 minutes and up to 1 hour, stirring once or twice. Remove the turkey from the marinade, then stir the cornstarch into the marinade and set it aside.

2. Heat the oil in a wok or large frying pan and stir-fry the turkey for 2 minutes. Add the sugar snap peas, bell pepper strips, and the garlic. Stir-fry for 1 minute. Add the papaya and reserved marinade. Simmer for 3 minutes, stirring often.

3. Serve the stir-fry spooned over the rice and sprinkled with the remaining 2 tablespoons of chopped mint.

◆ *PER SERVING: About 482 cals, 81 cals from fat, 9g total fat, 1g sat fat, 63mg chol, 289mg sodium, 6g total carbs, 5g fiber, 35g prot*

STIR-FRYING

Stir-frying is one of the quickest preparation methods and takes only a few minutes if you prepare the ingredients ahead of time. Traditional stir-frying is done in a wok set over a hot flame or in an electric wok set at a high temperature, and requires very little fat because the high heat and constant stirring of the food sears in moisture and flavor. Stir-fried vegetables retain more nutrients than those prepared by other cooking methods because the vegetables are quickly cooked in very little liquid. A large skillet can double as a wok for most recipes.

◆ Cut up all ingredients to approximately the same size for even cooking.
◆ Add ingredients according to the length of time they need to cook; quick-cooking items go in last.

◆ You can make substitutions within general categories in recipes—seafood for poultry and meat, for example—as long as the total quantity remains about the same.
◆ Consider color and texture in choosing ingredients for a stir-fry.
◆ You can turn many stir-fries, served over rice or pasta, into a complete meal.

Basil Chicken and Sweet Pepper Packets

Makes 6 servings

When you cook small cuts of poultry or fish in parchment or foil packets, you steam the food in its own juices, sealing the flavors in. Open the packets and a wonderful fragrance greets each diner. Accompany these attractive individual main courses with Baked Herbed Polenta (page 281) and Fennel Baked with Tomatoes and Onions (page 432). For dessert have Almond Anise Biscotti (page 477).

1½ pounds chicken breast cutlets, thinly sliced
2 garlic cloves, minced
1 tablespoon chopped fresh oregano or
   1 teaspoon dried
1 tablespoon chopped fresh marjoram or
   1 teaspoon dried
¼ teaspoon dried red pepper flakes
¼ teaspoon salt, plus ¼ teaspoon
¼ teaspoon black pepper, plus ⅛ teaspoon
3 tablespoons balsamic vinegar
1 tablespoon extra-virgin olive oil
¼ cup thinly sliced basil leaves, plus
   2 tablespoons
1 red bell pepper, seeded and thinly sliced
1 yellow bell pepper, seeded and thinly sliced
1 green bell pepper, seeded and thinly sliced

continued

1. Preheat the oven to 425 degrees. Cut six 12x15-inch rectangles of parchment paper or aluminum foil. Fold the parchment or foil rectangles in half from the short end. Cut out a large half heart along the fold, like a valentine. When unfolded, the six hearts should measure about 14 inches wide and 12 inches long.

2. Divide the chicken slices among the hearts, placing them on one side of the heart. Dividing the ingredients among the packets, sprinkle with the garlic, oregano, marjoram, pepper flakes, and ¼ teaspoon each of salt and black pepper. Drizzle with the balsamic vinegar and olive oil. Sprinkle with ¼ cup of the basil, then top with the red, yellow, and green pepper slices. Finally, sprinkle with the remaining ¼ teaspoon salt, ⅛ teaspoon black pepper, and remaining 2 tablespoons of basil.

3. Fold each heart over to make a half heart, then crimp the edges neatly to seal the packet completely. (This recipe can be prepared up to 4 hours ahead and refrigerated. Remove the packets from the refrigerator at least half an hour before baking.)

4. Place the packets on a baking sheet and bake until the parchment is puffed and lightly browned (the foil will not puff) and the chicken is white throughout, 10 to 12 minutes.

◆ *PER SERVING: About 176 cals, 35 cals from fat, 4g total fat, 1g sat fat, 66mg chol, 255mg sodium, 7g total carbs, 1g fiber, 27g prot*

Turkey Cutlets and Cranberry-Kumquat Relish

Makes 4 servings

Kumquats give a pleasantly tart character to this warm relish. If kumquats aren't available, chop a small, unpeeled, thin-skinned seedless orange or a small clementine. Serve this Thanksgiving-inspired main dish with Fabulous Garlic Mashed Potatoes (page 419), Gingered Carrot Purée (page 429), and Bulgur Pilaf with Leeks, Currents, and Pine Nuts (page 277).

1 cup fresh cranberries

4 kumquats, quartered

1 tablespoon sugar

1 pound thinly sliced turkey breast cutlets

Salt and black pepper to taste

4 teaspoons unsalted butter

¼ cup chopped shallots

1½ teaspoons chopped fresh sage or
    ½ teaspoon dried sage

½ cup orange juice

½ cup cranberry juice cocktail

1. In a food processor, coarsely chop the cranberries and kumquats and add the sugar. Set aside.

2. Season the turkey with salt and pepper. Heat the butter in a large, preferably non-stick skillet. Cook the turkey over medium-high heat, turning once or twice, until pale golden and cooked through, about 5 minutes total. Remove the turkey from the skillet. Add the shallots and sage to the drippings in the skillet, reduce the heat to medium-low and cook, stirring, for 1 minute. Stir in the orange and cranberry juices, then add the chopped cranberry mixture. Simmer, uncovered, stirring occasionally, until the cranberries have softened slightly and the sauce is a bit reduced. Salt and pepper to taste and serve.

◆ *PER SERVING: About 233 cals, 50 cals from fat, 6g total fat, 3g sat fat, 74mg chol, 59mg sodium, 19g total carbs, 3g fiber, 29g prot*

Turkey and Tarragon Tomato Salsa

Makes 4 servings

The salsa in this recipe is tasty spooned over grilled swordfish or even heaped on a thick slice of bread. Yellow tomatoes add attractive color to the salsa but, if you can't find them, simply substitute more fresh red tomatoes. Round out the meal with Sautéed Zucchini Shreds with Herbed Yogurt (page 436) and Quick Creamy Polenta (page 273).

½ cup defatted lower-sodium
   chicken broth or white wine
2 garlic cloves, minced
¼ cup dry-pack sun-dried
   tomatoes (about 1 ounce)
½ pound ripe red tomatoes, seeded
   and coarsely chopped
½ pound ripe yellow tomatoes,
   seeded and coarsely chopped
½ cup thinly sliced scallions

2 tablespoons chopped fresh
   tarragon
½ teaspoon salt, plus additional
   to taste
¼ teaspoon black pepper, plus
   additional to taste
1½ tablespoons extra-virgin
   olive oil, plus ½ tablespoon
1 pound turkey breast steaks, cut
   about ½ inch thick

1. In a small saucepan, bring the broth, garlic, and sun-dried tomatoes to a simmer. Remove them from the heat and let them stand until they are plumped and softened, about 20 minutes. Coarsely chop the sun-dried tomatoes, then transfer them and the broth to a medium bowl. Add the fresh red and yellow tomatoes, scallions, tarragon, ½ teaspoon salt, ¼ teaspoon pepper, and 1½ tablespoons olive oil. Stir to blend. Let the salsa stand at least 15 minutes at room temperature or refrigerate up to 8 hours, but return to room temperature before serving.

continued

2. Prepare a medium-hot barbecue fire or preheat a gas grill. Rub the turkey with the remaining ½ tablespoon of oil and season with salt and pepper. Grill, turning once, until the turkey is white throughout, 8 to 10 minutes total.

3. Serve the turkey with the room-temperature salsa spooned over the top.

◆ *PER SERVING: About 222 cals, 79 cals from fat, 9g total fat, 1g sat fat, 63mg chol, 406mg sodium, 8g total carbs, 0g fiber, 30 g prot*

Garden Vegetable and Turkey Meat Loaf

Makes 8 servings

Meat loaf is a perennial family favorite, and this one made with turkey is really tasty. The secret ingredients are the yogurt and vegetables, which keep the loaf wonderfully moist. You can substitute other vegetables that you have on hand if you keep the total amount of vegetables to about 2½ cups. Leftover turkey loaf makes great sandwiches.

Vegetable oil spray
2 teaspoons vegetable oil
½ cup finely chopped onion
½ cup finely chopped carrots
½ cup finely chopped red bell pepper
1 garlic clove, minced
½ cup thinly sliced scallions including
   green tops
½ cup freshly cooked or frozen corn kernels
2 pounds ground turkey
1½ cups fresh whole-wheat bread crumbs
½ cup bottled chili sauce, plus ¼ cup
½ cup nonfat plain yogurt
2 egg whites
1½ teaspoons dried sage
1 teaspoon dried savory
1 teaspoon dried thyme
½ teaspoon ground celery seed
½ teaspoon salt
½ teaspoon black pepper

1. Preheat the oven to 350 degrees. Coat a 5x9-inch loaf pan with vegetable oil spray. In a large, preferably nonstick skillet, heat the oil over medium-low heat. Cook the onion, carrots, and bell pepper, stirring often, until just softened, about 4 minutes. Add the garlic and cook, stirring, for 1 minute. Transfer the vegetables to a mixing bowl and let cool.

2. Add the scallions, corn, turkey, bread crumbs, ½ cup chili sauce, yogurt, egg whites, sage, savory, thyme, celery seed, salt, and pepper to the mixing bowl. Use your hands to gently but thoroughly mix the ingredients together.

3. Transfer the mixture to the prepared pan. (This recipe can be prepared up to 4 hours ahead and refrigerated. Remove from the refrigerator at least 30 minutes before baking.)

4. Bake for 30 minutes. Spread the ¼ cup of chili sauce over the loaf and bake until a meat thermometer inserted into the center registers 165 degrees and the loaf is firm, about 30 minutes longer. Let stand in the pan for 5 to 10 minutes before slicing and serving.

◆ *PER SERVING: About 253 cals, 87 cals from fat, 10g total fat, 2g sat fat, 92mg chol, 622mg sodium, 17g total carbs, 2g fiber, 25g prot*

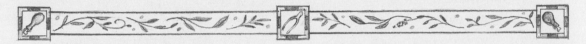

Grilled Duck with Citrus Honey Salsa

Makes 4 servings

This salsa is also very good with grilled turkey steaks, chicken breasts, or any kind of fish steak. Serve the duck with Spicy Thai Rice with Chopped Peanuts (page 280), then tame the heat with a basket of Moist Banana Muffins (page 126) and a green salad.

1 lemon	¼ teaspoon salt
1 seedless orange	4 skinless boneless duck breast
½ pink grapefruit	halves (about 1 pound total)
¼ cup chopped red onion	2 teaspoons olive oil, preferably
3 tablespoons chopped cilantro	extra virgin
1 teaspoon minced jalapeño pepper	½ teaspoon ground coriander
1 tablespoon honey	Salt and black pepper to taste

1. Grate 1 teaspoon of peel from the lemon and 2 teaspoons from the orange. Squeeze 2 teaspoons of juice from the lemon. Place the peels and the juice in a medium bowl. Peel and section the orange and the grapefruit, taking care to discard all of the white pith. Add the fruit sections, onion, cilantro, jalapeño, honey, and salt to the mixing bowl. Stir to blend well. Let stand for 30 minutes at room temperature or refrigerate from 1 to 6 hours. Return to room temperature before serving.

2. Prepare a medium-hot barbecue fire or preheat a gas grill. Rub the duck with the oil, then sprinkle with the coriander and salt and pepper to taste. *continued*

3. Grill the duck, turning once, until no longer pink, a total of 8 to 10 minutes.

4. Serve the duck with the salsa spooned over the top.

◆ *PER SERVING: About 182 cals, 37 cals from fat, 4g total fat, 1g sat fat, 130mg chol, 242mg sodium, 12g total carbs, 3g fiber, 24g protein*

Sesame Turkey and Asparagus Stir-Fry

Makes 4 servings

Asparagus is the quintessential springtime vegetable, and tastes delicious when stir-fried with a little sesame and lemon. Hoisin sauce can be found in Asian markets.

1 cup defatted lower-sodium
  chicken broth

1½ tablespoons reduced-sodium
  soy sauce

1 tablespoon hoisin sauce

1 tablespoon fresh lemon juice

2 teaspoons cornstarch

2 teaspoons toasted Asian sesame
  oil

1 pound skinless boneless turkey
  breast cutlets, cut into thin strips

3 tablespoons sesame seeds

1 tablespoon vegetable oil

1 yellow bell pepper, seeded and
  cut into thin strips

½ pound pencil-thin asparagus,
  trimmed and cut into 1½-inch
  diagonal pieces

2 garlic cloves, minced

1 teaspoon grated lemon peel

½ teaspoon dried red pepper flakes

4 cups cooked brown or white rice

¼ cup thinly sliced scallions
  including green tops

1. In a small bowl, combine the broth, soy sauce, hoisin sauce, lemon juice, cornstarch, and sesame oil. Sprinkle the turkey on both sides with the sesame seeds, patting them in with your hands. Cut the turkey across the grain into ½-inch strips.

2. In a nonstick wok or large skillet, heat the vegetable oil and stir-fry the turkey over medium-high heat for 3 minutes. Use a slotted spoon to remove the turkey from the wok. Add the bell pepper and stir-fry for 1 minute. Add the asparagus and stir-fry for 1 minute. Add the garlic, lemon peel, and pepper flakes and stir-fry for 30 seconds. Add the broth mixture and cook for 2 minutes. Return the turkey to the pan and cook for 2 minutes.

3. Serve the turkey and vegetables over the rice and sprinkled with the scallions.

◆ *PER SERVING: About 476 cals, 113 cals from fat, 13g total fat, 2g sat fat, 63mg chol, 360mg sodium, 56g total carbs, 6g fiber, 37g prot*

Apple-Sage Glazed Game Hens

Makes 4 servings

Glazed game hen halves make an attractive main course for a dinner party. Serve them with puréed winter squash, steamed brussels sprouts or cauliflower, and Braised Wild Rice with Cranberries (page 278) for an elegant autumn meal. Ask the butcher to halve the game hens.

2 Cornish game hens (1 to 1¼ pounds each), cut in half with backbones discarded

1 tablespoon chopped fresh sage, plus 2 teaspoons, or 1 teaspoon dried sage, plus ½ teaspoon

½ teaspoon salt

½ teaspoon ground black pepper

2 teaspoons olive oil

3 tablespoons minced shallots

¼ cup apple jelly

1 tablespoon cider vinegar

2 teaspoons Dijon mustard

1 teaspoon Worcestershire sauce

1 tart apple, peeled, cored, and sliced into rings

1. Use your hands to flatten the hen halves somewhat, then use your fingers to loosen the breast and thigh skin of the hen halves. In a small bowl, combine 1 tablespoon fresh chopped sage (or 1 teaspoon dried sage) with the salt and pepper. Use your fingers to rub the mixture as evenly as possible under the skin to season the meat. Refrigerate the hens, covered, for at least 1 hour, up to 4 hours.

2. In a small saucepan, heat the oil and cook the shallots over medium heat, stirring constantly, for 1 minute. Add the jelly, vinegar, mustard, Worcestershire, and remaining 2 teaspoons chopped fresh sage (or ½ teaspoon dried sage). Simmer, stirring to melt the jelly, about 2 minutes. (The sauce can be made up to 4 hours ahead and kept at room temperature. Reheat to use.)

3. Preheat the oven to 450 degrees. Place the hens in a shallow roasting pan, skin side up. Brush with some of the glaze and roast for 10 minutes. Turn the hens, brush again, and roast for 10 minutes. Turn and brush again, then roast until the juices run clear when pricked, about 15 minutes more. About 8 minutes before the hens are done, brush the apples with some of the glaze and set in the roasting pan to cook along with the hens. The apples should soften a bit.

4. Remove and discard the skin from the hens. Serve them garnished with the roasted apple slices.

◆ *PER SERVING: About 259 cals, 70 cals from fat, 8g total fat, 2g sat fat, 80mg chol, 420mg sodium, 20g total carbs, 1g fiber, 27g prot*

Poultry Glossary

Because of its versatility and modest cost, chicken occupies more space in the super-market than all types of meat combined. Turkey is gaining popularity fast because it can be even lower in fat—and cost—than chicken. You can now buy turkey as the whole bird, in parts, or as sausage—even as bologna and bacon. And, as supermarkets increase their range of products, game birds—from ducks to goose to quail—will become more widely available than ever. Poultry is graded A, B, or C by the United States Department of Agriculture (USDA) according to flavor and tenderness; grade A is the best and most common. Here is a brief glossary of poultry sizes and parts:

Chicken

(Per a 3-ounce, cooked, boneless, skinless serving of light meat—120 calories and 2 grams of fat; per a 3-ounce, cooked, boneless, skinless serving of dark meat—158 calories and 8 grams of fat.)

TYPE	DESCRIPTION, WEIGHT, AND NUMBER OF SERVINGS	COOKING TIPS AND TIME
Young roaster	Whole bird, 5 to 8 pounds, with high proportion of meat to bone; usually sold with neck and giblets; 8 to 10 servings.	Roast with or without stuffing 2 to 2½ hours at 350 to 400 degrees.
Broiler/fryer	Whole bird, 3 to 4½ pounds, usually sold without neck or giblets; 5 to 6 servings.	Roast at 350 degrees 1 to 1½ hours or cut up and use the bony parts for soup stock.
Halves and splits	Whole broiler cut in half through the backbone, usually sold without neck or giblets; 2 to 3 servings.	Bake, broil, or grill for 45 minutes to 1 hour.
Cut up	Whole broiler cut into 6 or 8 pieces, usually sold without neck or giblets; 5 to 6 servings.	Bake, grill, braise, or panfry for 40 to 50 minutes.
Thighs	Portion of leg above knee joint (available skinless and boneless); 1 or 2 per 1 serving.	Cook bone-in 30 to 45 minutes and boneless 18 to 22 minutes.
Drumsticks	Portion of leg below knee joint (available skinless); 2 per 1 serving.	Cook 30 to 40 minutes.
Split breasts	Whole breasts cut in half, usually with ribs removed (available skinless and boneless); 1 per 1 serving.	Bake, grill, panfry, or poach for 30 to 40 minutes for bone-in and 15 to 18 minutes for boneless.
Cutlets	Thinly sliced portions of boneless, skinless breasts or thighs; 4 ounces raw per serving.	Grill, broil, or panfry for 5 to 7 minutes.
Wings	Whole wing, including all sections; 6 ounces raw (with skin and bones) per serving.	Grill, broil, bake, or use for soup stock (to be defatted after cooking) for 20 to 30 minutes.
Ground	Usually made from skinless, boneless breast and thigh meat; often interchangeable with, but softer and more moist than, ground turkey; 4 ounces raw per serving.	Use in meat loaf or chili; cook until white throughout.

Turkey

(Per a 3-ounce, cooked, boneless, skinless serving of light meat—112 calories and 2 grams of fat;
per a 3-ounce, cooked, boneless, skinless serving of dark meat—153 calories and 6 grams of fat.)

TYPE	DESCRIPTION, WEIGHT, AND NUMBER OF SERVINGS	COOKING TIPS AND TIME
Roaster	Whole bird, 8 to 24 pounds; young (smaller) turkeys are more tender, but larger ones have a higher meat-to-bone ratio; ½ to ¾ pound (uncooked bone-in weight) per serving.	Roast at 350 degrees for smaller birds and 325 degrees for larger ones 20 to 30 minutes per pound; thermometer inserted into thigh should read 180 degrees when done.
Bone-in breast	Available as whole or half, 4 to 8 pounds; 6 ounces raw (with bone and skin) per serving.	Roast at 350 degrees 20 minutes per pound; thermometer inserted into breast should read 180 degrees when done.
Boneless roast	Tied boneless breast (with or without skin) weighing 2 to 3½ pounds; 4 ounces raw per serving.	Roast at 350 degrees 20 minutes per pound; thermometer inserted into roast should read 170 degrees when done.
Cutlets	Thinly sliced, boneless, skinless breast meat; 4 ounces raw per serving.	Use interchangeably with chicken or veal cutlets; grill, broil, or panfry for 5 to 10 minutes.
Drumsticks	Portion of leg below the knee joint, ½ to 1½ pounds each; 6 ounces raw (with skin and bones) per serving.	Roast at 350 degrees 30 to 45 minutes per pound.
Thighs	Portion of leg above the knee joint, ½ to 1½ pounds each; 6 ounces raw (with skin and bones) per serving.	Roast or braise 30 to 40 minutes per pound.
Wings	Whole wings or first joints called drummettes, ½ to 1¼ pounds each; 8 ounces raw (with skin and bones) per serving.	Roast or stew 30 to 40 minutes per pound.
Ground	Mixture of white and dark meat and skin or white meat only; fat content varies—check the label carefully; 4 ounces raw per serving.	Use in burgers, meat loaf, and chili; cook until white throughout.
Sausages	Ground turkey seasoned like traditional sausages, bologna, and salami; fat content varies among brands; 4 ounces raw and 3 ounces cooked per serving.	Use like traditional counterparts.
Bacon	Turkey meat processed to look and taste like bacon; 3 ounces raw per serving.	Cook like bacon.

Common Game Birds

(Calories and fat vary according to type of bird and whether wild or farm raised. Discard skin before eating in all cases.)

TYPE	DESCRIPTION, WEIGHT, AND NUMBER OF SERVINGS	COOKING TIPS AND TIME
Cornish game hen	Small bird, 1 to 1½ pounds; 3 ounces cooked per serving.	Roast at 400 to 450 degrees 1 hour for whole birds and 35 minutes for halves or quarters.
Duck	Breasts are the leanest and meatiest part of the bird; 3 ounces cooked per serving.	Roast or panfry 13 to 15 minutes until no trace of pink remains; discard skin and fat before serving.
Goose, squab, quail	Weight and fat vary according to species and whether farm raised or wild; 3 ounces cooked per serving.	Roast at 350 to 400 degrees about 20 minutes per pound.

CHAPTER TEN

Seafood

Seafood offers a wide range of flavors and textures. Many varieties of fish—sole, haddock, cod—are so delicate that they leave only the slightest trace of flavor. Others, including firm-fleshed fish like swordfish and salmon, have a more assertive taste and texture. And the briny flavor of clams, mussels, and shrimp is the telltale sign of their saltwater home. Whether you prefer flaky or firm, mild or strong tasting, you'll find an abundance of fish, shellfish, and crustaceans to choose from.

Foods from the sea have long been associated with healthful eating. Almost all are extremely low in fat. For example, a 3-ounce serving of shrimp, lobster, haddock, or grouper supplies less than 2 grams of fat, compared to 6 grams in a serving of top sirloin, one of the leanest cuts of beef. While higher-fat fish like salmon and trout have about as much fat as many cuts of beef, the fat in the fish is unsaturated. In fact, the unsaturated omega-3 fatty acids in fish may even have health benefits. So higher-fat fish can certainly have a place in today's low-fat diets. And no need for most people to fear the cholesterol in shellfish like lobster, shrimp, and crawfish—these crustaceans have very little saturated fat so they are unlikely to affect your blood cholesterol…unless you drench them in butter.

Ounce for ounce, seafood is lower in calories than poultry or meat because it has little fat to contribute to the calorie count. Many varieties, particularly mildly flavored white-fleshed fish, also have a high water content. So don't be surprised to find that a Pyramid-sized 3-ounce serving of unadorned fish has less than 200 calories. Of course, these are far too few calories to make a full meal—all the more reason to add an array of tasty side dishes to boost your meal's calorie and nutrient content.

While frying is quick and lends a distinctive flavor and juiciness to fish, clams, and other foods from the sea, it is the highest-fat cooking method. You can create an equally delicious crispy coating with far less fat and fewer calories by breading and baking your fish, as in the Crackling Fish Sticks recipe (page 355). Poaching produces fish that is moist and tender, imparting just a hint of flavor from the poaching liquid. Grilling works well for strong-tasting, firm fish—the flesh holds together during the grilling process. Grill fish with just a light brushing of oil and a sprinkle of salt and pepper or marinate it ahead of time to add flavor. Shellfish and crustaceans are particularly well suited to the gentle simmering of a stew, as in Sausalito Cioppino (page 360), or the oven heat of a baked casserole, as in Crawfish and Tasso Jambalaya (page 359).

Toppings and sauces lend personality to your seafood dishes. Salsa imparts a taste of the tropics, especially when you make it with summery melon, as in the Grouper with Cantaloupe-Lime Salsa (page 369). Creamy sauces cool and enrich a dish. Of course, sour cream– or mayonnaise-based sauces, such as tartar sauce, are high in fat—even a small portion might contain more calories and fat than the fish you serve it with. Find out how to lighten them up without losing flavor by trying Lemon Tartar Sauce (page 355) or Dilled Cucumber Yogurt Sauce (page 369). For a new, healthier twist on an old favorite, serve herb-infused broth with your lobster instead of butter.

Fish dishes that please kids go far beyond just fish sticks and fried shrimp. Grilled fish and vegetable kebabs, like Skewered Swordfish and Summer Squash (page 366), are both tasty and fun. For a more elegant meal, cook seafood and vegetables in a packet as in Seafood Printemps en Papillotes (page 370) and watch the excitement in your children's eyes as they unwrap their "secret" meal. Encourage your kids to try local fish dishes while on a seaside vacation, where the ocean breezes and get-away spirit make everything taste so good. Once you get home, you can recreate vacation meals like Baltimore Crab Cakes (page 358), Herb-Steamed Mussels (page 375), and Cape Cod Baked Stuffed Clams (page 357).

Make fish a regular part of your weekly menu—its reputation for good flavor and good health is well-deserved.

Tuna and Celery Bread Pudding

Makes 6 servings

Assemble this casserole a few hours ahead of time, then pop it into the oven for a terrific informal dinner party main course. You can also substitute canned salmon, which contains a lot of calcium, for the tuna in this versatile casserole. Serve with Summer Harvest Ratatouille (page 426), a crisp romaine salad, and a basket of rolls.

Vegetable oil spray
2 eggs
2 egg whites
1½ cups low-fat milk
1½ teaspoons dry mustard
1 teaspoon dried savory
¼ teaspoon ground celery seed
¼ teaspoon salt
¼ teaspoon black pepper
⅛ teaspoon cayenne pepper

⅛ teaspoon grated nutmeg
8 slices whole-wheat bread
2 cans (6½ ounces each) solid white tuna packed in water, drained
½ cup chopped celery
½ cup chopped scallions
1 jar (4 ounces) chopped pimiento
1 cup (4 ounces) shredded reduced-fat Swiss cheese

1. Preheat the oven to 350 degrees. Coat a 7x11-inch baking dish with vegetable oil spray. In a mixing bowl, whisk together the eggs, whites, milk, mustard, savory, ground celery seed, salt, pepper, cayenne, and nutmeg.

2. Place half of the bread slices in the prepared baking dish, cutting them to fit into the bottom of the dish. Sprinkle with the tuna and celery, and half each of the scallions, pimiento, and cheese. Make another layer with the rest of the bread, then sprinkle with the remaining scallions, pimiento, and cheese. Carefully pour the milk and egg mixture over the bread, coating all the slices. Use the back of a spoon or a spatula to push the bread down into the milk. (The casserole can be assembled to this point about 4 hours ahead, covered, and refrigerated. Remove from the refrigerator 30 minutes before baking.)

3. Bake the bread pudding, uncovered, until it puffs and the top is golden brown, 40 to 45 minutes. Cut into squares and serve.

◆ *PER SERVING: About 286 cals, 80 cals from fat, 9g total fat, 1g sat fat, 109mg chol, 706mg sodium, 21g total carbs, 5g fiber, 31g prot*

Crackling Fish Sticks

Makes 4 servings

These fish sticks have a lot of crunch without all the fat of regular fish sticks. Crusty Oven "Fries" (page 417) and sliced tomatoes sprinkled with herbs round out the meal nicely.

3 tablespoons low-fat mayonnaise	1 tablespoon grated lemon peel
1 tablespoon lemon juice	1 pound orange roughy or other
¼ teaspoon liquid hot pepper	whitefish fillets
sauce	½ cup Lemon Tartar Sauce
4 cups cornflakes	(recipe follows)

1. Preheat the oven to 500 degrees. In a small, shallow dish, stir together the mayonnaise, lemon juice, and hot pepper sauce. Crush the cornflakes to make coarse crumbs using a rolling pin or a food processor. Add the lemon peel and mix. Transfer the crumbs to a plate. Cut the fish crosswise into ¾-inch strips.

2. Brush the fish lightly with the mayonnaise mixture, then dip it into the crumbs to coat completely. Place the fish sticks on a baking sheet, leaving at least 1 inch between each stick. Sprinkle the tops with any remaining crumbs.

3. Bake the fish sticks, without turning, until they are opaque in the center and the crumbs are golden brown, 14 to 16 minutes. Serve with the tartar sauce (recipe follows).

◆ *PER SERVING (without sauce): About 204 cals, 41 cals from fat, 5g total fat, 1g sat fat, 22mg chol, 435mg sodium, 21g total carbs, 1g fiber, 18g prot*

LEMON TARTAR SAUCE

Makes about ½ cup (4 servings)

Serve this sauce with Crackling Fish Sticks (above), Baltimore Crab Cakes (page 358), or Southern-"Fried" Lemon Pepper Catfish (recipe follows), as well as any plain broiled, baked, or oven-fried fish.

⅓ cup low-fat mayonnaise	1 teaspoon drained small	1½ teaspoons grated lemon
3 tablespoons pickle relish	capers	peel
		1½ teaspoons lemon juice

In a small bowl, whisk together all of the ingredients. Cover and refrigerate for at least 30 minutes or up to 3 days before using.

Per serving: About 78 cals, 59 cals from fat, 7g total fat, 1g sat fat, 0mg chol, 293mg sodium, 4g total carbs, 0g fiber, 0g prot

Southern-"Fried" Lemon Pepper Catfish

Makes 6 servings

The "frying" in this recipe is done in the oven, and you'll never miss the fat or the splatters. Steamed greens, Calico Coleslaw (page 97), and Yogurt Corn Bread (page 125) complete this updated version of the classic Southern fish fry.

Vegetable oil spray
1 cup low-fat buttermilk
½ to 1 teaspoon liquid hot pepper
   sauce to taste
1½ pounds catfish or other firm
   mild whitefish fillets, cut into
   6 pieces

½ cup yellow cornmeal
½ cup all-purpose flour
1 tablespoon grated lemon peel
¾ teaspoon coarsely ground black
   pepper
½ teaspoon salt
Lemon wedges for garnish

1. Coat a large baking sheet with vegetable oil spray. In a shallow dish just large enough to hold the fish in a single layer, stir together the buttermilk and hot pepper sauce. Add the fish, turning to coat. Let stand at room temperature for 15 to 20 minutes, turning once or twice.

2. Preheat the oven to 500 degrees. In another shallow dish, combine the cornmeal, flour, lemon peel, pepper, and salt. Remove the fish from the buttermilk and dip it into the cornmeal mixture to coat it completely.

3. Arrange the fish on the prepared baking sheet, leaving at least 1 inch between each fillet. Lightly coat the tops of the fish fillets with vegetable oil spray.

4. Bake the fish, without turning, until it is opaque throughout and the coating is golden brown and crisp, 12 to 14 minutes. Serve immediately garnished with lemon wedges.

◆ *PER SERVING: About 238 cals, 81 cals from fat, 9g total fat, 2g sat fat, 53mg chol, 250mg sodium, 18g total carbs, 1g fiber, 20g prot*

SEAFOOD SAFETY

The three most important things you can do to ensure seafood safety at home are buying from a reliable source, storing it properly in the refrigerator, and cooking it within a day or two of purchase.

Eating raw seafood causes very little illness, but don't take the chance unless you are sure about where the seafood came from and how it was handled. The federal government checks the quality and

safety of seafood sold in the United States. If you catch your own fish, know the quality of the water in the area and find out whether local authorities determine it to be safe.

Cape Cod Baked Stuffed Clams

Makes 4 servings

Practically every restaurant along the New England shore specializes in baked stuffed clams. You can bake the iron-rich clams on shell-shaped dishes, available in kitchen specialty stores, on well-scrubbed shells from fresh, hard-shell clams, or in a casserole dish. Serve with Summer Harvest Ratatouille (page 426) and Yogurt Corn Bread (page 125).

3 cups fresh French bread crumbs
1½ tablespoons olive oil,
   preferably extra virgin
¾ cup finely chopped onion
¾ cup finely chopped celery
6 garlic cloves, minced
1½ teaspoons grated lemon peel
¼ teaspoon salt
¼ teaspoon dried red pepper
   flakes
⅓ cup chopped fresh basil

2 tablespoons chopped fresh
   marjoram or 2 teaspoons dried
2 tablespoons chopped fresh thyme
   or 2 teaspoons dried
1½ cups drained chopped fresh
   clams or 3 cans (6½ ounces
   each) chopped clams, drained,
   juice reserved
3 tablespoons chopped parsley,
   plus 3 tablespoons
⅓ cup grated Parmesan cheese
Lemon wedges for garnish

1. Preheat the oven to 400 degrees. In a medium, preferably nonstick frying pan, toss the crumbs over medium heat until lightly toasted, about 2 minutes. Transfer the crumbs to a large mixing bowl.

2. In the same skillet, heat the oil and cook the onion and celery over medium heat, stirring often, until the vegetables soften, about 5 minutes. Add the garlic, lemon peel, salt, and pepper flakes and cook, stirring, for 1 minute. Transfer the vegetable mixture to the mixing bowl with the bread crumbs and stir in the basil, marjoram, thyme, clams, and 3 tablespoons of the parsley. Add enough reserved clam juice to moisten the stuffing. (This recipe can be prepared a day ahead to this point and refrigerated. Return to room temperature before proceeding.)

3. Spoon the stuffing into 8 clam baking shells, 24 hard-shell clam shells, or a shallow casserole dish. Sprinkle with the cheese and the remaining 3 tablespoons of parsley. Bake, uncovered, until heated through and the top is browned and crisp, about 15 minutes.

4. Serve garnished with the lemon wedges.

◆ *PER SERVING: About 303 cals, 91 cals from fat, 10g total fat, 3g sat fat, 47mg chol, 643mg sodium, 29g total carbs, 1g fiber, 23g prot*

Baltimore Crab Cakes

Makes 4 servings

The secret of good crab cakes is to combine the mixture as gently as possible so that the crab will not lose moisture or break up too much. For the best crab cakes, use vacuum-packed fresh lump crabmeat, although the far less pricey canned white crabmeat makes delicious cakes, too. Look for seafood seasoning in the spice section of the grocery store.

1 egg

3 egg whites

3 tablespoons low-fat mayonnaise

1 tablespoon lemon juice

2½ teaspoons Worcestershire
　sauce

2 teaspoons Maryland-style
　seafood seasoning

¾ teaspoon dry mustard

¼ teaspoon cayenne pepper

3 cups fresh French bread crumbs,
　plus 1½ cups

½ cup finely chopped scallions

½ cup finely chopped red bell
　pepper

¾ pound vacuum-packed fresh
　lump crabmeat or 3 cans
　(6 ounces each) white crabmeat,
　drained and picked over for
　cartilage

Vegetable oil spray

Lemon wedges for garnish

Lemon Tartar Sauce (optional)

1. In a large mixing bowl, whisk together the egg, egg whites, mayonnaise, lemon juice, Worcestershire, seafood seasoning, mustard, and cayenne. Add 3 cups bread crumbs, the scallions, and the bell pepper and mix well. Add the crabmeat and toss gently to mix.

2. Coat a baking sheet with vegetable oil spray. Use your hands to gently form the crab mixture into 8 cakes, each about ½ inch thick. Spread the remaining 1½ cups of bread crumbs on a plate. Dip the crab cakes into the crumbs to lightly coat both sides. The cakes will be fragile; re-form them if they begin to fall apart. Place the crab cakes on the prepared baking sheet. (This recipe can be made up to 4 hours ahead and refrigerated. Remove from the refrigerator 30 minutes before broiling.)

3. Turn on the broiler. Broil the crab cakes about 5 inches from the heat source until golden and crisp on one side, 3 to 4 minutes. Use a spatula to carefully turn the crab cakes and broil until golden and crisp on the other side, 3 to 4 minutes longer.

4. Serve with the lemon wedges and Lemon Tartar Sauce (page 355), if desired.

◆ *PER SERVING: About 326 cals, 76 cals from fat, 8g total fat, 2g sat fat, 138mg chol, 751mg sodium, 34g total carbs, 1g fiber, 27g prot*

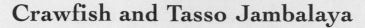

Crawfish and Tasso Jambalaya

Makes 6 servings

Jambalaya is a great party dish; it can be mostly made ahead and then served right from the baking dish. If you can't get crawfish tails, which are usually available frozen, substitute medium or large shrimp. Tasso is a spicy Cajun ham, but any really good smoked ham will do nicely. If you like, you can also add some chicken to the jambalaya. Although crawfish and shrimp are higher in cholesterol than other seafood, they have almost no fat.

1 tablespoon olive oil
¼ pound (about 1 cup) diced
    tasso or smoked ham
1 large onion, chopped
1 large green bell pepper, seeded
    and chopped
2 celery ribs, chopped
3 garlic cloves, minced
1½ teaspoons dried thyme

1½ cups raw long-grain rice
1½ cups bottled clam juice
2 cans (14½ ounces each)
    stewed tomatoes
1 pound crawfish tails or medium
    shrimp, shelled and deveined
½ cup thinly sliced scallions
Liquid hot pepper sauce, to taste

1. Preheat the oven to 350 degrees. In a large skillet, heat the oil and cook the tasso, onion, bell pepper, and celery over medium heat, stirring constantly until the meat is golden brown and the vegetables are softened, about 5 minutes. Add the garlic and thyme and cook for 1 minute. Add the rice and cook, stirring, for 1 minute. Transfer the mixture to a shallow 3-quart casserole, such as a 9x13-inch baking dish. (The jambalaya can be made up to 4 hours in advance to this point and refrigerated. Return to room temperature before proceeding.)

2. Stir the clam juice and 1 cup of water into the rice mixture. Cover tightly with foil and bake for 30 minutes. Gently stir in the tomatoes and juices, then arrange the crawfish on top, pushing them down into the jambalaya. Re-cover the casserole and continue to bake until the rice is tender and the shellfish are opaque and cooked through, about 15 minutes.

3. Stir in about half of the scallions and season to taste with hot pepper sauce. Sprinkle the jambalaya with the remaining scallions.

◆ *PER SERVING: About 461 cals, 48 cals from fat, 5g total fat, 1g sat fat, 99mg chol, 1441mg sodium, 77g total carbs, 6g fiber, 24g prot*

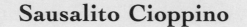

Sausalito Cioppino

Makes 6 servings

Cioppino is the classic fish stew that in San Francisco nearly always contains Dungeness crab, along with other Pacific fish and shellfish. This recipe also includes clams, which are rich in iron, but you could use whatever fresh seafood is available. Serve it with lots of sourdough or French bread to sop up the broth.

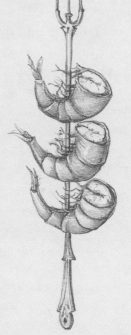

1 tablespoon extra-virgin olive oil

1 medium onion, chopped

1 green bell pepper, seeded and chopped

2 large garlic cloves, finely chopped

1 can (14½ ounces) stewed tomatoes

1 cup fish broth or bottled clam juice

½ cup dry red or white wine

1 teaspoon dried marjoram

1 teaspoon dried thyme

¼ teaspoon dried red pepper flakes

1 bay leaf, broken in half

18 clams, such as littlenecks, in the shell, scrubbed

½ pound firm fish, such as halibut or monkfish,
    cut into 1-inch chunks

18 large shrimp, peeled and deveined

1 pound cooked Dungeness crab claws or ½ pound
    Dungeness or other lump crabmeat

2 tablespoons chopped flat-leaf parsley

1. Heat the oil in a 4- or 5-quart pot. Cook the onion and green pepper over medium heat for 4 minutes. Add the garlic and cook until the vegetables are softened, 1 to 2 minutes more. Add the tomatoes, fish broth, wine, marjoram, thyme, pepper flakes, and bay leaf. Partially cover the pan and simmer over medium-low heat for 20 minutes. Discard the bay leaf.

2. Add the clams and fish. Cover the pan and simmer for 5 minutes. Add the shrimp, crab, and parsley. Simmer until the shrimp turn pink and the clams open, 2 to 3 minutes. Serve in shallow soup bowls.

◆ *PER SERVING: About 150 cals, 36 cals from fat, 4g total fat, 1g sat fat, 52mg chol, 626mg sodium, 9g total carbs, 1g fiber, 18g prot*

Sole Rolls Florentine

Makes 4 servings

This quick-and-easy, yet sophisticated dish is rich in fiber, iron, and vitamins A and C. Serve it with an orzo pilaf, Mixed Mushroom Sauté with Tarragon (page 438), and a salad of delicate greens. Add Citrus Chiffon Cake (page 455) for dessert.

1 pound fresh spinach, washed and trimmed

Olive oil spray

12 small lemon or gray sole fillets (about 1½ pounds)

Salt and black pepper to taste

1 tablespoon dried herbes de Provence, plus 1 teaspoon

1 cup white wine

¾ cup French bread crumbs

½ tablespoon butter, melted, plus ½ tablespoon

1. Preheat the oven to 450 degrees. Steam the spinach in a small amount of water until wilted, about 3 minutes. Drain the spinach and squeeze out as much liquid as possible. (You can cook the spinach a day ahead and refrigerate it. Return it to room temperature before proceeding.)

2. Coat a shallow 2-quart casserole, such as a 7x11-inch baking dish, with olive oil spray.

3. Lay the fish fillets flat on a work surface. Sprinkle each lightly with salt and pepper, and ¼ teaspoon of the herbes de Provence. Divide the spinach among the fish, laying it flat on the fillets. Starting at a short side, roll up each fillet into a cylinder. Arrange, seam side down, in the prepared baking dish. Sprinkle with the remaining 1 teaspoon of herbes de Provence. Pour the wine around the fish. In a small bowl, toss the bread crumbs with ½ tablespoon of the butter. Sprinkle the crumbs over the fish rolls.

4. Bake, uncovered, until the fish is opaque and the topping is browned and crisp, about 15 minutes. Use a slotted spoon to place the fish fillets on plates. Strain the sauce into a small skillet. Bring to a boil, then reduce the heat to low and whisk in the remaining ½ tablespoon of butter.

5. Spoon the sauce over the fish and serve.

◆ *PER SERVING: About 203 cals, 48 cals from fat, 5g total fat, 2g sat fat, 87mg chol, 331mg sodium, 6g total carbs, 9g fiber, 32g prot*

Poached Turbot with Sorrel Sauce

Makes 4 servings

Sorrel is a tender, spring green with a tart, lemony flavor. Be sure to choose young sorrel; mature leaves tend to be stronger tasting and slightly bitter. If sorrel isn't available, substitute young spinach leaves. The easiest way to cut the leaves is to roll several into a cylinder, then thinly slice the roll with a small knife.

1½ pounds turbot or other fish fillets, cut into 8 pieces	2 tablespoons all-purpose flour
White pepper to taste	2 cups thinly sliced sorrel leaves
2 cups bottled clam juice	1 cup low-fat (1 percent) milk
6 thin lemon slices	½ teaspoon grated lemon peel
1½ tablespoons unsalted butter	¼ teaspoon ground mace
¼ cup chopped shallots	1 tablespoon lemon juice
	Salt and pepper to taste

1. Season the fish lightly with white pepper. Place the fillets in a skillet. Pour the clam juice over the fish and add enough water to just cover the fillets. Add the lemon slices. Place the skillet over medium heat and bring to a simmer. Reduce the heat to low. Cover the skillet and poach the fish until it becomes opaque, 6 to 8 minutes. Use a slotted spoon to remove the fish from the skillet. Raise the heat to high and boil the poaching liquid until it is reduced by about a third, about 3 minutes. Strain the liquid and reserve 1 cup.

2. Melt the butter in a medium, preferably nonstick skillet, and cook the shallots over medium heat for 1 minute. Stir in the flour and cook, stirring, for 2 minutes. Add the sorrel, milk, lemon peel, mace, and reserved poaching liquid. Bring to a boil, stirring until lightly thickened and bubbly. Stir in the lemon juice and season with salt and pepper. Return the fish to the pan and simmer gently for 2 minutes to reheat the fish.

3. Serve the fish immediately with the sauce spooned over it.

◆ *PER SERVING: About 267 cals, 95 cals from fat, 11g total fat, 4g sat fat, 96mg chol, 548mg sodium, 10g total carbs, 1g fiber, 32g prot*

WILD VERSUS FARM-RAISED SEAFOOD

More and more fish and seafood are farm raised in this country. Catfish, trout, and mussels are among the most common farm-raised seafood, but new varieties are being farmed every day. The advantages of farm raising are better quality control and a more uniform size. The disadvantage is a slightly more bland taste and a higher fat content because fish and other seafood that are farm raised lead more leisurely lives than do their wild cousins.

Sesame-Glazed Tuna

Makes 4 servings

This is a simple way to prepare fish with a Japanese flair. Serve the tuna with Japanese-style "sticky" rice and Broccoli and Carrot Stir-Fry with Garlic (page 431). Finish with frozen yogurt or Fresh Apricot Soufflé (page 450). You can use halibut, swordfish, or shark steaks in place of the tuna.

¼ cup reduced-sodium soy sauce

1½ tablespoons mirin or sherry

1 tablespoon honey

2 teaspoons sesame oil

1 tablespoon rice wine vinegar

1 pound tuna steaks, about ¾ inch
  thick, cut into 4 pieces

2 tablespoons sesame seeds

1. Preheat the oven to 450 degrees. In a small bowl, stir together the soy sauce, mirin, honey, and sesame oil. Remove and set aside half of the mixture for the glaze. Stir the vinegar into the remaining soy mixture, and reserve to use as the dipping sauce. (You can prepare the glaze and sauce several hours ahead and reserve them at room temperature.)

2. Place the pieces of fish on a baking sheet and brush the tops with the soy glaze. Sprinkle with the sesame seeds. Bake, brushing once or twice with the remaining glaze, until the fish is opaque and the sesame seeds are lightly toasted, 8 to 10 minutes.

3. Serve the fish with the vinegar-soy dipping sauce.

◆ *PER SERVING: About 202 cals, 50 cals from fat, 6g total fat, 1g sat fat, 51mg chol, 570mg sodium, 7g total carbs, 1g fiber, 29g prot*

HOW TO CHOOSE FRESH SEAFOOD

To buy good, fresh seafood, you need to know your market and your fish dealer. The waters from which a fish comes and the way it is handled from catch to cooking make all the difference. A reliable fish dealer will get the best quality from the best sources. Whether you buy from a small fish store or a large supermarket, try to build a relationship with the salesperson. Here are the basics to look for when buying seafood:

◆ The store always should be scrupulously clean, from floors to counters, and the fish should either be packed on ice or kept in a refrigerator. All fish and shellfish should smell fresh.

◆ Whole fresh fish should have bright skin, clear eyes, lively looking flesh with no brown spots, and red to pink gills.

◆ Fresh fish steaks and fillets are best cut to order. If they are pre-cut, their surface should look clear and bright, and the flesh should be firm and not mushy (ask the fish dealer to press on the flesh so you can see its texture).

◆ Clams, oysters, and mussels in the shell should be well iced or refrigerated and have closed shells when you buy them.

◆ Shellfish out of the shell, such as scallops, should be glistening and moist.

◆ Frozen fish or shellfish should be free of white spots that indicate freezer burn. Others should be well wrapped and should show no signs of previous thawing and refreezing.

Broiled Citrus and Herb Trout

Makes 4 servings

Broiling is one of the nicest ways to prepare trout. The skin imparts flavor to the fish, and so does the bed of herbs in this recipe. Trout season occurs in spring, so serve the fish with springlike steamed Lemon and Honey-Glazed Baby Carrots (page 430), Herbed Brown Rice Pilaf (page 275), and a watercress salad.

4 small whole boneless rainbow trout
   (about 8 ounces each)
4 teaspoons extra-virgin olive oil
Salt and freshly ground black
   pepper to taste
1 bunch fresh tarragon
1 bunch fresh thyme
1 small bunch flat-leaf parsley
2 limes, thinly sliced

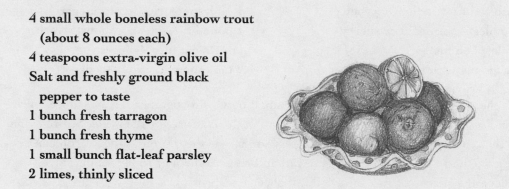

1. Brush or rub the fish skin and cavities with the oil. Season with salt and pepper. Chop 2 tablespoons each of the tarragon, thyme, and parsley. Sprinkle the chopped herbs evenly in the cavities of the trout. Top the herbs with overlapping slices of lime, reserving 4 slices for garnish.

2. Turn on the broiler. Place half of the remaining whole herbs on a baking sheet or broiler pan. Arrange the trout on top of the herbs and broil, about 4 inches from the heat source, until the skin is brown, about 5 minutes. Using a spatula, carefully turn the trout and broil until the skin on the other side is browned and the fish is opaque, about 4 minutes longer.

3. Serve the trout garnished with the remaining whole herbs and reserved lime slices.

◆ *PER SERVING: About 244 cals, 93 cals from fat, 10g total fat, 2g sat fat, 97mg chol, 49mg sodium, 0g total carbs, 0g fiber, 35g prot*

THE 10-MINUTE COOKING RULE

The most common mistake in cooking fish is overcooking. A good rule of thumb, which works with all cooking methods, is to cook the fish 10 minutes for every inch of thickness, measured at the thickest point. If you will be cooking a fish in a sauce, in a crust, or in parchment, measure it when it is completely sauced, breaded, or wrapped for cooking. Fish is done when it is opaque throughout. If it flakes, it is probably overcooked.

Sautéed Red Snapper Maque Choux

Makes 4 servings

Maque choux is a highly seasoned Cajun corn dish, which usually contains bell pepper, celery, onions, and tomatoes. It's great on its own, but also makes a terrific, vitamin C– and iron-rich cooked "salsa" for sautéed fish fillets, especially red snapper or trout. Team this dish with Braided Semolina Bread (page 115) or crusty French bread.

2 tablespoons yellow cornmeal

2 tablespoons all-purpose flour

¼ teaspoon salt, plus additional to taste

⅛ teaspoon cayenne pepper, plus additional to taste

1 pound skinless red snapper fillets, cut into 4 pieces

1 tablespoon extra-virgin olive oil, plus ½ tablespoon

¼ cup (about 1 ounce) slivered smoked ham

⅓ cup chopped green bell pepper

⅓ cup chopped celery

⅓ cup chopped onion

½ cup fresh, canned, or frozen corn kernels

1 cup seeded and diced plum tomatoes

½ cup bottled clam juice or white wine

1 tablespoon chopped fresh or 1 teaspoon dried thyme

1. Preheat the oven to 300 degrees. On a shallow plate, combine the cornmeal, flour, ¼ teaspoon salt, and ⅛ teaspoon cayenne. Dip the fish into the mixture to lightly coat both sides. Set aside.

2. In a large, preferably nonstick skillet, heat 1 tablespoon of the oil and cook the fish over medium-high heat until browned, about 4 minutes. Use a spatula to carefully turn the fish. Cook the fish until it is browned and nearly opaque, about 4 minutes longer. Remove the fish to a baking sheet and keep it warm in the preheated oven while making the sauce.

3. Add the remaining ½ tablespoon of oil to the skillet and cook the ham, pepper, celery, and onion over medium heat, stirring until the vegetables soften, about 5 minutes. Add the corn, tomatoes, clam juice, and thyme. Cover the pan and simmer over medium-low heat for 5 minutes. Season to taste with salt and cayenne pepper.

4. Serve the fish with the sauce spooned over it.

◆ *PER SERVING: About 239 cals, 68 cals from fat, 8g total fat, 1g sat fat, 46mg chol, 462mg sodium, 15g total carbs, 2g fiber, 27g prot*

Skewered Swordfish and Summer Squash

Makes 4 servings

You can substitute tuna, salmon, or halibut, which are especially well suited to skewering, in this recipe. You can also use green or yellow peppers. Serve Molasses and Pepper Grilled Sweet Potato Slices (page 424) along with the kebabs.

¼ cup plain nonfat yogurt
¼ cup reduced-fat sour cream
2 tablespoons chopped cilantro
3 tablespoons fresh lime juice
1 tablespoon extra-virgin olive oil
2 teaspoons chili powder
1 teaspoon ground cumin
1¼ pounds swordfish steaks, cut
   into 1-inch chunks

1 large red bell pepper, seeded and
   cut into 8 pieces
1 medium yellow summer squash
   (about 6 ounces), cut into
   8 chunks
8 thick scallions, trimmed with
   2 inches of green intact
4 cups cooked brown or white rice
Cilantro sprigs for garnish

1. In a small bowl, stir together the yogurt, sour cream, and cilantro. Refrigerate until ready to use, up to 8 hours. Prepare a medium-hot barbecue fire, preheat a gas grill, or turn on the oven broiler.

2. In a shallow dish just large enough to hold the fish, combine the lime juice, oil, chili powder, and cumin. Add the fish, turning to coat. Refrigerate for 15 to 20 minutes. Remove the fish from the marinade and add the vegetables, turning and rubbing to coat with the marinade left in the dish. Thread the fish and vegetables onto 4 long metal skewers, placing the scallions at the ends.

3. Grill or broil, turning once or twice, until the fish is opaque throughout and the vegetables are tender and lightly charred, 8 to 10 minutes.

4. Arrange the skewers over the rice, dollop the fish with the sour cream sauce, and garnish with cilantro sprigs. For a buffet, remove the fish and vegetables from the skewers and arrange on top of the rice.

◆ *PER SERVING: About 446 cals, 102 cals from fat, 11g total fat, 2g sat fat, 50mg chol, 150mg sodium, 55g total carbs, 6g fiber, 31g prot*

CHOOSING SHELLFISH

Here is a handy guide to help you select the freshest shellfish you can find.

◆ **CLAMS, MUSSELS, AND OYSTERS IN THE SHELL:** Buy live shellfish in the shell on the day you will be cooking them. Store them, loosely wrapped in paper or in a bowl so they can breathe, in the refrigerator. Choose shellfish that have closed, unbroken shells, and discard any that do not open after cooking. Clean the shells by scrubbing well with a stiff brush. Pull the beards off of mussel shells.

◆ **CLAMS, MUSSELS, AND OYSTERS OUT OF THE SHELL:** Choose fresh-smelling, plump oysters or mussels. Clams are often available chopped, either fresh, frozen, or canned. All types are acceptable if of good quality.

◆ **SHRIMP:** Raw shrimp should have firm, shiny shells. Black spots and an iodine odor are signs of aging. Most raw shrimp have been previously frozen. Cooked shrimp should be firm and bright in color with no hint of mushiness.

◆ **SCALLOPS:** Choose bay or sea scallops that are milky white, firm, moist, and sweet smelling. They are usually sold out of the shell.

◆ **LOBSTERS:** Live lobsters should be lively and active, whether sold on ice or in a tank. Refrigerate them in a paper or plastic bag with airholes and cook within a few hours. Cooked lobster meat is available fresh, pasteurized, canned, or frozen.

◆ **CRABS:** Live crabs should be active and lively at the time of purchase. The fish dealer will kill and clean soft-shell crabs for you. You should cook them shortly after purchase. Cooked crabmeat is available fresh, pasteurized, canned, or frozen.

SARDINES AND SALMON ARE CALCIUM RICH

Sardines and salmon, commonly bought in cans, should be shelf staples for their flavor and versatility. Because they are usually canned with bones, both are good sources of calcium, as well as protein, vitamins, and other minerals. The fish bones soften during the canning process so they are perfectly edible. A 3-ounce serving of canned sardines or salmon with bones has as much calcium as 6 ounces of milk.

Anchovies, a tasty addition to pasta dishes and salads, are another good source of calcium. Most canned seafood contains added salt, so you may not need to add salt to the recipe. Here are some ideas for using these nutri-ent-packed canned fish:

◆ Substitute salmon for canned tuna in salads, sandwiches, or casseroles.

◆ Add sardines or anchovies to tomato-based pasta sauces or pasta and potato salads.

◆ Garnish green salads with sardines or anchovies.

◆ Layer sardines or salmon on sliced tomatoes and sweet onions for a quick-and-easy main-dish salad.

◆ Make anchovy or salmon bruschetta by brushing olive oil and garlic on toasted bread along with thinly sliced tomatoes and a sprin-kling of capers, topped with fish.

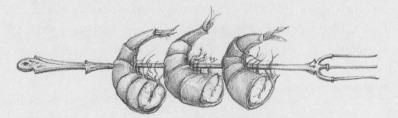

Grilled Salmon with Dilled Cucumber Yogurt Sauce

Makes 8 servings

A "side" or whole fillet of salmon, arranged on a bed of herbs and lavishly garnished with cucumber, makes a stunning presentation for a party. It's also easy to prepare. You can use individual salmon fillets in this dish if you prefer. A Belgian endive and radicchio salad and Herbed Brown Rice Pilaf (page 275) are colorful buffet accompaniments.

Oak wood chips, optional

1 whole salmon fillet (about 2½ pounds)
2 teaspoons olive oil
1 teaspoon coarsely ground black pepper

¼ teaspoon salt
1 bunch fresh dill
1 lemon, thinly sliced
1 cucumber, thinly sliced
2 teaspoons small capers, drained
1 cup Dilled Cucumber Yogurt Sauce (recipe follows)

1. If you like your salmon to have a smoky flavor, use oak wood chips in the grill. Soak them in cold water for at least 30 minutes. Prepare a medium-hot barbecue fire, then use tongs to push the coals to one side and place the wood chips over the coals.

2. Rub the salmon with the oil, then season with the pepper and salt. Place the salmon, skin side up, on the grill rack on the side away from the coals. Grill about 7 minutes, then use a large spatula to carefully loosen the fish from the grill and turn, skin side down. Grill until the fish is opaque, about 7 minutes longer.

3. Spread the dill on a large platter. Use 2 spatulas to carefully remove the fish from the grill and set it on the bed of dill. Garnish with the lemon, cucumber slices, and capers. Spoon a little of the Dilled Cucumber Yogurt Sauce (recipe follows) onto the fish and serve the remainder separately.

◆ *PER SERVING (without sauce): About 276 cals, 149 cals from fat, 17g total fat, 3g sat fat, 84mg chol, 178mg sodium, 2g total carbs, 0g fiber, 29g prot*

Note: If you don't want to grill the fish, roast it in a 450-degree oven, skin side down, without turning, for about 15 minutes until cooked through.

DILLED CUCUMBER YOGURT SAUCE

Makes about 1 cup (8 servings)

This cooling sauce is good with any plain grilled fish.

½ cup nonfat plain yogurt
¼ cup reduced-fat mayonnaise

⅓ cup seeded and coarsely
chopped cucumber

3 tablespoons snipped fresh dill
½ teaspoon grated lemon peel
Salt and white pepper to taste

In a bowl, stir together the yogurt, mayonnaise, cucumber, dill, and lemon peel. Season with salt and white pepper. Let stand 15 minutes at room temperature or refrigerate up to 4 hours before serving.

Per serving: About 34 cals, 23 cals from fat, 3g total fat, 1g sat fat, 0mg chol, 66mg sodium, 2g total carbs, 0g fiber, 1g prot

Grouper with Cantaloupe-Lime Salsa

Makes 4 servings

This refreshing salsa is terrific over any grilled fish, or chicken breasts, and adds vitamins A and C to the dish. A romaine lettuce salad with Basic Creamy Dressing (page 75), corn on the cob, and a basket of Herbed Focaccia (page 118) or crusty peasant bread complete the meal.

1 small cantaloupe, seeded and
diced (about 2 cups)
½ cup chopped red onion
¼ cup chopped fresh cilantro
1 small jalapeño, seeded and
minced
3 tablespoons fresh lime juice
1 teaspoon grated lime peel

½ teaspoon black pepper, plus
additional to taste
¼ teaspoon salt, plus additional to
taste
⅛ teaspoon curry powder
1½ pounds grouper or other mild
firm fish fillets
1½ tablespoons vegetable oil

1. In a medium bowl, stir together the melon, onion, cilantro, jalapeño, lime juice and peel, ½ teaspoon pepper, ¼ teaspoon salt, and the curry powder. Let stand at room temperature for 15 minutes.

2. Prepare a medium-hot barbecue fire, preheat a gas grill, or turn on the oven broiler. Brush the fish with the oil and season it with salt and pepper. Grill or broil the fish for 3 minutes. Use a spatula to turn it carefully, and cook until opaque, about 3 minutes longer.

3. Serve the fish with the salsa spooned over it.

◆ *PER SERVING: About 243 cals, 64 cals from fat, 7g total fat, 1g sat fat, 62mg chol, 226mg sodium, 10g total carbs, 1g fiber, 34g prot*

Seafood Printemps en Papillotes

Makes 4 servings

Basic Baked Rice Pilaf (page 274), Grilled Tofu Caesar Salad (page 91), and dinner rolls round out this spring dinner. Rhubarb Fool (page 445) is the right seasonal finish.

1 pound skinless salmon fillets, cut crosswise into ¾-inch strips	½ teaspoon black pepper
¼ pound small bay scallops or peeled and deveined shrimp	1 tablespoon lemon juice
1 tablespoon chopped fresh tarragon	1 tablespoon orange juice
1 teaspoon grated lemon peel	2 teaspoons extra-virgin olive oil
1 teaspoon grated orange peel	¼ pound small snow peas, strings removed
½ teaspoon salt	2 carrots, cut into 2½- by ¼-inch strips
	⅓ cup thinly sliced scallions

1. Preheat the oven to 425 degrees. Cut 4 pieces of parchment paper or aluminum foil into 12x15-inch rectangles. Fold in half from the short end and cut out a large half-heart along the fold, like a valentine. When unfolded, the hearts should measure about 14 inches wide and 12 inches long.

2. Divide the salmon and scallops among the hearts, placing them on one long side of each. Sprinkle with the tarragon, lemon and orange peels, salt, and pepper. Drizzle with the lemon and orange juices and the oil. Scatter the snow peas, carrots, and scallions over the seafood. Fold the heart over and crimp the edges neatly to seal completely.

3. Place the packets on a baking sheet and bake until the parchment is puffed and lightly browned and the seafood is opaque, about 10 minutes.

◆ *PER SERVING: About 182 cals, 59 cals from fat, 7g total fat, 1g sat fat, 32mg chol, 409mg sodium, 8g total carbs, 2g fiber, 23g prot*

COOKING EN PAPILLOTE

Cooking in paper, or en papillote, is a classic French technique in which the food is oven steamed in the wrapper. Parchment paper is the classic wrapper because it puffs up and makes a lovely table presentation. Cut it into a heart shape, then fold it in half and seal it with the ingredients inside. You can use aluminum foil, although it isn't as pretty. Choose very quick-cooking (under 20 minutes) foods to cook en papillote—thin chicken breast or fish fillets, shellfish, and vegetables. Sprinkled with herbs and a touch of liquid, butter, or oil, the ingredients steam together and concentrate their flavors.

Vietnamese Steamed Fish in Spicy Broth

Makes 4 servings

You can steam nearly any whitefish or shellfish in this aromatic broth. Try this combination of grouper and shrimp, or use whatever is freshest in your area. Lemongrass and fish sauce are available in Asian markets and well-stocked supermarkets.

1 cup bottled clam juice
½ cup reduced-fat canned coconut
   milk
3 tablespoons bottled fish sauce
   (nam pla)
1 tablespoon fresh lime juice
1 tablespoon thinly sliced fresh
   lemongrass or 1 teaspoon grated
   lemon peel
3 thin slices fresh ginger
3 lime slices, plus additional for
   garnish

3 sprigs cilantro, plus additional
   for garnish
2 garlic cloves, slivered
1 teaspoon seeded and minced
   jalapeño pepper
½ teaspoon curry powder
⅔ pound large shrimp (about 20),
   peeled and deveined
½ pound grouper or other
   whitefish fillets, cut crosswise
   into 1-inch strips

1. In a shallow saucepan or covered skillet, bring the clam juice, coconut milk, fish sauce, lime juice, lemongrass, ginger, lime slices, cilantro, garlic, jalapeño, and curry powder to a simmer. Add the shrimp and grouper. Cover the pan and simmer until the shrimp and fish are opaque, 5 to 6 minutes. Use a slotted spoon to remove the seafood to a shallow rimmed platter.

2. Bring the sauce to a boil and reduce by about one fourth, 4 to 5 minutes. Strain the sauce over the seafood and garnish with lime slices and cilantro sprigs.

◆ *PER SERVING: About 151 cals, 31 cals from fat, 3g total fat, 1g sat fat, 108mg chol, 927mg sodium, 6g total carbs, 0g fiber, 23g prot*

WHAT ARE OMEGA-3 FATTY ACIDS?

Some fish that are higher in fat—salmon, bluefish, mackerel, herring, sardines, anchovies—are also rich in omega-3 fatty acids. These fatty acids reduce blood clotting in humans and may have other benefits that protect against heart disease, though the research is not conclusive. The bottom line is that including fish in your diet, in Food Guide Pyramid portions, is a healthy choice. Fish has other nutrients as well, so don't substitute fish oil supplements for the real thing.

Scallops and Grapefruit Gratinée

Makes 4 servings

Sea scallops have a wonderful sweetness that balances tart grapefruit. A spinach salad and Bulgur Pilaf with Leeks, Currants, and Pine Nuts (page 277) are tasty with this dish. Grapefruit makes the recipe rich in vitamin C and also adds a bit of fiber.

1 cup bottled clam juice

¼ cup dry sherry

4 whole cloves or ⅛ teaspoon ground cloves

4 whole peppercorns or ¼ teaspoon coarsely ground pepper

4 whole allspice or ⅛ teaspoon ground allspice

1 pound sea scallops

1 grapefruit, preferably pink, peeled and sectioned

4 teaspoons unsalted butter

1 cup fresh French bread crumbs

4 tablespoons grated Parmesan cheese

1. In a medium saucepan, bring the clam juice, sherry, cloves, peppercorns, and allspice to a simmer. Add the scallops and simmer, uncovered, until the scallops are just opaque, 2 to 3 minutes. Use a slotted spoon to transfer the scallops to a shallow 1½-quart gratin or baking dish or 4 individual gratin dishes. Place the grapefruit sections around the scallops. Bring the poaching liquid to a boil and reduce to about ½ cup. Whisk in the butter, then pour the sauce over the scallops and grapefruit. (This recipe can be prepared 2 hours ahead to this point and refrigerated. Return to room temperature before proceeding.)

2. Turn on the broiler. Toss the bread crumbs with the cheese and sprinkle over the scallops and grapefruit. Broil, about 4 inches from the heat source, until the crumbs are browned and the juices are bubbly, 1 to 2 minutes.

◆ *PER SERVING: About 237 cals, 70 cals from fat, 8g total fat, 4g sat fat, 64mg chol, 564mg sodium, 17g total carbs, 5g fiber, 26g prot*

FAT AND CHOLESTEROL IN SEAFOOD

Almost all commonly available seafood is relatively low in fat, particularly compared to red meat. The fat in fish varies a lot according to the season and the diet and maturity of the fish. Lobster and shrimp have quite a bit of cholesterol, but they contain very little fat and almost no saturated fat. So you don't have to avoid eating seafood because fat and cholesterol are not much of a problem. Preparation, cooking method, and sauces add most of the fat.

Stir-Fried Scallops and Vegetables

Makes 4 servings

Small bay scallops, which take only a few seconds to cook, are perfect for stir-frying. If you substitute shrimp or sea scallops, increase the cooking time to 2 or 3 minutes overall.

1 pound bay scallops
2 tablespoons mirin or dry sherry
1 tablespoon cornstarch
2 tablespoons reduced-sodium soy sauce
2 tablespoons bottled oyster sauce
⅓ cup bottled clam juice
1 tablespoon rice wine vinegar
1½ tablespoons vegetable oil
¼ pound sugar snap peas or
   snow peas, trimmed
1 small red bell pepper, seeded
   and thinly sliced
2 garlic cloves, minced
1 tablespoon grated fresh ginger
¼ teaspoon dried hot pepper flakes
4 cups cooked brown or white rice
¼ cup thinly sliced scallions

1. In a small bowl, toss the scallops with the mirin. Let stand for 15 minutes. Dissolve the cornstarch in the soy sauce, then stir in the oyster sauce, clam juice, vinegar, and ⅓ cup of water. Reserve.

2. In a wok or large, preferably nonstick skillet, heat the vegetable oil and stir-fry the sugar snap peas and bell pepper over high heat for 1 minute. Add the garlic, ginger, and hot pepper flakes and stir-fry for 30 seconds. Add the cornstarch mixture and simmer, stirring, for 1 minute. Add the scallops and mirin. Simmer until the scallops are opaque, less than 1 minute.

3. To serve, spoon the stir-fry over the rice. Sprinkle with the scallions.

◆ *PER SERVING: About 419 cals, 76 cals from fat, 8g total fat, 1g sat fat, 48mg chol, 1008mg sodium, 56g total carbs, 5g fiber, 29g prot*

Shrimp and Clams Espagnole

Makes 4 servings

Ladle the shellfish and sauce over pasta or serve lots of crusty French or Italian bread so your family can mop up the savory sauce. Clams are a delicious, rich source of iron. This Spanish-style sauce is also good with shrimp or mussels. Serve with Eggplant Roasted with Garlic and Herbs (page 428).

3 tablespoons slivered almonds

2 slices French bread (about ½ inch thick), torn into pieces

1 tablespoon extra-virgin olive oil

4 garlic cloves, minced

1 jar (7 ounces) roasted red peppers, drained

2 tablespoons sherry or red wine vinegar

¼ to ½ teaspoon cayenne pepper to taste

1 can (14½ ounces) stewed tomatoes, undrained

½ pound large shrimp, peeled and deveined (about 12 shrimp)

2 dozen clams in the shell, scrubbed

1 cup bottled clam juice

2 tablespoons chopped fresh basil, plus 2 tablespoons

1. In a small skillet, toss the almonds and bread in the oil over medium heat until golden, 1 to 2 minutes. Add the garlic, reduce the heat to medium-low, and cook, stirring, for 30 seconds.

2. Transfer the almonds, bread pieces, oil, and garlic to a food processor. Process to a coarse purée. Add the peppers, sherry, and cayenne and purée. Transfer the mixture to a saucepan and add the tomatoes. Simmer the sauce for 5 minutes.

3. In a large pot, steam the shrimp and clams in the clam juice until the clam shells open, about 5 minutes. (Discard any clams that do not open.) Remove the seafood to a shallow platter or 4 plates. Strain the liquid into the simmering sauce and add the 2 tablespoons chopped basil. Simmer for an additional 5 minutes.

4. To serve, pour the sauce over the seafood and sprinkle with the remaining 2 tablespoons chopped basil.

◆ *PER SERVING: About 311 cals, 71 cals from fat, 8g total fat, 1g sat fat, 85mg chol, 1025mg sodium, 36g total carbs, 3g fiber, 21g prot*

Herb-Steamed Mussels

Makes 4 servings

Most mussels on the market today are farm raised. They are relatively uniform in size and have little or no grit. Though a bit more bland than native mussels, they are pleasantly sweet and easy to clean. Serve with Braided Semolina Bread (page 115) for dipping into the broth.

1½ tablespoons extra-virgin olive oil

1 cup thinly sliced leeks

2 anchovy fillets, chopped

4 large garlic cloves, minced

¼ teaspoon dried hot pepper flakes

4 pounds fresh mussels, scrubbed
  and debearded (see note)

1 cup dry white wine

1 cup bottled clam juice

1 tablespoon chopped fresh marjoram
  or 1 teaspoon dried

1 tablespoon chopped fresh oregano or
  1 teaspoon dried

¼ cup chopped flat-leaf parsley

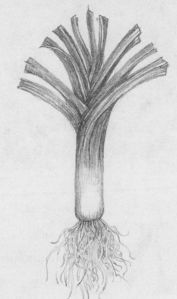

1. In a medium skillet, heat the oil and cook the leeks over medium-low heat, stirring until softened, about 5 minutes. Add the anchovies, garlic, and hot pepper flakes, and cook 1 minute. (This recipe can be prepared up to 2 hours ahead to this point. Reserve at room temperature.)

2. Place the mussels, wine, clam juice, marjoram, and oregano in a large pot or Dutch oven. Cover the pan and bring to a boil. Cook until the mussels open, 5 to 7 minutes. (Discard any mussels that do not open.)

3. Use tongs to transfer the mussels to shallow rimmed platters or soup bowls. Strain the cooking liquid into the skillet with the sauce. Boil the mixture over high heat until slightly reduced, about 3 minutes. Stir in the parsley.

4. To serve, ladle the hot broth over the mussels.

◆ *PER SERVING: About 217 cals, 72 cals from fat, 8g total fat, 1g sat fat, 33mg chol, 539mg sodium, 11g total carbs, 1g fiber, 15g prot*

Note: Fresh mussel shells have fuzzy beards. To remove, pull beard off the shell.

CHAPTER ELEVEN

Meat

Meat has traditionally been the centerpiece of the dinner plate, symbolizing success, well-being, and prosperity. And, for many people, nothing matches the taste of a sizzling steak on the grill or the delectable flavor of a juicy cut of pork or veal. Red meat—beef, veal, pork, and lamb—is also packed with important nutrients.

Meat is a top source of protein, which makes up about 25 percent of every ounce of cooked meat. The protein in meat is known as a "complete" protein because it supplies all of the essential amino acids needed to build and repair muscle. Beef, lamb, veal, and pork also supply iron and zinc—two minerals not found in abundance in many other foods. And the iron in red meat is easier for your body to absorb than the iron in plant foods such as vegetables and legumes, and iron-fortified grain foods like bread and cereal.

Today's red meat is lower in fat than ever before. Over the past few decades, cattle and hogs have been bred to be leaner, so most cuts of meat have less marbling. The 1-inch fat border around a steak that was common years ago is nowhere to be found today. Pick one of the cuts that are naturally the leanest (beef bottom round, top sirloin, pork tenderloin, lamb shank), trim the surrounding fat, and you'll get maximum taste with minimum fat.

In general, people eat large portions of meat—much more than the 3-ounce, palm-sized portion recommended in the Food Guide Pyramid—so calories and fat can add up quickly. If the 3-ounce cooked meat portion in most of this chapter's recipes looks skimpy at first glance, you're probably now eating far more protein than you need. Remember that you can choose to double the portion, and have meat at just one meal of the day. Better yet, shift the focus from meat as the centerpiece of your plate to meat as a side dish or condiment, rounding out your plate with more grains and vegetables. The best bet with meat is to select lean cuts, eat them in smaller portions, and use low-fat cooking methods.

The recipes in this chapter will help you to serve meats in their proper proportion by combining them with other delicious ingredients. Add a family-pleasing twist by serving the Ginger-Sesame Beef and Broccoli Stir-Fry (page 384) over pasta instead of rice. Veal and Mushroom Stew in Acorn Squash Halves (page 386) is hard to match for its abundance of fall vegetables. You can literally turn the Food Guide Pyramid upside down with Tex-Mex Beef Pie with Cornmeal Biscuit Topping (page 380), which has its grains on top. Or crown a dish with mashed potatoes, as in Contemporary Shepherd's Pie (page 382). Liven up your summer grilling by pairing lamb with firm summer fruits like nectarines, as in Curried Lamb and Fruit on Skewers (page 398) or stuff your skewers with vegetables from the garden, as in the Herb-Smoked Steak with Grilled Vegetables (page 388).

Meat should be cooked to doneness, without any trace of pink, to kill potentially harmful bacteria. Cooking to doneness can make meat a bit dry and less tender, so marinate your meat ahead of time to keep it as soft and moist as possible, or use cooking methods like stewing.

Meat definitely has a place in today's healthful diets, whether you choose an exotically seasoned Moroccan dish like Marrakech Orange and Spice-Braised Lamb Shanks (page 378) or an all-American favorite like pork chops, pot roast, or chili. Just look for dishes that deliver both great flavor and good nutrition.

Marrakech Orange and
Spice-Braised Lamb Shanks

Makes 4 servings

When lamb shanks are braised in seasoned liquid for a couple of hours, the meat becomes meltingly tender and infused with fragrant spice. Yellow rice accompanies this Moroccan-style stew, so all you need to add is Chunked Tomato, Fennel, and Chickpea Salad (page 98) for an unusual dinner that is perfectly suited to entertaining.

⅓ cup all-purpose flour

½ teaspoon salt, plus ¾ teaspoon

½ teaspoon black pepper, plus additional to taste

4 lamb shanks, about ¾ pound each, well trimmed

2 teaspoons olive oil

1 large onion, chopped

4 garlic cloves, finely chopped

2 cups defatted lower-sodium beef broth

½ cup red wine

¼ cup fresh orange juice

2 tablespoons chopped fresh oregano
   or 2 teaspoons dried

1 bay leaf, broken in half

1 cinnamon stick, broken in half

¾ teaspoon ground coriander seed

2 cups peeled pearl onions (see note)

1 pound carrots, peeled and cut into 2-inch lengths

1 tablespoon coarsely grated orange peel

1½ cups raw long-grain white rice

1 teaspoon powdered turmeric

½ cup chopped parsley, preferably flat leaf

1. Combine the flour, salt, and pepper in a paper or plastic bag. Add the shanks and shake to coat.

2. Heat the oil in a large, preferably nonstick skillet or Dutch oven. Sear the lamb shanks over medium-high heat until they are browned on all sides, about 8 minutes. Add the chopped onion, reduce the heat to low, and cook, stirring, until it begins to soften and brown, about 4 minutes. Add the garlic and cook, stirring, for 1 minute.

3. Pour in the broth, wine, orange juice, and 1 cup of water. Raise the heat to high and cook, stirring up any browned bits that cling to the bottom of the pot, until the liquid boils. Add the oregano, bay leaf, cinnamon stick, and coriander. Reduce the heat to low and cook, covered, until the meat is just tender, 1½ to 2 hours. Skim off any fat that rises to the surface. (You can make the recipe up to 2 days ahead to this point. Refrigerate and scrape off the fat. Reheat before proceeding.)

4. Add the pearl onions, carrots, and orange peel. Simmer, partially covered, until the vegetables are tender, 20 to 30 minutes. Remove the bay leaf and cinnamon stick. Skim off any additional fat and correct the seasoning if necessary.

5. Meanwhile, in a large saucepan, bring 3 cups of water and ¾ teaspoon of salt to a boil. Add the rice and turmeric and stir. Reduce the heat to low and cook, covered, until the rice is tender and the liquid is absorbed, about 20 minutes. Fluff with a fork and transfer to a serving platter or individual plates.

6. Serve the lamb shanks and vegetables over the rice and sprinkle with the parsley.

◆ *PER SERVING: About 677 cals, 104 cals from fat, 12g total fat, 3g sat fat, 99mg chol, 818mg sodium, 95g total carbs, 7g fiber, 42g prot*

Note: You can substitute the same quantity of frozen pearl onions. (Do not defrost the onions before using.)

Tex-Mex Beef Pie with Cornmeal Biscuit Topping

4 servings

A small amount of cornmeal in the biscuit dough adds an interesting texture and a lovely golden hue to the "crust" for this pie that is flavored with the seasonings of the American Southwest. Serve with a big salad made with mixed lettuces tossed with Basic Creamy Dressing (page 75). Try adding a tablespoon of chopped fresh cilantro to the dressing.

Beef and Vegetable Mixture:
1 pound lean ground beef
1 large onion, chopped
1 green bell pepper, seeded and
    chopped
3 garlic cloves, finely chopped
1 tablespoon chili powder
2 teaspoons ground cumin
2 teaspoons dried oregano
1 can (16 ounces) stewed tomatoes
    with juice, preferably Mexican
    style
1 cup fresh or frozen corn kernels

Cornmeal Biscuit Topping:
¾ cup all-purpose flour
1 tablespoon yellow cornmeal
¾ teaspoon baking powder
¼ teaspoon baking soda
¼ teaspoon salt
1½ tablespoons vegetable
    shortening
½ cup nonfat buttermilk

1. In a large skillet, cook the beef with the onion, green pepper, and garlic over medium heat, stirring to break the meat into smaller pieces, until it is browned. Spoon off any excess fat.

2. Add the chili powder, cumin, and oregano and cook, stirring, for 1 minute. Add the tomatoes, breaking them up into smaller chunks with the side of a spoon if necessary, along with the corn and ¾ cup of water. Bring to a boil, reduce the heat to medium, and simmer for about 10 minutes until slightly reduced and thickened. Transfer to a 9-inch-square baking dish. (The recipe can be made 1 day ahead to this point and refrigerated. Return to room temperature before adding the topping.)

3. Preheat the oven to 375 degrees. For the topping, combine the flour, cornmeal, baking powder, baking soda, and salt in a medium-sized bowl. Add the shortening and rub with your fingers until the mixture resembles coarse crumbs. Stir in the buttermilk to make a soft dough. On a lightly floured surface, roll or pat the dough into an 8-inch square and place it over the prepared beef mixture. Use a small knife to cut several slashes so steam can escape. Bake the pie uncovered in the preheated oven until it is hot, the filling bubbles around the edges, and the biscuit topping is golden brown, about 20 minutes.

4. Cut the pie into squares to serve.

◆ *PER SERVING: About 480 cals, 188 cals from fat, 21g total fat, 7g sat fat, 71mg chol, 584mg sodium, 46g total carbs, 5g fiber, 27g prot*

Quick Spring Lamb Stew

Makes 4 servings

Lean lamb doesn't need to be simmered for a long time to become tender, so it is ideal for this quickly made stew. Add a green salad tossed with Basic Vinaigrette (page 74) and some crusty whole-wheat rolls for an easy yet elegant meal. Consider Fresh Apricot Soufflé (page 450) or Cranberry-Orange Parfaits (page 448) for dessert.

1 pound lean boneless lamb, well
    trimmed, cut into ¾-inch pieces
½ teaspoon salt, plus additional
    to taste
½ teaspoon black pepper, plus
    additional to taste
3 tablespoons all-purpose flour
2 teaspoons olive oil
4 garlic cloves, finely chopped

2½ cups defatted lower-sodium
    beef broth
1½ pounds boiling potatoes,
    peeled and cut into 1-inch pieces
1 pound peeled baby carrots
1½ tablespoons chopped fresh
    thyme or 2 teaspoons dried
2 cups fresh or frozen green peas

1. Season the lamb with the salt and pepper and toss with the flour. Heat the oil in a large, preferably nonstick skillet with a lid or in a Dutch oven. Add the lamb and cook over medium-high heat until it is well browned on all sides, 5 to 8 minutes. Add the garlic and cook, stirring, for 30 seconds.

2. Add the broth, potatoes, carrots, and thyme. Bring to a boil, reduce the heat to medium-low, and cook, covered, until the vegetables are tender, about 20 minutes.

3. Add the peas and simmer uncovered over medium heat until the peas are tender. Fresh peas take about 8 minutes to cook; frozen peas take about 3 minutes. Adjust the seasoning, adding salt and pepper to taste if necessary.

◆ *PER SERVING: About 386 cals, 61 cals from fat, 7g total fat, 2g sat fat, 43mg chol, 391mg sodium, 58g total carbs, 8g fiber, 25g prot*

Contemporary Shepherd's Pie

Makes 4 servings

The British invented shepherd's pie as a way to use leftovers from the Sunday roast of lamb; now it's a well-loved classic. This version, which uses lean ground lamb topped with tangy buttermilk mashed potatoes, makes a wonderful winter supper. Serve it with Mixed Mushroom Sauté with Tarragon (page 438), a salad, and a basket of whole-grain bread.

2 pounds russet or all-purpose potatoes, peeled and cut into 2- to 3-inch chunks	1½ teaspoons dried rosemary
¾ cup nonfat buttermilk	1 teaspoon dried thyme
Salt and ground pepper to taste	⅛ teaspoon grated nutmeg
¾ pound lean ground lamb	1 tablespoon flour
1 large onion, chopped	1¼ cups defatted lower-sodium beef broth
3 garlic cloves, finely chopped	1 cup diced carrots
	1 teaspoon butter, melted

1. Put the potatoes in a saucepan filled with enough lightly salted water to cover, and cook until they are tender, 15 to 20 minutes. Drain, return the potatoes to the saucepan, and place the pan over low heat for about 1 minute until the potatoes are thoroughly dry. Add the buttermilk and whip the potatoes with a potato masher or handheld electric mixer until they are fluffy and smooth. Season with salt and pepper to taste and set aside. (You can substitute about 3 cups of leftover mashed potatoes if you have them on hand.)

2. Meanwhile, in a large skillet, cook the lamb with the onion and garlic over medium heat, stirring, until the meat browns, about 10 minutes. Spoon off any excess fat. Stir in the rosemary, thyme, and nutmeg. Sprinkle the flour over the meat and cook, stirring, for 2 minutes. Gradually stir in the broth and add the carrots. Cover, reduce the heat to medium-low, and cook until the carrots are almost tender, about 10 minutes. Salt and pepper to taste.

3. Preheat the oven to 375 degrees. Transfer the lamb mixture to a 9-inch-square baking dish and let cool for 10 minutes. Spread the potatoes over the top, using a fork to make peaks in the potatoes. (The recipe can be made a few hours ahead to this point and refrigerated. Return to room temperature before baking.)

4. Brush the potatoes with the melted butter and bake uncovered until the stew is bubbly around the edges and the potatoes are golden brown on top, 30 to 40 minutes.

5. Cool slightly and serve from the pan.

◆ *PER SERVING: About 439 cals, 131 cals from fat, 15g total fat, 6g sat fat, 65mg chol, 169mg sodium, 54g total carbs, 5g fiber, 23g prot*

Marvelous Mustard Meat Loaf

Makes 6 servings

Combine ground beef with lean ground turkey to produce a meat loaf that is satisfying yet lower in fat than the traditional version. Rolled oats add substance and a sweet, nutlike flavor while mustard contributes some zip. Round out the dinner with baked sweet potatoes, Cauliflower with Cumin and Fresh Ginger (page 435), and some whole-grain bread.

¾ pound lean ground beef

¾ pound lean ground turkey

1¼ cups rolled oats, regular or
    quick cooking

1 small onion, chopped

½ cup chopped parsley

2 garlic cloves, finely chopped

2 egg whites, lightly beaten

1½ tablespoons Dijon mustard

1 teaspoon dried savory

½ teaspoon salt

½ teaspoon black pepper

½ teaspoon Worcestershire sauce

Vegetable or olive oil spray

1. Preheat the oven to 375 degrees. In a large bowl, combine all of the ingredients except the oil spray. Use your hands to gently but thoroughly mix the ingredients until they are well combined.

2. Spray an 8½x4½-inch loaf pan with oil spray. Transfer the meat mixture to the pan, patting it in evenly.

3. Bake uncovered until the meat is browned on top, shrinks away from the sides of the pan, and the juices run clear when pierced with the tip of a sharp knife, about 1 hour.

4. Drain off any fat that has accumulated in the bottom of the pan. Slice and serve.

◆ *PER SERVING: About 273 cals, 115 cals from fat, 13g total fat, 4g sat fat, 81mg chol, 369mg sodium, 13g total carbs, 0g fiber, 25g prot*

STORING GROUND MEAT

Ground meats are highly perishable. Use the following tips to maintain the quality of ground meats and prevent illness:

◆ Bring ground meat from the supermarket to your refrigerator at home as quickly as possible.

◆ When handling ground meat, be sure that your hands and any utensils and surfaces that come into contact with the meat are clean.

◆ Store ground meat in the refrigerator for no longer than 2 days; wrap the meat in plastic wrap and place a plate underneath it to catch any drippings.

◆ For longer storage, wrap the ground meat in freezer-weight wrap or plastic bags and freeze. Frozen ground meat will keep for 2 to 3 months.

◆ Thaw frozen meat wrapped, on a plate, in the refrigerator. Cook the meat as soon as it is thawed.

◆ You can store leftovers made with cooked ground meat in the refrigerator for 2 to 3 days or freeze them for 1 month.

Ginger-Sesame Beef and Broccoli Stir-Fry

Makes 4 servings

The distinctive, toasty flavor of sesame seeds and Asian sesame oil permeates this stir-fry. As a change of pace, spoon the meat and vegetables over hot, cooked thin-strand noodles. Garnish the dish with cherry tomatoes and chopped fresh cilantro.

Sauce Mixture:
1 tablespoon cornstarch
1 cup defatted lower-sodium beef
  broth
2 tablespoons reduced-sodium soy
  sauce
2 tablespoons dry sherry
½ teaspoon toasted sesame oil
½ teaspoon hot chili oil
½ teaspoon dried red pepper
  flakes

Beef and Vegetable Mixture:
2 tablespoons sesame seeds
¾ pound lean beef round or
  sirloin, well trimmed and cut
  into thin strips

½ teaspoon black pepper
1 teaspoon vegetable oil, plus
  1 teaspoon
6 cups broccoli florets and thinly
  sliced broccoli stems
1 bunch scallions, cut diagonally
  into 1-inch pieces
2 garlic cloves, finely chopped
2 tablespoons minced fresh ginger
Salt to taste
8 ounces vermicelli or angel hair
  pasta, cooked and drained
12 cherry tomatoes, stemmed and
  halved
¼ cup chopped fresh cilantro

1. For the sauce mixture, in a small bowl, whisk the cornstarch with the broth, soy sauce, sherry, sesame oil, chili oil, pepper flakes, and ¼ cup water. Set aside.

2. Toast the sesame seeds in a small skillet over medium heat, stirring occasionally, until pale golden and fragrant, about 5 minutes. Set aside.

3. Season the beef on all sides with the pepper. Heat 1 teaspoon of the oil in a large skillet or wok over high heat. Add the beef and stir-fry until the meat is seared, 2 to 3 minutes. Remove with a slotted spoon and set aside.

4. Add the remaining 1 teaspoon of oil to the pan. Add the broccoli and stir-fry until it is crisp-tender, about 2 minutes. Add the scallions and stir-fry for 1 minute. Add the garlic and ginger and stir-fry for 30 seconds.

5. Reduce the heat to medium. Stir the sauce mixture and add it to the pan. Cook, stirring almost constantly, until the sauce comes to a boil, thickens, and turns translucent, about 3 minutes. Stir in the beef and any accumulated juices and heat through. Season with salt to taste.

6. To serve, spoon the meat and vegetable mixture over the hot cooked noodles and sprinkle with the sesame seeds. Top with the cherry tomatoes and sprinkle with the cilantro.

◆ *PER SERVING: About 515 cals, 114 cals from fat, 13g total fat, 3g sat fat, 62mg chol, 384mg sodium, 63g total carbs, 9g fiber, 38g prot*

MEAT NOW PLAYS A SUPPORTING ROLE

Meat traditionally has been given a starring role on menus. But because many meats are high in fat, they should play more of a supporting role as flavor enhancers or condiments in dishes. You should also serve smaller portions of meats. Still an excellent source of protein, iron, and zinc, meat is a delicious, high-flavor complement to such foods as grains, pastas, and beans.

THE LEANEST CUTS OF MEAT

The beef, pork, and lamb available in stores today are leaner than ever, but you should know which cuts are naturally leaner. Generally, the loin, tenderloin, round, and flank cuts are leaner than the shoulder, rib, or sirloin. Ground beef that is labeled "extra lean" is just that, it contains the least amount of fat—no more than 5 percent.

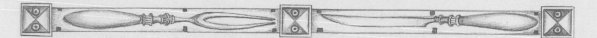

Veal and Mushroom Stew
in Acorn Squash Halves

Makes 4 servings

Serve this stew in acorn squash halves for some sophisticated dinner party fare. Add Gingered Carrot Purée (page 429), a salad of arugula and tender lettuces, and some crusty French bread to complete this wonderful (and mostly do-ahead) meal.

3 tablespoons all-purpose flour

½ teaspoon salt, plus additional to taste

½ teaspoon black pepper, plus additional to taste

1 pound veal stew meat (leg or shoulder),
   cut in 1½-inch cubes

1 tablespoon olive oil, plus 1 teaspoon

½ pound fresh mushrooms, preferably shiitake,
   thinly sliced

1 large leek, white and pale green parts only,
   thinly sliced

2 tablespoons coarsely chopped shallots

1 cup dry white wine

3 cups defatted lower-sodium chicken broth

1 bay leaf, broken in half

4 carrots, peeled and sliced

2 medium white turnips (about ¾ pound),
   peeled and cut in 1-inch cubes

1½ tablespoons chopped fresh sage or
   2 teaspoons dried

2 acorn squash, about 1 pound each, halved
   and seeds removed

2 teaspoons butter, melted

4 teaspoons maple syrup

2 teaspoons grainy Dijon mustard

3 tablespoons chopped parsley, preferably flat leaf

Sprigs of fresh sage for garnish, optional

1. Combine the flour, salt, and pepper in a plastic or paper bag. Add the veal and shake gently until the meat is lightly coated with the seasoned flour.

2. Heat 1 tablespoon of the oil in a large, preferably nonstick skillet with a lid or in a Dutch oven. Add the veal, in two batches if necessary, and cook over medium heat until browned on all sides. Remove with a slotted spoon to a plate.

3. Add the remaining teaspoon of oil to the pan. Add the mushrooms and cook, stirring frequently, until they begin to brown, about 5 minutes. Add the leek and shallots and cook for 2 minutes. Add the wine, raise the heat to high, and cook, stirring up any browned bits that cling to the bottom of the pan, until reduced by about one third.

4. Return the meat to the pan and add the broth and the bay leaf. Bring to a boil, reduce the heat to low, and cook, covered, until the veal is almost tender, about 35 minutes. (This recipe can be prepared ahead to this point and refrigerated, covered, for 2 days, or frozen for up to 1 month. Remove the bay leaf before freezing. Reheat before proceeding.)

5. Add the carrots, turnips, and sage to the stew. Simmer partially covered over medium heat until the vegetables and meat are tender, 20 to 25 minutes. (Serve immediately or set aside at room temperature for up to 1 hour while the squash cooks.)

6. About 1 hour before serving, cook the squash. Preheat the oven to 400 degrees. Arrange the squash halves cut sides up in a baking dish. Brush with the melted butter and maple syrup and sprinkle with salt and pepper. Pour ¼ cup water in the bottom of the pan and bake the squash uncovered until tender when pierced with a knife, 40 to 50 minutes. (Or, arrange squash in a glass baking dish, cover with plastic wrap, and microwave on high, rotating the dish two or three times, until the squash halves are tender, 10 to 20 minutes.)

7. Reheat the stew if necessary. Remove and discard the bay leaf halves and whisk the mustard into the sauce. Place a squash half on each dinner plate and fill the centers with the stew, allowing it to spill over the sides a bit. Sprinkle with the parsley. Garnish with the sage sprigs, if desired.

◆ *PER SERVING: About 509 cals, 111 cals from fat, 12g total fat, 4g sat fat, 120mg chol, 544mg sodium, 64g total carbs, 10g fiber, 40g prot*

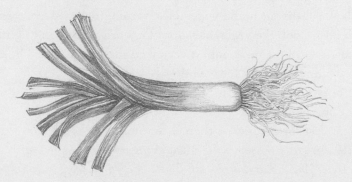

Herb-Smoked Steak with Grilled Vegetables

Makes 6 servings

You can vary the vegetables for this summery grilled meal according to what looks best at the market—baby eggplant, pattypan squashes, or any color of sweet bell pepper.

⅓ cup defatted lower-sodium chicken broth

3 tablespoons balsamic vinegar

2 teaspoons olive oil

2 garlic cloves, finely chopped

1 tablespoon chopped fresh oregano or 1 teaspoon dried

½ teaspoon salt

½ teaspoon black pepper

1½ pounds top round steak, cut about 1 inch thick

Vegetable oil spray

8 branches fresh oregano, plus additional for garnish

1 zucchini (about 8 ounces), cut into long diagonal slices

1 yellow crookneck squash (about 8 ounces), cut into long diagonal slices

1 large red onion, cut into crosswise slices about ¼ inch thick

1 small red bell pepper, seeded and cut into 6 slices

1 small yellow bell pepper, seeded and cut into 6 slices

8 ounces Italian bread, cut into ¾-inch-thick slices

1. In a small bowl, whisk together the broth, vinegar, oil, garlic, oregano, salt, and pepper. Spoon 2 tablespoons of the marinade into a shallow dish just large enough to hold the meat. Place the meat in the marinade, turn to coat completely, and set aside in a cool room for 1 hour or refrigerate for up to 8 hours, turning occasionally.

2. Prepare a medium-hot barbecue fire. Make sure the grill rack is well seasoned or coat it with vegetable oil spray. Soak the oregano branches in water for 10 minutes.

3. Brush the cut vegetables with some of the marinade. Distribute the oregano branches over the hot coals. Grill the meat and vegetables, turning once or twice and brushing with more of the marinade. Cook the vegetables until they are tender and lightly charred at the edges, 5 to 7 minutes. Grill the meat until it is cooked the way you like it, 7 to 8 minutes for medium-rare, a few minutes longer for well-done.

4. Brush the bread lightly with the remaining marinade and grill until lightly toasted, 30 seconds to 1 minute per side.

5. Let the meat rest for 5 minutes, then slice thinly across the grain. Heap the vegetables onto the grilled bread, and serve the meat alongside, garnished with the oregano.

◆ *PER SERVING: About 326 cals, 74 cals from fat, 8g total fat, 2g sat fat, 71mg chol, 459mg sodium, 30g total carbs, 2g fiber, 32g prot*

MEAT GRILLING TIPS

◆ Lightly coat the grill rack with nonstick vegetable oil spray before setting it over the coals.

◆ Let the grill rack heat for at least 5 minutes over the hot coals before cooking on it. Food tends to stick to a cold rack.

◆ Trim all excess fat from meat

before grilling to lower the fat content and to reduce the chance of grill flare-ups.

◆ Turn meat with tongs or a spatula while grilling to avoid piercing the surface, which allows juices to escape.

◆ Brush on thick or sweet sauces

during the last 5 or 10 minutes of grilling time to prevent burning.

◆ Grilling is a dry-heat cooking method, so lean meat can dry out if left too long on the grill. Check it after the minimum recommended cooking time; remove the meat as soon as it is done.

Pork Chops Braised in Cider

Makes 4 servings

In this dish, pork chops are simmered to a succulent tenderness with sage and apple cider. Spiced Applesauce (recipe follows) is the ideal accompaniment. Add Greens with Bacon and Onion (page 437) and noodles tossed with poppy seeds for a super supper.

4 center-cut bone-in pork chops, 1½ to 2 pounds total

½ teaspoon salt

¼ teaspoon black pepper

2 teaspoons vegetable oil

1 large onion, thinly sliced

1 celery rib, thinly sliced

¾ cup apple cider

1½ tablespoons chopped fresh sage or 2 teaspoons dried leaf sage

1 tablespoon cider vinegar

1. Season the pork chops with the salt and pepper. Heat the oil in a large, preferably nonstick skillet with a lid. Sauté the pork chops over medium-high heat until well browned, about 4 minutes per side. Transfer to a plate. Pour off any excess fat, but leave the drippings in the pan.

2. Add the onion and celery to the skillet and cook, stirring occasionally, until softened, about 5 minutes. Stir in the cider, sage, and vinegar and return the pork chops and any accumulated juices to the skillet. Bring to a boil, reduce the heat to low, and cook covered until the meat is tender, about 25 minutes.

3. Serve the pork chops with the braising liquid spooned over the top with Spiced Applesauce (recipe follows) alongside, if desired.

◆ *PER SERVING: About 250 cals, 118 cals from fat, 13g total fat, 4g sat fat, 66mg chol, 337mg sodium, 13g total carbs, 1g fiber, 20g prot*

SPICED APPLESAUCE

Makes 4 servings

This slightly tart spiced applesauce is a natural accompaniment to pork chops or almost any other pork dish.

6 tart apples, such as Granny Smith, peeled, cored, and cut into quarters

1 tablespoon sugar
Half a cinnamon stick
2 whole cloves

2 teaspoons fresh lemon juice
½ teaspoon grated lemon peel

1. In a medium-large saucepan, combine the apples, sugar, cinnamon stick, cloves, and 2 tablespoons of water. Bring to a boil, reduce the heat to low, and cook, covered, stirring occasionally, until the apples are very tender, about 20 minutes.

2. Remove the whole spices and beat the apples with a wooden spoon to make a chunky sauce. Stir in the lemon juice and peel.

Per serving: About 122 cals, 5 cals from fat, 1g total fat, 0g sat fat, 0mg chol, 0mg sodium, 32g total carbs, 3g fiber, 0g prot

Pork Pot Roast with Root Vegetables and Thyme

Makes 4 servings

Fabulous Garlic Mashed Potatoes (page 419) topped with some snipped chives along with Chicory, Arugula, and Orange Salad Siciliana (page 103) are excellent accompaniments to this savory pot-roasted pork.

2 teaspoons olive oil
1 large or 2 small pork tenderloins (1 pound total), well trimmed
¼ teaspoon salt
¼ teaspoon black pepper
2 teaspoons chopped fresh thyme, plus 2 tablespoons (see note)
4 carrots, peeled and cut into 1-inch pieces
3 parsnips, peeled and cut into 1-inch pieces

2 white turnips, peeled and cut in 1-inch chunks
3 garlic cloves, finely chopped
½ teaspoon sugar
2 cups defatted lower-sodium chicken broth
1 bay leaf, broken in half
1 tablespoon Dijon mustard
Branches of fresh thyme for garnish

1. Heat the oil in a large, preferably nonstick skillet with a lid or in a Dutch oven. If the meat is too long to fit comfortably into the pot, cut it in half. Sprinkle the salt, pepper, and 2 teaspoons thyme onto the tenderloin, pressing it into the sides. Sauté the pork over medium-high heat until browned on all sides, 6 to 8 minutes total. Remove to a plate.

2. Add the carrots, parsnips, turnips, and garlic to the pan and sprinkle with the sugar. Cook over medium heat, stirring occasionally, until the vegetables begin to caramelize and soften, about 5 minutes. Add the broth, remaining 2 tablespoons of thyme, and the bay leaf, and return the meat and any accumulated juices to the pan. Simmer, covered, over low heat until the vegetables are tender and the pork is no longer pink in the center, 25 to 30 minutes.

3. Remove the meat to a platter. Discard the bay leaf halves. Stir the mustard into the sauce and simmer over medium-high heat until lightly thickened, about 3 minutes.

4. Cut the pork on the diagonal into ¾-inch-thick slices and arrange them on a platter. Spoon the sauce and vegetables over the meat, garnish with the thyme branches, and serve.

◆ *PER SERVING: About 298 cals, 68 cals from fat, 8g total fat, 2g sat fat, 81mg chol, 368mg sodium, 29g total carbs, 7g fiber, 29g prot*

Note: You can substitute 1 teaspoon chopped dried thyme, plus 2 teaspoons, for the fresh thyme.

COOKING PORK

To eliminate all risk of trichinosis (a worm larvae infection), cook pork to an internal temperature of 160 degrees. But, as with all lean cuts of meat, you should cook lean pork until it's done and not overcooked, or it will be dry and less flavorful.

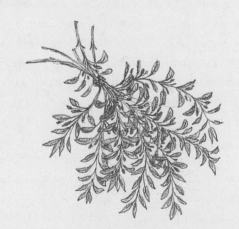

Maple-Mustard Pork on Mashed "Sweets"

Makes 4 servings

Mashed sweet potatoes make a delicious bed for these maple- and mustard-flavored pork medallions. Garlicky Broccoli Rabe (page 413) would be a terrific side dish, along with a basket of crusty whole-wheat rolls.

Sweet Potatoes:

2 pounds sweet potatoes
½ cup orange juice, plus 1 to 2 tablespoons additional if necessary
2 tablespoons reduced-fat sour cream
2 teaspoons brown sugar
¼ teaspoon grated mace or nutmeg
Salt and freshly ground black pepper to taste

Maple-Mustard Pork:

1 pound pork tenderloin, well trimmed, cut crosswise into ¾-inch slices
½ teaspoon salt
½ teaspoon black pepper, preferably coarsely ground
2 teaspoons olive oil
¼ cup chopped shallots
1¼ cups defatted lower-sodium chicken broth
3 tablespoons maple syrup
2 tablespoons balsamic vinegar
1 tablespoon Dijon mustard

1. Peel the sweet potatoes and cut them into 2- to 3-inch chunks. Cover them completely in lightly salted boiling water. Cook until they are tender, about 20 minutes.

2. Drain the sweet potatoes, return them to the saucepan, and add the ½ cup orange juice, sour cream, brown sugar, and mace. Mash with a large fork, adding more juice if necessary to make a slightly textured purée. Salt and pepper to taste.

3. Meanwhile, sprinkle the pork with the salt and pepper. Heat the oil in a large, non-stick skillet. Cook the pork over medium heat until browned on both sides and no longer pink inside, about 4 minutes per side. Remove to a platter.

4. Add the shallots and cook, stirring, for 1 minute. Add the broth, bring to a boil, and cook until somewhat thickened and reduced, 3 to 4 minutes. Whisk in the maple syrup, vinegar, and mustard. Return the pork and any accumulated juices to the pan and simmer until heated through, about 1 minute.

5. Spoon the sweet potatoes onto plates and serve the meat and sauce over the top.

◆ *PER SERVING: About 422 cals, 71 cals from fat, 8g total fat, 2g sat fat, 83mg chol, 549mg sodium, 58g total carbs, 6g fiber, 30g prot*

Pork with Cranberry-Orange-Pear Sauce

Makes 4 servings

The fruit sauce in this dish sings with the flavors of the fall season, and also happens to be a rich source of fiber and vitamin C. Herbed Brown Rice Pilaf (page 275) and Summer Harvest Ratatouille (page 426) would be just the right accompaniments to extend the autumn theme.

1 pound pork tenderloin, well trimmed,
   cut crosswise into ¾-inch slices
½ teaspoon salt
¼ teaspoon black pepper
1½ teaspoons dried leaf sage
2 teaspoons olive oil, plus 1 teaspoon
1 large onion, chopped
4 firm pears (any type), peeled,
   cored, and chopped
⅔ cup fresh orange juice
⅓ cup fresh cranberries
¼ teaspoon powdered ginger
½ teaspoon grated orange peel

1. Sprinkle the pork slices with the salt, pepper, and sage, rubbing the seasonings into the meat. In a large nonstick skillet, heat 2 teaspoons of the olive oil over medium-high heat. Cook the pork, in two batches if necessary, until browned on both sides, about 4 minutes total. Remove to a plate.

2. Add the remaining 1 teaspoon of oil to the skillet. Add the onion and cook over medium heat, stirring frequently, until it begins to brown and soften, about 5 minutes. Add the pears, orange juice, cranberries, and ginger. Simmer, uncovered, until the cranberries begin to soften and burst, about 5 minutes. Stir in the orange peel.

3. Return the pork and any accumulated juices to the skillet. Cook over medium heat until the meat loses any trace of pink in the center and the sauce is somewhat reduced and thickened, about 5 minutes.

4. Serve the pork medallions with the sauce spooned over the top.

◆ *PER SERVING: About 321 cals, 75 cals from fat, 8g total fat, 2g sat fat, 81mg chol, 328mg sodium, 36g total carbs, 6g fiber, 27g prot*

Fiery Grilled Pork Tenderloin

Makes 6 servings

This pork is stuffed with a piquant seasoning mixture that you can adapt to your own personal heat index by adjusting the amount of jalapeño peppers. It's a delicious summer dish, especially if you add some Molasses and Pepper Grilled Sweet Potato Slices (page 424), Curried Waldorf Salad (page 104), and a basket of crusty bread.

½ cup nonfat plain yogurt

¾ teaspoon paprika

¾ teaspoon ground cumin

2 pork tenderloins, about
    12 ounces each, well trimmed

¾ teaspoon salt

½ teaspoon black pepper

5 garlic cloves, finely chopped

1 to 2 jalapeño peppers, finely
    chopped

Vegetable oil spray

1. In a shallow dish just large enough to hold the pork, stir together the yogurt, paprika, and cumin.

2. Cut each pork tenderloin lengthwise halfway through the meat and open it up like a book. Sprinkle all sides of the pork with the salt and pepper, then sprinkle the garlic and jalapeños over the cut sides of the meat. Fold the tenderloins back into their original shape and press so that the sides adhere to each other. Place in the yogurt marinade, turning to coat completely. Cover loosely and refrigerate for 1 to 3 hours, turning once or twice. Return to room temperature before cooking.

3. Prepare a medium-hot charcoal fire or preheat a gas grill. Spray the grill rack lightly with vegetable oil spray. Grill the pork, turning occasionally and brushing with the marinade, until the meat is browned outside and no longer pink inside, 15 to 20 minutes.

4. Let the meat sit for 5 minutes; then slice and arrange it on a platter.

◆ *PER SERVING: About 152 cals, 38 cals from fat, 4g total fat, 1g sat fat, 81mg chol, 346mg sodium, 1g total carbs, 0g fiber, 25g prot*

THE "NEW" PORK

Today, pork is a great deal leaner than it was in years past. According to the USDA, farmers reduced the fat content of the average cut of pork by more than 50 percent from 1963 to 1983. While some cuts, such as spareribs, remain relatively fatty, the loin—particularly the tenderloin—has most benefited from the breeding of leaner hogs. A 3-ounce cooked portion of tenderloin now compares favorably to skinless chicken breast in fat, cholesterol, and calories.

Five-Alarm Firehouse Chili

Makes 6 servings

This Texas-style chili is made with cubed beef and five kinds of spicy seasonings (black pepper, paprika, cayenne, red pepper flakes, and chipotle pepper). You can adjust any of these spices for more or less heat, but the dried red pepper flakes carry the most punch.

1½ pounds top or bottom beef
    round, well trimmed and
    cut into ½-inch cubes
½ teaspoon salt
¾ teaspoon black pepper
2 teaspoons olive oil
5 garlic cloves, finely chopped
1 tablespoon paprika
1 teaspoon ground cumin
1 teaspoon dried oregano
¼ teaspoon cayenne pepper
1 bay leaf
1 can (28 ounces) crushed plum
    tomatoes in purée

¼ to ½ teaspoon dried red
    pepper flakes
1 chipotle pepper packed in adobo
    sauce, minced
1 teaspoon sugar
1 can (19 ounces) red kidney
    beans, rinsed and drained, or
    2 cups cooked kidney beans
1 tablespoon flour
2 tablespoons cornmeal
6 cups cooked white rice
1½ cups chopped sweet white or
    red onion

1. Sprinkle the beef on all sides with the salt and pepper. Heat the oil in a Dutch oven or other large pot. Cook the meat over medium heat, stirring frequently, until it loses its pink color, about 5 minutes. Add the garlic, paprika, cumin, oregano, and cayenne and cook, stirring, for 1 minute. Add 2½ cups of water and the bay leaf, cover, and simmer over low heat until the meat is almost tender, about 1 hour.

2. Add the tomatoes, red pepper flakes, chipotle, sugar, and kidney beans. Simmer over medium heat, uncovered, until the meat is tender, 30 to 45 minutes.

3. Whisk the flour and cornmeal with ½ cup of water. Gradually stir the flour mixture into the chili and simmer until the chili thickens, about 10 minutes. Remove the bay leaf. Taste and adjust the seasonings if necessary.

4. Serve the chili spooned over the hot rice and sprinkle with the chopped onions.

◆ *PER SERVING: About 536 cals, 62 cals from fat, 7g total fat, 2g sat fat, 76mg chol, 700mg sodium, 74g total carbs, 7g fiber, 42g prot*

Canadian Bacon and Garlic Greens

Makes 4 main-dish servings (6 side-dish servings)

Canadian bacon is the smoked and cured eye of the pork loin, so it's a fairly lean cut of meat. Like ham, it's very flavorful and tastes wonderful with vitamin-rich cooked greens. Stewed tomatoes and Feather-Light Buttermilk Drop Biscuits (page 131) are excellent accompaniments.

2 pounds tender young mustard,
   collard, or turnip greens,
   washed and trimmed (see note)
4 teaspoons butter
¾ pound sliced Canadian bacon
3 garlic cloves, finely chopped
¾ cup defatted lower-sodium chicken broth
2 teaspoons sugar
1½ teaspoons cider vinegar
¼ teaspoon liquid hot pepper sauce

1. Bring a large pot of lightly salted water to a boil. Add the greens and cook until tender, 10 to 15 minutes. Drain the greens into a colander, pressing out as much liquid as possible, transfer them to a cutting board, and chop them.

2. Heat the butter in a large, preferably nonstick skillet. Add the Canadian bacon and cook over medium heat, turning once, until the meat is tinged with brown around the edges and heated through, 5 to 7 minutes. Remove to a warm plate, leaving the drippings in the pan.

3. Add the garlic to the skillet and cook, stirring, for 1 minute. Add the greens, broth, and sugar. Simmer, stirring occasionally, until the greens are heated through and most of the liquid is absorbed, 3 to 5 minutes. Stir in the vinegar and hot pepper sauce.

4. Spoon the greens onto serving plates, top with the Canadian bacon, and serve.

◆ *PER MAIN-DISH SERVING: About 163 cals, 78 cals from fat, 9g total fat, 4g sat fat, 41mg chol, 896mg sodium, 6g total carbs, 2g fiber, 16g prot*

Note: You can substitute two packages (10 ounces each) of frozen greens. Cook according to package directions.

Lamb with White Beans and Rosemary

Makes 4 servings

Rosemary infuses this delectable French-style blend of lamb, white beans, tomatoes, and wine. Some crusty French rolls and a salad of bitter greens, such as escarole tossed with Basic Vinaigrette (page 74), are all you need to complete a simple but satisfying meal.

1 pound lean boneless lamb, well trimmed, cut into 1½-inch cubes

¼ teaspoon salt, plus additional to taste

½ teaspoon black pepper, plus additional to taste

2 teaspoons olive oil

5 garlic cloves, finely chopped

2 cans (15 ounces each) white beans, rinsed and drained, or 3 cups cooked white beans

1 can (28 ounces) plum tomatoes with juice

1 cup dry white wine

1 cup defatted lower-sodium chicken broth

2 tablespoons chopped fresh rosemary or 1 tablespoon crumbled dried

2 teaspoons sugar

1. Season the lamb on all sides with the salt and pepper. Heat the oil in a large, preferably nonstick skillet with a lid or in a Dutch oven. Add the meat and sear over medium-high heat until nicely browned, about 6 minutes. Add the garlic and cook, stirring, for 1 minute.

2. Add the beans, tomatoes, wine, broth, rosemary, and sugar. Bring to a boil, breaking the tomatoes into smaller chunks with the side of a spoon. Simmer the stew, uncovered, over medium heat until the meat is no longer pink inside and the sauce is somewhat reduced and thickened, 20 to 25 minutes.

3. Season to taste with additional salt and pepper if necessary. Spoon onto rimmed plates or into shallow soup bowls to serve.

◆ *PER SERVING: About 363 cals, 78 cals from fat, 9g total fat, 2g sat fat, 57mg chol, 921mg sodium, 42g total carbs, 12g fiber, 31g prot*

Curried Lamb and Fruit on Skewers

Makes 4 servings

Calcium-rich yogurt makes a terrific marinade for grilling because it tenderizes lean meat and helps protect it from the intense barbecue fire. Its milk proteins also promote browning. In this dish, the sugar in the nectarines caramelizes, creating an interesting interplay of sweet and savory flavors. These kabobs make a particularly enticing meal when served with Summer Harvest Ratatouille (page 426) and a basket of pita.

¾ cup nonfat plain yogurt
2 teaspoons fresh lime juice
2 teaspoons minced fresh ginger
2 garlic cloves, finely chopped
2 teaspoons curry powder
¼ teaspoon salt
¼ teaspoon black pepper
¼ teaspoon cayenne pepper
1 pound very lean boneless lamb,
    cut into 1½-inch cubes
Vegetable oil spray
1 red onion, cut in 2-inch chunks
2 nectarines, pitted and cut in 6 wedges each

1. In a shallow dish just large enough to hold the lamb, stir together the yogurt, lime juice, ginger, garlic, curry powder, salt, pepper, and cayenne. Add the lamb cubes and stir to coat completely. Cover and refrigerate for at least 2 hours and up to 8 hours.

2. Prepare a medium-hot charcoal fire or preheat a gas grill. Make sure the grill rack is well seasoned or spray lightly with vegetable oil spray.

3. Thread the lamb, onion, and nectarine wedges onto metal skewers and brush with the marinade.

4. Grill, turning occasionally and brushing with any remaining marinade, until the lamb is nicely browned outside and pink inside, and the nectarines and onions are soft and lightly caramelized, about 8 minutes. Remove from the skewers to serve.

◆ *PER SERVING: About 200 cals, 50 cals from fat, 6g total fat, 2g sat fat, 58mg chol, 212mg sodium, 15g total carbs, 2g fiber, 22g prot*

Teriyaki Flank Steak with Shiitakes

Makes 6 servings

The honey in the teriyaki sauce helps caramelize the outside of this marinated flank steak to a crusty, flavorful goodness. Cut the meat into very thin slices and serve with grilled, skewered mushrooms and scallions.

⅓ cup reduced-sodium soy sauce

⅓ cup dry sherry

1 tablespoon vegetable oil

2 teaspoons honey

3 garlic cloves, minced

1 tablespoon grated fresh ginger

⅓ cup chopped scallions, plus

12 whole scallions

1½ pounds flank steak, well trimmed

12 shiitake mushrooms

1. In a shallow dish just large enough to hold the meat, combine the soy sauce, sherry, oil, honey, garlic, ginger, and chopped scallions, whisking until the honey is dissolved. Add the flank steak and turn to coat both sides. Cover and refrigerate for at least 6 hours and up to 24 hours, turning occasionally.

2. Prepare a hot charcoal fire or preheat a gas grill. Remove the meat from the marinade and pat it dry with paper towels. Trim the whole scallions, leaving 2 inches of the green tops. Toss the scallions and mushrooms in the marinade to coat, then thread onto metal skewers.

3. Grill the meat, turning once, to the desired degree of doneness, 8 to 10 minutes for rare, 12 to 15 minutes for medium-rare to medium. Let the meat sit for 5 minutes before cutting into thin slices at a sharp diagonal across the grain.

4. Meanwhile, grill the skewered mushrooms and scallions at the edge of the grill until the vegetables soften and the edges are charred, about 4 minutes.

5. Arrange the meat on a platter, place the skewered vegetables on top, and serve.

◆ *PER SERVING: About 154 cals, 51 cals from fat, 6g total fat, 2g sat fat, 23mg chol, 265mg sodium, 8g total carbs, 1g fiber, 15g prot*

MARINADE SAFETY

If you're going to use a marinade as a sauce, set aside a portion of the marinade before adding the raw meat to it to prevent bacteria from contaminating the sauce. If you want to use leftover marinade as a table sauce, bring it to a boil in a saucepan over high heat. Boil it for 3 minutes to kill any potentially harmful bacteria transferred from the raw meat.

Moorish Lamb and Dried Fruit Tagine

Makes 8 servings

In Morocco, a tagine is an earthenware vessel used to cook this rich stew. You can make this dish in a large, heavy pot. Made with lamb and sweet dried fruits, this tagine is permeated with the savory spices of North Africa.

1 teaspoon olive oil, preferably
   extra virgin
2 medium onions, thinly sliced
5 garlic cloves, finely chopped
2 teaspoons ground coriander
1½ teaspoons ground cumin
¾ teaspoon powdered ginger
¼ teaspoon cayenne pepper
2 pounds lean boneless shoulder of
   lamb, well trimmed, cut in
   2-inch cubes
½ teaspoon salt

½ teaspoon black pepper
2 cups defatted lower-sodium beef
   broth
2 cups defatted lower-sodium
   chicken broth
2 cinnamon sticks
¾ cup pitted prunes
¾ cup dried apricots
1 lemon
8 cups cooked couscous or brown
   rice

1. Heat the oil in a Dutch oven. Add the onions and cook over medium-high heat, stirring frequently, until they begin to soften, about 5 minutes. Add the garlic, coriander, cumin, ginger, and cayenne and stir to mix well.

2. Season the lamb with the salt and pepper, add to the pot, and stir to coat. Add the beef broth and chicken broth, bring to a boil, and add the cinnamon sticks. Reduce the heat to low and simmer, covered, for 1 hour. Spoon off any fat that rises to the surface.

3. Add the prunes and apricots and simmer over medium heat, uncovered, for 30 minutes. Remove the peel from the lemon in several long strips. Squeeze 2 tablespoons of juice from the lemon. Add the peel and the juice to the tagine and continue to simmer until the lamb is very tender and the liquids have been reduced to a saucelike consistency, 15 to 30 minutes. Adjust the seasonings if necessary. Remove the cinnamon sticks and lemon peel.

4. Serve the tagine spooned over the hot cooked couscous.

◆ *PER SERVING: About 455 cals, 89 cals from fat, 10g total fat, 3g sat fat, 66mg chol, 216mg sodium, 64g total carbs, 11g fiber, 28g prot*

Roast Pork Tenderloin with Lemon and Fennel

Makes 6 servings

In this roasted pork tenderloin, both the bulb and seed of the fennel are used—so if you love fennel's distinctive licorice flavor, this recipe will appeal to you. Serve the meat and sauce with plain egg noodles or fettucine pasta and Garlicky Broccoli Rabe (page 413).

2 teaspoons fennel seeds

1 teaspoon olive oil, plus 2 teaspoons

3 garlic cloves, plus 1 garlic clove, finely chopped

2 teaspoons grated lemon peel

½ teaspoon salt, plus additional to taste

¾ teaspoons pepper, plus additional to taste

2 pork tenderloins (about ¾ pound each), trimmed of fat and membrane

1 medium fennel bulb (about ¾ pound), trimmed and thinly sliced (fronds reserved for garnish if desired)

1 teaspoon sugar

½ cup defatted lower-sodium chicken broth

¼ cup dry white wine

1 tablespoon lemon juice

1. Preheat the oven to 425 degrees. Coarsely crush the fennel seeds in a spice grinder or with a mortar and pestle or chop with a large knife. In a small bowl, combine the fennel seeds with 1 teaspoon oil, 3 of the chopped garlic cloves, the lemon peel, salt, and pepper. Rub this seasoning mixture over both pork tenderloins.

2. Heat the remaining 2 teaspoons of oil in a large nonstick skillet. Cook the pork over medium-high heat until browned on all sides, about 5 minutes. Transfer the meat to a shallow roasting pan, leaving the drippings in the skillet. Place the pan in the preheated oven and roast until the meat registers 160 degrees on a meat thermometer inserted into the thickest part, 20 to 25 minutes. Remove to a platter and let the meat sit for about 10 minutes before slicing.

continued

3. Add the sliced fennel to the skillet and cook over medium heat, stirring frequently, until it begins to brown lightly and soften, 10 to 15 minutes. Add the garlic, sprinkle with the sugar, and cook, stirring, for 1 minute. Add the broth and wine, bring to a boil, and simmer until the liquids are slightly reduced and the fennel is tender, about 5 minutes. Stir in the lemon juice and season with salt and pepper to taste.

4. Cut the pork across the grain into ½-inch-thick slices and serve with the fennel mixture spooned over the top. Garnish with the reserved fennel fronds if desired.

◆ *PER SERVING: About 199 cals, 60 cals from fat, 7g total fat, 2g sat fat, 59mg chol, 271mg sodium, 7g total carbs, 0g fiber, 26g prot*

Savory Beef Stew with Paprika and Herbs

Makes 8 servings

Sweetly pungent paprika lends a rosy glow to this long-simmering beef stew. It's the perfect do-ahead party dish. Serve it with a big salad of tender lettuces and radicchio and a basket of Herbed Focaccia (page 118).

4 tablespoons all-purpose flour

1 tablespoon paprika, preferably sweet Hungarian

½ teaspoon salt

½ teaspoon black pepper

2 pounds top round of beef, well trimmed, cut in 1½-inch cubes

2 teaspoons olive oil, plus 1 teaspoon

1 large onion, chopped

2 leeks, white and pale green parts only, thinly sliced

1 large carrot, thinly sliced

1 celery rib, thinly sliced

4 garlic cloves, finely chopped

3 cups defatted lower-sodium beef broth

1 cup dry red wine

1 can (16 ounces) plum tomatoes with juice

3 tablespoons fresh thyme or 1 tablespoon dried

1 tablespoon chopped fresh savory or 1 teaspoon dried

1 bay leaf

1 pound baby carrots

2 cups peeled fresh or frozen small pearl onions

½ pound large mushrooms, sliced

1 teaspoon sugar

2 teaspoons lemon juice

2 pounds waxy potatoes, peeled and cut in 2-inch chunks

½ cup chopped parsley, preferably flat leaf

1. Combine the flour, paprika, salt, and pepper in a paper or plastic bag. Add the meat, about half at a time, and shake to coat with the seasoned flour. Reserve the remaining flour.

2. Heat 2 teaspoons of the oil in a Dutch oven. Cook the beef, about half at a time, over medium-high heat, until browned on all sides, about 10 minutes. Remove with a slotted spoon to a plate, leaving the drippings in the pan.

3. Add the onion, leeks, carrot, celery, and garlic. Cook, stirring frequently, until they soften, about 8 minutes. Stir in the remaining flour and cook, stirring, for 2 minutes.

4. Return the meat and any accumulated juices to the pan. Add the broth, wine, tomatoes, thyme, savory, and bay leaf. Bring to a boil, stirring to break up the tomatoes into smaller pieces with the side of a spoon. Reduce the heat to low and simmer, covered, until the meat is almost tender, 1½ to 2 hours. Skim off any fat that has accumulated on the surface. (The recipe can be prepared ahead to this point and refrigerated for up to 2 days, or frozen for 1 month. Reheat before proceeding.)

5. Add the carrots and onions and simmer, uncovered, over medium heat, until the vegetables are tender, about 20 minutes.

6. Heat the remaining 1 teaspoon of oil in a large skillet. Add the sliced mushrooms and cook over medium-high heat, stirring frequently, until somewhat softened and lightly browned, about 6 minutes. Sprinkle with sugar and lemon juice. Scrape the mushrooms into the stew pot and simmer for 5 minutes.

7. Shortly before serving, cook the potatoes in a large pot of boiling salted water until tender, about 15 minutes. Drain well.

8. Serve the stew spooned over the potatoes. Sprinkle with the parsley.

◆ *PER SERVING: About 424 cals, 69 cals from fat, 8g total fat, 2g sat fat, 76mg chol, 401mg sodium, 49g total carbs, 6g fiber, 37g prot*

Apple and Pork Stir-Fry
with Cashews and Ginger

Makes 4 servings

This tasty sweet-and-tart pork and apple stir-fry is high in fiber and vitamin C. Fragrant ground coriander seed adds a pleasing hint of spice. If you don't have any on your shelf, season the meat with ½ teaspoon of grated mace or nutmeg instead.

Sauce:

4 teaspoons cornstarch

1 cup apple juice

2 tablespoons reduced-sodium soy sauce

2 tablespoons white wine vinegar

½ teaspoon dried red pepper flakes

Meat and Vegetables:

¾ pound well-trimmed pork tenderloin, cut into thin strips

1 teaspoon ground coriander seed

½ teaspoon black pepper

1 teaspoon vegetable oil, plus 1 teaspoon

1 large (8 to 10 ounces) tart apple, such as Granny Smith, cored and thinly sliced

1 medium onion, cut into ½-inch slices

1 red bell pepper, seeded and sliced

2 garlic cloves, finely chopped

1 tablespoon finely chopped fresh ginger

Salt to taste

4 cups cooked brown or white rice

¼ cup lightly toasted cashews, chopped

1. For the sauce, whisk the cornstarch, apple juice, soy sauce, vinegar, pepper flakes, and ⅓ cup water in a small bowl. Set aside.

2. Season the meat on all sides with the coriander and pepper.

3. Heat 1 teaspoon of the oil in a large skillet or wok over medium-high to high heat. Stir-fry the pork until seared, 2 to 3 minutes. Remove with a slotted spoon to a plate.

4. Add the remaining 1 teaspoon of oil to the pan. Add the apple, onion, and red pepper and stir-fry until lightly browned on the edges and beginning to soften, about 2 minutes. Add the garlic and ginger and stir-fry for 30 seconds.

5. Reduce the heat to medium. Stir the sauce and add it to the pan, along with the pork and any accumulated juices. Cook, stirring almost constantly, until the sauce comes to a boil, thickens, and turns translucent, about 3 minutes. Season with salt to taste.

6. To serve, spoon the stir-fry over the hot rice and sprinkle with the chopped cashews.

◆ *PER SERVING: About 503 cals, 105 cals from fat, 12g total fat, 3g sat fat, 60mg chol, 327mg sodium, 74g total carbs, 7g fiber, 27g prot*

SAVORY SPICES

You can use spices to flavor and enhance savory meat dishes, including some spices that are traditionally used in desserts. Store spices tightly covered in a dark, cool place. Replace spices once a year; they lose flavor and pungency over time. When you can, buy whole spices and grind or grate them yourself. To release the most flavor, toast whole or ground spices in a small dry skillet for about 1 minute before using. Common savory spices are:

◆ **ALLSPICE**: Fragrant berries, available whole or ground. Named for the combined flavors of cinnamon, cloves, and nutmeg. Used in chutneys, relishes, and pickles, and as the principal spice in Jamaican "jerk" seasoning.

◆ **ANISE**: Seeds of a herbaceous plant, also known as aniseed, with a distinct licorice flavor. Available whole or ground and used in breads, stews, and occasionally in tomato sauces.

◆ **CARDAMOM**: Fragrant lemon-cinnamon flavor, available as seeds and ground. Used in seed form in Indian cooking; popular in Scandinavian breads and desserts.

◆ **CAYENNE PEPPER**: Spicy red pepper, available dried and ground. Used to flavor savory dishes in the United States and around the world. Use sparingly; it is fiery hot.

◆ **CHILI POWDER**: Sometimes made solely from ground dried chiles (labeled "pure chili powder"), but more often a combination of ground chiles mixed with cumin, oregano, garlic, salt, and other spices. Varies from mild to very hot. Used to flavor many savory meat and vegetable dishes.

◆ **CINNAMON**: The woody bark of a tree, with a sweet-sharp flavor and aroma, available in rolled sticks and ground. Used ground as a flavoring for desserts in Europe; used in the Middle East and India to flavor stews, curries, and other savory meat and vegetable dishes.

◆ **CLOVES**: The dried, unopened buds of an evergreen tree native to Southeast Asia, available both whole and ground and often used as a dessert spice. As a savory seasoning, whole cloves often stud the surface of a whole ham or pork and can be stuck into an onion to flavor stocks or sauces. Also used as a component of pickling spice for pickles and chutney.

◆ **CORIANDER SEED**: The ground seed of the cilantro plant has a sweet, nutty flavor. Popular in Middle Eastern cooking and in pork, lamb, and rice dishes. Used in baked desserts. Available as whole seed for pickling spice.

◆ **CUMIN**: Pungent, aromatic seed, available whole or ground. Used extensively in Indian, Mexican, and Middle Eastern cooking. The unique, slightly bitter flavor of cumin has become popular as a characteristic flavor of American Southwest cooking.

◆ **CURRY POWDER**: A blend of spices that usually includes turmeric, cumin, coriander, cardamom, fenugreek, cinnamon, hot red pepper, and ginger. Used in soups, salads, stews, and Indian curries. Ranges from mild to spicy.

◆ **FENNEL**: Seeds from the fennel plant with an aniselike flavor. Used extensively in Italian cooking.

◆ **FILÉ POWDER**: Made from the dried, ground leaves of the North American sassafras tree. Used as both a flavoring and thickening agent in Creole cooking; essential in Louisiana Filé gumbo.

◆ **GINGER**: The root of a plant, available fresh, preserved, crystallized, and powdered. Used powdered or crystallized in Europe as a sweet spice, and fresh or pickled in Asia and India to flavor stir-fries and curries.

◆ **JUNIPER**: The ripe, dried berries of an evergreen tree, with an aromatic, spicy-pine flavor. Gives gin its characteristic taste; frequently used in marinades for game.

◆ **MACE**: The dried casing of a nutmeg seed, with a flavor milder than nutmeg, having a hint of cinnamon. Used to flavor seafood and chicken dishes, curries, and savory sauces.

◆ **NUTMEG**: A large, hard, whole seed of the fruit of a nutmeg tree, with a pleasing, sweetly pungent flavor. Best freshly grated. Used as a savory seasoning in curries and cream sauces and to flavor vegetable dishes.

◆ **PAPRIKA**: A bright red powder spice ground from dried, aromatic sweet red peppers. Used as flavoring; adds color to savory dishes, such as custards. Ranges from mild to hot. Sweet Hungarian paprika is the most flavorful. Paprika can turn brown and lose flavor quickly, so replace it frequently.

◆ **SAFFRON**: The dried stigmas of a crocus plant, with an intense flavor and orange color, available as whole threads or ground. Whole threads, crumbled before using, have a stronger flavor than ground. Used in French bouillabaisse and Spanish paella and many North American and Indian dishes.

◆ **TURMERIC**: Made from a ground root with a yellow-orange color and a mild, faintly bitter flavor. Used in curry powder; can also be used as a flavoring on its own.

CHAPTER TWELVE

Vegetables

Vegetables are packed with nutrients, linked to a host of health benefits, and low in calories. Yet many people still remember being forced, bribed, or coerced as children into eating every last pea on their plates. And some vegetables' strong flavors, pungent aromas, and off colors after cooking are enough to drive away even the most health-conscious eater. But, when well prepared, vegetables can look and taste so good your family will ask for more.

As a group, vegetables are quite diverse. Many are green and leafy, like lettuce and spinach. Others—carrots, turnips, and parsnips—are the edible roots of plants. Broccoli, cabbage, and cauliflower may not look alike but they all belong to the family of cruciferous vegetables. Some say tomatoes belong in the fruit group but, in fact, they share a plant family with eggplant and peppers. Corn, peas, and potatoes, considered starches in many diet plans, count as vegetables on the Food Guide Pyramid.

If you think that healthy eating means consuming tons of vegetables, think again. The Food Guide Pyramid recommends three to five servings a day, and a serving equals half a cup of cooked or raw vegetables or a cup of lettuce. So you can easily meet the three-serving minimum with carrots and celery sticks at lunch and any of the recipes in this chapter plus a green salad at dinner.

Vegetables supply a wide array of nutrients, including vitamin A, vitamin C, folic acid, and fiber. Each vegetable is different in its combination of vitamins and minerals, so think variety when you shop.

An easy way to achieve variety is to shop for color, because the color of the vegetable usually signals its nutritional content. For example, white vegetables, like cauliflower and potatoes, supply vitamin C; dark green, leafy vegetables, such as kale, spinach, and collards, contain both vitamin C and vitamin A. On the other hand, winter squash, sweet potatoes, carrots, and other orange vegetables are rich in vitamin A but have little vitamin C (with the exception of sweet potatoes). So if you vary the color, you will vary the nutrients and stand the best chance of getting all the benefits that vegetables have to offer.

Cook vegetables in ways that make the most of their flavor and nutrition. For maximal nutrition, use as little water as possible and cook quickly—although slow roasting caramelizes the natural sugars in onions, winter squash, and carrots, giving them a rich, sweet taste. Cook broccoli and other strongly flavored vegetables with the pot lid off or slightly ajar to allow pungent-smelling gases to escape. Get to know which seasonings enhance the flavor of vegetables. Spices like cinnamon, nutmeg, and ginger bring out the sweetness of carrots and sweet potatoes. Chives are a natural match for potatoes, as in the Golden Scalloped Potatoes with Chives (page 420).

Go meatless at least once in a while with a vegetable main dish. Broccoli Pie à la Grecque (page 410), paired with bread and a side salad, makes a great summer meal. Perk up a cold, dreary evening with Acorn Squash with Wild Mushroom–Cranberry Stuffing (page 414). When serving a vegetable main dish, remember to include enough side dishes to round out the meal and satisfy an appetite.

Many parents don't believe it, but kids can love vegetables. Prepare dishes made with sweet vegetables, like Gingered Carrot Purée (page 429) or a plain baked sweet potato. Think white potatoes—mashed as in Fabulous Garlic Mashed Potatoes (page 419), baked into "fries" like Crusty Oven "Fries" (page 417), or baked plain and served with an assortment of low-fat toppings. Most importantly, if you show that you enjoy eating vegetables, your child will learn to enjoy them too.

Thai Stir-Fry with Ginger and Mint

Makes 4 main-dish servings

The lively flavors, colors, and textures that make Thai food so popular perk up this sprightly stir-fry. You can pass a bottle of Asian hot sauce at the table to spice up this dish.

2 cups vegetable broth or defatted
    lower-sodium chicken broth
1 tablespoon fish sauce (nam pla)
1 tablespoon reduced-sodium soy
    sauce
2 teaspoons cornstarch
2 tablespoons vegetable oil, plus
    1 teaspoon
½ pound firm tofu, well drained,
    cut in ¾-inch cubes
½ pound unpeeled eggplant,
    trimmed and cut in ¾-inch cubes
    (see note)

½ pound slender zucchini,
    trimmed and sliced ½ inch
    thick
1 small red bell pepper, seeded and
    coarsely chopped
4 garlic cloves, finely chopped
2 tablespoons minced fresh ginger
2 jalapeño peppers, minced
4 cups cooked white rice,
    preferably jasmine rice
2 cups fresh bean sprouts
1 cup chopped fresh mint
Mint sprigs for garnish

1. In a small bowl, stir together the broth, fish sauce, soy sauce, and cornstarch.

2. Heat 2 tablespoons of the oil in a large skillet or wok. Add the tofu and stir-fry over high heat until the cubes are golden on all sides, about 4 minutes. Remove to a plate using a slotted spoon.

3. Add the remaining 1 teaspoon of oil to the pan. Add the eggplant, zucchini, and pepper and stir-fry over high heat until the vegetables begin to brown and soften, about 4 minutes. Add the garlic, ginger, and jalapeño peppers and stir-fry for 1 minute.

4. Stir the broth mixture to recombine and add it to the pan, along with the reserved tofu. Simmer uncovered over medium heat until the sauce thickens somewhat and the eggplant is tender, about 5 minutes.

5. Spoon the vegetable mixture over the rice. Scatter the bean sprouts over the top, sprinkle with the mint, garnish with the mint sprigs, and serve immediately.

◆ *PER SERVING: About 472 cals, 145 cals from fat, 16g total fat, 2g sat fat, 0mg chol, 647mg sodium, 66g total carbs, 4g fiber, 20g prot*

Note: Use either a small, dark-skinned eggplant or a slender Japanese eggplant.

ABOUT NAM PLA (ASIAN FISH SAUCE)

This pungent, slightly salty and sweet sauce is the single most essential ingredient in Thai and other Southeast Asian cuisines.

Made from an extract of anchovies and sea salt, the sauce is aged and refined to a clear, amber liquid. Nam pla is now widely

available in the Asian food section of most supermarkets.

Curried Winter Vegetable and Tofu Stew

Makes 4 main-dish servings

Pita bread, a salad of spinach leaves tossed with Basic Vinaigrette (page 74), and Pumpkin Pecan Bars (page 457) are excellent accompaniments to this colorful meatless stew that glows with the richly complex flavor of curry. Curry powder loses its pungency over time, so be sure to replace yours about once a year.

2 teaspoons vegetable oil

1 red onion, cut into chunks

5 teaspoons curry powder

¾ pound unpeeled red potatoes, cut in 1-inch chunks

½ pound cauliflower florets

½ pound broccoli florets

½ pound baby carrots

1 small red bell pepper, seeded and cut in rough 1-inch chunks

3 cups vegetable broth or defatted lower-sodium chicken broth

1 cup reduced-fat coconut milk

¾ pound regular or firm tofu, drained, cut in 1-inch cubes

½ teaspoon dried red pepper flakes

3 tablespoons fresh lime juice

2 teaspoons sugar

Salt and black pepper to taste

1. Heat the oil in a large saucepan or Dutch oven. Add the onion and cook over medium-high heat, stirring frequently, until it begins to soften, about 3 minutes. Stir in the curry powder and cook, stirring, for 1 minute. Add the potatoes, cauliflower, broccoli, carrots, and red pepper and stir to coat with the curry mixture. Add the broth and coconut milk and bring to a boil over high heat. Reduce the heat, cover, and cook until the potatoes and carrots are almost tender, about 15 minutes.

2. Add the tofu and red pepper flakes and simmer, uncovered, over medium heat until the vegetables are tender and the broth has thickened slightly, about 5 minutes. Stir in the lime juice and sugar and season the stew with salt and pepper to taste.

◆ *PER SERVING: About 356 cals, 126 cals from fat, 14g total fat, 3g sat fat, 0mg chol, 142mg sodium, 45g total carbs, 5g fiber, 20g prot*

Broccoli Pie à la Grecque

Makes 6 main-dish servings

This rich-tasting, herb-flecked pie, a source of iron, is also rich in vitamins A and C and calcium. Serve it with Chunked Tomato, Fennel, and Chickpea Salad (page 98) and a loaf of seeded Italian bread.

2 cups (6 ounces) broccoli florets, coarsely chopped

Olive oil or vegetable oil spray

2 whole eggs

2 egg whites

1 cup part-skim ricotta cheese

½ cup crumbled feta cheese

1 cup low-fat (1 percent) milk

1¼ cups chopped scallions

⅓ cup chopped fresh mint

3 tablespoons chopped fresh dill or 2 teaspoons dried

2 tablespoons chopped fresh oregano or 1 teaspoon dried

½ teaspoon salt

½ teaspoon black pepper

1½ cups cubed French or Italian bread

Dill sprigs for garnish

1. Cook the broccoli in a pot of lightly salted boiling water until it is bright green and crisp-tender, about 3 minutes. Drain into a colander, rinse under cold water, and press gently to remove excess moisture.

2. Preheat the oven to 350 degrees. Lightly coat a 1½-quart deep-dish pie plate or an 8x8-inch glass baking dish with olive oil or vegetable oil spray.

3. In a large bowl, whisk together the eggs, egg whites, ricotta, and feta. Whisk in the milk and add the scallions, mint, dill, oregano, salt, and pepper, stirring gently to combine.

4. Spoon the broccoli into the prepared dish in an even layer and arrange the bread cubes on top. Pour in the custard mixture, stirring gently to distribute the ingredients, making sure the bread is soaked. Bake, uncovered, in the center of the preheated oven until the custard is set and the top of the pie is flecked with brown, 20 to 30 minutes, depending on the size and shape of the baking dish.

5. Cut into wedges or squares to serve, garnished with the dill sprigs.

◆ *PER SERVING: About 202 cals, 94 cals from fat, 10g total fat, 6g sat fat, 104mg chol, 580mg sodium, 13g total carbs, 2g fiber, 15g prot*

Baked Potatoes with Spicy Chili Bean Topping

Makes 4 main-dish servings

Not only does this delightfully spicy, sweet-tart sauce make a terrific topping for fluffy baked potatoes, but it's also an excellent sauce for pasta. To round out this supper, add some warm corn tortillas and a salad made with spinach and red cabbage tossed with Basic Creamy Dressing (page 75).

4 large (about 10 ounces each) russet (or baking) potatoes, scrubbed

¼ pound lean ground pork

1 medium onion, chopped

1 small green bell pepper, seeded and chopped

3 garlic cloves, finely chopped

1½ tablespoons chili powder

2 teaspoons ground cumin

¼ teaspoon cayenne pepper

1 can (14 to 16 ounces) stewed tomatoes

1 cup bottled or canned tomato sauce

1 can (19 ounces) pinto or kidney beans, rinsed and drained, or 2 cups cooked beans

2 tablespoons brown sugar

2 tablespoons cider vinegar

Salt and black pepper to taste

1. Preheat the oven to 425 degrees. Prick the potatoes in two or three places with a skewer or small knife. Place the potatoes directly on the oven rack and bake until soft in the center when pierced, 1 to 1¼ hours.

2. Meanwhile, in a large, preferably nonstick skillet, cook the pork over medium heat with the onion, green pepper, and garlic, stirring to break the meat into smaller pieces, until the pork is no longer pink and the vegetables are softened, about 10 minutes. Add the chili powder, cumin, and cayenne and cook, stirring, for 1 minute. Add the tomatoes, tomato sauce, beans, brown sugar, and vinegar. Bring to a boil over high heat, reduce the heat to medium-low and simmer, uncovered, for 15 to 20 minutes, until the sauce reduces and thickens slightly and the flavors blend. If the sauce is too thick, add up to ½ cup water as it cooks. Season with salt and pepper to taste.

3. Make deep crisscross cuts in the top of each potato and gently squeeze to expose the flesh and make a cavity for the sauce. Spoon the sauce into and over each potato and serve.

◆ *PER SERVING: About 589 cals, 30 cals from fat, 3g total fat, 1g sat fat, 13mg chol, 1409mg sodium, 124g total carbs, 6g fiber, 20g prot*

QUICKENED-UP BAKED POTATOES

Large potatoes cooked in a conventional oven take an hour or more to bake until the insides are soft, dry, and fluffy, and the thick outer skins almost crisp and chewy. In a microwave oven, you can cook potatoes in about 15 minutes but, because moisture is trapped inside, the resulting texture and flavor are more like those of a steamed potato than a baked one. To shorten overall cooking times, while retaining the texture and taste of a well-baked potato, try this combination technique. Prick three or four potatoes, depending on the size of your microwave, and place them between two layers of paper towels. Microwave them on high, rotating twice, for 8 to 12 minutes, until they can be pierced with a small, sharp knife. Transfer the potatoes to a preheated 425-degree oven and bake, turning over once, until they are tender, 20 to 25 minutes.

Spaghetti Squash with Sun-Dried Tomato Sauce

Makes 4 main-dish servings

The flesh of the spaghetti squash looks like long-strand pasta. After cooking it, you have to scrape or "comb" it out of its yellow shell with a fork. Then sauce the long, slightly crunchy, mildly sweet strands just like spaghetti. This sun-dried tomato sauce is a particularly delicious complement. Add a basket of Herbed Focaccia (page 118), a green salad, and Amaretti Baked Pears (page 442) for a truly terrific supper.

1 large spaghetti squash, about
  3 pounds
½ cup slivered or chopped dry
  pack sun-dried tomatoes
1 tablespoon olive oil
1 medium onion, chopped
3 garlic cloves, finely chopped
½ teaspoon dried oregano
1 can (16 ounces) crushed tomatoes
½ cup dry white wine

2 tablespoons freshly grated
  Parmesan cheese, preferably
  imported
2 teaspoons sugar
¼ cup chopped parsley, preferably
  flat leaf
2 tablespoons slivered fresh basil
Salt and black pepper to taste
1 cup part-skim ricotta cheese

1. Preheat the oven to 375 degrees. Pierce the uncut squash in several places with a skewer or sharp knife. Place on a rimmed baking sheet and bake, uncovered, turning once, until tender when pierced with a skewer, 1 to 1½ hours (see note).

2. To rehydrate the tomatoes, place them in a small bowl and cover with ½ cup boiling water. Set aside until softened, about 15 minutes, reserving the liquid.

3. Heat the oil in a large skillet. Add the onion and cook over medium heat, stirring frequently, until softened, about 4 minutes. Add the garlic and oregano and cook, stirring, for 1 minute. Add the crushed tomatoes, wine, Parmesan cheese, sugar, sun-dried tomatoes, and soaking water. Bring to a boil, reduce the heat to medium-low, and simmer, uncovered, until the sauce reduces and thickens and the flavors blend, 15 to 20 minutes. Stir in the parsley and basil. Season with salt and pepper to taste.

4. Cut the cooked squash in half lengthwise and scoop out and discard the seeds. Use a fork to scrape the strands of flesh out of the skin. Place the squash on a platter, spoon the sauce over it, and top with spoonfuls of the ricotta.

◆ *PER SERVING: About 281 cals, 93 cals from fat, 10g total fat, 4g sat fat, 21mg chol, 563mg sodium, 32g total carbs, 6g fiber, 14g prot*

Note: To cook in a microwave, carefully cut the squash in half lengthwise and scoop out the seeds. Place the halves, cut sides down, in a microwave-safe baking dish. Cover with plastic wrap and microwave on high for 15 to 20 minutes, rotating the dish twice, until the squash softens.

Garlicky Broccoli Rabe

Makes 4 side-dish servings

Broccoli rabe is a flowering variety of broccoli. The whole plant—stems, leaves, and flowering buds—is edible and delicious, particularly when you blanch it to get rid of some of its bitterness.

1 large bunch (about 1½ pounds) broccoli rabe	¼ teaspoon dried red pepper flakes
1 tablespoon extra-virgin olive oil	Salt and freshly ground black pepper to taste
3 garlic cloves, finely chopped	

1. Cut the broccoli rabe stems and buds into 1- to 2-inch lengths. Add them to a large pot of salted boiling water and cook, uncovered, at a rolling boil for 4 to 5 minutes until almost tender. Drain into a colander.

2. Heat the oil in a large skillet. Add the garlic and cook over medium heat, stirring, until fragrant but not brown, about 1 minute. Add the broccoli rabe and red pepper flakes. Cook, stirring, until the broccoli rabe is heated through and tender, 2 to 3 minutes. Season with salt and black pepper to taste before serving.

◆ *PER SERVING: About 81 cals, 36 cals from fat, 4g total fat, 1g sat fat, 0mg chol, 45mg sodium, 9g total carbs, 6g fiber, 5g prot*

Acorn Squash with Wild Mushroom–Cranberry Stuffing

Makes 4 main-dish servings

After you scoop the seeds out of a split acorn squash, you'll have a shell that is ideal for stuffing. This savory bread stuffing blends earthy mushrooms with tart dried cranberries and crunchy pecans. It's substantial enough to serve as a main dish, particularly when paired with Lentil Stew with Rosemary (page 301) or Four-Bean Ranch Salad (page 94). Candied Gingerbread (page 462) makes a tasty dessert.

2 acorn squash, about 1¾ pounds each,
    halved lengthwise and seeded
Salt and black pepper to taste
½ cup apple juice
1 cup dried cranberries or currants
1 tablespoon olive oil
2 teaspoons butter, plus 1 tablespoon
1 medium onion, chopped
½ pound fresh wild mushrooms, such as
    shiitake, trimmed and chopped
¼ cup vegetable broth or defatted
    lower-sodium chicken broth
2 cups fresh whole-wheat bread crumbs
¼ cup chopped pecans
1 egg, lightly beaten
2 teaspoons dried sage

1. Preheat the oven to 425 degrees. Sprinkle the squash with salt and pepper and arrange in a baking dish cut sides down. Bake, uncovered, in the preheated oven for about 25 minutes, until the squash begins to soften (see note). Remove from the oven and turn cut sides up to fill.

2. Bring the apple juice to a boil in a small saucepan. Remove from the heat, add the cranberries, and set aside until they soften, about 10 minutes.

3. Meanwhile, heat the oil and 2 teaspoons of the butter in a large skillet. Add the onion, mushrooms, and broth and cook over medium to medium-high heat, stirring frequently, until the mushrooms begin to soften and most of the liquid evaporates, about 5 minutes. Add the bread crumbs and pecans and cook, stirring, until the crumbs brown lightly and the nuts are lightly toasted, 3 to 4 minutes. Mix in the cranberries and soaking liquid and add the egg, tossing to combine well. Season with the sage, and salt and pepper to taste.

4. Fill the partially cooked squash with the bread crumb mixture, mounding it into the cavities. Melt the remaining 1 tablespoon of butter and drizzle it over the crumbs.

5. Return the squash to the oven and bake until the squash is tender and the stuffing is heated throughout and lightly browned on top, 20 to 25 minutes.

◆ *PER SERVING: About 411 cals, 139 cals from fat, 15g total fat, 4g sat fat, 66mg chol, 240mg sodium, 65g total carbs, 17g fiber, 8g prot*

Note: The squash can be partially cooked in a microwave oven. Place it in a microwave-safe dish, cut sides down, cover with plastic wrap, and bake, rotating the dish twice, until the squash partially softens, 10 to 15 minutes.

Blackened Scallions

Makes 4 side-dish servings

Scallions take beautifully to grilling over an outdoor fire. Finished with a drizzle of seasoned broth and vinegar, they make an ideal accompaniment to any grilled meat.

2 bunches large scallions	¼ teaspoon liquid hot pepper
1 tablespoon extra-virgin olive oil	sauce
2 tablespoons defatted lower-sodium chicken broth	¼ teaspoon salt
	¼ teaspoon pepper
1 tablespoon red wine vinegar	¼ teaspoon sugar

1. Prepare a medium-hot barbecue fire or preheat a gas grill. Trim off the scallion roots and all but about 6 inches of the green tops. Brush the scallions with the olive oil.

2. Place the scallions crosswise on the grill so they cannot fall through, and grill, turning with tongs, until the scallions soften and some of the edges turn black, 3 to 4 minutes. Remove to a platter.

3. In a small bowl, whisk the chicken broth with the vinegar, hot pepper sauce, salt, pepper, and sugar. Drizzle over the scallions and serve.

◆ *PER SERVING: About 85 cals, 31 cals from fat, 3g total fat, 0g sat fat, 0mg chol, 138mg sodium, 14g total carbs, 0g fiber, 0g prot*

Spring Vegetable Frittata

Makes 4 main-dish servings

Frittatas, which you can eat warm or at room temperature, are great for supper, lunch, or even brunch. Make this one in the spring when asparagus is plentiful. It not only tastes delicious, but is rich in vitamins A and C. It's also a good source of fiber, calcium, and iron.

½ pound slender asparagus

2 teaspoons olive oil

1 carrot, cut into small dice

1 cup thinly sliced scallions

1 large garlic clove, finely chopped

1 cup frozen peas

1½ cups cooked orzo or other
    pasta (see note)

4 eggs (see note)

4 egg whites

½ cup part-skim ricotta cheese

3 tablespoons slivered fresh basil

½ teaspoon salt

½ teaspoon black pepper

3 tablespoons grated part-skim
    mozzarella cheese

1. Cut off and discard the tough stem ends of the asparagus. Slice the asparagus tips about 1 inch long and cut the remaining stems into ½-inch lengths.

2. Heat the oil in a large (10- to 11-inch) oven-proof skillet. Add the asparagus and carrot along with 2 tablespoons of water and cook, covered, over medium heat, stirring frequently, until the vegetables are crisp-tender, about 5 minutes. Add the scallions and garlic, and cook, stirring, for 1 minute. Add the peas and cooked orzo and cook, stirring, until heated through, about 2 minutes.

3. Whisk the eggs and egg whites with the ricotta, basil, salt, and pepper until blended. Pour the egg mixture over the vegetable mixture in the pan, stir gently to combine, and cover. Cook over low heat until the eggs are almost set, 7 to 10 minutes.

4. Turn on the broiler.

5. Sprinkle the frittata with the mozzarella. Place under the broiler, about 5 inches from the heat, and broil until the cheese melts and the top of the frittata is flecked golden brown, about 2 minutes. Watch carefully to prevent burning.

6. Cut into wedges and serve.

◆ *PER SERVING: About 279 cals, 100 cals from fat, 11g total fat, 4g sat fat, 225mg chol, 492mg sodium, 24g total carbs, 4g fiber, 20g prot*

Note: Use leftover cooked orzo or cook ½ cup (about 3 ounces) dried orzo in boiling salted water until al dente, about 9 minutes. You can substitute 1½ cups of liquid egg substitute for the fresh eggs and egg whites if you like.

Crusty Oven "Fries"

Makes 4 side-dish servings

Your whole family will love these baked "fries," which are much lower in fat than the deep-fried originals. They go well with just about any sandwich, especially Sage and Onion Turkey Burgers (page 183) or the stylish Springtime Chicken and Watercress Sandwich (page 187).

Vegetable or olive oil spray
1½ pounds unpeeled russet or
    all-purpose potatoes, scrubbed
1 tablespoon vegetable oil
½ teaspoon salt, plus additional
    to taste
¼ teaspoon paprika
¼ teaspoon black pepper

1. Preheat the oven to 425 degrees and position a rack in the upper level of the oven. Lightly coat a rimmed baking sheet with oil spray.

2. Cut each potato lengthwise into ½-inch-thick slices; stack the slices and cut into ½-inch-wide strips. Place the potatoes in a colander, run them under cold water to rinse off some of the starch, and pat them dry on several layers of paper towels. Transfer the potatoes to the prepared baking sheet.

3. In a small bowl, combine the oil, salt, paprika, and pepper and drizzle over the potatoes. Using your hands, toss the potatoes with the flavored oil until they are evenly coated, and spread them out on the baking sheet in a single layer.

4. Bake for 20 minutes. Use a spatula to turn and redistribute the potatoes; return to the oven and continue to bake until the potatoes are golden brown, 15 to 20 minutes longer. Serve immediately, seasoned with additional salt if necessary.

◆ *PER SERVING: About 217 cals, 32 cals from fat, 4g total fat, 0g sat fat, 0mg chol, 280mg sodium, 43g total carbs, 4g fiber, 4g prot*

Stuffed Summer Squash Provençal

Makes 4 main-dish servings (6 side-dish servings)

These stuffed summer squash involve a bit of work, but they taste absolutely delicious and make a particularly spectacular presentation on a festive buffet. Serve them as a meatless main dish with Four-Bean Ranch Salad (page 94) or Minted Couscous Greek Salad (page 99), or as a side dish to accompany baked ham or other meat.

2 pounds small zucchini or yellow crookneck summer squash
Salt and freshly ground black pepper to taste
2 teaspoons olive oil
3 garlic cloves, finely chopped
3 anchovy fillets, chopped
2 cups seeded and chopped fresh tomatoes
1 cup fresh white bread crumbs
1 egg, lightly beaten
¼ cup slivered fresh basil, plus 2 tablespoons
2 tablespoons chopped fresh oregano
3 cups canned or bottled tomato sauce
½ teaspoon dried red pepper flakes
2 tablespoons chopped flat-leaf parsley, plus 2 tablespoons
2 tablespoons freshly grated Parmesan cheese

1. Cut off the squash stems and cut the squash in half lengthwise. Use a teaspoon or grapefruit spoon to scoop out the pulp, leaving a sturdy shell. Chop the pulp and set aside. Sprinkle the squash shells with salt and pepper and arrange in a baking dish.

2. Heat the oil in a large, preferably nonstick skillet. Add the garlic and anchovies and cook over medium heat, mashing the anchovies to make a paste, about 1 minute. Add the tomatoes and reserved squash pulp, raise the heat to high, and cook, stirring frequently, until the vegetables soften and most of the liquid evaporates, about 6 minutes. Remove the pan from the heat and stir in the bread crumbs, egg, ¼ cup basil, and oregano. Season with several grindings of black pepper. Spoon the stuffing into the squash cavities. (This recipe can be prepared ahead to this point. Cover and refrigerate for up to 4 hours.)

3. Preheat the oven to 350 degrees. In a bowl, stir together the tomato sauce, remaining 2 tablespoons of basil, red pepper flakes, and 2 tablespoons of parsley. Pour the tomato sauce around the stuffed squash in the baking dish. Sprinkle the cheese over the squash. Cover the pan with foil and bake in the preheated oven for 20 minutes. Uncover and continue to bake until the squash is tender and the stuffing is lightly browned, about 20 minutes longer.

4. Serve the squash hot or warm, directly from the baking dish or transferred to a large platter, with some of the sauce spooned over the top. Sprinkle with the remaining chopped parsley before serving.

◆ *PER MAIN-DISH SERVING: About 197 cals, 53 cals from fat, 6g total fat, 2g sat fat, 58mg chol, 1509mg sodium, 29g total carbs, 7g fiber, 9g prot*

Fabulous Garlic Mashed Potatoes

Makes 4 side-dish servings

Flavored with just a hint of garlic, thinned with chicken broth, and enriched with reduced-fat sour cream, these potatoes are everybody's favorite side dish, particularly when there is any sauce or gravy on the menu. As a variation, try stirring in about ¼ cup of snipped chives or scallions, or any combination of minced fresh herbs.

2½ pounds russet potatoes, peeled and cut into 2-inch chunks

3 garlic cloves, peeled

1 teaspoon salt, plus additional to taste

⅔ cup defatted lower-sodium chicken broth

¼ cup reduced-fat sour cream

¼ teaspoon freshly ground black pepper

⅛ teaspoon grated nutmeg

1. Place the potatoes and garlic in a large saucepan and add enough water to cover. Bring to a boil over high heat and add 1 teaspoon salt. Reduce the heat to medium, cover, and cook until the potatoes are tender, about 15 minutes. Drain the potatoes, return them to the pot, and place over low heat for about 1 minute until thoroughly dry. Transfer to a large bowl, or leave them in the saucepan to mash.

2. Add the broth to the potatoes and mash with a potato masher or handheld electric mixer to make a fairly smooth purée. Add the sour cream and continue to mash until the potatoes are light and fluffy. Season with pepper, nutmeg, and salt to taste.

◆ *PER SERVING: About 238 cals, 12 cals from fat, 1g total fat, 0g sat fat, 5mg chol, 567mg sodium, 52g total carbs, 3g fiber, 5g prot*

Golden Scalloped Potatoes with Chives

Makes 6 side-dish servings

Yukon Gold potatoes add their appealing, buttery yellow hue to these rich-tasting scalloped potatoes. Their creamy sauce (achieved without adding any cream) makes them an ideal side dish with broiled chicken, meat, or fish.

Olive or vegetable oil spray
1 garlic clove, split
1 teaspoon butter
1 medium onion, thinly sliced
½ teaspoon salt, plus additional
   to taste
½ teaspoon black pepper, plus
   additional to taste

2½ pounds Yukon Gold potatoes,
   peeled and thinly sliced
   (see note)
2 tablespoons flour
2 cups low-fat milk
1 cup defatted lower-sodium
   chicken broth
3 tablespoons snipped chives

1. Preheat the oven to 375 degrees. Lightly coat a 2-quart baking dish with oil spray and rub with the cut sides of the garlic clove.

2. Melt the butter in a medium-sized skillet. Add the onion and cook over medium heat, stirring frequently, until it begins to soften, about 4 minutes. Add the salt and pepper and stir to combine.

3. Cover the bottom of the baking dish with about one third of the potatoes. Spread with half the onion mixture and sprinkle with half the flour. Make another layer of potatoes and spread with the remaining onions and flour. Top with a layer of potatoes.

4. Heat the milk and broth to a simmer in a saucepan and pour over the potatoes. The liquid should come just to the top of the potatoes. Sprinkle with salt and pepper.

5. Bake, uncovered, until the potatoes are soft and most of the liquid is absorbed, 50 to 60 minutes. Sprinkle with chives before serving.

◆ *PER SERVING: About 193 cals, 17 cals from fat, 2g total fat, 1g sat fat, 5mg chol, 247mg sodium, 38g total carbs, 3g fiber, 7g prot*

Note: If you can't find Yukon Gold potatoes, you can substitute all-purpose potatoes, decreasing the flour in the recipe to 1 tablespoon.

New Potatoes and Peas with Mustard Glaze

Makes 4 side-dish servings

A zesty wine and mustard glaze coats new red potatoes and spring peas to make a side dish that is a fitting partner for thinly sliced smoked ham or broiled salmon.

1¾ pounds small red new
   potatoes (see note)
1 cup fresh or frozen peas
3 tablespoons dry white wine
¼ cup finely chopped shallots
2 tablespoons Dijon mustard
1 tablespoon vegetable oil

¼ teaspoon salt, plus additional
   to taste
¼ teaspoon freshly ground black
   pepper
¼ cup chopped parsley, preferably
   flat leaf

1. Cook the potatoes in a large pot of boiling salted water until tender, 10 to 15 minutes. If using fresh peas, add them to the potatoes during the last 5 minutes of cooking time; if using frozen, add during the last 2 minutes. Drain the peas and potatoes into a colander and do not wash the saucepan.

2. Add the wine and shallots to the saucepan, bring to a boil over high heat, and boil until the liquid is reduced by half, about 2 minutes. Remove from the heat and whisk in the mustard, oil, salt, and pepper.

3. Return the potatoes and peas to the cooking pot and toss with the mustard glaze to coat thoroughly. Add the parsley and toss again before serving.

◆ *PER SERVING: About 285 cals, 38 cals from fat, 4g total fat, 1g sat fat, 0mg chol, 330mg sodium, 55g total carbs, 1g fiber, 7g prot*

Note: If you can't get small red potatoes, cut larger red potatoes into 1½-inch chunks.

VEGETABLE "COLOR GROUPS" AND GOOD NUTRITION

The more colorful your vegetable bin, the more nutritious your diet. For example, carrots, sweet potatoes, butternut squash, and other orange-colored vegetables supply vitamin A in the form of beta carotene, a plant pigment that your body converts into active vitamin A. The dark green, leafy vegetables—spinach, kale, and other greens—also provide vitamin A, along with vitamin C. On the other hand, white vegetables like potatoes and cauliflower supply no vitamin A but plenty of vitamin C. And tomatoes are rich in a pigment called lycopene, one of many phytochemicals, which are plant chemicals that may protect against certain types of cancer and other diseases.

Parsley-Parmesan Potato Cake

Makes 4 side-dish servings

This potato cake is tempting paired with Lentil Stew with Rosemary (page 301), but it's also delicious as an accompaniment to a vegetable or meat stew, such as Quick Spring Lamb Stew (page 381) or Easy Chicken Cacciatore (page 336).

Olive or vegetable oil spray
2 pounds russet, all-purpose, or
 Yukon gold potatoes
⅔ cup skim milk
1 egg white
2 teaspoons butter

3 tablespoons grated Parmesan
 cheese, preferably imported,
 plus 1 tablespoon
2 tablespoons chopped parsley,
 preferably flat leaf
Salt to taste
⅛ teaspoon paprika

1. Lightly coat a shallow 2-quart baking dish with oil spray. Peel the potatoes and cut into rough 2- to 3-inch chunks. Cook in a large saucepan of boiling, salted water until fork tender, 15 to 20 minutes. Drain the potatoes, return to the saucepan, and cook over low heat for about 1 minute until thoroughly dry. Transfer to a large bowl or leave in the saucepan to mash.

2. In a small bowl, whisk the milk with the egg white. Mash the potatoes with a potato masher, then gradually beat in the milk mixture and the butter with a wooden spoon to make a fairly smooth purée. Stir in 3 tablespoons of the cheese and the parsley and season with salt to taste. Spoon into the prepared pan, smooth the top, and sprinkle with the remaining 1 tablespoon of cheese and dust with the paprika. (The casserole can be made several hours ahead to this point and held at room temperature for 2 to 3 hours or refrigerated overnight.)

3. If the potatoes are freshly made and warm, turn on the broiler and place the casserole under the heat until the top is flecked with brown and the cheese melts, about 2 minutes. If cool, preheat the oven to 425 degrees, cover the casserole with foil, and bake until nearly heated through, 10 to 15 minutes. Uncover and bake until the top is flecked with brown, about 15 minutes longer.

4. To serve, cut into squares and remove from the pan with a small spatula.

◆ *PER SERVING: About 235 cals, 37 cals from fat, 4g total fat, 2g sat fat, 11mg chol, 448mg sodium, 42g total carbs, 3g fiber, 8g prot*

Glazed Gratin of Yams, Potatoes, and Turnips

Makes 6 side-dish servings

This hearty root vegetable casserole goes beautifully with any roast meat or poultry. Try it with Sunday Supper Roast Chicken (page 320) or Marvelous Mustard Meat Loaf (page 383).

Olive or vegetable oil spray
1 tablespoon butter
1 large onion, chopped
2 teaspoons grated orange peel
½ teaspoon salt
½ teaspoon black pepper
1 pound all-purpose or russet
  potatoes, peeled and thinly sliced
1 large (12 ounces) orange-fleshed
  yam or sweet potato, peeled and thinly sliced
1 medium (8 ounces) white turnip, peeled and thinly sliced
1 cup defatted lower-sodium chicken broth
½ cup dry vermouth or white wine
½ cup orange juice
2 teaspoons granulated sugar

1. Preheat the oven to 375 degrees. Lightly coat a 2-quart baking dish with oil spray.

2. Melt the butter in a medium skillet. Add the onion and cook over medium heat, stirring often, until softened, about 5 minutes. Stir in the orange peel and salt and pepper.

3. In the bottom of the prepared baking dish, make a layer of about one third of the sliced potatoes, yams, and turnips. Spread with about half the onion mixture. Repeat with another layer of the three root vegetables, then onions, and finish with a layer of root vegetables.

4. In a small saucepan, bring the chicken broth, wine, and orange juice to a boil. Pour the liquid over the potatoes and sprinkle with the sugar. Cover the casserole with foil and bake in the preheated oven for 20 minutes. Uncover and continue to bake until the vegetables are tender and most of the liquid is absorbed, 40 to 50 minutes longer.

5. Serve from the casserole dish.

◆ *PER SERVING: About 148 cals, 20 cals from fat, 2g total fat, 1g sat fat, 5mg chol, 234mg sodium, 30g total carbs, 4g fiber, 3g prot*

Molasses and Pepper Grilled Sweet Potato Slices

Makes 4 side-dish servings

This grilling method intensifies the natural sweetness of dark orange–fleshed sweet potatoes. If you have cold, leftover sweet potatoes, you can slice them about ½ inch thick and grill them the same way. These potatoes are delicious with grilled meat, such as Fiery Grilled Pork Tenderloin (page 394).

Vegetable oil spray
1¾ to 2 pounds orange-fleshed
sweet potatoes
3 tablespoons molasses
1 tablespoon vegetable oil
1 tablespoon fresh lemon juice
½ teaspoon grated lemon peel
½ teaspoon salt
½ teaspoon coarsely ground
black pepper

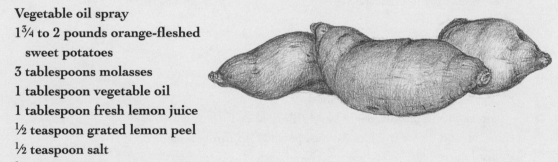

1. Prepare a medium barbecue fire or preheat a gas grill. Spray the grill rack with cooking oil spray. Peel the sweet potatoes and cut them lengthwise into slices about ⅛ inch thick.

2. In a small bowl, stir together the molasses, oil, lemon juice, lemon peel, salt, and pepper. Brush the mixture onto both sides of the potato slices.

3. Grill the potatoes, turning occasionally with a wide spatula, until they are golden brown, crisp on the outside, and tender inside, about 10 minutes.

◆ *PER SERVING: About 217 cals, 32 cals from fat, 4g total fat, 0g sat fat, 0mg chol, 283mg sodium, 45g total carbs, 5g fiber, 3g prot*

SWEET POTATOES AND YAMS

There are two types of sweet potatoes—one with a light skin and pale, firm flesh, and the more common darker-skinned variety with the soft orange-red flesh. The latter is sometimes referred to as a Louisiana yam, but a true yam is a starchy tuber native to Africa that isn't available in this country. Lighter-skinned sweet potatoes have a delicate flesh and are in season only in the fall. The darker sweet potato is richer, hardier, and available year-round. Both types of sweet potatoes are rich in vitamins A and C, along with fiber and several minerals.

GRILLING VEGETABLES

Almost all vegetables can be successfully cooked on a grill. Place them directly on the grill rack, cut into small pieces, and thread them together onto skewers to grill.

Vegetables need to be protected from the flame and from sticking to the grill rack with a light coating of oil applied before grilling. To minimize the amount of oil used, try dunking the vegetables in an oil/water bath of 1 tablespoon of oil to 1 quart of water before cooking. You can also spritz the vegetables lightly with vegetable oil spray or rub oil directly onto them.

Grill vegetables over medium or moderate heat, watching carefully so they don't get overly charred. Cooking times vary a lot depending on the type of grill and fire, the position of the vegetables on the grill, and the weather. Delicate, tender vegetables—such as asparagus, bell pepper slices, broccoli spears, mushrooms, onions, scallions, sliced summer squash, and tomatoes—usually cook in about 4 to 8 minutes. Denser vegetables—such as baby carrots, beet wedges, corn in the husk, sliced eggplant, fennel wedges, small leeks, and sliced sweet potatoes—take longer to cook, about 6 to 15 minutes. Very hard vegetables—such as white potatoes, turnips, and winter squash slices—come out best if you parboil them until they're almost tender before grilling for a few minutes.

POTATOES

When served without toppings that add fat, potatoes are relatively low in calories. A 7-ounce white potato eaten with the skin contains about 220 calories. It's also high in fiber, rich in vitamin C, and contains small amounts of folic acid.

When buying potatoes, choose ones that are firm, unblemished, and free of sprouts. Potatoes stored in a cool, dark, well-ventilated place at about 50 degrees Fahrenheit will keep for 3 to 4 weeks. Potatoes that have a slight green tinge to the skin from prolonged light exposure contain solanine, a bitter alkaloid that can be toxic if eaten in large quantities. Cut away any green parts before cooking.

Potato varieties differ primarily in the amount of starch they contain (see chart), so buy potatoes according to how you plan to use them. New potatoes are just very young potatoes of any variety, with a high moisture content, thin skin, and waxy flesh.

NAME (COMMON NAME)	DESCRIPTION	COOKING USES/ TECHNIQUES
HIGH STARCH		
RUSSETS (Idahos or Idaho bakers—though also grown in Maine, Nova Scotia, and the Pacific Northwest)	Long, slightly rounded ends; thick, rough brown skin with numerous eyes; very low moisture; fluffy, floury interior when cooked	Baking, mashing, frying
MEDIUM STARCH (ALL-PURPOSE POTATOES)		
EASTERN ROUND WHITES (Maine potatoes, Kennebecs, Acadias)	Medium-sized; dark thick skins; flesh has higher water content than russets	All-purpose—boiling, mashing, baking, roasting, scalloped
YUKON GOLDS (yellow finns)	Medium-sized; light brown skin; yellowish-gold flesh; moisture content is higher than eastern round whites	Scalloped, stews, potato salads
CALIFORNIA LONG WHITES	Long, slightly rounded ends; smooth, very pale brown skin; high moisture content; almost waxy texture	Boiled, scalloped, potato salads
LOW STARCH (BOILING POTATOES)		
RED BLISS (round reds)	Small to medium; smooth red skin; waxy; high moisture content	Best for potato salad; boiled; stews

Summer Harvest Ratatouille

Makes 4 side-dish servings

Make this classic Provençal vegetable stew at the height of summer when gardens and produce stands overflow with fresh vegetables. The yellow crookneck squash is a nontraditional ingredient in the recipe, but it contributes a welcome splash of sunny color.

1 tablespoon olive oil
1 large onion, thinly sliced
4 garlic cloves, chopped
1 small eggplant (about ¾ pound),
   cut into ¾-inch cubes (see note)
1 small zucchini, sliced
1 small yellow crookneck squash,
   sliced

1 green or red bell pepper, seeded
   and chopped
1 teaspoon dried oregano
½ teaspoon salt or to taste
½ teaspoon black pepper
1 pound fresh plum tomatoes,
   coarsely chopped
½ cup slivered fresh basil

1. Heat the oil in a large skillet. Add the onion and cook over medium heat, stirring occasionally, until it begins to soften, about 5 minutes. Add the garlic and cook for 1 minute. Add the eggplant, zucchini, squash, and bell pepper to the skillet and cook, stirring, for 3 minutes. Season with the oregano, salt, and pepper. Cover, reduce the heat to low, and simmer until the vegetables are soft, about 20 minutes.

2. Add the tomatoes, raise the heat to medium-high, and simmer, uncovered, until the tomatoes soften and produce liquid, about 10 minutes. Stir in the basil. (This recipe can be made up to 2 days ahead and refrigerated or frozen.)

◆ *PER SERVING: About 110 cals, 38 cals from fat, 4g total fat, 1g sat fat, 0mg chol, 276mg sodium, 17g total carbs, 4g fiber, 3g prot*

Note: If the eggplant is large with many seeds, sprinkle it lightly with salt and place in a colander to drain for 30 minutes. Rinse under cold water and pat dry on paper towels. This step will remove any excess bitterness.

PEPPERS

A lively profusion of colorful peppers has exploded onto the market. Peppers are low in calories (about 30 calories per half a cup) and are an excellent source of vitamin C. The amount of vitamin A varies with the color of the pepper. Green peppers have almost no vitamin A, yellow peppers supply just a little, while red peppers contain more than 20 percent of the daily value.

Peppers are either sweet or hot. Generally, the smaller and more tapered the chili, the hotter it is. Most of the heat is concentrated in the pepper's ribs. Use rubber gloves when cutting chiles to avoid their stinging heat, and do not rub your eyes, nose, or mouth afterward.

Many chili peppers are sold dried. Dried chiles have lost most of their nutritional value. They have an almost indefinite shelf life if stored in a cool, dry place; they must be reconstituted in liquid before use. The flavor of dried chiles is concentrated, and the heat usually remains in the peppers.

NAME (COMMON NAME)	DESCRIPTION	COOKING USES
SWEET		
BELL PEPPERS (green, red, yellow, orange, purple)	Meaty texture; mild flavor; purple peppers are the ripest and the sweetest; green peppers are the most bitter; peppers of other colors range in between	Raw in salads, sandwiches, salsas, and relishes; cooked in stews, soups, sauces, and casseroles; seeds and ribs removed
ITALIAN PEPPERS (Cubanelles)	Mild flavor; pale green to yellow-green; tapered; somewhat twisted; 4 to 6 inches long x 2 inches wide	Sautéed; a good substitute for bell peppers
HOT (CHILI PEPPERS—LISTED FROM MILDEST TO HOTTEST)		
POBLANOS	Mildly hot; 5 inches long; tapered; black-green skin	Chiles rellenos
JALAPEÑOS	1½ to 2 inches long; straight; tapered round tip; hot; dark green	Chopped in salsas, nachos, or guacamole
SERRANOS	Hotter than jalapeños if ribs are not removed; smooth green skin; long and thin with a pointed end	In all Mexican dishes where jalapeños can be used
CAYENNE PEPPERS	Same heat range as serranos, with especially hot ribs; about 2 inches long; red, or green and red; thin; pointed	Fresh in Indian and Chinese dishes; substitute for jalapeños or serranos in Mexican cooking
HABAÑEROS (Scotch bonnet)	Extremely hot; light green when immature; ripens to orange; lantern shape; 1 inch long x 1 inch wide; scalloped edges	Finely chopped in Mexican, Jamaican, and Haitian dishes
DRIED		
CHIPOTLES (dried and smoked jalapeños)	Hot; distinctive smoky flavor; light brown; wrinkled	Sauces; soak in hot water for 30 minutes to soften
ANCHOS (dried poblanos)	Medium-hot; deep reddish-brown wrinkled shiny skin	Purée in Mexican sauces; soak in hot water for 30 minutes to soften
PASTILLAS (Chiles negro, dried chilaca peppers)	Mild with ribs removed, hot used whole; long; slender; blackish; wrinkled	Toasted and ground for salsas and sauces

Eggplant Roasted with Garlic and Herbs

Makes 4 side-dish servings

Fiber-rich eggplant caramelizes and develops a mellow, smoky flavor when roasted. This side dish makes a tantalizing accompaniment to Lentil, Spinach, and Meat Loaf (page 292), or any leftover roast meat or chicken.

Olive or vegetable oil spray
2 pounds eggplant, stems trimmed
   and cut into ½-inch
   lengthwise slices (see note)
2 tablespoons extra-virgin olive oil
3 large garlic cloves, finely chopped
2 tablespoons finely chopped flat-leaf parsley
2 teaspoons finely chopped fresh rosemary or
   1½ teaspoons crumbled dried rosemary
½ teaspoon salt
Freshly ground black pepper to taste
2 teaspoons balsamic vinegar

1. Preheat the oven to 400 degrees. Position an oven rack in the top third of the oven. Coat a rimmed baking sheet with oil spray.

2. Arrange the eggplant slices on the baking sheet. In a small bowl, combine the oil with the garlic, parsley, rosemary, and salt. Brush the top sides of the eggplant with the mixture, making sure that the garlic and herbs are distributed evenly over the surface.

3. Roast the eggplant on the top oven rack until the flesh is golden brown and very soft, 25 to 30 minutes. Remove from the oven, grind a generous amount of pepper over the eggplant slices, and drizzle with the vinegar.

4. Serve hot, warm, or at room temperature.

◆ *PER SERVING: About 121 cals, 65 cals from fat, 7g total fat, 1g sat fat, 0mg chol, 274mg sodium, 14g total carbs, 6g fiber, 2g prot*

Note: You can also use slender, pale purple Japanese eggplant. Remove the stems, cut in half lengthwise, and make crosshatches in the cut sides of the eggplant, cutting almost down to the skin. Arrange on the baking sheet cut sides up and follow the rest of the recipe as written.

Gingered Carrot Purée

Makes 4 side-dish servings

You can easily transform carrots, which are rich in vitamin A, into this velvety, ginger-spiked purée in a food processor. If you don't have a processor, pass the cooked carrots through a food mill or coarse sieve, and then beat in the seasonings. Try this smooth purée with Crispy Mustard Crumb Baked Chicken (page 329).

1½ pounds carrots (about
    12 slender carrots), peeled and
    cut into 1-inch pieces
1 tablespoon butter
2 teaspoons grated orange peel
1 teaspoon powdered ginger

1 teaspoon sugar
2 tablespoons orange juice
¼ teaspoon black pepper
⅛ teaspoon grated nutmeg
Salt to taste

1. Steam the carrots in a large steamer basket set over lightly salted boiling water until very tender, 25 to 30 minutes, or cook in a saucepan of lightly salted boiling water over medium heat, until very tender, about 20 minutes. Drain well.

2. In a food processor, process the carrots, in two batches if necessary, with the butter, orange peel, ginger, and sugar, to make a textured purée. Add the orange juice and process until smooth. Season with the pepper, nutmeg, and salt to taste.

3. Serve immediately or return to the saucepan to reheat gently over low heat before serving.

◆ *PER SERVING: About 109 cals, 29 cals from fat, 3g total fat, 2g sat fat, 8mg chol, 355mg sodium, 20g total carbs, 4g fiber, 2g prot*

PURÉEING VEGETABLES FOR YOUR BABY

Almost any cooked vegetable can be puréed and used as baby food. Some of the vegetables that are first introduced into an infant's diet are carrots, peas, spinach, beets, squash, and sweet potatoes. (Check with your pediatrician before adding anything new to your child's diet.) Stronger-flavored vegetables, such as broccoli and other cruciferous vegetables, are usually best introduced later.

To purée vegetables, first rinse them thoroughly under cold running water and peel them, if necessary. Cook the vegetables by steaming, boiling, or microwaving them until tender. Purée the vegetables in a food processor or blender, or mash them with a fork, adding small amounts of the cooking water to thin the purée, if necessary.

Lemon and Honey-Glazed Baby Carrots

Makes 4 side-dish servings

Baby carrots, which are already trimmed and washed, are sold in plastic bags in the produce section of your supermarket. They are an excellent convenience food and they taste wonderful with this sweet-sharp lemon and honey glaze. Serve them with Sole Rolls Florentine (page 361) or Canadian Bacon and Garlic Greens (page 396).

1½ pounds baby carrots

⅔ cup dry white wine, apple juice, or white grape juice

1½ tablespoons honey

2 teaspoons butter

½ teaspoon salt, plus additional to taste

2 strips lemon peel

2 tablespoons lemon juice

Freshly ground black pepper to taste

1. In a large nonstick skillet, combine the carrots, wine, honey, butter, salt, and lemon peel. Add enough water to barely cover the carrots. Bring to a boil, reduce the heat to medium, and simmer uncovered, stirring occasionally, until the carrots are tender and most of the liquid has evaporated, about 15 minutes. Add more water if necessary to prevent scorching. If any liquid remains, raise the heat and boil it until it cooks down to make a syrupy glaze.

2. Discard the lemon peel. Sprinkle the lemon juice over the carrots and stir. Add salt and pepper to taste and serve.

◆ *PER SERVING: About 117 cals, 20 cals from fat, 2g total fat, 1g sat fat, 5mg chol, 347mg sodium, 25g total carbs, 4g fiber, 2g prot*

EAT YOUR CARROTS!

Mom was right. Carrots are a nutritious food, supplying fiber, beta carotene (which the body converts to vitamin A), potassium, and other nutrients. Carrots are an extremely versatile vegetable. They are delicious eaten raw or grated in salads and slaws. Cooked carrots add color, texture, and a sweet flavor to stews. They also make wonderful side dishes seasoned in various ways or mashed to make a smooth purée. Whole baby carrots, available in plastic bags in the produce section, make an excellent instant snack for children.

Broccoli and Carrot Stir-Fry with Garlic

Makes 4 side-dish servings

In this recipe, broccoli florets and thinly sliced carrots are quickly stir-fried and then lightly steamed until crisp-tender. A shower of garlic and herbs finishes this deliciously nutritious side dish. If you use the broccoli stems, cut them into thin slices. You can use this recipe as a basic guide, substituting other vegetables such as cauliflower, asparagus, peppers, fennel, halved brussels sprouts, or green beans.

2 teaspoons olive oil

6 cups broccoli florets, cut from
  1 bunch of broccoli

2 carrots, peeled and cut into
  ¼-inch diagonal slices

3 garlic cloves, thinly sliced

1 tablespoon chopped fresh
  oregano or ¾ teaspoon dried

Salt and freshly ground black
  pepper to taste

1. Heat the oil in a large, preferably nonstick skillet. Add the broccoli and carrots and stir-fry over high heat until the vegetables begin to brown on the edges, about 2 minutes.

2. Add ¼ cup of water, reduce the heat to medium-low, and cook, covered, until the vegetables are crisp-tender, 2 to 3 minutes.

3. Uncover, raise the heat to medium-high. Add the garlic and oregano and stir-fry the mixture until the water evaporates and the garlic is fragrant and turns a pale golden brown, about 1 minute. Season with salt and pepper to taste and serve immediately.

◆ *PER SERVING: About 105 cals, 29 cals from fat, 3g total fat, 0g sat fat, 0mg chol, 73mg sodium, 16g total carbs, 9g fiber, 7g prot*

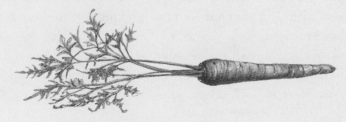

Fennel Baked with Tomatoes and Onions

Makes 4 servings

Raw bulb fennel has a crisp texture and a distinctively aniselike taste. When baked, it melts to a silken softness, and its flavor becomes richer. By sprinkling the baked vegetables in this recipe with the chopped green fennel fronds, you restore a bit of the licorice "bite." This dish is terrific with a simple broiled fish such as halibut.

1 tablespoon olive oil, preferably extra virgin

2 medium fennel bulbs (about 1 pound), reserve the fronds for garnish

1 large onion, sliced

2 medium tomatoes, seeded and coarsely chopped

½ teaspoon salt, plus additional to taste

¼ teaspoon freshly ground black pepper, plus additional to taste

2 tablespoons balsamic vinegar

1. Preheat the oven to 400 degrees. Pour the oil into a 7x11-inch baking dish. Trim the base of the fennel bulbs. Cut across the top to remove the darker green portion of the stalks and the fernlike fronds. Discard the stalks and chop and reserve ½ cup of the fronds for a garnish, if desired. Cut each fennel bulb in half lengthwise, then cut crosswise into slices about ¾ inch wide.

2. Combine the fennel in the baking dish with the onion and tomatoes. Sprinkle with salt and pepper and toss to coat evenly with the oil.

3. Cover the pan with foil and bake, stirring once or twice, until the fennel is almost tender when pierced with a fork, about 35 minutes. Uncover and continue to bake until the juices reduce and thicken slightly, about 10 minutes.

4. Before serving, drizzle with the vinegar, season with additional salt and pepper to taste, and sprinkle with the reserved fennel fronds.

◆ *PER SERVING: About 127 cals, 42 cals from fat, 5g total fat, 1g sat fat, 0mg chol, 67mg sodium, 20g total carbs, 1g fiber, 3g prot*

INTRODUCING THE ONION FAMILY

Onions are one of the most commonly used flavoring ingredients in the world. The onion family includes garlic, leeks, shallots, and chives as well as onions. Here are some of the most common types of onions and their uses:

◆ **GARLIC:** Grown and eaten all over the world, particularly in warmer climates, the volatile oils in garlic are what give it its potent, pungent flavor. It consists of a bulb or head made up of 12 to 14 individual cloves, each wrapped in a papery skin. Garlic can be eaten both raw and cooked. The more finely chopped, the more oils are released and the more pungent the garlic tastes. When cooked, it loses most of its sharp taste and takes on a mellower quality.

◆ **YELLOW AND WHITE ONIONS:** Medium to large, with fairly thick skins and a sharp, strong flavor. These onions keep well for several months and are the most common cooking varieties; they can also be used raw.

◆ **SPANISH ONIONS:** Very large, round, yellow onions with a crisp texture, and slightly higher water content and milder flavor than yellow and white onions. Spanish onions can be used either raw or cooked.

◆ **RED ONIONS:** Medium to large onions with purple-red skin and a mild, slightly sweet flavor similar to Spanish onions. Red onions are best used raw because they become watery and lose their bright color when cooked.

◆ **BOILING ONIONS:** About 1¼ to 2 inches in diameter, boiling onions are simply a smaller version of yellow or white onions and are ideal for cooking whole or in stews.

◆ **PEARL ONIONS:** These onions are a smaller version of the boiling onion and are also good in soups and stews.

◆ **SHALLOTS:** Small, oval, and brown-skinned, shallots are a mild-flavored onion used raw in salads and dressings and cooked to flavor sauces.

◆ **FRESH, SWEET ONIONS:** Large, juicy, mild onions with a high sugar content that are harvested in the spring or early summer and sold soon after harvest. Sweet onions are marketed under regional names such as Vidalia, Maui, and Walla Walla. Because of their sugar content, they caramelize easily when cooked and are also delicious eaten raw in salads or on sandwiches.

◆ **SCALLIONS:** Also called green onions or spring onions, these onions are harvested when young, while the bulbs are slender and the green tops are still intact. Sold in bunches, scallions are mild in flavor and can be used both cooked and raw.

◆ **LEEKS:** Resembling a large scallion, leeks are almost always eaten cooked. They have a mellow, mildly earthy, onion flavor. Leeks must be cleaned thoroughly to remove hidden grit and dirt before using.

◆ **CHIVES:** This member of the onion family has pretty purple or white flowers and fine, tubular, grasslike leaves. The green leaves, which have a subtle onion flavor, can be chopped or snipped and used to flavor or garnish many dishes including soups, sauces, salads, and eggs.

TO COOK CORN

Sweet, fresh corn on the cob is one of the glories of summer. Cook corn using one of these methods:

◆ In a large pot of boiling water: Add a pinch of sugar or a spoonful of milk to sweeten the water (do not add salt, it toughens the kernels), and cook the husked ears at a rapid boil until the juices are no longer milky when a kernel is pierced with a knife, 2 to 10 minutes, depending on the size and age of the corn (older corn needs to cook longer).

◆ In a microwave oven: Husk the ears, arrange side by side in a microwave-safe dish, add 2 to 3 tablespoons of water, and cover the dish with plastic wrap. Cook on high power, rotating the dish two or three times, until the corn is tender, 4 to 10 minutes, depending on the number and size of the ears. Let stand for 2 to 3 minutes before stripping off the husks and silk. You can also microwave corn in the husk; just remove a few of the outer leaves. The remaining leaves are full of water and will keep the corn moist. Corn is delicious and plump when prepared this way, and you don't lose any nutrients to the cooking water.

◆ On the grill: Peel back the husks and remove the corn silk. Pull the husks back up over the ears and soak the corn in cold water for 15 minutes. Place the corn directly on the grill rack and cook, turning occasionally, until the husks are charred and the kernels are tender, 10 to 15 minutes.

Roasted Winter Vegetables and Whole Garlic

Makes 6 side-dish servings

When slowly roasted, the vegetables in this side dish caramelize and become sweet while the garlic softens and mellows. You can substitute other firm vegetables such as white potatoes or sweet potatoes, bulb fennel, or pearl onions. This side dish makes the most of Apple-Sage Glazed Game Hens (page 349) or other roast poultry or meat.

1 pound carrots (about 8 slender
    carrots), peeled and cut in
    2-inch pieces
1 pound white turnips (about 4
    small-medium turnips), peeled
    and cut in 2-inch chunks
1 pound winter squash such as
    Hubbard or butternut, peeled
    and cut in 2-inch chunks
2 tablespoons olive oil
1 teaspoon dried thyme or 2 tablespoons
    chopped fresh thyme
Salt and freshly ground black pepper to taste
1 whole head of garlic

1. Preheat the oven to 400 degrees. In a large, shallow roasting pan, combine the carrots, turnips, and squash. Drizzle with the olive oil and sprinkle with the dried thyme (if using fresh thyme, add later in recipe), salt, and pepper, and toss until the vegetables are well coated with oil. Break the garlic into individual cloves, removing and discarding as much of the excess papery outer skin as possible. Add to the roasting pan and toss with the vegetables.

2. Roast the vegetables uncovered for 10 minutes. Reduce the heat to 350 degrees and continue to cook, stirring once or twice with a metal spatula, until the vegetables are tender and lightly caramelized, 40 to 50 minutes. If using fresh thyme, sprinkle it over the vegetables during the last 5 minutes of cooking.

3. Season to taste with additional salt and pepper before serving. Squeeze the garlic out of its skin and combine it with the other vegetables.

◆ *PER SERVING: About 111 cals, 43 cals from fat, 5g total fat, 1g sat fat, 0mg chol, 58mg sodium, 18g total carbs, 5g fiber, 2g prot*

Cauliflower with Cumin and Fresh Ginger

Makes 4 side-dish servings

In this Indian-inspired recipe, the cauliflower florets cook slowly with the fragrant spices, becoming a rich amber color as they absorb the aromatic seasonings. At the end, sprinkle the vegetable with dark green chopped cilantro to make a very pretty dish to serve to friends or family.

1 medium-large head of cauliflower (about 3 pounds), trimmed and broken into florets	¾ teaspoon cumin seeds, coarsely crushed in a mortar and pestle or spice mill
1 tablespoon vegetable oil	1 garlic clove, finely chopped
1 tablespoon minced fresh ginger	Salt and pepper to taste
2 teaspoons curry powder	2 tablespoons chopped cilantro

1. Arrange the cauliflower florets in a large steamer basket and steam over lightly salted boiling water until crisp-tender, about 5 minutes.

2. Heat the oil in a large, preferably nonstick skillet. Add the ginger, curry powder, and cumin, and cook over medium heat, stirring, until the spices are fragrant, about 1 minute. Add the garlic and cook, stirring, for 1 minute. Add the cauliflower and stir to coat with the spice mixture.

3. Add ½ cup of water to the pan and season the cauliflower with salt and pepper. Bring to a boil, reduce the heat to low, and cook covered, stirring occasionally, until the cauliflower is very tender, about 20 minutes. If the water begins to boil away, add more water, 1 tablespoon at a time, to prevent the spices from burning.

4. Sprinkle with the cilantro before serving.

◆ *PER SERVING: About 90 cals, 40 cals from fat, 4g total fat, 0g sat fat, 0mg chol, 106mg sodium, 10g total carbs, 9g fiber, 7g prot*

THE CRUCIFEROUS FAMILY

Cruciferous vegetables include broccoli, broccoflower, brussels sprouts, cabbage, cauliflower, chard, kale, mustard greens, rutabagas, and turnips. All are high in fiber, vitamins, and minerals.

Researchers are examining many promising chemical compounds in cruciferous vegetables that seem to confer health benefits. For example, broccoli contains several compounds that may have cancer-fighting properties. Other cruciferous vegetables, such as turnips, are also being studied for their potential to prevent or combat disease.

Sautéed Zucchini Shreds with Herbed Yogurt

Makes 4 side-dish servings

In this dish, zucchini is shredded and some of its excess liquid removed to concentrate and intensify its flavor. The zucchini shreds are then sautéed with a bit of garlic and finished with a cooling swirl of herbed yogurt.

1 pound zucchini
½ teaspoon salt, plus additional
   to taste
½ cup nonfat plain yogurt
2 tablespoons chopped fresh mint
2 tablespoons chopped fresh dill
¼ teaspoon cayenne pepper

2 teaspoons olive oil
1 garlic clove, finely chopped
3 tablespoons defatted lower-
   sodium chicken broth
Freshly ground black pepper
   to taste

1. Cut off the zucchini stems and coarsely grate the zucchini with a hand grater or chop it in a food processor. Transfer to a colander, sprinkle with ½ teaspoon salt, and let stand for 30 minutes. Press the zucchini with the palm of your hand to extract the excess liquid. Transfer to paper towels and pat dry.

2. In a small bowl, stir together the yogurt, mint, dill, and cayenne pepper.

3. Heat the oil in a large, preferably nonstick skillet. Add the zucchini and cook over medium-high heat, stirring almost constantly, until softened and lightly tinged with brown, 4 to 5 minutes. Add the garlic and chicken broth and cook, stirring, for 1 minute. Season with salt and black pepper to taste.

4. Serve the zucchini with the herbed yogurt spooned over the top.

◆ *PER SERVING: About 53 cals, 21 cals from fat, 2g total fat, 0g sat fat, 1mg chol, 292mg sodium, 6g total carbs, 1g fiber, 2g prot*

KEEPING NUTRIENTS IN COOKED VEGETABLES

Vegetables retain the most nutrients when you cook them for the shortest time in the least amount of water. Some vitamins are destroyed by heat; other vitamins and minerals leach into cooking water. Microwaving preserves vitamins and minerals because it cooks the vegetables quickly using small amounts of water. Steaming is another good method to prevent nutrient loss. Add any leftover vegetable cooking water to soups and stews to boost their nutrient content.

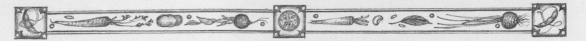

Greens with Bacon and Onion

Makes 4 side-dish servings

The classic, irresistible combination of greens and bacon is lightened up and updated in this recipe. Try it as a side dish to Kentucky Bean and Vegetable Stew (page 309).

2 pounds turnip, collard, kale, mustard, or other greens, stemmed, washed, and coarsely chopped

1 slice (about 1 ounce) bacon, chopped

1 medium onion, chopped

½ cup defatted lower-sodium chicken broth

2 teaspoons cider vinegar

Salt and freshly ground black pepper to taste

1. Cook the greens in a large pot of salted water, covered, over medium heat until almost tender, 7 to 9 minutes. Drain into a colander.

2. Cook the bacon in a large, preferably nonstick skillet over medium heat until crisp, about 6 minutes. Remove with a slotted spoon, leaving the drippings in the pan. Add the onion and cook, stirring frequently, until it softens, about 4 minutes. Stir in the greens, add the broth, and cook, covered, until the greens are tender, about 5 minutes.

3. Add the vinegar, toss to combine, and season with salt and pepper to taste. Serve topped with the cooked bacon bits.

◆ *PER SERVING: About 98 cals, 14 cals from fat, 2g total fat, 0g sat fat, 2mg chol, 83mg sodium, 19g total carbs, 9g fiber, 5g prot*

Mixed Mushroom Sauté with Tarragon

Makes 4 side-dish servings

You can use one type of mushroom or any combination for this deliciously versatile side dish that tastes wonderful with almost any meat.

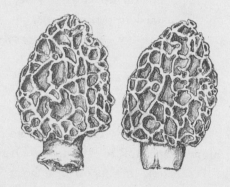

1 tablespoon olive oil, preferably extra virgin
½ pound domestic mushrooms, quartered
½ pound fresh wild mushrooms, such as
   morels, shiitake, or oyster mushrooms,
   trimmed and sliced (see note)
¼ cup finely chopped shallots
½ cup dry white wine
2 tablespoons chopped fresh tarragon
   or 1 teaspoon dried
Salt and freshly ground black pepper to taste
2 tablespoons chopped parsley, preferably flat leaf

1. Heat the oil in a large, preferably nonstick skillet. Add the mushrooms and cook over medium-high heat, stirring frequently, until they produce liquid and begin to soften and brown, about 4 minutes. Add the shallots and cook, stirring, for 1 minute. Add the wine and tarragon to the skillet. Cook, uncovered, over medium heat until most of the liquid is reduced and absorbed and the mushrooms are tender, 2 to 3 minutes.

2. Season with salt and pepper to taste and sprinkle with the parsley before serving.

◆ *PER SERVING: About 90 cals, 33 cals from fat, 4g total fat, 0g sat fat, 0mg chol, 9mg sodium, 5g total carbs, 0g fiber, 4g prot*

Note: If the shiitakes are large and the stems are very tough, discard the stems.

FRESH, FROZEN, AND CANNED VEGETABLES

Fresh and frozen vegetables compare well nutritionally, as long as they have been handled properly from harvest to table. To prevent nutrient loss, try to cook fresh vegetables as soon after harvest as possible, because light, air, and heat destroy vitamins over time.

Frozen vegetables should stay well frozen until you cook them. If a box of vegetables looks like it was frozen on a slant or a bag contains large icy clumps of vegetables, the contents have probably been thawed and refrozen; the vegetables may have lost nutrients.

Canned vegetables are higher in sodium than fresh or frozen unless they have been processed without salt. Otherwise, they may be comparable nutritionally to cooked vegetables. The canning liquid contains some of the nutrients leached out from the vegetables.

MUSHROOMS

Numerous varieties of mushrooms, both cultivated and wild, now appear in markets nationwide. Although mushrooms are relatively nutrient-poor, their intense, earthy taste enhances the flavor of many dishes. Raw mushrooms have only about 12 calories per half cup.

Although the flavors of mushrooms range from delicate to robust, all need the same care in handling. Buy only dry and firm mushrooms with tight caps and gills. Refrigerate them in a paper bag or loosely wrapped in a paper towel (plastic traps too much moisture), and cook them within 2 to 3 days. Mushrooms absorb liquid, so, instead of rinsing them under running water, wipe them clean with damp paper towels. If the stems are tough, remove them, then trim and cut the caps as needed.

NAME (COMMON NAME)	WILD OR CULTIVATED/ AVAILABLE DRIED	DESCRIPTION/FLAVOR	COOKING USES/TECHNIQUES
BUTTON MUSHROOMS (cultivated, domestic, white, common)	Cultivated only	Commonly available; small to large; snow white or fawn-colored; tightly closed caps; short stems/mild flavor	All-purpose; sauces, salads, gravies, stuffings/cooked or raw
CÈPES (porcini, boletus)	Wild/dried	Large reddish-brown caps (2 to 6 inches in diameter); white or creamy-brown stem/earthy, smoky flavor	Stews or risottos/ sautéed
CHANTERELLE (girolles)	Wild or cultivated/ dried	Trumpet-shaped; deep golden-orange; small to large (1 to 4 inches); delicate texture/peppery when raw, apricotlike when cooked	Poultry or fish/cook slowly over low heat
CREMINI (Roman)	Cultivated only	Related to button mushroom but large brown cap/more intense flavor	Use like button mushroom
ENOKI (enok)	Wild or cultivated	Snow-white clusters of long, thin stems with tiny caps/delicate, mild flavor	Salads or sandwiches/ raw or briefly stir-fried
MORELS	Wild/dried	Beige to dark brown; long, spongy, conical cap; hollow stems; earthy perfume; appears in early spring/nutlike flavor	Sauces, gravies, with eggs
OYSTER MUSHROOMS (Pleurottes)	Wild or cultivated/dried	Ruffled, fan-shaped caps; gray, beige, or white; soft, silky texture/mild flavor	Meats such as sausages and roast pork/sautéed
PORTOBELLO	Wild or cultivated	Dark brown; large caps (up to 8 inches in diameter)/woodsy, meaty taste	Marinated, grilled, or broiled (whole) or sautéed (sliced)
STRAW MUSHROOMS	Wild/canned	Small; light brown oval cap; springy texture/mild flavor	Use in Asian stir-fries
WOOD EAR MUSHROOMS (tree ear, cloud ear)	Cultivated/ dried	Dark brown; flower-shaped caps; crunchy texture; no stems/mild flavor	Use in Asian stir-fries and vegetable dishes
SHIITAKE (Japanese mushrooms)	Wild in Japan, cultivated in North America/dried	Parasol-shaped brown-black caps (2 to 4 inches); creamy gills and stems/ intense, woodsy, meaty flavor	Use in sauces, gravies, stews, or casseroles; stems used to flavor stock

CHAPTER THIRTEEN

Desserts

Many a meal would be incomplete without dessert, that little something sweet that lends a final touch to mealtime. What would a birthday or holiday be without a special dessert to celebrate the occasion? We start life out with a natural sweet tooth, and it stays with us all our lives.

Fresh fruit, brimming with vitamins, minerals, and fiber, makes dessert guilt-free. And nothing beats the flavor, texture, and juiciness of fruit when it's at the height of ripeness. For simple elegance, serve fruit alone or tossed with other fruits to bring out the flavor, as in Cranberry-Orange Parfaits (page 448). Poached fruits, with their softer texture and mellower flavor, are a simple, light, and extremely versatile partner for a simple cookie or a slice of Classic Angel Cake (page 453). In many countries around the world, dessert would not be dessert without fruit.

But think again if you believe that fruit is the *only* healthful dessert. In fact, you can make many traditional desserts in a way that improves their nutritional profile without sacrificing flavor. Take rice pudding, for example. By just switching the whole milk in your favorite traditional recipe to low-fat or skim milk, you will lower both the fat and calories considerably. Try the Bombay Rice Pudding recipe (page 465) in this chapter for an unusual but delicious and healthful treat.

Cakes are a little trickier to modify because most need butter, margarine, or another type of fat for flakiness and moistness. The key is to find recipes that substitute other moist ingredients for some (but not all) of the fat. For example, the mashed bananas in the Banana Spice Cake with Seafoam Icing (page 458) add so much texture and flavor that you'd never know the cake is lower in fat.

The many tasty lower-fat dairy products on the market make it a breeze to create healthier versions of classic desserts. Low-fat ricotta cheese makes a deliciously smooth—and very low-fat—filling for Strawberry-Ricotta Cake Roll (page 460). A combination of low-fat cottage cheese and Neufchâtel (lower-fat) cream cheese in Orange Marmalade–Glazed Cheesecake (page 464) replaces the full-fat cream cheese that is traditionally used. And instead of apple pie with full-fat ice cream, try Date and Cranberry Baked Apples (page 449) topped with a dollop of reduced-fat ice cream or frozen yogurt.

You can even make luscious chocolate desserts with less fat and fewer calories. The secret is to use highly flavored ingredients like cocoa powder, which has very little fat, small amounts of high-quality chocolate, and coffee powder. All contribute their intense flavors to Double Chocolate Brownies (page 475), a dessert that also uses applesauce for moistness. Hot Fudge Soufflé (page 476) combines cocoa, cinnamon, and vanilla for high-impact flavor. After eating either of these desserts, any chocoholic will leave the table entirely satisfied.

Feel free to adapt this chapter's recipes to your own tastes. Make Raspberry Coulis (page 455) with a different berry or serve Candied Gingerbread (page 462) with the Warm Citrus Sauce (page 463) or a different sauce. The possibilities are limitless.

Many of the desserts in this chapter count as a Food Guide Pyramid serving of fruit. But, unless a dessert is made almost exclusively from fruit, it will count as a tip-of-the-Pyramid food to be eaten in moderation. Here's where you can benefit from increasing your activity. The more calories you burn, the more extra calories you have to spend. Certainly some of those calories can be spent on a tasty dessert.

Healthful eating means saying yes to dessert— but a new type of dessert that is lower in fat and nutritious as well as delicious.

Amaretti Baked Pears

Makes 4 servings

Marsala wine and pears make a wonderful combination for a sophisticated dessert, but orange juice is very pleasing too. Amaretti are crunchy Italian cookies. Because a food processor can overprocess the cookies, it's best to crush them in a plastic bag using a rolling pin.

4 small ripe but firm pears, such as
   Bosc or Anjou (about 1½ pounds)
1 tablespoon fresh lemon juice
½ cup marsala or orange juice
1½ teaspoons unsalted butter,
   cut into small pieces

2 tablespoons light brown sugar
⅛ teaspoon ground cinnamon
6 tablespoons (about 1½ ounces)
   coarsely crushed amaretti
   cookies

1. Preheat the oven to 350 degrees. Peel and core the pears, then cut them in half lengthwise (see note). Brush the pears with lemon juice and set them in a 9x9-inch or other similar size shallow baking dish. Pour the marsala over and around the pears. Scatter the butter over the pears. In a small bowl, combine the brown sugar, cinnamon, and amaretti crumbs, then sprinkle them over the pears.

2. Bake the pears, uncovered, until they are tender and the pan juices are thickened, about 40 to 45 minutes. Baste several times with the pan juices. (The pears can be baked ahead and kept at room temperature for up to 2 hours.) Serve warm or at room temperature with the pan juices spooned over them.

◆ *PER SERVING: About 253 cals, 59 cals from fat, 7g total fat, 2g sat fat, 8mg chol, 28mg sodium, 45g total carbs, 5g fiber, 3g prot*

Note: The pears can also be baked whole. Peel them, but leave the stem intact. Cut off a small slice from the bottom so the pears will stand upright. Increase the baking time to 50 to 60 minutes.

BROWN BAGGING FOR RIPENESS

Some fruits—such as peaches, pears, apricots, mangoes, papayas, and melons (except watermelon)—are often picked and shipped when underripe.

You can ripen them at home by placing them in a loosely closed paper bag and letting them stand for a day or so. The bag traps the ethylene gas that fruits naturally

give off, hastening the ripening. Do not ripen fruit in an airtight plastic bag because moisture will accumulate and the fruit will quickly spoil.

Almond Meringues with Purple Plum Compote

Makes 6 servings

This fancy autumn dessert is easy to make. You can vary the dessert with the season using Double Strawberry Sauce (page 461) in spring or Raspberry Coulis (page 455) in summer. The meringues are also good filled with frozen yogurt or sorbet.

Meringues:

3 egg whites, brought to room
   temperature
½ teaspoon cream of tartar
Pinch of salt
1 teaspoon vanilla
½ teaspoon almond extract
¾ cup granulated sugar

Purple Plum Compote:

6 ripe purple plums, pitted and
   sliced
6 tablespoons granulated sugar
3 tablespoons brandy or orange
   juice
¾ tablespoon grated lemon peel

1. For the meringues, preheat the oven to 275 degrees. Using a 3-inch biscuit cutter or cardboard circle, trace six circles on parchment paper, leaving at least 2 inches in between each. Place the parchment paper on a large baking sheet.

2. In a large bowl, beat the egg whites until frothy, about 3 to 5 minutes. Add the cream of tartar and salt and beat until soft peaks form. Add the vanilla and almond extract, then beat in the sugar, 2 tablespoons at a time, until the meringue is stiff and glossy.

3. Dab a little meringue under the corners of the parchment to "glue" it to the baking sheet. Spoon the meringue into a pastry bag fitted with a plain ½-inch tip or use a spoon to form the meringue nests. Pipe or spoon the meringue to the edges of the traced circles, building up the sides and depressing the center.

4. Bake the meringues until they are straw colored and no longer sticky to the touch, 35 to 40 minutes. (The meringues will expand during baking.) Turn off the heat and let the meringues dry in the oven for 1 hour. Transfer the baking sheet to a rack and let the meringues cool completely. Carefully peel the parchment paper from the meringues. (The meringues can be made 2 days ahead and stored, tightly covered, at room temperature.)

5. For the compote, combine the plums, sugar, brandy, and lemon peel in a bowl, stirring to dissolve the sugar. Let the compote stand at least 30 minutes at room temperature or refrigerate up to 3 hours before using.

6. To serve, place the meringues on dessert plates and spoon in the compote.

◆ *PER SERVING: About 212 cals, 4 cals from fat, 0g total fat, 0g sat fat, 0mg chol, 50mg sodium, 47g total carbs, 1g fiber, 2g prot*

Blackberry-Peach Cobbler

Makes 6 servings

If you can't get blackberries, try blueberries in this wonderful, old-fashioned cobbler. In fact, nearly any berries except strawberries will make a good cobbler, especially when you pair them with peaches.

Vegetable oil spray

Filling:
2 cups fresh or thawed frozen
   blackberries
2 cups peeled and thinly sliced
   peaches (about 4 or 5 peaches)
⅔ cup granulated sugar
1 tablespoon cornstarch
2 teaspoons lemon juice
⅛ teaspoon cinnamon

Dough:
1 cup all-purpose flour
3 tablespoons granulated sugar,
   plus 1 teaspoon
1 teaspoon baking powder
½ teaspoon baking soda
⅛ teaspoon salt
1 tablespoon cold unsalted butter,
   cut into 6 pieces
¾ teaspoon grated lemon peel
½ cup low-fat buttermilk
1 tablespoon vegetable oil

1. Preheat the oven to 400 degrees. Coat a deep, 9-inch pie plate with vegetable oil spray.

2. For the filling, combine the blackberries, peaches, sugar, cornstarch, lemon juice, and cinnamon in a mixing bowl. Stir to mix well, then spoon into the prepared pie plate.

3. For the dough, whisk together the flour, 3 tablespoons sugar, the baking powder, baking soda, and salt in a mixing bowl. Using a pastry blender or two knives, cut the butter into the flour mixture until it becomes crumbly. Stir in the lemon peel. Whisk together the buttermilk and oil in a small bowl. Pour the liquid into the dry ingredients in the bowl. Use a large fork to stir the mixture just until the dough is combined and moistened. Turn the dough out onto a lightly floured work surface. Roll or pat it into a rough 8-inch circle. Lift the dough circle and lay it over the fruit in the dish. The dough will be soft and may tear; simply pinch and patch the tears together (the dough is supposed to look "cobbled"). Prick the dough in several places with the tines of a fork, then sprinkle the top with the remaining 1 teaspoon sugar.

4. Bake the cobbler until the fruit is bubbly and the dough turns golden brown, 25 to 30 minutes. Let cool, then serve slightly warm or at room temperature.

◆ *PER SERVING: About 291 cals, 44 cals from fat, 5g total fat, 2g sat fat, 6mg chol, 233mg sodium, 60g total carbs, 5g fiber, 4g prot*

THE ROLE OF FAT IN BAKING

Fat tenderizes baked goods and adds flavor and moisture. It makes pastry flaky, cakes tender, and cookies crisp or chewy. But all fats are not alike, so you can't use them interchangeably in baking. Reduced-fat butters and margarines, which contain more air or water than regular fats, are usually not suitable for baking in conventional recipes. Here are the baking properties of commonly used fats:

◆ **BUTTER:** Unsalted butter is best in baking because It has a more consistent flavor. Use only regular stick butter unless the recipe specifies otherwise. Do not use whipped butter, which has air in it, or "light" butter, which has added water. Butter has about 107 calories and 12 grams of fat (8 grams of saturated fat) per tablespoon.

◆ **MARGARINE:** You can substitute regular stick margarine for butter in most recipes, although the flavor will be different. Margarine also tends to be "greasier," which you will especially note in cookies. Do not use whipped or "light" margarine in baking. Margarine has about 100 calories and 11 grams of fat (2 grams of saturated fat) per tablespoon.

◆ **SOLID VEGETABLE SHORTENING:** You can often substitute shortening for butter in baking, although it will not always produce the same texture. Shortening produces chewier cookies and flakier pie crusts, but adds no real flavor of its own. Butter-flavored shortening can be used in place of regular shortening. Shortening has about 110 calories and 12 grams of fat (3 grams of saturated fat) per tablespoon.

◆ **VEGETABLE OIL:** Oils usually cannot be substituted for solid fat in recipes. Vegetable oil has about 120 calories and 14 grams of fat (1 gram of saturated fat), depending on the type of oil.

Rhubarb Fool

Makes 4 servings

A fool is an English dessert, made from fruit purée swirled through whipped cream or custard. This lightened version features rhubarb and low-fat vanilla yogurt.

1 pound fresh or thawed frozen
rhubarb stalks, trimmed and cut
into ½-inch slices
½ cup granulated sugar
½ cup orange juice

¼ teaspoon ground mace
3 tablespoons orange liqueur or
additional orange juice
2 cups low-fat vanilla yogurt

1. In a nonreactive saucepan, bring the rhubarb, sugar, orange juice, and mace to a simmer, stirring to dissolve the sugar. Partially cover the pan and simmer over medium-low heat, stirring occasionally until the rhubarb is very soft and mushy, 5 to 7 minutes. Stir in the liqueur. Let the purée cool completely.

2. In four stemmed goblets or dessert dishes, alternate two or three layers of the yogurt and rhubarb mixture. Gently cut through the layers and swirl with a knife. Serve immediately or refrigerate up to 1 hour before serving.

◆ *PER SERVING: About 284 cals, 11 cals from fat, 1g total fat, 0g sat fat, 5mg chol, 45mg sodium, 61g total carbs, 2g fiber, 5g prot*

Banana Berry Smoothie

Makes 2 servings

This treat can be served as a dessert, snack, or even breakfast. Vary the yogurt and berry flavors for even more versatility. This smoothie is a super way to use extra-ripe bananas.

2 ripe soft bananas
1 teaspoon fresh lemon juice, plus
   1 tablespoon
1 cup plain low-fat yogurt
1 cup sliced fresh or frozen
   unsweetened strawberries
3 tablespoons honey
1 tablespoon orange juice
2 whole strawberries for garnish

1. Peel and slice the bananas. Sprinkle them with 1 teaspoon lemon juice, then place them in a sturdy plastic bag and freeze them until solid, about 2 hours or up to 24 hours.

2. Place the frozen banana pieces, yogurt, strawberries, honey, orange juice, and remaining lemon juice in a blender or food processor. Process to make a thick purée.

3. Pour the smoothie into two tall glasses, garnish with the whole berries, and serve.

◆ *PER SERVING: About 308 cals, 24 cals from fat, 3g total fat, 1g sat fat, 7mg chol, 83mg sodium, 68g total carbs, 4g fiber, 8g prot*

MAKING FRUIT SORBET

You can make nearly any fruit into a terrific sorbet. Peel and cut 1 pound of nectarines, peaches, melons, or very ripe bananas into 1-inch chunks; cut 1 pound of unpeeled plums into 1-inch chunks; or stem 3 cups of strawberries and spread the fruit on a baking sheet. Freeze until firm.

Make a simple syrup by boiling ⅔ cup water with ⅓ cup sugar, stirring until the sugar dissolves and the syrup is clear, about 2 minutes. Let cool. (The syrup can be stored in the refrigerator up to 3 months.) In a food processor, process the fruit with 2 teaspoons lemon juice. Then slowly pour in the syrup, and process to make a coarse purée. Serve immediately or refreeze up to 24 hours, then reprocess briefly to break up any ice crystals. Coarsely purée the sorbet again if it has hardened too much.

THE SCOOP ON FROZEN DESSERTS

In general, all types of ice cream and frozen yogurt are interchangeable in recipes. Those with a lower milk-fat content melt faster and crystallize more when refrozen. Sherbet and sorbet are equivalent, but sorbet crystallizes more and melts faster. You can sometimes, but not always, substitute gelato and frozen tofu for ice cream or sherbet.

NAME	PERCENT OF MILK FAT	DESCRIPTION
REGULAR ICE CREAM	10 to 20 percent	Nuts, crushed cookies, or candy bars in the ice cream increase the calorie and fat content
REDUCED-FAT ICE CREAM	At least 25 percent less fat than regular ice cream	
LIGHT ICE CREAM	At least 50 percent less fat than regular ice cream	
LOW-FAT ICE CREAM (ICE MILK)	3 grams of fat or less per ½-cup serving	
NONFAT ICE CREAM	Less than 0.5 grams of fat per ½-cup serving	
FROZEN YOGURT	Fat content labeling subject to same standards as ice cream	Because of the active cultures, tends to have more sugar in it than ice cream
SHERBET	Between 1 and 2 percent	Usually flavored with fruit
SORBET, GRANITA, OR FRUIT ICE	Fat free	Similar to sherbet, but contains no dairy products; texture varies according to the amount of fruit and sugar
GELATO	No official standard	Semifrozen ice cream–like dessert that contains milk, cream, egg yolks, flavoring, and sweeteners
FROZEN TOFU	No official standard	Dairy-free and cholesterol-free but not necessarily low in fat

MAKE A GOOD THING GOOD FOR YOU

◆ Make a frozen yogurt parfait with toasted oatmeal or unsweetened ready-to-eat breakfast cereal.
◆ Spoon sliced or puréed berries over puddings or frozen yogurt.

◆ Dip bananas into low-fat granola and freeze.
◆ Make graham cracker sandwiches with peanut butter and pure fruit spread.

◆ Sandwich banana slices between vanilla wafers.
◆ Sweeten and flavor plain yogurt with puréed fresh fruit.

Cranberry-Orange Parfaits

Makes 8 servings

Though it contains ingredients reminiscent of the cold weather holidays, this dessert makes a refreshing finale to summer meals. It is rich in vitamin C and is a source of both fiber and calcium, so serve it often.

12 ounces fresh or frozen cranberries (3 cups)

¼ cup dried cranberries or cherries

1 cup granulated sugar

1½ cups orange juice

3 tablespoons finely chopped candied ginger,
   plus 1 tablespoon for garnish

2 teaspoons grated orange peel

6 tablespoons cranberry or orange
   liqueur or additional orange juice

1 quart low-fat vanilla frozen yogurt

1. Place the fresh and dried cranberries, sugar, orange juice, 3 tablespoons ginger, and orange peel in a heavy, nonreactive saucepan. Bring to a boil, stirring constantly to dissolve the sugar. Reduce the heat to medium-low and simmer, partially covered, until all the berries have popped and the sauce is lightly thickened, 8 to 10 minutes. Remove from the heat and stir in the liqueur. Let cool to room temperature. (You can make the sauce up to 3 days ahead and refrigerate it. Return it to room temperature to use, thinning with a little orange juice if it becomes too thick.)

2. To assemble the parfaits, place three alternate layers each of frozen yogurt and cranberry mixture in tall sherbet or parfait glasses. Sprinkle the tops of the parfaits with the remaining 1 tablespoon candied ginger.

◆ *PER SERVING: About 311 cals, 10 cals from fat, 1g total fat, 0g sat fat, 5mg chol, 43mg sodium, 69g total carbs, 3g fiber, 4g prot*

SUGAR: USE THE REAL THING

Unless a recipe has been specifically developed for artificial sweeteners, you cannot substitute them for sugar in baking. Brown sugar can sometimes, but not always, be substituted for granulated sugar. Honey cannot be used as a substitute because it is a liquid.

Date and Cranberry Baked Apples

Makes 6 servings

To make chopping dates easier, first sprinkle the cutting board with a little granulated sugar, or snip the dates into small pieces with sharp scissors dampened and dipped in sugar. You can substitute other dried fruits, but cranberries seem just right for this warm fall-like dessert. For baking, use a juicy apple that keeps its shape, such as Golden Delicious, Cortland, Rome Beauty, Gala, or Crispin. This is a dessert that the whole family will love.

Vegetable oil spray
6 large juicy baking apples
2 tablespoons dark brown sugar
¼ cup chopped dates
¼ cup chopped dried cranberries
2 tablespoons finely chopped
    crystallized ginger
½ teaspoon ground cinnamon

½ teaspoon grated lemon peel
1½ tablespoons unsalted butter,
    cut into 6 pieces
1 cup orange juice
¼ cup honey
1 tablespoon lemon juice
Low-fat sour cream or vanilla or
    lemon yogurt (optional)

1. Preheat the oven to 375 degrees. Coat a 9x13-inch baking dish with vegetable oil spray. Core the apples and peel them about halfway down.

2. In a small bowl, mix together the brown sugar, dates, cranberries, ginger, cinnamon, and lemon peel. Divide the mixture evenly among the apples, spooning it into the core cavities. Top each apple with a piece of butter. Arrange the apples in the prepared baking dish.

3. In a small saucepan, heat the orange juice, honey, and lemon juice, stirring until the honey melts. Pour around the apples.

4. Bake the apples, uncovered. Spoon the pan juices over the apples until they are tender but not mushy when pierced with a knife tip, 40 to 45 minutes.

5. Remove the pan from the oven and continue to spoon the juices over the apples two or three times to glaze them as they cool to lukewarm. (The apples can be baked several hours ahead and kept at room temperature. Reheat slightly in the oven or in a microwave oven before serving.)

6. To serve, spoon the apples and juices into shallow dessert dishes. Serve the apples slightly warm, with a dollop of sour cream or yogurt, if desired.

◆ *PER SERVING: About 271 cals, 33 cals from fat, 4g total fat, 2g sat fat, 8mg chol, 6mg sodium, 64g total carbs, 7g fiber, 1g prot*

Fresh Apricot Soufflé

Makes 6 servings

The fragrance of ripe apricots is very enticing. Look for them from June through September. At other times of the year, make this fat-free soufflé with dried or canned apricots (see note). All supply vitamins A and C.

1½ pounds fresh apricots, pitted and
   quartered, but not peeled
¾ cup granulated sugar, extra for
   dusting, plus 2 tablespoons
2 tablespoons orange liqueur,
   plus 1 tablespoon
2 tablespoons cornstarch
3 tablespoons cold orange juice
Vegetable oil spray
5 egg whites
¼ teaspoon cream of tartar

1. Place all but one of the apricots in a medium saucepan and barely cover them with water. Cover the pot and simmer over medium-low heat until the apricots are soft, about 8 minutes. Remove the apricots using a slotted spoon, and purée them in a food processor or blender with ¾ cup of the sugar and 2 tablespoons of the liqueur.

2. Measure out ¾ cup of the purée. Chop the one remaining apricot and stir it into the purée along with the remaining 1 tablespoon of orange liqueur. Set aside at room temperature to use as a sauce.

3. In the saucepan used to cook the apricots, stir the cornstarch into the cold orange juice until dissolved. Stir in the remaining apricot purée. Cook, stirring over medium-low heat until the purée just comes to a boil. Remove from the heat and let cool to room temperature. (This recipe can be prepared to this point up to 4 hours ahead. Reserve at room temperature.)

4. Preheat the oven to 350 degrees. Lightly coat a 1½-quart soufflé dish with nonstick vegetable oil spray. Dust with granulated sugar.

5. Beat the egg whites until frothy in a large mixing bowl. Add the cream of tartar, and beat until soft peaks form. Add 2 tablespoons of the sugar, and beat just until stiff peaks form. Fold the egg whites into the apricot base until no streaks of white remain. Spoon into the prepared soufflé dish.

6. Place the soufflé dish in a baking pan and fill the pan half full with hot water. Bake the soufflé until it puffs up and has a rich, golden-brown top, 30 to 35 minutes.

7. Serve the hot soufflé immediately with the room-temperature apricot sauce spooned over it.

◆ *PER SERVING: About 208 cals, 4 cals from fat, 0g total fat, 0g sat fat, 0mg chol, 48mg sodium, 46g total carbs, 2g fiber, 4g prot*

Note: To make this recipe from canned apricots, drain and purée 2 cans (1 pound each) of apricots in light syrup. Reduce the sugar to ⅓ cup. To make it with dried apricots, simmer ½ pound of dried apricots in 1 cup of water until soft, about 15 minutes. Purée them with the cooking liquid and 1 tablespoon of sugar.

DRIED AND CANNED FRUIT

Dried fruit is simply fruit with the moisture removed, and canned fruit is cooked fruit that is sometimes sweetened. Both dried and canned fruit retain most of the same nutrients as their fresh counterparts. Drying fruit intensifies the natural flavors and sugars, giving an almost candylike taste that makes a nutritious snack.

Among the more common dried fruits are raisins, which are dried grapes, and prunes, which are dried plums. Apricots, peaches, figs, apples, currants, and pineapples are also commonly available dried. Dark and sweet cherries, as well as cranberries and blueberries are becoming increasingly obtainable; you can substitute them whenever a recipe calls for raisins. Canned fruit tends to be quite sweet, although many fruits are now canned in juice without added sugar. The liquid used in the canning process tends to dilute the fruit flavor, so intensely flavored fruits—such as apricots, figs, and pineapple—make the most satisfying canned products.

HOW TO SLIM DOWN YOUR BAKING

It is easy to shave both calories and fat from baked goods by using the following hints:

◆ Coat baking pans with vegetable oil spray instead of butter or shortening.
◆ Use low-fat or skim milk in place of whole milk.

◆ In a recipe calling for at least 2 whole eggs, substitute 2 egg whites for one of the whole eggs.
◆ Use "light" sour cream or low-fat yogurt in place of sour cream.
◆ Use puréed fruits (such as prunes or applesauce) for up to half of the fat called for in a recipe (you may need to experiment—this substitution does not work in all recipes).
◆ Make angel food or chiffon cakes instead of butter cakes.
◆ Choose fluffy, meringue-type frostings instead of buttercream frostings.

Red, White, and Blueberry Shortcakes

Makes 8 servings

Of course you'll want to serve this dessert on the Fourth of July—and it's also good any other day of the year. It should become a year-round favorite.

Filling:

2 pints fresh strawberries,
**   stemmed and hulled**

1 pint fresh blueberries

½ cup sugar

2 teaspoons lemon juice

Shortcakes:

Vegetable oil spray

3 cups all-purpose flour, plus extra
**   for kneading**

⅓ cup sugar, plus 2 teaspoons

1 tablespoon baking powder

2 teaspoons baking soda

½ teaspoon salt

2 tablespoons unsalted butter, cut
**   into small pieces**

1¼ cups low-fat buttermilk,
**   plus 1 tablespoon**

1½ tablespoons vegetable oil

2 cups Chantilly Cream
**   (recipe follows)**

1. For the filling, set aside eight of the best-looking strawberries for a garnish. Crush half of the remaining strawberries with a fork and slice the other half. Place all of the strawberries in a mixing bowl. Add half of the blueberries. Place the remaining blueberries in a heavy saucepan along with the sugar and lemon juice. Stir over medium-low heat, crushing the berries with the back of a spoon, until the berries simmer and release their juices, and the sugar dissolves to form a syrup, about 5 minutes. Add the cooked berries to the berries in the bowl. Let stand at room temperature for 20 minutes or refrigerate up to 8 hours.

2. For the shortcakes, preheat the oven to 425 degrees. Lightly coat a baking sheet with vegetable oil spray. In a mixing bowl, whisk together the flour, ⅓ cup of the sugar, baking powder, baking soda, and salt. Use your fingertips to work the butter into the flour until crumbly. Make a well in the center and pour in 1¼ cups of the buttermilk and the oil. Stir with a fork just until combined to make a slightly sticky dough. Do not overmix.

3. Flour your hands and gather the dough into a ball. Knead the dough 10 times on a lightly floured surface, then pat or roll it to a 1 inch thickness. Using a 3-inch round cookie or biscuit cutter, cut out eight shortcakes and transfer them to the baking sheet, leaving 2 inches in between each. Brush the shortcakes with the remaining 1 tablespoon of buttermilk and sprinkle with the remaining 2 teaspoons of sugar.

4. Bake the shortcakes until golden, 12 to 16 minutes. Transfer the shortcakes to a rack to cool slightly.

5. To serve, split the warm shortcakes and place the bottoms on dessert plates. Spread with some of the Chantilly Cream; spoon on the berries and juices and replace the short-cake tops. Spoon on more Chantilly Cream and serve.

◆ *PER SERVING (without cream): About 363 cals, 60 cals from fat, 7g total fat, 2g sat fat, 9mg chol, 631mg sodium, 70g total carbs, 4g fiber, 7g prot*

CHANTILLY CREAM
Makes 2 cups (8 servings)

This creamy topping is slightly tangy—a perfect finishing touch for any dessert, particularly with Red, White, and Blueberry Shortcakes (page 452).

1⅓ cups nonfat vanilla yogurt

⅔ cup nonfat sour cream

⅛ teaspoon vanilla or almond extract

1. In a small bowl, gently stir together the yogurt, sour cream, and vanilla.
2. Serve immediately or refrigerate up to 24 hours.

Per serving: About 42 cals, 0 cals from fat, 0g total fat, 0g sat fat, 1mg chol, 36mg sodium, 8g total carbs, 0g fiber, 3g prot

Classic Angel Cake
Makes 12 servings

This great American cake has been enormously popular since the 19th century, but it's also a dessert for the 21st century because it is fat and cholesterol free, and tastes heavenly. Dress it up with Raspberry Coulis (recipe follows), Double Strawberry Sauce (page 461), or a scoop of frozen yogurt.

1 cup sifted cake flour (not self rising)
¾ cup sifted granulated sugar, plus ¾ cup
12 large egg whites
1 teaspoon cream of tartar
¼ teaspoon salt
1½ teaspoons vanilla
1½ teaspoons lemon juice
½ teaspoon almond extract

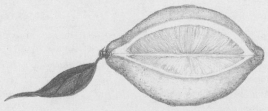

continued

1. Preheat the oven to 325 degrees.

2. In a small bowl, combine the flour with ¾ cup of the sugar. Whisk the flour/sugar mixture for about 5 seconds, then transfer it to a flour sifter set over wax paper or over the mixing bowl.

3. In a large mixing bowl, beat the egg whites at low speed just until they are frothy, 1 to 2 minutes. Add the cream of tartar and the salt and beat at medium speed until the whites form very soft, billowy mounds, about 2 minutes. With the mixer remaining at medium speed, beat in the remaining ¾ cup of sugar, 1 tablespoon at a time, until all the sugar is added and the whites are shiny and form soft peaks. (Do not overbeat the whites.) Add the vanilla, lemon juice, and almond extract. Beat for a few seconds until it is just blended.

4. Sift the flour mixture over the egg whites, about 3 tablespoons at a time, and use a wide rubber spatula to gently fold it in until just blended. Gently scrape the batter into an ungreased 9½-inch angel food cake pan (preferably one with a removable bottom and "feet"), smoothing the top. Tap the pan on the counter a couple of times to release any large air bubbles in the batter.

5. Bake the cake in the lower third of the oven until it turns golden brown and the top springs back when firmly pressed, 50 to 60 minutes.

6. If the cake pan has feet, invert the pan onto them. If not, invert the pan over the neck of a bottle so that air can circulate all around it. Allow the cake to cool completely for 2 to 3 hours before removing it from the pan.

7. To unmold, run a thin knife around the edges, being careful not to dislodge the golden crust. Release the cake from the pan, then run the knife the same way around the removable bottom to release the cake from it. Set the cake on a rack, bottom side up, and cool it completely for another hour or more. (The cake can be made up to a day ahead and stored, covered, at room temperature. Or it can be frozen for 1 month.)

8. Using a serrated knife, cut the cake with a gentle sawing motion, or cut slices by sawing with a taut thread.

◆ *PER SERVING: About 150 cals, 1 cal from fat, 0g total fat, 0g sat fat, 0mg chol, 100 mg sodium, 33g total carbs, 0g fiber, 4g prot*

ANGEL FOOD ADD-ONS

Angel food, the only truly fat-free cake, presents a wide-range of dessert possibilities. Try these variations of the basic recipes:

◆ Substitute 2 tablespoons unsweetened cocoa for 2 tablespoons cake flour.

◆ Substitute ½ cup sifted brown sugar for ½ cup granulated sugar.

◆ Add 1 teaspoon orange, anise, lemon, or mint extract, or orange flower water or rose water.

◆ Add 1 tablespoon grated lemon, lime, or orange peel.

Try these variations after the cake is baked:

◆ Dollop with low-fat yogurt.

◆ Glaze with marmalade or fruit-only preserves.

◆ Hollow out the cake to form a shell and fill it with berries or sliced peaches or nectarines.

◆ Slice and toast the cake and serve it with puddings or fruit compotes.

RASPBERRY COULIS

Makes about 2 cups (8 servings)

Frozen unsweetened raspberries are far more economical than fresh ones. They're the best choice if you are going to purée the berries anyway. This combination of frozen and fresh berries produces an irresistible dessert sauce with lots of uses, from a topping for frozen yogurt to a garnish for Classic Angel Cake (page 453).

1 bag (12 ounces) frozen and thawed unsweetened raspberries (about 1½ cups)

2 tablespoons almond or orange liqueur, rum, or orange juice

⅓ cup granulated sugar
1½ cups fresh raspberries

1. In a food processor, purée the frozen raspberries with the liqueur and the sugar. Strain through a sieve, pressing hard on the seeds with the back of a spoon to extract as much purée as possible.
2. Refrigerate the purée until chilled or up to 3 days. Just before using, stir in the fresh berries.

Per serving: About 68 cals, 2 cals from fat, 0g total fat, 0g sat fat, 0mg chol, 1mg sodium, 15g total carbs, 0g fiber, 1g prot

Citrus Chiffon Cake

Makes 16 servings

This towering cake makes a spectacular presentation as a party dessert. It is far lighter than the usual chiffon cake, but has the same golden color and silky texture. Serve it plain or topped with Raspberry Coulis (above).

Cake:
1½ cups cake flour
 (not self rising)
¾ cup granulated sugar, plus
 ¾ cup
1 teaspoon baking powder
10 large egg whites, brought to
 room temperature
¾ teaspoon cream of tartar
¼ teaspoon salt
3 egg yolks
2 tablespoons orange juice

1 tablespoon fresh lemon juice
1 tablespoon fresh lime juice
3 tablespoons grated orange peel
2 teaspoons grated lemon peel
2 tablespoons grated lime peel
1 teaspoon vanilla

Glaze:
1 large orange
1 large lemon
1 large lime
1 cup confectioners' sugar

continued

1. Preheat the oven to 350 degrees. In a mixing bowl, whisk together the flour, ¾ cup of the sugar, and the baking powder.

2. In a large bowl, beat the egg whites with an electric mixer until frothy. Add the cream of tartar and salt, and beat just until soft peaks form. With the mixer at medium speed, beat in the remaining ¾ cup of sugar, 2 tablespoons at a time, until the whites are shiny and hold firm, but do not form dry peaks. In a small bowl, whisk together the egg yolks, fruit juices and peels, and the vanilla. Pour the liquid over the beaten egg whites and fold in by hand, using a wide rubber spatula just until no streaks remain. By hand, sift about 3 tablespoons of the flour/sugar mixture over the whites. Fold in with the spatula. Repeat the sifting and folding until you use all of the flour/sugar mixture. Spoon the batter into a 9½- or 10-inch angel food cake pan (preferably one with a removable bottom and "feet"), smoothing the top. Rap the pan on the counter to release any large air bubbles.

3. Bake the cake until the top turns golden and springs back when firmly pressed, 45 to 50 minutes. If the cake pan has feet, invert the pan onto them. If not, invert the pan over the neck of a bottle so that air can circulate all around it. Allow the cake to cool completely for 2 to 3 hours before removing it from the pan.

4. To unmold, run a thin knife around the edges, being careful not to dislodge the golden crust. Release the cake from the pan, then cut the same way around the removable bottom to release it. Set the cake on a rack, bottom side up, and cool it completely for another hour or more. (The cake can be made up to a day ahead and stored, covered, at room temperature. Or it can be frozen for up to 1 month.)

5. For the glaze, use a zesting tool or grater to make long thread peels from the orange, lemon, and lime. Squeeze 2 teaspoons of juice from each of the fruits. In a small bowl, whisk the juices into the confectioners' sugar to make a smooth glaze. Spoon the glaze over the top of the cooled cake, allowing it to drip down the sides. Immediately sprinkle the top of the cake with the grated peels. Let the cake stand for at least 30 minutes for the glaze to set.

6. Using a serrated knife, cut the cake with a gentle sawing motion.

◆ *PER SERVING: About 160 cals, 10 cals from fat, 1g total fat, 0g sat fat, 40mg chol, 92mg sodium, 34g total carbs, 0g fiber, 4g prot*

USEFUL BAKING TIPS

◆ Instead of greasing the pan, coat it with vegetable oil spray or line with parchment paper.

◆ If using glass baking dishes, reduce the oven temperature by 25 degrees, but bake for about the same length of time. Glass is a better heat conductor than metal, but metal promotes better browning of crusts.

◆ Bake cakes, pies, and cookies on a rack placed in the lower half of the oven unless the recipe directs otherwise. If you are baking two sheets of cookies at the same time, switch the placement of the pans halfway through baking.

◆ Test for cake doneness with a toothpick. When inserted, it should come out clean with no crumbs.

◆ Cool baked goods on a rack, unless directed otherwise. The rack will allow all-around air circulation for even cooling.

◆ Measure dry ingredients by dipping a dry measuring cup or spoon into the ingredient, then level off the ingredient with the back of a knife or spatula.

Pumpkin Pecan Bars

Makes 16 bar cookies

These golden bar cookies will evoke warm memories of Thanksgiving dinner and pumpkin pie, and they are a wonderful holiday dessert. Be sure to use unsweetened pumpkin purée and not sweetened pie filling. Pumpkin is filled with beta carotene, so these bars not only taste good but are good for you.

Vegetable oil spray
4 tablespoons unsalted butter
¾ cup packed light brown sugar
⅔ cup unsweetened canned
 pumpkin purée
1 egg
2 egg whites

⅔ cup all-purpose flour
1½ teaspoons pumpkin pie spice
 (see note)
¾ teaspoon baking powder
¼ teaspoon baking soda
½ cup dried cranberries
½ cup chopped pecans

1. Preheat the oven to 375 degrees. Coat a 9-inch square baking pan with vegetable oil spray.

2. In a medium saucepan, melt the butter and brown sugar, stirring until smooth. Remove from the heat and whisk in the pumpkin purée. Let the mixture cool until lukewarm, then whisk in the egg and egg whites until blended.

3. In a mixing bowl, whisk together the flour, pumpkin pie spice, baking powder, and baking soda. Stir in the cranberries and nuts to coat with flour. Add the flour mixture to the pumpkin mixture and stir until combined. Spoon into the prepared baking pan.

4. Bake until the top is golden brown, firm to the touch, and a toothpick inserted into the center comes out clean, about 25 minutes. Transfer the pan to a rack and let cool. Cut into 16 bars and serve. (These bars can be stored in an airtight container for up to 3 days, or frozen up to a month.)

◆ *PER COOKIE: About 128 cals, 50 cals from fat, 6g total fat, 2g sat fat, 21mg chol, 53mg sodium, 19g total carbs, 2g fiber, 2g prot*

Note: If you don't have pumpkin pie spice, substitute ¾ teaspoon ground cinnamon, ½ teaspoon ground ginger, and ½ teaspoon grated nutmeg.

Banana Spice Cake with Seafoam Icing

Makes 14 servings

This is a terrific cake for a birthday party or any other special occasion. An inexpensive nutmeg grater and a jar of whole nutmegs are a worthwhile investment—the taste of freshly ground nutmeg is pleasantly startling.

Vegetable oil spray
2½ cups sifted cake flour
2 teaspoons ground cinnamon
2 teaspoons baking powder
1½ teaspoons baking soda
1 teaspoon grated nutmeg
¾ teaspoon salt
¾ teaspoon ground allspice
½ teaspoon ground ginger
¼ teaspoon ground cloves
2 tablespoons unsalted butter
3 egg whites
¼ teaspoon cream of tartar
¾ cup sugar, plus 1 cup

1 cup puréed ripe bananas
  (about 2 bananas)
¼ cup vegetable oil
1 tablespoon grated orange peel
1½ teaspoons vanilla
1 egg yolk
¾ cup nonfat buttermilk
Seafoam Icing
1 banana, thinly sliced and lightly
  brushed with lemon juice
  (optional)
3 tablespoons finely chopped
  toasted walnuts (optional)
  (see note)

1. Preheat the oven to 350 degrees. Coat two 9-inch round cake pans with nonstick vegetable oil spray. Line the bottoms of the pans with wax paper and coat the paper with the nonstick spray.

2. In a large mixing bowl, blend together the flour, cinnamon, baking powder, baking soda, nutmeg, salt, allspice, ginger, and cloves. In a small saucepan, melt the butter over medium heat, swirling the pan until the butter turns nutty brown. Pour into a small bowl and let cool slightly.

3. In a large bowl, use an electric mixer to beat the egg whites at low speed until frothy. Add the cream of tartar, increase speed to medium, and beat until soft peaks form. Slowly beat in ¾ cup sugar, 2 tablespoons at a time, just until peaks become firm (about 3 to 5 minutes total). Remove the mixture to another bowl, but do not wash the mixing bowl.

4. Place the banana purée, oil, orange peel, vanilla, egg yolk, melted butter, and remaining 1 cup of sugar into the mixing bowl. Beat until smooth. With mixer at low speed, add the buttermilk and the flour mixture alternately in two batches each, beating just until blended. Add a heaping spoonful of the egg white mixture, and beat a few seconds to lighten batter. Fold in the remaining egg white mixture.

5. Divide the batter evenly between the two pans and bake until the cakes have browned and risen, 28 to 30 minutes (test to see if a toothpick inserted into the center comes out clean). Let the layers cool in the pans on a rack for 10 minutes, then turn out onto the racks, peel off the wax paper, and let cool completely.

6. Place one cake layer on a serving plate and frost the top with about 1½ cups Seafoam Icing (recipe follows). Arrange all but five banana slices on the icing, then cover with a thin layer of more icing. Add the second cake layer. Frost the top and sides of the cake with remaining icing, swirling and making peaks. Arrange the reserved banana slices on top and sprinkle with the walnuts, if desired.

◆ *PER SERVING (without icing or garnish): About 249 cals, 57 cals from fat, 6g total fat, 2g sat fat, 20mg chol, 328mg sodium, 46g total carbs, 1g fiber, 3g prot*

Note: Toast the walnuts on a small baking sheet or piece of aluminum foil in a 350-degree oven until lightly browned and fragrant, 4 to 6 minutes.

SEAFOAM ICING

Makes enough to generously frost a 2- or 3-layer, 9-inch round cake

If you want a light, lavishly frosted cake, this icing is a great choice. The delicate and fluffy icing tastes best when freshly made, so make and serve the cake on the same day.

1½ cups light brown sugar	⅓ cup cold water	¾ teaspoon grated nutmeg
3 egg whites	1 tablespoon dark molasses	1 teaspoon vanilla

1. Place all of the ingredients except the vanilla in the top of a double boiler set over simmering water. Beat with a handheld electric mixer until the mixture quadruples in volume and becomes very fluffy, about 7 minutes.

2. Remove the top of the double boiler from the heat, add the vanilla, and continue to beat until the frosting cools and thickens to spreading consistency, about 3 minutes.

Per serving: About 97 cals, 0 cals from fat, 0g total fat, 0g sat fat, 0mg chol, 22mg sodium, 24g total carbs, 0g fiber, 1g prot

Strawberry-Ricotta Cake Roll

Makes 6 servings

Orange flower water and rose water are delicate, old-fashioned flavorings that you can find in specialty stores, pharmacies, and Indian or Mediterranean markets. Both lend an exotic flavor to desserts; choose either one for this delicate cake roll.

Cake:

½ cup cake flour (not self rising)

6 tablespoons granulated sugar, plus 6 tablespoons

6 egg whites, brought to room temperature

½ teaspoon cream of tartar

⅛ teaspoon salt

1½ teaspoons orange flower water or rose water

¾ teaspoon vanilla

¾ teaspoon fresh lemon juice

1 tablespoon confectioners' sugar

Filling:

1 cup part-skim ricotta cheese

¼ cup confectioners' sugar

⅓ cup all-fruit strawberry preserves

1 tablespoon orange juice

½ teaspoon orange flower water or rose water

1 tablespoon confectioners' sugar

1½ cups Double Strawberry Sauce (recipe follows)

1. Preheat the oven to 325 degrees. Line a 10x15-inch jelly roll pan with parchment paper. Sift the flour and 6 tablespoons of granulated sugar into a small bowl.

2. In a mixing bowl, use an electric mixer to beat the egg whites until frothy. Add the cream of tartar and salt and beat just until soft peaks form. Beat in the remaining 6 table-spoons sugar, 2 tablespoons at a time, until the whites are shiny and hold firm but do not form dry peaks. Beat in the orange flower water, vanilla, and lemon juice. Sift about 3 table-spoons of the flour/sugar mixture over the whites. Fold into the batter, using a large rub-ber spatula. Repeat until you use all of the flour/sugar mixture.

3. Spoon the batter into the prepared jelly roll pan, smoothing the top. Bake until the top is lightly colored and bounces back when pressed lightly, 22 to 25 minutes.

4. Immediately run a small knife around the edges of the cake to loosen them from the sides. Lay a tea towel on a counter and dust it lightly with 1 tablespoon confectioners' sugar. Invert the cake onto the prepared tea towel. Remove the pan and carefully peel off the parchment paper. Let the cake cool slightly for about 5 minutes, then roll it up from the long side, rolling the tea towel up with the cake (the tea towel will be inside the rolled cake). Let the cake cool completely for at least 1 hour. (The cake can be made early in the day and stored, covered with plastic wrap, at room temperature.)

5. While the cake is cooling, make the filling. In a mixing bowl, whisk together the ricotta cheese, ¼ cup confectioners' sugar, preserves, orange juice, and orange flower water.

6. To assemble the dessert, carefully unroll the cake, removing the tea towel. Spread the filling over the cake to within ½ inch of the edges, then roll the cake up again. Use two large spatulas to transfer the cake to a serving platter, seam side down. (The cake can be assembled up to 4 hours before serving and refrigerated, covered.)

7. Just before serving, dust the cake roll with 1 tablespoon confectioners' sugar. Cut the cake into diagonal slices and serve with some Double Strawberry Sauce spooned around each slice.

◆ *PER SERVING: About 250 cals, 13 cals from fat, 1g total fat, 0g sat fat, 0mg chol, 276mg sodium, 51g total carbs, 0g fiber, 8g prot*

DOUBLE STRAWBERRY SAUCE

Makes about 3 cups

All-fruit strawberry preserves and a spark of fresh lemon juice intensify the flavor of fresh strawberries in this luscious sauce. You can substitute whole raspberries or blackberries in the same proportions. The sauce is tasty spooned over the Strawberry-Ricotta Cake Roll (page 460), and is equally delicious on Classic Angel Cake (page 453).

1 pint fresh strawberries, hulled and sliced

¼ cup all-fruit strawberry preserves
2 tablespoons granulated sugar

2 teaspoons fresh lemon juice
2 teaspoons chopped fresh mint (optional)

1. In a bowl, stir together the berries, preserves, sugar, and lemon juice, and mint, if using. Let stand at least 15 minutes or up to 1 hour at room temperature, stirring occasionally to draw out the strawberry juices. (The sauce can be made up to a day ahead and refrigerated.)
2. Serve immediately or refrigerate up to 8 hours.

Per serving: About 29 cals, 1 cal from fat, 0g total fat, 0g sat fat, 0mg chol, 0mg sodium, 7g total carbs, 0g fiber, 0g prot

Candied Gingerbread

Makes 9 servings

Candied, ground, and fresh ginger all lend their distinctive flavors to this dark, moist, homespun dessert that supplies a lot of iron. Serve it just out of the oven with Warm Citrus Sauce (recipe follows) ladled over it, and you will surely be asked for seconds.

Vegetable oil spray

1½ cups all-purpose flour

½ cup packed light brown sugar

1¼ teaspoons baking soda

1 teaspoon ground ginger

1 teaspoon ground cinnamon

½ teaspoon grated nutmeg

½ teaspoon ground cloves

⅛ teaspoon salt

½ cup dark molasses

½ cup orange juice

1 egg

2 egg whites

3 tablespoons vegetable oil

¼ cup finely chopped crystallized
  ginger

1 teaspoon grated fresh ginger

1 teaspoon vanilla

1¼ cups Warm Citrus Sauce
  (recipe follows)

1. Preheat the oven to 350 degrees. Coat an 8- or 9-inch square baking pan with vegetable oil spray. In a mixing bowl, whisk together the flour, brown sugar, baking soda, ground ginger, cinnamon, nutmeg, cloves, and salt. Use your fingers to break up any clumps of sugar, if necessary. In a large mixing bowl, use an electric mixer or a wooden spoon to beat together the molasses, orange juice, egg, egg whites, oil, crystallized and fresh gingers, and the vanilla. Add the dry ingredients and mix on low speed or beat with the spoon until blended.

2. Transfer the batter to the prepared baking pan. Bake until a toothpick inserted into the center of the cake comes out clean, about 30 minutes. Let the cake cool on a rack for about 15 minutes before serving warm with the Warm Citrus Sauce. (The cake can be stored, covered, for up to a day and served at room temperature.)

◆ *PER SERVING: About 235 cals, 49 cals from fat, 5g total fat, 1g sat fat, 24mg chol, 247mg sodium, 43g total carbs, 1g fiber, 4g prot*

WARM CITRUS SAUCE

Makes about 1¼ cups (10 servings)

Serve this versatile sauce over Candied Gingerbread (page 462). It's also tempting as a dip for hunks of Classic Angel Cake (page 00) or fresh strawberries, banana chunks, or fresh pineapple spears.

½ cup granulated sugar
1 tablespoon cornstarch
¾ cup orange juice

¼ cup fresh lemon juice
1 teaspoon grated orange peel
1 teaspoon grated lemon peel

2 tablespoons bourbon or dark rum (optional)
1½ teaspoons unsalted butter

1. Whisk together the sugar and cornstarch in a medium saucepan. Whisk in the orange and lemon juices and peels. Whisk constantly over medium heat until the sauce thickens and boils. Cook, whisking constantly, for 1 minute more. Strain the hot sauce into a small bowl and gently whisk in the bourbon, if using, and the butter until the butter melts.

2. Let the sauce cool until it is just warm before using. (The sauce can be made up to 3 days ahead and refrigerated. Reheat gently before using.)

Per serving: About 57 cals, 6 cals from fat, 1g total fat, 0g sat fat, 2mg chol, 1mg sodium, 13g total carbs, 0g fiber, 0g prot

SWEET SPICES

NAME	FORM AVAILABLE	FLAVOR/AROMA	COOKING USES
ALLSPICE	Whole berries or ground	A blend of cinnamon, nutmeg, and cloves	Baked goods, fruit desserts, chutneys, pickles, relishes; the principal spice in Jamaican "jerk" seasoning
ANISE	Whole seeds or ground	Distinct licorice flavor	Cookies, cakes, breads, stews, tomato sauces
CARDAMOM	Whole pods, whole seeds, or ground	Haunting sweet flavor	Cakes, breads, coffee, custards, sweet sauces, meatballs, curry; used in cooking from India to Scandinavia
CINNAMON	Whole sticks or ground	Sharp, spicy flavor and heady aroma	Breads, cookies, cakes, some vegetables and curry; used in Indian and Mexican dishes
CLOVE	Whole or ground	Pungent and potent flavor	Baked goods, meats, sauces, beverages, chutneys, pickles
GINGER	Fresh, preserved, crystallized, or ground	Tangy and aromatic	Cookies, cakes, stir-fries, soups, stews, curries
MACE	Whole blades or ground	Mild nutmeg flavor with a hint of cinnamon	Baked goods, sweet sauces, seafood, chicken dishes, curry, sauces
NUTMEG	Whole or grated	Pleasing sweet flavor and aroma	Baked goods, fruit desserts, milk-based beverages, some vegetables
VANILLA	Whole beans or extract	Sweet, creamy flavor	Sauces, custards, baked goods, desserts

Orange Marmalade–Glazed Cheesecake

Makes 12 servings

This delicate yet rich cheesecake is an excellent party dessert because it serves a crowd and can be made ahead of time.

1 cup graham cracker crumbs

3 tablespoons granulated sugar, plus 1 cup

2 teaspoons unsalted butter, melted

1 container (1 pound) low-fat cottage cheese

8 ounces Neufchâtel or light cream cheese

6 tablespoons all-purpose flour

¼ teaspoon salt

1 egg

3 egg whites

1 tablespoon fresh lemon juice

1 tablespoon grated lemon rind

2 teaspoons vanilla

½ cup orange marmalade

1 seedless orange, peeled and thinly sliced crosswise

1. Preheat the oven to 325 degrees. In a small bowl, combine the graham cracker crumbs, 3 tablespoons sugar, and butter. Press the mixture into an 8-inch springform pan.

2. In a food processor, process the cottage and softened Neufchâtel cheese until smooth. Add the flour, salt, egg, egg whites, lemon juice and rind, vanilla, and remaining 1 cup sugar. Process just until smooth. Pour into the prepared pan. Place the pan on a baking sheet.

3. Bake the cheesecake for 55 minutes. Turn off the oven and let the cheesecake cool in the oven with the door opened slightly for 1 hour. Cool the cheesecake completely on a rack. Unlatch the sides of the pan and use a small knife to carefully separate the cheesecake from the pan, then reclose the pan sides with the cheesecake still resting inside of the pan.

4. Melt the marmalade in a small pan over medium-low heat. Let it cool to lukewarm, then brush about half of the marmalade over the cooled cheesecake. Arrange the orange slices over the marmalade, then brush the orange slices with the remaining marmalade.

5. Refrigerate, covered, until the glaze is set, at least 1 hour and up to 24 hours.

6. To serve, remove the sides of the pan and cut the cheesecake into wedges.

◆ *PER SERVING: About 261 cals, 54 cals from fat, 6g total fat, 3g sat fat, 28mg chol, 378mg sodium, 44g total carbs, 2g fiber, 9g prot*

Bombay Rice Pudding

Makes 6 servings

Basmati rice, rose water, pistachios, and dried fruits combine to make this exotic dessert, which tastes good after a spicy Indian dish, such as Chicken Vindaloo (page 338). If you can't find rose water, substitute ½ teaspoon almond or anise extract for a different but equally delicious flavor.

⅔ cup basmati rice

⅓ cup granulated sugar

2 eggs

2¼ cups low-fat milk

⅓ cup chopped dried apricots or
    other dried fruits

1 teaspoon vanilla

1 teaspoon rose water

3 tablespoons coarsely chopped
    dry-roasted pistachios

1. Combine the rice and 1¾ cups water in a medium saucepan. Cover and bring to a boil, then reduce the heat to low and cook until the liquid is just absorbed, about 15 minutes. Let the rice cool slightly.

2. In a mixing bowl, whisk together the sugar and eggs, then whisk in the milk. Stir a spoonful of the hot rice into the milk mixture, then pour the milk mixture into the pan with the rice. Add the apricots.

3. Cook, stirring often over medium-low heat, until the pudding thickens to a creamy consistency, about 10 minutes. Do not allow the pudding to come to a full boil. Stir in the vanilla and rose water.

4. Serve the pudding warm or at room temperature in shallow dishes, sprinkled with the pistachios.

◆ *PER SERVING: About 224 cals, 43 cals from fat, 5g total fat, 1g sat fat, 75mg chol, 69mg sodium, 38g total carbs, 1g fiber, 8g prot*

TOASTING NUTS AND SEEDS

Toasting nuts and seeds gives them a deeper, richer flavor. Large amounts of nuts or seeds (more than ½ cup) are best toasted in a single layer on a baking sheet or piece of aluminum foil in a 350-degree oven until they become fragrant and turn a shade darker. The timing varies from 2 to 15 minutes, but burning can easily occur, so watch the nuts or seeds carefully and stir them occasionally to promote even toasting. Small amounts of nuts and seeds can be toasted by tossing in a skillet set over medium heat. Watch them carefully and stir constantly. Whether you bake them or toss them in a skillet, remove the toasted nuts or seeds as soon as they are done or they will begin to burn on the hot baking sheet or skillet.

Deep-Dish Apple Pie

Makes 8 servings

The secret to a great apple pie is using more than one kind of apple. The bottom crust of a fruit pie often gets soggy and underbaked. This recipe solves the problem by skipping it entirely. The terrific top crust bakes to a richly caramelized crispness.

Pastry:

1¼ cups all-purpose flour

2 teaspoons granulated sugar

¼ teaspoon salt

3 tablespoons cold unsalted
   butter, cut into 8 pieces

2 tablespoons vegetable oil

1 teaspoon cider vinegar

2 to 3 tablespoons ice water

Filling:

¾ cup granulated sugar

2 tablespoons all-purpose flour

½ teaspoon grated lemon peel

¼ teaspoon ground cinnamon

¼ teaspoon ground nutmeg

4 cups thinly sliced pared and cored
   tart crisp apples, such as Granny Smith
   (about 1¼ pounds apples)

2 cups thinly sliced pared and cored sweet crisp
   apples, such as Golden Delicious
   (about ¾ pound apples)

1 tablespoon fresh lemon juice

2 teaspoons low-fat milk

2 teaspoons granulated sugar

1. To make the pastry in a food processor, pulse together the flour, sugar, and salt. Distribute the butter over the flour and pulse until fine crumbs form. With the motor running, pour in the oil, vinegar, and 2 tablespoons ice water. Process just until the dough begins to form a ball, adding up to 1 tablespoon more water if the dough seems too dry. Stop processing just as soon as the dough gathers together; do not overprocess. To make the pastry by hand, whisk together the flour, sugar, and salt in a large mixing bowl. Use two knives to cut in the butter until the mixture forms fine crumbs. Add the oil, vinegar, and ice water and stir just until combined to form a dough. Transfer the dough to a piece of plastic wrap, flatten into a ½-inch-thick disk, and wrap and refrigerate the dough for 30 minutes to 1 hour.

2. Preheat the oven to 425 degrees. To make the filling, stir together the sugar, flour, lemon peel, cinnamon, and nutmeg. Add the apples and lemon juice and toss to coat the apples with the sugar mixture. Spoon the apples into a deep 9-inch pie plate or pan.

3. Remove the pastry disk from the refrigerator. Between sheets of plastic wrap, roll the dough to a rough 11-inch circle. Remove the top sheet of plastic wrap and invert the pastry onto the apples. Peel off the remaining plastic wrap. Fold the pastry edges under, then press the pastry to the edge of the pie plate and crimp the edges.

4. Make several slits in the pastry to allow steam to escape. Brush the pastry with the milk and sprinkle with the granulated sugar.

5. Bake the pie for 15 minutes, then reduce the oven temperature to 350 degrees and continue to bake until the pastry turns a rich golden brown and the apples are tender and bubbly, 35 to 40 minutes longer.

6. Cool the pie on a rack for at least 1 hour before serving warm or at room temperature.

◆ *PER SERVING: About 277 cals, 74 cals from fat, 8g total fat, 3g sat fat, 12mg chol, 69mg sodium, 50g total carbs, 2g fiber, 2g prot*

THE APPLE OF YOUR PIE

The most common baking apples found in supermarkets are Granny Smith and Golden Delicious; both are fine for pies and general baking. The most common eating apple is the Red Delicious. But hundreds of varieties of apples are available. Most of them are marketed only in the home region and they are often fresher and more flavorful than the apples available in a supermarket. Here are some apples that you can substitute for the most commonly available types.

◆ **GRANNY SMITH** (crisp, tart, with bright green skin): Cortland, Empire, Greening, Pippin, Northern Spy, York, Winesap; good for pies, baking, and in combination with sweeter apples for sauces

◆ **GOLDEN DELICIOUS** (slightly sweet, crisp, and juicy, with yellow to pale green skin): Crispin, Ginger Gold, Gravenstein, Macoun, Rome Beauty; good for baking, sauces, and in combination with tart apples for baking

◆ **RED DELICIOUS** (crisp, sweet and juicy, with deep red skin): Gala, Fuji, McIntosh; good for eating by hand, but McIntosh also good for sauces

CHOCOLATE CHOICES

Few foods have evoked as much folklore and mystique as chocolate. Cacao trees, whose pods contain chocolate liquor, have been cultivated in Central and South America since ancient times. Even then, the bitter drink made from the pods was thought to have aphrodisiac powers and was an important part of many rituals. Originally used only as a beverage, chocolate became popular to eat only in the nineteenth century. Brought to Europe by explorers of the New World, chocolate-making has become high art in many countries. You can buy chocolate in different forms, but they are generally not interchangeable in recipes.

Unsweetened cocoa is the powder left after most of the cocoa butter has been extracted from chocolate liquor. Dutch-process cocoa has been treated with an alkali agent, which makes it darker and gives it a different flavor than American cocoa powder. Both cocoas are interchangeable but, if a recipe calls for American or Dutch-process cocoa by name, try to use the cocoa the recipe calls for to get the best taste. Cocoa delivers a lot of chocolate flavor for few calories and little fat, about 11 calories and 0.5 grams of fat per tablespoon.

Unsweetened chocolate is hardened pure chocolate liquor without any sweeteners; it is not suitable for eating plain. Also called baking chocolate and available in bars, it contains about 147 calories and 16 grams of fat per ounce.

Semisweet and bittersweet chocolates are made of chocolate liquor with varying amounts of sugar, vanilla, and emulsifiers added. They are available in blocks or as chips. Depending on the brand and the sweetness, they contain about 135 calories and 9 grams of fat per ounce.

Milk chocolate consists of hardened pure chocolate liquor with added milk solids, sugar, vanilla, and emulsifiers. Generally eaten in candy bars, it is also available as chips and contains about 148 calories and 9 grams of fat per ounce.

White chocolate isn't really chocolate at all because most of the cocoa butter has been removed and replaced by another fat. Containing sugar, milk solids, and vanilla, white chocolate comes in bars for eating or baking, where it lends a smooth richness and just a hint of chocolate flavor. It has about 162 calories and 9 grams of fat per ounce.

Updated Old-Fashioned Chocolate Pudding

Makes 4 servings

The secret to rich flavor lies in the chocolates. Look for European-style Dutch-process cocoa and premium-quality bittersweet chocolate, which give a smoother and richer taste for the same amount of fat and calories.

½ cup granulated sugar
¼ cup unsweetened cocoa,
   preferably Dutch process
2½ tablespoons cornstarch
⅛ teaspoon salt
2 cups skim milk

½ ounce semisweet chocolate,
   chopped
1½ teaspoons vanilla
½ cup Chantilly Cream
   (optional)

1. In a heavy saucepan, whisk together the sugar, cocoa, cornstarch, and salt. Gradually whisk in about half of the milk until smooth, then whisk in the remainder.

2. Cook over medium-low heat, stirring constantly until the pudding thickens and comes to a boil, 5 to 8 minutes. Cook, stirring, 1 minute more.

3. Remove the pudding from the heat and add the chocolate and vanilla. Allow the pudding to stand 1 minute to melt the chocolate, then stir gently just until smooth.

4. Pour the pudding into a serving bowl. Place a piece of plastic wrap directly on the surface to prevent a "skin" from forming. Refrigerate at least 1 hour and up to 8 hours.

5. Serve the pudding with Chantilly Cream (page 453) dolloped on top, if desired.

◆ *PER SERVING: About 191 cals, 17 cals from fat, 2g total fat, 1g sat fat, 2mg chol, 134mg sodium, 41g total carbs, 0g fiber, 5g prot*

Mocha Walnut Brownie Pudding

Makes 9 servings

Almost like magic, this dessert bakes into a warm, fudgy brownie in a pool of rich chocolate sauce. Serve it plain or with a scoop of vanilla frozen yogurt.

⅓ cup walnut pieces
Vegetable oil spray
¾ cup all-purpose flour
¾ cup granulated sugar
5 tablespoons unsweetened cocoa,
  plus 4 tablespoons
1½ teaspoons instant coffee
  powder
1½ teaspoons baking powder

½ teaspoon baking soda
¼ teaspoon salt
¼ teaspoon ground cinnamon
½ cup skim milk
1 tablespoon unsalted butter,
  melted
1 teaspoon vanilla
⅓ cup packed dark brown sugar
1⅔ cup boiling water

1. Preheat the oven to 350 degrees. Toast the walnuts on a baking sheet, stirring occasionally, about 5 minutes. Let cool. Coat a 9x9-inch baking pan with vegetable oil spray.

2. In a large mixing bowl, whisk together the flour, sugar, 5 tablespoons cocoa, coffee powder, baking powder, baking soda, salt, and cinnamon. Stir in the nuts. In a small bowl, stir together the milk, butter, and vanilla. Add the liquid to the dry ingredients and stir until just blended. (The batter will be stiff.) Spread the batter evenly into the prepared pan.

3. In a small bowl, stir together the brown sugar and remaining 4 tablespoons cocoa. Sprinkle evenly over the batter. Pour the boiling water over the top. Do not stir.

4. Bake the pudding until the top is glazed and turns a crusty dark brown, about 35 minutes. Cool the dessert in the pan on a rack for about 20 minutes. Serve warm.

◆ *PER SERVING: About 190 cals, 41 cals from fat, 5g total fat, 1g sat fat, 4mg chol, 204mg sodium, 37g total carbs, 1g fiber, 4g prot*

Oatmeal Raisin Cookies

Makes about 5 dozen cookies

Toasting the oats is the secret to the great taste of these cookies. In this recipe, applesauce replaces some of the fat without replacing the cookies' old-fashioned richness.

3 cups rolled oats, regular or quick
Vegetable oil spray
2 cups all-purpose flour
1 teaspoon ground cinnamon
½ teaspoon baking powder
1 teaspoon baking soda
½ teaspoon salt
1 cup granulated sugar
½ cup packed light brown sugar
½ cup unsweetened applesauce
2 eggs
¼ cup vegetable oil
1 cup raisins

1. Preheat the oven to 375 degrees. Spread the oats onto a baking sheet and toast, stirring often, until they turn a shade darker and become mildly fragrant, 5 to 8 minutes. Let the oats cool. Do not turn the oven off. Coat two baking sheets with vegetable oil spray. (If you have only one baking sheet, make the cookies in several batches, but let the sheet cool in between each batch.)

2. In a small bowl, whisk together the flour, cinnamon, baking powder, baking soda, and salt. Set aside.

3. In a large mixing bowl, use an electric mixer to beat the granulated and brown sugars, applesauce, eggs, and oil until fluffy. By hand or with the mixer at low speed, blend in the dry flour mixture. Stir in the oats and raisins until well blended.

4. Drop the dough by rounded teaspoons, 1½ inches apart, onto the prepared baking sheets. Bake until lightly browned, 10 to 12 minutes. Transfer the cookies to a rack to cool completely. (The cookies are best served on the day of baking, but can be frozen for up to a month.)

◆ *PER COOKIE: About 69 cals, 12 cals from fat, 1g total fat, 0g sat fat, 7mg chol, 45mg sodium, 13g total carbs, 0g fiber, 1g prot*

Cinnamon Raisin Bread Pudding

Makes 8 servings

This is a particularly easy bread pudding that will become an immediate family favorite. The Vanilla Custard Sauce (recipe follows) is an elegant topping for a special occasion.

Vegetable oil spray
5 cups torn cinnamon raisin
   bread (about 8 slices)
3 eggs
1 egg white
½ cup granulated sugar,
   plus 2 tablespoons
2½ cups skim milk
1 teaspoon vanilla
2 cups Vanilla Custard Sauce (optional)

1. Preheat the oven to 325 degrees. Coat a shallow 3-quart (such as a 9x13-inch) baking dish with vegetable oil spray. Spread the bread in the dish.

2. In a mixing bowl, whisk together the eggs, egg white, ½ cup sugar, milk, and vanilla. Pour over the bread, pressing down so that the bread is submerged. Let the bread stand for 10 minutes. Sprinkle the top of the pudding with the remaining 2 tablespoons of sugar.

3. Bake the pudding for 40 minutes, then increase the oven temperature to 400 degrees and bake an additional 10 to 15 minutes until the top is golden brown and puffed. Serve immediately with Vanilla Custard Sauce, if desired. (The pudding will deflate as it cools and will taste like French toast.)

◆ *PER SERVING (without custard sauce): About 190 cals, 28 cals from fat, 3g total fat, 1g sat fat, 81mg chol, 171mg sodium, 33g total carbs, 0g fiber, 7g prot*

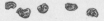

VANILLA CUSTARD SAUCE

Makes about 2 cups (8 servings)

Crème anglaise, or English custard sauce, is a classic and versatile dessert sauce. This lower-fat version is especially good if you use real vanilla beans as flavoring. You can vary the custard by adding a few drops of anise, orange, or almond extract, or a tablespoon or so of rum, bourbon, or flavored liqueur. It is delicious with Cinnamon Raisin Bread Pudding (page 471), Candied Gingerbread (page 462), Deep-Dish Apple Pie (page 466), or poached fruit.

5 tablespoons granulated sugar
1 tablespoon cornstarch
⅛ teaspoon salt

½ cup low-fat milk, plus
1½ cups
1 vanilla bean, split lengthwise

1 egg, beaten

1. In a medium saucepan, whisk together the sugar, cornstarch, and salt. Whisk in ½ cup of the milk until the mixture is smooth, then whisk in the remaining 1½ cups milk. Scrape the seeds from the vanilla bean into the mixture, then add the bean.

2. Cook the milk mixture over medium heat, stirring constantly, until the mixture thickens and comes to a boil. Whisk about one fourth of the hot liquid into the beaten egg, then return it to the saucepan. Cook, stirring constantly, for 1 minute, but do not let the custard boil. Let the sauce cool, stirring gently once or twice to prevent a skin from forming, then discard the vanilla bean. Refrigerate the sauce until ready to serve, up to 2 days.

3. Serve chilled.

Per serving: About 69 cals, 11 cals from fat, 1g total fat, 1g sat fat, 29 mg chol, 72mg sodium, 12g total carbs, 0g fiber, 3g prot

Iced Cocoa Cloud Cookies

Makes about 4 dozen cookies

Dutch-process cocoa gives a deep chocolate flavor to these chocolate-dipped meringues, but regular cocoa also works well. Store these cookies in an airtight container or they will lose their crispness.

½ cup slivered almonds
⅓ cup granulated sugar, plus
  ⅔ cup
⅓ cup unsweetened cocoa,
  preferably Dutch process
3 tablespoons cornstarch
½ teaspoon ground cinnamon

4 egg whites
¼ teaspoon cream of tartar
Pinch of salt
1 teaspoon vanilla
¼ teaspoon almond extract
1½ ounces semisweet chocolate,
  chopped

1. Preheat the oven to 350 degrees. Spread the almonds on a baking sheet and toast them, stirring once or twice, until pale golden and fragrant, 5 to 8 minutes. Let them cool.

2. Lower the oven temperature to 200 degrees. Line two large baking sheets with parchment paper.

3. In a food processor, process the nuts with ⅓ cup of the sugar, pulsing until the nuts are finely chopped. Add the cocoa, cornstarch, and cinnamon, and process a few seconds to blend. Set aside. You can also finely chop the nuts by hand and stir in the sugar, cocoa, cornstarch, and cinnamon.

4. In a large mixing bowl, use an electric mixer to beat the egg whites until frothy. Add the cream of tartar and salt, and beat until soft peaks form. Gradually beat in the remaining ⅔ cup sugar, 2 tablespoons at a time, until firm peaks form. Add the vanilla and almond extract. Use a large rubber spatula to fold the cocoa mixture into the beaten whites, until just blended, with a few streaks of white remaining.

5. Drop the batter by teaspoonfuls onto the parchment-lined baking sheets, or use a pastry bag and a ½-inch plain tip to pipe the batter onto the baking sheets, leaving 1 inch in between each cookie. Bake the cookies for 1½ hours, alternating the position of the baking sheets in the oven halfway through the baking time. Turn the oven off and let the cookies cool on the baking sheets in the oven for 1 hour. Carefully peel the parchment paper away from the cookie bottoms and set the cookies on a large piece of parchment or waxed paper.

6. Melt the chocolate in a small custard cup in a microwave oven or in a small pan set over hot water. Use a small pastry brush to thinly coat the flat side of the cookies with the chocolate. Let the cookies stand on the wax paper, chocolate side up, until the chocolate has set. (These cookies can be stored in an airtight container for up to 5 days.)

◆ *PER COOKIE: About 32 cals, 9 cals from fat, 1g total fat, 0g sat fat, 0mg chol, 8mg sodium, 6g total carbs, 0g fiber, 1g prot*

MERINGUE MANAGEMENT

Meringues are egg whites beaten with sugar to varying degrees of stiffness. You can use an electric mixer or a handheld whisk to make all sorts of meringues. Be sure that the mixing bowl and the utensils are completely grease-free or the egg whites will not form peaks. Soft meringues, used as toppings for pies and other desserts as well as the base for angel food and chiffon cakes, are beaten to soft peaks that hold their shape but drape over when you raise the beater or whisk. Firm meringues, which contain a higher proportion of sugar and are used for cookies or pastries, are beaten to stiff or firm peaks that stay upright when you raise the beater or whisk. Italian meringues, which can be either soft or firm, are made by beating hot sugar syrup into stiffly beaten egg whites. Do not overbeat egg whites or they will be too dry and stiff to fold into other ingredients or pipe or spoon into shapes. If you have accidentally overbeaten egg whites, add one unbeaten white for every four overbeaten whites, then beat them again for a few seconds until peaks form. Meringues should be cooked before eating, because there is real risk of salmonella contamination in raw egg whites. If the recipe calls for an uncooked meringue, you can use powdered egg whites, also called meringue powder, available in specialty cooking and baking shops or by mail from baking supply catalogs.

Glazed Citrus and Spice Crisps

Makes about 40 cookies

These wonderfully fragrant cookies contain no shortening, so they are soft as they come out of the oven, but cool to a crackly crispness. Their flavor actually improves with age. They keep nicely for up to 3 weeks, making for a terrific holiday gift for teachers and neighbors.

Dough:
1¾ cups all-purpose flour
1 teaspoon ground cinnamon
1 teaspoon ground allspice
¾ teaspoon grated nutmeg
½ teaspoon ground cloves
¼ teaspoon ground mace
¼ teaspoon salt
¼ teaspoon baking soda
¼ teaspoon freshly ground black
  pepper
½ cup honey
½ cup dark brown sugar

1 egg
1 teaspoon grated lemon peel
1 teaspoon grated orange peel

Glaze:
¼ cup confectioners' sugar
1½ teaspoons fresh lemon juice
1½ teaspoons orange juice
½ teaspoon grated lemon peel
½ teaspoon grated orange peel

Vegetable oil spray

1. For the cookie dough, whisk together the flour, cinnamon, allspice, nutmeg, cloves, mace, salt, baking soda, and pepper in a bowl. In a large mixing bowl, whisk together the honey, brown sugar, egg, and lemon and orange peels until blended and smooth. Add the flour mixture to the honey mixture and mix with a spoon or an electric mixer to make a soft and sticky dough. Transfer the dough to a large sheet of wax paper or plastic wrap and shape into a flat, ½-inch-thick disk. Wrap and refrigerate at least 6 hours or up to 3 days.

2. For the glaze, whisk together the confectioners' sugar, lemon and orange juices, and lemon and orange peels in a small bowl until smooth. Cover and set aside at room temperature until ready to use, up to 2 hours.

3. Preheat the oven to 350 degrees. Lightly coat two large baking sheets with vegetable oil spray. (If you have only one baking sheet, bake the cookies in two batches.)

4. Divide the dough in half. Keep one portion refrigerated and roll the other portion to a ¼ inch thickness on a floured surface with a floured rolling pin. Use a pastry wheel or a small sharp knife to cut the dough into 1¼x2-inch rectangles. Transfer the cookies to the prepared baking sheet, spacing them about 1 inch apart. Repeat with the remaining dough.

5. Bake the cookies, one sheet at a time, until the edges are lightly colored and the cookies are firm, 8 to 10 minutes. Transfer the cookies to a rack and, while they are still very warm, brush the tops with the glaze. Let the cookies stand until the glaze has set, about 1 hour. You can eat the cookies immediately, but they are best if stored a day or two before eating. Store the cookies in an airtight tin for up to 3 weeks.

◆ *PER COOKIE: About 48 cals, 2 cals from fat, 0g total fat, 0g sat fat, 5mg chol, 24mg sodium, 11g total carbs, 0g fiber, 1g prot*

Double Chocolate Brownies

Makes 16 squares

The combination of cocoa and semisweet chocolate gives a rich, deep flavor to these brownies—and a bit of applesauce replaces some of the fat. Serve the brownies at room temperature or slightly warm from the pan, with a scoop of vanilla or raspberry yogurt.

Vegetable oil spray
1 cup all-purpose flour
½ cup Dutch-process
   unsweetened cocoa
½ teaspoon instant coffee
½ teaspoon baking powder
¼ teaspoon salt
3 tablespoons butter

1 ounce (1 square) semisweet
   chocolate, finely chopped
2 tablespoons smooth applesauce
1 cup and 2 tablespoons of
   granulated sugar
1 egg
2 egg whites
1 teaspoon vanilla

1. Preheat the oven to 350 degrees. Coat an 8x8-inch baking pan with vegetable oil spray.

2. In a mixing bowl, whisk together the flour, cocoa, coffee, baking powder, and salt. In a 2- or 3-quart saucepan, melt the butter. Remove the pan from the heat and stir in the chocolate until melted, then stir in the applesauce and sugar until blended. In a small bowl, whisk together the egg, egg whites, and vanilla. Whisk the egg mixture into the saucepan, then add the dry ingredients and stir until blended and smooth.

3. Spread the batter evenly into the prepared pan and bake until the brownies are just firm and begin to pull away from the edges, 20 to 25 minutes. Do not overbake.

4. Let the brownies cool at least 10 minutes in the pan on a rack, then cut into squares and serve.

◆ *PER SQUARE: About 123 cals, 30 cals from fat, 3g total fat, 2g sat fat, 19mg chol, 79mg sodium, 23g total carbs, 0g fiber, 2g prot*

Hot Fudge Soufflé

Makes 6 servings

Chocolate and cinnamon have had a long and satisfying relationship. In fact, many cooks think that cinnamon actually intensifies the flavor of chocolate. That fact, combined with this recipe's easy preparation and sophisticated presentation, will put it near the top of your dessert list.

Vegetable oil spray	Pinch of salt
2 teaspoons granulated sugar, plus	1 cup cold skim milk
⅓ cup, plus ⅓ cup	2 egg yolks
⅓ cup unsweetened Dutch	1 teaspoon vanilla
process cocoa	5 egg whites
1 tablespoon all-purpose flour	½ teaspoon cream of tartar
¾ teaspoon ground cinnamon	1 tablespoon powdered sugar

1. Preheat the oven to 425 degrees. Coat a deep 9-inch pie plate with vegetable oil spray. Dust with 2 teaspoons sugar. Set aside.

2. In a medium saucepan, whisk together ⅓ cup sugar, the cocoa, flour, cinnamon, and salt. Slowly whisk in the milk until smooth. Cook, whisking constantly over medium heat, until the mixture thickens and comes to a boil, 3 to 5 minutes. Remove from the heat. In a medium bowl, whisk together the egg yolks and vanilla. Whisk the hot chocolate mixture into the yolks until smooth. Set aside.

3. In a large mixing bowl, beat the egg whites with an electric mixer on medium-low speed until frothy. Add the cream of tartar, increase the speed to medium-high and beat until soft peaks form, 3 to 5 minutes. Increase speed to high and beat in the rest of the sugar, 1 tablespoon at a time, until firm (but not dry) peaks form, 3 to 5 minutes.

4. Stir about one fourth of the beaten whites into the chocolate mixture to lighten it. Then use a large spatula to fold the chocolate mixture into the whites until just incorporated. Spoon the soufflé into the prepared dish and bake 15 minutes or until the soufflé is almost doubled in height and feels firm around the edges but still somewhat jiggly in the center.

5. Dust the top of the soufflé with powdered sugar and serve immediately by spooning onto dessert plates.

◆ *PER SERVING: About 162 cals, 20 cals from fat, 2g total fat, 1g sat fat, 72mg chol, 73mg sodium, 31g total carbs, 0g fiber, 6g prot*

Almond Anise Biscotti

Makes about 2 dozen cookies

Biscotti get their characteristic crunchy texture from a double baking—first shaped into a log and baked until firm, then sliced and baked again until very crisp. Unless they have lots of nuts, most traditional biscotti are low in fat, though some of the American bakery versions contain butter or shortening. Anise is a classic flavor for biscotti in Italy.

⅓ cup sliced almonds	½ teaspoon baking soda
Vegetable oil spray	¼ teaspoon salt
2 cups all-purpose flour, plus	2 eggs
¼ cup, if needed	2 egg whites
1 cup granulated sugar	¾ teaspoon vanilla
1 tablespoon anise seeds	½ teaspoon almond extract
1 teaspoon baking powder	¼ teaspoon anise extract (optional)

1. Preheat the oven to 325 degrees. Toast the almonds on a baking sheet, stirring often until golden and fragrant, 8 to 10 minutes. Let cool. Coat a large baking sheet with vegetable oil spray.

2. In a mixing bowl, whisk together 2 cups flour, the sugar, anise seeds, baking powder, baking soda, and salt. Stir in the almonds. In a small bowl, lightly whisk together the eggs, whites, vanilla, almond extract, and anise extract, if using. Add the liquid to the dry ingredients and mix with a wooden spoon or electric mixer to make a sticky dough.

3. Place the dough on a well-floured surface and use your floured hands to shape it into a 13-inch log. (If the dough is too sticky to shape, knead in up to ¼ cup of flour.) Transfer the log to the prepared baking sheet and flatten it to a cylinder about 1½ inches thick and 2½ inches wide.

4. Bake until the cylinder is just firm and very lightly colored, 25 to 30 minutes. Remove from the oven and reduce the oven temperature to 300 degrees. Let cool for 10 minutes, then transfer it to a cutting board and use a sharp knife to cut it into diagonal ½-inch slices. Place the slices on the baking sheet, cut sides up, and bake for 12 minutes. Turn the slices over and bake an additional 10 minutes until pale golden brown.

5. Transfer the biscotti to racks to cool completely. Store at room temperature, tightly covered, for up to 2 weeks.

◆ *PER COOKIE: About 90 cals, 12 cals from fat, 1g total fat, 0g sat fat, 18mg chol, 74mg sodium, 17g total carbs, 0g fiber, 2g prot*

Fruits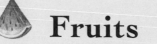

"To everything there is a season" is especially notable for fruits. There is little better than a crisp apple in October except perhaps a plump, juicy strawberry in June. This chart shows how to chose, store, and use the best fruit of the season.

NAME/ NUTRITIONAL INFO	HOW TO BUY/PEAK SEASON	HOW TO STORE OR RIPEN
Apple 80 calories per medium apple; source of fiber	Firm; crisp; without blemishes or soft spots/autumn	Store in a cool place or refrigerate for up to 1 month without the apples touching each other
Apricot 40 calories per two medium apricots; source of vitamin A	Golden to orange yellow; lush; plump; should yield slightly to pressure/June-July	Ripen in a paper bag, then refrigerate up to 3 days
Banana 105 calories per medium banana; source of vitamin C, fiber, and potassium	Solid yellow; firm skins/year round	Ripen at room temperature and eat raw within 2 days or purée overripe fruit and use in baking or yogurt smoothies
Blackberry 35 calories per ½ cup; source of fiber; rich in vitamin C	Plump; firm; dry; deeply colored; no bruises/June-September	Purchase ripe and refrigerate in a shallow container 1 to 2 days or freeze on a baking sheet and store in plastic bags
Blueberry 40 calories per ½ cup; source of vitamin C	Plump; firm; deep blue with a silver hue/June-August	Purchase ripe and refrigerate in a shallow container up to 3 days
Cantaloupe 30 calories per ½ cup; rich in vitamins A and C	Heavy; well-netted skin; no stem; perfumed aroma/July-September	Ripen at room temperature until skin yields to pressure and eat within 2 days or refrigerate up to 3 days
Cherry 60 calories per ½ cup	Bright red, burgundy, or white, depending on variety; firm; unblemished; fresh-looking stems/June-July	Refrigerate up to 4 days or pit and freeze in a single layer and store in plastic bags
Cranberry 25 calories per ½ cup; source of vitamin C	Plump; firm; bright to deep red/October-December	Refrigerate or freeze in plastic bags
Grape 55 calories per ½ cup; source of vitamin C	Firm; plump; dry; well attached to stem; bright red, green, or purple/August-November	Store in refrigerator up to 5 days or freeze in plastic bags for frozen snacks
Grapefruit 40 calories per ½ grapefruit; rich in vitamin C	Firm; heavy; no bruises or brown spots; white or pink flesh, depending on variety/December-March	Refrigerate up to 1 month
Honeydew melon 30 calories per ½ cup; rich in vitamin C	Heavy; firm; greenish white to pale yellow; slightly soft at blossom end; perfumed fragrance/August-September	Ripen at room temperature and store in refrigerator up to 5 days

NAME/ NUTRITIONAL INFO	HOW TO BUY/PEAK SEASON	HOW TO STORE OR RIPEN
Kiwifruit 60 calories per medium kiwifruit; source of potassium; rich in vitamin C	Fuzzy greenish brown skin; plump; yields to pressure; perfumed fragrance/year round	Ripen at room temperature and refrigerate up to 4 days
Lemon 15 calories per medium lemon; rich in vitamin C	Firm and heavy; bright yellow/ year round, but at peak in winter	Refrigerate up to 2 weeks
Lime 20 calories per medium lime; rich in vitamin C	Firm; heavy; shiny deep green/ year round	Refrigerate up to 2 weeks
Mango 135 calories per medium mango; source of fiber and potassium; rich in vitamins A and C	Firm; heavy; yields to pressure; yellow-orange skin with tinges of red or green/spring-summer	Ripen at room temperature and refrigerate up to 5 days
Nectarine 65 calories per medium nectarine; source of vitamins A and C and potassium	Plump; smooth golden skin with tinges of pink or red; firm; yields to pressure/June-August	Ripen in a paper bag then refrigerate up to 5 days
Orange 70 calories per medium orange; source of potassium; rich in vitamin C and fiber	Firm; heavy; shiny orange skin; no bruises or brown spots/year round (peak December-April)	Refrigerate up to 1 month
Papaya 25 calories per ½ cup; rich in vitamin C	Smooth green-yellow skin; firm; yields to pressure/March-August	Ripen in a paper bag at room temperature then refrigerate up to 5 days
Peach 35 calories per medium peach	Firm; plump; slightly fuzzy golden or reddish-golden skin; no bruises/ May-September	Ripen in paper bag at room temperature then refrigerate up to 5 days
Pear 100 calories per medium pear; source of vitamin C and fiber	Unblemished; pale green, golden, or red, depending on variety; firm; yields to pressure/September-November	Ripen in paper bag at room temperature then refrigerate up to 4 days
Pineapple 75 calories per ½ cup; rich in vitamin C	Plump; firm; heavy; shiny tips and leaves/year round	Purchase ripe and refrigerate up to 5 days
Plum 35 calories per medium plum; source of vitamin C	Plump; firm; bright green, yellow, red, or purple; should yield to pressure/July-September	Purchase ripe and refrigerate up to 5 days
Strawberry 20 calories per ½ cup; rich in vitamin C	Firm; no blemishes; bright or deep red; fresh leaves/March-July	Refrigerate in a shallow container for 1 to 2 days
Watermelon 25 calories per ½ cup; source of vitamin C	Firm; shiny; heavy; red or yellow flesh, depending on variety/June-September	Buy ripe and refrigerate up to 3 days

GLOSSARY

◆ **ADOBO:** a marinade of Spanish origin, now popular from the Caribbean to the Philippines; varies according to the region, but usually contains orange, garlic, cumin, and oregano.

◆ **AIOLI:** a Mediterranean garlic mayonnaise sauce or dip.

◆ **AL DENTE:** properly cooked pasta that is still firm in the center; means "to the tooth" in Italian.

◆ **AL FORNO:** Italian foods baked or roasted in ovens, especially wood-fired ovens.

◆ **ANDOUILLE:** a garlicky, peppery Cajun pork sausage.

◆ **BAGUETTE:** a long, slim French bread loaf.

◆ **BLANCH:** to briefly cook in boiling water.

◆ **BRAISE:** to cook meat, poultry, or vegetables in a small amount of liquid in a heavy, covered pot, such as a Dutch oven.

◆ **CALAMARI:** small squid.

◆ **CAPONATA:** a Sicilian relish that usually contains eggplant, garlic, raisins, and spices.

◆ **CARAMELIZE:** to cook to a rich, golden color; can refer to sugar used in desserts or meat or vegetables cooked in butter or oil.

◆ **CORNICHON:** French term for small pickles or gherkins.

◆ **CROSTINI:** lightly toasted Italian bread slices, sometimes rubbed with the cut side of a garlic clove after toasting.

◆ **CROTTINS:** small goat cheeses.

◆ **CROÛTES:** large croutons made by toasting thin slices of Italian bread; can be floated in soups or used as a base for other foods, such as grilled tenderloin steaks.

◆ **CRUDITÉS:** the French term for raw or blanched vegetables cut up for hors d'oeuvres, sometimes served with a dip.

◆ **DEGLAZE:** to form the basis for a sauce by adding liquid to the flavorful, browned bits of meat, poultry, or seafood left in a pan and then simmering.

◆ **DICE:** to cut into small, even pieces; large dice are about ½ inch in diameter and small dice are ¼ inch or less.

◆ **FOLD:** to gently combine ingredients with a flat spatula; usually refers to cake batters, whipped cream, or beaten egg whites.

◆ **FRA DIAVOLO:** a peppery, spicy, usually tomato-based sauce; means "brother of the devil" in Italian.

◆ **FRISÉE:** a tender, slightly bitter, curly salad green of the chicory family.

◆ **HARISSA:** a very hot, chili-based spice mixture used in Eastern Mediterranean cooking.

◆ **HERBES DE PROVENCE:** a classic French herb mixture that usually includes rosemary, marjoram, thyme, sage, anise, and savory.

◆ **JULIENNE:** to cut vegetables into very thin strips less than ⅛ inch thick and about 1½ inches long.

◆ **LAVASH:** a very large and thin Mediterranean flatbread; soft lavash can be rolled for sandwiches and hard lavash is used like a cracker.

◆ **LEMONGRASS:** a tall, green plant with a woody stem, long slender leaves, and a mild lemon taste; minced stems are used as an herb in Southeast Asian cooking.

◆ **MÂCHE:** a salad green with small, oval, dark green leaves and a slightly bitter flavor; also known as lamb's lettuce.

◆ **MALFADI:** leftover scraps of fresh pasta dough that can be cooked and sauced much like fettucine or other similar noodles.

◆ **MARINATE:** to soak food in a seasoned liquid to add flavor and tenderize.

◆ **MESCLUN:** a mixture of tender young salad greens.

◆ **MI-FUN:** Asian rice noodles; also spelled mee-fun or mi-fin.

◆ **NAM PLA:** a salty-sweet sauce refined from anchovy paste that is one of the essential condiments and flavorings of Southeast Asian cooking.

◆ **NONREACTIVE:** describes pots and pans that do not cause adverse chemical reactions to foods cooked in them. (Cast iron transfers metallic flavors to foods that have a high acid content, and aluminum can cause eggs and egg-based sauces to turn gray.)

◆ **OLIVADE:** a paste made from puréed olives; may contain other ingredients, such as garlic or herbs; also known as tapenade.

◆ **PANCETTA:** unsmoked, salt-cured Italian bacon.

◆ **PARBOIL:** to partially cook in boiling or simmering liquid; similar to blanching but the food is cooked longer.

◆ **PECORINO:** a sharp, tangy sheep's-milk cheese from central and southern Italy; usually grated and used like Parmesan cheese; also called pecorino romano.

◆ **POACH:** to cook in barely simmering liquid.

◆ **PROSCIUTTO:** Italian ham that is salt-cured and air-dried but not smoked; also called Parma ham.

◆ **RAITA:** an Indian relish consisting of plain yogurt mixed with chopped vegetables, such as cucumbers or tomatoes, and seasoned with herbs and spices.

◆ **REDUCE:** to cook and thicken a liquid until it decreases in quantity from evaporation to concentrate its flavors.

◆ **ROCKET:** a common nickname for the peppery salad green arugula.

◆ **ROUILLE:** a spicy, mayonnaiselike sauce from the French Mediterranean, traditionally served with bouillabaisse or other fish soups.

◆ **SAI-FUN:** Asian noodles made from mung bean starch and water.

◆ **SAUTÉ:** to sear in a small amount of fat over relatively high heat.

◆ **SIMMER:** to boil gently, so that the liquid barely bubbles.

◆ **SOBA:** Japanese buckwheat-flour noodles; available fresh or dried.

◆ **SOFRITO:** a mixture of cooked onions, peppers, garlic, and sometimes tomatoes that forms the base for many dishes in Spanish and Spanish-Caribbean cuisines.

◆ **SOMEN:** thick Japanese wheat-flour noodles; usually eaten in a broth or with a dipping sauce.

◆ **STIR-FRY:** to cook over very high heat using little fat while stirring almost constantly; often done in a wok.

◆ **TAGINE:** in Eastern Mediterranean cooking, refers to both an earthenware baking dish with a conical lid and the spiced stew that is cooked in it.

◆ **TAHINI:** ground sesame seed paste; an essential ingredient in hummus and other Middle Eastern dishes.

◆ **TOMATILLO:** a bright green fruit covered with a papery husk; has a tart, lemony flavor and is used in Southwestern and Mexican cuisines; also known as the Mexican green tomato.

◆ **VINDALOO:** a very spicy, tart Indian curry sauce, often made with a small amount of vinegar.

AMA FAMILY HEALTH COOKBOOK

Recipes Containing Important Vitamins and Minerals

This chart shows which recipes in this cookbook are good sources of vitamin A, vitamin C, calcium, iron, or fiber.

*   supplies 10% to 19% of the daily value
** supplies at least 20% of the daily value

Recipe	Vitamin A	Vitamin C	Calcium	Iron	Fiber
Appetizers and Snacks					
Mini Pita Pizza Wedges		**			
Herbed Cheese Dip and Crudité Color Wheel	**	**			
Smoked Salmon Yogurt Cheese Dip with Winter Crudités	*	**	*		*
Buffalo Chicken Strips		*	*		
Pico de Gallo Salsa		**			
Chile con Queso with Dippers	**	**			*
Crispy Garlic Potato Skins		*		*	*
Tomatillo Salsa		**			
Black Olivade Crostini				*	
Sun-Dried Tomato Crostini	**	*			
Sicilian Caponata		**			
Spiced Baba Ghanouj					*
Pickled Vegetable Medley	**	**			
Three-Alarm Texas Black Bean "Caviar"		**			*
White Bean "Pesto" with Garden Vegetables		**		*	*
Salads					
Classic Southern Chicken Salad		**			
Thai Grilled Chicken and Broccoli on Napa Cabbage Salad	*	**		*	*
Wild Rice, Turkey, and Grape Salad		**	*	*	*
Steakhouse Salad	*	**	*	**	*
Greek Barbecued Lamb and Spring Greens Salad	**	**	*		
Marinated Scallop, Lima Bean, and Corn Salad	*	**		*	*
Grilled Salade Niçoise	**	**	*	**	*

Recipe	Source of				
	Vitamin A	Vitamin C	Calcium	Iron	Fiber
Salads (continued)					
Grilled Shrimp, Black Bean, and Mango Salad	✿✿	✿✿	✿	✿✿	✿✿
Tropical Vinaigrette		✿			
Lemon, Tuna, and White Bean Salad	✿	✿✿	✿✿	✿✿	✿✿
Peppery Jambalaya Seafood Salad	✿✿	✿✿	✿	✿✿	✿
Seashell Macaroni and Salmon Salad	✿✿	✿✿	✿✿	✿✿	✿
Grilled Tofu Caesar Salad	✿✿	✿✿	✿✿	✿✿	✿
Tortellini and Cilantro Pesto Salad		✿✿	✿✿	✿	
Cilantro Pesto	✿	✿✿	✿	✿	
Old-Fashioned Potato Salad		✿✿			✿
Four-Bean Ranch Salad		✿		✿	✿✿
Family Reunion Macaroni Salad	✿✿	✿✿		✿	
Shredded Carrot, Jicama, and Currant Slaw	✿✿	✿✿			
Calico Coleslaw	✿✿	✿✿			
Chunked Tomato, Fennel, and Chickpea Salad	✿	✿✿	✿	✿	
Minted Couscous Greek Salad	✿✿	✿✿	✿	✿	✿✿
Mint Vinaigrette		✿			
Herbed and Spiced Tabbouleh	✿	✿✿		✿	✿✿
Tuscan Bread and Roasted Pepper Salad		✿✿	✿		
Chicory, Arugula, and Orange Salad Siciliana	✿✿	✿✿	✿		✿✿
Curried Waldorf Salad		✿✿			✿
Vietnamese Grilled Vegetable Salad	✿	✿✿	✿	✿	✿
Breads					
Marvelous Multigrain Bread				✿	✿
Super Sandwich Bread					✿
Braided Semolina Bread				✿	✿
Basic Pizza Dough				✿✿	✿✿
Cranberry Pumpkin Bread	✿✿				
Morning Glory Breakfast Muffins	✿✿	✿			✿
Dried Cran-Raspberry Quick Jam		✿✿			✿
Blueberry Corn Muffins			✿		
Oven-Baked Orange French Toast	✿	✿✿	✿	✿	✿
Whole-Wheat Yogurt Waffles			✿✿	✿	✿
Crunchy Oat Waffles			✿✿	✿	
Giant Cornmeal Flapjacks			✿✿	✿	
Buckwheat Buttermilk Silver Dollar Pancakes			✿		

Recipe	Source of				
	Vitamin A	Vitamin C	Calcium	Iron	Fiber
Soups					
Basic Vegetable Broth	✿✿				
Garden Patch Gazpacho	✿	✿✿			✿
Creamy Iced Cantaloupe Soup	✿✿	✿✿	✿		
Very Cool Beet and Berry Borscht		✿✿	✿		
Day-After-Thanksgiving Turkey Noodle Soup	✿✿	✿✿	✿	✿✿	✿✿
Favorite Neoclassic Chicken Noodle Soup	✿✿	✿✿		✿✿	✿✿
Creamy Broccoli and Leek Bisque	✿✿	✿✿	✿✿	✿	✿
Family-Style Vegetable Beef Alphabet Soup	✿✿	✿✿		✿✿	✿
Nantucket Clam Chowder	✿	✿✿	✿✿	✿✿	✿
Clam Chowder Manhattan Style	✿✿	✿✿	✿	✿✿	✿
Sweet Corn and Shrimp Chowder	✿	✿✿	✿✿	✿	✿
Herbed Minestrone	✿✿	✿✿	✿✿		✿✿
Quick Cuban Black Bean Soup with Garnishes	✿✿	✿✿	✿✿	✿✿	✿✿
Moroccan Lamb, Chickpea, and Vegetable Soup	✿	✿✿	✿	✿✿	✿✿
Split Pea Soup with Ham Bits and Dilled Yogurt	✿✿	✿✿	✿	✿✿	✿✿
Tuscan Cannellini and Escarole Soup	✿✿	✿✿	✿✿	✿✿	✿✿
Spicy Mixed Bean Soup with Turkey Sausage		✿✿		✿✿	✿
Sweet Potato and Squash Soup	✿✿	✿✿			✿
Scottish Turkey, Leek, and Barley Soup	✿✿	✿✿	✿	✿✿	✿✿
Tortellini Soup with Greens and Mushrooms	✿✿	✿✿	✿✿	✿✿	
Hot and Sour Tofu and Rice Soup	✿	✿✿	✿✿	✿✿	✿
Cambodian Chicken, Rice, and Garlic Soup		✿✿		✿✿	
Japanese Vegetable Noodle Soup with Wasabi	✿✿	✿✿		✿✿	✿
Spicy Thai Noodle Soup with Shrimp and Lime		✿✿	✿	✿✿	
Classic Wonton Soup				✿✿	
Sandwiches, Burgers, Pizzas, and Tacos					
Contemporary Club Sandwich	✿	✿✿		✿	✿
Egg Salad Bagelwich	✿	✿	✿	✿✿	
Panfried Fish Po' Boy	✿	✿✿	✿	✿	
Western Omelet Sandwich	✿✿	✿✿	✿✿	✿	
Roast Beef Lavash Rolls	✿	✿	✿	✿	✿✿
Tuna Salad Roll-Ups		✿✿			✿✿
Mediterranean-Style Tuna Melt		✿	✿✿	✿	
Sage and Onion Turkey Burgers			✿	✿	

Recipe	Source of				
	Vitamin A	Vitamin C	Calcium	Iron	Fiber
Sandwiches (continued)					
Black Bean and Radish Burgers		*	*	**	**
Falafel Pitas with Chutney and Yogurt		**		*	**
Tomato-Lemon Chutney	**	**			
Springtime Chicken and Watercress Sandwich	*	**		*	
Grilled Portobello Mushroom and Arugula Sandwich		*	*	**	**
Soft Tacos with Turkey	*	**	**	**	
Huevos Rancheros Tostadas	*	*	**	*	
Warm Fruit Salsa	*	**			*
Steak and Charred Onion Fajitas		**	*	**	
Pork and Unfried Bean Burritos		*	*	*	
Baked Cheese and Bean Quesadillas	*	*	**	**	*
Basil and Ripe Tomato Bruschetta		**		**	**
Personalized Pita Pizzas	**	**			
Antipasto Pan Pizza	*	*	**	**	**
New Mexican White Clam Pizza	*	**	*	**	**
Roasted Vegetable Baguette		**		*	*
Spinach and Cheese Calzone	**	**	**	**	**
Athenian Lamb Gyros	**	**	*	*	
Pasta					
Double Tomato Sauce	**	**	*		**
Basic Marinara Sauce	**	**			
Basic Bolognese Sauce	**	**	*		
Basil Pesto			*		
Sun-Dried Tomato Pesto			*		
Pasta with Lightened Pesto Sauce				*	
Freshened Fettuccine Alfredo	*		**	*	
Contemporary Pasta Carbonara		*	*	**	
Pasta Primavera with Mustard Cream	**	**	*	**	*
Light-and-Easy Turkey Tetrazzini	*	*	*	**	
Summer Formal Bow Ties	*	**	*	**	
Straw and Hay with Peas and Pancetta	**	**	**	**	
Modern Macaroni and Cheddar	**	**	**	*	
Angel Hair Arrabbiata	**	**	**	**	
Cincinnati Chili Spaghetti	*	**		**	*
Shellfish Lasagne	*	**	*	**	

Recipe	Source of				
	Vitamin A	Vitamin C	Calcium	Iron	Fiber
Pasta (continued)					
Roasted Summer Vegetable Lasagne	✿✿	✿✿	✿✿	✿	✿✿
Santa Fe Spaghetti Pie	✿	✿✿	✿✿	✿	✿
Spinach and Two-Cheese Stuffed Shells	✿✿	✿✿	✿✿	✿✿	
Fruited Noodle Kugel	✿		✿	✿	
Linguine with Herbed Clam Sauce	✿	✿✿	✿	✿✿	
Calamari Fra Diavolo	✿	✿✿	✿	✿✿	
Dilled Salmon and Pasta Frittata	✿✿	✿✿	✿✿	✿	✿
Radiatore with Peppers, Chard, and Gorgonzola	✿✿	✿✿	✿✿	✿✿	✿✿
Curried Penne with Cauliflower and Peas	✿	✿✿	✿	✿✿	✿
Rigatoni and Savory Bean Sauce	✿✿	✿✿	✿✿	✿✿	✿✿
Ziti with Roasted Potatoes, Tomatoes, and Leeks	✿	✿✿	✿	✿✿	
Orrechiette with Broccoli Rabe and Beans		✿✿	✿✿	✿✿	✿✿
Whole-Wheat Fettuccine with Mushrooms	✿✿			✿✿	✿
Penne with Sausage and Autumn Vegetables	✿✿	✿✿	✿	✿✿	✿✿
Fusilli with Moroccan Lamb and Chickpeas	✿✿	✿✿	✿✿	✿✿	✿✿
Cold Sesame Noodles	✿✿	✿✿	✿	✿✿	✿✿
Shrimp and Tofu Pad Thai	✿✿	✿✿	✿	✿✿	✿
Sizzling Pork and Black Bean Sauce		✿✿		✿	
Hot-and-Sour Chicken Noodle Stir-Fry	✿✿	✿✿		✿✿	✿✿
Simplified Sukiyaki	✿✿	✿✿		✿✿	
Rice and Grains					
Honey-Orange Breakfast Oatmeal with Bananas		✿✿	✿	✿	
Fruited Barley and Rice Breakfast Bake	✿	✿✿		✿	✿✿
Spiced Pear and Coconut Breakfast Couscous			✿		✿✿
Homemade Crunchy Granola				✿	
Turkish Bulgur with Chicken and Eggplant	✿	✿✿		✿	✿✿
Spinach and Mushroom Polenta "Lasagne"	✿✿	✿	✿✿	✿✿	✿
Cajun "Dirty" Rice	✿✿	✿✿		✿✿	
Garlic-Lemon Rice with Shrimp and Snow Peas	✿	✿✿	✿	✿✿	
Spoon Bread, Garlic Greens, and Smoked Ham	✿✿	✿✿	✿✿	✿	✿✿
Herbed Broccoli and Rice Frittata	✿✿	✿✿	✿✿	✿	✿
Baked Grits Cakes with Shiitake Gravy	✿	✿✿		✿✿	
Barley "Risotto" with Clams and Tomatoes	✿	✿✿	✿	✿✿	✿✿
Fennel and Prosciutto Risotto		✿✿	✿	✿✿	
Wild Mushroom and Herb Risotto	✿	✿✿	✿✿	✿✿	

Recipe	Source of				
	Vitamin A	Vitamin C	Calcium	Iron	Fiber
Rice and Grains (continued)					
Cuban-Style Saffron Rice with Smoked Ham and Peas	❀	❀❀	❀	❀❀	❀❀
Classic Moroccan Chicken and Vegetable Couscous	❀❀	❀❀	❀	❀❀	❀❀
Tunisian Couscous Pilaf with Chickpeas, Almonds, and Dates	❀	❀❀	❀	❀❀	❀❀
Contemporary Paella	❀	❀❀		❀❀	
Greek Chicken, Artichokes, and Brown Rice		❀❀		❀❀	❀❀
Kasha with Lamb Tidbits	❀❀	❀❀		❀❀	❀❀
Quinoa, Beef, and Sweet Potato Casserole	❀❀	❀❀		❀❀	❀❀
Shredded Turkey and Chiles with Hominy Stew	❀❀	❀❀	❀	❀	❀❀
Quick Creamy Polenta				❀	
Basic Baked Rice Pilaf				❀❀	
Herbed Brown Rice Pilaf		❀			❀
Southwest Rice and Corn Pilaf	❀	❀❀		❀	❀
Bulgur Pilaf with Leeks, Currants, and Pine Nuts		❀❀	❀	❀❀	❀❀
Braised Wild Rice with Cranberries		❀			❀
Curried Basmati Rice and Peas with Ginger		❀		❀	❀
Spicy Thai Rice and Chopped Peanuts		❀❀		❀	
Baked Herbed Polenta				❀	
Beans					
Family-Style Bean and Tortilla Casserole	❀❀	❀❀	❀❀	❀	❀❀
Black Bean Patties with Dill		❀❀	❀	❀❀	❀❀
Chunky Yogurt Sauce			❀		
Unfried Beans				❀	
Lentil, Spinach, and Meat Loaf	❀❀	❀		❀	❀
Mixed Baked Beans with Maple		❀		❀	❀❀
Smoky Black Bean and Pork Chili	❀	❀❀	❀	❀❀	❀❀
White Beans and Greens Casserole	❀❀	❀❀	❀❀	❀❀	❀❀
Quick Cassoulet		❀❀	❀	❀❀	❀❀
Jamaican Rice and Beans with Thyme	❀	❀❀		❀❀	❀
Cuban Black Beans and Rice	❀❀	❀❀	❀	❀❀	❀❀
Tropical Salsa		❀❀			❀
Turkish Red Lentils and Rice	❀❀	❀❀	❀	❀❀	
Lentil, Spinach, and Potato Ragout	❀❀	❀❀	❀❀	❀❀	❀❀
Spiced Split Peas on Jasmine Rice	❀	❀❀		❀❀	❀❀
Cooling Cucumber Raita			❀		

Recipe	Source of				
	Vitamin A	Vitamin C	Calcium	Iron	Fiber
Beans (continued)					
Black Bean and Yam Stew Sofrito	*	**	*	**	**
Fava Beans with Fennel and New Potatoes	**	**	*	**	**
Tuscan-Style Ribollita	**	**	**	**	**
Kentucky Bean and Vegetable Stew	**	**	**	**	**
Hoppin' John with Colorful Garnishes		**	*	**	**
French Quarter Red Beans and Rice		**		**	**
Lentils and Rice with Blackened Onions	**	**	**	**	**
Turkey and White Bean Chili Verde	*	**	*	*	**
Chickpea-Cilantro Stew with Cumin Croûtes	*	**	**	**	**
Poultry					
Kale, Corn Bread, and Cranberry Dressing	**	**	*		*
Exotic Fruit and Nut Bulgur Dressing	**	**		*	**
Easy Amish Country Chicken Noodle Stew	**	**		**	**
Country-Style Chicken and Dumplings	**	**	*	*	
Garlic-Braised Chicken and New Potatoes		**		*	
Company Chicken and Wild Rice Bake	**	**		*	*
All-American Barbecued Chicken		*		*	
Chinese Grilled Five-Spice Chicken		*			
Tuscan Grilled Chicken and Roasted Garlic Aioli	*	*	*	**	*
Tandoor-Style Chicken Nuggets	*	**		*	*
Easy Chicken Cacciatore		*		**	
Roasted Lebanese Chicken		**		*	
Chicken Vindaloo	*	**		**	
Chicken and Summer Vegetable Tagine		**		*	**
Chicken Adobo		*			
Turkey Stir-Fry with Ginger and Mint	**	**		*	**
Basil Chicken and Sweet Pepper Packets		**			
Turkey Cutlets with Cranberry-Kumquat Relish	*	**			*
Turkey and Tarragon Tomato Salsa	*	**			
Garden Vegetable and Turkey Meat Loaf	**	**	*		
Grilled Duck with Citrus Honey Salsa		**		**	*
Sesame Turkey and Asparagus Stir-Fry		**	*	*	**
Apple-Sage Glazed Game Hens	*			*	

Recipe	Source of				
	Vitamin A	Vitamin C	Calcium	Iron	Fiber
Seafood					
Tuna and Celery Bread Pudding	✿	✿✿	✿	✿	✿
Crackling Fish Sticks	✿✿	✿✿			
Cape Cod Baked Stuffed Clams	✿	✿✿	✿✿	✿✿	
Baltimore Crab Cakes	✿	✿✿	✿	✿	
Crawfish and Tasso Jambalaya	✿✿	✿✿	✿✿	✿✿	✿✿
Sausalito Cioppino	✿	✿✿		✿✿	
Sole Rolls Florentine	✿✿	✿✿	✿	✿✿	✿✿
Poached Turbot with Sorrel Sauce	✿✿	✿✿	✿	✿✿	
Sesame-Glazed Tuna				✿	
Broiled Citrus and Herb Trout		✿✿	✿	✿✿	
Sautéed Red Snapper Maque Choux		✿✿		✿✿	
Skewered Swordfish and Summer Squash	✿✿	✿✿	✿	✿	✿✿
Grilled Salmon with Dilled Cucumber Yogurt Sauce		✿✿			
Grouper with Cantaloupe-Lime Salsa	✿✿	✿✿		✿	
Seafood Printemps en Papillotes	✿✿	✿✿		✿	
Vietnamese Steamed Fish in Spicy Broth		✿✿	✿	✿✿	
Scallops and Grapefruit Gratinée	✿	✿✿	✿✿	✿✿	✿
Stir-Fried Scallops and Vegetables	✿	✿✿	✿	✿✿	✿✿
Shrimp and Clams Espagnole	✿✿	✿✿	✿✿	✿✿	
Herb-Steamed Mussels		✿✿		✿✿	
Meat					
Marrakech Orange and Spice-Braised Lamb Shanks	✿✿	✿✿	✿	✿✿	✿✿
Tex-Mex Beef Pie with Cornmeal Biscuit Topping	✿	✿✿	✿	✿✿	✿✿
Quick Spring Lamb Stew	✿✿	✿✿		✿✿	✿✿
Contemporary Shepherd's Pie	✿✿	✿✿	✿	✿	✿✿
Marvelous Mustard Meat Loaf		✿		✿	
Ginger-Sesame Beef and Broccoli Stir-Fry	✿✿	✿✿	✿	✿✿	✿✿
Veal and Mushroom Stew in Acorn Squash Halves	✿✿	✿✿	✿✿	✿✿	✿✿
Herb-Smoked Steak with Grilled Vegetables		✿✿		✿✿	
Braised Pork Chops		✿✿			✿
Pork Pot Roast with Root Vegetables and Thyme	✿✿	✿✿	✿	✿✿	✿✿
Maple-Mustard Pork on Mashed "Sweets"	✿✿	✿✿		✿	✿✿
Pork with Cranberry-Orange-Pear Sauce		✿✿		✿	✿✿
Five-Alarm Firehouse Chili	✿✿	✿✿	✿	✿✿	✿✿
Canadian Bacon and Garlic Greens	✿✿	✿✿			

Recipe	Source of				
	Vitamin A	Vitamin C	Calcium	Iron	Fiber
Meat (continued)					
Lamb with White Beans and Rosemary	✿	✿✿	✿	✿✿	✿✿
Curried Lamb and Fruit on Skewers		✿	✿	✿	
Teriyaki Flank Steak with Shiitakes		✿			
Moorish Lamb and Dried Fruit Tagine	✿			✿✿	✿✿
Roast Pork Tenderloin with Lemon and Fennel		✿			
Savory Beef Stew with Paprika and Herbs	✿✿	✿✿	✿	✿✿	✿✿
Apple and Pork Stir-Fry with Cashews and Ginger	✿	✿✿		✿	✿✿
Vegetables					
Thai Stir-Fry with Ginger and Mint	✿✿	✿✿	✿✿	✿✿	✿
Curried Winter Vegetable and Tofu Stew	✿✿	✿✿	✿✿	✿✿	✿✿
Broccoli Pie à la Grecque	✿✿	✿✿	✿✿	✿	✿
Baked Potatoes with Spicy Chili Bean Topping	✿✿	✿✿	✿✿	✿✿	✿✿
Spaghetti Squash with Sun-Dried Tomato Sauce	✿✿	✿✿	✿✿	✿	✿✿
Garlicky Broccoli Rabe	✿✿	✿✿			✿✿
Acorn Squash with Wild Mushroom–Cranberry Stuffing	✿	✿✿		✿	✿✿
Blackened Scallions	✿	✿			
Spring Vegetable Frittata	✿✿	✿✿	✿	✿	✿
Crusty Oven "Fries"		✿✿		✿	✿
Stuffed Summer Squash Provençal	✿✿	✿✿	✿	✿✿	✿✿
Fabulous Garlic Mashed Potatoes		✿✿			✿
Golden Scalloped Potatoes with Chives		✿✿	✿		✿
New Potatoes and Peas with Mustard Glaze	✿	✿✿		✿	
Parsley-Parmesan Potato Cake		✿✿	✿		✿
Glazed Gratin of Yams, Potatoes, and Turnips	✿✿	✿✿			✿
Molasses and Pepper Grilled Sweet Potato Slices	✿✿	✿✿			✿✿
Summer Harvest Ratatouille	✿	✿✿			✿
Eggplant Roasted with Garlic and Herbs		✿			✿✿
Gingered Carrot Purée	✿✿	✿✿			✿
Lemon and Honey-Glazed Baby Carrots	✿✿	✿✿			✿
Broccoli and Carrot Stir-Fry with Garlic	✿✿	✿✿	✿	✿	✿✿
Fennel Baked with Tomatoes and Onions		✿✿			
Roasted Winter Vegetables and Whole Garlic	✿✿	✿✿			✿✿
Cauliflower with Cumin and Fresh Ginger		✿✿		✿	✿✿
Sautéed Zucchini Shreds with Herbed Yogurt		✿			

Recipe	Source of				
	Vitamin A	Vitamin C	Calcium	Iron	Fiber
Vegetables (continued)					
Greens with Bacon and Onion	✿✿	✿✿			✿✿
Mixed Mushroom Sauté with Tarragon	✿				
Desserts					
Amaretti Baked Pears		✿			✿✿
Almond Meringues with Purple Plum Compote		✿			
Blackberry-Peach Cobbler		✿✿	✿		✿
Rhubarb Fool		✿✿	✿✿		
Banana Berry Smoothie		✿✿	✿✿		✿
Cranberry-Orange Parfaits		✿✿	✿		✿
Date and Cranberry Baked Apples		✿✿			✿✿
Fresh Apricot Soufflé	✿✿	✿✿			
Red, White, and Blueberry Shortcakes		✿✿	✿✿	✿	✿
Raspberry Coulis		✿✿			
Pumpkin Pecan Bars	✿✿				
Banana Spice Cake with Seafoam Icing				✿	
Double Strawberry Sauce		✿✿			
Candied Gingerbread		✿	✿	✿✿	
Warm Citrus Sauce		✿			
Orange Marmalade–Glazed Cheesecake	✿	✿			
Bombay Rice Pudding	✿		✿	✿	
Updated Old-Fashioned Chocolate Pudding			✿	✿	
Mocha Walnut Brownie Pudding				✿	
Cinnamon Raisin Bread Pudding			✿		
Hot Fudge Soufflé	✿			✿	

Index

H

Liquid and Dry Measure Equivalents

a pinch = less than $\frac{1}{8}$ teaspoon (dry)

a dash = a few drops

3 teaspoons = 1 tablespoon = $\frac{1}{2}$ ounce

2 tablespoons = 1 ounce (liquid)

1 jigger = 3 tablespoons = $1\frac{1}{2}$ ounces

4 tablespoons = 2 ounces (liquid) = $\frac{1}{4}$ cup

$5\frac{1}{3}$ tablespoons = $\frac{1}{3}$ cup

8 tablespoons = 4 ounces = $\frac{1}{2}$ cup = $\frac{1}{4}$ pound

16 tablespoons = 8 ounces = 1 cup = $\frac{1}{2}$ pound

32 tablespoons = 16 ounces = 2 cups = 1 pound

64 tablespoons = 32 ounces = 1 quart = 2 pounds

1 cup = 8 ounces (liquid) = $\frac{1}{2}$ pint

2 cups = 16 ounces (liquid) = 1 pint

4 cups = 32 ounces (liquid) = 2 pints = 1 quart

16 cups = 128 ounces (liquid) = 4 quarts = 1 gallon

1 quart = 2 pints (dry)

4 quarts = 1 gallon (liquid) = $3\frac{3}{4}$ liters

8 quarts = 1 peck (dry) = $7\frac{1}{4}$ kilograms (liquid)

4 pecks = 1 bushel (dry)